ISO	International Organization for Standardization
LAP-B	Link Access Protocol—Balanced
LRC	Longitudinal Redundancy Check
NBS	National Bureau of Standards
NRZ	Nonreturn to Zero
OSI	Open Systems Interconnection
PAD	Packet Assembler/Disassembler
PBX	Private Branch Exchange
PCM	Pulse Code Modulation
PDN	Public Data Network
PDU	Protocol Data Unit
PM	Phase Modulation
PSK	Phase-Shift Keying
QPSK	Quadrature Phase-Shift Keying
RF	Radio Frequency
SAP	Service Access Point
SCA	Subsidiary Communications Authorization
SCPC	Single Channel per Carrier
SDLC	Synchronous Data Link Control
SS/TDMA	Satellite-Switched Time-Division Multiple Access
TCP	Transmission Control Protocol
TDM	Time-Division Multiplexing
TDMA	Time-Division Multiple Access
TMS	Time Multiplex Switching
TPDU	Transport Protocol Data Unit
TSI	Time Slot Interchange
UDP	User Datagram Protocol
VAN	Value-Added Network
VRC	Vertical Redundancy Check
VTP	Virtual Terminal Protocol

Data and Computer Communications

WILLIAM STALLINGS, Ph.D.

DATA AND COMPUTER COMMUNICATIONS

Macmillan Publishing Company

New York

Collier Macmillan Publishers

London

Macmillan Publishing Company
866 Third Avenue, New York, New York 10022

Collier Macmillan Canada, Inc.

Library of Congress Cataloging in Publication Data

Stallings, William.
  Data and computer communications.

  Includes bibliographies and index.
  1. Data transmission systems.   2. Computer networks.
I. Title.
TK5105.S73   1985   384   84-7914

Printing: 6 7 8   Year: 6 7 8 9 0 1 2

ISBN   0-02-415440-7

To my loving wife, Tricia

PREFACE

The 1970's and early 1980's saw a merger of the fields of computer science and data communications that profoundly changed the technology, products, and companies of the now combined computer-communications industry. Although the consequences of this revolutionary merger are still being worked out, it is safe to say that the revolution occurred, and any investigation of the field of data communications must be made within this new context.

Objectives

It is the ambitious purpose of this book to provide a unified view of the broad field of data and computer communications. The organization of the book reflects an attempt to break this massive subject into comprehensible parts and to build, piece by piece, a survey of the state of the art. The book emphasizes basic principles and topics of fundamental importance concerning the technology and architecture of data and computer communications.

The book explores the key topics in the field in the following general categories:

- *Principles:* Although the scope of this book is broad, there are a number of basic principles that appear repeatedly as themes which unify this field. Examples are multiplexing, flow control, and error control. The book highlights these principles and contrasts their application in specific areas of technology.
- *Design approaches:* The book examines alternative approaches to meeting specific communication requirements. The discussion is bolstered with examples from existing implementations.

- *Standards:* Standards have come to assume an increasingly important, not to say dominant, role in this field. An understanding of the current status and future direction of the technology is not possible without a comprehensive discussion of the role and nature of the related standards.

The subject, and therefore this book, is highly technical. Nevertheless, an attempt has been made to make the book self-contained. Part I, in particular, draws upon the disciplines of probability and electrical engineering, but the emphasis is on results rather than derivations. In general, a building-block approach is taken. The principles of data communications are carefully and thoroughly explored. These principles are then applied to the complex systems found in communication networks and computer-communications architectures.

Intended Audience

The book is intended for a broad range of readers interested in data and computer communications:

- *Students and professionals in data processing and data communications:* This book is intended as both a textbook for study and a basic reference volume for this exciting and complex field.
- *Designers and implementers:* The book discusses the critical design issues and explores alternative approaches to meeting user requirements.
- *Computer and communication system customers and managers:* The book provides the reader with an understanding of what features and structure are needed in a communications capability, as well as a knowledge of current and evolving standards. This information provides a means of assessing specific implementations and vendor offerings.

Plan of the Text

The book is organized to clarify the unifying and differentiating concepts underlying the field of data and computer communications. It is divided into three parts:

I   *Data communications:* This part is concerned primarily with the exchange of data between two directly-connected devices. Within this restricted environment, the key aspects of transmission, interfacing, link control, and multiplexing are examined.

II *Data communication networking:* This part examines the internal mechanisms by which communication networks provide a data transfer service for attached devices.

III *Computer communications architecture:* This part explores both the architectural principles and the specific mechanisms required for the exchange of data among computers, terminals and other data processing devices.

The organization of the chapters is as follows:

1. *Introduction:* Provides an overview of the book as well as a discussion of the roles of the various standards-making organizations.
2. *Data transmission:* Explores the behavior of signals propagated through a transmission medium.
3. *Data encoding:* Describes the techniques used for encoding analog and digital data as either analog or digital signals.

4. *Digital data communication techniques:* Examines interfacing and synchronization issues.
5. *Data link control:* Describes the techniques used for converting an unreliable transmission link into a reliable communications link.
6. *Multiplexing:* Examines frequency-division multiplexing and both synchronous and statistical time-division multiplexing.
7. *Communication networking techniques:* Serves as an overview to Part II.
8. *Circuit switching:* Discusses circuit-switching mechanisms and network design.
9. *Packet switching:* Examines the mechanisms of packet switched networking, including routing, traffic control, and error control.
10. *Radio and satellite networks:* Explores design and performance issues for antenna-based communication networks.
11. *Local networks:* Examines alternative approaches in the areas of transmission medium, topology, and medium access control technique.
12. *Protocols and architecture:* Defines communications protocols and motivates the need for a communications architecture.
13. *Network access protocols:* Examines techniques for accessing circuit-switched, packet-switched, and local networks.
14. *Internetworking:* Explores alternative techniques for communicating across multiple networks.
15. *Transport protocols:* Provides a detailed analysis of the most complex and important class of communications protocols.
16. *Process/application protocols:* Provides examples of higher-layer protocols.
17. *Integrated services digital network:* A preview of the network which represents the culmination of the computer-communications revolution.

The three parts of the book have been written to be sufficiently independent so that shorter courses could also be conducted using this book. For example, a course on fundamentals of data communications would cover just Part I. A course on communications networks could cover Part II and Chapter 17. A course on communications architecture and the OSI model could cover Chapters 4, 5, 7, and Part III.

In addition, the book includes an extensive glossary, a list of frequently-used acronyms, and a bibliography. Each chapter includes problems and suggestions for further reading.

The book is suitable for self-study and can be covered in a two-semester course.

Related Materials

Computer Communications: Architectures, Protocols, and Standards (IEEE Computer Society Press, 1985) is a companion to this text, covering topics in Chapters 4 and 5 and Part III. It contains reprints of many of the key references used herein. The IEEE Computer Society Press is at P. O. Box 80452, Worldway Postal Center, Los Angeles, CA 90080; telephone (714) 821-8380.

A set of videotape courses specifically designed for use with *Data and Computer Communications* is available from the Association for Media-Based Continuing Education for Engineers, Inc., 500 Tech Parkway NW, Suite 200A, Atlanta, Georgia 30313; telephone (404) 894-3362.

Acknowledgments

Many people have helped me during the preparation of this book. I would like to particularly acknowledge and thank the following people. K. C. Houston provided me with the opportunity to pursue this fascinating field. John Burruss, John Carson, Randall Frank, William Franta, Hal Folts, Govind Gupta, Stanislow Kesler, Ralph Martinez, and Robert Pokress reviewed all or a portion of the manuscript. Macmillan provided me with not one but three excellent editors: Sally Elliott, Peter Gordon, and Maria Colligan. Alice Wilding-White of A Way With Words, Inc., who typed the manuscript, and John Travis of Macmillan, who managed the book's production, once again did the job in record time. And finally, I thank my wife Tricia, who knew what we were getting into this time.

W.S.

CONTENTS

CHAPTER 1

Introduction

THE COMPUTER-COMMUNICATIONS REVOLUTION

The 1970s and early 1980s saw a merger of the fields of computer science and data communications that profoundly changed the technology, products, and companies of the now combined computer-communications industry. Although the consequences of this revolutionary merger are still being worked out, it is safe to say that the revolution has occurred, and any investigation of the field of data communications must be made within this new context.

The computer-communications revolution has produced several remarkable facts:

- There is no fundamental difference between data processing (computers) and data communications (transmission and switching equipment).
- There are no fundamental differences among data, voice, and video communications.
- The lines between single-processor computer, multi- processor computer, local network, metropolitan network, and long-haul network have blurred.

The result has been a growing overlap of the computer and communications industries, from component fabrication to system integration. The forthcoming result is the development of integrated systems that transmit and process all types

1

of data and information. Both the technology and the technical standards organizations are driving toward a single public system that integrates all communications and makes virtually all data and information sources around the world easily and uniformly accessible.

It is the ambitious purpose of this book to provide a unified view of the broad field of data and computer communications. The organization of the book reflects an attempt to break this massive subject into comprehensible parts and to build, piece by piece, a survey of the state of the art. This introductory chapter begins with a general model of communications. Then, a brief discussion introduces each of the three major parts of this book. Next, the all-important role of standards is introduced. Finally, a brief outline of the rest of the book is provided.

1-2

A COMMUNICATIONS MODEL

We begin our study with a simple model of communications. A block diagram of this model appears as Figure 1-1.

The fundamental purpose of data communications is to exchange information between two agents. In Figure 1-1, the information to be exchanged is a message labeled m. This information is represented as data g and is generally presented to a transmitter in the form of a time-varying signal, $g(t)$.

The terms data and information are defined in Table 1-1. These definitions seem rather academic, but for our purpose they might be given the following interpretation: data can be identified; data can be described; data do not necessarily represent something physical in terms of the measurable world; but above all data can be and should be used, namely for producing information. They also imply that data to one person may appear as information to another. Information is born when data are interpreted. To exchange information, then, requires access to elements of data and the ability to transmit them.

Returning now to Figure 1-1, the signal $g(t)$ is to be transmitted. Generally, the signal will not be in a form suitable for transmission and must be converted to a signal $s(t)$ that is in some sense matched to the characteristics of the transmission medium. The signal is then transmitted across the medium. On the other end, a signal $r(t)$, which may differ from $s(t)$, is received. This signal is then converted by a receiver into a form suitable for output. The converted signal $\tilde{g}(t)$, or data $\tilde{g}$, is an approximation or estimate of the input. Finally, the output device presents the estimated message, $\tilde{m}$, to the destination agent.

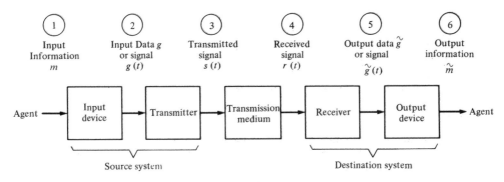

FIGURE 1-1. Simplified communications block diagram.

TABLE 1-1 Data and Information

Data	A representation of facts, concepts, or instructions in a formalized manner suitable for communication, interpretation, or processing by human beings or by automatic means
Information	The meaning that a human being assigns to data by means of the conventions applied to those data

Source: [ANSC82].

This simple narrative conceals a wealth of technical complexity. To attempt to elaborate, we present two examples, one using electronic mail, the other a telephone conversation.

For the case of electronic mail, consider that that input device and transmitter are components of a personal computer. The agent is a user who wishes to send a message to another user, for example, ''The meeting scheduled for March 25 is canceled'' (m). This string of characters is the information. The user activates the electronic mail package on the personal computer and enters the message via the keyboard (input device). The character string is briefly buffered in main memory. We can view it as a sequence of characters (g) or, more literally, a sequence of bits (g) in memory. The personal computer is connected to some transmission medium, such as a local network or a telephone line, by an I/O device (transmitter), such as a local network transceiver or a modem. The input data are transferred to the transmitter as a sequence of bits $[g(t)]$ or, more literally, a sequence of voltage shifts $[g(t)]$ on some communications bus or cable. The transmitter is connected directly to the medium and converts the incoming bits $[g(t)]$ into a signal $[s(t)]$ suitable for transmission; specific alternatives will be described in Chapter 3.

The transmitted signal $s(t)$ presented to the medium is subject to a number of impairments, discussed in Chapter 2, before it reaches the receiver. Thus the received signal $r(t)$ may differ to some degree from $s(t)$. The receiver will attempt to estimate the nature of $s(t)$, based on $r(t)$ and its knowledge of the medium, producing a sequence of bits $\tilde{g}(t)$. These bits are sent to the output personal computer, where they are briefly buffered in memory as a block of bits or characters ($\tilde{g}$). In many cases, the destination system will attempt to determine if an error has occurred and, if so, cooperate with the source system to eventually obtain a complete, error-free block of data. These data are then presented to the user via an output device, such as a printer or screen. The message ($\tilde{m}$) as viewed by the user will usually be an exact copy of the original message (m).

A variation is worth mentioning. The agent at either end may be a computer process rather than a human user. For example, messages might be stored on disk or tape to be automatically sent when a certain condition occurs (e.g., in the evening, when phone rates are lower). Or a message might be received when the user is unavailable and stored on disk or tape for later retrieval.

Now consider a telephone conversation. The agent in this case is the speaker, who generates a message (m) in the form of sound waves. The sound waves are converted by the telephone into electrical signals of the same frequency. These signals are transmitted without modification over the telephone line. Hence the input signal $g(t)$ and the transmitted signal $s(t)$ are identical. The signal $s(t)$ will suffer some distortion over the medium, so that $r(t)$ will not be identical to $s(t)$. Nevertheless, the signal $r(t)$ is converted back into a sound wave with no attempt at correction or improvement of signal quality. Thus $\tilde{m}$ is not an exact replica of

TABLE 1-2 Communication Tasks

Transmission system utilization
Interfacing
Signal generation
Synchronization
Exchange management
Error detection and correction
Flow control
Addressing
Routing
Recovery
Message formatting
Protection
System management

m. However, the received sound message is generally comprehensible to the listener.

Again, we mention a variation. In so-called digital telephones, the input signal $g(t)$ is digitized (i.e., converted into a sequence of bits). It is this sequence of bits, in the form of a sequence of voltage shifts, that is transmitted as $s(t)$.

These two examples give some idea of the nature of data communications. Another view is expressed in Table 1-2, which lists key tasks that must be performed in a data communications system. The list is somewhat arbitrary: Elements could be added; items on the list could be merged; and some items represent several tasks that are performed at different "levels" of the system. However, the list as it stands is suggestive of the scope of this book.

The first item, *transmission system utilization*, refers to the need to make efficient use of transmission facilities that are typically shared among a number of communicating devices. Various techniques (referred to as *multiplexing*) are used to allocate the total capacity of a transmission medium among a number of users. Congestion control techniques may be required to assure that the system is not overwhelmed by excessive demand for transmission services.

In order to communicate, a device must *interface* with the transmission system. All the forms of communication discussed in this book depend, at bottom, on the use of electromagnetic signals propagated over a transmission medium. Thus, once an interface is established, *signal generation* is required for communication. The properties of the signal, such as form and intensity, must be such that they are (1) capable of being propagated through the transmission system, and (2) interpretable as data at the receiver.

Not only must the signals be generated to conform to the requirements of the transmission system and receiver, but there must be some form of *synchronization* between transmitter and receiver. The receiver must be able to determine when a signal begins to arrive and when it ends. It must also know the duration of each signal element.

Beyond the basic matter of deciding on the nature and timing of signals, there are a variety of requirements for communication between two parties that might be collected under the term *exchange management*. If data are to be exchanged in both directions over a period of time, the two parties must cooperate. For example, for two parties to engage in a telephone conversation, one party must dial the number of the other, causing signals to be generated that result in the ringing of the called phone. The called party completes a connection by lifting the receiver. For data processing devices, more will be needed than simply establishing a connection; certain conventions must be decided upon. These conventions may include: whether both devices may transmit simultaneously or must take turns, the amount of data to be sent at one time, the format of the data, and what to do if certain contingencies such as an error arise.

The next two items might have been included under exchange management, but seem important enough to list separately. *Error detection and correction* are required in circumstances where errors cannot be tolerated. This is usually the case with data processing systems. For example, in transferring a file from one computer to another, it is simply not acceptable for the contents of the file to be accidentally altered. *Flow control* is required to assure that the source does not overwhelm the destination by sending data faster than they can be processed and absorbed.

Next, we mention the related but distinct concepts of *addressing* and *routing*. When a transmission facility is shared by more than two devices, a source system must somehow indicate the identity of the intended destination. The transmission system must assure that the destination system, and only that system, receives the data. Further, the transmission system may itself be a network through which various paths may be taken. A specific route through this network must be chosen.

Recovery is a concept distinct from that of error correction. Recovery techniques are needed in situations in which an information exchange, such as a data base transaction or file transfer, is interrupted due to a fault somewhere in the system. The objective is either to be able to resume activity at the point of interruption or at least to restore the state of the systems involved to the condition prior to the beginning of the exchange.

Message formatting has to do with an agreement between two parties as to the form of the data to be exchanged or transmitted. For example, both sides must use the same binary code for characters.

Frequently, it is important to provide some measure of *protection* in a data communications system. The sender of data may wish to be assured that only the intended receiver actually receives the data. And the receiver of data may wish to be assured that the received data have not been altered in transit and that the data actually come from the purported sender.

Finally, a data communications facility is a complex system that cannot create or run itself. *System management* capabilities are needed to configure the system, monitor its status, react to failures and overloads, and plan intelligently for future growth.

Thus we have gone from the simple idea of data communication between source and destination, to a six-stage model (Figure 1-1) of data communications, to a rather formidable list of data communications tasks. In this book, we further elaborate this list of tasks to describe and encompass the entire set of activities that can be classified under data and computer communications.

1-3

DATA COMMUNICATIONS

This book is organized into three parts. The first part deals primarily with the portion of Figure 1-1 between points 2 and 5. For want of a better name, we have given Part I the title Data Communications, although that term arguably encompasses some or even all of the topics of Parts II and III.

Since the purpose of this chapter is merely to preview the remainder of the book, little needs to be added to the discussion of the preceding section to introduce Part I. The topics that will be covered are:

- Data transmission.
- Data encoding.
- Digital data communication techniques.
- Data link control.
- Multiplexing.

Data transmission deals with the portion of Figure 1-1 between points 3 and 4. As was mentioned, the received signal will differ from the transmitted signal due to distortions, or transmission impairments. These distortions are in large part determined by the nature of the transmission medium used. *Data encoding* is the process of transforming input data or signals into signals that can be transmitted. The encoding technique is tailored to the method of data transmission to optimize performance.

The next two topics, *digital data communications techniques* and *data link control*, move the discussion from the simple transmission of data signals to true data communications. Referring again to Figure 1-1, the objective is to transfer data from the input device to the output device, with these two devices cooperating to minimize or eliminate error and to coordinate their actions. We will see that some rather complex techniques are required to achieve these objectives.

Finally, *multiplexing* refers to a variety of techniques used to make more efficient use of a transmission facility. In many cases, the capacity of a transmission facility exceeds the requirements for the transfer of data between two devices. That capacity can be shared among multiple transmitters by multiplexing a number of signals onto the same medium. In this case, the actual transmission path is referred to as a *circuit* or *link*, and the portion of capacity dedicated to each pair of transmitter/ receivers is referred to as a *channel*.

1-4

DATA COMMUNICATION NETWORKING

In its simplest form data communication takes place between two devices that are directly connected by some form of point-to-point transmission medium. Often, however, it is impractical for two devices to be directly, point-to-point connected. This is so for one (or both) of the following contingencies:

- The devices are very far apart. It would be inordinately expensive, for example, to string a dedicated link between two devices thousands of miles apart.
- There is a set of devices, each of which may require a link to many of the others at various times. Examples are all of the telephones in the world and all of the terminals and computers owned by a single organization. Except for the case of a very few devices, it is impractical to provide a dedicated wire between each pair of devices.

The solution to this problem is to attach each device to a *communication network*. Figure 1-2 illustrates this concept in a general way. We have a collection of devices that wish to communicate; we will refer to them generically as *stations*. The stations may be computers, terminals, telephones, or other communicating devices. Each

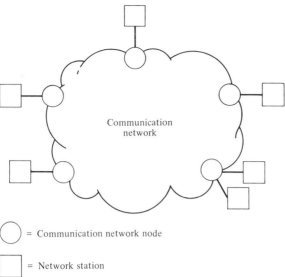

= Communication network node

= Network station

FIGURE 1-2. Interconnection via a communication network.

station attaches to a network *node*. The set of nodes to which stations attach is the boundary of a communication network that is capable of transferring data between pairs of stations.

Communication networks may be categorized based on the architecture and techniques used to transfer data. In this book we will be concerned with the following types of communication networks:

- Switched networks.
  - Circuit-switched networks.
  - Packet-switched networks.
- Broadcast networks.
  - Packet radio networks.
  - Satellite networks.
  - Local networks.

In a *switched communication network* (Figure 1-3), data are transferred from source to destination through a series of intermediate nodes. These nodes (including the boundary nodes) are not concerned with the content of the data; rather, their purpose is to provide a switching facility that will move the data from node to node until they reach their destination.

In a *circuit-switched network*, a dedicated communications path is established between two stations through the nodes of the network. That path is a connected sequence of physical links between nodes. On each link, a logical channel is dedicated to the connection. Data generated by the source station are transmitted along the dedicated path as rapidly as possible. At each node, incoming data are routed or switched to the appropriate outgoing channel without delay. The most common example of circuit switching is the telephone network.

A quite different approach is used in a *packet-switched network*. In this case, it is not necessary to dedicate transmission capacity along a path through the network. Rather, data are sent out in a sequence of small chunks, called *packets*. Each packet

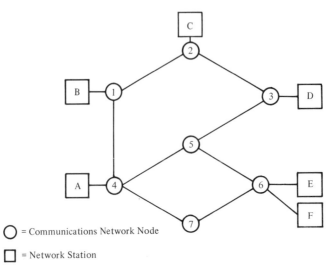

O = Communications Network Node

□ = Network Station

FIGURE 1-3. Generic switching network.

is passed through the network from node to node along some path leading from source to destination. At each node, the entire packet is received, stored briefly, and then transmitted to the next node. Packet-switched networks are commonly used for terminal-to-computer and computer-to-computer communications.

With a *broadcast communication network*, there are no intermediate switching nodes (Figure 1-4). At each station, there is a transmitter/receiver that communicates over a medium shared by other stations. A transmission from any one station is broadcast to and received by all other stations. A simple example of this is a CB radio system, in which all users tuned to the same channel may communicate. We will be more concerned with networks used to link terminals and computers. In the latter case, data are often transmitted in packets. Since the medium is shared, only one station at a time can transmit a packet.

Two similar types of broadcast networks are packet radio networks and satellite networks. In both cases, stations transmit and receive via antenna, and all stations share the same channel or radio frequency. In a *packet-radio network*, stations are within transmission range of each other, and broadcast directly to each other. In a *satellite network*, data are not transferred directly from transmitter to receiver but are relayed via satellite: each station transmits to the satellite and receives from the satellite.

Another common instance of broadcasting is the *local network*. A local network is a communication network that is confined to a small area, such as a single building or a small cluster of buildings. The two most common types of local networks are depicted in Figure 1-4c and d. In a *bus local network*, all stations are attached to a common wire or cable. A transmission by any one station propagates the length of the medium in both directions and can be received by all other stations. The *ring local network* consists of a closed loop, with each station attached to a repeating element. A transmission from any station circulates around the ring past all other stations, and can be received by each station as it goes by.

Each of these types of communication network, in its own fashion, overcomes the problems cited at the beginning of this section. A detailed discussion of these networks comprises Part II of this book.

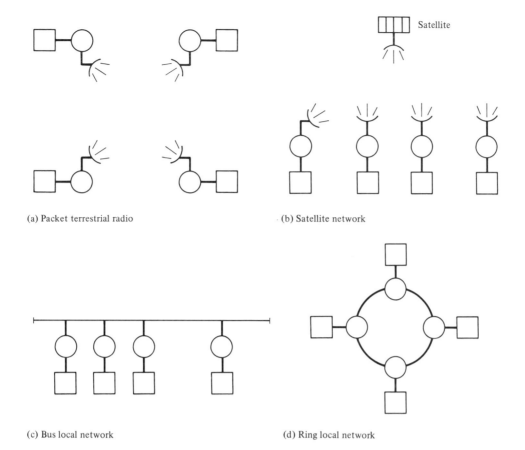

(a) Packet terrestrial radio   (b) Satellite network

(c) Bus local network   (d) Ring local network

FIGURE 1-4. Broadcast communication networks.

1-5

COMPUTER COMMUNICATIONS ARCHITECTURE

As we have mentioned, the term "data communications" as used in this book refers primarily to the area between points 2 and 5 of Figure 1-1. That is, it is concerned with the transfer of a signal or set of data between two points, with no regard for the meaning or intent of those data. Similarly, communication networks are concerned primarily with such a data transfer, again with no regard for data content.

However, when computers, terminals, and/or other data processing devices exchange data, the scope of concern is much broader. Consider, for example, the transfer of a file between two computers. There must be a data path between the two computers, either directly (Figure 1-1) or via a communication network (Figure 1-2). But more is needed. Typical tasks to be performed:

1. The source system must either activate the direct data communication path, or inform the communication network of the identity of the desired destination system.
2. The source system must ascertain that the destination system is prepared to received data.

3. The file transfer application on the source system must ascertain that the file management program on the destination system is prepared to accept and store the file.
4. If the file formats used on the two systems are incompatible, one or the other system must perform a format translation function.

It is clear that there must be a high degree of cooperation between the two computer systems. The exchange of information between computers for the purpose of cooperative action is generally referred to as *computer communications*. Similarly, when two or more computers are interconnected via a communication network, the set of computer stations is referred to as a *computer network*. Since a similar level of cooperation is required between a user at a terminal and a computer, these terms are often used when some of the communicating entities are terminals.

In discussing computer communications and computer networks, two concepts are paramount:

- Protocols.
- Computer-communications architecture.

A protocol is used for communication between entities in different systems. The terms "entity" and "system" are used in a very general sense. Examples of entities are user application programs, file transfer packages, data-base management systems, electronic mail facilities, and terminals. Examples of systems are computers, terminals, and remote sensors. Note that in some cases the entity and the system in which it resides are coextensive (e.g., terminals). In general, an *entity* is anything capable of sending or receiving information, and a *system* is a physically distinct object that contains one or more entities. For two entities to communicate successfully, they must "speak the same language." What is communicated, how it is communicated, and when it is communicated must conform to some mutually acceptable conventions between the entities involved. The conventions are referred to as a *protocol*, which may be defined as a set of rules governing the exchange of data between two entities. The key elements of a protocol are:

- *Syntax:* includes such things as data format and signal levels.
- *Semantics:* includes control information for coordination and error handling.
- *Timing:* includes speed matching and sequencing.

Having introduced the concept of a protocol, we can now introduce the concept of a computer communications architecture. We make the observation that the task of communicating between two entities on different systems is too complicated to be handled by a single process or module. Figure 1-5 returns again to the file transfer application. Tasks 3 and 4, listed above, might be performed by an application-oriented protocol implemented in a file transfer package. For the two file transfer packages to exchange data, each invokes a network services module, which performs task 2 and exchanges data with its local file transfer module. To perform task 2, the two network services modules employ a system-to-system protocol. Finally, to actually transfer the data, the network services module must perform task 1, by engaging in a network access protocol with the boundary node of the communication network. Thus, instead of a single protocol, there is a structured set of protocols that implement the communication function. That structure is referred to as a *computer-communications architecture*.

As suggested by Figure 1-5, the various elements of the structured set of protocols are layered, or form a hierarchy. This is even more clearly indicated in Figure 1-6, which depicts the *open systems interconnection* (OSI) model. The OSI

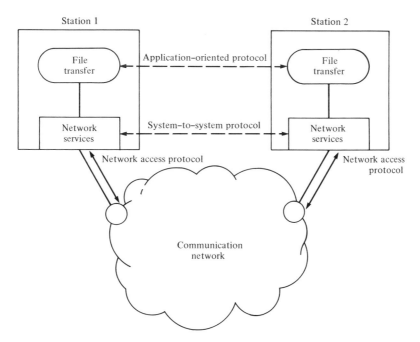

FIGURE 1-5.   Example of computer communications architecture.

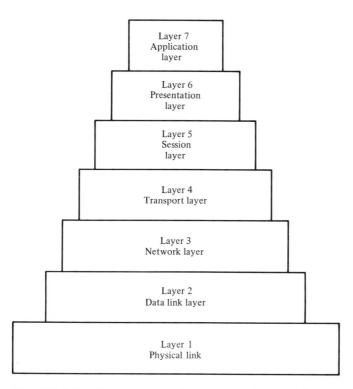

FIGURE 1-6.   Open systems interconnection model.

TABLE 1-3 The OSI Layers

1. Physical	Concerned with transmission of unstructured bit stream over physical medium; deals with the mechanical, electrical, functional, and procedural characteristics to access the physical medium
2. Data link	Provides for the reliable transfer of information across the physical link; sends blocks of data (frames) with the necessary synchronization, error control, and flow control
3. Network	Provides upper layers with independence from the data transmission and switching technologies used to connect systems; responsible for establishing, maintaining, and terminating connections
4. Transport	Provides reliable, transparent transfer of data between end points; provides end-to-end error recovery and flow control
5. Session	Provides the control structure for communication between applications; establishes, manages, and terminates connections (sessions) between cooperating applications
6. Presentation	Provide independence to the application processes from differences in data representation (syntax)
7. Application	Provides access to the OSI environment for users and also provides distributed information services

model was developed by the International Organization for Standardization as a model of a computer communications architecture. Table 1-3 briefly defines the functions performed at each layer. The intent of the OSI model is that protocols be developed to perform the functions of each layer. Part III of this book will examine protocols in detail, and make use of this model for that purpose.

1-6

STANDARDS-MAKING ORGANIZATIONS

It has long been accepted in the communications industry that standards are required to govern the physical, electrical, and procedural characteristics of communication equipment. In the past, this view has not been embraced by the computer industry. Whereas communication equipment vendors recognize that their equipment will generally interface to and communicate with other vendors' equipment, computer vendors have traditionally attempted to monopolize their customers. The proliferation of computers and distributed processing has made that an untenable position. Computers from different vendors must communicate with each other and, with the ongoing evolution of protocol standards, customers will no longer accept special-purpose protocol conversion software development. The day is quickly coming when standards will permeate all of the areas of technology discussed in this book.

Throughout the book, especially in Part III, we will describe the most important standards that are in use or being developed for various aspects of data and computer communications. Some of the standards-making bodies that are most important to our discussion:

- *International Organization for Standardization (ISO):* voluntary, nontreaty organization whose members are designated standards bodies of participating nations, and nonvoting observer organizations. One of ISO's technical committees (TC97) is concerned with information systems. This committee developed the OSI model and is developing protocol standards at various layers of the model.

- *International Telegraph and Telephone Consultative Committee (CCITT):* U.N. treaty organization made up primarily of the Postal, Telegraph, and Telephone (PTT) authorities of the member countries. The U.S. representative is the Department of State. As its name indicates, CCITT is involved in a broad range of communication areas. The organization works closely with ISO on communication protocol standards.

- *American National Standards Institute (ANSI):* nonprofit, nongovernmental organization composed of manufacturers, users, communications carriers, and other interested organizations. It is the national clearinghouse for voluntary standards in the United States. It is also the U.S.-designated voting member of the ISO. ANSI's interests roughly parallel those of ISO.

- *National Bureau of Standards (NBS):* part of the Department of Commerce. It issues Federal Information Processing Standards (FIPS) for equipment sold to the federal government. The Department of Defense (DOD) need not, and frequently does not, comply. The concerns of NBS are broad, encompassing the areas of interest of both CCITT and ISO. NBS is attempting to satisfy federal government requirements with standards that, as far as possible, are compatible with international standards.

- *Federal Telecommunications Standards Committee (FTSC):* interagency advisory board responsible for establishing standards (FED-STD) for federal procurements to assure interoperability of government-owned communications equipment. FTSC tends to concentrate on standards corresponding to the lower layers of the OSI model, whereas NBS is more focused on higher layers. However, there is an unresolved area of overlap between the two sets of standards.

- *Defense Communications Agency (DCA):* promulgates communications-related military standards (MIL-STD). DOD feels that its requirements in some areas are unique, and this is reflected in DCA standards that are unlike those used elsewhere.

- *Electronics Industries Association (EIA):* trade association of electronics firms and a member of ANSI. It is concerned primarily with standards that fit into OSI layer 1 (physical).

- *Institute of Electrical and Electronics Engineers (IEEE):* professional society and also a member of ANSI. Their concerns have been primarily with the lowest two layers of the OSI model (physical and data link).

- *European Computer Manufacturers Association (ECMA):* composed of computer suppliers selling in Europe, including the European divisions of some American companies. It is devoted exclusively to the cooperative development of standards applicable to computer technology. ECMA serves as a nonvoting member of CCITT and ISO and also issues its own standards. Because of the rapidity of their efforts, they have had considerable influence on OSI work.

Table 1-4 lists some of the standards developed by these organizations. At a first reading, the standards indicated will be unfamiliar. However, this table will serve as a handy reference as the book proceeds.

There are a number of advantages and disadvantages to the standards-making process. We list here the most striking ones. The principal advantages of standards are:

- A standard assures that there will be a large market for a particular piece of equipment or software. This encourages mass production, and in some cases,

TABLE 1-4 Standards and Standards—Making Organizations

Organization	Areas of Interest	Standards
International Organization for Standardization (ISO)	OSI model, layers 4–7	Transport, session
International Telegraph and Telephone Consultative Committee (CCITT)	Communications networks, telematics	X.25, X.75, X.21
National Bureau of Standards (NBS)	Layers 2–7	Transport
Defense Communications Agency (DCA)	Layers 3–7	TCP, IP
Institute of Electrical and Electronic Engineers (IEEE)	Layers 1 and 2	IEEE 802
American National Standards Institute (ANSI)	Layers 1–7	X3T9.5
Electronics Industries Association (EIA)	Layer 1	RS-232-C, RS-449
Federal Telecommunications Standards Committee (FTSC)	Layers 1–3	Encryption
European Computer Manufacturers Association (ECMA)	Layers 1–7	Input to ISO

the use of large-scale- integration (LSI) or very-large-scale-integration (VLSI) techniques, resulting in lower costs.

• A standard allows products from multiple vendors to communicate, giving the purchaser more flexibility in equipment selection and use.

The principal disadvantages are:

• A standard tends to freeze the technology. By the time a standard is developed, subjected to review and compromise, and promulgated, more efficient techniques are possible.

• There are multiple standards for the same thing. This is not a disadvantage of standards per se, but of the current way things are done. Fortunately, in recent years the various standards-making organizations have begun to cooperate more closely. Nevertheless, there are still areas where multiple conflicting standards exist.

1-7

OUTLINE OF THE BOOK

This chapter, of course, serves as an introduction to the entire book. A brief synopsis of the remaining chapters follows.

Data Transmission

The principles of data transmission underlie all of the concepts and techniques presented in this book. To understand the need for encoding, multiplexing, switching, error control, and so on, the reader must understand the behavior of data signals propagated through a transmission medium. Chapter 2 provides an understanding of the distinction between digital and analog data and digital and analog transmission. Concepts of attenuation and noise are introduced, and the various transmission media described.

Data Encoding

Data come in both analog (continuous) and digital (discrete) form. For transmission, input data (point 2, Figure 1-1) must be encoded as an electrical signal (point 3, Figure 1-1) that is tailored to the characteristics of the transmission medium. Both analog and digital data can be represented by either analog or digital signals; each of the four cases is discussed in Chapter 3.

Digital Data Communication Techniques

In Chapter 4 the emphasis shifts from data transmission to data communications. For two devices linked by a transmission medium to exchange digital data, a high degree of cooperation is required. Typically, data are transmitted one bit at a time over the medium. The timing (rate, duration, spacing) of these bits must be the same for transmitter and receiver. Two common communication techniques—asynchronous and synchronous—are explored. This chapter also looks at techniques for detecting bit errors. Finally in this chapter, we look at transmission line interfaces. Typically, digital data devices do not attach to and signal across a transmission medium directly. Rather, this process is mediated through a standardized interface.

Data Link Control

True cooperative exchange of digital data between two devices requires some form of data link control. Chapter 5 examines the fundamental techniques common to all data link control protocols, and then examines the most commonly used protocols.

Multiplexing

Transmission facilities are, by and large, expensive. It is often the case that two communication stations will not utilize the full capacity of a data link. For efficiency, it should be possible to share that capacity. The generic term for such sharing is multiplexing.

Chapter 6 concentrates on the three most common types of multiplexing techniques. The first, frequency-division multiplexing (FDM), is the most widespread and is familiar to anyone who has ever used a radio or television set. The second is a particular case of time-division multiplexing (TDM) often known as synchronous TDM. This is commonly used for multiplexing digitized voice streams. The third type is another form of TDM that is more complex but potentially more efficient than synchronous TDM; it is referred to as statistical or asynchronous TDM.

Communication Networking Techniques

Chapter 7 serves as an overview of Part II. The two switched communication network techniques mentioned earlier, circuit switching and packet switching, as well as the less well known message switching, are introduced and compared. The discussion gives insight into the relative performance of these techniques. Broadcast networks are also introduced, and relevant access techniques are discussed.

Circuit Switching

Any treatment of the technology and architecture of circuit-switched networks must of necessity focus on the internal operation of a single switch. This is in contrast to packet-switched networks, which are best explained by the collective behavior of the set of switches that make up a network. Thus Chapter 8 begins by examining digital switching concepts, including space- and time-division switching. This leads to a discussion of the devices most commonly used to build circuit-switched local networks (although these are rarely thought of as "true" local networks): digital data switches. We are then ready to look at the computerized branch exchange, which supports both digital data devices and telephones. Finally, the concepts of a multinode circuit-switched network are discussed using the public telecommunications network as an example.

Packet Switching

There are three main technical problems associated with a packet-switched network, and each is examined in Chapter 9:

- *Routing:* Since the source and destination station are not directly connected, the network must route each packet, from node to node, through the network.
- *Traffic control:* The amount of traffic entering and transiting the network must be regulated for efficient, stable, and fair performance.
- *Error control:* Inevitably, packets will be lost in the network. Some networks ignore this contingency; most take measures to at least partially alleviate the suffering of the attached stations.

The key features in each of the foregoing areas are presented, and the discussion is supported by examples from specific systems currently in operation.

Radio and Satellite Networks

Chapter 10 begins the discussion of broadcast networks by looking at the related technologies of packet-radio and satellite networks. In each case, the overall architecture is examined, followed by a detailed discussion of the techniques by which the common transmission capacity is shared.

Local Networks

The nature of a local network is determined primarily by three factors: transmission medium, topology, and the technique used to share access to the transmission medium. The bulk of Chapter 11 is devoted to these topics, together with a look at local network performance. Throughout, reference is made to standards developed for local networks by two committees: IEEE 802 and ANS X3T9.5. These are described briefly at the end of the chapter.

Protocols and Architectures

Chapter 12 introduces the subject of computer-communications architecture and motivates the need for a layered architecture with protocols defined at each layer. Protocols are defined and the important constituent elements discussed. The Open Systems Interconnection (OSI) model is introduced and justified.

Although the OSI model is almost universally accepted as the framework for discourse in this area, there is another point of view which grows out of the extensive research and practical experience of ARPANET. This viewpoint, which is characterized by a hierarchy of protocols, is also presented.

Both of the foregoing viewpoints describe the communications function in terms of an architecture, which specifies protocols and their interrelationships. To lend concreteness to the discussion, two commercial architectures are presented: IBM's SNA and DEC's DNA.

Network Access Protocols

When two stations communicate across a network, a network access protocol between station and network is needed. The requirements for such a protocol differ significantly for circuit-switched, packet-switched, and broadcast networks. After a review of general principles, each of these three cases is examined in Chapter 13 using a specific protocol standard.

Internetworking

Packet-switched and packet broadcasting networks grew out of a need to allow the computer user to have access to resources beyond that available in a single system. In a similar fashion, the resources of a single network are often inadequate to meet users' needs. Because the networks that might be of interest exhibit so many differences, it is impractical to consider merging them into a single network. Rather, what is needed is the ability to interconnect various networks so that any two stations on any of the constituent networks can communicate. This ability is referred to as internetworking, and protocols have been developed for this purpose. Chapter 14 includes an examination of the requirements for an internetworking capability and the various approaches that can be taken to satisfy those requirements. Then several standardized protocols are examined.

Transport Protocols

The transport protocol (OSI layer 4) is the keystone of the whole concept of a computer communications architecture. It can also be one of the most complex of protocols. Chapter 15 examines the mechanisms of transport protocols and the services they provide. The two major standardization efforts for transport protocols are also described.

Process/Application Protocols

The higher layers of a communications architecture are those most visible to the ultimate user. They must support a wide variety of process and application requirements. This is a broad subject, and only a representative sample of techniques are examined in Chapter 16.

Integrated Services Digital Network

The *integrated services digital network* (ISDN) is a projected worldwide public telecommunications network that will service a wide variety of user needs. The ISDN will be defined by the standardization of user interfaces, and will be implemented as a set of digital switches and paths supporting a broad range of traffic types and employing many of the concepts discussed in this book.

Because the ISDN does not yet exist and is defined only by an evolving set of standards (being developed on a truly massive scale, both in terms of content and participants), Chapter 17 can only suggest the likely characteristics of the future ISDN.

PART I

DATA
COMMUNICATIONS

This first part of the book deals with the transfer of data between two devices that are directly connected; that is, the two devices are linked by a single transmission path rather than a network.

Chapter 2 looks at the key aspects of data transmission. A distinction is drawn between the concepts of analog and digital, in the context of data, signaling, and transmission. The effect of impairments and choice of medium on transmission are also examined. Chapter 3 then reviews the various means of encoding data for transmission.

With Chapter 4, the text moves from the simple transmission of data to the additional processing required to achieve true data communications. This chapter introduces some of the basic data communication processing techniques. Chapter 5 examines data link control procedures, which are designed to turn an unreliable transmission medium into a reliable data link. Chapter 6 examines various methods of multiplexing data signals to achieve more efficient utilization of the transmission medium

Data Transmission

The successful transmission of data depends principally on two factors: the quality of the signal being transmitted and the characteristics of the transmission medium. The objective of this chapter is to provide the reader with an intuitive feeling for the nature of these two factors.

The first section presents some concepts and terms from the field of electrical engineering. This should provide sufficient background to deal with the remainder of the chapter. Section 2-2 clarifies the use of the terms "analog" and "digital." Either analog or digital data may be transmitted using either analog or digital signals. Furthermore, it is common for intermediate processing to be performed between source and destination, and this processing has either an analog or digital character.

Section 2-3 looks at the various impairments that may introduce errors into the data during transmission. The chief impairments are attenuation, delay distortion, and the various forms of noise.

Finally, Section 2-4 looks at the most common types of transmission media, and the behavior of signals on those media.

2-1

CONCEPTS AND TERMINOLOGY

In this section we introduce some concepts and terms that will be referred to throughout the rest of the chapter and, indeed, throughout Part I.

Transmission Terminology

Data transmission occurs between transmitter and receiver over some *transmission medium*. The medium may be *hardwire*, which physically guides the transmitted signal; examples are twisted-pair telephone wires, coaxial cables, and fiber optic cables. With *softwire* media, the signal is not physically confined; examples are propagation through air, vacuum, and seawater.

The term *direct link* is used to refer to the transmission path between two devices if signals propagate directly from transmitter to receiver with no intermediate devices, other than amplifiers or repeaters used to increase signal strength. Both parts of Figure 1-1 depicts a direct link. Note that this term can apply to both hardwire and softwire media.

A hardwire transmission medium is *point-to-point* if it provides a direct link between two devices and those are the only two devices sharing the medium (Figure 2-1a). In a *multipoint* hardwire configuration, more than two devices share the same medium (Figure 2-1b).

A channel or transmission medium may be simplex, half-duplex, or full duplex. In *simplex* transmission, signals are transmitted in only one direction; one station is transmitter and the other is receiver. In *half-duplex* operation, both stations may transmit, but only one at a time. In *full-duplex* operation, both stations may transmit simultaneously. In the latter case, the medium is carrying signals in both directions at the same time. How this can be is explained in due course.

We should note that the definitions just given are the ones in common use in the United States (ANSI definitions). In Europe (CCITT definitions), the term "simplex" is used to correspond to half-duplex as defined above, and "duplex" is used to correspond to full-duplex as defined above.

Frequency, Spectrum, and Bandwidth

At point 3 in Figure 1-1, a signal is generated by the transmitter and transmitted over a medium. The signal is a function of time, but it can also be expressed as a

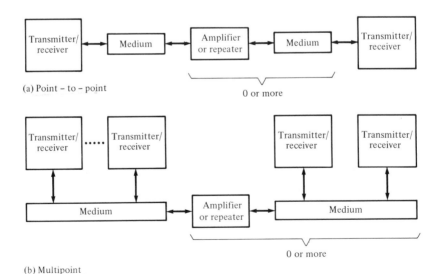

FIGURE 2-1. Hardware transmission configurations.

Amplitude (volts)

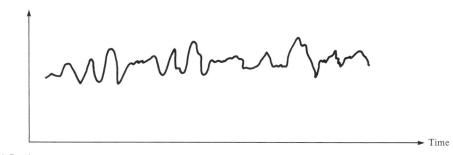

Time

(a) Continuous

Amplitude

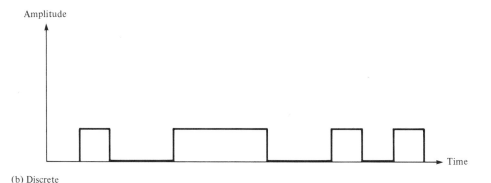

Time

(b) Discrete

FIGURE 2-2. Continuous and discrete signals.

function of frequency; that is, the signal consists of components of different frequencies. It turns out that the "frequency-domain" view of a signal is far more important to an understanding of data transmission than a "time domain" view. Both views are introduced below.

Time-Domain Concepts.   We begin by looking at a signal as a function of time. A signal $s(t)$ is *continuous* if

$$\lim_{t \to a} s(t) = s(a)$$

for all a. In words, there are no breaks or discontinuities in the signal. A signal is *discrete* if it takes on only a finite number of values. Figure 2-2 shows examples of both kinds of signals. The continuous signal might represent speech, and the discrete signal might represent binary 1's and 0's.

A signal $s(t)$ is *periodic* if and only if

$$s(t + T) = s(t) \quad -\infty < t < +\infty$$

where the constant T is the *period* of the signal (T must be the smallest value that satisfies the equation). Otherwise, a signal is aperiodic.

Figure 2-3 displays portions of two periodic signals, the sine wave and the square wave. Three important characteristics of a periodic signal are amplitude, frequency, and phase. The *amplitude* is the instantaneous value of a signal at any time. Since the signals discussed in this book are all electrical or electromagnetic waves, am-

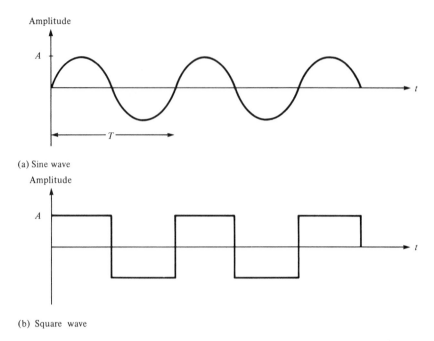

(a) Sine wave

(b) Square wave

FIGURE 2-3.   Examples of periodic signals.

plitude is measured in volts. The *frequency* is the inverse of the period $(1/T)$, or the number of repetitions of the period per second; it is expressed in cycles per second, or hertz (Hz). *Phase* is a measure of the relative position in time within a single period of a signal. As an example, Figure 2-4 shows two signals that are out of phase by $\pi/2$ radians (2π radians $= 360° = 1$ period).

Thus we can express a sinusoid as

$$s(t) = A \sin(2\pi ft + \theta)$$

where A is the maximum amplitude, f is the frequency, and θ is the phase. Note that the sine wave in Figure 2-3 can be expressed as either

$$s(t) = A \sin(2\pi ft)$$

or

$$s(t) = A \cos(2\pi ft - \pi/2)$$

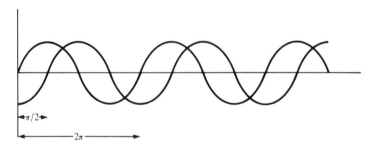

FIGURE 2-4.   Example of a phase difference.

Frequency Domain Concepts. So far, we have viewed a signal as a function of time. But any signal can also be viewed as a function of frequency. For example, the signal

$$s(t) = \sin 2\pi\, ft + 1/3\sin 3(2\pi f)t + 1/5\sin 5(2\pi f)t$$

is shown in Figure 2-5. The components of this signal are just sine waves of frequencies f, $3f$, and $5f$. Indeed, it can be shown, using a discipline known as Fourier analysis, that any signal is made up of components at various frequencies, where each component is a sinusoid. For the interested reader, this subject is pursued in Appendix 2A at the end of this chapter.

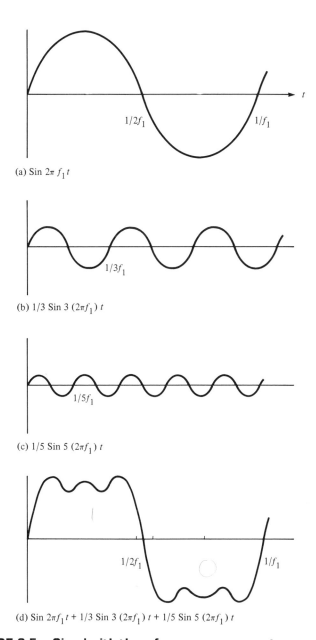

(a) Sin $2\pi\, f_1 t$

(b) 1/3 Sin 3 $(2\pi f_1)\, t$

(c) 1/5 Sin 5 $(2\pi f_1)\, t$

(d) Sin $2\pi f_1 t + 1/3$ Sin 3 $(2\pi f_1)\, t + 1/5$ Sin 5 $(2\pi f_1)\, t$

FIGURE 2-5. Signal with three frequency components.

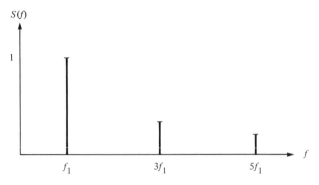

(a) $s(t) = \text{Sin } 2\pi f_1 t + 1/3 \text{ Sin } 3 \ (2\pi f_1) \ t + 1/5 \text{ Sin } 5 \ (2\pi f_1) \ t$

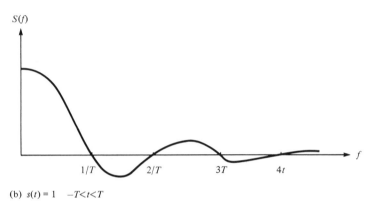

(b) $s(t) = 1 \quad -T < t < T$

FIGURE 2-6. Frequency-domain representations.

So, we can say that for each signal there is a time-domain function $s(t)$ that specifies the amplitude of the signal at each instant of time. Similarly, there is a frequency-domain function $S(f)$ that specifies the constituent frequencies of the signal. Figure 2-6a shows the frequency-domain function for the signal of Figure 2-5. Note that in this case, $S(f)$ is discrete. Figure 2-6b shows the frequency domain function for a single square pulse that has value 1 between $-T/2$ and $T/2$, and 0 elsewhere. Note that $S(f)$ is continuous, and that it has nonzero values indefinitely, although the magnitude of the frequency components becomes smaller for larger f. This is not uncommon for real signals.

The *spectrum* of a signal is the range of frequencies that it contains. For the signal of Figure 2-5, the spectrum extends from f_1 to $5f_1$. The *absolute bandwidth* of a signal is the width of the spectrum. In the case above, the bandwidth is $4f_1$. Many signals, such as that of Figure 2-6b, have an infinite bandwidth. However, most of the energy in the signal is contained in a relatively narrow band of frequencies. This band is referred to as the *effective bandwidth*, or just *bandwidth*.

There is a direct relationship between data rate and bandwidth: the higher the data rate of a signal, the greater its bandwidth. Looked at the other way, the greater the bandwidth of a signal, the higher the data rate that can be transmitted using the signal. As a very simple example, consider again Figure 2-5d. Suppose that we let a positive pulse represent binary 1 and a negative pulse represent binary 0. Then the signal represents the binary stream 1010. . . The duration of each pulse is $1/2f_1$, thus the data rate is $2f_1$ bits per second (bps). We have already observed

Amplitude

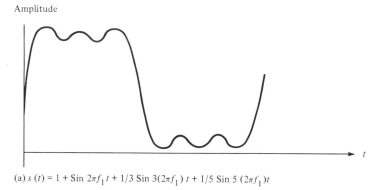

(a) $s(t) = 1 + \text{Sin } 2\pi f_1 t + 1/3 \text{ Sin } 3(2\pi f_1) t + 1/5 \text{ Sin } 5 (2\pi f_1)t$

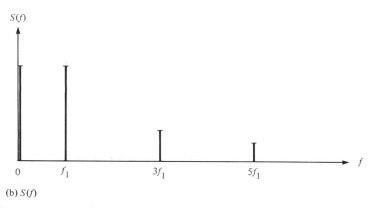

(b) $S(f)$

FIGURE 2-7. Signal with dc component.

that the bandwidth is $4f_1$. For $f_1 = 1000$ Hz, the data rate is 2000 bps and the bandwidth is 4000 Hz. Doubling either the data rate or the bandwidth doubles the other parameter.

Another observation worth making is this: If we think of the bandwidth of a signal as being centered about some frequency, referred to as the *center frequency*, then the higher the center frequency, the higher the potential data rate. Consider that if a signal is centered at 2000 Hz, its maximum possible bandwidth is 4000 Hz. As the center frequency increases, so does the potential bandwidth, and hence the potential data rate.

One final term to define is *dc component*. If a signal includes a component of zero frequency, that component is a direct current (dc) or constant component. For example, Figure 2-7 shows the result of adding a dc component to the signal of Figure 2-5. With no dc component, a signal has an average amplitude of zero. With a dc component, it has a frequency term at $f = 0$, and a nonzero average value.

Signal Strength

An important parameter in any transmission system is the strength of the signal being transmitted. As a signal propagates along a transmission medium, there will be a loss, or *attenuation*, of signal strength. To compensate, amplifiers may be inserted at various points to impart a gain in signal strength.

It is customary to express gains, losses, and relative levels in decibels because:

- Signal strength often falls off logarithmically, so loss is easily expressed in terms of the decibel, which is a logarithmic unit.
- Gains and losses in a cascaded transmission path can be calculated with simple addition and subtraction.

The decibel is a measure of the difference in two power levels:

$$N_{dB} = 10\log_{10} \frac{P_1}{P_2}$$

where

N_{dB} = number of decibels
$P_{1,2}$ = power values
$\log_{10}$ = logarithm to the base 10 (from now on, we will simply use log to mean $\log_{10}$)

For example, if a signal with a power of 10 mw is inserted onto a transmission line and the measured power some distance away is 5 mw, the loss can be expressed as

$$LOSS = 10\log(5/10) = 10(-0.3) = -3 \text{ dB}$$

Note that the decibel is a measure of relative, not absolute, difference. A loss from 1000 w to 500 w is also a -3dB loss.

The decibel is also used to measure the difference in voltage, taking into account that power is proportional to the square of the voltage:

$$P = \frac{V^2}{R}$$

where

P = power dissipated across resistance R
V = voltage across resistance R

Thus

$$N_{dB} = 10 \log \frac{P_1}{P_2} = 10 \log \frac{V_1^2/R}{V_2^2/R} = 20 \log \frac{V_1}{V_2}$$

Decibel values refer to relative magnitudes or changes in magnitude, not to an absolute level. It is convenient to be able to refer to an absolute level of power or voltage in decibels so that gain and losses may be easily calculated. Thus several derived units are in common use.

The dBW (decibel-watt) is used extensively in microwave applications. The value of 1 w is selected as reference and defined to be 0 dBW. The absolute decibel level of power in dBW is defined as:

$$Power(dBW) = 10 \log \frac{Power(W)}{1 W}$$

For example, a power of 1000 w is 30 dBW. A power of 1 mw is -30 dBW.

The dBmV (decibel-millivolt) is used in video applications and is an absolute decibel unit with 0 dBmV equivalent to 1 mV. Thus

$$\text{Voltage(dBmV)} = 20 \log_{10} \frac{\text{Voltage(mV)}}{1 \text{ mV}}$$

The voltage levels are assumed to be across a 75-ohm resistance.

The decibel is convenient for determining overall gain or loss in a system. For example, consider a point-to-point link that consists of a transmission line with a single amplifier part way along. If the loss on the first portion of line is 13 dB, the gain of the amplifier is 30 dB, and the loss on the second portion of line is 40 dB, then the overall gain (loss) is $-13 + 30 - 40 = -23$ dB. If the original signal strength is -30 dBW, the received signal strength is -53 dBW.

2-2

ANALOG AND DIGITAL DATA TRANSMISSION

In transmitting data from a source to a destination, one must be concerned with the nature of the data, the actual physical means used to propagate the data, and what processing or adjustments may be required along the way to assure that the received data are intelligible. For all of these considerations, the crucial point is whether we are dealing with analog or digital entities.

The terms *analog* and *digital* correspond, roughly, to continuous and discrete, respectively. These two terms are used frequently in data communications in at least three contexts:

- Data.
- Signaling.
- Transmission.

We discussed data, as distinct from information, in Chapter 1. For present purposes, we define *data* as entities that convey meaning. *Signals* are electric or electromagnetic encoding of data. *Signaling* is the act of propagating the signal along a suitable medium. Finally, *transmission* is the communication of data by the propagation and processing of signals. In what follows, we try to make these abstract concepts clear, by discussing the terms "analog" and "digital" in these three contexts.

Data

The concepts of analog and digital data are simple enough. *Analog data* take on continuous values on some interval. For example, voice and video are continuously varying patterns of intensity. Most data collected by sensors, such as temperature and pressure, are continuous-valued. *Digital data* take on discrete values; examples are text and integers.

The most familiar example of analog data is audio or acoustic data, which, in the form of sound waves, can be perceived directly by human beings. Figure 2-8 shows the acoustic spectrum for human speech. Frequency components of speech may be found between 20 Hz and 20 kHz. Although much of the energy in speech is concentrated at the lower frequencies, tests have shown that frequencies up to 600 to 700 Hz add very little to the intelligibility of speech to the human ear. The dashed line more accurately reflects the intelligibility or emotional content of speech.

Another common example of analog data is video. Here it is easier to characterize the data in terms of the viewer (destination) of the TV screen rather than the original

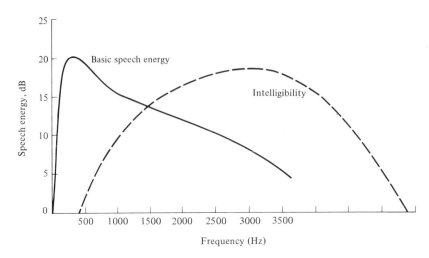

FIGURE 2-8. Acoustic spectrum for speech. Source: [FREE81]

scene (source) that is recorded by the TV camera. To produce a picture on the screen, an electron beam scans across the surface of the screen from left to right and top to bottom. For black-and-white television, the amount of illumination produced (on a scale from black to white) at any point is proportional to the intensity of the beam as it passes that point. Thus at any instant in time the beam takes on an analog value of intensity to produce the desired brightness at that point on the screen. Further, as the beam scans, the analog value changes. Thus the video image can be viewed as a time-varying analog signal.

Figure 2-9a depicts the scanning process. At the end of each scan line, the beam is swept rapidly back to the left (horizontal retrace). When the beam reaches the bottom, it is swept rapidly back to the top (vertical retrace). The beam is turned off (blanked out) during the retrace intervals.

To achieve adequate resolution, the beam produces a total of 483 horizontoal lines at a rate of 30 complete scans of the screen per second. Tests have shown that this rate will produce a sensation of flicker rather than smooth motion. However, the flicker is eliminated by a process of interlacing, as depicted in Figure 2-9b. The electron beam scans across the screen starting at the far left, very near the top. The beam reaches the bottom at the middle after $241\frac{1}{2}$ lines. At this point, the beam is quickly repositioned at the top of the screen and, beginning in the middle, produces an additional $241\frac{1}{2}$ lines interlaced with the original set. Thus the screen is refreshed 60 times per second rather than 30, and flicker is avoided. Note that the total count of lines is 525. Of these, 42 are blanked out during the vertical retrace interval, leaving 483 actually visible on the screen.

A familiar example of digital data is text or character strings. While textual data are most convenient for human beings, they cannot, in character form, be easily stored or transmitted by data processing and communications systems. Such systems are designed for binary data. Thus a number of codes have been devised by which characters are represented by a sequence of bits. Perhaps the earliest common example of this is the Morse code. Today, the most commonly used code in the United States is the ASCII (American Standard Code for Information Interchange) code (Table 2-1) promulgated by ANSI. ASCII is also widely used outside the United States. Each character in this code is represented by a unique 7-bit pattern;

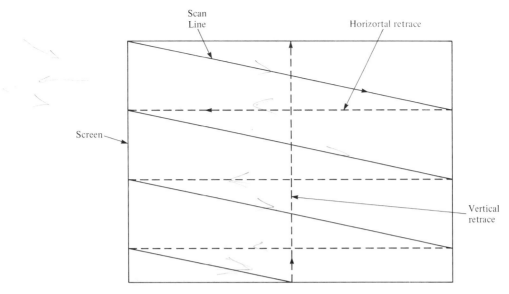

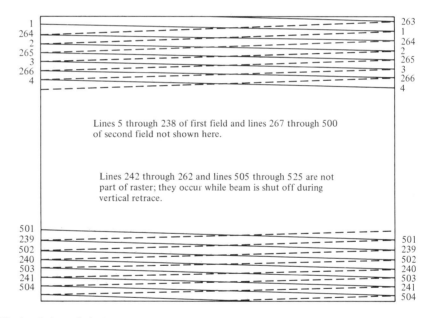

(a) Composition of a TV field

Lines 5 through 238 of first field and lines 267 through 500 of second field not shown here.

Lines 242 through 262 and lines 505 through 525 are not part of raster; they occur while beam is shut off during vertical retrace.

(b) Video interlacing technique

FIGURE 2-9. TV picture production.

thus 128 different characters can be represented. This is a larger number than is necessary, and some of the patterns represent ''control'' characters. Some of these control characters have to do with controlling the printing of characters on a page. Others are concerned with communications procedures and will be discussed later. ASCII-encoded characters are almost always stored and transmitted using 8 bits per character (a block of 8 bits is referred to as an *octet* or a *byte*). The eighth bit

TABLE 2-1 U.S. ASCII Codes[a]

b7→					0	0	0	0	1	1	1	1
b6→					0	0	1	1	0	0	1	1
b5→					0	1	0	1	0	1	0	1
b_4↓	b_3↓	b_2↓	b_1↓	Column → / Row ↓	0	1	2	3	4	5	6	7
0	0	0	0	0	NUL	DLE	SP	0	@	P	`	p
0	0	0	1	1	SOH	DC1	!	1	A	Q	a	q
0	0	1	0	2	STX	DC2	"	2	B	R	b	r
0	0	1	1	3	ETX	DC3	#	3	C	S	c	s
0	1	0	0	4	EOT	DC4	$	4	D	T	d	t
0	1	0	1	5	ENQ	NAK	%	5	E	U	e	u
0	1	1	0	6	ACK	SYN	&	6	F	V	f	v
0	1	1	1	7	BEL	ETB	´	7	G	W	g	w
1	0	0	0	8	BS	CAN	(	8	H	X	h	x
1	0	0	1	9	HT	EM	)	9	I	Y	i	y
1	0	1	0	10	LF	SUB	*	:	J	Z	j	z
1	0	1	1	11	VT	ESC	+	;	K	[	k	{
1	1	0	0	12	FF	FS	,	<	L	\	l	|
1	1	0	1	13	CR	GS	—	=	M	]	m	}
1	1	1	0	14	SO	RS	.	>	N	^	n	~
1	1	1	1	15	SI	US	/	?	O	_	o	DEL

[a]This is the U.S. national version of CCITT alphabet number 5. The control characters are explained on page 33.

NUL (Null): No character. Used for filling in time or filling space on tape when there is no data.

SOH (Start of Heading): Used to indicate the start of a heading which may contain address or routing information.

STX (Start of Text): Used to indicate the start of the text and so also indicates the end of the heading.

ETX (End of Text): Used to terminate the text which was started with STX.

EOT (End of Transmission): Indicates the end of a transmission, which may have included one or more "texts" with their headings.

ENQ (Enquiry): A request for a response from a remote station. It may be used as a "WHO ARE YOU?" request for a station to identify itself.

ACK (Acknowledge): A character transmitted by a receiving device as an affirmation response to a sender. It is used as a positive response to polling messages.

BEL (Bell): Used when there is need to call human attention. It may control alarm or attention devices.

BS (Backspace): Indicates movement of the printing mechanism or display cursor backwards in one position.

HT (Horizontal Tab): Indicates movement of the printing mechanism or display cursor forward to the next preassigned "tab" or stopping position.

LF (Line Feed): Indicates movement of the printing mechanism or display cursor to the start of the next line.

VT (Vertical Tab): Indicates movement of the printing mechanism or display cursor to the next of a series of preassigned printing lines.

FF (Form Feed): Indicates movement of the printing mechanism or display cursor to the starting position of the next page, form, or screen.

CR (Carriage Return): Indicates movement of the printing mechanism or display cursor to the starting position of the same line.

SO (Shift Out): Indicates that the code combinations which follow shall be interpreted as *outside* of the standard character set until a SHIFT IN character is reached.

SI (Shift In): Indicates that the code combinations which follow shall be interpreted according to the standard character set.

DLE (Data Link Escape): A character which shall change the meaning of one or more contiguously following characters. It can provide supplementary controls, or permits the sending of data characters having any bit combination.

DC1, DC2, DC3 and DC4 (Device Controls): Characters for the control of ancillary devices or special terminal features.

NAK (Negative Acknowledgment): A character transmitted by a receiving device as a negative response to a sender. It is used as a negative response to polling messages.

SYN (Synchronous/Idle): Used as a synchronous transmission system to achieve synchronization. When no data is being sent a synchronous transmission system may send SYN characters continuously.

ETB (End of Transmission Block): Indicates the end of a block of data for communication purposes. It is used for blocking data where the block structure is not necessarily related to the processing format.

CAN (Cancel): Indicates that the data which precedes it in a message or block should be disregarded (usually because an error has been detected).

EM (End of Medium): Indicates the physical end of a card, tape, or other medium, or the end of the required or used portion of the medium.

SUB (Substitute): Substituted for a character that is found to be erroneous or invalid.

ESC (Escape): A character intended to provide code extension in that it gives a specified number of contiguously following characters an alternate meaning.

FS (File Separator):
GS (Group Separator):
RS (Record Separator):
US (United Separator):
Information separators to be used in an optional manner except that their hierarchy shall be FS (the most inclusive) to US (the least inclusive).

SP (Space): A nonprinting character used to separate words, or to move the the printing mechanism or display cursor forward by one position.

DEL (Delete): Used too obliterate unwanted characters (for example, on paper tape by punching a hole in *every* bit position).

is a parity bit used for error detection. This bit is set such that the total number of binary 1s in each octet is always odd (odd parity) or always even (even parity). Thus a transmission error which changes a single bit can be detected.

Signals

In a communications system, data are propagated from one point to another by means of electric signals. An *analog signal* is a continuously varying electromagnetic wave that may be propagated over a variety of media, depending on spectrum; examples are wire media, such as twisted pair and coaxial cable, fiber optic cable, and atmosphere or space propagation. A *digital signal* is a sequence of voltage pulses that may be transmitted over a wire medium; for example, a constant positive voltage level may represent binary 1 and a constant negative voltage level may represent binary 0.

In what follows, we first look at some specific examples of signal types, and then discuss the relationship between data and signals.

Examples. Let us return to our three examples of the preceding subsection. For each example, we will describe the signal and estimate its bandwidth.

In the case of acoustic data (voice), the data can be represented directly by an electromagnetic signal occupying the same spectrum. However, there is a need to compromise between the fidelity of the sound as transmitted electrically and the cost of transmission, which increases with increasing bandwidth. Although, as mentioned, the spectrum of speech is approximately 20 Hz to 20 kHz, a much narrower bandwidth will produce acceptable voice reproduction. The standard spectrum for a voice signal is 300 to 3400 Hz. This is adequate for voice reproduction, minimizes required transmission capacity, and allows the use of rather inexpensive telephone sets. Thus the telephone transmitter converts the incoming acoustic voice signal into an electromagnetic signal over the range 300 to 3400 Hz. This signal is then transmitted through the telephone system to a receiver, which reproduces an acoustic signal from the incoming electromagnetic signal [ATT61].

Now, let us look at the video signal which, interestingly, consists of both analog and digital components. To produce a video signal, a TV camera, which performs similar functions to the TV receiver, is used. One component of the camera is a photosensitive plate, upon which a scene is optically focused. An electron beam sweeps across the plate from left to right and top to bottom, in the same fashion as depicted in Figure 2-9 for the receiver. As the beam sweeps, an analog electric signal is developed proportional to the brightness of the scene at a particular spot.

Now we are in a position to describe the video signal. Figure 2-10a shows three lines of a video signal; in this diagram, white is represented by a small positive voltage and black by a much larger positive voltage. So, for example, line 3 is at a medium gray level most of the way across with a blacker portion in the middle. Once the beam has completed a scan from left to right, it must retrace to the left edge to scan the next line. During this period, the picture should be blanked out (on both camera and receiver). This is done with a digital "horizontal blanking pulse." Also, to maintain transmitter-receiver synchronization, a synchronization (sync) pulse is sent between every line of video signal. This horizontal sync pulse rides on top of the blanking pulse, creating a staircase-shaped digital signal between adjacent analog video signals. Finally, when the beam reaches the bottom of the screen, it must return to the top, with a somewhat longer blanking interval required.

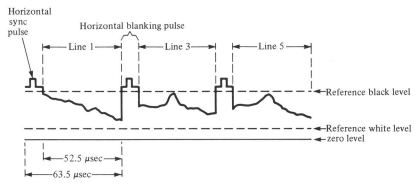

(a) Horizontal lines of video

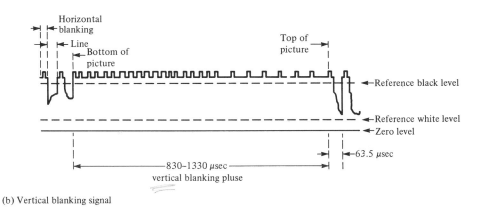

(b) Vertical blanking signal

FIGURE 2-10. **Video signal (different scales for a and b).**

This is shown in Figure 2-10b. The vertical blanking pulse is actually a series of synchronization and blanking pulses, whose details need not concern us here.

Next, consider the timing of the system. We mentioned that a total of 483 lines are scanned at a rate of 30 complete scans per second. This is an approximate number taking into account the time lost during the vertical retrace interval. The actual U.S. standard is 525 lines, but of these about 42 are lost during vertical retrace. Thus the horizontal scanning frequency is 525 lines $\div \frac{1}{30}$ s/scan = 15,750 lines per second, or 63.5 μs/line. Of this 63.5 μs, about 11 μs are allowed for horizontal retrace, leaving a total of 52.5 μs per video line.

Finally, we are in a position to estimate the bandwidth required for the video signal. To do this we must estimate the upper (maximum) and lower (minimum) frequency of the band. We use the following reasoning to arrive at the maximum frequency: The maximum frequency would occur during the horizontal scan if the scene were alternating between black and white as rapidly as possible. We can estimate this maximum value by considering the resolution of the video image. In the vertical dimension, there are about 485 lines, so the maximum vertical resolution would be 485. Experiments have shown [CUNN80] that the actual subjective resolution is about 70% of that number, or about 339 lines. In the interest of a balanced picture, the horizontal and vertical resolutions should be about the same. Since the ratio of width to height of a TV screen is 4:3, the horizontal resolution

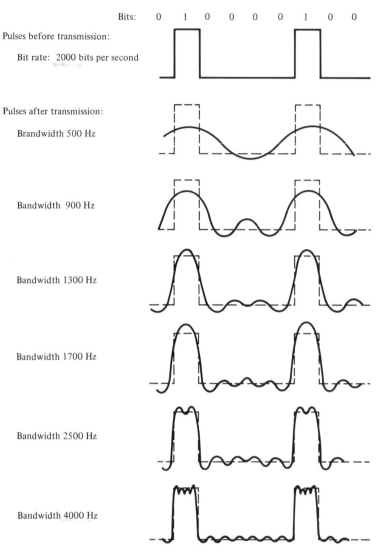

FIGURE 2-11. Effect of bandwidth on a digital signal.

should be about $\frac{4}{3} \times 339 = 452$ lines. As a worst case, a scanning line would be made up of 452 elements alternating black and white. The scan would result in a wave with each cycle of the wave consisting of one higher (black) and one lower (white) voltage level. Thus there would be $452/2 = 266$ cycles of the wave in 52.5 μs, for a maximum frequency of about 4 MHz. This rough reasoning, in fact, is fairly accurate. Thus the maximum frequency is 4 MHz. The lower limit will be a dc or zero frequency, where the dc component corresponds to the average illumination of the scene (the average value by which the signal exceeds the reference white level). Thus the bandwidth of the video signal is approximately 4 MHz − 0 = 4 MHz.

The foregoing discussion did not consider color or audio components of the signal. It turns out that with these included, the bandwidth remains about 4 MHz.

Finally, the third example described above is the general case of binary digital data. A commonly used signal for such data uses two constant (dc) voltage levels, one level for binary 1 and one level for binary 0. (In Chapter 3, we shall see that this is but one alternative, referred to as NRZ.) Again, we are interested in the bandwidth of such a signal. This will depend, in any specific case, on the exact shape of the waveform, and the sequence of 1's and 0's. We can obtain some understanding by considering Figure 2-11. As can be seen, the greater the bandwidth of the signal, the more faithfully it represents a digital pulse stream. For a data rate of x bits per second, the representation is quite as good at a bandwidth of x hertz and is very good at $2x$ hertz.

Data and Signals. In the foregoing discussion, we have looked at analog signals used to represent analog data and digital signals used to represent digital data. Generally, analog data are a function of time and occupy a limited frequency spectrum; such data can be represented by an electromagnetic signal occupying the same spectrum. Digital data can be represented by digital signals, with a different voltage level for each of the two binary digits.

As Figure 2-12 illustrates, these are not the only possibilities. Digital data can also be represented by analog signals by use of a *modem* (modulator/demodulator).

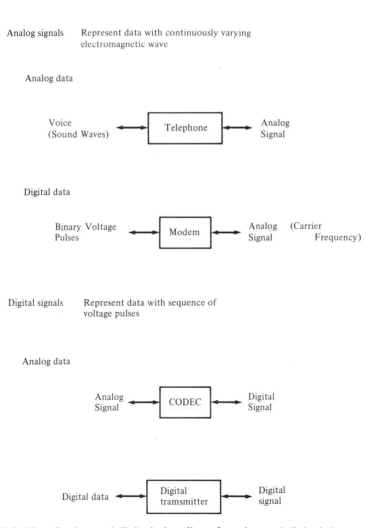

FIGURE 2-12. Analog and digital signaling of analog and digital data.

The modem converts a series of binary (two-valued) voltage pulses into an analog signal by encoding the digital data onto a *carrier frequency*. The resulting signal occupies a certain spectrum of frequency centered about the carrier and may be propagated across a medium suitable for that carrier. The most common modems represent digital data in the voice spectrum and hence allow those data to be propagated over ordinary voice-grade telephone lines. At the other end of the line, the modem demodulates the signal to recover the original data.

In an operation very similar to that performed by a modem, analog data can be represented by digital signals. The device that performs this function for voice data is a *codec* (coder-decoder). In essence, the codec takes an analog signal that directly represents the voice data and approximates that signal by a bit stream. At the receiving end, the bit stream is used to reconstruct the analog data.

Thus Figure 2-12 suggests that data may be encoded into signals in a variety of ways. We will return to this topic in Chapter 3.

Transmission

A final distinction remains to be made. Both analog and digital signals may be transmitted on suitable transmission media. The way these signals are treated is a function of the transmission system. Table 2-2 summarizes the methods of data transmission. *Analog transmission* is a means of transmitting analog signals without regard to their content; the signals may represent analog data (e.g., voice) or digital data (e.g., binary data that pass through a modem). In either case, the analog signal will become weaker (attenuate) after a certain distance. To achieve longer distances, the analog transmission system includes amplifiers that boost the energy in the signal. Unfortunately, the amplifier also boosts the noise components. With amplifiers cascaded to achieve long distances, the signal becomes more and more distorted. For analog data, such as voice, quite a bit of distortion can be tolerated and the the data remain intelligible. However, for digital data, cascaded amplifiers will introduce errors.

Digital transmission, in contrast, is concerned with the content of the signal. A digital signal can be transmitted only a limited distance before attenuation endan-

TABLE 2-2 Analog and Digital Transmission

	Analog Transmission	Digital Transmission
a. Treatment of Signals		
Analog signal	Is propagated through amplifiers; same treatment for both analog and digital data	Assumes digital data; at propagation points, data in signal are recovered, new analog signal is generated
Digital signal	Not used	Repeaters retransmit new signal; same treatment for both analog and digital data
b. Possible Combinations		
Analog data	Analog signal	Digital signal
Digital data	Analog signal	Digital signal Analog signal

gers the integrity of the data. To achieve greater distances, repeaters are used. A repeater receives the digital signal, recovers the pattern of 1's and 0's, and retransmits a new signal. Thus the attenuation is overcome.

The same technique may be used with an analog signal if it is assumed that the signal carries digital data. At appropriately spaced points, the transmission system has repeaters rather than amplifiers. The repeater recovers the digital data from the analog signal and generates a new, clean analog signal. Thus noise is not cumulative.

The question naturally arises as to which is the preferred method of transmission. The answer being supplied by the telecommunications industry and its customers is digital, this despite an enormous investment in analog communications facilities. Both long-haul telecommuncations facilities and intrabuilding services are gradually being converted to digital transmission and, where possible, digital signaling techniques. The most important reasons:

- *Digital technology:* The advent of large-scale integration (LSI) and very large-scale integration (VLSI) technology has caused a continuing drop in the cost and size of digital circuitry. Analog equipment has not shown a similar drop.
- *Data integrity:* With the use of repeaters rather than amplifiers, the effects of noise and other signal impairments are not cumulative. Thus it is possible to transmit data longer distances and over lesser quality lines by digital means while maintaining the integrity of the data. This is explored in Section 2-3.
- *Capacity utilization:* It has become economical to build transmission links of very high bandwidth, including satellite channels and optical fiber. A high degree of multiplexing is needed to effectively utilize such capacity, and this is more easily and cheaply achieved with digital (time-division) rather than analog (frequency-division) techniques. This is explored in Chapter 6.
- *Security and privacy:* Encryption techniques can be readily applied to digital data and analog data that have been digitized.
- *Integration:* By treating both analog and digital data digitally, all signals have the same form and can be treated similarly. Thus economies of scale and convenience can be achieved by integrating voice, video, and digital data.

2-3

TRANSMISSION IMPAIRMENTS

In Section 2-2, in discussing analog and digital signals, we were interested in the bandwidth adequate to *construct* a signal. Unfortunately, such bandwidth may be insufficient, or at least may allow the introduction of error, when we attempt to *transmit* the signal. While the signal is being transmitted, it is subject to a number of impairments. The most important of these are

- Attenuation and attenuation distortion.
- Delay distortion.
- Noise.

Attenuation

The strength of a signal falls off with distance over any transmission medium. For hardwire media, this reduction in strength, or attenuation, is generally logarithmic and thus is typically expressed as a constant number of decibels per unit distance.

For software media, attenuation is a more complex function of distance and the makeup of the atmosphere. Attenuation introduces three considerations for the transmission engineer. First, a received signal must have sufficient strength so that the electronic circuitry in the receiver can detect and interpret the signal. Second, the signal must maintain a level sufficiently higher than noise to be received without error. Third, attenuation is an increasing function of frequency.

The first and second problems are dealt with by attention to signal strength and the use of amplifiers or repeaters. For a point-to-point link, the signal strength of the transmitter must be strong enough to be received intelligibily, but not so strong as to overload the circuitry of the transmitter, which would cause a distorted signal to be generated. Beyond a certain distance, the attenuation is unacceptably great, and repeaters or amplifiers are used to boost the signal from time to time. These problems are more complex for multipoint lines where the distance from transmitter to receiver is variable.

The third problem is particularly noticeable for analog signals. Because the attenuation varies as a function of frequency, the received signal is distorted, reducing intelligibility. To overcome this problem, techniques are available for equalizing attenuation across a band of frequencies. This is commonly done for voice-grade telephone lines by using loading coils that change the electrical properties of the line; the result is to smooth out attenuation effects. Another approach is to use amplifiers that amplify high frequencies more than lower frequencies.

An example is shown in Figure 2-13a which shows attenuation as a function of frequency for a typical leased line. In the figure, attenuation is measured relative to the attenuation at 1000 Hz. A 1000-Hz tone of a given power level is applied to the input, and the power, P_{1000}, is measured at the output. For any other frequency f, the procedure is repeated and the relative attenuation in decibels is

$$N_f = 10 \log_{10} \frac{P_f}{P_{1000}}$$

The solid line in Figure 2-13a shows attenuation without equalization. As can be seen, frequency components at the upper end of the voice band are attenuated much more than those at lower frequencies. It should be clear that this will result in a distortion of the received speech signal. The dashed line shows the effect of equalization. Overall attenuation is increased, but the flattened response curve improves the quality of voice signals. It also allows higher data rates to be used for digital data that are passed through a modem.

Attenuation distortion is much less of a problem with digital signals. As we have seen, the strength of a digital signal falls off rapidly with frequency (Figure 2-6b); most of the content is concentrated near the fundamental frequency or bit rate of the signal.

Delay Distortion

Delay distortion is a phenomenon peculiar to hardwire transmission media. The distortion is caused by the fact that the velocity of propagation of a signal through a hardwire medium varies with frequency. For a bandlimited signal, the velocity tends to be highest near the center frequency, and fall off toward the two edges of the band. Thus various frequency components of a signal will arrive at the receiver at different times.

This effect is referred to as delay distortion, since the received signal is distorted

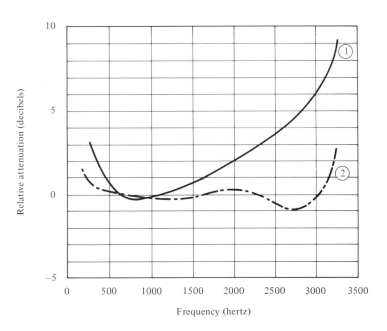

(a) Attenuation

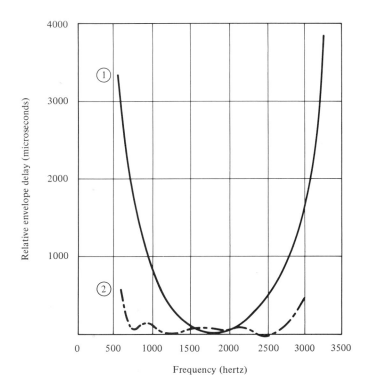

(b) Delay distortion

FIGURE 2-13. Attenuation and delay distortion curves for a voice channel.

due to variable delay in its components. Delay distortion is particularly critical for digital data. Consider that a sequence of bits is being transmitted, using either analog or digital signals. Because of delay distortion, some of the signal components of one bit position will spill over into other bit positions, causing *intersymbol interference*, which is a major limitation to maximum bit rate over a transmission channel.

Equalizing techniques can also be used for delay distortion. Again using a leased telephone line as an example, Figure 2-13b shows the effect of equalization on delay as a function of frequency.

Noise

For any data transmission event, the received signal will consist of the transmitted signal, modified by the various distortions imposed by the transmission system, plus additional unwanted signals that are inserted somewhere between transmission and reception. The latter, undesired signals are referred to as noise. It is noise that is the major limiting factor in communications system performance.

Types of Noise.   Noise may be divided into four categories [FREE81]:

- Thermal noise.
- Intermodulation noise.
- Crosstalk.
- Impulse noise.

Thermal noise is due to thermal agitation of electrons in a conductor. It is present in all electronic devices and transmission media and is a function of temperature. Thermal noise is uniformly distributed across the frequency spectrum and hence is often referred to as white noise. Thermal noise cannot be eliminated and therefore places an upper bound on communications system performance. The amount of thermal noise to be found in a bandwidth of 1 Hz in any device or conductor is

$$N_0 = kT$$

where

N_0 = noise power density, watts/hertz
k = Boltzmann's constant = 1.3803×10^{-23} J/°K
T = temperature, degrees Kelvin

The noise is assumed to be independent of frequency. Thus the thermal noise in watts present in a bandwidth of W hertz can be expressed as

$$N = kTW$$

or, in decibel-watts:

$N = 10 \log k + 10 \log T + 10 \log W$
$N = -228.6 \text{ dbW} + 10 \log T + 10 \log W$

When signals at different frequencies share the same transmission medium, the result may be *intermodulation noise*. The effect of intermodulation noise is to produce signals at a frequency which is the sum or difference of the two original frequencies or multiples of those frequencies. For example, the mixing of signals at frequencies f_1 and f_2 might produce energy at the frequency $f_1 + f_2$. This derived signal could interfere with an intended signal at the frequency $f_1 + f_2$.

Intermodulation noise is produced when there is some *nonlinearity* in the transmitter, receiver, or intervening transmission system. Normally, these components behave as linear systems; that is, the output is equal to the input times a constant. In a nonlinear system, the output is a more complex function of the input. Such nonlinearity can be caused by component malfunction or the use of excessive signal strength. It is under these circumstances that the sum and difference terms occur.

Crosstalk has been experienced by anyone who, while using the telephone, has been able to hear another conversation; it is an unwanted coupling between signal paths. It can occur by electrical coupling between nearby twisted pair or, rarely, coax cable lines carrying multiple signals. Crosstalk can also occur when unwanted signals are picked up by microwave antennas; although highly directional, microwave energy does spread during propagation. Typically, crosstalk is of the same order of magnitude as, or less than, thermal noise.

All of the types of noise discussed so far have reasonably predictable and reasonably constant magnitudes. Thus it is possible to engineer a transmission system to cope with them. *Impulse noise*, however, is noncontinuous, consisting of irregular pulses or noise spikes of short duration and of relatively high amplitude. It is generated from a variety of causes, including external electromagnetic disturbances, such as lightning, and faults and flaws in the communications system.

Impulse noise is generally only a minor annoyance for analog data. For example, voice transmission may be corrupted by short clicks and crackles with no loss of intelligibility. However, impulse noise is the primary source of error in digital data communication. For example, a sharp spike of energy of 0.01 s duration would not destroy any voice data, but would wash out about 50 bits of data being transmitted at 4800 bps. Figure 2-14 is an example of the effect on a digital signal. Here the noise consists of a relatively modest level of thermal noise plus occasional spikes of impulse noise. The digital data are recovered from the signal by sampling the received waveform once per bit time. As can be seen, the noise is occasionally sufficient to change a 1 to a 0 or a 0 to a 1.

The Signal-to-Noise Ratio. The most important parameter in determining the performance of a transmission system is the signal-to-noise (S/N) ratio, which is just the ratio of the power in a signal to the power contained in the noise that is present. Typically, this ratio is measured at a receiver, since it is at this point that an attempt is made to process the signal and eliminate the unwanted noise. For convenience, this ratio is often reported in decibels:

$$(S/N)_{dB} = 10 \log \frac{\text{signal power}}{\text{noise power}}$$

This expresses the amount, in decibels, that the intended signal exceeds the noise level. A high S/N will mean a high-quality signal and a low number of required intermediate repeaters.

The signal-to-noise ratio is especially important in the transmission of digital data, in that it determines the upper bound on the achievable data rate. A result from information theory is that the maximum channel capacity, in bits per second, obeys

$$C = W \log_2(1 + S/N)$$

where W is bandwidth of the channel in hertz. As an example, consider a voice

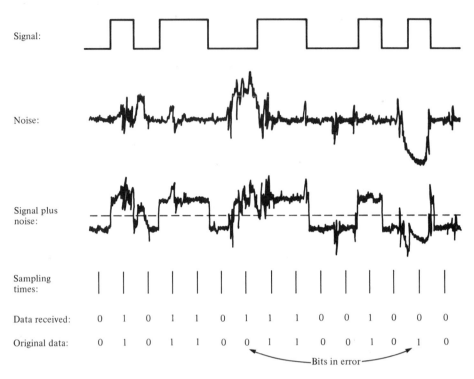

Data transmitted: 0 1 0 1 1 0 0 1 1 0 0 1 0 1 0

Signal:

Noise:

Signal plus noise:

Sampling times:

Data received: 0 1 0 1 1 0 1 1 1 0 0 1 0 0 0

Original data: 0 1 0 1 1 0 0 1 1 0 0 1 0 1 0

—Bits in error—

FIGURE 2-14. Effect of noise on a digital signal.

channel being used, via modem, to transmit digital data. Assume a bandwidth of 3100 Hz. A typical value of S/N for a voice-grade line is 30 dB, or a ratio of 1000:1. Thus

$$C = 3100 \log_2(1 + 1000)$$
$$= 30{,}894 \text{ bps}$$

This represents the theoretical maximum that can be achieved. In practice, however, only much lower rates are achieved. One reason for this is that the formula assumes white noise, such as thermal noise. Impulse noise is not accounted for, nor are attenuation and delay distortion.

By comparison, another formulation, due to Nyquist, assumes a noiseless channel and develops a limit based on intersymbol interference, such as is produced by delay distortion. For a system with bandwidth W, the maximum data rate using binary signaling elements (two voltage levels) is $2W$. Thus for $W = 3100$ Hz, $C = 6200$ bps. However, as we shall see in Chapter 3, signals with more than two levels can be used and the formulation becomes

$$C = 2W \log_2 M$$

where M is the number of discrete signal or voltage levels. Thus, for $M = 8$, a value used with some modems, C becomes 18,300 bps.

Finally, we mention a parameter related to S/N that is more convenient for determining digital data rates and error rates. The parameter is the ratio of signal energy per bit to noise energy per hertz, E_b/N_0. Consider a signal, digital or analog, that contains binary digital data transmitted at a certain bit rate R. Recalling that 1 w = 1 J/s, the energy per bit in a signal is given by $E_b = ST_b$, where S is the signal power and T_b is the time required to send one bit. The data rate R is just $R = 1/T_b$. Thus

$$\frac{E_b}{N_0} = \frac{S/R}{N_0} = \frac{S}{\mathrm{kTR}}$$

or, in decibel notation

$$\frac{E_b}{N_0} = S - 10 \log R + 228.6 \text{ dbW} - 10 \log T$$

The ratio E_b/N_0 is important because the bit error rate for digital data is a (decreasing) function of this ratio. Given a value of E_b/N_0 needed to achieve a desired error rate, the parameters in the formula above may be selected. Note that as the bit rate R increases, the transmitted signal power, relative to noise, must increase to maintain the required E_b/N_0.

Let us try to grasp this result intuitively by considering again Figure 2-14. The signal here is digital, but the reasoning would be the same for an analog signal. In several instances, the noise is sufficient to alter the value of a bit. Now, if the data rate were doubled, the bits would be more tightly packed together, and the same passage of noise might destroy two bits. Thus, for constant signal and noise strength, an increase in data rate increases the error rate.

EXAMPLE. For binary phase-shift keying (defined in Chapter 3), $E_b/N_0 = 8.4$ dB is required for a bit error rate of 10^{-4} (probability of error $= 10^{-4}$). If the effective noise temperature is 290°K (room temperature) and the data rate is 2400 bps, what received signal level is required?

We have

$$8.4 = S(\text{dbW}) - 10 \log 2400 + 228.6 \text{ dBW} - 10 \log 290$$

$$= S(\text{dBW}) - (10)(3.38) + 228.6 - (10)(2.46)$$

$$S = -161.8 \text{ dBW}$$

■

2-4 TRANSMISSION MEDIA

The transmission medium is the physical path between transmitter and receiver in a data transmission system. Transmission media may be classified as hardwire or softwire. Examples of *hardwire* media are twisted pair, coaxial cable, and optical fiber cable. Examples of *softwire* media are air, vacuum, and seawater.

The characteristics and quality of data transmission are determined both by the nature of the signal and the nature of the medium. In the case of hardwire media, the medium itself is more important in determining the limitations of transmission. Table 2-3 contains typical characteristics for hardwire media, including the total data rate that the medium can support, the bandwidth the medium can transmit, and the required repeater spacing for digital transmission.

TABLE 2-3   Point-to-Point Transmission Characteristics of Hardware Media

Transmission Medium	Total Data Rate	Bandwidth	Repeater Spacing
Twisted pair	1 Mbps	250 kHz	2–10 km
Coaxial cable	500 Mbps	350 MHz	1–10 km
Optical fiber	1 Gbps	1 GHz	10–100 km

For softwire media, the spectrum or frequency band of the signal produced by the transmitting antenna is more important than the medium in determining transmission characteristics. As we have already mentioned, the higher the center frequency of a signal, the greater the potential bandwidth and hence data rate. Another property of signals transmitted by antenna is *directionality*. In general, at lower frequencies signals are omnidirectional; that is, the signal propagates in all directions from the antenna. At higher frequencies, it is possible to focus the signal into a directional beam.

Two general ranges of frequencies are of interest in this discussion. Microwave frequencies cover a range of about 2 to 40 GHz. At these frequencies, highly directional beams are possible, and microwave is quite suitable for point-to-point transmission. We will refer to signals in the range 30 MHz to 1 GHz as radio waves. Omnidirectional transmission is used and signals at these frequencies are suitable for broadcast applications.

The reader should also be aware of a finer subdivision of the electromagnetic spectrum defined by the International Telecommunications Union, and shown in Table 2-4. The table also summarizes key characteristics of each band. Microwave covers part of the UHF and all of the SHF bands, and radio covers the VHF and part of the UHF band. Note that this is a restricted use of the term ''radio'' that is appropriate for the concerns of this book.

In this section we examine the three most important hardwire media—twisted pair, coaxial cable, and optical fiber—as well as the three most important softwire transmission techniques—terrestrial and satellite microwave, and radio. In all cases, we describe the systems physically, then briefly discuss applications, and finally look at transmission characteristics.

Twisted Pair

Physical Description.   A twisted pair consists of two insulated copper wires arranged in a regular spiral pattern. A wire pair acts as a single communication link. Typically, a number of these pairs are bundled together into a cable by wrapping them in a tough protective sheath. Over longer distances, cables may contain hundreds of pairs. The twisting of the individual pairs minimizes electromagnetic interference between the pairs. The wires in a pair have thicknesses of from 0.015 to 0.056 in.

Uses.   By far the most common transmission medium for both analog and digital data is twisted pair. It is the backbone of the telephone system as well as the workhorse for intrabuilding communications.

TABLE 2-4 Characteristics of Softwire Communications Bands

Frequency Band	Name	Analog Data		Digital Data		Principal Applications
		Modulation	Bandwidth	Modulation	Data Rate	
30–300 kHz	LF (low frequency)	Generally not practical		ASK, FSK, MSK	0.1–100 bps	Navigation
300–3000 kHz	MF (medium frequency)	AM	To 4 kHz	ASK, FSK, MSK	10–1000 bps	Commercial AM radio
3–30 MHz	HF (high frequency)	AM, SSB	To 4 kHz	ASK, FSK, MSK	10–3000 bps	Shortwave radio CB radio
30–300 MHz	VHF (very high frequency)	AM, SSB; FM	5 kHz to 5 MHz	FSK, PSK	To 100 kbps	VHF television FM radio
300–3000 MHz	UHF (ultra high frequency)	FM, SSB	To 20 MHz	PSK	To 10 Mbps	UHF Television Terrestrial Microwave
3–30 GHz	SHF (super high frequency)	FM	To 500 MHz	PSK	To 100 Mbps	Terrestrial microwave Satellite microwave
30–300 GHz	EHF (extremely high frequency)	FM	To 1 GHz	PSK	To 750 Mbps	Experimental short point-to-point

In the telephone system, individual telephone sets are connected to the local telephone exchange or "end office" by twisted-pair wire. These are referred to as "local loops." Within an office building, telephone service is often provided by means of a private branch exchange (PBX). The PBX will be discussed in detail in Chapter 8. Essentially, it is an on-premise telephone exchange system that services a number of telephones within a building. It provides for intrabuilding calls via extension numbers and outside calls by trunk connection to the local end office. Within the building, the telephones are connected to the PBX via twisted pair. For both of the systems just described, twisted pair has primarily been a medium for voice traffic between subscribers and their local telephone exchange office. Digital data traffic can also be carried over moderate distances. For modern digital PBX systems, data rates of about 64 kbps are achievable using digital signaling. Local loop connections typically require a modem, with a maximum data rate of 9600 bps. However, twisted pair is used for long-distance trunking applications and data rates of 1 Mbps or more may be achieved.

Twisted pair is also the medium of choice for a low-cost microcomputer local network within a building. This application is discussed in Chapter 11.

Transmission Characteristics. Wire pairs may be used to transmit both analog and digital signals. For analog signals, amplifiers are required about every 5 to 6 km. For digital signals, repeaters are used every 2 or 3 km.

Compared to other transmission media, twisted pair is limited in distance, bandwidth, and data rate. Figure 2-15 shows that the attenuation for twisted pair is a very strong function of frequency. Other impairments are also severe for twisted pair. The medium is quite susceptible to interference and noise because of its easy coupling with electromagnetic fields. For example, a wire run parallel to an ac power line will pick up 60-Hz energy. Impulse noise also easily intrudes into twisted pair.

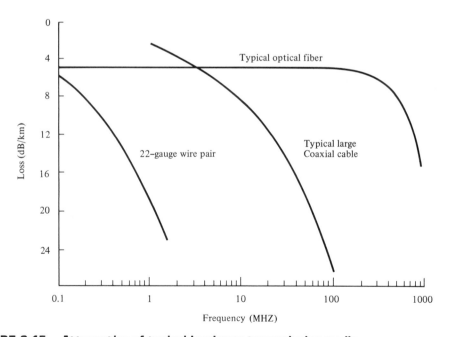

FIGURE 2-15. Attenuation of typical hardware transmission media.

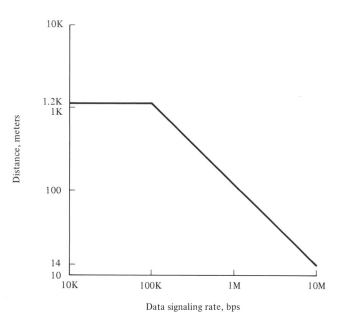

FIGURE 2-16. **Twisted-pair cable length vs. data rate for balanced transmission (RS-422).**

Several measures are taken to reduce impairments [PICK83c]. Shielding the wire with metallic braid or sheathing reduces interference. The twisting of the wire reduces low-frequency interference, and the use of different twist lengths in adjacent pairs reduces crosstalk. Another technique is the use of a balanced transmission line. With an unbalanced line, one wire is at ground potential; with balanced transmission, both wires are above ground potential, carrying signals with equal amplitude but opposite phase.

For point-to-point analog signaling, a bandwidth of up to about 250 kHz is possible. For voice transmission, such as the local loop, the attenuation is about 1 dB/km over the voice frequency range. A common standard for telephone lines is a maximum loss of 6 dB; hence a 6 km section of line represents an upper limit on the distance that can be covered. For digital point-to-point lines, data rates of up to a few Mbps are possible. Figure 2-16 shows the achievable data rate versus distance for a common balanced electrical signaling technique, the EIA standard RS-422.

Coaxial Cable

Physical Description. Coaxial cable, like twisted pair, consists of two conductors, but it is constructed differently to permit it to operate over a wider range of frequencies (Figure 2-17). It consists of a hollow outer cylindrical conductor which surrounds a single inner wire conductor. The inner conductor can be either solid or stranded; the outer conductor can be either solid or braided. The inner conductor is held in place by either regularly spaced insulating rings or a solid dialectric material. The outer conductor is covered with a jacket or shield. A single coaxial cable has a diameter of from 0.4 to about 1 in.

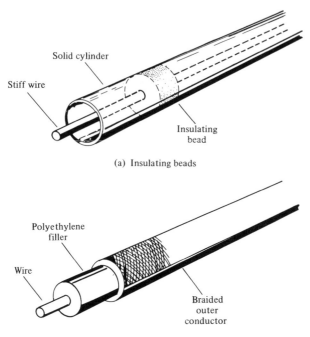

Solid cylinder

Stiff wire

Insulating
bead

(a) Insulating beads

Polyethylene
filler

Wire

Braided
outer
conductor

(b) Solid dielectric

FIGURE 2-17. Coaxial cable construction.

Uses. Coaxial cable is perhaps the most versatile transmission medium and is enjoying increasing utilization in a wide variety of applications. The most important of these are:

- Long-distance telephone and television transmission.
- Television distribution.
- Local area networks.
- Short-run system links.

Coaxial cable is an important part of the long-distance telephone network. Although it faces increasing competition from optical fiber, microwave, and satellite, coaxial cable will remain a prevalent carrier for the forseeable future. Using frequency-division multiplexing (FDM, see Chapter 6), a coaxial cable can carry over 10,000 voice channels simultaneously. Cable is also used for long-distance television transmission.

Coaxial cable is also spreading rapidly as a means of distributing TV signals to individual homes—cable TV. From its modest beginnings as Community Antenna Television (CATV), designed to provide service to remote areas, cable TV will eventually reach almost as many homes as the telephone. A CATV system can carry dozens of TV channels at ranges up to a few tens of miles.

An equally explosive growth area for coaxial cable is local area networks (Chapter 11). It is the medium of choice for many local network systems. Coaxial cable can support a large number of devices with a variety of data and traffic types, over distances that encompass a single building or a complex of buildings.

Finally, coaxial cable is commonly used for short-range connections between devices. Using analog signaling, coaxial cable is used to transmit radio or TV signals. With digital signaling, coaxial cable can be used to provide high-speed I/O channels on computer systems.

Transmission Characteristics.   Coaxial cable is used to transmit both analog and digital signals. Long-distance systems may be either analog or digital. CATV is analog, and both analog and digital techniques have been used for local networks.

As can be seen from Figure 2-15, coaxial cable has superior frequency characteristics to twisted pair, and can hence be used effectively at higher frequencies and data rates. Because of its shielded, concentric construction, coaxial cable is much less susceptible to interference and crosstalk than twisted pair. The principle constraints on performance are attenuation, thermal noise, and intermodulation noise. The latter is present only when several channels (FDM) or frequency bandwidths are in use on the cable.

Figure 2-18 is an instructive look at the engineering constraints faced in transmission systems. To achieve proper signal quality, a certain signal-to-noise (S/N) ratio must be maintained on the cable. The engineer has two variables to play with: signal power and amplifier spacing. The S/N can be raised by spacing amplifiers closely to boost signal frequency. However, it is desirable to maximize amplifier spacing to reduce cost and because amplifiers introduce nonlinearities. S/N can be increased, of course, by boosting S. This will work, however, only in a region of operation where the dominant noise source is thermal noise, which is relatively constant independent of the signal. When a number of signals in adjacent bandwidths are being carried on the cable, intermodulation noise increases as signal power increases. This phenomenon is seen clearly in Figure 2-18. Figure 2-18b is derived from 2-18a, and shows that, as the spacing between amplifiers increases, the maximum attainable S/N declines and, further, that increasing signal power is required to achieve the maximum.

For long distance transmission of analog signals, amplifiers are needed every few kilometers, with closer spacing required if higher frequencies are used. The usable spectrum for analog signaling extends to about 400 MHz. For digital signaling, repeaters are needed every kilometer or so, with closer spacing needed for higher data rates. On experimental systems, data rates as high as 800 Mbps have been achieved with a repeater spacing of 1.6 km [KASA83].

Optical Fiber

Physical Description.   An optical fiber is a thin (50 to 100 μm), flexible medium capable of conducting an optical ray. Various glasses and plastics can be used to make optical fibers [ITT75]. The lowest losses have been obtained using fibers of ultrapure fused silica. Ultrapure fiber is difficult to manufacture; higher-loss multicomponent glass fibers are more economical and still provide good performance. Plastic fiber is even less costly and can be used for short-haul links, for which moderately high losses are acceptable.

For a single optical fiber, the glass or plastic fiber, having a high index of refraction, is surrounded by a cladding layer of a material with slightly lower index. The cladding layer isolates the fiber and prevents crosstalk with adjacent fibers. Fiber optic cable consists of a bundle of fibers, sometimes with a steel core for stability. Stacked ribbon cable is an alternative method of bundling; the cable consists of a stack of flat ribbons, each with a single row of fibers [MOKH81].

Uses.   One of the most significant technological breakthroughs in data transmission has been the development of practical fiber optic communications systems [SCHW84]. Optical fiber already enjoys considerable use in long-distance tele-

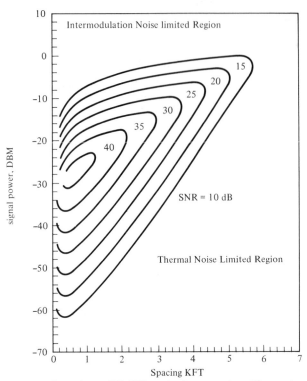

(a) Dependence of T1 SNR on signal power and amplifier spacing for systems using 0.375-in cables. The bandwidth occupied by each channel is 1.5 MHz. System length is 20 mi.

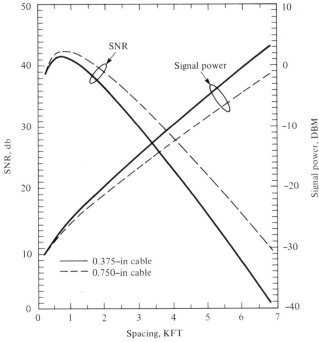

(b) Maximum attainable SNR and the corresponding signal power. as a function of spacing. The bandwidth for each channel is 1.5 MHz.

FIGURE 2-18. **Dependence of S/N on signal power and amplifier spacing for coaxial cable.**

communications and its use in military applications is growing. The continuing improvements in performance and decline in prices, together with the inherent advantages of optical fiber, will result in new areas of application, such as local networks and short-haul video distribution. The following characteristics distinguish optical fiber from twisted pair and coaxial cable.

- *Greater bandwidth:* The potential bandwidth, and hence data rate, of a medium increases with frequency. At the immense frequencies of optical fiber, data rates of 2 Gbps over tens of kilometers have been demonstrated. Compare this to the practical maximum of hundreds of Mbps over about 1 km for coaxial cable and just a few Mbps over 1 km for twisted pair.
- *Smaller size and lighter weight:* Optical fibers are considerably smaller than coaxial cable or bundled twisted-pair cable—at least an order of magnitude smaller in diameter for comparable data transmission capacity. For cramped conduits in buildings and underground along public right-of-way, the advantage of small size is considerable. The corresponding reduction in weight reduces structural support requirements.
- *Lower attenuation:* Attenuation is significantly lower for optical fiber than for coaxial cable or twisted pair (Figure 2-15), and is constant over a wide range.
- *Electromagnetic isolation:* Optical fiber systems are not affected by external electromagnetic fields. Thus the system is not vulnerable to interference, impulse noise, or crosstalk. By the same token, fibers do not radiate energy, causing little interference with other equipment and providing a high degree of security from eavesdropping; in addition, fiber is inherently difficult to tap.
- *Greater repeater spacing:* Fewer repeaters mean lower cost and fewer sources of error. Bell Labs has successfully tested a 119-km repeaterless link at 420 Mbps with a bit error rate of 10^{-9} [MIER83]. Coaxial and twisted-pair systems generally have repeaters every few kilometers.

Transmission Characteristics. Optical fiber transmits a signal-encoded beam of light by means of total internal reflection. Total internal reflection can occur in any transparent medium that has a higher index of refraction than the surrounding medium. In effect, the optical fiber acts as a waveguide for frequencies in the range 10^{14} to 10^{15} Hz, which covers the visible spectrum and part of the infrared spectrum.

Figure 2-19a shows the principle of optical fiber transmission. Light from a source enters the cylindrical glass or plastic core. Rays at shallow angles are reflected and propagated along the fiber; other rays are absorbed by the surrounding material. This form of propagation is called multimode, referring to the variety of angles that will reflect. When a fiber core radius is reduced, fewer angles will reflect. By reducing the radius of the core to the order of a wavelength, only a single angle or mode can pass: the axial ray. Table 2-5 compares these two modes. The reason for the superior performance of single-mode is this. With multimode transmission, multiple propagation paths exist, each with a different path length and hence time to traverse the fiber. This causes signal elements to spread out in time and limits the rate at which data can be accurately received. Since there is a single transmission path with single-mode transmission, such distortion cannot occur. Finally, by varying the index of refraction of the core, a third type of transmission, known as multimode graded index, is possible. This type is intermediate between the other two in characteristics. The variable refraction has the effect of focusing the rays more efficiently than ordinary multimode.

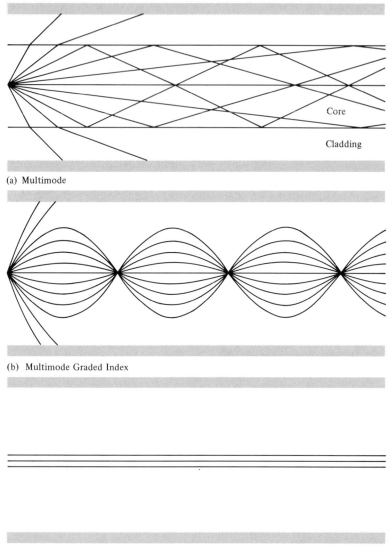

Absorptive jacket

Core

Cladding

(a) Multimode

(b) Multimode Graded Index

(c) Single mode

FIGURE 2-19. Optical fiber transmission modes.

TABLE 2-5   Comparison of Single-Mode and Multimode Optical Fiber

Single-Mode	Multimode
Used for long distances and high data rates	Used for short distances and low data rates
Expensive	Inexpensive
Narrow core: requires laser light source	Wide core: gathers light well
Difficult to terminate	Easy to terminate
Minimum dispersion: very efficient	Large dispersion: inefficient

Two different types of light source are used in fiber optic systems: the *light-emitting diode* (LED) and the *injection laser diode* (ILD). The LED is a solid-state device that emits light when a current is applied. The ILD is a solid-state device that works on the laser principle in which quantum electronic effects are stimulated to produce a superradiant beam of narrow bandwidth. The LED is less costly, operates over a greater temperature range, and has a longer operational life. The ILD is more efficient and can sustain greater data rates.

The detector used at the receiving end to convert the light into electrical energy is a *photodiode*. Two solid-state devices have been used: the PIN detector and the APD detector. The PIN photodiode has a segment of intrinsic (I) silicon between the P and N layers of a diode. The APD, avalanche photodiode, is similar in appearance but uses a stronger electric field. Both devices are basically photon counters. The PIN is less expensive and less sensitive than the APD.

Of course, only analog signaling is possible in optical fiber, since only light waves may be transmitted. With appropriate modulation, either digital or analog data may be carried.

Terrestrial Microwave

Physical Description. The most common type of microwave antenna is the parabolic "dish." A typical size is about 10 ft in diameter. The antenna is fixed rigidly and focuses a narrow beam to achieve line-of-sight transmission to the receiving antenna. Microwave antennas are usually located at substantial heights above ground level in order to extend the range between antennas and to be able to transmit over intervening obstacles. With no intervening obstacles, the maximum distance between antennas conforms to

$$d = 7.14 \sqrt{Kh} \tag{2-1}$$

where d is the distance between antennas in kilometers, h is the antenna height in meters, and K is an adjustment factor to account for the fact that microwaves are bent or refracted with the curvature of the earth and will hence propagate farther than the optical line of sight. A good rule of thumb is $K = \frac{4}{3}$ [FREE80]. So, for example, two microwave antennas at a height of 100 m may be as far as $7.14 \times \sqrt{133} = 82$ km apart. To achieve long-distance transmission, a series of microwave relay towers is used, and point-to-point microwave links are strung together over the desired distance.

Uses. The primary use for terrestrial microwave systems is in long-haul telecommunications service, as an alternative to coaxial cable for transmitting television and voice. Like coaxial cable, microwave can support high data rates over long distances. The microwave facility requires far fewer amplifiers or repeaters than coaxial cable for the same distance, but requires line-of-sight transmission. Microwave is commonly used for both voice and television transmission.

Another increasingly common use of microwave is for short point-to-point links between buildings [RUSH82]. This can be used for closed-circuit TV or as a data link between local networks.

Finally, a potential use for terrestrial microwave is for providing digital data transmission in small regions (radius <10 km). This concept has been termed "local data distribution" and would provide an alternative to phone lines for digital networking [ROCH79].

TABLE 2-6 Typical Digital Microwave Performance

Band (GHz)	Bandwidth (MHz)	Data Rate (Mbps)
2	7	12
6	30	90
11	40	90
18	220	274

Source: [PICK83a].

Transmission Characteristics.   As Table 2-4 indicates, microwave transmission covers a substantial portion of the spectrum. Common frequencies used for transmission are in the range 2 to 40 GHz. The higher the frequency used, the higher the potential bandwidth and therefore the higher the potential data rate. Table 2-6 indicates bandwidth and data rate for some typical systems.

As with any transmission system, a main source of loss for microwave is attenuation. For microwave (and radio frequency), the loss can be expressed as

$$L = 10 \log \left(\frac{4\pi d}{\lambda} \right)^2 \; dB \tag{2-2}$$

TABLE 2-7 Principal Microwave Bands Authorized for Fixed Telecommunications in the United States (1979)

Band Name	Range (GHz)	Maximum Channel Bandwidth (MHz)	Necessary Spectral Efficiency (bits/Hz)	Type of Service
2 GHz	1.71 – 1.85	—		Federal government
2 GHz	1.85 – 1.99	8		Private; local government
2 GHz	2.11 – 2.13	3.5	2	Common carrier (shared)
2 GHz	2.13 – 2.15	0.8/1.6		Private; local government
2 GHz	2.15 – 2.16	10		Private; multipoint
2 GHz	2.16 – 2.18	3.5	2	Common carrier
2 GHz	2.18 – 2.20	0.8/1.6		Private; local government
2 GHz	2.20 – 2.29	—		Federal government
2 GHz	2.45 – 2.50	0.8		Private; local government (shared)
4 GHz	3.70 – 4.20	20	4.5	Common carrier; satellite
6 GHz	5.925– 6.425	30	3	Common carrier; satellite
6 GHz	6.525– 6.875	5/10		Private; shared
7–8 GHz	7.125– 8.40	—		Federal government
10 GHz	10.550–10.680	25		Private
11 GHz	10.7 –11.7	50	2.25	Common carrier
12 GHz	12.2 –12.7	10/20		Private; local government
13 GHz	13.2 –13.25	25		Common carrier; private
14 GHz	14.4 –15.25	—		Federal government
18 GHz	17.7 –19.7	220		Common carrier; shared
18 GHz	18.36 –19.04	50/100		Private; local government
22 GHz	21.2 –23.6	50/100		Private; common carrier
31 GHz	31.0 –31.2	50/100		Private; common carrier
38 GHz	36.0 –38.6	—		Federal government
40 GHz	38.6 –40.0	50		Private; common carrier
	Above 40.0	—		Developmental

where d is the distance and λ is the wavelength, in the same units. Thus loss varies as the square of the distance. This is in contrast to twisted pair and coaxial cable where the loss varies logarithmically with distance (linear in decibels). Thus repeaters or amplifiers may be placed farther apart for microwave systems—10 to 100 km is typical. Attenuation is increased with rainfall. The effects become noticeable above 10 GHz.

Another source of impairment for microwave is interference. With the growing popularity of microwave, transmission areas overlap and interference is always a danger. Thus the assignment of frequency bands is strictly regulated.

Table 2-7 shows the authorized microwave frequency bands as regulated by the FCC. The most common bands for common carrier long-haul communications are the 4-GHz and 6-GHz bands. With increasing congestion at these frequencies, the 11-GHz band is now coming into use. The 12-GHz band is used as a component of the cable TV system [CUNN80]. Microwave links are used to provide TV signals to local CATV installations; the signals are then distributed to individual subscribers via coaxial cable. The FCC has reserved the 10-GHz band for local data distribution, called the Digital Termination Service. Finally, we mention that higher-frequency microwave is being used for short point-to-point links between buildings [RUSH82]. Typically, the 22-GHz band is used. The higher microwave frequencies are less useful for longer distance because of increased attenuation, but are quite adequate for shorter distances. In addition, at the higher frequencies, antennas are smaller and cheaper.

Satellite Microwave

Physical Description. A communication satellite is, in effect, a microwave relay station. It is used to link two or more ground-based microwave transmitter/receivers, known as earth stations or ground stations. The satellite receives transmissions on one frequency band (uplink), amplifies (analog transmission) or repeats (digital transmission) the signal, and transmits it on another frequency (downlink). A single orbiting satellite will operate on a number of frequency bands, called *transponder channels*, or simply *transponders*.

Figure 2-20 depicts in a general way two common uses of communications satellites. In the first, the satellite is being used to provide a point-to-point link between two distant ground-based antennas. In the second, the satellite provides communication between one ground-based transmitter and a number of ground-based receivers. In fact, these depictions are only suggestive of the ways in which satellites are used, a subject that we explore in Chapter 10.

For a communication satellite to function effectively, it is generally required that it remain stationary with respect to its position over the earth. Otherwise, it would not be within the line of sight of its earth stations at all times. To remain stationary, the satellite must have a period of rotation equal to the earth's period of rotation. This match occurs at a height of 35,784 km.

Two satellites using the same frequency band, if close enough together, will interfere with each other. To avoid this, current standards require a 4° spacing (angular displacement as measured from the earth) in the 4/6-GHz band, and a 3° spacing at 12/14 GHz. Thus, the number of possible satellites is quite limited.

Uses. The communication satellite is a technological revolution as important as fiber optics [PRIT84]. Communications satellites are being used today to handle

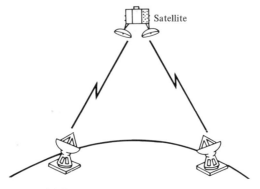

(a) Point-to-point link via satellite microwave

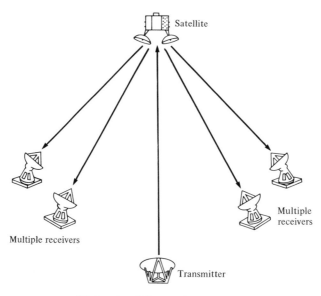

(b) Broadcast link via satallite microwave

FIGURE 2-20. Satellite communications configurations.

telephone, telex, and television traffic over long distances. Satellite is the optimum medium for high-usage international trunks and is competitive with terrestrial microwave and coaxial cable for many long-distance intranational links.

Transmission Characteristics.   The optimum frequency range for satellite transmission is in the range 1 to 10 GHz. Below 1 GHz, there is significant noise from natural sources, including galactic, solar, and atmospheric noise, and human-made noise from various electronic devices. Above 10 GHz, the signal is severely attenuated by atmospheric absorption and precipitation.

Most satellites providing point-to-point service today use a frequency bandwidth in the range 5.925 to 6.425 GHz for transmission from earth to satellite (uplink) and a bandwidth in the range 3.7 to 4.2 GHz for transmission from satellite to earth (downlink). This combination is referred to as the 4/6 GHz band. Note that the uplink and downlink frequencies differ. For continuous operation without interference, a satellite cannot transmit and receive on the same frequency. Thus data received from a ground station on one frequency must be transmitted back on another.

The 4/6 GHz band is within the optimum zone of 1 to 10 GHz, but has become saturated. Other frequencies in that range are unavailable because of sources of interference operating at those frequencies, usually terrestrial microwave. Therefore, the 12/14 GHz band is being developed (uplink: 14 to 14.5 GHz; downlink: 11.7 to 12.2 GHz). At this frequency range, attenuation problems must be overcome. However, smaller and cheaper earth-station receivers can be used. It is anticipated that this band will also saturate, and use is projected for the 19/29 GHz band (uplink: 27.5 to 31.0 GHz; downlink: 17.7 to 21.2 GHz). This band experiences even greater attenuation problems, but will allow greater bandwidth (2500 MHz versus 500 MHz) and even smaller and cheaper receivers.

Several peculiar properties of satellite communications should be noted. First, because of the long distance involved, there is a propagation delay of about 240 to 300 ms from transmission from one earth station to reception by another earth station. This delay is noticeable in ordinary telephone conversations. It also introduces problems in the areas of error control and flow control, which we discuss in later chapters. Second, satellite microwave is inherently a broadcast medium. Many stations can transmit to the satellite, and a transmission from a satellite can be received by many stations.

Radio

Physical Description. The principal difference between radio and microwave is that radio is omnidirectional and microwave is focused. Thus radio does not require dish-shaped antennas, and the antennas need not be rigidly mounted to a precise alignment.

Uses. Radio is a general term sometimes used to encompass all the frequency bands of Table 2-4. We use it in a more restricted sense to cover the VHF and part of the UHF band: 30 MHz to 1 GHz. This range covers FM radio and UHF and VHF television. In addition to these traditional uses, new applications have grown up in this band, and we mention several of these briefly.

A well-known use of radio for digital data communications is packet radio, which is discussed in Chapter 10. A packet radio system uses ground-based antennas to link multiple sites in a data transmission network. A more recent digital application is the teletext service. This service inserts character data in the vertical blanking interval in a conventional TV signal. Television sets equipped with a special decoder can receive and display the text.

A recent application for voice is based on a concept known as cellular radio. With cellular radio, a given frequency may be simultaneously used by a number of transmitters in the same area. The principle is explained below.

Finally, a service akin to teletext can be provided using a frequency-division multiplexed carrier known as *subsidiary communications authorization* (SCA). This service is used for one-way broadcast of messages and information.

Transmission Characteristics. The range 30 MHz to 1 GHz is a very effective one for broadcast communications. Unlike the case for lower-frequency electromagnetic waves, the ionosphere is transparent to radio waves above 30 MHz. Thus transmission is limited to the line of sight and distant transmitters will not interfere with each other due to reflection from the atmosphere. Unlike the higher frequencies of the microwave region, radio waves are less sensitive to attenuation from rainfall. For digital data communications, the primary drawback of this frequency range is that lower data rates are achievable: in the kilobit rather than the megabit range.

As a line-of-sight propagation technique, radio obeys Equation (2-1); that is, the maximum distance between transmitter and receiver is slightly more than the optical line of sight, or $7.14\sqrt{Kh}$. As with microwave, the amount of attenuation due simply to distance obeys Equation (2-2), namely $10 \log \left(\dfrac{4\pi d}{\lambda}\right)^2$ dB. Because of the longer wavelength, radio waves suffer relatively less attenuation.

A prime source of impairment for radio waves is multipath interference. Reflection from land, water, and natural or human-made objects can create multiple paths between antennas. This effect is frequently evident when TV reception displays multiple images as a plane passes by.

The transmission characteristics of radio used for broadcast communications are straightforward. The first such system was the ALOHA system in Hawaii [ABRA70]. Two frequency bands were used, one at 407.35 MHz for transmitting from users' terminals to a central controller and one at 413.475 MHz for transmission in the opposite direction; the bandwidth on both channels was 100kHz, with the data rate of 9600 bps. Transmission is in the form of short bursts of data called packets. The point-to-point range is about 30 km; repeaters were used to extend the system to a radius of about 500 km. A similar system is in operation in Montreal [ROUL81] using frequencies in the 220-MHz range. A system with mobile stations has been developed by the Printer Terminal Corp. [FOR81] using frequencies between 450 and 510 MHz.

Teletext is a one-way broadcast data service that may be embedded into a television signal. Teletext data are inserted into the vertical blanking intervals, which occur 60 times per second. The use of teletext is discussed further in Chapter 16.

Cellular radio is a technique that was developed to increase the capacity available for mobile radio telephone service [FLOO82]. The problem is this: With conventional radio telephone service, only 25 channels are available. Service is provided through a high-power transmitter/receiver that has an effective radius of about 80km. Thus only 25 channels are available in an area of about 20,000 km². The solution to this problem is to decrease the power of the transmitter/receiver, to no more than about 100 w. Because the range of such a system is small, on the order of a few kilometers at most, an area can be divided into cells, each one serviced by its own antenna (Figure 2-21). Each cell is allocated a set of frequencies, and is served by a cell node, consisting of transmitter, receiver, and control unit. Adjacent cells are assigned different frequencies to avoid interference or crosstalk. However, cells sufficiently distant from each other can use the same frequencies; it is expected that each frequency can be reused 20 or more times within a metropolitan area. The FCC has allocated two 20-MHz bands in the range 800 to 900 MHz for cellular radio. This bandwidth will support 333 full-duplex 60-kHz channels, each of which can be reused. Eventually thousands of channels will be provided in a given service area.

The initial application of cellular radio is for voice traffic [GODI83]. A mobile phone user is assigned a frequency in a particular cell. If the user moves to a new cell, the frequency is switched. Perhaps by the late 1980s, data applications will also be supported via cellular radio [MIER82b]. Such a scheme would provide modest data rates (9.6 kbps) and probably would be used by fixed-position terminals as an alternative to phone lines.

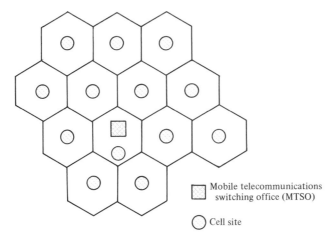

FIGURE 2-21. **Cellular radio layout.**

The SCA service makes use of available capacity on commercial FM radio channels. The FM band extends from 88 to 108 MHz, with each channel having a bandwidth of 200 kHz. Within that bandwidth, there is a subchannel which is not used for transmitting the FM radio signal and may be used for SCA transmission. For stereophonic stations, the SCA bandwidth is 22kHz wide, and data rates up to 9600 bps have been achieved [ANDE81].

2-5

RECOMMENDED READING

There are a large number of books on data transmission for the reader to choose from. [FREE81] provides readable and thorough coverage of all the topics in this chapter. [BELL82a] is a more difficult treatment, recommended for those with an electrical engineering background. Descriptive coverage can be found in [CHOU83] and [MART76]. A mathematical treatment of signal transmission is provided in [COUC83]. A detailed study of Fourier analysis can be found in [ZIEM83].

2-6

PROBLEMS

2-1 **a.** For the multipoint configuration of Figure 2-1, only one device at a time can transmit. Why?

  b. There are two methods of enforcing the rule that only one device can transmit. In the centralized method, one station is in control and can either transmit or allow a specified other station to transmit. In the decentralized method, the stations jointly cooperate in taking turns. What do you see as the advantages and disadvantages of the two methods?

2-2 Figure 2-10 indicates that the vertical blanking pulse has a duration of 830 to 1330 μs. What is the total number of visible lines for each of these two figures?

2-3 For a video signal, what increase in horizontal resolution is possible if a bandwidth of 5 MHz is used? What increase in vertical resolution is possible? Treat the two questions separately; that is, the increased bandwidth is to be used to increase either horizontal or vertical resolution, but not both.

2-4   **a.** Suppose that a digitized TV picture is to be transmitted from a source that uses a matrix of 480×500 picture elements (pixels), where each pixel can take on one of 32 intensity values. Assume that 30 pictures are sent per second. (This digital source is roughly equivalent to broadcast TV standards that have been adopted.) Find the source rate R (bps).

     b. Assume that the TV picture is to be transmitted over a channel with 4.5-MHz bandwidth and a 35-dB signal-to-noise ratio. Find the capacity of the channel (bps).

     c. Discuss how the parameters given in part (a) could be modified to allow transmission of color TV signals without increasing the required value for R.

2-5   Figure 2-5 shows the effect of eliminating higher-harmonic components of a square wave and retaining only a few lower harmonic components. What would the signal look like in the opposite case; that is, retaining all higher harmonics and eliminating a few lower harmonics?

2-6   What is the channel capacity for a teleprinter channel with a 300-Hz bandwidth and a signal-to-noise ratio of 3 dB?

2-7   A digital signaling system is required to operate at 9600 bps.

     a. If a signal element encodes a 4-bit word, what is the minimum required bandwidth of the channel?

     b. Repeat part (a) for the case of 8-bit words.

2-8   The relationship between frequency f and wavelength λ is $\lambda f = c$, where c is the speed of light (3×10^8 m/s). Determine the wavelength ranges for the frequency bands of Table 2-4.

2-9   If an amplifier has a 30-dB gain, what voltage ratio does the gain represent?

2-10 An amplifier has an output of 20 W. What is its output in dBW?

2-11 A periodic bandlimited signal has only three frequency components: dc, 100 Hz, and 200 Hz. In sine-cosine form:

$$x(t) = 12 + 15\cos 200\pi t + 20\sin 200\pi t$$
$$- 5\cos 400\pi t - 12\sin 400\pi t$$

Express the signal in amplitude/phase form.

APPENDIX 2A

FOURIER ANALYSIS

2A-1 Fourier Series Representation of Periodic Signals

With the aid of a good table of integrals, it is a remarkably simple task to determine the frequency-domain nature of many signals. We begin with periodic signals. Any periodic signal can be represented as a sum of sinusoids; known as a Fourier series:

$$x(t) = \sum_{n=0}^{\infty} a_n \cos(2\pi nf_0 t) + \sum_{n=1}^{\infty} b_n \sin(2\pi nf_0 t)$$

where f_0 is the inverse of the period of the signal ($f_0 = 1/T$). The frequency of f_0 is referred to as the *fundamental frequency*; multiples of f_0 are referred to as *harmonics*. Thus a periodic signal with period T consists of the fundamental frequency $f_0 = 1/T$ plus harmonics of that frequency. If $a_0 \neq 0$, then $x(t)$ has an additional *dc component*.

The values of the coefficients are calculated as follows:

$$a_0 = \frac{1}{T} \int_0^T x(t) dt$$

$$a_n = \frac{2}{T} \int_0^T x(t) \cos(2\pi nf_0 t) \, dt$$

$$b_n = \frac{2}{T} \int_0^T x(t) \sin(2\pi nf_0 t) \, dt$$

This form of representation, known as the *sine-cosine representation*, is the easiest form to compute, but suffers from the fact that there are two components at each frequency. A more meaningful representation, the *amplitude-phase representation*, takes the form

$$x(t) = c_0 + \sum_{n=1}^{\infty} c_n \cos(2\pi f_0 t + \theta_n)$$

This relates to the earlier representation as follows:

$$c_0 = a_0$$

$$c_n = \sqrt{a_n^2 + b_n^2}$$

$$\theta_n = -\tan^{-1}\left(\frac{b_n}{a_n}\right)$$

Examples of the Fourier series for periodic signals are shown in Figure 2-22.

2A-2 Fourier Transform Representation of Aperiodic Signals

For a periodic signal, we have seen that its spectrum consists of discrete frequency components, at the fundamental frequency and its harmonics. For an aperiodic signal, the spectrum consists of a continuum of frequencies. This spectrum can be defined by the Fourier transform. For a signal $x(t)$ with a spectrum $X(f)$, the following relationships hold:

$$x(t) = \int_{-\infty}^{\infty} X(f) e^{j2\pi ft} df$$

$$X(f) = \int_{-\infty}^{\infty} x(t) e^{-j2\pi ft} dt$$

Figure 2-23 presents some examples of Fourier transform pairs.

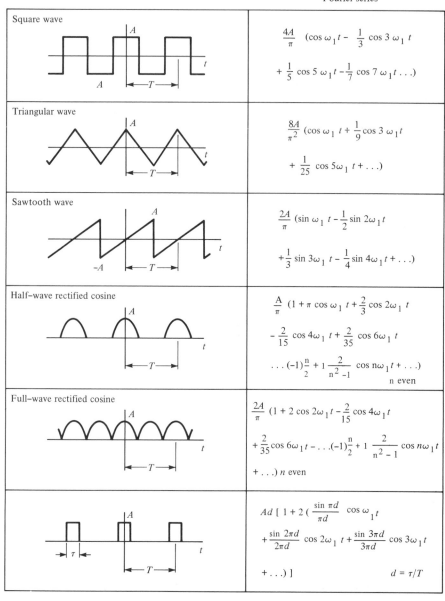

Square wave	$\dfrac{4A}{\pi}$ $(\cos \omega_1 t - \dfrac{1}{3} \cos 3\omega_1 t$ $+ \dfrac{1}{5} \cos 5\omega_1 t - \dfrac{1}{7} \cos 7\omega_1 t \dots)$
Triangular wave	$\dfrac{8A}{\pi^2}$ $(\cos \omega_1 t + \dfrac{1}{9} \cos 3\omega_1 t$ $+ \dfrac{1}{25} \cos 5\omega_1 t + \dots)$
Sawtooth wave	$\dfrac{2A}{\pi}$ $(\sin \omega_1 t - \dfrac{1}{2} \sin 2\omega_1 t$ $+ \dfrac{1}{3} \sin 3\omega_1 t - \dfrac{1}{4} \sin 4\omega_1 t + \dots)$
Half-wave rectified cosine	$\dfrac{A}{\pi}$ $(1 + \pi \cos \omega_1 t + \dfrac{2}{3} \cos 2\omega_1 t$ $- \dfrac{2}{15} \cos 4\omega_1 t + \dfrac{2}{35} \cos 6\omega_1 t$ $\dots (-1)^{\frac{n}{2}} + 1 \dfrac{2}{n^2 - 1} \cos n\omega_1 t + \dots)$ n even
Full-wave rectified cosine	$\dfrac{2A}{\pi}$ $(1 + 2 \cos 2\omega_1 t - \dfrac{2}{15} \cos 4\omega_1 t$ $+ \dfrac{2}{35} \cos 6\omega_1 t - \dots (-1)^{\frac{n}{2}} + 1 \dfrac{2}{n^2 - 1} \cos n\omega_1 t$ $+ \dots) \; n \text{ even}$
	$Ad [1 + 2 (\dfrac{\sin \pi d}{\pi d} \cos \omega_1 t$ $+ \dfrac{\sin 2\pi d}{2\pi d} \cos 2\omega_1 t + \dfrac{\sin 3\pi d}{3\pi d} \cos 3\omega_1 t$ $+ \dots)]$ $d = \tau/T$

FIGURE 2-22. **Some common periodic signals and their Fourier series.**

2A-3 Power Spectral Density and Bandwidth

The absolute bandwidth of any time-limited signal is infinite. In practical terms, however, most of the power in a signal will be concentrated in some finite band, and the effective bandwidth will consist of that portion of the spectrum that contains most of the power. To make this concept precise, we need to define the power spectral density.

First, we observe the power in the time domain. A function $x(t)$ usually specifies a signal in terms of either voltage or current. In either case, the instantaneous

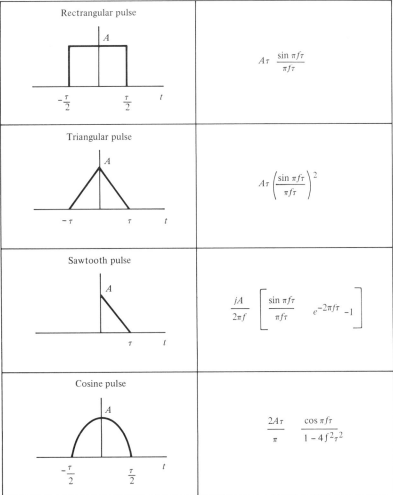

FIGURE 2-23.   Some common signals and their Fourier transforms.

power in the signal is proportional to $|x(t)|^2$. We define the average power of a time-limited signal as

$$P = \frac{1}{t_2 - t_1} \int_{t_1}^{t_2} |x(t)|^2 \, dt$$

For a periodic signal the average power in one period is

$$P = \frac{1}{T} \int_{0}^{T} |x(t)|^2 \, dt.$$

We would like to know the distribution of power as a function of frequency. For periodic signals, this is easily expressed in terms of the coefficients of the amplitude-phase Fourier series. The power spectral density $S(f)$ obeys

$$S(f) = \tfrac{1}{2} \sum_{n=0}^{\infty} |C_n|^2 \, \delta(f - nf_0)$$

The power spectral density $S(f)$ for aperiodic functions is more difficult to define. In essence, it is obtained by defining a "period" T_0 and allowing T_0 to increase without limit.

For a continuous valued function $S(f)$, the power contained in a band of frequencies, $f_1 < f < f_2$, is

$$P = 2 \int_{f_2}^{f_1} S(f) \, df$$

For a periodic waveform, the power through the first j harmonics is

$$P = \tfrac{1}{2} \sum^{j} |C_n|^2$$

With these concepts, we can now define the half-power bandwidth, which is perhaps the most common bandwidth definition. The half-power bandwidth is the interval between frequencies at which $S(f)$ has dropped to half of its maximum value of power, or 3 dB below the peak value.

CHAPTER 3

Data Encoding

In Chapter 2 a distinction was made between analog and digital *data* and analog and digital *signals*. Figure 2-12 suggested that either form of data could be encoded into either form of signal.

Figure 3-1 is another depiction that emphasizes the process involved. For digital signaling, a data source $g(t)$, which may be either digital or analog, is encoded into a digital signal $x(t)$. The actual form of $x(t)$ depends on the encoding technique, and is chosen to optimize use of the transmission medium. For example, the encoding may be chosen to conserve bandwidth or to minimize errors.

The basis for analog signaling is a continuous constant-frequency signal known as the carrier signal. The frequency of the carrier signal is chosen to be compatible with the transmission medium being used. Data may be transmitted using a carrier signal by *modulation*. Modulation is the process of encoding source data onto a *carrier signal* with frequency f_c. All modulation techniques involve operation on one or more of the three fundamental frequency-domain parameters:

- Amplitude.
- Frequency.
- Phase.

The input signal $m(t)$ may be analog or digital and is called the *modulating signal*

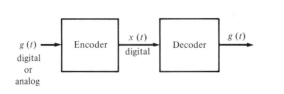
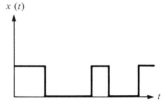

(a) Encoding onto a digital signal

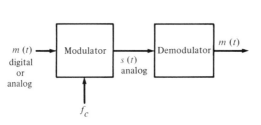
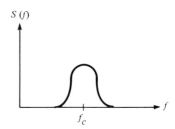

(b) Modulation onto an analog signal

FIGURE 3-1.   Encoding and modulation techniques.

or *baseband signal*. The result of modulating the carrier signal is called the *modulated signal s(t)*. As Figure 3-1b indicates, $s(t)$ is a bandlimited (bandpass) signal. The location of the bandwidth on the spectrum is related to f_c and is often centered on f_c. Again, the actual form of the encoding is chosen to optimize some characteristic of the transmission.

Each of the four possible combinations depicted in Figure 3-1 is in widespread use. The reasons for choosing a particular combination for any given communication task vary. We list here some representative reasons:

- *Digital data, digital signal:* In general, the equipment for encoding digital data into a digital signal is less complex and less expensive than digital-to-analog modulation equipment.
- *Analog data, digital signal:* Conversion of analog data to digital form permits the use of modern digital transmission and switching equipment. The advantages of the digital approach were outlined in Section 2-1.
- *Digital data, analog signal:* Some transmission media, such as optical fiber and the softwire media, will only propagate analog signals.
- *Analog data, analog signal:* Analog data in electrical form can be transmitted as baseband signals easily and cheaply. This is done with voice transmission over voice-grade lines. One common use of modulation is to shift the bandwidth of a baseband signal to another portion of the spectrum. In this way multiple signals, each at a different position on the spectrum, can share the same transmission medium. This is known as frequency-division multiplexing.

We now examine the techniques involved in each of these four combinations.

DIGITAL DATA, DIGITAL SIGNALS

A digital signal is a sequence of discrete, discontinuous voltage pulses. Each pulse is a *signal element*. Binary data are transmitted by encoding each data bit into signal elements. In the simplest case, there is a one-to-one correspondence between bits and signal elements. An example is shown in Figure 2-14, in which binary 0 is represented by a lower voltage level and binary 1 by a higher voltage level. As we shall see in this section, a variety of other encoding schemes are also used.

First, we define some terms. If the signal elements all have the same algebraic sign, that is, all positive or negative, then the signal is *unipolar*. In *polar* signaling, one logic state is represented by a positive voltage level, and the other by a negative voltage level. The *data signaling rate*, or just *data rate*, of a signal is the rate, in bits per second, that data are transmitted. The *duration* or length of a bit is the amount of time it takes for the transmitter to emit the bit; for a data rate R, the bit duration is $1/R$. The *modulation rate*, in contrast, is the rate at which signal level is changed. This will depend on the nature of the digital encoding, as explained below. The modulation rate is expressed in *bauds*, which means signal elements per second. Finally, the terms *mark* and *space*, for historical reasons, refer to the binary digits 1 and 0, respectively.

The tasks involved in interpreting digital signals at the receiver can be summarized by again referring to Figure 2-14. First, the receiver must know the timing of each bit. That is, the receiver must know with some accuracy when a bit begins and ends. Second, the receiver must determine whether the signal level for each bit position is high (1) or low (0). In Figure 2-14, these tasks are performed by sampling each bit position in the middle of the interval and comparing the value to a threshold. Because of noise and other impairments, there will be errors, as shown.

What factors determine how successful the receiver will be in interpreting the incoming signal? We saw in Chapter 2 that three factors are important: the signal-to-noise ratio (or, better, E_b/N_o), the data rate, and the bandwidth. With other factors held constant, the following statements are true:

- An increase in data rate increases bit error rate (the probability that a bit is received in error).
- An increase in S/N decreases bit error rate.
- An increase in bandwidth allows an increase in data rate.

There is another factor that can be used to improve performance, and that is the encoding scheme. The encoding scheme is simply the mapping from data bits to signal elements. A variety of approaches have been tried. In what follows, we describe some of the more common ones; they are defined in Table 3-1 and depicted in Figure 3-2. They can be categorized as follows

- Nonreturn to zero (NRZ).
- Return to zero (RZ).
- Biphase.
- Delay modulation.
- Multilevel binary.

Before describing these techniques, let us consider the ways of evaluating or comparing the various techniques. [LIND73] lists five evaluation factors.

TABLE 3-1 Definition of Digital Signal Encoding Formats

Nonreturn to zero—level (NRZ-L)
  1 = high level
  0 = low level
Nonreturn to zero—mark (NRZ-M)
  1 = transition at beginning of interval
  0 = no transition
Nonreturn to zero—space (NRZ-S)
  1 = no transition
  0 = transition at beginning of interval
Return to zero (RZ)
  1 = pulse in first half of bit interval
  0 = no pulse
Biphase—level (Manchester)
  1 = transition from high to low in middle of interval
  0 = transition from low to high in middle of interval
Biphase—mark
  Always a transition at beginning of interval
  1 = transition in middle of interval
  0 = no transition in middle of interval
Biphase—space
  Always a transition at beginning of interval
  1 = no transition in middle of interval
  0 = transition in middle of interval
Differential Manchester
  1 = no transition at beginning of interval
  0 = transistion at beginning of interval
  Always a transition in middle of interval
Delay modulation (Miller)
  1 = transition in middle of interval
  0 = no transition if followed by 1
      Transition at end of interval if followed by 0
Bipolar
  1 = pulse in first half of bit interval, alternating polarity from pulse to pulse
  0 = no pulse

- *Signal spectrum:* Several aspects of the spectrum are important. A lack of high-frequency components means that less bandwidth is required for transmission. On the other hand, a lack of a direct-current (dc) component is also desirable. With a dc component to the signal, there must be direct physical attachment of transmission components; with no dc component, alternating-current (ac) coupling via transformer is possible. This provides excellent electrical isolation, reducing interference.
- *Signal synchronization capability:* We mentioned the need to determine the beginning and end of each bit position. This is no easy task and may require a separate clock lead to synchronize transmitter and receiver. Some coding schemes avoid this problem.
- *Signal error-detecting capability:* We will discuss various error-detection techniques in Chapter 4. However, some primitive error-detection capability can be provided simply by the nature of the encoding.

70

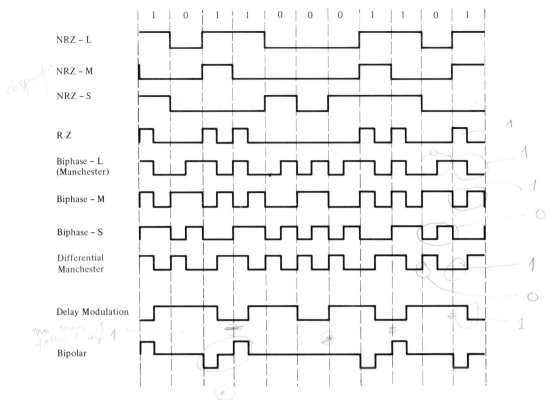

FIGURE 3-2. Digital signal encoding formats.

- *Signal interference and noise immunity:* Certain codes exhibit superior performance in the presence of noise. This is usually expressed by the bit error rate.
- *Cost and complexity:* Although digital logic continues to drop in price, this factor should not be ignored.

We now turn to discussion of the various techniques.

Nonreturn to Zero (NRZ)

The NRZ codes share the property that the voltage level is constant during a bit interval; there is no transition (no return to a zero voltage level). These are the simplest codes to implement and the simplest of these is NRZ-L (e.g., Figure 2-14). NRZ-L is generally the code used to generate or interpret digital data by data processing terminals and other devices. If a different code is to be used for transmission, it is typically generated from an NRZ-L signal by the transmission system (in terms of Figure 1-1, NRZ-L is $g(t)$ and the encoded signal is $s(t)$).

There are also mark (NRZ-M) and space (NRZ-S) versions of the NRZ signal. These have an advantage for transmission in that they are differential codes. In *differential encoding,* the signal is decoded by comparing the polarity of adjacent signal elements rather than the absolute value of a signal element. One benefit of this scheme is that it may be more reliable to detect a transition in the presence of

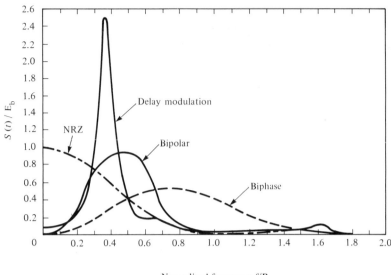

FIGURE 3-3. Spectral density of various digital signal encoding schemes.

noise than to compare a value to a threshold. Another benefit is that with a complex transmission system, it is easy to lose the sense of the polarity of the signal. For example, on a multidrop twisted-pair line, if the leads from an attached device to the twisted pair are accidentally inverted, all 1's and 0's will be inverted. This cannot happen with differential encoding.

The NRZ codes are easiest to engineer and in addition, make efficient use of bandwidth. This latter property is illustrated in Figure 3-3, which compares the spectra of various encoding schemes. In the figure, frequency is normalized to the data rate. As can be seen, most of the energy in NRZ signals is between dc and half the bit rate. For example, if an NRZ code is used to generate a signal with a data rate of 9600 bps, most of the energy in the signal would be concentrated between dc and 4800 Hz.

The main limitations of NRZ signals are the presence of the dc component and the lack of synchronization capability. To picture the problem with the latter, consider that with a long string of 1's for NRZ-L or NRZ-S, the output is a constant voltage. Any drift between transmitter and receiver cannot be corrected based on the signal alone.

Return to Zero (RZ)

With this code, we first see the distinction between data rate and modulation rate. The bit rate, as with all of these codes, is $1/t_B$, where t_B = bit duration. However, the minimum-size signal element is the pulse for a binary 1, which is one-half the length of the bit interval. Hence the maximum modulation rate (achieved by a string of 1s) for RZ signals is $2/t_B$.

The return to zero (RZ) convention provides no improvement over NRZ techniques. Because the modulation rate is higher than with NRZ, the bandwidth of the signal is greater. The same problems of dc component and no synchronization (with a string of 0's) remain. Because of its simplicity, RZ is used on some elementary transmitting and recording equipment, but is not the technique of choice for most applications.

Biphase

The term "biphase" is used to designate biphase-L (Manchester), biphase-M, biphase S, and differential Manchester. Biphase schemes are intended to overcome the disadvantages of NRZ and RZ signal encoding techniques. All of the biphase schemes require at least one transition per bit time and may have as many two transitions. Thus the maximum modulation rate is twice that for NRZ and the bandwidth is correspondingly greater. To compensate for this, the biphase schemes have several advantages:

- *Synchronization:* Because there is a predictable transition during each bit time, the receiver can synchronize on that transition. For Manchester and differential Manchester, there is always a transition in the middle of the bit interval. For biphase-M and biphase-S, there is always a transition at the beginning of a bit time. For this reason, the biphase codes are known as self-clocking codes.
- *No dc component:* Biphase codes have no dc component, yielding the benefits described earlier.
- *Error detection:* The absence of an expected transition can be used to detect errors. Noise on the line would have to invert both the signal before and after the expected transition to cause an undetected error.

As can be seen from Figure 3-3, the bulk of the energy in biphase codes is between one-half and one times the bit rate. Thus the bandwidth is reasonably narrow and contains no dc component. Also note that all but the Manchester code are differential.

Biphase codes are popular techniques for data transmission. Although NRZ is still most widely used in data communication systems, Manchester code is gaining ground rapidly [SAND82]. Already it is common in magnetic tape recording and as an input signal for fiber optic modulation systems. Both Manchester and differential Manchester appear in local network standards (discussed in Chapter 11).

Delay Modulation

An interesting alternative to the biphase technique is delay modulation, also known as Miller coding. With Miller, there is at least one transition per two bit times (the worst case is the 101 pattern), and there is never more than one transition per bit. Thus Miller coding has some synchronization capability, but requires a lower modulation rate and less bandwidth than biphase.

Figure 3-3 shows that the bandwidth for Miller is significantly less than either biphase or NRZ. This figure is somewhat misleading, however [SEVE80]. For worst-case bit patterns, Miller can have a significant dc component and greater bandwidth than NRZ.

Finally, we present Figure 3-4, which compares the theoretical bit error rate as a function of S/N for Miller, Manchester, NRZ and RZ. As can be seen, Manchester and NRZ have identical performance, which is about 3 dB better than Miller. Put another way, at a given S/N ratio, the bit error rate for NRZ and Manchester is significantly less than Miller.

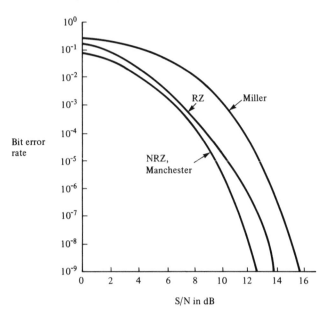

FIGURE 3-4. Theoretical bit error rate for various digital encoding schemes.

This difference in performance falls out of the derivation of the probability of error in white noise, which can be found in [LIND73], but we can give an intuitive explanation here. At the receiver, a decision must be made whether a received bit interval contains 1 or 0. In the case of NRZ and Manchester, there are only two elementary pulse waveforms to choose from. This is also true of RZ, but RZ makes inefficient use of signal time: either a half-pulse or no pulse. The Miller code uses four elementary pulse waveforms, making the decision even more difficult.

Multilevel Binary

A somewhat different category of encoding is multilevel binary, which uses more than two signal levels. Figure 3-2 show a popular example of this, bipolar. Bipolar is widely used by Bell for T1-PCM carriers (this is a digitized voice format, explained below).

As can be seen from Figure 3-3, bipolar has a bandwidth centered on one-half the bit rate. There is no dc component, which is an advantage. On the other hand, there is no synchronization capability. Bipolar provides some error-detection capability, since successive 1's must have opposite signs.

3-2

DIGITAL DATA, ANALOG SIGNALS

We turn now to the case of transmitting digital data using analog signals. The most familiar use of this transformation is for transmitting digital data through the public telephone network. The telephone network was designed to receive, switch, and transmit signals in the voice-frequency range of about 300 to 3400 Hz. It is not at present suitable for handling digital signals from the subscriber locations (although this is beginning to change). Thus digital devices are attached to the network via a *modem* (modulator-demodulator), which converts digital data to analog signals, and vice versa.

For the telephone network, modems are used which produce signals in the voice-frequency range. The same basic techniques are used for modems that produce signals at higher frequencies (e.g., microwave). This section introduces these techniques and provides a brief discussion of the performance characteristics of the alternative approaches.

Encoding Techniques

We mentioned that modulation involves operation on one or more of the three characteristics of a carrier signal: amplitude, frequency, and phase. Accordingly, there are three basic encoding or modulation techniques for transforming digital data into analog signals, as illustrated in Figure 3-5.

- Amplitude-shift keying (ASK).
- Frequency-shift keying (FSK).
- Phase-shift keying (PSK).

In all these cases, the resulting signal occupies a bandwidth centered on the carrier frequency.

In ASK, the two binary values are represented by two different amplitudes of the carrier frequency. Commonly, one of the amplitudes is zero; that is, one binary

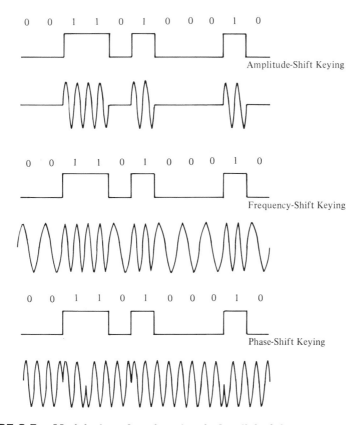

FIGURE 3-5. Modulation of analog signals for digital data.

digit is represented by the presence, at constant amplitude, of the carrier, the other by the absence of the carrier. The resulting signal is

ASK
$$s(t) = \begin{cases} A \cos(2\pi f_c t + \theta_c) & \text{binary 1} \\ 0 & \text{binary 0} \end{cases}$$

where the carrier signal is $A \cos(2\pi f_c t + \theta_c)$. ASK is susceptible to sudden gain changes and is a rather inefficient modulation technique. On voice-grade lines, it is typically used only up to 1200 bps.

In FSK, the two binary values are represented by two different frequencies near the carrier frequency. The resulting signal is

FSK
$$s(t) = \begin{cases} A \cos(2\pi f_1 t + \theta_c) & \text{binary 1} \\ A \cos(2\pi f_2 t + \theta_c) & \text{binary 0} \end{cases}$$

where f_1 and f_2 are typically offset from the carrier frequency f_c by equal but opposite amounts.

Figure 3-6 shows an example of the use of FSK for full-duplex operation over a voice-grade line. The figure is a specification for the Bell System 108 series modems. Recall that a voice-grade line will pass frequencies in the approximate range 300 to 3400 Hz, and that full-duplex means that signals are transmitted in both directions at the same time. To achieve full-duplex transmission, this bandwidth is split at 1700 Hz. In one direction (transmit or receive), the frequencies used to represent 1 and 0 are centered on 1170 Hz, with a shift of 100 Hz on either side. The effect of alternating between those two frequencies is to produce a signal whose spectrum is indicated as the shaded area on the left in Figure 3-6. Similarly, for the other direction (receive or transmit) the modem uses frequencies shifted 100 Hz to each side of a center frequency of 2125 Hz. This signal is indicated by the shaded area on the right in Figure 3-6. Note that there is little overlap and thus little interference.

FSK is less susceptible to error than ASK. On voice grade lines, it is typically used up to 1200 bps. It is also commonly used for high-frequency (3 to 30 MHz) radio transmission. It can also be used at even higher frequencies on local networks that use coaxial cable.

In PSK, the phase of the carrier signal is shifted to represent data. Figure 3-5c

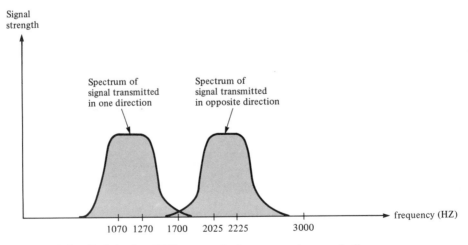

FIGURE 3-6. Full-duplex FSK transmission on a voice-grade line.

is an example of a two-phase system. In this system, a binary 0 is represented by sending a signal burst of the same phase as the previous signal burst sent. A binary 1 is represented by sending a signal burst of opposite phase to the preceding one. This is known as differential PSK, since the phase shift is with reference to the previous bit transmitted rather than to some constant reference signal. The resulting signal is

$$s(t) = \begin{cases} A \cos(2\pi f_c t + \pi) & \text{binary 1} \\ A \cos(2\pi f_c t) & \text{binary 0} \end{cases}$$

with the phase measured relative to the previous bit interval.

More efficient use of bandwidth can be achieved if each signaling element represents more than one bit. For example, instead of a phase shift of 180°, as allowed in PSK, a common encoding technique, known as *quadrature phase-shift keying* (QPSK) uses phase shifts of multiples of 90°.

$$s(t) = \begin{cases} A \cos(2\pi f_c t + 45°) & 11 \\ A \cos(2\pi f_c t + 135°) & 10 \\ A \cos(2\pi f_c t + 225°) & 00 \\ A \cos(2\pi f_c t + 315°) & 01 \end{cases}$$

Thus each signal element represents two bits rather than one.

This scheme can be extended. It is possible to transmit bits three at a time using eight different phase angles. Further, each angle can have more than one amplitude. For example, a standard 9600 bps modem uses 12 phase angles, four of which have two amplitude values (Figure 3-7). A thorough review of these and other techniques can be found in [OETT79].

This latter example points out very well the difference between the data rate R (in bps) and the modulation rate D (in bauds) of a signal. Let us assume that this scheme is being employed with NRZ-L digital input. The data rate is $R = 1/t_B$ where t_B is the width of each NRZ-L bit. However, the encoded signal contains $l = 4$ bits in each signal element using $L = 16$ different combinations of amplitude and phase. The modulation rate can be seen to be $R/4$, since each change of signal

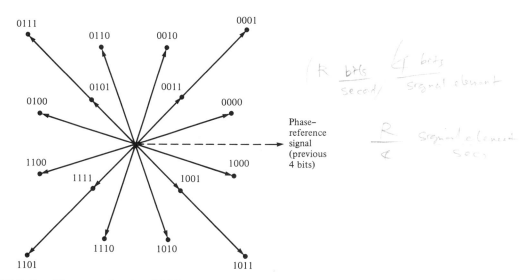

FIGURE 3-7. Phase angles for 9600 bit-per-second transmission.

element communicates four bits. Thus the line signaling speed is 2400 bauds, but the data rate is 9600 bps. This is the reason that higher bit rates can be achieved over voice-grade lines by employing more complex modulation schemes.

In general,

$$\frac{9600}{4}, \frac{2400}{} \quad D = \frac{R}{l} = \frac{R}{\log_2 L}$$

where

  D = modulation rate, bauds
  R = data rate, bps
  L = number of different signal elements
  l = number of bits per signal element

The above is complicated when an encoding technique other than NRZ is used. For example, we saw that the maximum modulation rate for RZ signals is $2/t_B$. Thus D for RZ is greater than D for NRZ. This to some extent counteracts the reduction in D achieved by using multilevel signal modulation techniques.

Performance

In looking at the performance of various digital-to-analog modulation schemes, the first parameter of interest is the bandwidth of the modulated signal. This depends on a variety of factors; including the definition of bandwidth used and the filtering technique used to create the bandpass signal. We will use some straightforward results from [COUC83]; a more detailed analysis can be found in [AMOR80].

The transmission bandwidth B_T for ASK is of the form

$$\text{ASK and PSK} \quad B_T = (1 + r)R$$

where R is the bit rate and r is related to the technique by which the signal is filtered to establish a bandwidth for transmission; typically $0 < r < 1$. Thus the bandwidth is directly related to the bit rate. The formula above is also valid for PSK.

For FSK, the bandwidth can be expressed as

$$B_T = 2\Delta F + (1 + r)R$$

where $\Delta F = f_2 - f_c = f_c - f_1$ is the offset of the modulated frequency from the carrier frequency. When very high frequencies are used, the ΔF term dominates. For example, one of the standards for FSK signaling on a coaxial cable multipoint local network uses $\Delta F = 1.25$ MHz, $f_c = 5$ MHz, and $R = 1$ Mbps. In this case $B_T \approx 2\Delta F = 2.5$ MHz. In the example of the preceding section for the Bell 108 modem, $\Delta F = 100$ Hz, $f_c = 1170$ Hz (in one direction), and $R = 300$ bps. In this case $B_T \approx (1 + r)R$, which is the range 300 to 600 Hz.

With multilevel signaling, significant improvements in bandwidth can be achieved. In general

$$B_T = \left(\frac{1 + r}{l}\right)R = \left(\frac{1 + r}{\log_2 L}\right)R$$

where l is the number of bits encoded per signal element and L is the number of different signal elements.

Table 3-2 shows the ratio of data rate to transmission bandwidth for various

TABLE 3-2 Data Rate to Transmission Bandwidth Ratio for Various Digital-to-Analog Encoding Schemes

	$r = 0$	$r = 0.5$	$r = 1$
ASK	1.0	0.67	0.5
FSK			
Wideband ($\Delta F \gg R$)	~0	~0	~0
Narrowband ($\Delta F \approx f_c$)	1.0	0.67	0.5
PSK	1.0	0.67	0.5
Multilevel signaling			
$L = 4, l = 2$	2.00	1.33	1.00
$L = 8, l = 3$	3.00	2.00	1.50
$L = 16, l = 4$	4.00	2.67	2.00
$L = 32, l = 5$	5.00	3.33	2.50

schemes. This ratio is also referred to as the bandwidth efficiency. As the name suggests, this parameter measures the efficiency with which bandwidth can be used to transmit data. The advantage of multilevel signaling methods now becomes clear.

Of course, the discussion above refers to the spectrum of the input signal to a communications line. Nothing has yet been said of performance in the presence of noise. Figure 3-8 summarizes some results based on reasonable assumptions concerning the transmission system [COUC83]. Here bit error rate is plotted as a function of the ratio E_b/N_o defined in Chapter 2. Of course, as that ratio increases, the bit error rate drops. Further, PSK and QPSK are about 3 dB superior to ASK and FSK.

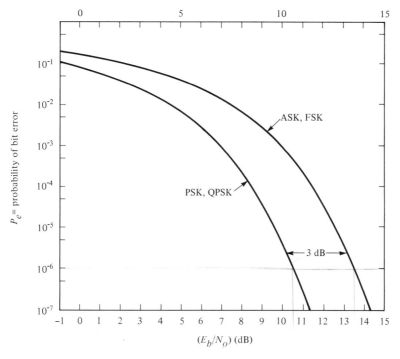

FIGURE 3-8. Bit error rate of various digital-to-analog encoding schemes.

This information can now be related to bandwidth efficiency. Recall that

$$\frac{E_b}{N_0} = \frac{S}{N_0 R}$$

The parameter N_0 is the noise power density in watts/hertz. Hence, the noise in a signal with bandwidth B_T is $N = N_0 B_T$. Substituting, we have

$$\frac{E_b}{N_0} = \frac{S}{N}\frac{B}{R}$$

For a given signaling scheme, the bit error rate can be reduced by increasing E_b/N_0, which can be accomplished by increasing the bandwidth or decreasing the data rate: in other words, by reducing bandwidth efficiency.

EXAMPLE. What is the bandwidth efficiency for FSK, ASK, PSK, and QPSK for a bit error rate of 10^{-7} on a channel with a S/N of 12 dB?

We have

$$\frac{E_b}{N_0} = 12 \text{ dB} - \left(\frac{R}{B}\right)\text{dB}$$

For FSK and ASK, from Figure 3-8,

$$\frac{E_b}{N_0} = 14.2 \text{ dB}$$

$$\left(\frac{R}{B}\right)\text{dB} = -2.2 \text{ dB}$$

$$\frac{R}{B} = 0.6$$

For PSK, from Figure 3-8

$$\frac{E_b}{N_0} = 11.2 \text{ dB}$$

$$\left(\frac{R}{B}\right)\text{dB} = 0.8 \text{ dB}$$

$$\frac{R}{B} = 1.2$$

The result for QPSK must take into account that the baud rate $D = R/2$. Thus

$$\frac{R}{B} = 2.4$$

As the example above shows, ASK and FSK exhibit the same bandwidth efficiency, PSK is better, and even greater improvement can be achieved with multilevel signaling.

It is worthwhile to compare these bandwidth requirements with those for digital signaling. A good approximation is

$$B_T = 0.5(1 + r)D$$

where D is the modulation rate. For NRZ, $D = R$, and we have

$$\frac{R}{B} = \frac{2}{1+r}$$

Thus digital signaling is in the same ballpark, in terms of bandwidth efficiency, as ASK, FSK, and PSK. Significant advantage for analog signaling is seen with multilevel techniques.

3-3

ANALOG DATA, DIGITAL SIGNALS

In this section we examine the process of transforming analog data into digital signals. Strictly speaking, it might be more correct to refer to this as a process of converting analog data into digital data, which process is known as *digitization*. Once analog data have been converted into digital data, a number of things can happen. The three most common:

1. The digital data can be transmitted using NRZ-L. In this case, we have in fact gone directly from analog data to a digital signal.
2. The digital data can be encoded as a digital signal using a code other than NRZ-L. Thus an extra step is required.
3. The digital data can be converted into an analog signal, using one of the modulation techniques discussed in Section 3-2.

This last, seemingly curious, procedure is illustrated in Figure 3-9, which shows voice data that are digitized and then converted to an analog ASK signal. This allows digital transmission in the sense defined in Chapter 2. The voice data, because it has been digitized can be treated as digital data, even though transmission requirements (e.g., use of microwave) dictate that an analog signal be used.

The device used for converting analog data into digital form for transmission, and subsequently recovering the original analog data from the digital is known as a *codec* (coder-decoder). In this section we examine the two principal techniques used in codecs, pulse code modulation and delta modulation. The section closes with a discussion of comparative performance.

Pulse Code Modulation

Pulse Code Modulation (PCM) is based on the sampling theorem, which states [ITT75]:

> "If a signal $f(t)$ is sampled at regular intervals of time and at a rate higher than twice the highest significant signal frequency, then the samples contain

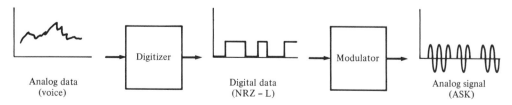

| Analog data | Digital data | Analog signal |
| (voice) | (NRZ – L) | (ASK) |

FIGURE 3-9. Digitizing analog data.

all the information of the original signal. The function $f(t)$ may be reconstructed from these samples by the use of a low-pass filter.''

For the interested reader, a proof is provided in Appendix 3A. If voice data are limited to frequencies below 4000 Hz, a conservative procedure for intelligibility, 8000 samples per second would be sufficient to completely characterize the voice signal. Note, however, that these are analog samples.

This is illustrated in Figure 3-10a and b. The original signal is assumed to be bandlimited with a bandwidth of B. Samples are taken at a rate $2B$, or once every $1/2B$ seconds. These samples are represented as narrow pulses whose amplitude is proportional to the value of the original signal. This process is known as *pulse amplitude modulation* (PAM). By itself, this technique has commercial applicability. It is used, for example, in Bell's Dimension PBX products.

However, the most significant fact about PAM is that it is the first step toward PCM, as depicted in Figure 3-10c. To produce PCM data, the PAM samples are quantized. That is, the amplitude of each PAM pulse is approximated by an n-bit

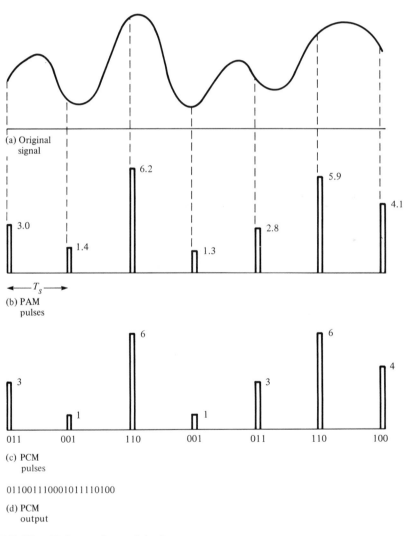

FIGURE 3-10.   Pulse-code modulation.

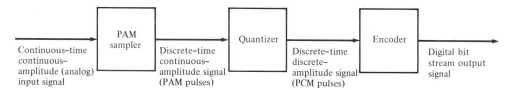

FIGURE 3-11. Analog-to-digital conversion.

integer. In the example, $n = 3$. Thus $8 = 2^3$ levels are available for approximating the PAM pulses.

Figure 3-11 illustrates the process, starting with a continuous-time, continuous-amplitude (analog) signal, a digital signal is produced. The digital signal consists of blocks of n bits, where each n-bit number is the amplitude of a PCM pulse. On reception, the process is reversed to reproduce the analog signal. Notice, however, that this process violates the terms of the sampling theorem. By quantizing the PAM pulse, the original signal is now only approximated and cannot be recovered exactly. This effect is known as *quantizing error* or *quantizing noise*. The signal-to-noise ratio for quantizing noise can be expressed as [BELL82a]

$$\frac{S}{N} = 6n + 1.8 \text{ dB}$$

Thus each additional bit used for quantizing increases S/N by 6 dB.

Typically, the PCM scheme is refined using a technique known as *nonlinear encoding*, which means, in effect, that the quantization levels are not equally spaced. The problem with equal spacing is that the mean absolute error for each sample is the same, regardless of signal level. Consequently, lower-amplitude values are relatively more distorted. By using a greater number of quantizing steps for signals of low amplitude, and a smaller number of quantizing steps for signals of large amplitude, a marked reduction in overall signal distortion is achieved (e.g., see Figure 3-12).

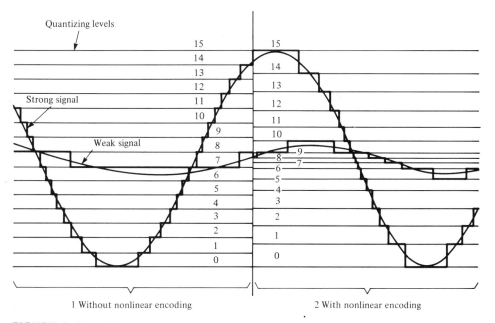

FIGURE 3-12. Effect of nonlinear coding.

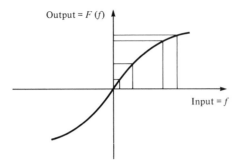

FIGURE 3-13.   Typical companding function.

The same effect can be achieved by using uniform quantizing but companding (*compressing-expanding*) the input analog signal. Companding is a process that compresses the intensity range of a signal by imparting more gain to weak signals than to strong signals on input. At output, the reverse operation is performed. Figure 3-13 is a typical companding function.

Nonlinear encoding can significantly improve the PCM S/N ratio. For voice signals, improvements of 24 to 30 dB have been achieved [FREE81].

Delta Modulation (DM)

A variety of techniques have been used to improve the performance of PCM or to reduce its complexity. A discussion of the various approaches that have been taken for voice data can be found in [CROC83]. Here we mention one of the most popular alternatives to PCM: delta modulation (DM).

With DM, the analog data are approximated by a staircase function that moves up or down by one quantization level at each sampling time. An example is shown in Figure 3-14c, where the staircase function is overlaid on the original analog waveform. The important characteristic of this staircase function is that it is binary: At each sampling time, the function moves up or down a constant amount. Thus the output of the DM process is a single binary digit for each sample. In essence, a bit stream is produced by approximating the derivative of an analog signal rather than its amplitude. A 1 is generated if the staircase function is to go up during the next interval; a 0 is generated otherwise.

The transition (up or down) that occurs at each sampling instant is chosen so that the staircase function tracks the original analog waveform as closely as possible. Figure 3-15 illustrates the logic of the process, which is essentially a feedback mechanism. For transmission, the following occurs. At each sampling instant, the analog input is compared to the most recent value of the approximating staircase function. If the value of the sampled waveform exceeds that of the staircase function, a 1 is generated; otherwise, a 0 is generated. This binary value is transmitted as the next output digit. It is also used to determine the next value of the reconstructed waveform or staircase function. The constant value δ is added to the function for a value of 1; the value δ is subtracted for a value of 0. Figure 3-15b shows how the binary stream generated using DM is used at reception to construct the approximating staircase function.

There are two important parameters in a DM scheme, the size of the step assigned to each binary digit, δ, and the sampling rate. As Figure 3-14c illustrates, δ must

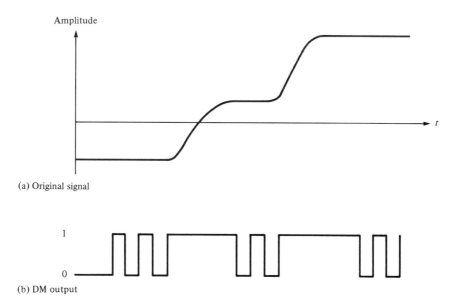

(a) Original signal

(b) DM output

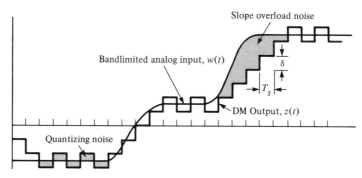

(c) Reconstructed wave form (compared to original)

FIGURE 3-14.   Example of delta modulation (DM).

be chosen to produce a balance between two types of errors or noise. When the analog waveform is changing very slowly, there will be *quantizing noise*. This noise increases as δ is increased. On the other hand, when the analog waveform is changing more rapidly than the staircase can follow, there is *slope overload noise*. This noise increases as δ is decreased.

It should be clear that the accuracy of the scheme can be improved by increasing the sampling rate. However, this increases the data rate of the output signal.

The principal advantage of DM over PCM is the simplicity of its implementation. In general, PCM exhibits better S/N characteristics at the same data rate [COUC83].

Performance

Good voice reproduction via PCM can be achieved with 128 quantization levels, or 7-bit coding ($2^7 = 128$). A voice signal, conservatively, occupies a bandwidth

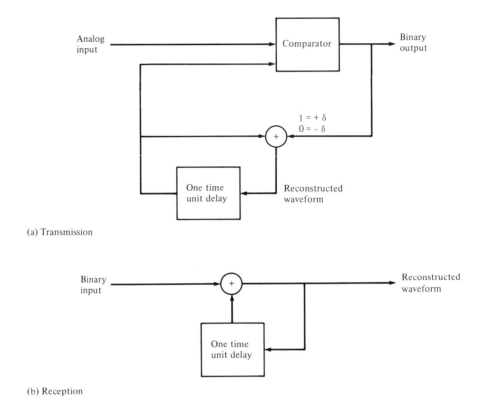

(a) Transmission

(b) Reception

FIGURE 3-15. Delta modulation.

of 4 kHz. Thus, according to the sampling theorem, samples should be taken at a rate of 8000 samples per second. This implies a data rate of $8000 \times 7 = 56$ kbps for the PCM-encoded digital data.

Consider what this means from the point of view of bandwidth requirement. An analog voice signal occupies 4 kHz. A 56-kbps digital signal will require on the order of at least 28 kHz! Even more severe differences are seen with higher bandwidth signals. For example, a common PCM scheme for color television uses 10-bit codes, which works out to 92 Mbps for a 4.6-MHz bandwidth signal. In spite of these numbers, digital techniques continue to grow in popularity for transmitting analog data. The principal reasons for this are:

- Because repeaters are used instead of amplifiers, there is no additive noise.
- As we shall see, time-division multiplexing (TDM) is used for digital signals instead of the frequency-division multiplexing (FDM) used for analog signals. With TDM, there is no intermodulation noise, whereas we have seen that this is a concern for FDM.
- The conversion to digital signaling allows the use of the more efficient digital switching techniques, discussed in Chapter 8.

Furthermore, techniques are being developed to provide more efficient codes. In the case of voice, a reasonable goal appears to be in the neighborhood of 4 kbps [HASK81]. With video, advantage can be taken of the fact that from frame to frame, most picture elements will not change. Interframe coding techniques should allow the video requirement to be reduced to about 15 Mbps, and for slowly

DATA ENCODING

changing scenes, such as found in a video teleconference, down to 1.5 Mbps or less [NETR80, KANE80b].

As a final point, we mention that in many instances, the use of a telecommunications system will result in both digital-to-analog and analog-to-digital processing. The overwhelming majority of local terminations into the telecommunications network is analog, and the network itself uses a mixture of analog and digital techniques. Thus digital data at a user's terminal may be converted to analog by a modem, subsequently digitized by a codec, and perhaps suffer repeated conversions before reaching its destination.

Because of the above, telecommunication facilities handle analog signals that represent both voice and digital data. The characteristics of the waveforms are quite different. Whereas voice signals tend to be skewed to the lower portion of the bandwidth (Figure 2-8), analog encoding of digital signals has a more uniform spectral content over the bandwidth and therefore contains more high-frequency components. Studies have shown that, because of the presence of these higher frequencies, PCM-related techniques are preferable to DM-related techniques for digitizing analog signals that represent digital data [ONEA80].

3-4

ANALOG DATA, ANALOG SIGNALS

Modulation has been defined as the process of combining an input signal $m(t)$ and a carrier at frequency f_c to produce a signal $s(t)$ whose bandwidth is (usually) centered on f_c. For digital data, the motivation for modulation should be clear: when only analog transmission facilities are available, modulation is required to convert the digital data to analog form. The motivation when the data are already analog is less clear. After all, voice signals are transmitted over telephone lines at their original spectrum (referred to as baseband transmission). There are two principal reasons:

- A higher frequency may be needed for effective transmission. For softwire transmission, it is virtually impossible to transmit baseband signals; the required antennas would be many kilometers in diameter.
- Modulation permits frequency-division multiplexing, an important technique explored in Chapter 6.

In this section we look at the principle techniques for modulation using analog data: amplitude modulation (AM), frequency modulation (FM), and phase modulation (PM). As before, the three basic characteristics of a signal are used for modulation.

Amplitude Modulation

Amplitude modulation (AM) is the simplest form of modulation, and is depicted in Figure 3-16. Mathematically, the process can be expressed as

$$s(t) = [1 + n_a x(t)]\cos 2\pi f_c t$$

where $\cos 2\pi f_c t$ is the carrier and $x(t)$ is the input signal to be modulated, both normalized to unity amplitude. The parameter n_a, known as the *modulation index*, is the ratio of the amplitude of the input signal to the carrier. Corresponding to our

(a) Sinusoidal modulating wave

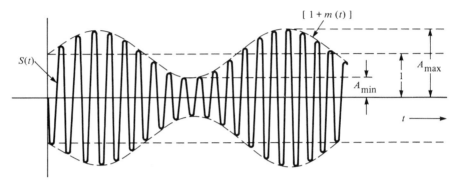

(b) Resulting AM signal

FIGURE 3-16. Amplitude modulation.

previous notation, the modulating signal is $m(5) = n_a x(t)$. The "l" in the equation above is a dc component that prevents loss of information, as explained below. This scheme is also known as double sideband transmitted carrier (DSBTC).

EXAMPLE.   Derive an expression for $s(t)$ if $x(t)$ is the amplitude-modulating signal $\cos 2\pi f_m t$.
   We have:

$$s(t) = [1 + n_a \cos 2\pi f_m t] \cos 2\pi f_c t$$

By trigonometric identity, this may be expanded to:

$$s(t) = \cos 2\pi f_c t + \frac{n_a}{2} \cos 2\pi (f_c - f_m)t + \frac{n_a}{2} \cos 2\pi (f_c + f_m)t$$

The resulting signal has a component at the original carrier frequency plus a pair of components each spaced f_m hertz from the carrier.   ∎

   From the equation above and Figure 3-16, it can be seen that AM involves the multiplication of the input signal by the carrier. The envelope of the resulting signal is $[1 + n_a x(t)]$ and, as long as $n_a < 1$, the envelope is an exact reproduction of the original signal. If $n_a > 1$, the envelope will cross the time axis and information is lost.
   It is instructive to look at the spectrum of the AM signal. An example is shown in Figure 3-17. The spectrum consists of the original carrier plus the spectrum of the input signal translated to f_c. The portion of the spectrum for $|f| > |f_c|$ is the *upper sideband,* and the portion for $|f| < |f_c|$ is the *lower sideband.* Both the upper

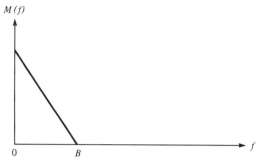

(a) Spectrum of modulating signal

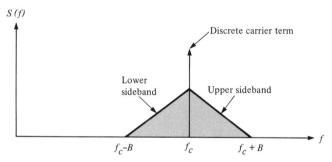

(b) Spectrum of AM signal with carrier at f_c

FIGURE 3-17. Spectrum of an AM signal.

and lower sidebands are replicas of the original spectrum $M(f)$, with the lower sideband being frequency-reversed. As an example, consider a voice signal with a bandwidth that extends from 300 to 3000 Hz being modulated on a 60-kHz carrier. The resulting signal contains an upper sideband of 60.3 to 63 kHz, a lower sideband of 57 to 59.7 kHz, and the 60-Hz carrier. An important relationship is

$$P_t = P_c \left(1 + \frac{n_a^2}{2} \right)$$

where P_t is the total transmitted power in $s(t)$ and P_c is the transmitted power in the carrier. We would like n_a as large as possible so that most of the signal power is used to actually carry information. However, n_a must remain below 1.

It should be clear that $s(t)$ contains unnecessary components, since each of the sidebands contains the complete spectrum of $m(t)$. A popular variant of AM, known as single sideband (SSB), takes advantage of this fact by sending only one of the sidebands, eliminating the other sideband and the carrier. The principal advantages of this approach are:

- Only half the bandwidth is required, that is, $B_T = B$, where B is the bandwidth of the original signal. For DSBTC, $B_T = 2B$.
- Less power is required since no power is used to transmit the carrier or the other sideband. Another variant is double sideband suppressed carrier (DSBSC) which filters out the carrier frequency and sends both sidebands. This saves some power but uses as much bandwidth as DSBTC.

The disadvantage of suppressing the carrier is that the carrier can be used for synchronization purposes. For example, suppose that the original analog signal is an ASK waveform encoding digital data. The receiver needs to know the starting point of each bit time to interpet the data correctly. A constant carrier provides a clocking mechanism by which to time the arrival of bits. A compromise approach is vestigial sideband (VSB), which uses one sideband and a reduced-power carrier.

Angle Modulation

Frequency modulation (FM) and *phase modulation* (PM) are special cases of *angle modulation*. The modulated signal is expressed as

$$s(t) = A_c \cos[2\pi f_c t + \phi(t)]$$

For phase modulation, the phase is proportional to the modulating signal:

$$\phi(t) = n_p m(t)$$

where n_p is the phase modulation index.

For frequency modulation, the derivative of the phase is proportional to the modulating signal:

$$\phi'(t) = n_f m(t)$$

where n_f is the frequency modulation index.

The definitions above may be clarified if we consider the following. The phase of $s(t)$ at any instant is just $2\pi f_c t + \phi(t)$. The instantaneous phase deviation from the carrier signal is $\phi(t)$. In PM, this instantaneous phase deviation is proportional to $m(t)$. Since frequency can be defined as the rate of change of phase of a signal, the instantaneous frequency of $s(t)$ is

$$2\pi f_i(t) = \frac{d}{dt} [2\pi f_c t + \phi(t)]$$

$$f_i(t) = f_c + \frac{1}{2\pi} \phi'(t)$$

and the instantaneous frequency deviation from the carrier frequency is $\phi'(t)$, which in FM is proportional to $m(t)$.

Figure 3-18 illustrates amplitude, phase, and frequency modulation by a sine wave. The shapes of the FM and PM signals are very similar. Indeed, it is impossible to tell them apart without knowledge of the modulation function.

Several observations about the FM process are in order. The peak deviation ΔF can be seen to be

$$\Delta F = \frac{1}{2\pi} n_f A_m \qquad \text{Hz}$$

where A_m is the maximum value of $m(t)$. Thus an increase in the magnitude of $m(t)$ will increase ΔF, which, intuitively, should increase the transmitted bandwidth B_T. However, as should be apparent from Figure 3-18, this will not increase the average power level of the FM signal, which is $A_c^2/2$. This is distinctly different from AM, where the level of modulation affects the power in the AM signal but does not affect its bandwidth.

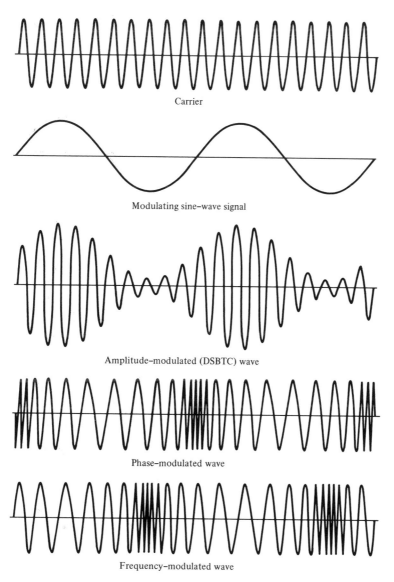

Carrier

Modulating sine–wave signal

Amplitude–modulated (DSBTC) wave

Phase–modulated wave

Frequency–modulated wave

FIGURE 3-18. Amplitude, phase, and frequency modulation of a sine-wave carrier by a sine-wave signal.

EXAMPLE.   Derive an expression for $s(t)$ if $\phi(t)$ is the phase-modulating signal $n_p \cos 2\pi f_m t$. Assume that $A_c = 1$. This can be seen directly to be

$$s(t) = \cos[2\pi f_c t + n_p \cos 2\pi f_m t]$$

The instantaneous phase deviation from the carrier signal is $n_p \cos 2\pi f_m t$. The phase angle of the signal varies from its unmodulated value in a simple sinusoidal fashion, with the peak phase deviation equal to n_p.

The expression above can be expanded using Bessel's trigonometric identities:

$$s(t) = \sum_{n=-\infty}^{\infty} J_n(n_p) \cos\left(2\pi f_c t + 2\pi n f_m t + \frac{n\pi}{2}\right)$$

where $J_n(n_p)$ is the nth order Bessel function of the first kind. Using the property

$$J_{-n}(x) = (-1)^n J_n(x)$$

this can be rewritten as

$$s(t) = J_0(n_p) \cos 2\pi f_c t + \sum_{n=1}^{\infty} J_n(n_p) \left[\cos \left(2\pi(f_c + nf_m)t + \frac{n\pi}{2} \right) \right.$$
$$\left. + \cos \left(2\pi(f_c - nf_m)t + \frac{(n+2)\pi}{2} \right) \right]$$

The resulting signal has a component at the original carrier frequency plus a set of sidebands displaced from f_c by all possible multiples of f_m. For $n_p \ll 1$, the higher-order terms fall off rapidly. ∎

EXAMPLE.   Derive an expression for $s(t)$ if $\phi'(t)$ is the frequency-modulating signal $-n_f \sin 2\pi f_m t$. The form of $\phi'(t)$ was chosen for convenience. We have

$$\phi(t) = -\int n_f \sin 2\pi f_m t \, dt = \frac{n_f}{2\pi f_m} \cos 2\pi f_m t$$

Thus

$$s(t) = \cos \left[2\pi f_c t + \frac{n_f}{2\pi f_m} \cos 2\pi f_m t \right]$$

$$= \cos \left[2\pi f_c t + \frac{\Delta F}{f_m} \cos 2\pi f_m t \right]$$
∎

The instantaneous frequency deviation from the carrier signal is $-n_f \sin 2\pi f_m t$. The frequency of the signal varies from its unmodulated value in a simple sinusoidal fashion, with the peak frequency deviation equal to n_f rad/s.

The equation for the FM signal has the identical form as for the PM signal, with $\Delta F/f_m$ substituted for n_p. Thus the Bessel expansion is the same.

As with AM, both FM and PM result in a signal whose bandwidth is centered at f_c. However, we can now see that the magnitude of that bandwidth is very different. Amplitude modulation is a linear process and produces frequencies that are the sum and difference of the carrier signal and the components of the modulating signal. Hence, for AM:

$$B_T = 2B$$

However, angle modulation includes a term of the form $\cos(\phi(t))$ which is nonlinear and will produce a wide range of frequencies. In essence, for a modulating sinusoid of frequency f_m, $s(t)$ will contain components at $f_c + f_m$, $f_c + 2f_m$, and so on. In the most general case, infinite bandwidth is required to transmit an FM or PM signal. As a practical matter, a very good rule of thumb, known as Carson's rule [COUC83], is:

$$B_T = 2(\beta + 1)B$$

where

$$\beta = \begin{cases} n_p A_m \text{ for PM} \\ \dfrac{\Delta F}{B} = \dfrac{n_f A_m}{2\pi B} \quad \text{for FM} \end{cases}$$

We can rewrite the formula for FM as

$$B_T = 2\Delta F + 2B$$

Thus both FM and PM require greater bandwidth than AM.

3-5

RECOMMENDED READING

A good analysis of digital data, digital signal schemes can be found in [LIND73]. [TUGA82] and [SEVE80] also provides some insights. The latter is concerned with the use of these codes for magnetic tape recording, but the discussion is valid in the data transmission context. A great deal has been written about analog modulation schemes for digital data. [OETT79] is a good survey. [RODE82] contains a lengthy and systematic analysis. [DAVE72] examines specifically modems for voice-grade lines. Other worthwhile sources are [FREE81], [BELL82a], and [MART76]. [MART76] also contains a readable introduction to PCM. More in-depth looks at digitization of analog signals can be found in [FREE81] and [COUC83]. [SAIN84] is a brief survey of a variety of voice digitization techniques. Finally, the literature on the various analog modulation schemes for analog data is almost limitless; [BELL82a] is a concise overview of the subject.

3-6

PROBLEMS

3-1 Which of the signals of Table 3-1 use differential encoding?

3-2 Develop algorithms for generating each of the codes of Table 3-1 from NRZ-L.

3-3 A modified NRZ code known as *enhanced-NRZ* (E-NRZ) is sometimes used for high density magnetic tape recording. E-NRZ encoding entails separating the NRZ-L data stream into 7-bit words; inverting bits 2, 3, 6, and 7; and adding one parity bit to each word. The parity bit is chosen to make the total number of 1's in the 8-bit word an odd count. What are the advantages of E-NRZ over NRZ-L? Any disadvantages?

3-4 Assume a typical binary sequence and show that if the corresponding polar and unipolar signal have the same peak-to-peak amplitude, the polar signal has less power (an advantage) than the unipolar signal.

3-5 A common modification of the bipolar code is *bipolar with 6-zero substitution* (B6ZS). This code substitutes either $0 + - 0 - +$ or $0 - + 0 + -$ for blocks of six consecutive zeros, according as the last transmitted pulse was $+$ or $-$. What might be the purpose of such a scheme? How can the original data be reliably recovered?

3-6 For the bit stream 01001110, sketch the waveforms for each of the codes of Table 3-1.

3-7 Derive an expression for baud rate D as a function of bit rate R for QPSK using the digital encoding techniques of Table 3-1.

3-8 What S/N ratio is required to achieve a bandwidth efficiency of 5.0 for ASK, FSK, PSK, and QPSK? Assume that the required bit error rate is 10^{-6}.

3-9 An NRZ-L signal is passed through a filter with $r = 0.5$ and then modulated onto a carrier. The data rate is 2400 bps. Evaluate the bandwidth for ASK and FSK. For FSK assume that the two frequencies used are 50 kHz and 55 kHz.

3-10 Assume that a telephone line channel is equalized to allow bandpass data transmission over a frequency range of 600 to 3000 Hz. The available bandwidth is 2400 Hz with a center frequency of 1800 Hz. For $r = 1$, evaluate the required bandwidth for 2400 bps QPSK and 4800-bps, eight-level multilevel signaling. Is the bandwidth adequate?

3-11 Why should PCM be preferable to DM for encoding analog signals that represent digital data?

3-12 Are the modem and the codec functional inverses (i.e., could an inverted modem function as a codec, or vice versa)?

3-13 The signal of Problem 2-11 is quantized using 10-bit PCM. Find the signal-to-quantization noise ratio.

3-14 Consider an audio signal with spectral components in the range 300 to 3000 Hz. Assume that a sampling rate of 7 kHz will be used to generate a PCM signal.
a. For $S/N = 30$ dB, what is the number of uniform quantization levels needed?
b. What data rate is required?

3-15 Find the step size δ required to prevent slope overload noise as a function of the frequency of the highest-frequency component of the signal. Assume that all components have amplitude A.

3-16 A PCM encoder accepts a signal with a full-scale voltage of 10 V and generates 8-bit codes using uniform quantization. The maximum normalized quantized voltage is $1 - 2^{-8}$. Determine: (a) normalized step size, (b) actual step size in volts, (c) actual maximum quantized level in volts, (d) normalized resolution, (e) actual resolution, and (f) percentage resolution.

3-17 A carrier with a frequency of 100 kHz is amplitude-modulated with the signal

$$x(t) = 10 \cos 2\pi \times 10^3 t + 8 \cos 4\pi \times 10^3 t + 6 \cos 8\pi \times 10^3 t.$$

a. List the frequencies appearing at the output of the modulator.
b. Develop an expression for the DSBTC output $y(t)$. Assume that the carrier has the form $\cos 2\pi \times 10^5 t$.

3-18 An AM broadcast station operates at its maximum allowed total output of 50 kW and 95% modulation ($n_a = 0.95$). How much of its transmitted power conveys information?

3-19 The carrier $c(t) = A_c \sin 2\pi f_c t$ is to be amplitude-modulated by input $m(t) = A_m \sin 2\pi f_m t$. Derive a simplified expression for the modulated signal $s(t)$.

3-20 A modulated RF waveform is given by $s(t) = 500 \cos [2\pi f_c t + 20 \cos 2\pi f_1 t]$, where $f_1 = 1$ kHz and $f_c = 100$ MHz.

   a. If the phase modulation index is 100 rad/V, find the expression for the phase modulation voltage $m(t)$. What is its peak value and frequency?

   b. If the frequency modulation index is 10^6 rad/V-s, find the frequency modulation voltage $m(t)$. What is its peak value and frequency?

APPENDIX 3A

PROOF OF THE SAMPLING THEOREM

The sampling theorem can be restated as follows. *Given:*

- $x(t)$ is a bandlimited signal with bandwidth f_h.
- $p(t)$ is a sampling signal consisting of pulses at intervals $T_s = 1/f_s$, where f_s is the sampling frequency.
- $x_s(t) = x(t)p(t)$ is the sampled signal.

Then, $x(t)$ can be recovered exactly from $x_s(t)$ if and only if $f_s \geq 2f_h$.
Proof:

Since $p(t)$ consists of a uniform series of pulses, it is a periodic signal and can be represented by a Fourier series:

$$p(t) = \sum_{n=-\infty}^{\infty} P_n e^{j2\pi n f_s t}$$

We have

$$x_s(t) = x(t)p(t)$$

$$= \sum_{n=-\infty}^{\infty} P_n x(t) e^{j2\pi n f_s t}$$

Now consider the Fourier transform of $x_s(t)$:

$$X_s(f) = \int_{-\infty}^{\infty} x_s(t) e^{-j2\pi f t} \, dt$$

Substituting for $x_s(t)$, we have

$$X_s(f) = \int_{-\infty}^{\infty} \sum_{n-\infty}^{\infty} P_n x(t) e^{j2\pi n f_s t} \, e^{-j2\pi f t} \, dt$$

Rearranging yields

$$X_s(f) = \sum_{n=-\infty}^{\infty} P_n \int_{-\infty}^{\infty} x(t) e^{-j2\pi(f-nf_s)t} \, dt$$

From the definition of the Fourier transform, we can write

$$X(f - nf_s) = \int_{-\infty}^{\infty} x(t) e^{-j2\pi(f-nf_s)t} \, dt$$

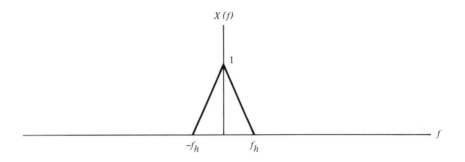

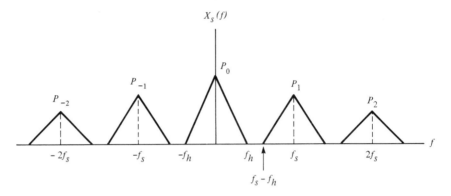

FIGURE 3-19. Spectrum of a sampled signal.

where $X(f)$ is the Fourier transform of $x(t)$. Substituting this into the preceding equation, we have

$$X_s(f) = \sum_{n=-\infty}^{\infty} P_n X(f - nf_s)$$

This last equation has an interesting interpretation, which is illustrated in Figure 3-19, where we assume without loss of generality that the bandwidth of $x(t)$ is in the range 0 to f_h. The spectrum of $x_s(t)$ is composed of the spectrum of $x(t)$ plus the spectrum of $x(t)$ translated to each harmonic of the sampling frequency. Each of the translated spectra is multiplied by the corresponding coefficient of the Fourier series of $p(t)$. Now, if $f_s > 2f_h$, these various translations do not overlap, and the spectrum of $x(t)$, multiplied by P_o, appears in $X_s(f)$. By passing $X_s(f)$ through a bandpass filter with $f < f_s$, the spectrum of $x(t)$ is recovered. In equation form,

$$X_s(f) = P_0 X(f) \qquad -f_s < f < f_s$$

CHAPTER 4

Digital Data Communication Techniques

In Chapters 2 and 3, we have been concerned primarily with the attributes of data transmission, such as the characteristics of data signals and transmission media, the encoding of signals, and transmission performance. In this chapter we shift our emphasis from data transmission to data communications.

For two devices linked by a transmission medium to exchange data, a high degree of cooperation is required. Typically, data are transmitted one bit at a time over the medium. The timing (rate, duration, spacing) of these bits must be the same for transmitter and receiver. Two common techniques—asynchronous and synchronous—are explored in Section 4-1. Next, we look at the problem of bit errors. As we have seen, data transmission is not an error-free process and some means of accounting for these errors is needed. In Section 4-2 we look at several error-detection techniques. Finally in this chapter, we look at transmission line interfaces. Typically, digital data devices do not attach to and signal across a transmission medium directly. Rather, this process is mediated through a standardized interface.

Another topic relating to these three is that of data link control. This is sufficiently important to warrant a separate chapter, and is explored in Chapter 5.

4-1

ASYNCHRONOUS AND SYNCHRONOUS TRANSMISSION

In this book we are concerned with serial transmission of data; that is, data are transferred over a single communications path rather than a parallel set of lines, as is sometimes done in I/O devices and internal computer signal paths. With serial transmission, signaling elements are sent down the line one at a time. Each signaling element may be:

- *Less than one bit:* This is the case, for example, with Manchester coding.
- *One bit:* NRZ-L and FSK are digital and analog examples, respectively.
- *More than one bit:* QPSK is an example.

For simplicity in the following discussion, we assume one bit per signaling element unless otherwise stated. The discussion is not materially affected by this assumption.

It was mentioned in Chapter 1 that synchronization is one of the key tasks of data communications. A transmitter is sending a message one bit at a time through a medium to a receiver. The receiver must recognize the beginning and end of a block of bits. It must also know the duration of each bit so that it can sample the line with the proper timing to read each bit.

A typical case is that the receiver will attempt to sample the medium at the center of each bit time. The receiver will time its samples at intervals of one bit time. If there is a timing difference of, say, 5% between transmitter and receiver, the first sampling by the receiver will be 0.05 of a bit time away from the center of the bit. At the end of the tenth sampling, the receiver may be in error. For smaller timing differences, the error would occur later, but eventually the receiver will be out of step with the transmitter unless they are somehow synchronized.

Two approaches are common for synchronization. The first is called, oddly enough, asynchronous transmission. In this scheme, bits are sent one character at a time, where each character is five to eight bits in length. Timing or synchronization must only be maintained within each character; the receiver has the opportunity to resynchronize at the beginning of each new character. The alternative is the more difficult synchronous transmission in which larger blocks of bits are sent as a unit, and the receiver must maintain synchronization with the transmitter for a longer period of time.

We should mention that there is a hierarchy of synchronization tasks:

- *Bit synchronization:* recognizing the start and end of each bit.
- *Character or word synchronization:* recognizing the start and end of each character or other small unit of data.
- *Block or message synchronization:* recognizing the start and end of large units of data.

The distinction among these three should become clear as the discussion proceeds.

Asynchronous Transmission

One solution to the synchronization problem is to send very small blocks of bits and to resynchronize at the beginning of each block. An old technique, known as start-stop or *asynchronous* transmission, does just that. Asynchronous transmission is character-oriented in nature and characters of from 5 to 8 bits are used.

The technique is easily explained with reference to Figure 4-1. When no character is being transmitted the line between transmitter and receiver is in an "idle" state. The definition of idle is by convention, but typically is equivalent to the signaling element for binary 1. Thus for NRZ-L signaling, idle would be the presence of voltage (and current) on the line. The beginning of a character is

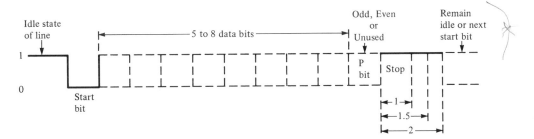

(a) Data character format

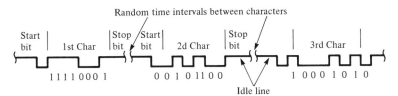

(b) 8 – bit asynchronous bit stream

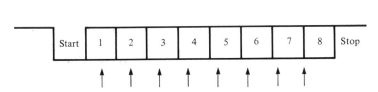

(c) Effect of timing error

FIGURE 4-1.   Asynchronous transmission.

signaled by a start bit with a value of binary 0. This is followed by the character, which consists of from 5 to 8 data bits and, in some cases, a parity bit. The parity bit is set by the transmitter such that the total number of 1's in the character, including the parity bit, is even. This bit is used by the receiver for error detection, as discussed in Section 4-2. The last bit of the character is followed by a stop bit, which is a binary 1. A minimum length for the stop bit is specified and this is usually 1, 1.5, or 2 times the duration of an ordinary bit. No maximum value is specified. Since the stop bit is the same as the idle state, the transmitter will continue to transmit the stop bit until it is ready to send the next character.

If a steady stream of characters is sent, the interval between characters is uniform and equal to the stop bit. For example, if the stop bit has unit length and the ASCII characters ABC are sent (without parity bit) the pattern is 01000001100100001101100001 . . . 1111. The start bit (0) starts the timing sequence for the next eight elements, which are the 7-bit ASCII code and the stop bit. In the idle state, the receiver looks for a transition from 1 to 0 to begin the character, and then samples the input signal at one-bit intervals for seven intervals. It then looks for the next 1-to-0 transition, which will occur no sooner than one bit time.

The timing requirements for this scheme are modest. For example, ASCII characters are typically sent as 8-bit units, including the parity bit. If the receiver is 5% slower or faster than the transmitter, the eighth information bit will be displaced by 45%, and still be correctly identified. Figure 4-1c shows the effect of a timing error of sufficient magnitude to cause an error in reception.

An error such as this actually results in two errors. First, the last sampled bit is incorrectly received. Second, the bit count may now be out of alignment. If bit 7 is a 1 and bit 8 is a 0, bit 8 could be mistaken for a start bit. This condition is termed a *framing error*, as the character plus start and stop bits is sometimes referred to as a *frame*. A framing error can also occur if some noise condition causes the false appearance of a start bit during the idle state.

Asynchronous communication is simple and cheap but requires an overhead of two to three bits per character. For example, for a 7-bit code, using a 1-bit-long stop bit, two out of every nine bits convey no information but are there merely for synchronization; thus the overhead is $2/9 = 0.22$. Of course, the percentage overhead could be reduced by sending larger blocks of bits between the start and stop bits. However, as Figure 4-1c indicates, the larger the block of bits, the greater the cumulative timing error. To use larger blocks of bits successfully, a different form of synchronization, known as synchronous transmission, is used.

Synchronous Transmission

A more efficient means of communication is synchronous transmission. In this mode, blocks of characters or bits are transmitted without start and stop codes, and the exact departure or arrival time of each bit is predictable. To prevent timing drift between transmitter and receiver, their clocks must somehow be synchronized. One possibility is to provide a separate clock line between transmitter and receiver. Otherwise, the clocking information must be embedded in the data signal. For digital signals, this can be achieved with biphase encoding. For analog signals, a number of techniques can be used; the carrier frequency itself can be used to synchronize the receiver based on the phase of the carrier.

With synchronous transmission, there is another level of synchronization required, to allow the receiver to determine the beginning and end of a block of data. To achieve this, each block begins with a *preamble* bit pattern and generally ends with *postamble* bit pattern. These patterns are control information rather than data. In addition, other control information is included that is used in the data link control procedures discussed in Chapter 5. The data plus control information is called a *frame*. The exact format of the frame depends on whether the transmission scheme is character-oriented or bit-oriented.

With *character-oriented* transmission, the block of data is treated as a sequence of characters (usually 8-bit characters). All control information is in character form. The frame begins with one or more "synchronization characters" (Figure 4-2a). The synchronization character, usually called *SYN*, is a unique bit pattern that signals the receiver that this is the beginning of a block. The postamble is another unique character used in some schemes. The receiver thus is alerted to an incoming block of data by the SYN characters and accepts data until the postamble character is seen. The receiver can then look for the next SYN pattern. Alternatively, another approach is to include frame length as part of the control information. The receiver then looks for a SYN character, determines frame length, reads the indicated number of characters, and then looks for the next SYN character to start the next frame.

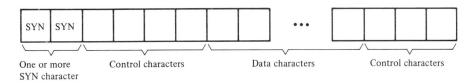

One or more
SYN character
Control characters
Data characters
Control characters

(a) Character – oriented frame

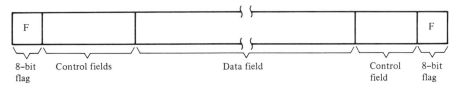

8–bit
flag
Control fields
Data field
Control
field
8–bit
flag

(b) Bit – oriented frame

FIGURE 4-2. Synchronous transmission.

With *bit-oriented* transmission, the block of data is treated as a sequence of bits. Neither data nor control information needs to be interpreted in units of 8-bit characters. As with character-oriented schemes, a special bit pattern signals the beginning of a block. In bit-oriented transmission, this preamble is eight bits long and is referred to as a flag. The same flag is also used as a postamble (Figure 4-2b). The receiver looks for the occurrence of the flag pattern to signal start of frame. This is followed by some number of control fields, then a variable-length data field, more control fields, and finally the flag is repeated. The differences between this approach and the character-oriented approach depend on details of the formats and the interpretation of the control information. This subject is explored in Chapter 5.

For sizable blocks of data, synchronous transmission is far more efficient than asynchronous. Asynchronous transmission requires 20% or more overhead. The control information in synchronous transmission is typically less than 100 bits. For example, one of the more common bit-oriented schemes, HDLC, contains 48 bits of control information (including the flags). Thus for a 1000-bit message, the overhead is only $48/1048 \times 100\% = 4.6\%$.

4-2

ERROR DETECTION TECHNIQUES

In earlier chapters we talked about transmission impairments and the effect of data rate and S/N on bit error rate. Regardless of the design of the transmission system, there will be errors. And, while thermal noise errors may be reduced to vanishingly small rates, bursty impulse noise may still result in substantial errors.

When a frame is transmitted, three classes of probabilities can be defined at the receiving end:

- *Class 1* (P_1): A frame arrives with no bit errors.
- *Class 2* (P_2): A frame arrives with one or more undetected bit errors.
- *Class 3* (P_3): A frame arrives with one or more detected bit errors but no undetected bit errors.

First consider the case when no means are taken to detect errors. Then the probability of detected errors (P_3) is zero. To express the remaining probabilities, assume that the probability that any given bit is in error, P_B, is constant and independent of bit position. Then we have   *probability of error*

$$P_1 = (1 - P_B)^{N_f}$$
$$P_2 = 1 - P_1$$

where N_f is the number of bits per frame.

Figure 4-3a illustrates these equations and shows how the probability of erroneous frames increases drastically with bit error probability. Consider the rather

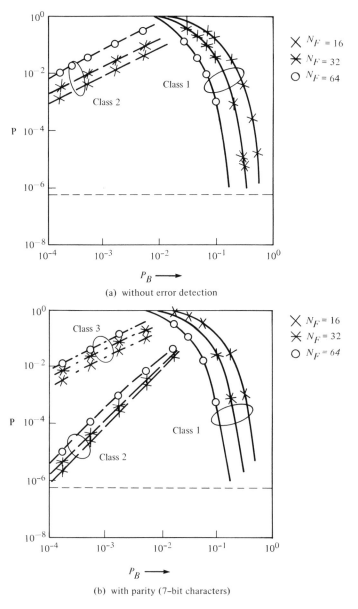

(a) without error detection

(b) with parity (7-bit characters)

FIGURE 4-3. **Probability of frame error without and with parity bits.**

modest requirement that at most one frame with an undetected bit error should occur per day on a continuously used 300 bps channel. If the frame length is 16 bits, this requirement means that at most one frame out of 1.62×10^6 has an error ($P_2 = 0.6 \times 10^{-6}$). A typical P_B for a public telephone line using a 300 bps modem is 10^{-4}. The resulting value of P_2 can be seen to be about three orders of magnitude too large to meet our requirement.

This is the kind of result that motivates the use of error-detection techniques. All of these techniques operate on the following principle: For a given frame of bits, additional bits that constitute an *error-detecting code*, are added by the transmitter. This code is calculated as a function of the other transmitted bits. The receiver performs the same calculation and compares the two results. A detected error occurs if and only if there is a mismatch. Thus P_3 is the probability that if a frame contains errors, the error-detection scheme will detect that fact. P_2 is known as the *residual error rate*, and is the probability that an error will be undetected despite the use of an error-detection scheme. A number of specific techniques follow this general rule. We will examine the three most common ones:

- Parity bit.
- Longitudinal redundancy check.
- Cyclic redundancy check.

Of course, the detection of an error does no good unless some action is taken to correct the error. One approach is to use an error-detection technique that generates sufficient information that errors can be corrected by the receiver. This technique is known as an error-correcting code, and is reviewed briefly in this section. A far more common procedure is for the receiver to notify the transmitter that an error has been detected and to request a retransmission. This is an element of data link control and will be examined in Chapter 5.

Parity Checks

The simplest bit error detection scheme is to append a parity bit to the end of each word in the frame. A typical example is ASCII transmission, in which a parity bit is attached to each 7-bit ASCII character. The value of this bit is selected so that the word has an even number of 1's (even parity) or an odd number of 1's (odd parity). Typically even parity is used for asynchronous transmission and odd parity for synchronous transmission. So, for example, if the transmitter is transmitting an ASCII G (1110001) and using odd parity, it will append a 1 and transmit 11100011. The receiver examines the received character and if the total number of 1's is odd, assumes that no error has occurred. If one bit or any odd number of bits is erroneously inverted during transmission (e.g., 11000011), then, clearly, the receiver will detect an error. Note, however, that if two (or any even number of) bits are inverted, an undetected error occurs!

Again the probabilities are easily expressed:

$$P_1 = (1 - P_B)^{N_B N_C}$$

$$P_2 = \sum_{k=1}^{N_C} \binom{N_C}{k} \left[\sum_{j=2,4,\ldots}^{N_B} \binom{N_B}{j} P_B^j (1 - P_B)^{(N_B - j)} \right]^k$$
$$[(1 - P_B)^{N_B}]^{(N_C - k)}$$

$$P_3 = 1 - P_2 - P_1$$

where

N_B = number of bits per character (including the parity bit)

N_C = number of characters per frame

These three probabilities are illustrated in Figure 4-3b ($N_F = N_B \times N_C$). The parity bit dramatically reduces the probability of accepting a message with undetected errors (P_2), while the probability of receiving a correct message does not change significantly. For a bit error rate of 10^{-4}, the value of P_2 now approaches the requirements of the preceding example. For longer frames, however, this is still not sufficient.

The problem with the use of the parity bit is that noise impulses are often long enough to destroy more than one bit, particularly at high data rates. Figure 4-4 shows the probability of a second error bit within X bits of a first error bit on a 1200-bps voice-grade line. Thus the formulation used above for P_2 is too conservative.

A substantial improvement can be achieved by using a second set of parity bits, as illustrated in Figure 4-5. The frame is viewed as a block of characters arranged in two dimensions. To each character is appended a parity bit, as before. In addition, a parity bit is generated for each bit position across all characters. That is, an additional character is generated in which the Ith bit of the character is a parity bit for the Ith bit of all other characters in the block. This can be expressed mathematically using the exclusive-or $\oplus$ operation. The exclusive-or of two binary digits is 0 if both digits are 0 or both are 1. If the digits differ, the result is 1. Let us call the parity bit at the end of each character the row parity bit. Then

$$R_j = b_{1j} \oplus b_{2j} \oplus \cdots b_{nj}$$

where

R_j = parity bit of jth character

b_{ij} = ith bit in jth character

n = number of bits in a character

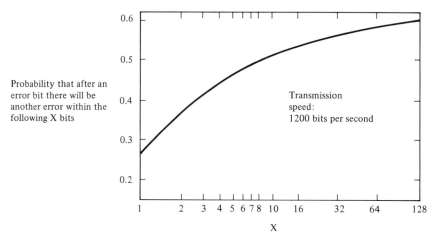

FIGURE 4-4.

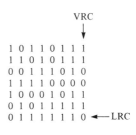

	bit 1	bit 2		bit n	Parity bit
Character 1	b_{11}	b_{21}		b_{n1}	R_1
Character 2	b_{12}	b_{22}		b_{n2}	R_2
Character m	b_{1m}	b_{2m}		b_{nm}	R_m
Parity check character	C_1	C_2		C_n	C_{n+1}

(a) Format

VRC
↓
```
1 0 1 1 0 1 1 1
1 1 0 1 0 1 1 1
0 0 1 1 1 0 1 0
1 1 1 1 0 0 0 0
1 0 0 0 1 0 1 1
0 1 0 1 1 1 1 1
0 1 1 1 1 1 1 0  ←── LRC
```

(b) Example

FIGURE 4-5. Vertical and longitudinal redundancy checks.

This equation generates even parity. For the parity check character:

$$C_i = b_{i1} \oplus b_{i2} \oplus \cdots \oplus b_{in}$$

where

C_i = ith bit of parity check character

m = number of characters in a frame

In this format, the parity bits at the end of each character are referred to as the vertical redundancy check (VRC), and the parity check character is referred to as the longitudinal redundancy check (LRC).

Measurements indicate that the use of both VRC and LRC reduces the error rate compared to simple VRC by two to four orders of magnitude [MART70]. However, even this scheme is not foolproof. Consider the case of bits 1 and 3 in character 1 being in error. When the receiver generates the parity bit for character 1, it will match the received parity bit, and no error is detected. However, when it generates the parity check character, bits 1 and 3 will differ from those of the received parity check character, and the error is detected. Now suppose that, in addition, bits 1 and 3 of character 5 are also in error. Not only do the parity bits for character 1 and 5 fail to detect errors, but the parity check character also fails to detect them. Thus some patterns of even numbers of errors remain undetected.

Cyclic Redundancy Checks

To achieve further improvement a very powerful but easily implemented technique, known as *cyclic redundancy check* (CRC) can be used. The procedure can be explained as follows. Given a k-bit frame or message, the transmitter generates an n-bit sequence, known as a *frame check sequence* (FCS) so that the resulting frame, consisting of $k + n$ bits is exactly divisible by some predetermined number. The receiver then divides the incoming frame by the same number and, if there is no remainder, assumes that there was no error.

To clarify the above, we present the procedure in several ways:

- Modulo 2 arithmetic.
- Polynomials.
- Shift registers and exclusive-or gates.

First, we work with binary numbers and modulo 2 arithmetic. Modulo 2 arithmetic uses binary addition with no carries, which is just the exclusive-or operation.

EXAMPLES

$$
\begin{array}{r}
1111 \\
+\,1010 \\
\hline
0101
\end{array}
\qquad
\begin{array}{r}
11001 \\
\times\quad 11 \\
\hline
11001 \\
11001 \\
\hline
101011
\end{array}
\qquad \blacksquare
$$

Now define:

$T = (k + n)$-bit frame to be transmitted, with $n < k$
$M = k$-bit message, the first k bits of T
$F = n$-bit FCS, the last n bits of T
$P = $ pattern of $n + 1$ bits; this is the predetermined divisor mentioned above

We would like T/P to have no remainder. It should be clear that

$$T = 2^n M + F$$

That is, by multiplying M by 2^n, we have in effect shifted it to the left by n bits and padded out the result with 0's. Adding F gives us the concatenation of M and F, which is T. Now we want T to be exactly divisible by P. Suppose that we divided $2^n M$ by P:

$$\frac{2^n M}{P} = Q + \frac{R}{P} \qquad (4\text{-}1)$$

There is a quotient and a remainder. Since division is binary, the remainder is always one bit less than the divisor. We will use this remainder as our FCS. Then

$$T = 2^n M + R$$

Question: Does this R satisfy our condition? To see that it does, consider

$$\frac{T}{P} = \frac{2^n M + R}{P}$$

substituting equation (4-1), we have

$$\frac{T}{P} = Q + \frac{R}{P} + \frac{R}{P}$$

However, any binary number added to itself modulo 2 yields zero. Thus

$$\frac{T}{P} = Q + \frac{R + R}{P} = Q$$

There is no remainder, and therefore T is exactly divisible by P. Thus the FCS is easily generated. Simply divide $2^n M$ by P and use the remainder as the FCS. On reception, the receiver will divide T by P and will get no remainder if there have been no errors.

A simple example of the procedure is now presented:

1. Given

$$\text{Message } M = 110011 \text{ (6 bits)}$$
$$\text{Pattern } P = 11001 \text{ (5 bits)}$$
$$\text{FCS } R = \text{to be calculated (4 bits)}$$

2. The message is multiplied by 2^4, yielding 1100110000.
3. This product is divided by P:

```
                     100001←Q
        P→11001 1100110000←2^n M
                11001
                ─────
                10000
                11001
                ─────
                 1001←R
```

4. The remainder is added to $2^n M$ to give $T = 1100111001$, which is transmitted.
5. If there are no errors, the receiver receives T intact. The received frame is divided by P:

```
                    100001
        11001 1100111001
              11001
              ─────
               11001
               11001
               ─────
               00000
```

Since there is no remainder, it is assumed that there have been no errors.

The pattern P is chosen to be one bit longer than the desired FCS, and the exact bit pattern chosen depends on the type of errors expected. At minimum, both the high- and low-order bits of P must be 1.

The occurrence of an error is easily expressed. An error results in the reversal of a bit. Mathematically, this is equivalent to taking the exclusive-or of the bit and 1: $0 + 1 = 1$; $1 + 1 = 0$. Thus the errors in an $(n + k)$-bit frame can be represented by an $(n + k)$-bit field with 1's in each error position. The resulting frame T_r can be expressed as

$$T_r = T \oplus E$$

where

T = transmitted frame
E = error pattern with 1's in positions where errors occur
T_r = received frame

The receiver will fail to detect an error if and only if T_r is divisible by P, that is, if and only if E is divisible by P. Intuitively, this seems an unlikely occurrence.

A second way of viewing the CRC process is to express all values as polynomials in a dummy variable X with binary coefficients. The coefficients correspond to the bits in the binary number. Thus for $M = 110011$, we have $M(X) = X^5 + X^4 + X + 1$, and for $P = 11001$, we have $P(X) = X^4 + X^3 + 1$. Arithmetic operations are again modulo 2. The CRC process can now be described as:

1. $\dfrac{X^n M(X)}{P(X)} = Q(X) + \dfrac{R(X)}{P(X)}$

2. $T(X) = X^n M(X) + R(X)$

An error $E(X)$ will only be undetectable if it is divisible by $P(X)$. It can be shown [PETE61] that all of the following are not divisible by $P(X)$ and hence are detectable:

1. All single-bit errors.
2. All double-bit errors, as long as $P(X)$ has a factor with at least three terms.
3. Any odd number of errors, as long as $P(X)$ contains a factor $(X + 1)$.
4. Any burst error for which the length of the burst is less than the length of the FCS.
5. Most larger burst errors.

The first assertion is clear. A single-bit error can be represented by $E(X) = X^i$ for some i. We have said that for $P(X)$ both the first and last terms must be nonzero. Thus $P(X)$ has at least two terms and cannot divide the one-term $E(X)$. Similarly, a two-bit error can be represented by $E(X) = X^i + X^j = X^i(1 + X^{j-i})$ for some i and j with $i > j$. Thus $P(X)$ must divide either X^i or $(1 + X^{j-i})$. We have shown that it does not divide X^i, and it can be shown [PETE61] that it does not divide $(1 + X^{j-i})$ except for very large values of $j - i$, beyond the practical frame length. To see the third assertion, assume that $E(X)$ has an odd number of terms and is divisible by $(X + 1)$. Then we can express $E(X)$ as $E(X) = (X + 1)F(X)$. Then $E(1) = (1 + 1)F(1) = 0$ since $1 + 1 = 0$. But $E(1)$ will be 0 if and only if $E(X)$ contains an even number of terms. For the fourth assertion, we define a burst of length j as a string of bits beginning and ending with 1 and containing intervening 1's and 0's. This can be represented as $E(X) = X^i(X^{j-1} + \ldots + 1)$ where i expresses how far the burst is shifted from the right-hand end. We know that $P(X)$ does not divide X^i. For $j < n$, where n is the length of the FCS, $P(X)$ will not divide the second factor, since $P(X)$ is of higher order.

Finally, it can be shown that if all error patterns are considered equally likely, then for a burst of length $r + 1$, the probability that $E(X)$ is divisible by $P(X)$ is $1/2^{r-1}$, and for a longer burst, the probability is $1/2^r$ [PETE61].

Four versions of $P(X)$ are widely used:

$$
\begin{aligned}
\text{CRC-12} &= X^{12} + X^{11} + X^3 + X^2 + 1 \\
\text{CRC-16} &= X^{16} + X^{15} + X^2 + 1 \\
\text{CRC-CCITT} &= X^{16} + X^{12} + X^5 + 1 \\
\text{CRC-32} &= X^{32} + X^{26} + X^{23} + X^{22} + X^{16} + X^{12} + X^{11} \\
&\quad + X^{10} + X^8 + X^7 + X^5 + X^4 + X^2 + X + 1
\end{aligned}
$$

The CRC-12 system is used for transmission of streams of 6-bit characters and generates a 12-bit FCS. Both CRC-16 and CRC-CCITT are popular for 8-bit characters, in the United States and Europe respectively, and both result in a 16-bit

FCS. This would seem adequate for most applications, although CRC-32 is specified as an option in some point-to-point synchronous transmission standards. The local network standards committee (IEEE-802), evidently a suspicious lot, has specified the use of CRC-32, which generates a 32-bit FCS. This CRC is also used in some DOD applications.

As a final representation, Figure 4-6 shows that the CRC process can be easily implemented with shift registers and exclusive-or gates. In a transmitter, the shift registers are initialized to all 0's. As each bit of M is transmitted, it is also applied to the point marked A in the figure, and a shifting pulse is applied to the register. The figure shows the state of the system after 16 bits have been transmitted. After the last bit of M is transmitted, the shift register contains the FCS, or R, which can then be transmitted.

At the receiver, the same logic is used. As each bit of M arrives it is inserted into the shift register at A. If there have been no errors, the shift register should contain the bit pattern for R at the conclusion of M. The transmitted bits of R now

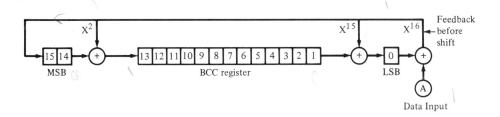

Shift no.	15 14	BCC register (13 ... 1)			
Start	0 0	0 0 0 0 0 0 0 0 0 0 0 0 0	0	–	1
1	1 0	1 0 0 0 0 0 0 0 0 0 0 0 0	1	1 LSB	1
2	1 1	1 1 0 0 0 0 0 0 0 0 0 0 0	1	0	1
3	1 1	0 1 1 0 0 0 0 0 0 0 0 0 0	1	0	1
4	1 1	0 0 1 1 0 0 0 0 0 0 0 0 0	1	0	1
5	1 1	0 0 0 1 1 0 0 0 0 0 0 0 0	1	0	1
6	1 1	0 0 0 0 1 1 0 0 0 0 0 0 0	1	0	1
7	1 1	0 0 0 0 0 1 1 0 0 0 0 0 0	1	0	1
8	1 1	0 0 0 0 0 0 1 1 0 0 0 0 0	1	0	1
9	1 1	0 0 0 0 0 0 0 1 1 0 0 0 0	1	0	1
10	1 1	0 0 0 0 0 0 0 0 1 1 0 0 0	1	0	1
11	1 1	0 0 0 0 0 0 0 0 0 1 1 0 0	1	0	1
12	1 1	0 0 0 0 0 0 0 0 0 0 1 1 0	1	0	1
13	1 1	0 0 0 0 0 0 0 0 0 0 0 1 1	1	0	1
14	1 1	0 0 0 0 0 0 0 0 0 0 0 0 1	0	0	0
15	0 1	1 0 0 0 0 0 0 0 0 0 0 0 0	1	0	1
16	1 0	0 1 0 0 0 0 0 0 0 0 0 0 0	1	0 MSB	1

Arrows indicate exclusive-or of data bit and LSB of BCC register prior to shift

└─ Block check character (bcc)   └─ 16 bit data word

NOTES:

▫ = BCC register stage

⊕ = Exclusive-or

CRC-16 Polynomial = $X^{16} + X^{15} + X^2 + 1$

LSB = Least significant bit of register (sent first)

MSB = Most significant bit of register (sent last)

FIGURE 4-6. CRC-16 implemented with shift registers and exclusive-or gates.

begin to arrive, and the effect is to zero out the register so that, at the conclusion of reception, the register contains all 0's.

The shift register implementation makes clear the power of the CRC algorithm. Due to the feedback arrangement, the state of the shift register depends, in a complex way, on the past history of bits presented. Thus it will take an extremely rare combination of errors to fool the system. Further, it is evident that the CRC algorithm is easy to implement in hardware.

Forward Error Correction

In addition to error-detecting codes, there are also error-correcting codes. These are rarely used in data transmission, since retransmission schemes (see Chapter 5) are generally more efficient. Error-correcting codes are used in some situations where retransmission is impractical. Examples are broadcast situations in which there are multiple receivers for one transmission and space probes which essentially use simplex transmission. Error-correcting codes are referred to as *forward error correction* to indicate that the receiver, on its own, is correcting the error. Retransmission schemes, in contrast, are referred to as *backward error correction,* since the receiver feeds back information to the transmitter, which then retransmits data found to be in error.

As with error-detecting codes, an error-correcting code is calculated from the bits to be transmitted and is then added to the transmission. To achieve acceptable levels of error correction, the length of the code must be about the same as the length of the data, reducing the effective data rate by 50%. With a code of this relative length, a reduction in error rate by a factor of 10^2 to 10^3 is achieved.

The reader interested in such codes is referred to [BHAR83] and [MIER84]. A deeper analysis of both error-detecting and error-correcting codes is found in [GALL68].

4-3

INTERFACING

Most digital data processing devices are possessed of limited data transmission capability. Typically, they generate only digital signals, and these are usually NRZ-L or a variant. The distance across which they can transmit data is also limited. Consequently it is rare for such a device to attach directly to a transmission medium. The more common situation is depicted in Figure 4-7. The devices we are discussing, which include terminals and computers, are generically referred to as *data terminal equipment* (DTE). A DTE makes use of the transmission system through the mediation of *data circuit-terminating equipment* (DCE). An example of the latter is a modem (a good description of a variety of DCEs can be found in [HELD79]).

On one side, the DCE is responsible for transmitting and receiving bits, one at a time, over a transmission medium. On the other side, the DCE must interact with the DTE. In general, this requires both data and control information to be exchanged. This is done over a set of wires referred to as *interchange circuits.* For this scheme to work, a high degree of cooperation is required. The two DCEs must understand each other. That is, the receiver of each must use the same encoding

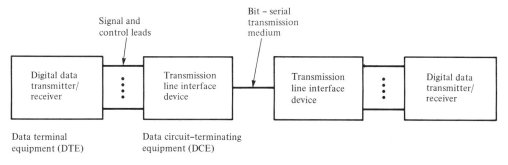

FIGURE 4-7. Generic interface to transmission medium.

scheme (e.g., Manchester, PSK) as the transmitter of the other. In addition, each DTE-DCE pair must be designed to have complementary interfaces and must be able to interact effectively. To ease the burden on data processing equipment manufacturers and users, standards have been developed that specify the exact nature of the interface between the DTE and the DCE. In contemporary parlance, these standards are known as physical layer protocols, and occupy layer 1 of the OSI model referred to in Chapter 1. In this section we examine the nature and functioning of this interface.

The interface has four important characteristics [BERT80]:

- Mechanical.
- Electrical.
- Functional.
- Procedural.

The *mechanical* characteristics pertain to the actual physical connection of the DTE and DCE. Typically, the signal and control leads are bundled into a cable with a terminator plug, male or female, at each end. The DTE and DCE must each present a plug of opposite gender at one end of the cable, effecting the physical connection. This is analogous to the situation for residential electrical power. Power is provided via a socket or wall outlet, and the device to be attached must have the appropriate plug (two-pronged, two-pronged polarized, three-pronged).

The *electrical* characteristics have to do with the voltage levels and timing of voltage changes. Both DTE and DCE must use the same code (e.g., NRZ-L), must use the same voltage levels to mean the same thing, and must use the same duration of signal elements. These characteristics determine the data rates and distances that can be achieved.

Functional characteristics specify the functions that are performed, by assigning meaning to the various interchange circuits. Functions can be classified into the broad categories of data, control, timing, and ground.

Procedural characteristics specify the sequence of events for transmitting data, based on the functional characteristics of the interface. Examples below should clarify this point.

A variety of standards for interfacing exist. This section presents the three most important:

- RS-232-C.
- RS-449/422-A/423-A.
- X.21.

RS-232-C

By far the most common interface standard is RS-232-C [EIA69, EIA71]. It is used to connect DTE devices to voice-grade modems for use on the public telecommunications system. It is also widely used for many other interconnection functions.

The *mechanical* specification for RS-232-C is illustrated in Figure 4-8. It calls for a 25-pin connector with a specific arrangement of leads. Thus in theory, a 25-wire cable could be used to connect the DTE to the DCE. In practice, far fewer interchange circuits are used.

The *electrical* characteristics specify the signaling between DTE and DCE. Digital signaling is used on all interchange circuits. The convention specified is that, with respect to a common ground, a voltage more negative than -3 V is interpreted

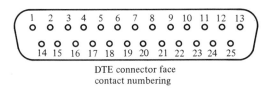

DTE connector face
contact numbering

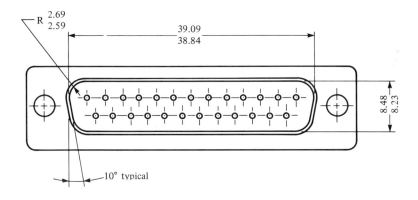

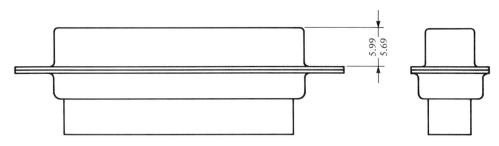

FIGURE 4-8.   RS-232-C connector (dimensions in mm.).

as binary 1 and a voltage more positive than $+3$ V is interpreted as binary 0. The interface is rated at a signal rate of <20 kbps and a distance of <15 m. Greater distance and data rates are possible with good design, but it is reasonable to assume that these limits apply in practice as well as in theory.

Table 4-1 summarizes the *functional* specification of the most important circuits. There is one data circuit in each direction, so full-duplex operation is possible. One ground lead is for protective isolation; the other serves as the return circuit for both data leads. Hence transmission is "unbalanced," with only one active wire. The timing signals provide clock pulses for synchronous transmission. When the DCE is sending data over circuit BB, it also sends 1-0 and 0-1 transitions on DD, with transitions timed to the middle of each BB signal element. When the DTE is sending data, either the DTE or DCE can provide timing pulses, depending on the circumstances. The control signals are explained by *procedural* specifications, and a few examples are given below.

The first example is for an asynchronous private line modem, also known as a

TABLE 4-1 RS-232-C Circuit Definitions

Name	Direction to:	Function
Data Signals		
Transmitted Data (BA)	DCE	Data generated by DTE
Received Data (BB)	DTE	Data received by DTE
Control Signals		
Request to Send (CA)	DCE	DTE wishes to transmit
Clear to Send (CB)	DTE	DCE is ready to transmit; response to request to send
Data Set Ready (CC)	DTE	DCE is ready to operate
Data Terminal Ready (CD)	DCE	DTE is ready to operate
Ring Indicator (CE)	DTE	Indicates that DCE is receiving a ringing signal on the communication channel
Carrier Detect (CF)	DTE	Indicates that DCE is receiving a carrier signal
Signal Quality Detector (CG)	DTE	Asserted when there is reason to believe there is an error in the received data
Data Signal Rate Selector (CH)	DCE	Asserted to select the higher of two possible data rates
Data Signal Rate Selector (CI)	DTE	Asserted to select the higher of two possible data rates
Timing signals		
Transmitter Signal Element Timing (DA)	DCE	Clocking signal, transitions to ON and OFF occur at center of each signal element
Transmitter Signal Element Timing (DB)	DTE	Clocking signal, as above; both leads relate to signals on BA
Receiver Signal Element Timing (DD)	DTE	Clocking signal, as above, for circuit BB
Ground		
Protective Ground (AA)	NA	Attached to machine frame and possibly external grounds
Signal Ground (AB)	NA	Establishes common ground reference for all circuits.

limited distance modem, used to connect two devices with a point-to-point link. The modem, as a DCE, requires only the following circuits:

- Signal ground (AB).
- Transmitted data (BA).
- Received data (BB).
- Request to send (CA).
- Clear to send (CB).
- Data set ready (CC).
- Carrier detect (CF).

The first three circuits have been reasonably well explained. When the DTE is ready to send data, it asserts Request to Send. The modem responds, when ready, with Clear to Send, thereby indicating that data may be transmitted over circuit BA. If the arrangement is half-duplex, then Request to Send also inhibits the receive mode. The Data Set Ready circuit is asserted when the modem is ready to operate. This lead should be asserted before the DTE attempts Request to Send. Finally, Carrier Detect indicates that the remote modem is transmitting. Note that it is not necessary to use timing circuits, since this is asynchronous transmission.

Figure 4-9 shows a state diagram of this operation. EIA divides the six major control circuits into two groups. Group A (CC, CD, CE) relates to the alerting and readiness of the equipment to operate, and group B (CA, CB, CF) relates to preparing the communications equipment to transmit and receive data. The ON and OFF states of these two groups are coded in octal as indicated. The coding also includes DTE power on for this operation.

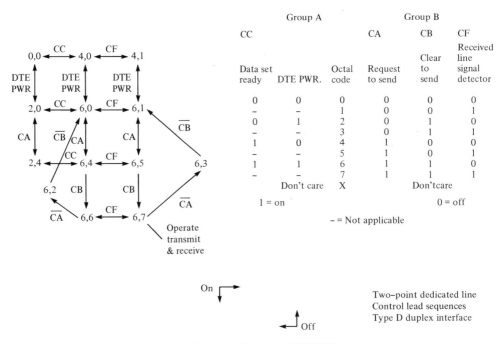

Group A			Group B		
CC			CA	CB	CF
Data set ready	DTE PWR.	Octal code	Request to send	Clear to send	Received line signal detector
0	0	0	0	0	0
–	–	1	0	0	1
0	1	2	0	1	0
–	–	3	0	1	1
1	0	4	1	0	0
–	–	5	1	0	1
1	1	6	1	1	0
–	–	7	1	1	1
Don't care	X			Don't care	

1 = on   0 = off

– = Not applicable

Two–point dedicated line
Control lead sequences
Type D duplex interface

FIGURE 4-9. RS-232-C state diagram. Source: [EIA71]

The circuits described so far are sufficient for private line modems used point-to-point, but additional circuits are required when the telephone network is to be used. Now, the initiator of a connection must call the destination station. Two additional leads are required.

- Data terminal ready (CD).
- Ring indicator (CE).

With the addition of these two leads, the DTE-modem system can effectively use the telephone lines in a way analogous to voice telephone usage. When a call is made, either manually or automatically, the telephone system sends a ringing signal. A telephone set would respond by ringing its bell; a modem responds by asserting Ring Indicator. A human being answers the call by lifting the handset; a DTE answers by asserting Data Terminal Ready. The person will then listen for another's voice and, if nothing is heard, hang up; the DTE will listen for Carrier Detect, which will be raised by the modem when a carrier is present, and if this circuit is not asserted, drop Data Terminal Ready. You might wonder how this last contingency could arise. One common way is if a person accidentally dials the number of a modem. This activates the DTE, but when no carrier tone comes through, the problem is resolved.

As an aside, it is instructive to consider situations in which the distances between devices are so close as to allow two DTEs to directly signal each other. In this case, the RS-232-C leads can still be used, but now no DCE equipment is provided. For the scheme to work, a *null modem* is needed, which interconnects leads in such a way as to fool both DTEs into thinking that they are connected to modems. The reasons for the particular connections in Figure 4-10 should be apparent if the reader has grasped the preceding discussion.

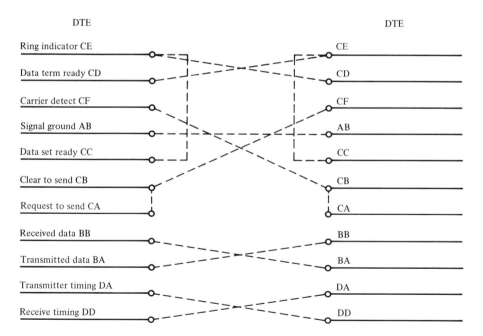

FIGURE 4-10. The null modem.

The most notable shortcoming of RS-232-C is its limited distance/speed characteristics. Also, in the case of its use with a modem, it provides very little DTE control of the modem. To make improvements in these areas, the Electronic Industries Association (EIA) issued a set of standards to replace the older standard: RS-449, RS-422-A, and RS-423-A [FOLT80c]. Although RS-232-C remains the most popular DTE-DCE interface, these new standards are finding increasingly widespread use. RS-449 defines the mechanical, functional, and procedural characteristics of the new interface; RS-422-A and RS-423-A define electrical characteristics. We turn first to RS-449.

RS-449 is similar to RS-232-C and is intended to exhibit a degree of interoperability with the older interface. Functionally, RS-449 retains all of the interchange circuits of RS-232-C, with the exception of protective ground, and adds 10 new circuits (Table 4-2). The most important of these are:

- *Terminal In Service (IS):* Indicates to the DCE that the DTE is operational. This allows an attached device to signal whether it is available to answer calls.
- *New Signal (NS):* Tells the DCE to prepare to acquire a new line signal. This improves overall response time on a polling line.
- *Select Frequency(SF):* When two modems communicate, the transmit frequency of one must be the receive frequency of the other (see Figure 3-6). This circuit allows selection of the frequency mode of the DCE in a multipoint configuration.
- *Local Loopback (LL):* Requests that the DCE loop signals from the local DTE (on SD) back to the same DTE (on RD). This checks the functioning of the local interface and DCE.
- *Remote Loopback (RL):* Requests that signals from the local DTE loop to the remote DCE and back. This tests the operation of the transmisssion channel and the remote DCE (Figure 4-11).
- *Test Mode (TM):* Indicates that local DCE is in a test condition. The ON condition is in response to a local LL, local or remote RL, or activation of a test condition by some other means.

Procedurally, RS-449, is similar to RS-232-C. Each circuit has a single function and communication is based on action-reaction pairs. For example, if the DTE turns on Request to Send, it then waits for the DCE to respond with Clear to Send. Mechanically, the RS-449 standard specifies a 37-pin connector for the basic interface and a separate 9-pin connector if a secondary channel is used. As with RS-232-C, in most cases only a few of these pins are used.

Thus RS-449 improves over RS-232-C by providing greater DTE control over the modem, if used. However, the major improvement is in the electrical characteristics of the new standard, and these are specified by RS-422-A and RS-423-A. Whereas RS-232-C was designed in the era of discrete electronic components, the new standards take advantage of the superior performance possibilities of integrated circuit technology. To understand these standards we need to define several modes of transmission.

In a conventional telephone system and indeed in most uses of twisted pair, signals are carried on a *balanced transmission* line consisting of two conductors. Signals are transmitted as a current that travels down one conductor and returns on the other; the two conductors form a complete circuit. For digital signals this technique is known as *differential signaling,* since the binary value depends on the

TABLE 4-2 RS-449 and RS-232-C Interchange Circuits

RS-449		RS-232C	
		AA	Protective Ground
SG	Signal Ground	AB	Signal Ground
SC	Send Common		
RC	Receive Common		
IS	Terminal in Service		
IC	Incoming Call	CE	Ring Indicator
TR*	Terminal Ready	CD	Data Terminal Ready
DM*	Data Mode	CC	Data Set Ready
SD*	Send Data	BA	Transmitted Data
RD*	Receive Data	BB	Received Data
TT*	Terminal Timing	DA	Transmitter Signal Element Timing (DTE source)
ST*	Send Timing	DB	Transmitter Signal Element Timing (DCE Source)
RT*	Receive Timing	DD	Receiver Signal Element Timing
RS*	Request to Send	CA	Request to Send
CS*	Clear to Send	CB	Clear to Send
RR*	Receiver Ready	CF	Received Line Signal Detector
SQ	Signal Quality	CG	Signal Quality Detector
NS	New Signal		
SF	Select Frequency		
SR	Signaling Rate Selector	CH	Data Signal Rate Selector (DTE source)
SI	Signaling Rate Indicator	CI	Data Signal Rate Selector (DCE source)
SSD	Secondary Send Data	SBA	Secondary Transmitted Data
SRD	Secondary Receive Data	SBB	Secondary Received Data
SRS	Secondary Request to Send	SCA	Secondary Request to Send
SCS	Secondary Clear to Send	SCB	Secondary Clear to Send
SRR	Secondary Receiver Ready	SCF	Secondary Received Line Signal Detector
LL	Local Loopback		
RL	Remote Loopback		
TM	Test Mode		
			Pins 9 and 10 Test Function
SS	Select Standby		
SB	Standby Indicator		

ᵃCategory I circuits.

direction of the voltage difference between the two conductors. *Unbalanced transmission* uses a single conductor to carry the signal, with ground providing the return path. There is also a third mode, known as current-mode transmission, in which two conductors are used and current is sent in one direction down either of the two conductors, depending on the binary value.

The balanced mode tolerates more, and produces less, noise than the unbalanced. Ideally, interference on a balanced line will act equally on both conductors and not affect the voltage difference. For this reason, unbalanced transmission is generally limited to coaxial cable or very short distances, such as used in RS-232-C.

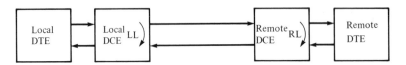

FIGURE 4-11. Local and remote loopback.

RS-423-A specifies unbalanced transmission and achieves the following rated performance: 3 kbps at 1000 m to 300 kbps at 10 m. This is a significant improvement over RS-232-C, which is a constant limit of 20 kbps up to 15 m. RS-422-A specifies balanced transmission and achieves even better performance: 100 kbps at 1200 m to 10 Mbps at 12 m; a graph of the rated performance was shown in Figure 2-16.

For lower performance and presumably lower cost, RS-423-A can be used on all RS-449 interchange circuits. Even for higher performance, most of the circuits carry low-speed control signals and do not need better electrical characteristics. Accordingly, 10 circuits have been designated as Category I and it is only these circuits that require RS-422-A for higher performance:

- Send data (SD).
- Receive data (RD).
- Terminal timing (TT).
- Send timing (ST).
- Receive timing (RT).
- Request to send (RS).
- Clear to send (CS).
- Receiver ready (RR).
- Terminal ready (TR).
- Data mode (DM).

Each of these circuits requires two wires for RS-422-A; twisted pair is used. Both the balanced and unbalanced leads are usually housed in the same cable sheath.

We should also point out that RS-422-A has a life of its own outside its use with RS-449. For example, a number of low-cost local networks use RS-422-A twisted pair in a multipoint configuration. This will be described in Chapter 11.

X.21

The benefits to be derived from RS-449 are achieved at the expense of extra circuits and connections. This is a rather expensive way to achieve results. An alternative would be to provide fewer circuits but to add more logic at the DTE and DCE interfaces. With the dropping costs of logic circuitry this is an attractive approach and the one taken for the X.21 standard [YANO81].

X.21 specifies a 15-pin connector but at present makes use of fewer leads than that. Table 4-3 summarizes the defined interface circuits. As with RS-232-C and RS-449, there is a transmit circuit in both directions (T and R). Now, however, these circuits may provide both user data and control information. In addition, there are two other circuits (C and I), one in each direction, for control and status information. These two circuits do not carry digital data streams, but may be either in an ON or an OFF state. X.21 is defined only for synchronous operation, for which a bit timing circuit is provided. These five circuits are sufficient for many

TABLE 4-3 X.21 Circuit Definitions

Name	Direction to:	Function
Signal Ground (G)	NA	
DTE Common Return (Ga)	DCE	
Transmit (T)	DCE	Used to convey both user data and network control information, depending on state of C and I
Receive (R)	DTE	Same as T in opposite direction
Control (C)	DCE	Provides control information to DCE (e.g., ON/OFF hook)
Indication (I)	DTE	Provides indicators to DTE (e.g., start of transparent data phase)
Signal Element Timing (S)	DTE	Provides bit timing
Byte Timing (B)	DTE	Provides byte (8-bit) timing

applications. A little-used byte timing signal is optional for synchronizing control characters.

Balanced and unbalanced modes, similar to RS-422-A and RS-423-A, are provided in the standard. Thus the same speed/distance levels can be achieved. In most cases, only the balanced mode is used on all circuits.

Most of the procedures defined for X.21 circuits have to do with operation over a circuit-switched communications network. Thus they are not properly part of a physical layer protocol, and a discussion is deferred until Chapter 13. Procedures associated with the readiness status of the DTE and DCE do, however, have a physical layer flavor and are presented here. Two states are defined for the DCE and three for the DTE:

- *DTE ready:* Indicates readiness to operate. This is signaled by a steady 1 on T and a control OFF (binary 1) on C.
- *DTE uncontrolled not ready:* Indicates that DTE is unable to enter operational phases because of an abnormal condition. The signals are T = 0, C = OFF.
- *DTE controlled not ready:* The DTE is operational but unable to accept calls. Signals are T = 010101 . . . and C = OFF.
- *DCE ready:* The DCE is ready to operate. Signals are R = 1 and I = OFF.
- *DCE not ready:* No service is available. Signals are R = 0 and I = OFF.

The various allowable combined states, called quiescent states, and possible transitions are shown in Figure 4-12. To ensure proper detection, X.21 requires that the DTE and DCE be prepared to send these signals for at least 24 bit intervals. Detection of the signals for 16 contiguous bit intervals is required.

X.21 represents a major improvement over RS-232-C and RS-449. It is more flexible and should cost less. The use of streams of control characters gives an unlimited set of options to meet future needs.

X.21 is a good example of the basic dilemma or paradox inherent in standards, a theme that will be echoed again in this book. Standards are needed to permit equipment built by various vendors and owned by various users to work together (referred to by DOD as "interoperability"). Standards also encourage the cost saving realized by efficient mass production techniques. Unfortunately, standards

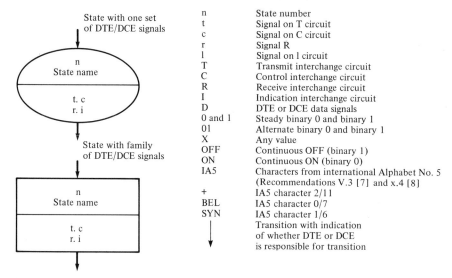

n   State number
t   Signal on T circuit
c   Signal on C circuit
r   Signal R
l   Signal on l circuit
T   Transmit interchange circuit
C   Control interchange circuit
R   Receive interchange circuit
I   Indication interchange circuit
D   DTE or DCE data signals
0 and 1   Steady binary 0 and binary 1
01   Alternate binary 0 and binary 1
X   Any value
OFF   Continuous OFF (binary 1)
ON   Continuous ON (binary 0)
IA5   Characters from international Alphabet No. 5
           (Recommendations V.3 [7] and x.4 [8]
+   IA5 character 2/11
BEL   IA5 character 0/7
SYN   IA5 character 1/6
           Transition with indication
           of whether DTE or DCE
           is responsible for transition

(a) Symbols used in the state diagram

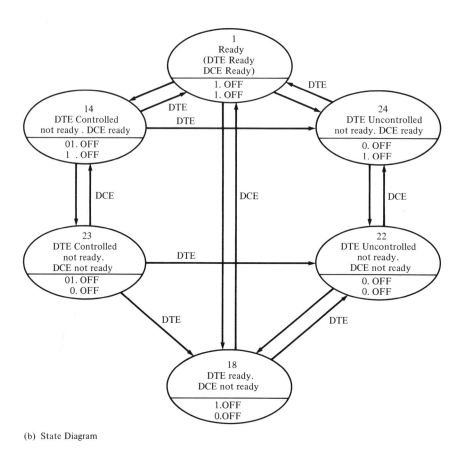

(b) State Diagram

FIGURE 4-12.   X.21 quiescent state diagram.

tend to freeze technology and become obsolete almost as soon as they are issued. In the case of physical interface standards, the following is a brief history. RS-449, RS-422-A, and RS-423-A were specifically developed as interim standards to improve performance over RS-232-C while awaiting a new and far more efficient standard, namely X.21. X.21 was expected to have a long lifetime and become *the* universal interface. Alas, time and events have overcome X.21 and it is now also considered interim. A newer, more efficient standard, using even fewer interchange circuits, is on the drawing boards. This new standard, as yet undefined, will be part of a more ambitious effort known as ISDN (see Chapter 17). In the meantime, users and manufacturers are faced with the prospect of relying on relatively inefficient interfaces such as RS-232-C or RS-449/422-A/423-A, or making a capital investment in an interface (X.21) which will soon be replaced.

4-4

RECOMMENDED READING

An excellent book that covers all of the topics of this chapter is [MCNA82]; the book has somewhat of an electrical engineering orientation but is nevertheless quite approachable and is as thorough as most readers could wish for. [PETE61] is a good presentation of CRC codes. [BERT80] discusses various physical-level interfaces. [MCCL83] discusses the physical-level interface from the point of view of its role in an overall communications architecture.

4-5

PROBLEMS

4-1 A data source produces 7-bit ASCII characters. Derive an expression for the maximum effective data rate (rate of ASCII data bits) over a B-bps line for the following:
  a. Asynchronous transmission, with a 1.5-unit stop bit and a parity bit.
  b. Bit-synchronous transmission, with a frame consisting of 48 control bits and 128 information bits. The information field contains 8-bit (parity included) ASCII characters.
  c. Same as part (b), except that the information field is 1024 bits.
  d. Character-synchronous transmission, with 9 control characters per frame and 16 or 128 information characters.
  e. Same as part (d), with 12 control characters per frame.

4-2 Demonstrate by example (write down a few dozen arbitrary bit patterns with start and stop bits) that a receiver that suffers a framing error on asynchronous transmission will eventually become realigned.

4-3 Using Figure 4-4, work out the probability of an undetected error in 7-bit character with one parity bit, given that at least one error has occurred.

4-4 In the VRC/LRC scheme, is the last bit of the parity check character generated horizontally (from the other bits in the character) or vertically (from the parity bit of all other characters)?

4-5 Consider a frame consisting of two characters of four bits each. Assume that the probability of bit error is 10^{-3} and that it is constant and independent for each bit.

a. What is P, the probability that the frame is received correctly?

b. Now add a parity bit to each character, but assume that parity bits are never in error. What is P?

c. Now add a parity check character, and again assume parity bits are never in error. What is P?

4-6 Using the CRC-CCITT polynomial, generate the 16-bit CRC code for the message consisting of a 1 followed by 15 0's.

4-7 Explain in words why the shift register implementation of CRC will result in all 0's at the receiver if there are no errors. Demonstrate by example.

4-8 Duplicate the contents of the shift register in Figure 4-6 using long division.

4-9 A modified CRC procedure is commonly used in communications standards. It is defined as follows:

$$\frac{X^{16} M(X) + X^k L(X)}{P(X)} = Q(X) + \frac{R(X)}{P(X)}$$

$$FCS = L(X) + R(X)$$

where

$L(X) = X^{15} + X^{14} + X^{13} + \ldots X + 1$
k = number of bits in M

a. Describe in words the effect of this procedure.

b. Can you explain the potential benefits?

c. Show a shift register implementation for $P(X) = X^{16} + X^{12} + X^5 + 1$.

4-10 Draw a timing diagram showing the state of all RS-232-C leads between two DTE-DCE pairs during the course of a data call on the switched telephone network.

4-11 Explain the operation of each null modem connection in Figure 4-10.

4-12 For the RS-449 RL circuit to function properly, what circuits must be logically connected?

CHAPTER 5

Data Link Control

Our discussion so far has concerned *sending signals over a transmission link*. For effective digital data communications much more is needed to control and manage the exchange. We want to convert the procedure above into one of *sending data over a data communications link*. This is done by adding a layer of control in each communicating device above the physical interfacing discussed in Chapter 4, referred to as *data link control* or *data link protocol*. When a data link control procedure is used, the transmission medium between stations is referred to as a *data link*.

To see the need for data link control, we list some of the requirements and objectives for effective data communication between two directly connected transmitting–receiving stations:

- *Frame synchronization:* Data are sent in blocks called frames. The beginning and end of each frame must be clearly identifiable.
- *Use of a variety of line configurations:* These are defined in Section 5-1.
- *Flow control:* The sending station must not send frames at a rate faster than the receiving station can absorb them.
- *Error control:* The bit errors introduced by the transmission system must be corrected.
- *Addressing:* On a multipoint line, the identity of the two stations involved in a transmission must be known.

- *Control and data on same link:* It is usually not desirable to have a separate communications path for control signals. Accordingly, the receiver must be able to distinguish control information from the data being transmitted.
- *Link management:* The initiation, maintenance, and termination of a sustained data exchange requires a fair amount of coordination and cooperation among stations. Procedures for the management of this exchange are required.

None of these requirements is satisfied by the physical interfacing techniques described in Chapter 4. We shall see in this chapter that a data link protocol that satisfies these requirements is a rather complex affair. To begin, some of the key features of data link control protocols are presented: line configuration control, flow control, and error control. In assessing flow and error control procedures, a novel method of comparing various approaches for various links is presented. This method is based on a parameter a, defined as the ratio of propagation delay to frame transmission time. We will have occasion to employ this parameter again in Part II.

Following these preliminaries, a specific data link protocol, HDLC, is discussed in some detail. HDLC is representative of modern data link protocols that use bit-oriented synchronous transmission. For the interested reader, the older and increasingly obsolete character-oriented protocols are discussed in Appendix 5A.

5-1

LINE CONFIGURATIONS

The three characteristics that distinguish various data link configurations are topology, duplexity, and line discipline.

Topology and Duplexity

The *topology* of a data link refers to the physical arrangement of stations on a link. This was discussed in Chapter 2. If there are only two stations, the link is *point-to-point*. If there are more than two stations, then it is a *multipoint* topology. Traditionally, a multipoint link has been used in the case of a computer (primary station) and a set of terminals (secondary stations). More recently, more complex versions of the multipoint topology are found in local networks (Figure 1-4c).

Traditional multipoint lines are made possible when the terminals are only transmitting a fraction of the time. Figure 5-1 illustrates the advantages of the multipoint configuration. If each terminal has a point-to-point link to its computer, then the computer must have one I/O port for each terminal. Also, there is a separate transmission line from the computer to each terminal. In a multipoint configuration, the computer needs only a single I/O port, saving hardware costs. Only a single transmission line is needed, which also saves costs.

The *duplexity* of a link refers to the direction and timing of signal flow. In *simplex* transmission, the signal flow is always in one direction. For example, an input device such as a card reader or remote sensor could be attached to a host so that the device could only transmit, and never receive. An output device such as a printer or actuator could be configured to only receive. Simplex is not in general use since it is not possible to send error or control signals back down the link to the data source. Simplex is similar to a one-lane, one-way bridge.

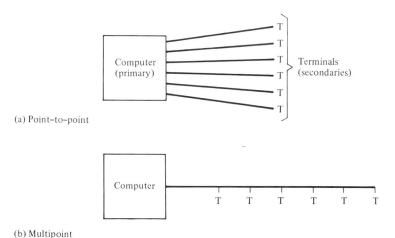

(a) Point–to–point

(b) Multipoint

FIGURE 5-1. Traditional computer/terminal configurations.

A *half-duplex* link can transmit and receive, but not simultaneously. This mode is also referred to as "two-way alternate," suggestive of the fact that two stations on a half-duplex link must alternate in transmitting. This is similar to a one-lane, two-way bridge. On a *full-duplex* link, two stations can simultaneously send and receive data from each other. Thus this mode is known as "two-way simultaneous" and may be compared to a two-lane, two-way bridge.

With digital signaling, which requires hardwire transmission, full-duplex usually requires two separate transmission paths (e.g., two twisted pair), while half-duplex requires only one. For analog signaling, duplexity depends on frequency, whether hardwire or softwire transmission is used. If a station transmits and receives on the same frequency, it must operate in half-duplex mode (exception: hardwire transmission using two separate, isolated conductors; this is rarely done). If a station transmits on one frequency and receives on another, it may operate in full-duplex mode (Figure 3-6).

A number of combinations of topology and duplicity are possible. Figure 5-2 depicts the most common configurations. The figure always shows a single primary station (P) and one or more secondary (S) stations (this point is explored when we discuss line discipline). For point-to-point links, the two possibilities are self explanatory. For multipoint links, three configurations are possible:

- Primary full-duplex, secondaries half-duplex (multi-multipoint).
- Both primary and secondaries half-duplex (multipoint half-duplex).
- Both primary and secondaries full-duplex (multipoint duplex).

Line Discipline

Some discipline is needed in the use of a transmission link. On a half-duplex line, only one station at a time should transmit. On either a half- or full-duplex line, a station should only transmit if it knows that the intended receiver is prepared to receive.

Point-to-Point Links. Line discipline is simple with a point-to-point link. Let us consider first a half-duplex link in which either station may initiate an exchange.

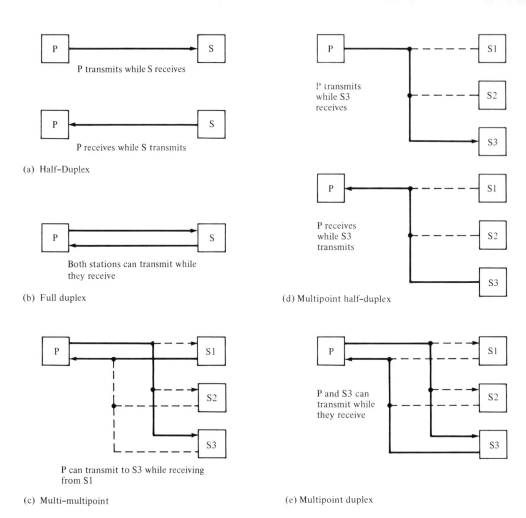

(a) Half–Duplex

(b) Full duplex

(c) Multi–multipoint

(d) Multipoint half–duplex

(e) Multipoint duplex

FIGURE 5-2. Data link configurations.

An example exchange is depicted in Figure 5-3. If either station wishes to send data to the other, it first performs an enquiry (depicted as enq) of the other station to see if it is prepared to receive. The second station responds with a positive acknowledgment (ack) to indicate that it is ready. The first station then sends some data, which the figure depicts as a frame. In asynchronous communication, the data would be sent as an asynchronous stream of characters. In any case, after some quantum of data is sent, the first station pauses to await results. The second station acknowledges successful receipt of the data (ack). The first station then sends an end of transmission message (eot) which terminates the exchange and returns the system to its initial state.

Several additional features are added to Figure 5-3 to provide for coping with errors. A negative acknowledgment (nak) is used to indicate that a station is not ready to receive, or that data were received in error. A station may fail to respond or respond with an invalid message. The result of these conditions is indicated by light lines in the figure; the heavy line is the normal sequence of communication events. If an unexpected event occurs, such as a nak or invalid reply, a station may retry its last action or may institute some error recovery procedure (erp).

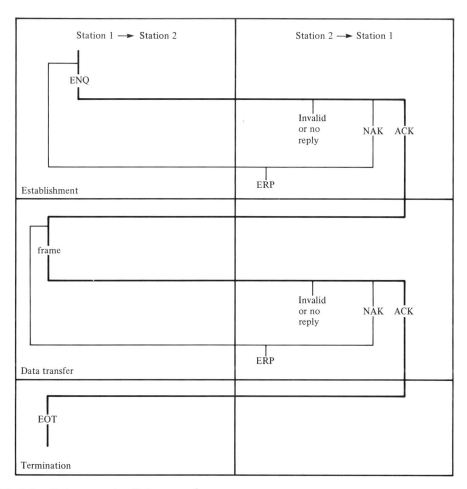

FIGURE 5-3. Point-to-point link control.

There are three distinct phases in this communication control procedure:

- *Establishment:* This determines which station is to transmit and which to receive, and that the receiver is prepared to receive.
- *Data Transfer:* The data are transferred in one or more acknowledged blocks.
- *Termination:* This terminates the logical connection (transmitter-receiver relationship).

These three phases, in some form, are a part of all line disciplines for both point-to-point and multipoint links.

Several refinements can be added to our discussion. The relationship described above was peer; that is, either station could initiate transmission. A common situation is to have one of the stations designated *primary* and the other *secondary*. The primary has the responsibility of initiating the exchange. This is a common situation when one station is a computer (primary) and the other is a terminal (secondary). Figure 5-3 depicts a sequence in which the primary has data to send to the secondary. If the secondary has data to send, it must wait for the primary to request the data, and only then enter a data transfer phase.

If the link is full-duplex, data and control messages can be transmitted in both directions simultaneously. We shall see the advantages of this when we discuss flow and error control.

Multipoint Links. The choice of line discipline for multipoint links depends primarily on whether there is a designated primary station or not. When there is a primary station, data are exchanged only between the primary and a secondary, not between two secondaries. The most common disciplines used in this situation are all variants of a scheme known as *poll and select*:

- *Poll:* The primary requests data from a secondary.
- *Select:* The primary has data to send and informs a secondary that data are coming.

Figure 5-4 illustrates these concepts. In Figure 5-4a, the primary polls a secondary by sending a brief polling message. In this case, the secondary has nothing to send and responds with some sort of nak message. The timing for this sequence is indicated. The total time is

$$T_N = t_{\text{prop}} + t_{\text{poll}} + t_{\text{proc}} + t_{\text{nak}} + t_{\text{prop}}$$

where

$$T_N = \text{total time to poll terminal with nothing to send}$$
$$t_{\text{prop}} = \text{propagation time} = t_1 - t_0 = t_5 - t_4$$
$$t_{\text{poll}} = \text{time to transmit a poll} = t_2 - t_1$$
$$t_{\text{proc}} = \text{time to process poll before acknowledging} = t_3 - t_2$$
$$t_{\text{nak}} = \text{time to transmit a negative acknowledgment} = t_4 - t_3$$

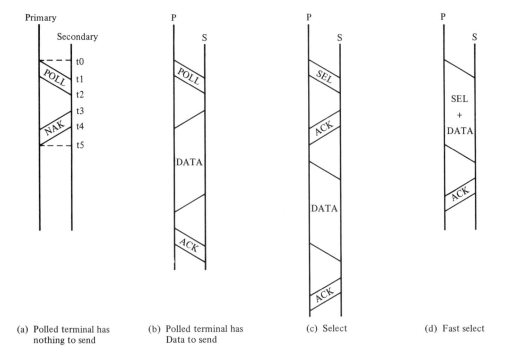

(a) Polled terminal has nothing to send

(b) Polled terminal has Data to send

(c) Select

(d) Fast select

FIGURE 5-4. Poll and select sequences.

Figure 5-4b depicts the case of a successful poll. The time here is

$$T_P = 3t_{\text{prop}} + t_{\text{poll}} + t_{\text{ack}} + t_{\text{data}} + 2t_{\text{proc}}$$

$$= T_N + t_{\text{prop}} + t_{\text{data}} + t_{\text{proc}}$$

Here we assume for simplicity that the processing time to respond to any message is a constant.

The most common form of polling is *roll-call polling*, in which the primary selectively polls each secondary in a predetermined sequence. In the simplest case, the primary polls each secondary in a round-robin fashion, $S_1, S_2, \ldots, S_n$, for all n secondaries and then repeats the sequence. The timing can be expressed as

$$T_c = nT_N + kT_D \tag{5-1}$$

where

T_c = time for one complete polling cycle

T_N = average time to poll a secondary exclusive of data transfer

T_D = time to transfer data = $t_{\text{prop}} + t_{\text{data}} + t_{\text{proc}}$

n = number of secondary stations

k = number of secondary stations with data to send during the cycle

Variants of roll-call polling permit priority handling by, for example, polling some stations more than once per cycle.

The select function is shown in Figure 5-4c. Note that four separate transmissions are required to transfer data from the primary to the secondary. An alternative technique is *fast select*. In this case, the selection message includes the data to be transferred (Figure 5-4d). The first reply from the secondary is an acknowledgment that indicates that the station was prepared to receive and did receive the data successfully. Fast selection is particularly well suited for applications where short messages are frequently transmitted and the transfer time for the message is not appreciably longer than the reply time.

The use of roll-call polling for other configurations is easily explained. In the case of multi-multipoint (Figure 5-2c), the primary can be sending a poll to one secondary at the same time that it is receiving a control message or data from another. For multipoint duplex, the primary can engage in full-duplex conversation with any of the secondaries.

It should be clear from Equation (5-1) that the overhead in polling each station can significantly increase response times if there are a large number of terminals (large n) or a long line (large t_{prop}). An improvement can be obtained by using *hub polling* (Figure 5-5). This technique requires secondary stations to participate actively in the polling operation. Two data paths with simultaneous transmission are required, and each secondary must be able to receive on both paths simultaneously. The operation is as follows. The primary sends a poll to the most remote secondary. If the secondary has data to transmit, it transmits the data to the primary, and then sends a poll to the next secondary in line. If the secondary has no data to send, it immediately sends a poll to the next secondary. The last secondary in line sends a poll to the primary which begins a new cycle. All during this process, the primary can be sending data to the secondaries on the line labeled "output."

Another form of line discipline is *contention*. In this mode, there is typically no primary but rather a collection of peer stations. A station can transmit if the line is free; otherwise, it must wait. This technique has found widespread use in local networks and satellite systems.

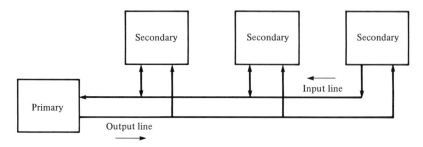

FIGURE 5-5. Hub polling.

A characteristic of all multipoint line disciplines is the need for addressing. In the case of roll-call polling, transmissions from the primary must indicate the intended secondary; transmissions from a secondary must identify the secondary. In a peer situation, both transmitter and receiver must be identified. Thus there are three cases:

- *Point-to-point:* no address needed.
- *Primary-secondary multipoint:* one address needed, to identify secondary.
- *Peer multipoint:* two addresses needed, to identify transmitter and receiver.

In practice, the first case is subsumed into the second, so that most data link control protocols require one address even for point-to-point transmission. This simplifies the demands on the station by allowing a single protocol to be used in both circumstances. The peer multipoint case is seen in local networks; this chapter will be concerned only with the first two cases, for which traditional data link control protocols were developed.

5-2

FLOW CONTROL

Flow control is a technique for assuring that a transmitting station does not over-whelm a receiving station with data. The receiver will typically allocate a data buffer with some maximum length. When data are received, it must do a certain amount of processing before it can clear the buffer and be prepared to receive more data.

The simplest form of flow control, known as *stop and wait*, works as follows. The receiver indicates its willingness to accept data by sending a poll or responding to a select. The sender than transmits its data. Following reception, the receiver must again indicate its willingness to accept data before more are sent. This procedure works fine, and indeed can hardly be improved on, when a message is sent as one contiguous block or frame of data. However, it is often the case that a transmitter will break a large block of data up into smaller blocks and send these one at a time. This is done for one or more of the following reasons:

- The longer the transmission, the more likely that there will be an error, ne-cessitating retransmission of the entire block. With smaller blocks, errors are less likely per block, and fewer data need be retransmitted.
- On a multipoint line, it is usually desirable not to permit one station to occupy the line for very long, thus causing long delays at the other stations.
- The buffer size of the receiver may be limited.

With the use of multiple frames for a single message, the simple procedure described above may be inadequate. We first explore the reason for this inadequacy, then show a technique for overcoming it.

The Effect of Propagation Delay and Transmission Rate

Let us determine the maximum potential efficiency of a half-duplex point-to-point line using the stop-and-wait scheme described above. Suppose that a long message is to be sent as a sequence of frames $f_1, f_2, \ldots, f_n$. For a polling procedure, the following events occur:

- Station S_1 sends a poll of station S_2.
- S_2 responds with f_1.
- S_1 sends an acknowledgment.
- S_2 sends f_2.
- S_1 acknowledges.

      •
      •
      •

- S_2 sends f_n.
- S_1 acknowledges.

The total time to send the data is

$$T_d = T_I + nT_F$$

where

$$T_I = \text{time to initiate sequence} = t_{\text{prop}} + t_{\text{poll}} + t_{\text{proc}}$$
$$T_F = \text{time to send one frame} = t_{\text{prop}} + t_{\text{frame}} + t_{\text{proc}} + t_{\text{prop}} + t_{\text{ack}} + t_{\text{proc}}$$

To simplify matters, we ignore a few terms. For a long sequence of frames, T_I is relatively small and can be dropped. Let us assume that the processing time between transmission and reception is negligible, and that the acknowledgment frame is very small. Then we can express T_D as

$$T_D = n(2t_{\text{prop}} + t_{\text{frame}})$$

Of that time, only $n \times t_{\text{frame}}$ is actually spent transmitting data and the rest is overhead. Thus the utilization or efficiency of the line is

$$U = \frac{n \times t_{\text{frame}}}{n(2t_{\text{prop}} + t_{\text{frame}})}$$

$$U = \frac{t_{\text{frame}}}{2t_{\text{prop}} + t_{\text{frame}}}$$

It is useful to define $a = t_{\text{prop}}/t_{\text{frame}}$. Then

$$U = \frac{1}{1 + 2a} \tag{5-2}$$

This is the maximum possible utilization of the link. We will see that the frame itself contains overhead bits, so actual utilization is lower. The parameter a is a constant if both t_{frame} and t_{prop} are constants. This is typically the case: Fixed-length frames are often used for all except the last frame in a sequence, and the propagation delay is constant for point-to-point links. An approximation for U can be obtained by using the maximum propagation time on a multipoint link.

To get some insight into Equation (5-2), let us derive a different expression for a. We have

$$a = \frac{\text{Propagation Time}}{\text{Transmission Time}} \qquad (5\text{-}3)$$

The propagation time is equal to the distance d of the link divided by the velocity of propagation V. For softwire transmission (except through seawater) V is the speed of light, 3×10^8 m/s. A typical value for hardwire media is 2×10^8 m/sec. The transmission time is equal to the length of the frame L divided by the data rate B, so

$$a = \frac{d/V}{L/B} = \frac{Bd}{VL}$$

Thus a is proportional to the data rate times the length of the medium. This term, $B \times d$, and hence a, is the single most important parameter determining the performance of a data link. A useful way of looking at a is that it represents the length of the medium in bits ($B \times d/V$) compared to the frame length.

With this interpretation of a in mind, Figure 5-6 validates Equation (5-2). In this figure, transmission time is normalized to 1. Hence the propagation time, by Equation (5-3), is a. First consider the case of $a < 1$; this is the case in which the "bit length" of the link is less than that of the frame. A station begins transmitting a frame at time t_0. At $t_0 + a$, the leading edge of the frame reaches the receiving station, while the sending station is still in the process of transmitting the frame. At $t_0 + 1$, the sending station has completed transmission. At $t_0 + 1 + a$, the

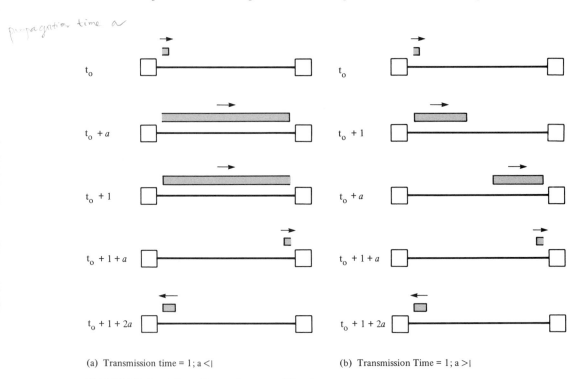

propagation time a

(a) Transmission time = 1; a <| (b) Transmission Time = 1; a >|

FIGURE 5-6.   The effect of *a* on utilization.

receiving station has received the entire frame and immediately transmits a small acknowledgment frame. This acknowledgment arrives back at the sending station at $t_0 + 1 + 2a$. Total elapsed time: $1 + 2a$. Total transmission time: 1. Hence utilization or efficiency is $1/(1 + 2a)$. The same result is achieved with $a > 1$, as illustrated in Figure 5-6b.

Let us consider a few examples. At one extreme is a satellite link. The round trip propagation time is about 270 ms. A typical digital transmission service is 56 kbps, and a 4000-bit frame is within the typical range. Thus transmission time equals $4000/56,000 = 71$ ms, and $a = 270/71 = 3.8$. From Equation (5-2) the maximum utilization is $1/(1 + 7.6) = 0.12$. This is about the smallest value of a that one might expect for a satellite link. Recent and proposed satellite services use much shorter transmission times: from 6 ms down to 125μs [EDEL82]. For this range, a is in the range 45 to 2160. Thus for the simple stop-and-wait acknowledgment protocol described above, efficiency could be as low as 0.0002! At the other extreme, in terms of distance, is the local network. Distances range from 0.1 to 10 km, with data rates of 0.1 to 10 Mbps. Using a value of $V = 2 \times 10^8$ m/s and a frame size of 500 bits, the value of a is in the range 10^{-4} to 1. Typical values are 0.01 to 0.1. For the latter range, utilization is in the range 0.83 to 0.98.

We can see that local networks are inherently quite efficient, whereas satellite links are not. As a final example, let us consider digital data transmission via modem over a voice-grade line. A practical upper bound on data rate is 9600 bps. We can again use $V = 2 \times 10^8$ m/s. Again, let us consider a 500-bit frame. Such transmission is used for distances anywhere from a few tens of meters to thousands of kilometers. If we pick, say, as a short distance $d = 100$ m, then $a = (9600 \text{ bps} \times 100 \text{ m})/(2 \times 10^8 \text{ m/s} \times 500 \text{ bits}) = 9.6 \times 10^{-6}$ and utilization is effectively unity. Even in a long-distance case, such as $d = 5000$ km, we have $a = (9600 \times 5 \times 10^6)/(2 \times 10^8 \times 500) = 0.48$ and efficiency equals 0.5.

efficiency increase when V is great L is small

We can conclude that, in some cases, the simple stop-and-wait acknowledgment procedure provides adequate line utilization. For those cases in which this is not the case, a more elaborate procedure is desirable. Such a procedure, universally accepted, is the sliding-window protocol.

The Sliding Window Protocol

The essence of the problem described so far is that only one frame at a time can be in transit. In situations where the bit length of the link is greater than the frame length ($a > 1$), serious inefficiencies result. The obvious solution is to allow multiple frames to be in transit at one time.

Let us examine how this might work for two stations, A and B, connected via full-duplex link. Station B allocates seven buffers for reception instead of the one discussed above. Thus B can accept seven frames, and A is allowed to send seven frames without waiting for an acknowledgment. To keep track of which frames have been acknowledged, each is labeled with a sequence number in the range 0 to 7 (modulo 8). B acknowledges a frame by sending an acknowledgment that includes the sequence number of the next frame expected. Thus, if B returns the sequence number 5, this acknowledges receipt of frame number 4, and says that B is now expecting frame number 5. This scheme can be used to acknowledge multiple frames. For example, B could receive frames 2, 3, and 4, but withhold acknowledgment until frame 4 arrives. By then returning sequence number 5, *B* acknowledges frames 2, 3, and 4 at one time. *A* maintains a list of sequence numbers that it is allowed to send and *B* maintains a list of sequence numbers that it is prepared to receive. Each of these lists can be thought of as a "window" of frames.

An example of operation is shown in Figure 5-7. Initially, *A* and *B* have seven-frame windows. After transmitting three frames with no acknowledgment, *A* has shrunk its window to four frames. When frame 2 is acknowledged, *A* is back up to seven frames. Later, *B* decides to restrict flow to three frames. This is easily accomplished by withholding acknowledgment.

The efficiency of the line now depends on both *N*, the window size, and *a*. For convenience, let us again normalize frame transmission time to a value of 1; thus the propagation time is *a*. Figure 5-8 illustrates the efficiency of a full-duplex point-to-point line. Station *A* begins to emit a sequence of frames at time t_0. The leading edge of the first frame reaches station *B* at $t_0 + a$. The first frame is entirely absorbed by $t_0 + a + 1$. Assuming negligible processing time, station *B* can

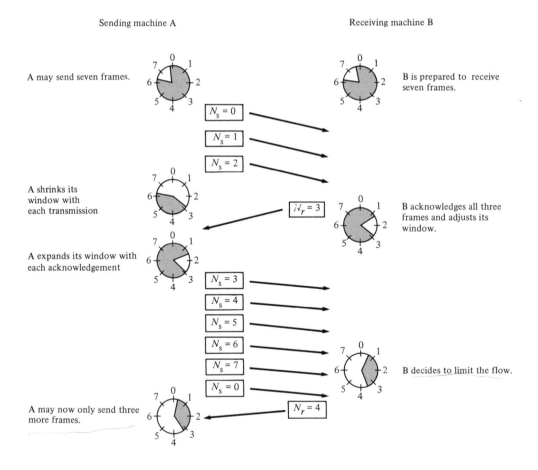

N_s = sequence number of frame sent
N_r = sequence number of next frame expected
Shaded part designates window

FIGURE 5-7. Example of a sliding-window protocol.

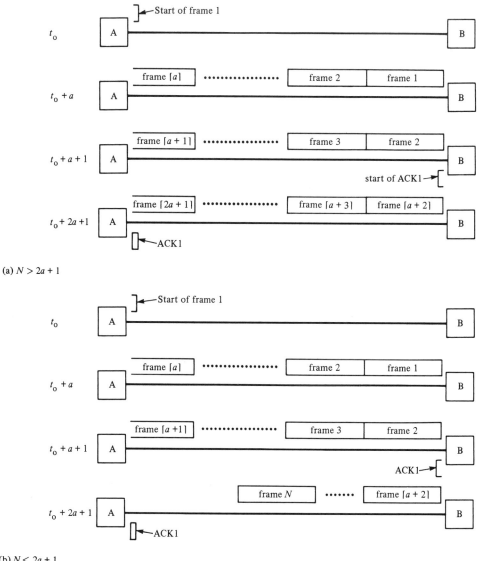

FIGURE 5-8. **Timing of a sliding-window protocol.**

[X] = smallest integer greater
than or equal to X

immediately acknowledge the first frame (ACK1). Let us also assume that the acknowledgment frame is so small that transmission time is negligible. Then the ACK1 reaches station A at $t_0 + 2a + 1$. There are two cases:

- *Case 1: $N > 2a + 1$.* The acknowledgment for frame 1 reaches station A before it has exhausted its window. Thus A can transmit continuously with no pause.
- *Case 2: $N < 2a + 1$.* Station A exhausts its window at $t_0 + N$ and cannot send additional frames until $t_0 + 2a + 1$. Thus the line utilization is N time units out of a period of $(2a + 1)$ time units.

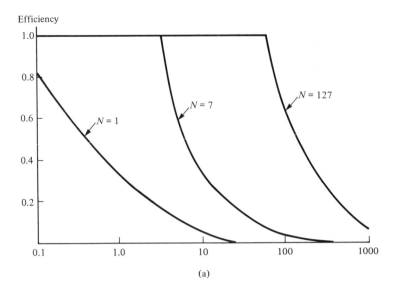

Efficiency

(a)

FIGURE 5-9. Line utilization as a function of window size.

From the above, we can state that

$$U = \begin{cases} 1 & N > 2a + 1 \\ \dfrac{N}{2a+1} & N < 2a + 1 \end{cases} \tag{5-4}$$

Typically, the sequence number is provided for in an n-bit field and the maximum window size is $N = 2^n - 1$ (not 2^n; this is explained in Section 5-3). Figure 5-9 shows the maximum efficiency achievable for window sizes of 1, 7, and 127 as a function of a. A window size of one, of course, corresponds to the simple protocol discussed earlier. A window size of seven (3 bits) should be adequate for most applications. A window size of 127 (7 bits) is adequate for some satellite links.

So far, we have discussed transmission in one direction only. If two stations exchange data, each needs to maintain two windows: one for transmit and one for receive. When this is the case, a technique known as *piggybacking* is often used. If a station has data to send and an acknowledgment to send, it sends both together in one frame, thus saving communications capacity. This technique works with either half-duplex or full-duplex links. For a multipoint link, the primary needs transmit and receive windows for each secondary.

5-3

ERROR CONTROL

Automatic Repeat Request

The most common techniques for error control are based on two functions:

- *Error detection:* One of the techniques discussed in Chapter 4, usually CRC, is used.
- *Automatic repeat request (ARQ):* When an error is detected, the receiver requests that the frame be retransmitted.

This is a straightforward approach that results in the conversion of an unreliable data link into a reliable one. Three versions of ARQ are in popular use

- Stop-and-wait ARQ.
- Go-back-N continuous ARQ.
- Selective-repeat continuous ARQ.

Stop-and-wait ARQ uses the simple stop-and-wait acknowledgment scheme described in Section 5-2 and is depicted in Figure 5-10a. The sending station transmits a single frame and then must await an acknowledgment. No other data frames can be sent until the receiving station's reply arrives at the transmitting station. The receiver sends a positive acknowledgment (ACK) if the frame is correct and a negative acknowledgment (NAK) otherwise.

The algorithm so far described does not cover all contingencies. The transmitted frame could be so corrupted by noise as not to be received, in which case the receiver will not acknowledge. To account for this possibility, the sender is equipped with a timer. After a frame is transmitted, the sender waits for an acknowledgment (ACK or NAK). If no recognizable acknowledgment is received by the time that the timer expires, then the same frame is sent again. Note that this system requires that the transmitter maintain a copy of a transmitted frame until an ACK is received for that frame.

One more refinement is needed. Consider the following situation. Station A sends a frame. The frame is received correctly by station B, which responds with an ACK. The ACK is damaged in transit and is not recognizable by A, which must resend the same frame. This duplicate frame arrives and is accepted by B. To avoid this problem, frames are alternately labeled with 0 or 1 and positive acknowledgments are of the form ACK0 or ACK1.

The principal advantage of stop-and-wait ARQ is its simplicity. Its principal disadvantage, as discussed in Section 5-2, is that this is an inefficient protocol for large a. The sliding-window technique introduced before can be adapted to provide more efficient line utilization. In this context, it is referred to as *continuous ARQ*.

One variant of continuous ARQ is known as *go-back-N ARQ*. In this technique, a station may send a series of frames determined by window size. If the receiving station detects an error on a frame, it sends a NAK for that frame. The receiving station will discard all future incoming frames until the frame in error is correctly received. Thus the transmitting station, when it receives a NAK, must retransmit the frame in error plus all succeeding frames.

Figure 5-10b shows the frame flow for go-back-N ARQ on a full-duplex line. While frames 2, 3, and 4 are being transmitted, from station A to station B, an ACK of the previously received frame 1 is going from B to A. Some time later, frame 2 is received in error. Frames 3, 4, and 5 are in transit. B sends a NAK2 to A which is received after frame 5 has been sent but before A has a chance to send frame 6. A must now retransmit frames 2, 3, 4, and 5, even though only frame 2 was in error. Again, note that station A must maintain a copy of each unacknowledged frame.

With go-back-N ARQ, it is not required that each individual frame be acknowledged. For example, station A sends frames 0, 1, 2, and 3. Station B responds with ACK0 after frame 0, but then does not respond to frames 1 and 2. After frame 3 is received, B issues ACK3, indicating that frame 3 and all previous frames are accepted.

We are now in a position to explain why a sequence space of 2^n can support a window size of only $2^n - 1$. It has to do with the interaction of error control and

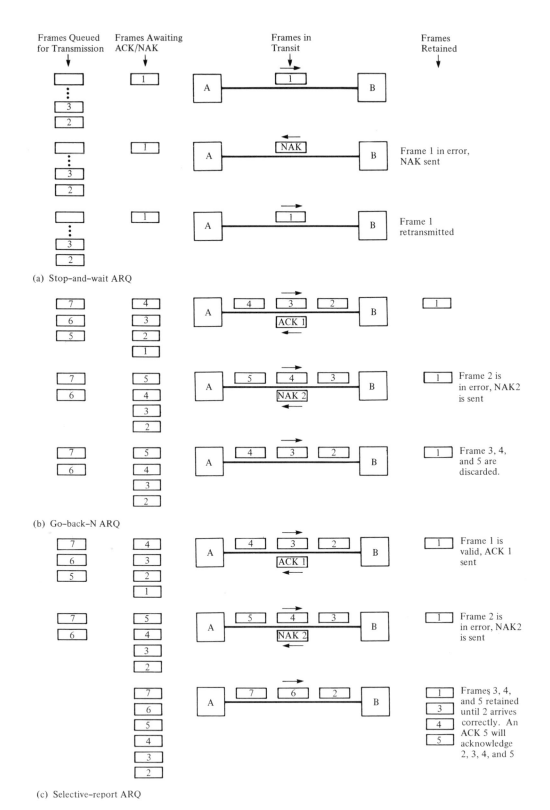

| Frames Queued for Transmission | Frames Awaiting ACK/NAK | Frames in Transit | Frames Retained |

(a) Stop-and-wait ARQ

Frame 1 in error, NAK sent

Frame 1 retransmitted

(b) Go-back-N ARQ

Frame 2 is in error, NAK 2 is sent

Frame 3, 4, and 5 are discarded.

(c) Selective-report ARQ

Frame 1 is valid, ACK 1 sent

Frame 2 is in error, NAK2 is sent

Frames 3, 4, and 5 retained until 2 arrives correctly. An ACK 5 will acknowledge 2, 3, 4, and 5

FIGURE 5-10. Automatic repeat request (ARQ) techniques.

acknowledgment. In most piggyback schemes, a station will send an acknowledgment with a frame, even if the acknowledgment has already been sent. This is because a fixed-length acknowledgment field of n bits is incorporated into the frame and some number must be put into the frame. This has the side benefit that in case the first ACK gets lost, the second ACK may get through. Now consider a case in which a station transmits frame 0 and gets an ACK0, and then transmits frame 1, 2, 3, 4, 5, 6, 7, 0 and gets another ACK0. This could mean that all eight frames were received correctly. It could also mean that all eight frames were lost in transit, and the receiving station is repeating its previous ACK0.

Selective repeat ARQ provides a more refined approach than go-back-N. The only frames retransmitted are those that receive a NAK. In Figure 5-10c, only frame 2 need be retransmitted. This would appear to be more efficient than the go-back-N approach. On the other hand, the receiver must contain storage to save post-NAK frames until the error frame is retransmitted, and the logic for reinserting the frame in the proper sequence. The transmitter, too, will require more complex logic to be able to send frames out of sequence. Because of such complications, the go-back-N algorithm is more commonly used.

The window-size requirement is more restrictive for selective-repeat than for go-back-N. We have seen that for 2^n sequence numbers, a window of $2^n - 1$ can be used for go-back-N. Now, consider the case of a three-bit field (sequence space is eight), and consider the following scenario:

1. Station A sends frames 0 through 6 to station B.
2. Station B receives and acknowledges all six frames.
3. Because of a long noise burst, all six acknowledgments (ACK0 through ACK6) are lost.
4. Station A times out and retransmits frame 0.
5. Station B has already advanced its window to accept frames 7, 0, 1, 2, 3, 4, 5. Thus it assumes that this is a new frame 0 and accepts it.

The problem with the foregoing scenario, for selective-repeat ARQ, is that there is an overlap between the sending and receiving windows. To overcome the problem, the maximum window size should be no more than half the range of sequence numbers. In the scenario above, if only four unacknowledged frames may be outstanding, no confusion can result.

Figure 5-11 compares the two approaches. In Figure 5-11a, the go-back-N technique is used and the window size is seven. The third frame (frame 2) is transmitted in error. Because of propagation delays, the effect of the error is that three good frames are sent and discarded. Using selective repeat, these frames are stored and acknowledged by the receiver.

Performance

It would appear that both go-back-N and selective repeat are more efficient than stop-and-wait. Let us develop some approximations to determine the degree of improvement to be expected.

First, consider stop-and-wait ARQ. With no errors, the maximum utilization is $1/(1 + 2a)$ as shown in Equation (5-2). Now, we must take into account the fact that some frames are repeated because of errors. To do this, note that the utilization U can be defined as

$$U = \frac{T_f}{T_t}$$

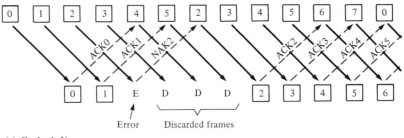

(a) Go-back-N

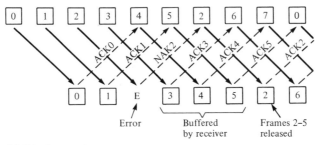

(b) Selective report

FIGURE 5-11. Examples of continuous ARQ.

where

T_f = time for transmitter to emit a single frame

T_t = total time that line is engaged in the transmission of a single frame

For error-free operation using stop-and-wait ARQ, we have

$$U = \frac{T_f}{T_f + 2T_p}$$

where T_p is the propagation time. Dividing by T_f and remembering that $a = T_p/T_f$, we again have Equation (5-2). Now, if errors occur, we must modify Equation (5-2) to

$$U = \frac{T_f}{N_r T_t}$$

where N_r is the expected number of transmissions of a frame. Thus for stop-and-wait ARQ we have

$$U = \frac{1}{N_r (1 + 2a)}$$

A simple expression for N_r can be derived by considering the probability P that a single frame is in error. If we assume that ACKs and NAKs are never in error, the probability that it will take exactly i attempts to transmit a frame successfully is $iP^{i-1}(1 - P)$. Thus

$$N_r = \sum_{i=1}^{\infty} iP^{i-1}(1 - P) = \frac{1}{1 - P}$$

and

$$Stop\text{-}and\text{-}wait: \quad U = \frac{1 - P}{1 + 2a}$$

DATA LINK CONTROL

For the sliding window protocol, we developed Equation (5-4) for error free operation, which is repeated here:

$$U = \begin{cases} 1 & N > 2a + 1 \\ \dfrac{N}{2a + 1} & N < 2a + 1 \end{cases}$$

For selective-repeat ARQ, we can use the same reasoning as applied to stop-and-wait ARQ. That is, the error-free equations must be divided by N_r. Again, $N_r = 1/(1 - P)$. So

Selective-repeat:

$$U = \begin{cases} 1 - P & N > 2a + 1 \\ \dfrac{N(1 - P)}{2a + 1} & N < 2a + 1 \end{cases}$$

The same reasoning will still apply for go-back-N ARQ, but we must be more careful in approximating N_r. Each error generates a requirement to retransmit K frames rather than just one frame. Thus

$$\begin{aligned} N_r &= E[\text{number of transmitted frames to successfully} \\ &\quad \text{transmit one frame}] \\ &= \sum_{i=1}^{\infty} f(i)P^{i-1}(1 - P) \end{aligned}$$

where $f(i)$ is the total number of frames transmitted if the original frame must be transmitted i times. This can be expressed as

$$\begin{aligned} f(i) &= 1 + (i - 1)K \\ &= (1 - K) + Ki \end{aligned}$$

Substituting yields

$$\begin{aligned} N_r &= (1 - K) \sum_{i=1}^{\infty} P^{i-1}(1 - P) + K \sum_{i=1}^{\infty} iP^{i-1}(1 - P) \\ &= 1 - K + \frac{K}{1 - P} \\ &= \frac{1 - P + KP}{1 - P} \end{aligned}$$

By studying Figure 5-8, the reader should conclude that K is approximately equal to $2a + 1$ for $N > (2a + 1)$, and $K = N$ for $N < (2a + 1)$. Thus

Go-back-N:

$$U = \begin{cases} \dfrac{1 - P}{1 + 2ap} & N > 2a + 1 \\ \dfrac{N(1 - P)}{(2a + 1)(1 - P + NP)} & N < 2a + 1 \end{cases}$$

Note that for $N = 1$, both selective-repeat and go-back-N reduce to stop and wait. Figure 5-12 compares these three error control techniques for a value of $P = 10^{-3}$. This figure and the equations are only approximations. For example, we have ignored errors in acknowledgment frames and, in the case of go-back-N, errors in retransmitted frames other than the frame initially in error. Nevertheless, the results are very close to those produced by a more careful analysis [MILL81].

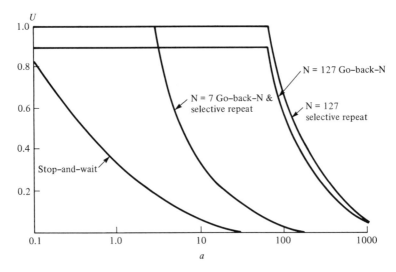

FIGURE 5-12. **Line utilization for various error control techniques ($p = 10^{-3}$).**

5·4

BIT-ORIENTED LINK CONTROL

Bit-oriented protocols are designed to satisfy a wide variety of data link requirements, including:

- Point-to-point and multipoint links.
- Half-duplex (two-way alternate) and full-duplex (two-way simultaneous) operation.
- Primary-secondary (e.g., host-terminal) and peer (e.g., computer-computer) interaction.
- Links with large (e.g., satellite) and small (e.g., short-distance direct connect) values of a.

In addition, these protocols are intended to satisfy the following objectives:

- *Code independence:* The user should be able to use any code set or bit patterns in the data to be transmitted.
- *Adaptability:* The format should support a variety of link types and an evolving set of requirements.
- *High efficiency:* The format should minimize overhead bits and permit efficient error and flow control.
- *High reliability:* The protocol should have a powerful set of error detection and recovery procedures.

DATA LINK CONTROL

The key to satisfying these requirements and objectives is to rely on positional significance and coded control fields. A structure is positionally significant when it is divided into fields each of which has a particular meaning and whose position is fixed relative to a frame delimiter. A coded control field is one in which different combinations of bits have specific meanings and in which positionally significant subfields are used. We will see that this approach leads to a compact control mechanism. It should be compared with the less efficient character-oriented schemes discussed in Appendix 5A.

A number of very similar bit-oriented protocols have achieved widespread use:

- *High-level data link control (HDLC):* developed by the International Organization for Standardization (ISO).
- *Advanced data communication control procedures (ADCCP):* developed by the American National Standards Institute (ANSI). With very minor exceptions, ADCCP has been adopted by the U.S. National Bureau of Standards (FIPS PUB 71-1) for use on federal government procurements, and by the Federal Telecommunications Standards Committee (FED-STD- 1003A) as the standard for the national-defense-related National Communications System.
- *Link access procedure, balanced (LAP-B):* adopted by the International Telegraph and Telephone Consultative Committee (CCITT) as part of its X.25 packet-switched network standard.
- *Synchronous data link control (SDLC):* used by IBM. This is not a standard, but is in widespread use.

There are virtually no differences between HDLC and ADCCP. LAP-B is a subset of HDLC. SDLC is also a subset of HDLC, but also includes several minor additional features [BROD83a]. The following discussion is based on HDLC.

Basic Characteristics

To satisfy the variety of requirements listed above, HDLC defines three types of stations, two link configurations, and three data transfer modes of operation. The three stations types are:

- *Primary station:* has the responsibility for controlling the operation of the link. Frames issued by the primary are called *commands*.
- *Secondary station:* operates under the control of the primary station. Frames issued by the secondary station(s) are called *responses*. The primary maintains a separate logical link with each secondary station on the line.
- *Combined station:* combines the features of primary and secondary stations. A combined station may issue both commands and responses.

The two link configurations are (Figure 5-13):

- *Unbalanced configuration:* used in point-to-point and multipoint operation. This configuration consists of one primary and one or more secondary stations and supports both full-duplex and half-duplex transmission.
- *Balanced configuration:* used only in point-to-point operation. This configuration consists of two combined stations and supports both full-duplex and half-duplex transmission.

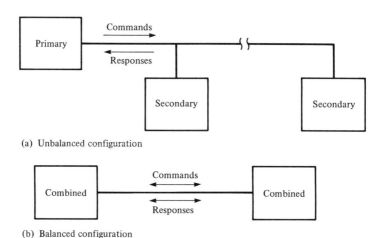

(a) Unbalanced configuration

(b) Balanced configuration

FIGURE 5-13. HDLC link configurations.

The three data transfer modes of operation are:

- *Normal response mode (NRM):* This is an unbalanced configuration. The primary may initiate data transfer to a secondary, but a secondary may only transmit data in response to a poll from the primary.
- *Asynchronous balanced mode (ABM):* This is a balanced configuration. Either combined station may initiate transmission without receiving permission from the other combined station.
- *Asynchronous response mode (ARM):* This is an unbalanced configuration. In this mode, the secondary may initiate transmission without explicit permission of the primary (i.e., send a response without waiting for a command). The primary still retains responsibility for the line, including initialization, error recovery, and logical disconnection.

The normal response mode is used on multidrop lines, in which a number of terminals are connected to a computer. The computer polls each terminal for input. NRM is also often used on point-to-point links, particularly if the link connects a terminal or other peripheral to a computer. The asynchronous balanced mode makes more efficient use of a full-duplex point-to-point link, since there is no polling overhead. The asynchronous response mode is rarely used; it is applicable to hub polling and other special situations in which a secondary may need to initiate transmission.

Frame Structure

HDLC uses synchronous transmission. All transmissions are in frames, and a single frame format suffices for all types of data and control exchanges.

Figure 5-14 depicts the structure of the HDLC frame. The frame has the following fields:

- *Flag:* 8 bits.
- *Address:* One or more octets.
- *Control:* 8 or 16 bits.
- *Data*: variable.
- *Frame check sequence (FCS):* 16 or 32 bits.
- *Flag:* 8 bits.

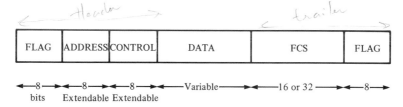

FLAG	ADDRESS	CONTROL	DATA	FCS	FLAG

←—8—→←—8—→←—8—→←——Variable——→←——16 or 32——→←—8—→
bits   Extendable Extendable

(a) Frame format

	1	2	3	4	5	6	7	8
I: Information	O		N(S)		P/F		N (R)	
S: Supervisory	1	O	S		P/F		N (R)	
U: Unnumbered	1	1	M		P/F		M	

N (S) = Send sequence number
N (R) = Receive sequence number
S = Supervisory function bits
M = Unnumbered function bits
P/F = Poll/final bit

(b) Control field format

1 2 3 4 5 6 7 8 9 10 11 12 13 14 15 16   8n
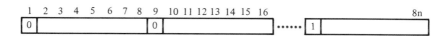

(c) Extended address field

	1	2	3	4	5	6	7	8	9	10	11	12	13	14	15	16
Information	0		N(S)						P/F				N(R)			
Supervisory	1	0	S		0	0	0	0	P/F				N(R)			

(d) Extended control fields

FIGURE 5-14. HDLC frame structure.

The flag, address, and control fields that precede the data field are known as a *header*. The FCS and flag fields following the data field are referred to as a *trailer*.

Flag Fields. Flag fields delimits the frame at both ends with the unique pattern 01111110. A single flag may be used as the closing flag for one frame and the opening flag for the next. All active stations attached to the link are continuously hunting for the flag sequence to synchronize on the start of a frame. While receiving a frame, a station continues to hunt for that sequence to determine the end of the frame. However, since the HDLC frame allows arbitrary bit patterns, there is no assurance that the pattern 01111110 will not appear somewhere inside the frame, thus destroying frame-level synchronization. To avoid this problem, a procedure known as *bit stuffing* is used. The transmitter will always insert an extra 0 bit after each occurrence of five 1's in the frame (with the exception of the flag fields). After detecting a starting flag, the receiver monitors the bit stream. When a pattern of five 1's appears, the sixth bit is examined. If this bit is 0, it is deleted. If the sixth bit is a 1 and the seventh bit is a 0, the combination is accepted as a flag. If the sixth and seventh bits are both 1, the sending station is signaling an abort condition.

With the use of bit stuffing, arbitrary bit patterns can be inserted into the data field of the frame. This property is known as *data transparency*.

Figure 5-15 shows an example of bit stuffing. Note that in the first two cases, the extra 0 is not strictly necessary for avoiding a flag pattern, but is necessary for the operation of the algorithm. The pitfalls of bit stuffing are also illustrated in this figure. When a flag is used as both an ending and starting flag, a 1-bit error merges two frames into one. Conversely, a 1-bit error inside the frame could split it in two.

Original pattern

1 1 1 1 1 1 1 1 1 1 1 1 0 1 1 1 1 1 1 0 1 1 1 1 1 1 0

After bit–stuffing

1 1 1 1 1 0 1 1 1 1 1 0 1 1 0 1 1 1 1 1 0 1 0 1 1 1 1 1 0 1 0

(a) Example

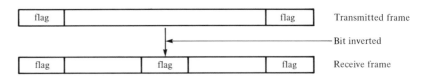

(b) An inverted bit splits a frame in two.

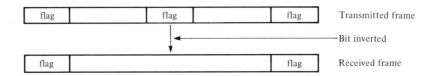

(c) An inverted bit merges two frames.

FIGURE 5-15.   Bit stuffing.

Address Field.   The address field is used to identify the secondary station that transmitted or is to receive the frame. This field is not needed for point-to-point links, but is always included for the sake of uniformity. An address is normally eight bits long but, by prior agreement, an extended format may be used in which the address length is a multiple of seven bits. The eighth bit in each octet is 1 or 0 according as it is or is not the last octet of the address field. The single octet address of 11111111 is interpreted as the all-stations address in both basic and extended formats. It is used to allow the primary to broadcast a frame for reception by all secondaries.

Control Field. HDLC defines three types of frames, each with a different control field format. *Information frames* (I-frames) carry the data to be transmitted for the station, known as *user data*. Additionally, flow and error control data using the ARQ mechanism, may be piggybacked on an information frame. *Supervisory frames* (S-frames) provide the ARQ mechanism when piggybacking is not used, and *unnumbered frames* (U-frames) provide supplemental link control functions. The first one or two bits of the control field serves to identify the frame type. The remaining bit positions are organized into subfields as indicated in Figure 5-14b and d. Their use is explained in the discussion of HDLC operation, below.

Note that the basic control field for S- and I-frames uses 3-bit sequence numbers. With the appropriate set-mode command, an extended control field can be used for S- and I-frames that employs 7-bit sequence numbers.

Data Field. The data field is present only in I-frames and some unnumbered frames. The field can contain any sequence of bits. Its length is undefined in the standard, but is generally limited by each implementation to a specified maximum. Frequently, the length must be a multiple of eight bits.

Frame Check Sequence Field. The frame check sequence is applied to the remaining bits of the frame, exclusive of flags. The normal FCS is the 16-bit CRC-CCITT defined earlier. An optional 32-bit FCS, using CRC-32, may be employed if the frame length or line reliability dictates this choice.

Operation

The operation of HDLC consists of the exchange of I-frames, S-frames, and U-frames between a primary and a secondary or between two primaries. The various commands and responses defined for these frame types are listed in Table 5-1. To describe HDLC operation, we will first discuss these three types of frames, and then give some examples.

Information Frames. The basic operation of HDLC involves the exchange of information frames (I-frames) containing user data. Each I-frame contains the sequence number of the transmitted frame as well as a piggybacked positive acknowledgment. The acknowledgment is the sequence of the *next* frame expected. A maximum window size of 7 or 127 is allowed.

The I-frame also contains a poll/final (P/F) bit. The bit is a poll bit for commands (from primary) and a final bit (from secondary) for responses. In normal response mode (NRM), the primary issues a poll giving permission to send by setting the poll bit to 1, and the secondary sets the final bit to 1 on the last I-frame of its response. In asynchronous response mode (ARM) and asynchronous balanced mode (ABM), the P/F bit is sometimes used to coordinate the exchange of S- and U-frames.

Supervisory Frames. The supervisory frame (S-frame) is used for flow and error control. Both go-back-N ARQ (REJ) and selective-repeat ARQ (SREJ) are allowed. The latter is rarely implemented because of the buffering requirements. A frame may be positively acknowledged with a receive ready (RR) when an I-frame is not available for piggybacking. In addition, a receive not ready (RNR) is used to accept a frame but request that no more I-frames be sent until a subsequent RR is used.

TABLE 5-1 HDLC Commands and Responses

Name	Function	Description
Information (I)	C/R	Exchange user data
Supervisory (S)		
Receive Ready (RR)	C/R	Positive acknowledgment; ready to receive I-frame
Receive Not Ready (RNR)	C/R	Positive acknowledgment; not ready to receive
Reject (REJ)	C/R	Negative acknowledgment; go back N
Selective Reject (SREJ)	C/R	Negative acknowledgment; selective repeat
Unnumbered (U)		
Set Normal Response/	C	Set mode; extended = two-octet control field
Extended Mode (SNRM/SNRME)		
Set Asynchronous Response/	C	Set mode; extended = two-octet control field
Extended Mode (SARM/SARME)		
Set Asynchronous Balanced/	C	Set mode; extended = two-octet control field
Extended Mode (SABM/SABME)		
Set Initialization Mode (SIM)	C	Initialize link control functions in addressed station
Disconnect (DISC)	C	Terminate logical link connection
Unnumbered Acknowledgment (UA)	R	Acknowledges acceptance of one of the above set-mode commands
Disconnected Mode (DM)	R	Secondary is logically disconnected
Request Disconnect (RD)	R	Request for DISC command
Request Initialization Mode (RIM)	R	Initialization needed; request for SIM command
Unnumbered Information (UI)	C/R	Used to exchange control information
Unnumbered Poll (UP)	C	Used to solicit control information
Reset (RSET)	C	Used for recovery; resets N(R), N(S)
Exchange Identification (XID)	C/R	Used to request/report identity and status
Test (TEST)	C/R	Exchange identical information fields for testing
Frame Reject (FRMR)	R	Reports receipt of unacceptable frame

The P/F bit on a supervisory frame may be employed as follows. The primary may set the P bit in an RR frame to poll the secondary. This is done when the primary has no I-frame upon which to piggyback the poll. The secondary responds with an I-frame if it has one; otherwise, it sends an RR with the F bit set to indicate that it has no data to send. The primary (combined station) may set the P bit in the RNR command to solicit the receive status of a secondary/combined station. The response will be an RR with the F bit set if the station can receive I-frames, and an RNR with the F bit set if the station is busy.

Unnumbered Frames. Unnumbered frames are used for a variety of control functions. As the name indicates, these frames do not carry sequence numbers and do not alter the sequencing or flow of numbered I-frames. We can group these frames into the following categories:

- Mode-setting commands and responses.
- Information transfer commands and responses.
- Recovery commands and responses.
- Miscellaneous commands and responses.

Mode-setting commands are transmitted by the primary/combined station to initialize or change the mode of the secondary/combined station. The secondary/combined station acknowledges acceptance by responding with an unnumbered acknowledgment (UA) frame; the UA has the F bit set to the same value as the received P bit. Once established, a mode remains in effect at a secondary station until the next mode-setting command is accepted, and at a combined station until the next mode-setting command is either accepted or transmitted and acknowledged.

The commands SNRM, SNRME, SARM, SARME, SABM, and SABME are self-explanatory. Upon acceptance of the command, the I-frame sequence numbers in both directions are set to 0. The set initialization mode (SIM) command is used to cause the addressed secondary/combined station to initiate a station specified procedure to initialize its data link control functions (e.g., accept a new program or update operational parameters). While in initialization mode, the required information is sent using unnumbered information (UI) frames. The disconnect command (DISC) is used to inform the addressed station that the transmitting station is suspending operation.

In addition to UA, there are several other responses related to mode setting. The disconnected mode (DM) response is sent in response to all commands to indicate that the responding station is logically disconnected. When sent in response to a mode-setting command, DM is a refusal to set the requested mode. The request initialization mode (RIM) response is used in response to a mode-setting command when the station is not ready and wishes to initialize. The request disconnect (RD) response is used to request a disconnect of the logical link.

Information transfer commands and responses are used to exchange information between stations. This is done primarily through the unnumbered information (UI) command/response. Examples of UI frame information are higher-level status, operational interruption, time of day, and link initialization parameters. The unnumbered poll (UP) command is used to solicit an unnumbered response, as a way of establishing the status of the addressed station.

Recovery commands and responses are used when the normal ARQ mechanism does not apply or will not work. The frame reject (FRMR) response is used to report an error in a received frame, such as:

- Invalid control field.
- Data field too long.
- Data field not allowed with received frame type.
- Invalid receive count (i.e., a frame is acknowledged that has not yet been sent).

The reset (RSET) command is used to clear the FRMR condition. RSET announces that the sending station is resetting its send sequence number, and the addressed station should reset its receive sequence number.

Finally, there are two *miscellaneous* command/responses that fit into no neat category. The exchange identification (XID) command/response is used for two stations to exchange station identification and the characteristics of the two stations. The actual information exchanged is implementation dependent. A recently added frame type is the test (TEST) command/response. A test command must be echoed with a test response at the earliest opportunity. This is a simple means of testing that the link and the addressed station are still functioning.

Examples.   Figure 5-16 contains a number of examples of HDLC operation for both point-to-point and multipoint links. The reader is urged to study this figure carefully.

(a) Point–to point duplex exchange

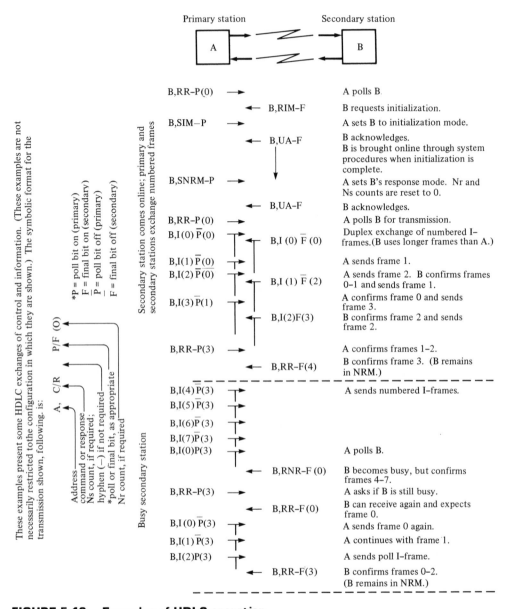

These examples present some HDLC exchanges of control and information. (These examples are not necessarily restricted to the configuration in which they are shown.) The symbolic format for the transmission shown, following, is:

A, C/R   P/F (O)

Address
command or response
Ns count, if required;
hyphen (–) if not required
*poll or final bit, as appropriate
Nr count, if required

*P = poll bit on (primary)
F = final bit on (secondary)
$\overline{P}$ = poll bit off (primary)
$\overline{F}$ = final bit off (secondary)

Secondary station comes online; primary and secondary stations exchange numbered frames

Busy secondary station

Primary station		Secondary station
A		B

B,RR–P(0) →		A polls B.
	← B,RIM–F	B requests initialization.
B,SIM–P →		A sets B to initialization mode.
	← B,UA–F	B acknowledges. B is brought online through system procedures when initialization is complete.
B,SNRM–P →		A sets B's response mode. Nr and Ns counts are reset to 0.
	← B,UA–F	B acknowledges.
B,RR–P(0) →		A polls B for transmission.
B,I(0) $\overline{P}$(0)	← B,I (0) $\overline{F}$ (0)	Duplex exchange of numbered I–frames.(B uses longer frames than A.)
B,I(1) $\overline{P}$(0)		A sends frame 1.
B,I(2) $\overline{P}$(0)	← B,I (1) $\overline{F}$ (2)	A sends frame 2. B confirms frames 0–1 and sends frame 1.
B,I(3) $\overline{P}$(1)		A confirms frame 0 and sends frame 3.
	← B,I(2)F(3)	B confirms frame 2 and sends frame 2.
B,RR–P(3) →		A confirms frames 1–2.
	← B,RR–F(4)	B confirms frame 3. (B remains in NRM.)

– –

B,I(4) $\overline{P}$(3)		A sends numbered I–frames.
B,I(5) $\overline{P}$(3)		
B,I(6) $\overline{P}$ (3)		
B,I(7) $\overline{P}$(3)		
B,I(0)P(3)		A polls B.
	← B,RNR–F (0)	B becomes busy, but confirms frames 4–7.
B,RR–P(3) →		A asks if B is still busy.
	← B,RR–F(0)	B can receive again and expects frame 0.
B,I (0) $\overline{P}$(3)		A sends frame 0 again.
B,I(1) $\overline{P}$(3)		A continues with frame 1.
B,I(2)P(3)		A sends poll I–frame.
	← B,RR–F(3)	B confirms frames 0–2. (B remains in NRM.)

– –

FIGURE 5-16.   Examples of HDLC operation.

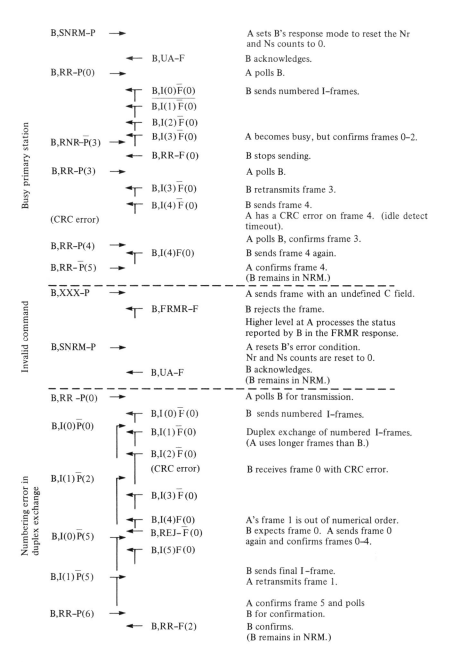

Busy primary station

B,SNRM-P →		A sets B's response mode to reset the Nr and Ns counts to 0.
	← B,UA-F	B acknowledges.
B,RR-P(0) →		A polls B.
	← B,I(0)$\overline{\text{F}}$(0)	B sends numbered I-frames.
	← B,I(1)$\overline{\text{F}}$(0)	
	← B,I(2)$\overline{\text{F}}$(0)	
B,RNR–$\overline{\text{P}}$(3) →	← B,I(3)$\overline{\text{F}}$(0)	A becomes busy, but confirms frames 0–2.
	← B,RR-F(0)	B stops sending.
B,RR-P(3) →		A polls B.
	← B,I(3)$\overline{\text{F}}$(0)	B retransmits frame 3.
	← B,I(4)$\overline{\text{F}}$(0)	B sends frame 4.
(CRC error)		A has a CRC error on frame 4. (idle detect timeout).
B,RR-P(4) →		A polls B, confirms frame 3.
	← B,I(4)F(0)	B sends frame 4 again.
B,RR–$\overline{\text{P}}$(5) →		A confirms frame 4. (B remains in NRM.)

Invalid command

B,XXX-P →		A sends frame with an undefined C field.
	← B,FRMR-F	B rejects the frame.
		Higher level at A processes the status reported by B in the FRMR response.
B,SNRM-P →		A resets B's error condition. Nr and Ns counts are reset to 0.
	← B,UA-F	B acknowledges. (B remains in NRM.)

Numbering error in duplex exchange

B,RR –P(0) →		A polls B for transmission.
	← B,I(0)$\overline{\text{F}}$(0)	B sends numbered I-frames.
B,I(0)$\overline{\text{P}}$(0)	← B,I(1)$\overline{\text{F}}$(0)	Duplex exchange of numbered I-frames. (A uses longer frames than B.)
	B,I(2)$\overline{\text{F}}$(0)	
	(CRC error)	B receives frame 0 with CRC error.
B,I(1)$\overline{\text{P}}$(2)	← B,I(3)$\overline{\text{F}}$(0)	
	← B,I(4)F(0)	A's frame 1 is out of numerical order.
B,I(0)$\overline{\text{P}}$(5)	← B,REJ–$\overline{\text{F}}$(0)	B expects frame 0. A sends frame 0 again and confirms frames 0–4.
	← B,I(5)F(0)	
B,I(1)$\overline{\text{P}}$(5)		B sends final I-frame. A retransmits frame 1.
B,RR-P(6) →		A confirms frame 5 and polls B for confirmation.
	← B,RR-F(2)	B confirms. (B remains in NRM.)

FIGURE 5-16. (continued)

(b) Multipoint duplex exchanges

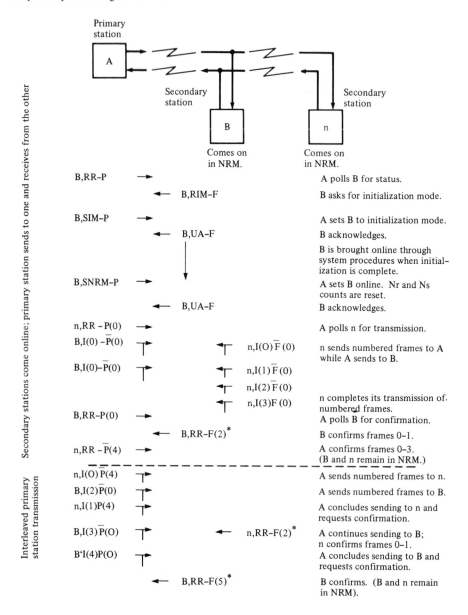

*If a secondary station has information to send, this confirmation may be in the I format.

FIGURE 5-16. (continued)

RECOMMENDED READING

There have been a number of survey articles on data link control, of which the following are recommended: [STUT72], [GRAY72], [CONA83], [LAM83]. [DOLL78], [CYPS78], and [MCNA82] also contain good discussions. Clear discussions of flow control and error control techniques can be found in [MART70] and [BLAC82]. [CONA80] discusses character-oriented protocols, while [CARL80], [WEIS83], and [DONN74] discuss bit-oriented protocols. The latter reference is specifically on SDLC. [BROD83b] is an excellent comparison of IBM's character-oriented (BSC) and bit-oriented (SDLC) protocols.

5-6

PROBLEMS

5-1   Draw a diagram similar to Figure 5-3 for the case in which the primary requests data from the secondary.

5-2   Derive an equation similar to Equation (5-1) for roll-call polling on a multi-multipoint line. Assume that t_0 is constant for all stations and that the primary does not send a poll until it is assured that the response of that poll will not arrive prior to the end of a transmission.

5-3   Derive an equation similar to Equation (5-1) for hub polling.

5-4   A channel has a data rate of 4 kbps and a propagation delay of 20 ms. For what range of frame sizes does stop-and-wait give an efficiency of at least 50%?

5-5   Why is it not necessary to have NAK0 and NAK1 for stop-and-wait ARQ?

5-6   It was stated that multiple-frame acknowledgment could not be used for selective-repeat ARQ. What about the following interpretation: ACK i means that frame i and all preceding frames are accepted except those that have been explicitly NAK'ed?

5-7   Consider the use of 1000-bit frames on a 1-Mbps satellite channel. What is the maximum link utilization for:
a. Stop-and-wait ARQ?
b. Continuous ARQ with a window size of 7?
c. Continuous ARQ with a window size of 127?
d. Continuous ARQ with a window size of 255?

5-8   Consider the following multipoint architecture, which consists of one primary and N equally spaced secondaries.

Let a = (propagation time)/transmission time), where the propagation time is from the primary to the farthest secondary.
a. Assume roll call polling. Also assume that the transmission time for the poll and that primary and secondary processing times are negligible. If every secondary is always ready to transmit, show that the line utilization is

$$U = \frac{1}{1 + a}$$

If only one station is ready to transmit during any polling cycle show that

$$U = \frac{1}{1 + aN}$$

b. Now consider the same architecture for hub polling. Show that if every secondary is always ready to transmit, the utilization can be approximated by

$$U = \frac{1}{1 + a/2 + a/N}$$

[Hint: Ignore the first station to be polled (from P) and derive the total time it takes for a typical secondary to be polled and transmit.] Now show that if only one station is ready to transmit in each cycle,

$$U = \frac{1}{1 + 2.5a}$$

5-9 In Figure 5-12, line utilization for go-back-N ARQ is greater for $N = 7$ than for $N = 127$ at values of a less than 3. How do you account for this?

as a increase an error occur at N = 127 is more damaging

5-10 It is clear that bit stuffing is needed for the address, data, and FCS fields of an HDLC frame. Is it needed for the control field?

5-11 Suggest improvements to the bit-stuffing algorithm to overcome the problems of a single-bit error.

5-12 Using the example bit string of Figure 5-15, show the signal pattern on the line using NRZ-L coding. Does this suggest a side benefit of bit stuffing?

5-13 Assume that the primary HDLC station in NRM has sent six I-frames to a secondary. The primary's N(S) count was three (011 binary) prior to sending the six frames. If the poll bit is on in the sixth frame, what will be the N(R) count back from the secondary after the last frame? (Assume error-free operation.)

5-14 Consider that several physical links connect two stations. We would like to use a "multilink HDLC" that makes efficient use of these links by sending frames on a FIFO basis on the next available link. What enhancements to HDLC are required?

APPENDIX 5A

CHARACTER-ORIENTED LINK CONTROL

Link control protocols have traditionally been character-oriented. Despite the development of more efficient and flexible bit-oriented protocols, the character-oriented techniques are still in widespread use. These techniques use specified "control characters" from a given character code set to delimit frames and to control data interchange.

There are two major categories of character-oriented link control protocols. The first delimits a frame by specified control characters at the beginning and end of the frame. The most common character-oriented scheme, BSC [IBM70], is in this category. The second category delimits a frame by specifying the number of characters, or bytes, of data that the frame contains. This is referred to as a byte-count protocol and DEC's Digital Data Communications Message Protocol (DDCMP) is the most common example. In this appendix, we explore the nature of character-oriented link control by examining these two protocols.

5A-1   Binary Synchronous Communications (BSC)

Binary Synchronous Communications (BSC) is a half-duplex protocol that transmits messages consisting of strings of characters. The protocol does not specify either the length or the code (e.g., ASCII) of the characters.

Control information is provided by special nonprinting characters used to convey control information. Bit combinations for these characters are found in character codes such as ASCII. Table 5-2 provides brief definitions of the BSC control characters. These fall into three categories:

- *Transmission block formatting:* used to delimit blocks and to divide messages into blocks (SYN, SOH, STX, ETB, ITB, ETX).
- *Station dialogue:* used to control the half-duplex exchange of data (ENQ, ACK0, ACK1, WACK, NAK, EOT, RVI).
- *Transparent mode control:* used to permit transfer of arbitrary data which might include the bit patterns of some control characters. The DLE character in combination with other control characters serves this function.

Transmission Block Formatting.   Two types of frame formats are used in BSC (Figure 5-17). Each frame begins with two or more SYN characters. The receiver will hunt for the bit pattern SYN SYN to synchronize at the beginning of a frame. The extra SYN character(s) improve the chances that the receiver will be able to synchronize in time.

One of the frame types, known as a ''transmission block,'' is used to transmit the data to be delivered by the BSC protocol. Each message is transmitted in one or more transmission blocks. The transmission block consists of three parts: header block, text block, and trailer. The header is optional and, if used, begins with an SOH character. The contents of the header are defined by the user. Polling and addressing on multipoint lines are handled by control frames and not by the header. The header might contain such information as message priority, addresses, time-stamps, and so on. The trailer is a two-character error detection field, which may be either a longitudinal redundancy check, (LRC) or a CRC.

The optional text block, prefaced by STX, contains the data to be transmitted. If the message is sent in a single frame, then the text block is terminated by ETX. A message may be broken up into smaller frames to satisfy communications re-quirements, in which case each text block except the last terminates with ETB, while the last is terminated with ETX. After each frame containing a text block ending with ETB or ETX, the line turns around for acknowledgment. It is some-times desirable to break the text block within a frame into smaller blocks. These are sent without a new STX but with their own BCC field. Thus after each trans-mission containing an ETB or ETX, the receiver checks the BCC and sends either a NAK or ACK. After a transmission containing ITB, the receiver checks the BCC but does not acknowledge. The next acknowledgment is a NAK if any of the blocks is in error.

Station Dialogue.   The station dialogue is in three phases: connection estab-lishment, message transfer, and connection termination. For a point-to-point link,

TABLE 5-2 BSC Control Characters

SYN	*Synchronous idle:* establishes and maintains synchronization.
SOH	*Start of heading:* precedes header block.
STX	*Start of text:* precedes text block.
ETB	*End of transmission block:* indicates end of a block of characters that started with SOH or STX and indicates that the block check character is next. ETB requires a response (ACK0, ACK1, NAK, WACK, or RVI).
ITB	*End of intermediate transmission block:* separates a message (header or text) for error-detection purposes without causing a reversal of transmission direction. The following block check is checked but the receiving station does not reply until a final block, ending in ETB or ETX, is received, at which time a negative acknowledgment is sent if any of the blocks were in error.
ETX	*End of text:* terminates a block started with SOH or STX. Its function is the same as ETB, plus it indicates that there are no more data blocks to be sent.
EOT	*End of transmission:* indicates end of a message transmission which may contain a number of blocks, including text and headings.
ENQ	*Enquiry:* used on point-to-point link to bid for line (select function). It is also used at the end of a poll or select sequence.
ACK0, ACK1	*Affirmative acknowledgment:* acknowledges error-free reception of previous block and readiness to accept next block.
WACK	*Wait-before-transmit positive acknowledgment:* indicates that previous block was received without error, but that the receiver is not ready for the next block.
NAK	*Negative acknowledgment:* indicates that previous block was received in error.
RVI	*Reverse interrupt:* is a positive acknowledgment that requests that the transmitting station terminate the current transmission because the receiving station has a high-priority message to send.
DLE	*Data link escape:* used to create WACK, ACK0, ACK1, and RVI. Also used to control transparent data transfer.
DLE STX	Initiates transparent text block.
DLE ETB	Terminates transparent text block.
DLE ETX	Terminates transparent text message.
DLE ITB	Terminates transparent intermediate text block.
DLE SYN	Maintains synchronization or as time-fill sequence for transparent mode.
DLE ENQ	Aborts current transparent transmission.
DLE DLE	Allows DLE character in transparent text.

connection establishment is performed using contention. If either station has a message to send, it seeks to acquire control of the line with

$$\text{SYN} \quad \text{SYN} \quad \text{ENQ}$$

One of the two stations is designated primary so that if both stations attempt to acquire control at the same time, only the primary may retry. Following a successful ENQ, the other station responds with one of the following:

SYN	SYN	ACK0	if ready to receive
SYN	SYN	NAK	if not ready
SYN	SYN	WACK	temporarily not ready, try later

Following receipt of an ACK0, the sending station sends one or more transmission

Control/response formats

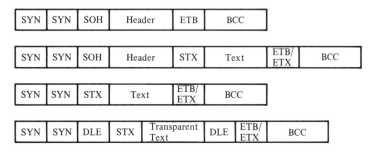

Text/header formats

FIGURE 5-17. BSC frame formats.

blocks. After each block (not counting ITB blocks as separate blocks), the receiving station responds with

SYN	SYN	ACK0,1	alternating affirmative acknowledgments
SYN	SYN	NAK	negative acknowledgment
SYN	SYN	WACK	affirmative acknowledgment, but receiver not ready for next block
SYN	SYN	RVI	affirmative acknowledgment, but receiver needs the line

During this exchange, the sending station may interject a temporary text delay (TTD) sequence:

SYN   SYN   STX   ENQ

which indicates that the sending station is not ready to transmit the next text block but wishes to retain the line. This prevents the receiving station from timing out and aborting the transmission dialogue. When the sending station has sent its last block, it relinquishes the line with

SYN   SYN   EOT

For multipoint lines, a poll and select procedure is used. The primary performs both poll and select with

SYN   SYN   EOT   SYN   SYN   [address]   ENQ

The address designates the secondary station, using uppercase for polling and lowercase for selection. A polled station responds with one of the following:

A transmission block
SYN   SYN   EOT   nothing to send
SYN   SYN   STX   ENQ   polled station is unable to transmit but wishes the primary to wait

The possible replies for a selected station are:

SYN	SYN	ACK0	ready to receive
SYN	SYN	NAK	not ready
SYN	SYN	WACK	temporarily not ready

Once a connection is established, the message transfer and connection termination phases proceed as in a point-to-point connection.

The discussion above describes the normal sequence followed during a dialogue. To handle exception conditions, BSC defines four timeouts.

- *Transmit timeout:* To maintain synchronization, the sequence SYN SYN is inserted once per second into transmission blocks.
- *Receive timeout:* A station will wait 3 s for a reply before assuming that the other station has failed.
- *Disconnect timeout:* This is used on a switched network (see Chapter 8). If a station is inactive for 20 seconds, it will disconnect.
- *Continue timeout:* A 2-second timeout is associated with TTD and WACK. A station is required to issue TTD or WACK within 2 s.

Transparent Mode Control. The description of BSC so far leaves one glaring deficiency: The text block must not contain certain BSC control characters since the receiver is scanning for them. These are ETB, ETX, and ITB. To overcome this problem, BSC allows a transparent mode. If a text block is preceded by DLE STX instead of just STX, the receiver will treat the text block as a transparent bit stream. This solves the problem mentioned above but raises three new ones.

First, there needs to be some way to identify the end of the text block; it cannot be truly transparent. The solution to this problem is to define DLE ETB, DLE ETX, and DLE ITB as transparent mode counterparts to ETB, ETX, and ITB. So the receiver will pass all characters in the text block except for these three pairs.

Unfortunately, the solution to this problem gives rise to a *second* problem. It is still possible that one of these three character pairs will appear in the text block. To overcome this problem the transmitter will insert a DLE in front of any DLE contained in the text block. When the receiver encounters DLE DLE, it discards the first DLE and treats the second as data.

A *third* problem also arises from the solution to the first. We have mentioned that SYN SYN is periodically inserted in a transmission block. These characters must be recognized and discarded by the receiver. To allow this, the transmitter uses DLE SYN in place of SYN SYN. Note that the solution to the second problem protects legitimate DLE SYN data sequences.

Summary. In recent years, the limitations of BSC and similar protocols have led to the introduction of more powerful data link control protocols, especially bit-oriented schemes. The major limitations of BSC are:

1. The lack of sequence numbers prevents efficient utilization of high-speed or long-distance lines.
2. BSC is half-duplex and cannot take advantage of full-duplex lines.
3. BSC depends on the character code being used. All devices on the line must use the same code, and different versions of BSC are required for different codes.
4. Error control is applied only to data, not to control fields.
5. BSC is not easily expandable. Each new control feature requires a new character.

6. With BSC, a sending station can monopolize the line, adversely affecting response time for other stations.
7. BSC does not support hub polling or fast select.
8. Transparent text procedures are unwieldy.

5A-2 Byte Count Protocols: DDCMP

One of the chief differences between DDCMP and BSC is that the former avoids the problems of data transparency. This is done by the simple expedient of specifying the length of the data field so that the receiver need not examine its contents. Other significant differences:

- Control information is bit-encoded rather than character-encoded, resulting in a significant overhead saving.
- The header, including addressing, is completely specified.

A feature comparison, in Table 5-3, summarizes other differences.

DDCMP uses only one frame format, depicted in Figure 5-18. Following two SYN characters, there is a Class character which designates one of three frame types: Data (SOH), Control (ENQ), or Maintenance (DLE).

The data frame is used to carry user data. The fields of the frame are defined as follows:

- *SOH:* identifies frame.
- *Count:* gives the length of the data field in bytes, from 1 to 16,383.
- *Sync:* indicates that frame will be followed by SYN characters.
- *Select:* used on half-duplex and multipoint lines to indicate that this is the last data frame.

TABLE 5-3 **Feature Comparison of Data Link Control Procedures**

Feature	BSC	DDCMP	HDLC
Transmission technique	Async/sync	Async/sync	Sync
Transmission mode	Half duplex	Half/full duplex	Half/full duplex
Framing			
Start	SYN SYN	SYN SYN	Flag
Stop	Characters	Count	Flag
Frame formats	Numerous	1 (three types)	1 (three types)
Control information	Header, control frames	Header (8 bytes)	Header (1–2 bytes)
Addressing	Contention or polling	Header	Header
Error detection	LRC, CRC-16, CRC-12	CRC-16	CRC-CCITT
Error checking	Transmission block only	Header and data field	Entire frame
Error control	Stop and wait	Go-back-N	Go-back-N or selective repeat
Flow control	WACK	Sliding window	Sliding window
Window size	1	255	7 or 127
Transparency	DLE	Count	Bit stuffing

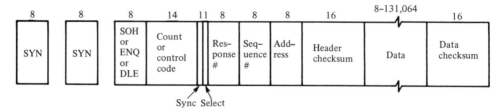

8	8	8	14	11	8	8	8	16	8–131,064	16
SYN	SYN	SOH or ENQ or DLE	Count or control code		Res- ponse #	Seq- uence #	Add- ress	Header checksum	Data	Data checksum

Sync Select

FIGURE 5-18. DDCMP frame format.

- *Response number:* is a piggybacked acknowledgment. This field contains the number of the last packet correctly received in sequence.
- *Sequence number:* is the number of this packet, using a sliding window with the range 0 to 255.
- *Address:* used to identify a secondary station on a multipoint line, for frames to and from the primary. On point-to-point links, this field is ignored.
- *Header checksum:* is a CRC-16 frame check sequence on the header. Because of the danger of loss of synchronization if the count field is damaged, the header gets its own checksum.
- *Data:* contains arbitrary sequence of bytes.
- *Data checksum:* is a CRC-16 FCS on the data field.

The control frame uses the same format as the data frame except that the data and data checksum fields are dropped. The remaining fields:

- *ENQ:* identifies frame.
- *Control code:* explained below.
- *Sync:* same as data frame.
- *Select:* not used.
- *Response number:* used in positive and negative acknowledgment messages.
- *Sequence number:* used with REP message, explained below.
- *Address:* same as data frame.
- *Header checksum:* same as data frame.

The control code is a bit pattern specifying one of a set of control messages:

- *ACK:* a positive acknowledgment, used when piggybacking is not convenient.
- *NAK:* a negative acknowledgment, using the go-back-N convention. The NAK implicitly acknowledges correct receipt of all frames up to the rejected one. NAK is also used to respond to REP.
- *REP:* used by sending station to ask for an acknowledgment to a specific frame. This is needed, for example, if an ACK or NAK was lost. The receiving station responds with ACK or NAK.
- *START:* used by station wishing to initialize receiving station.
- *STARTACK:* positive acknowledgment to a START.

There is also a maintenance frame, used to exchange data between DDCMP modules.

Turning back to the list of deficiencies for BSC listed above, it can be seen that a byte-count protocol overcomes most if not all of these problems. Nevertheless, this approach has been overtaken by bit-oriented protocols which not only remove the BSC deficiencies, but also are inherently more flexible and enjoy lower overhead.

CHAPTER 6

Multiplexing

In Chapter 5, we spent a lot of time trying to devise efficient techniques for utilizing a data link under heavy load. Specifically, with two devices connected by a point-to-point link, it was felt to be desirable to have multiple frames outstanding so that the data link not become a bottleneck between the stations. Now consider the opposite problem. Transmission facilities are, by and large, expensive. It is often the case that two communicating stations will not utilize the full capacity of a data link. For efficiency, it should be possible to share that capacity. The generic term for such sharing is multiplexing.

A simple example of multiplexing is the multidrop line. Here, a number of secondary devices (e.g., terminals) and a primary (e.g., host computer) share the same line. This has several advantages:

- The host computer needs only one I/O port for multiple terminals.
- Only one transmission line is needed.

These types of benefits are applicable in other contexts. In long-haul communications, a number of high-capacity coaxial, terrestrial microwave, and satellite facilities have been built. These facilities can carry large numbers of voice and data transmissions simultaneously using multiplexing.

This chapter concentrates on three types of multiplexing techniques. The first, frequency-division multiplexing (FDM), is the most widespread and is familiar to anyone who has ever used a radio or television set. The second is a particular case

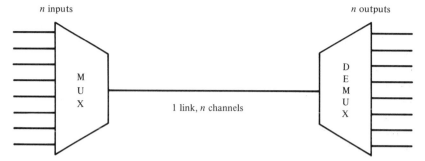

FIGURE 6-1. Multiplexing.

of time-division multiplexing (TDM) often known as synchronous TDM. This is commonly used for multiplexing digitized voice streams. The third type seeks to improve on the efficiency of synchronous TDM by adding complexity to the multiplexer. It is known by a variety of names, including:

- Statistical TDM.
- Asynchronous TDM.
- Intelligent TDM.

We shall refer to it as statistical TDM, since this label points out one of its chief properties.

Figure 6-1 depicts the multiplexing function generically. There are *n* inputs to a multiplexer. The multiplexer is connected by a single data link to a demultiplexer. The link is able to carry *n* separate *channels* of data. The multiplexer combines (multiplexes) data from the *n* input lines and transmits over a higher-capacity data link. The demultiplexer accepts the multiplexed data stream, separates (demultiplexes) the data according to channel, and delivers them to the appropriate output lines.

In addition to the three types of multiplexing listed above, there are other multiplexing techniques more properly termed medium access control techniques. A poll-and-select multipoint line is one example. Other examples are explored in Part II.

6-1

FREQUENCY-DIVISION MULTIPLEXING

Characteristics

Frequency-division multiplexing (FDM) is possible when the useful bandwidth of the medium exceeds the required bandwidth of signals to be transmitted. A number of signals can be carried simultaneously if each signal is modulated onto a different carrier frequency, and the carrier frequencies are sufficiently separated that the bandwidths of the signals do not overlap. A general case of FDM is shown in Figure 6-2a. Six signal sources are fed into a multiplexer, which modulates each signal onto a different frequency ($f_1, \ldots, f_6$). Each modulated signal requires a certain bandwidth centered around its carrier frequency, referred to as a *channel*. To prevent interference, the channels are separated by guard bands, which are unused portions of the spectrum.

The composite signal transmitted across the medium is analog. Note, however,

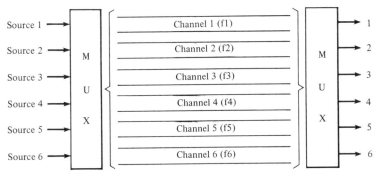

(a) Frequency-Division Multiplexing

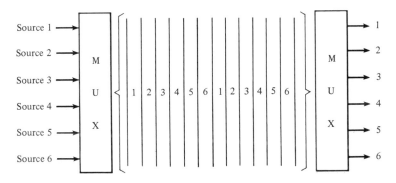

(b) Time-Division Multiplexing

FIGURE 6-2. FDM and TDM.

that the input signals may be either digital or analog. In the case of digital input, the techniques of Section 3-2 would be used to produce an analog signal centered at the desired frequency. In the case of an analog signal, such as voice, the techniques of Section 3-4 apply.

Figure 3-6, which shows full-duplex FSK transmission, is a simple example of FDM. Two signals are carried on the medium, one centered at 1170 Hz, the other at 2125 Hz. In this case, the signals propagate in opposite directions. More typically, FDM is used to refer to a situation in which multiple signals are carried in the same direction.

A familiar example of FDM is broadcast and cable television. The television signal discussed in Chapter 2 fits comfortably into a 6-MHz bandwidth. Figure 6-3 depicts the transmitted TV signal and its bandwidth. The black-and-white video signal is AM modulated on a carrier signal f_{cv}. Since the baseband video signal has a bandwidth of 4 MHz, we would expect the modulated signal to have a bandwidth of 8 MHz centered on f_{cv}. To conserve bandwidth, the signal is passed through a sideband filter so that most of the lower sideband is suppressed. The resulting signal extends from about $f_{cv} - 0.75$ MHz to $f_{cv} + 4.2$ MHz. A separate color subcarrier, f_{cc}, is used to transmit color information. This is spaced far enough from f_{cv} that there is essentially no interference. Finally, the audio portion of the signal is modulated on f_{ca}, outside the effective bandwidth of the other two signals. A bandwidth of 50 kHz is allocated for the audio signal. The composite signal fits into a 6-MHz bandwidth with the video, color, and audio signal carriers at 1.25 MHz, 4.799545 MHz, and 5.75 MHz above the lower edge of the band,

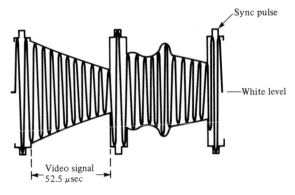

Sync pulse

—White level

Video signal
52.5 μsec

(a) Amplitude modulation with video signal

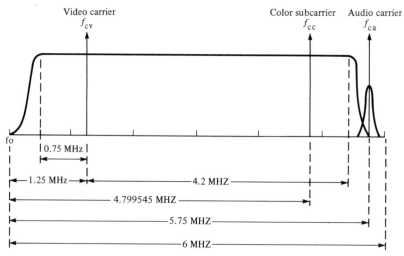

Video carrier
f_{cv}

Color subcarrier
f_{cc}

Audio carrier
f_{ca}

fo

0.75 MHz

1.25 MHz

4.2 MHZ

4.799545 MHZ

5.75 MHZ

6 MHZ

(b) Magnitude spectrum of RF video signal

FIGURE 6-3. Transmitted TV signal.

respectively. Thus multiple TV signals can be frequency-division multiplexed on a CATV cable, each with a bandwidth of 6 MHz. Given the enormous bandwidth of coaxial cable (as much as 500 MHz), dozens of TV signals can be simultaneously carried using FDM. Table 6-1 shows the most commonly used channel assignments. Of course, using radio-frequency propagation through the atmosphere is also a form of FDM; Table 6-2 shows the frequency allocation in the United States for broadcast television.

A generic depiction of an FDM system is shown in Figure 6-4. A number of analog or digital signals [$m_i(t)$, $i = 1, N$] are to be multiplexed onto the same transmission medium. Each signal $m_i(t)$ is modulated onto a carrier f_{sci}; since multiple carriers are to be used, each is referred to as a subcarrier. Any type of modulation may be used. The resulting analog, modulated signals are then summed to produce a composite signal $m_c(t)$. Figure 6-4b shows the result. The spectrum of signal $m_i(t)$ is shifted to be centered on f_{sci}. For this scheme to work, f_{sci} must be chosen so that the bandwidths of the various signals do not overlap. Otherwise, it will be impossible to recover the original signals.

TABLE 6-1 Cable TV Channel Frequency Allocation

Channel Designation	Frequency (MHz)
Low Band	
2	54–60
3	60–66
4	66–72
5	76–82
6	82–88
Mid Band	
A	120–126
B	126–132
C	132–138
D	138–144
E	144–150
F	150–156
G	156–162
H	162–168
I	168–174
High Band	
7	174–180
8	180–186
9	186–192
10	192–198
11	198–204
12	204–210
13	210–216
Super Band	
J	216–222
K	222–228
L	228–234
M	234–240
N	240–246
O	246–252
P	252–258
Q	258–264
R	264–270
S	270–276
T	276–282
U	282–288
V	288–294

Source: [CUNN80].

The composite signal may then be shifted as a whole to another carrier frequency by an additional modulation step. We will see examples of this below. This second modulation step need not use the same modulation technique as the first.

The composite signal has a total bandwidth B, where $B > \sum_{i=1}^{N} B_{sci}$. This analog signal may be transmitted over a suitable medium. At the receiving end, the composite signal is passed through N bandpass filters, each filter centered on f_{sci} and having a bandwidth B_{sci}, for $1 < i < N$. In this way, the signal is again split into its component parts. Each component is then demodulated to recover the original signal.

TABLE 6-2 Broadcast Television Channel Frequency Allocation

Channel Number	Band (MHz)	Channel Number	Band (MHz)	Channel Number	Band (MHz)
2	54–60	25	536–542	48	674–680
3	60–66	26	542–548	49	680–686
4	66–72	27	548–554	50	686–692
5	76–82	28	554–560	51	692–698
6	82–88	29	560–566	52	698–704
7	174–180	30	566–572	53	704–710
8	180–186	31	572–578	54	710–716
9	186–192	32	578–584	55	716–722
10	192–198	33	584–590	56	722–728
11	198–204	34	590–596	57	728–734
12	204–210	35	596–602	58	734–740
13	210–216	36	602–608	59	740–746
14	470–476	37	608–614	60	746–752
15	476–482	38	614–620	61	752–758
16	482–488	39	620–626	62	758–764
17	488–494	40	626–632	63	764–770
18	494–500	41	632–638	64	770–776
19	500–506	42	638–644	65	776–782
20	506–512	43	644–650	66	782–788
21	512–518	44	650–656	67	788–794
22	518–524	45	656–662	68	794–800
23	524–530	46	662–668	69	800–806
24	530–536	47	668–674		

Let us consider a simple example of transmitting three voice signals simultaneously over a medium. As was mentioned, the bandwidth of a voice signal is generally taken to be 4 kHz, with an effective spectrum of 300 to 3400 Hz (Figure 6-5a). If such a signal is used to amplitude-modulate a 64-kHz carrier, the spectrum of Figure 6-5b results. The modulated signal has a bandwidth of 8 kHz, extending from 60 to 68 kHz. To make efficient use of bandwidth, we elect to transmit only the lower sideband. Now, if three voice signals are used to modulate carriers at 64, 68, and 72 kHz, and only the lower sideband of each is taken, the spectrum of Figure 6-5c results.

This figure points out two problems that an FDM system must cope with. The first is crosstalk, which may occur if the spectra of adjacent component signals overlap significantly. In the case of voice signals, with an effective bandwidth of only 3100 Hz (300 to 3400), a 4 kHz bandwidth is adequate. The spectra of signals produced by modems for voiceband transmission also fit well in this bandwidth. Another potential problem is intermodulation noise, which was discussed in Chapter 2. On a long link, the nonlinear effects of amplifiers on a signal in one channel could produce frequency components in other channels.

Carrier Systems

The long-distance carrier system provided in the United States and throughout the world is designed to transmit voiceband signals over high-capacity transmission links, such as coaxial cable and microwave systems. The earliest, and still most

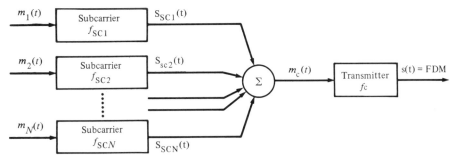

(a) Transmitter

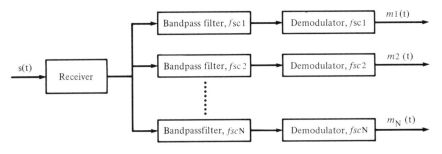

(b) Spectrum of composite signal (positive f)

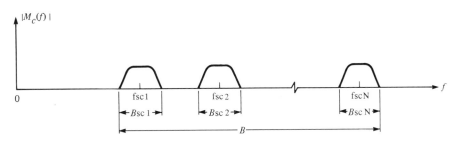

(c) Receiver

FIGURE 6-4. Frequency division multiplexing. Source: [COUC83]

common, technique for utilizing high-capacity links is FDM. In the United States, AT&T has designated a hierarchy of FDM schemes to accommodate transmission systems of various capacities. A similar, but unfortunately not identical, system has been adopted internationally under the auspices of CCITT (Table 6-3).

Figure 6-6 shows the first three levels of the AT&T-defined hierarchy. At the first level, 12 voice channels are combined to produce a *group* signal with a bandwidth of 12×4 kHz $= 48$ kHz, in the range 60 to 108 kHz. The signals are produced in a fashion similar to that described above, using subcarrier frequencies of from 64 to 108 kHz in increments of 4 kHz. The next basic building block is the 60-channel *supergroup*, which is formed by frequency-division multiplexing five group signals. At this step, each group is treated as a single signal with a 48 kHz bandwidth and is modulated by a subcarrier. The subcarriers have frequencies from 420 to 612 kHz in increments of 48 kHz. The resulting signal occupies 312 to 552 kHz.

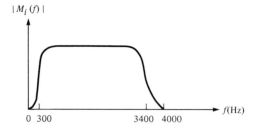

(a) Spectrum of $m_i(t)$, positive f

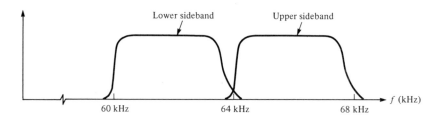

(b) Spectrum of $s_{SC1}(t)$ for f_{SC1} = 64 kHz

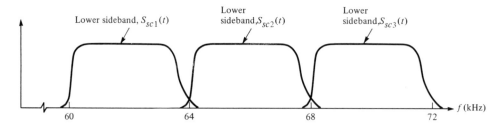

(c) Spectrum of composite signal using subcarriers at
64 kHz, 68kHz, and 72 kHz

FIGURE 6-5. FDM of three voiceband signals.

TABLE 6-3 North American and International FDM Carrier Standards

Number of Voice Channels	Bandwidth	Spectrum	AT&T	CCITT
12	48 kHz	60–108 kHz	Group	Group
60	240 kHz	312–552 kHz	Supergroup	Supergroup
300	1.232 MHz	812–2044 kHz		Mastergroup
600	2.52 MHz	564–3084 kHz	Mastergroup	
900	3.872 MHz	8.516–12.388 MHz		Supermaster group
$N \times 600$			Mastergroup multiplex	
3,600	16.984 MHz	0.564–17.548 MHz	Jumbogroup	
10,800	57.442 MHz	3.124–60.566 MHz	Jumbogroup multiplex	

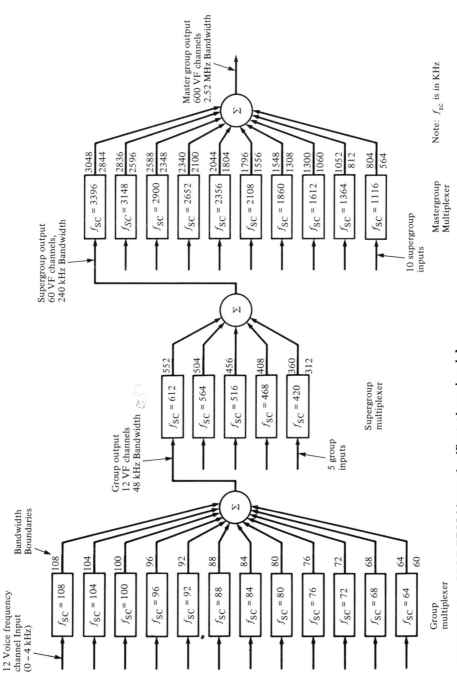

FIGURE 6-6. AT&T FDM hierarchy (first three levels).

169

There are several variations to supergroup formation. Each of the five inputs to the supergroup multiplexer may be a group channel containing 12 multiplexed voice signals. In addition, any signal up to 48 kHz wide whose bandwidth is contained within 60 to 108 kHz may be used as input to the supergroup multiplexer. As another variation, it is possible to directly combine 60 voiceband channels into a supergroup. This may reduce multiplex costs where an interface with existing group multiplex is not required.

The next level of the hierarchy is the *mastergroup* which combines 10 supergroup inputs. Again, any signal with a bandwidth of 240 kHz in the range 312 to 552 kHz can serve as input to the mastergroup multiplexer. The mastergroup has a bandwidth of 2.52 MHz and can support 600 voice frequency (VF) channels. Higher-level multiplexing is defined above the mastergroup, as shown in Table 6-3.

Note that the original voice or data signal may be modulated many times. For example, a data signal may be encoded using QPSK to form an analog voice signal. This signal could then be used to modulate a 76 kHz carrier to form a component of a group signal. This group signal could then be used to modulate a 516 kHz carrier to form a component of a supergroup signal. Each stage can distort the original data; this is so, for example, if the modulator/multiplexer contains nonlinearities or introduces noise.

6-2

SYNCHRONOUS TIME-DIVISION MULTIPLEXING

Characteristics

Synchronous time-division multiplexing is possible when the achievable data rate (sometimes, unfortunately, called bandwidth) of the medium exceeds the data rate of digital signals to be transmitted. Multiple digital signals (or analog signals carrying digital data) can be carried on a single transmission path by interleaving portions of each signal in time. The interleaving can be at the bit level or in blocks of bytes or larger quantities. For example, the multiplexer in Figure 6-2b has six inputs which might each be, say, 9.6 kbps. A single line with a capacity of at least 57.6 kbps (plus overhead capacity) could accommodate all six sources.

A generic depiction of a synchronous TDM system is depicted in Figure 6-7. A number of signals [$m_i(t)$, $i = 1, N$] are to be multiplexed onto the same transmission medium. The signals carry digital data and are generally digital signals. The incoming data from each source is briefly buffered. Each buffer is typically one bit or one character in length. The buffers are scanned sequentially to form a composite digital data stream $m_c(t)$. The scan operation is sufficiently rapid so that each buffer is emptied before more data can arrive. Thus the data rate of $m_c(t)$ must at least equal the sum of the data rates of the $m_i(t)$. The digital signal $m_c(t)$ may be transmitted directly, or passed through a modem so that an analog signal is transmitted. In either case, transmission is typically synchronous.

The transmitted data may have a format something like Figure 6-7b. The data are organized into frames. Each frame contains a cycle of time slots. In each frame, one or more slots is dedicated to each data source. The sequence of slots dedicated to one source, from frame to frame, is called a channel. The slot length equals the transmitter buffer length, typically a bit or a character.

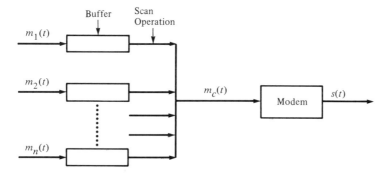

(a) Transmitter

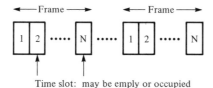

Time slot: may be empty or occupied

(b) TDM frames

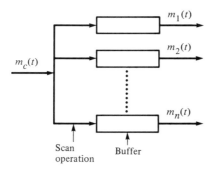

(c) Receiver

FIGURE 6-7. Synchronous time-division multiplexing.

The *character-interleaving* technique is used with asynchronous sources. Each time slot contains one character of data. Typically, the start and stop bits of each character are eliminated before transmission and reinserted by the receiver, thus improving efficiency. The *bit-interleaving* technique is used with synchronous sources and may also be used with asynchronous sources. Each time slot contains just one bit.

At the receiver, the interleaved data are demultiplexed and routed to the appropriate destination buffer. For each input source $m_i(t)$, there is an identical output source which will receive the input data at the same rate at which it was generated.

Synchronous TDM is called synchronous not because synchronous transmission is used, but because the time slots are preassigned to sources and fixed. The time slots for each source are transmitted whether or not the source has data to send.

This is, of course, also the case with FDM. In both cases, capacity is wasted to achieve simplicity of implementation. Even when fixed assignment is used, however, it is possible for a synchronous TDM device to handle sources of different data rates. For example, the slowest input device could be assigned one slot per cycle, while faster devices are assigned multiple slots per cycle.

TDM Link Control. The reader will note that the transmitted data stream depicted in Figure 6-7 does not contain the headers and trailers that we have come to associate with synchronous transmission. The reason is that the control mechanisms provided by a data link protocol are not needed. It is instructive to ponder this point, and we do so by considering two key data link control mechanisms: flow control and error control. It should be clear that, as far as the multiplexer and demultiplexer (Figure 6-1) are concerned, flow control is not needed. The data rate on the multiplexed line is fixed, and the multiplexer and demultiplexer are designed to operate at that rate. But suppose that one of the individual output lines attaches to a device that is temporarily unable to accept data? Should the transmission of TDM frames cease? Clearly not, since the remaining output lines are expecting to receive data at predetermined times. The solution is for the saturated output device to cause the flow of data from the corresponding input device to cease. Thus, for a while, the channel in question will carry empty slots, but the frames as a whole will maintain the same transmission rate.

The reasoning for error control is the same. It would not do to request retransmission of an entire TDM frame because an error occurs on one channel. The devices using the other channels do not want a retransmission nor would they know that a retransmission had been requested by some other device on another channel. Again, the solution is to apply error control on a per-channel basis.

How are flow control, error control, and other good things to be provided on a per-channel basis? The answer is simple: Use a data link control protocol such as HDLC on a per-channel basis. A simplified example is shown in Figure 6-8. We assume two data sources, each using HDLC. One is transmitting a stream of HDLC frames containing three octets of data, the other is transmitting HDLC frames containing four octets of data. For clarity, we assume that character-interleaved multiplexing is used, although bit interleaving is more typical. Notice what is happening. The octets of the HDLC frames from the two sources are shuffled together for transmission over the multiplexed line. The reader may initially be uncomfortable with this diagram, since the HDLC frames have lost their integrity

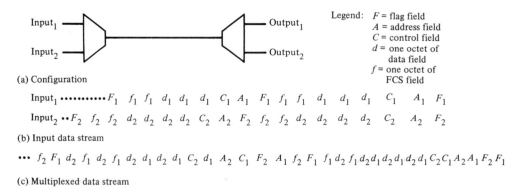

(a) Configuration

Legend: F = flag field
A = address field
C = control field
d = one octet of data field
f = one octet of FCS field

$\text{Input}_1 \cdots\cdots\cdots F_1 \ f_1 \ f_1 \ d_1 \ d_1 \ d_1 \ C_1 \ A_1 \ F_1 \ f_1 \ f_1 \ d_1 \ d_1 \ d_1 \ C_1 \ A_1 \ F_1$

$\text{Input}_2 \cdots F_2 \ f_2 \ f_2 \ d_2 \ d_2 \ d_2 \ d_2 \ C_2 \ A_2 \ F_2 \ f_2 \ f_2 \ d_2 \ d_2 \ d_2 \ d_2 \ C_2 \ A_2 \ F_2$

(b) Input data stream

$\cdots \ f_2 \ F_1 \ d_2 \ f_1 \ d_2 \ f_1 \ d_2 \ d_1 \ d_2 \ d_1 \ C_2 \ d_1 \ A_2 \ C_1 \ F_2 \ A_1 \ f_2 \ F_1 \ f_1 d_2 f_1 d_2 d_1 d_2 d_1 d_2 d_1 C_2 C_1 A_2 A_1 F_2 F_1$

(c) Multiplexed data stream

FIGURE 6-8. Use of data link control on TDM channels.

in some sense. For example, each frame check sequence (FCS) on the line applies to a disjointed set of bits. Even the FCS is not in one piece! However, the pieces are reassembled correctly before they are seen by the device on the other end of the HDLC protocol. In this sense, the multiplexing/demultiplexing operation is transparent to the attached stations; to each communicating pair of stations, it appears that they have a dedicated link.

One refinement is needed in Figure 6-8. Both ends of the line need to be a combination multiplexer/demultiplexer with a full-duplex line in between. Then each channel consists of two sets of slots, one traveling in each direction. The individual devices attached at each end can, in pairs, use HDLC to control their own channel. The multiplexer/demultiplexers need not be concerned with these matters.

Framing. So we have seen that a link control protocol is not needed to manage the overall TDM link. There is, however, a basic requirement for framing. Since we are not providing flag or SYNC characters to bracket TDM frames, some means is needed to assure frame synchronization. It is clearly important to maintain framing synchronization since, if the source and destination are out of step, data on all channels are lost.

Perhaps the most common mechanism for framing is known as *added-digit framing*. In this scheme, typically, one control bit is added to each TDM frame. An identifiable pattern of bits, from frame to frame, is used on this "control channel." A typical example is the alternating bit pattern, 101010. . . This is a pattern unlikely to be sustained on a data channel. Thus to synchronize, a receiver compares the incoming bits of one frame position to the expected pattern. If the pattern does not match, successive bit positions are searched until the pattern persists over multiple frames. Once framing synchronization is established, the receiver continues to monitor the framing bit channel. If the pattern breaks down, the receiver must again enter a framing search mode.

Pulse Stuffing. Perhaps the most difficult problem in the design of a synchronous time-division multiplexer is that of synchronizing the various data sources. If each source has a separate clock, any variation among clocks could cause loss of synchronization. Also, in some cases the data rates of the input data streams are not related by a simple rational number. For both these problems, a technique known as *pulse stuffing* is an effective remedy. With pulse stuffing, the outgoing data rate of the multiplexer, excluding framing bits, is higher than the sum of the maximum instantaneous incoming rates. The extra capacity is used by stuffing extra dummy bits or pulses into each incoming signal until its rate is raised to that of a locally generated clock signal. The stuffed pulses are inserted at fixed locations in the multiplexer frame format so that they may be identified and removed at the demultiplexer.

Example. An example, from [COUC83], illustrates the use of synchronous TDM to multiplex digital and analog sources. Consider that there are 11 sources to be multiplexed on a single link:

- *Source 1:* Analog, 2-kHz bandwidth.
- *Source 2:* Analog, 4-kHz bandwidth.
- *Source 3:* Analog, 2-kHz bandwidth.
- *Sources 4–11:* Digital, 7200 bps synchronous.

As a first step, the analog sources are converted to digital using PCM. Recall from Chapter 4 that PCM is based on the sampling theorem, which dictates that a signal be sampled at a rate equal to twice its bandwidth. Thus the required sampling rate is 4000 samples per second for sources 1 and 3, and 8000 samples per second for source 2. These samples, which are analog (PAM), must then be quantized or digitized. Let us assume that 4 bits are used for each analog sample. For convenience, these three sources will be multiplexed first, as a unit. At a scan rate of 4 kHz, one PAM sample each is taken from sources 1 and 2, and two PAM samples are taken from source 3 per scan. These four samples are interleaved and converted to 4-bit PCM samples. Thus a total of 16 bits is generated at a rate of 4000 times per second, for a composite bit rate of 64 kbps.

For the digital sources, pulse stuffing is used to raise each source to a rate of 8 kbps, for an aggregate data rate of 64 kbps. A frame can consist of multiple cycles of 32 bits, each containing 16 PCM bits and two bits from each of the eight digital sources. Figure 6-9 depicts the result.

Carrier Systems

As with FDM, synchronous TDM is used as part of the long-haul telecommunications system, and a hierarchy of TDM carriers has been developed. Table 6-4 shows the scheme used in North America (also used in Japan) plus the international (CCITT) standard.

The basis of the TDM hierarchy is the DS-1 transmission format (Figure 6-10) which multiplexes 24 channels. Each frame contains eight bits per channel plus a

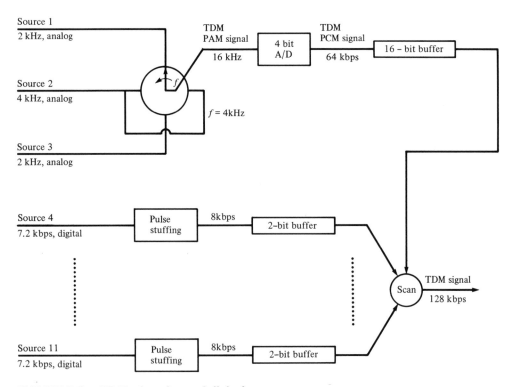

FIGURE 6-9. TDM of analog and digital sources.

TABLE 6-4 North American and International TDM Carrier Standards

(a) North American			(b) International (CCITT)		
Digital Signal Number	Number of Voice Channels	Data Rate (Mbps)	Level Number	Number of Voice Channels	Data Rate (Mbps)
DS-1	24	1.544	1	30	2.048
DS-1C	48	3.152	2	120	8.448
DS-2	96	6.312	3	480	34.368
DS-3	672	44.736	4	1920	139.264
DS-4	4032	274.176	5	7680	565.148

framing bit for 24 × 8 + 1 = 193 bits. For voice transmission, the following rules apply. Each channel contains one PCM word. As described earlier, PCM for voice assumes a 4-kHz bandwidth. Therefore, 8000 samples per second are taken. Therefore, each channel slot and hence each frame must repeat 8000 times per second. With a frame length of 193 bits, we have a data rate of 8000 × 193 = 1.544 Mbps. For five of every six frames, 8-bit PCM is used. For every sixth frame, each channel contains a 7-bit PCM word plus a signaling bit. The eighth bits form a stream for each voice channel which contains network control and routing information, for example, to establish a connection or terminate a call.

The same overall DS-1 format is used to provide digital data service. For compatibility with voice, the same 1.544-Mbps data rate is used. In this case 23 channels of data are provided. The twenty-fourth channel position is reserved for a special sync byte which allows faster and more reliable reframing following a framing error. Within each channel, seven bits per frame are used for data, with the eighth bit used to indicate whether the channel, for that frame, contains user data or system control data. With seven bits per channel, and since each frame is repeated 8000 times per second, a data rate of 56 kbps can be provided per channel. Lower data rates are provided using a technique known as subrate multiplexing. For this technique, an additional bit is robbed from each channel to indicate which

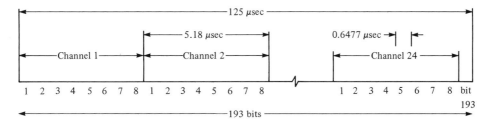

Notes:
  1. Bit 193 is a framing bit, used for synchronization.
  2. Voice channels:
      . 8-bit PCM used on five of six frames.
      . 7-bit PCM used on every sixth frame, bit 8
      of each channel is a signalling bit.
  3. Data channels:
      . Channel 24 used for signaling only in some schemes.
      . Bit 8 is a control bit.
      . Bits 1 – 7 used for 56 kbps service.
      . Bits 2 – 7 used for 9.6 kbps, 4.8 kbps, and 2.4 kbps service.

FIGURE 6-10. DS-1 transmission format.

subrate multiplexing speed is being provided. This leaves a total capacity per channel of 6 × 8000 = 48 kbps. This capacity is used to multiplex five 9.6-kbps channels, ten 4.8-kbps channels, or twenty 2.4-kbps channels. For example, if channel 2 is used to provide 9.6-kps service, then up to five data subchannels share this channel. The data for each subchannel appears as six bits in channel 2 in every fifth frame.

Finally, the DS-1 format can be used to carry a mixture of voice and data channels. In this case all 24 channels are utilized; no sync byte is provided.

Above this basic data rate of 1.544 Mbps, higher-level multiplexing is achieved by interleaving bits from DS-1 inputs. For example, the DS-2 transmission system combines four DS-1 inputs into a 6.312 Mbps stream. Data from the four sources are interleaved 12 bits at a time. Note that 1.544 × 4 = 6.176 Mbps. The remaining capacity is used for framing and control bits, and pulse stuffing. The reader interested in the details of this and other digital carrier TDM formats should consult [BELL82a].

As with FDM, a higher level of the TDM hierarchy is formed by multiplexing signals from the next lower level or by combination of those signals plus input at the appropriate data rate from other sources. Figure 6-11 illustrates this hierarchy. First, the DS-1 transmission rate is used to provide both a voice and data service. The data service is known as the Digital Data System (DDS). The DDS provides digital transmission service between customer data devices at data rates of from 2.4 to 56 kbps [SLAN81]. The service is available at customer premises over two twisted-pair lines. The advantage of this service is that it eliminates the need for modems.

The mastergroup codec performs a function known as *transmultiplexing*. It converts a 600-channel FDM signal into a TDM signal. This provides an interface between high-capacity digital and analog systems.

Figure 6-11 also specifies a number of transmission lines at the various data rates. These refer to Bell-provided carrier facilities. Table 6-5 lists some of these TDM facilities, as well as comparable FDM facilities. These facilities provide high-

TABLE 6-5 Capacity of Some Communication Carriers

Transmission Medium	Designation	Transmission	Number of Voice Channels	Operating Frequency (MHz)	Data Rate (Mbps)
Twisted pair	N3	Analog	24	0.172–0.268	
	T1	Digital	24		1.544
	T2	Digital	96		6.312
Coaxial cable	L1	Analog	600	0.006–2.79	
	L4	Analog	3600	0.564–17.55	
	L5	Analog	10,800	3.12–60.5	
	T4	Digital	4032		274.176
Optical fiber	FT3	Digital	672		44.736
Microwave	TD3	Analog	1200	3700–4200	
	TH1	Analog	1800	5925–6425	
	TN1	Analog	1800	10,700–11,700	
	11-GHz	Digital	672		44.736
	18-GHz	Digital	4032		274.176
Satellite	Intelsat V	Analog	~24,000	6/4-GHz band and 14/11-GHz band	

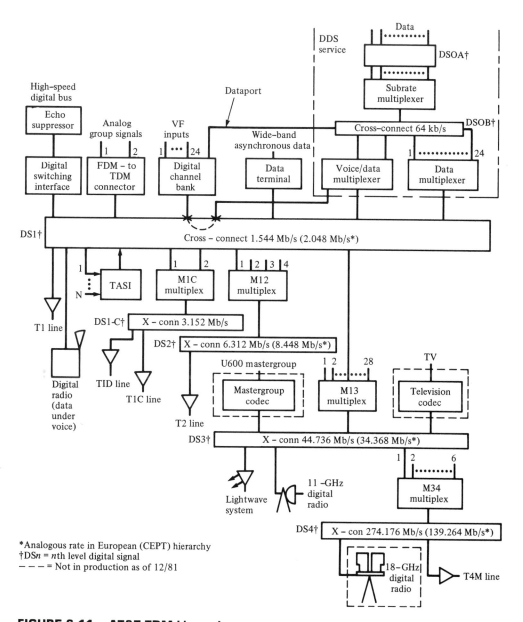

FIGURE 6-11. AT&T TDM hierarchy.

capacity transmission for today's long-haul telecommunications system. Each facility is given a designation that indicates the capacity provided. Thus the *T1 carrier* provides a 1.544-Mbps service, using the DS-1 transmission format. The column labeled transmission denotes whether an analog or digital transmission service is provided. As was mentioned in Chapter 2, analog service implies analog signaling, but a digital transmission service can be provided with either analog or digital service. For example, the T4 service uses digital signaling over coaxial cable, but the FT3 and 11-GHz digital services use analog signaling.

STATISTICAL TIME-DIVISION MULTIPLEXING

Characteristics

In a synchronous time-division multiplexer, it is generally the case that many of the time slots in a frame are wasted. A typical application of a synchronous TDM involves linking a number of terminals to a shared computer port. Even if all terminals are actively in use, most of the time there is no data transfer at any particular terminal.

An alternative to synchronous TDM is *statistical TDM*, also known as asynchronous TDM and intelligent TDM. The statistical multiplexer exploits this common property of data transmission by dynamically allocating time slots on demand. As with a synchronous TDM, the statistical multiplexer has a number of I/O lines on one side and a higher speed multiplexed line on the other. Each I/O line has a buffer associated with it. In the case of the statistical multiplexer, there are n I/O lines, but only k, where $k < n$, time slots available on the TDM frame. For input, the function of the multiplexer is to scan the input buffers, collecting data until a frame is filled, and then send the frame. On output, the multiplexer receives a frame and distributes the slots of data to the appropriate output buffers.

Because statistical TDM takes advantage of the fact that the attached devices are not all transmitting all of the time, the data rate on the multiplexed line is less than the sum of the data rates of the attached devices. Thus, a statistical multiplexer can use a lower data rate to support as many devices as a synchronous multiplexer. Alternatively, if a statistical multiplexer and a synchronous multiplexer both use a link of the same data rate, the statistical multiplexer can support more devices.

Figure 6-12 contrasts statistical and synchronous TDM. The figure depicts four data sources and shows the data produced in four time epochs (t_0, t_1, t_2, t_3). In the

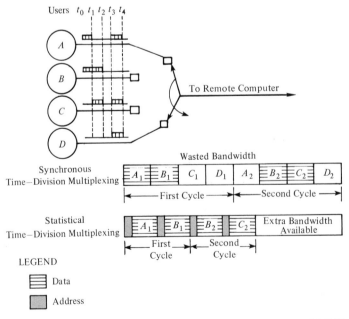

FIGURE 6-12. Synchronous TDM contrasted with statistical TDM.

case of the synchronous multiplexer, the multiplexer has an effective output rate of four times the data rate of any of the input devices. During each epoch, data are collected from all four sources and sent out. For example, in first epoch, sources C and D produce no data. Thus two of the four time slots transmitted by the multiplexer are empty.

In contrast, the statistical multiplexer does not send empty slots if there are data to send. Thus, during the first epoch, only slots for A and B are sent. However, the positional significance of the slots is lost in this scheme. It is not known ahead of time which source's data will be in any particular slot. Since data arrive from and are distributed to I/O lines unpredictably, address information is required to assure proper delivery. Thus there is more overhead per slot for statistical TDM since each slot carries an address as well as data.

The frame structure used by a statistical multiplexer has an impact on performance. Clearly, it is desirable to minimize overhead bits to improve throughput. Generally, a statistical TDM system will use a synchronous protocol such as HDLC. Within the HDLC frame, the data frame must contain control bits for the multiplexing operation. Figure 6-13 shows two possible formats [BACH83]. In the first case, only one source of data is included per frame. That source is identified by an address. The length of the data field is variable, and its end is marked by the end of the overall frame. This scheme can work well under light load, but is quite inefficient under heavy load.

A way to improve efficiency is to allow multiple data sources to be packaged in a single frame. Now, however, some means is needed to specify the length of data for each source. Thus the statistical TDM subframe consists of a sequence of data fields, each labeled with an address and a length. Several techniques can be used to make this approach even more efficient. The address field can be reduced by using relative addressing. That is, each address specifies the number of the current source relative to the previous source, modulo the total number of sources. So, for example, instead of an 8-bit address field, a 4-bit field might suffice.

Another refinement is to use a two-bit label with a length field [SEID78]. A

FLAG	Address	Control	Statistical TDM Sub frame	FCS	Flag

(a) Overall frame

(b) One source per frame

(c) Multiple sources per frame

FIGURE 6-13.   Statistical TDM frame formats.

value of 00, 01, or 10 corresponds to a data field of one, two, or three bytes; no length field is necessary. A value of 11 indicates that a length field is included.

Performance

We have said that the data rate of the output of a statistical multiplexer is less than the sum of the data rates of the inputs. This is allowable because it is anticipated that the average amount of input is less than the capacity of the multiplexed line. The difficulty with this approach is that, while the average aggregate input may be less than the multiplexed line capacity, there may be peak periods when the input exceeds capacity.

The solution to this problem is to include a buffer in the multiplexer to hold temporary excess input. Table 6-6 gives an example of the behavior of such systems. We assume 10 sources, each capable of 1000 bps, and we assume that the average input per source is 50% of its maximum. Thus, on average, the input load is 5000 bps. Two cases are shown: multiplexers of output capacity 5000 bps and 7000 bps. The entries of the table show the number of bits input from the 10 devices each millisecond and the output from the multiplexer. When the input exceeds the output, backlog develops that must be buffered.

There is clearly a trade-off here between the size of the buffer used and the data rate of the line. To minimize cost, we would like to use the smallest possible buffer and the smallest possible data rate, but a reduction in one requires an increase in the other. In this section we present some approximate measures that examine this trade-off. These are sufficient for most purposes. A more careful analysis can be found in [CHU73].

TABLE 6-6 Example of Statistical Multiplexer Performance

Input[a]	Capacity = 5000 bps		Capacity = 7000 bps	
	Output	Backlog	Output	Backlog
6	5	1	6	0
9	5	5	7	2
3	5	3	5	0
7	5	5	7	0
2	5	2	2	0
2	4	0	2	0
2	2	0	2	0
3	3	0	3	0
4	4	0	4	0
6	5	1	6	0
1	2	0	1	0
10	5	5	7	3
7	5	7	7	3
5	5	7	7	1
8	5	10	7	2
3	5	8	5	0
6	5	9	6	0
2	5	6	2	0
9	5	10	7	2
5	5	10	7	0

[a]Input = 10 sources, 1000 bps/source; average input rate = 50% of maximum.

Let us define the following parameters for a statistical time-division multiplexer:

N = number of input sources
R = data rate of each source, bps
M = effective capacity of multiplexed line, bps
α = mean fraction of time each source is transmitting,
   $0 < \alpha < 1$

$K = \dfrac{M}{NR}$ = ratio of multiplexed line capacity to total maximum input

In the above, we have defined M taking into account the overhead bits introduced by the multiplexer. That is, M represents the maximum rate at which data bits can be transmitted.

The parameter K is a measure of the compression achieved by the multiplexer. For example, for a given data rate M, if $K = 0.25$, there are four times as many devices being handled as by a synchronous time-division multiplexer using the same link capacity. The value of K can be bounded:

$$\alpha \le K \le 1$$

A value of $K = 1$ corresponds to a synchronous time-division multiplexer, since the system has the capacity to service all input devices at the same time. If $K < \alpha$, the input will exceed the multiplexer's capacity.

Some results can be obtained by viewing the multiplexer as a single-server queue. A queueing situation arises when a "customer" arrives at a service facility and, finding it busy, is forced to wait. The delay incurred by a customer is the time spent waiting in the queue plus the time for the service. The delay depends on the pattern of arriving traffic and the characteristics of the server. Table 6-7 summarizes

TABLE 6-7 Single-Server Queues with Constant Service Times (Poisson Arrivals)

Parameters:

λ = mean number of arrivals per second

s = service time for each arrival

ρ = utilization: fraction of time the server is busy

q = mean number of items in system (waiting and being served)

t_q = mean time an item spends in system

σ_q = standard deviation of q

Formulas:

$$\rho = \lambda s$$

$$q = \frac{\rho^2}{2(1 - \rho)} + \rho$$

$$t_q = \frac{s(2 - \rho)}{2(1 - \rho)}$$

$$\sigma_q = \frac{1}{1 - \rho} \sqrt{\rho - \frac{3\rho^2}{2} + \frac{5\rho^3}{6} - \frac{\rho^4}{12}}$$

results for the case of random (Poisson) arrivals and constant service time [MART72]. This model is easily related to the statistical multiplexer:

$$\lambda = \alpha\,NR$$

$$S = \frac{1}{M}$$

The average arrival rate λ, in bps, is the total potential input (NR) times the fraction of time α that each source is transmitting. The service time S, in seconds, is the time it takes to transmit one bit, which is $1/M$. Note that:

$$\rho = \lambda\,S = \alpha\,NR/M = \frac{\alpha}{K} = \frac{\lambda}{M}$$

The parameter ρ is the utilization or fraction of total link capacity being used. For example, if the capacity M is 50 kbps and $\rho = 0.5$, the load on the system is 25 kbps. The parameter q is a measure of the amount of buffer space being used in the multiplexer. Finally, t_q is a measure of the average delay encountered by an input source.

Figure 6-14 plots buffer size and delay as a function of utilization. Several interesting results emerge. First, note that the average buffer size being used de-

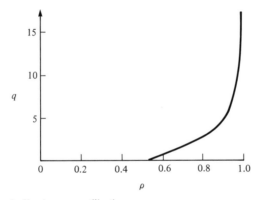

(a) Mean buffer size versus utilization

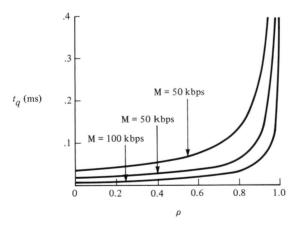

(b) Mean delay versus utilization

FIGURE 6-14. Buffer size and delay for a statistical multiplexer.

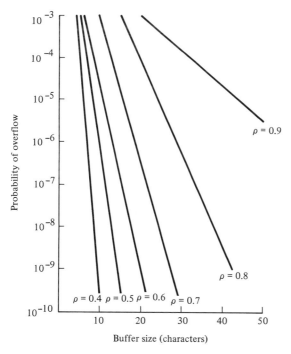

FIGURE 6-15. Probability of overflow as a function of buffer size.

pends only on ρ, and not directly on M. For example consider the following two cases:

Case I	Case II
$N = 10$	$N = 100$
$R = 100$ bps	$R = 100$ bps
$\alpha = 0.4$	$\alpha = 0.4$
$M = 500$ bps	$M = 5000$ bps

In both cases, the value of ρ is 0.8 and the mean buffer size is 2.4. Thus, proportionately, a smaller amount of buffer space per source is needed for multiplexers that handle a larger number of sources. Figure 6-14b also shows that the average delay will be smaller as the link capacity increases, for constant utilization.

So far, we have been considering average queue length, and hence the average amount of buffer capacity needed. Of course, there will be some fixed upper bound on the buffer size available. As Table 6-7 indicates, the variance of the queue size grows with utilization. Thus, at a higher level of utilization, a larger buffer is needed to hold the backlog. Even so, there is always a finite probability that the buffer will overflow. Figure 6-15, based on [CHU73], shows the strong dependence of overflow probability on utilization. This figure, plus Figure 6-14, suggest that utilization above about 0.8 is undesirable.

6-4

RECOMMENDED READING

A good overall discussion of multiplexing can be found in [DOLL78]. Description of FDM and TDM carrier systems can be found in [BELL82a] and [FREE81].

[SEID78] and [STIF83] are interesting presentations of statistical TDM principles, and [CHU73] provides a detailed mathematical analysis.

PROBLEMS

6-1 In Figure 6-6, why is it that the frequency of the carrier, f_{sc}, is not within the boundaries of the bandwidth of the modulated signal for group and supergroup inputs?

6-2 The information in four analog signals is to be multiplexed and transmitted over a telephone channel which has a 400- to 3100-Hz bandpass. Each of the analog baseband signals is bandlimited to 500 Hz. Design a communication system (block diagram) that will allow the transmission of these four sources over the telephone channel using
a. Frequency-division multiplexing with SSB subcarriers.
b. Time-division multiplexing using PCM.
Show the block diagrams of the complete system, including the transmission, channel, and reception portions. Include the bandwidths of the signals at the various points in the systems.

6-3 Draw the spectrum of the group signal of Figure 6-6.

6-4 In the DS-1 format, what is the control signal data rate for each voice channel?

6-5 Twenty-four voice signals are to be multiplexed and transmitted over twisted pair. What is the bandwidth required for FDM? Assuming a bandwidth efficiency of 1 bps/Hz, what is the bandwidth required for TDM using PCM?

6-6 Draw a block diagram similar to Figure 6-9 for a TDM PCM system that will accommodate four 300-bps, synchronous, digital inputs and one analog input with a bandwidth of 500 Hz. Assume that the analog samples will be encoded into 4-bit PCM words.

6-7 A character-interleaved time-division multiplexer is used to combine the data streams of a number of 110-bps asynchronous terminals for data transmission over a 2400-bps digital line. Each terminal sends characters consisting of 7 data bits, 1 parity bit, 1 start bit, and 2 stop bits. Assume that one synchronization character is sent every 19 data characters and, in addition, at least 3% of the line capacity is reserved for pulse stuffing to accommodate speed variations from the various terminals.
a. Determine the number of bits per character.
b. Determine the number of terminals that can be accommodated by the multiplexer.
c. Sketch a possible framing pattern for the multiplexer.

6-8 Assume that two 600-bps terminals, five 300-bps terminals, and a number of 150-bps terminals are to be time-multiplexed in a character-interleaved format over a 4800-bps digital line. The terminals send 10 bits/character and one synchronization character is inserted for every 99 data characters. All the terminals are asynchronous and 3% of the line capacity is allocated for pulse stuffing to accommodate variations in the terminal clock rates.

a. Determine the number of 150-bps terminals that can be accommodated.

b. Sketch a possible framing pattern for the multiplexer.

6-9 Find the number of the following devices that could be accommodated by a T1-type TDM line if 1% of the line capacity is reserved for synchronization purposes.

a. 110-bps teleprinter terminals

b. 300-bps computer terminals

c. 1200-bps computer terminals

d. 9600-bps computer output ports

e. 64-kbps PCM voice-frequency lines

How would these numbers change if each of the sources were operational an average of 10% of the time?

6-10 Ten 9600-bps lines are to be multiplexed using TDM. Ignoring overhead bits, what is the total capacity required for synchronous TDM? Assuming that we wish to limit average line utilization of 0.8, and assuming that each line is busy 50% of the time, what is the capacity required for statistical TDM?

6-11 For a statistical time-division multiplexer, define the following parameters

$$F = \text{frame length, bits}$$
$$OH = \text{overhead in a frame, bits}$$
$$L = \text{load of data in the frame, bps}$$
$$C = \text{capacity of link, bps}$$

a. Express F as a function of the other parameters. Explain why F can be viewed as a variable rather than a constant.

b. Plot F versus L for $c = 9.6$ kbps and values of $OH = 40, 80, 120$. Comment on the results and compare to Figure 6-14.

c. Plot F versus L for $OH = 40$ and values of $C = 9.6$ kbps and 7.2 kbps. Comment on the results and compare to Figure 6-14.

DATA COMMUNICATION NETWORKING

Part I dealt with the transfer of data between devices that are directly connected, generally by a point-to-point link. Often, however, this arrangement is impractical, and a data communication network is required to transmit data between devices. Chapter 7 explains why this is so and provides an overview of the remainder of Part II.

Communication networks can be categorized as follows:

- Switched Networks
  - Circuit-switched networks
  - Packet-switched networks
- Broadcast Networks
  - Packet radio networks
  - Satellite networks
  - Local networks

Packet radio and satellite networks exhibit many similarities and are treated in the same chapter. With that exception, each of these network types is presented and discussed in one chapter of Part II.

CHAPTER 7

Communication Networking Techniques

This chapter serves as an introduction and overview of all of Part II. We begin by showing that the problem of providing communications among a number of devices dictates some kind of communication network solution. Two generic approaches are possible: switched networks and broadcast networks. Following this introductory section the next three sections are devoted to introducing the three principal types of switched networks: circuit-switched, message-switched, and packet-switched. These three are then compared. The final section is an introduction to broadcast networks.

COMMUNICATION NETWORKS

In its simplest form, data communication takes place between two devices that are directly connected by some form of point-to-point transmission medium. Often, however, it is impractical for two devices to be directly, point-to-point connected. This is so for one (or both) of the following contingencies:

- The devices are very far apart. It would be inordinately expensive, for example, to string a dedicated line between two devices thousands of miles apart.
- There is a set of devices, each of which may require a link to many of the others at various times. Examples are all of the telephones in the world and all of the terminals and computers owned by a single organization.

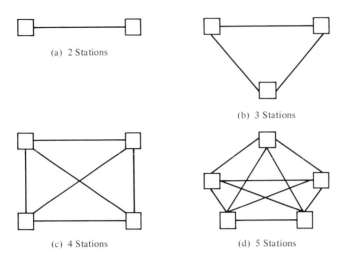

(a) 2 Stations

(b) 3 Stations

(c) 4 Stations

(d) 5 Stations

FIGURE 7-1. The problem with fully connected or mesh topology.

To see the problem raised by the second point, we need to consider the subject of topology. *Topology*, in this context, refers to the way in which multiple devices are interconnected via communication links. Consider the situation of multiple devices requiring multiple connections. Why not provide a direct point-to-point link between each pair of devices?

The problem with this approach is illustrated in Figure 7-1. Each device has a point-to-point link with each other device. This is referred to as a *fully connected* or mesh topology. If there are N devices, then $N(N - 1)/2$ full-duplex links are required, and each device requires $(N - 1)$ input/output (I/O) ports. Thus the cost

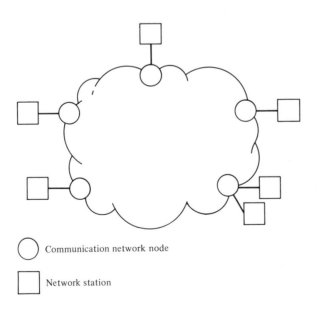

○ Communication network node

□ Network station

FIGURE 7-2. Interconnection via a communication network.

of the system, in terms of cable installation and I/O hardware, grows with the square of the number of devices.

The infeasibility of this approach is clear. The solution to the problem is to attach the devices to a *communication network*. Figure 7-2 illustrates this concept in a general way. We have a collection of devices that wish to communicate; we will refer to them generically as *stations*. The stations may be computers, terminals, telephones, or other communicating devices. Each station attaches to a network *node*. The set of nodes to which stations attach is the boundary of the communication network, which is capable of transferring data between pairs of attached stations. The communication network is not concerned with the content of the data exchanged between stations; its purpose is simply to move that data from source to destination.

Thus a communication network is a shared resource that addresses the problems cited earlier in this section. The network provides for the sharing of transmission facilities among many stations, which reduces the cost incurred by any pair of stations. Also, a single I/O port is needed by each station, rather than $N - 1$ ports.

Communication networks may be categorized based on the architecture and techniques used to transfer data. The following types of networks are in common use:

- Switched communication network.
  - Circuit-switched network.
  - Message-switched network.
  - Packet-switched network.
- Broadcast communication network.
  - Packet radio network.
  - Satellite network.
  - Local network.

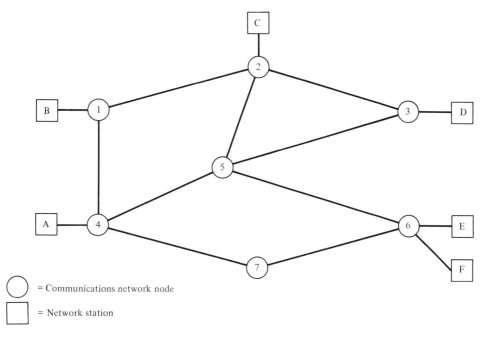

= Communications network node

= Network station

FIGURE 7-3. Generic switching network.

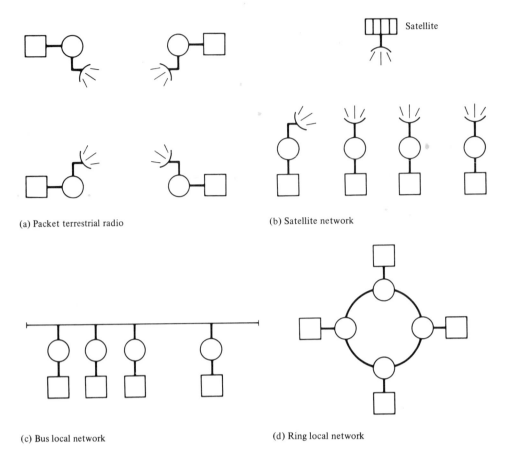

(a) Packet terrestrial radio

(b) Satellite network

(c) Bus local network

(d) Ring local network

FIGURE 7-4. Broadcast communication networks.

A *switched communication network* consists of an interconnected collection of nodes, in which data are transmitted from source to destination by being routed through the network of nodes. Figure 7-3 is a generic illustration of the concept. The nodes are connected by transmission paths. Data entering the network from a station are routed to its destination by being switched from node to node. For example, data from station *A* intended for station *F* are sent to node 4. They may then be routed via nodes 5 and 6 or nodes 7 and 6 to their destination. The classification of switched networks as circuit, message, or packet refers to the way in which the nodes switch data from one link to another on the way from source to destination. These techniques are discussed later in this chapter.

Several observations are in order:

1. Some nodes connect only to other nodes (e.g., 5 and 7). Their sole task is the internal (to the network) switching of data. Other nodes have one or more stations attached as well. In addition to their switching functions, such nodes accept data from and deliver data to the attached stations.
2. Node-station links are generally dedicated point-to-point links. Node-node links are usually multiplexed links, using either an FDM or TDM technique. For nodes that are some distance apart, the multiplexing significantly reduces

transmission costs, as compared to providing dedicated links between each pair of stations.

3. The topology of the network of nodes may be fully connected or partially connected. It is generally the latter, especially for large networks. However, it is always desirable to have more than one possible path through the network for each pair of stations. This enhances the reliability of the network.

With a *broadcast communication network*, there are no intermediate switching nodes. Each station is attached to a transmitter/receiver that communicates over a medium shared by other stations. In its simplest form, a transmission from any one station is broadcast to and received by all other stations. A simple example of this is a CB radio system, in which all users tuned to the same channel may communicate. Figure 7-4 illustrates types of broadcast networks; these will be discussed later in this chapter.

Again, several observations are in order:

1. Only a single I/O port is needed at each station, as with a switched communication network.

2. Since the transmission facility is shared, only a single station can successfully transmit at a time. This leads to the need for some mechanism for controlling access to the shared medium.

3. Interconnection capability is limited by the nature of the broadcast medium. This will become clear as various specific examples are explored.

Switched communication networks are explored in Sections 7-2 through 7-5 and in Chapters 8 and 9. Broadcast communication networks are explored in Section 7-6 and Chapters 10 and 11.

7-2

CIRCUIT SWITCHING

Communication via circuit switching implies that there is a dedicated communication path between two stations. That path is a connected sequence of links between nodes. On each physical link, a channel is dedicated to the connection. The most common example of circuit switching is the telephone network.

Communication via circuit switching involves three phases, which can be explained with reference to Figure 7-3.

1. *Circuit establishment:* Before any data can be transmitted, an end-to-end (station-to-station) circuit must be established. For example, station *A* sends a request to node 4 requesting a connection to station *E*. Typically, the link from *A* to 4 is a dedicated line, so that part of the connection already exists. Node 4 must find the next leg in a route leading to node 6. Based on routing information and measures of availability and perhaps cost, node 4 selects the link to node 5, allocates a free channel (using TDM or FDM) on that link and sends a message requesting connection to *E*. So far, a dedicated path has been established from *A* through 4 to 5. Since a number of stations may attach to 4, it must be able to establish internal paths from multiple stations to multiple nodes. How this is done is explained in Chapter 8. The remainder of the process proceeds similarly. Node 5 dedicates a channel to node 6 and internally ties that channel to the channel from node 4. Node 6 completes

the connection to *E*. In completing the connection, a test is made to determine if *E* is busy or is prepared to accept the connection.

2. *Data transfer:* Signals can now be transmitted from *A* through the network to *E*. The data may be digital (e.g., terminal to host) or analog (e.g., voice). The signaling and transmission may each be either digital or analog. In any case, the path is: *A*-4 link, internal switching through 4, 4-5 channel, internal switching through 5, 5-6 channel, internal switching through 6, 6-*E* link. Generally, the connection is full duplex, and data may be transmitted in both directions.

3. *Circuit disconnect:* After some period of data transfer, the connection is terminated, usually by the action of one of the two stations. Signals must be propagated to 4, 5, and 6 to deallocate the dedicated resources.

Note that the connection path is established before data transmission begins. Thus channel capacity must be reserved between each pair of nodes in the path, and each node must have available internal switching capacity to handle the requested connection. The switches must have the intelligence to make these allocations and to devise a route through the network.

Circuit switching can be rather inefficient. Channel capacity is dedicated for the duration of a connection, even if no data are being transferred. For a voice connection, utilization may be rather high, but it still does not approach 100%. For a terminal-to-computer connection, the capacity may be idle during most of the time of the connection. In terms of performance, there is a delay prior to data transfer for call establishment. However, once the circuit is established, the network is effectively transparent to the users. Data are transmitted at a fixed data rate with no delay other than the propagation delay through the transmission links. The delay at each node is negligible.

7-3

MESSAGE SWITCHING

Circuit switching is an appropriate and easily-used technique in the case of data exchanges that involve a relatively continuous flow, such as voice (telephone) and some forms of sensor and telemetry input. However, circuit switching does have two rather constraining constraints:

- Both stations must be available at the same time for the data exchange.
- Resources must be available and dedicated through the network between the two stations.

An alternative approach, which is generally appropriate to digital data exchange, is to exchange logical units of data, called *messages*. Examples of messages are telegrams, electronic mail, computer files, and transaction queries and responses. If one thinks of data exchange as a sequence of messages being transmitted in both directions between stations, then a very different approach, known as *message switching* can be used.

With message switching, it is not necessary to establish a dedicated path between two stations. Rather, if a station wishes to send a message it appends a destination address to the message. The message is then passed through the network from node to node. At each node, the entire message is received, stored briefly, and then transmitted to the next node.

In a circuit-switching network, each node is an electronic or perhaps electro-mechanical switching device (as described in Chapter 8) which transmits bits as fast as it receives them. A message-switching node is typically a general-purpose minicomputer, with sufficient storage to buffer messages as they come in. A message is delayed at each node for the time required to receive all bits of the message, plus a queueing delay waiting for an opportunity to retransmit to the next node.

Again using Figure 7.3, consider a message to be sent from A to E. Station A appends E's address to the message and sends it to node 4. Node 4 stores the message and determines the next leg of the route (say to 5). Then node 4 queues the message for transmission over the 4-5 link. When the link is available, the message is transmitted to node 5, which will forward the message to node 6, and finally to E. This system is also known as a *store-and-forward* message system. In some cases, the node to which the station attaches, or some central node, also files the message, creating a permanent record.

A number of advantages of this approach over circuit switching are listed in [MART76]:

- Line efficiency is greater, since a single node-to-node channel can be shared by many messages over time. For the same traffic volume, less total transmission capacity is needed. Because messages may be temporarily stored at any point en route, traffic peaks are smoothed out and need not be handled in real time.
- Simultaneous availability of sender and receiver is not required. The network can store the message pending the availability of the receiver.
- When traffic becomes heavy on a circuit-switched network, some calls are blocked; that is, the network refuses to accept any additional connection requests until the load on the network decreases. On a message-switched network, messages are still accepted, but delivery delay increases.
- A message-switching system can send one message to many destinations. Duplicate copies of the message are made, and each is sent to one of the requested destinations. This facility is not easily provided by a circuit-switched network.
- Message priorities can be established. Thus, if a node has a number of messages queued for transmission, it can transmit the higher-priority messages first. These messages will then experience less delay than lower-priority messages.
- Error control and recovery procedures on a message basis can be built into the network. Messages may be numbered and a copy filed for later retrieval in case the original fails to make it through the network.
- A message-switching network can carry out speed and code conversion. Two stations of different data rates can be connected since each connects to its node at its proper data rate. The message-switching network can also easily convert format (e.g., from ASCII to EBCDIC). These features are less often found in a circuit-switched system.
- Messages sent to inoperative terminals may be intercepted and either stored or rerouted to other terminals.

Table 7-1 summarizes the functions of a message-switching node. Note the focus on messages. Each message is treated as a separate entity and is subject to considerable processing.

TABLE 7-1   Functions Performed by a Message-Switching Node

1. The system accepts messages from destination terminals. The terminals are often teleprinters and paper-tape readers, but other devices may be used, such as card readers and special input keyboards. The system may also accept messages from other computers.

2. On receipt of a message it analyzes the message's header to determine the destination or destinations to which the message must be sent.

3. The system may analyze the header for a priority indication. This will tell the program that certain messages are urgent. They must jump any queues of messages and be sent to their destination immediately.

4. It may analyze the header for an indication that some processing of the message is necessary; for example, statistical information from the message may be gathered by the system.

5. The system detects any errors in transmission of the incoming message and requests a retransmission of faulty messages. This retransmission may be automatic.

6. It detects format errors in incoming messages insofar as possible. Types of format errors that may be picked up include the following:
   (a) *Address invalid:* The address to which the message is to be sent is not included in the computer's directory.
   (b) *Excessive addresses:* There are more than the given maximum number of addresses allowed.
   (c) *Incorrect format:* An invalid character appears in the message in an incorrect location.
   (d) A priority indicator is invalid.
   (e) *Originator code error:* The address of the originator is not included in the computer's list.
   (f) Incorrect character counts.

7. The system stores all the messages arriving and protects them from possible subsequent damage.

8. It takes messages from the store and transmits them to the desired addresses. One message may be sent to many different addresses. In doing this, it does not destroy the message held in the store. The store is thus a queuing area for messages received and messages waiting to be sent as well as a file in which messages are retained.

9. The system redirects messages from the store and sends them to the terminals requesting them. It may, for example, be asked to resend a message with a specified serial number or to send all messages from a given serial number.

10. Systems in use store messages in this manner for several hours or, on some systems, several days. Any message in the store is immediately accessible for this period of time.

11. The system may also maintain a permanent log of messages received. This will probably be done on a relatively inexpensive medium, such as magnetic tape, and not on a random-access file.

12. If messages are sent to a destination at which the terminal is temporarily inoperative, the system intercepts these messages. It may automatically reroute them to alternative terminals that are operative. On the other hand, it may store them until the inoperative terminal is working again.

13. It may intercept messages for other reasons. For example, the system may be programmed to send a message to the location of an important person, although he may be moving from one place to another. The person in question indicates his current location to the computer, and the computer diverts messages for him to that location. The system may handle messages on a priority

TABLE 7-1 (Cont.)

basis. There may be one urgent priority level so that these messages are sent before any others. Some systems have more than one level of priority, priority level 1 being transmitted before priority level 2, priority level 2 being transmitted before priority level 3, and so on. The system may notify the operator in the event that any priority queue becomes too great. A simple system may have no priority scheme, messages being handled on a first-in, first-out basis.

14. The system maintains an awareness of the status of lines and terminals. It is programmed to detect faulty operation on terminals where possible, to make a log of excessive noise on lines, and to notify its operator when a line goes out. The system maintains records of any faults it detects.

15. On a well-planned system the messages should be given serial numbers by the operator sending them. The computer checks the serial numbers and places new serial numbers on the outgoing messages. When serial numbers are used, the system can be designed to avoid the loss of any message. This is especially important in the event of a computer failure or of a switchover in a duplex system.

16. At given intervals, perhaps once an hour, the system may send a message to each terminal, quoting the serial number of the last message it received from that terminal. The terminal's operator then knows that the switching system is still on the air.

17. The system may conduct a statistical analysis of the traffic that it is handling.

18. It may be programmed to bill the users for the messages sent. It may, for example, make a small charge per character sent from each terminal and bill the terminal location appropriately.

19. It produces periodic reports of its operation for its operator. These may include reports on the status of all facilities, error statistics, reports giving the number of messages in each queue, message counts, and so on.

Source: [MART76].

The primary disadvantage of message switching is that it is not suited to real-time or interactive traffic. The delay through the network is relatively long and has relatively high variance. Thus it cannot be used for voice connections. Nor is it suited to interactive terminal-host connections.

7-4

PACKET SWITCHING

Packet switching represents an attempt to combine the advantages of message and circuit switching while minimizing the disadvantages of both [HEGG84]. In situations where there is a substantial volume of traffic among a number of stations, this objective is met.

Packet switching is very much like message switching. The principal external difference is that the length of the units of data that may be presented to the network is limited in a packet-switched network. A typical maximum length is 1000 to a few thousand bits. Message switching systems accommodate far larger messages.

From a station's point of view, then, messages above the maximum length must be divided into smaller units and sent out one at a time. To distinguish the two techniques, the data units in the latter system are referred to as *packets*. Another difference from message switching is that packets are typically not filed. A copy of a packet may be temporarily stored for error recovery purposes, but that is all.

Again using Figure 7-3 for an example, consider the transfer of a single packet. The packet contains data plus a destination address. Station *A* transmits the packet to 4, which stores it briefly and then passes it to 5, which passes it to 6, and on to *E*.

On its face, packet switching may seem a strange procedure to adopt, with no particular advantage over message switching. Remarkably, the simple expedient of limiting the maximum size of a data unit to a rather small length has a dramatic effect on performance. Before demonstrating this, we define two common procedures for handling entire messages over a packet-switched network.

The problem is this. A station has a message to send that is of length greater than the maximum packet size. It breaks the message into packets and sends these packets to its node. Question: How will the network handle this stream of packets? There are two approaches: datagram and virtual circuit. (*Note:* This section describes the use of datagrams and virtual circuits *internal* to the network. The somewhat different concept of *external* datagram and virtual-circuit service is introduced in Chapter 9.)

In the *datagram* approach, each packet is treated independently, just as each message is treated independently in a message-switched network. Let us consider the implications of this approach. Suppose that station *A* has a three-packet message to send to *E*. It pops the packets out, 1-2-3, to node 4. On *each* packet, node 4 must make a routing decision. Packet 1 comes in and node 4 determines that its queue of packets for node 5 is shorter than for node 7, so it queues the packet for node 5. Ditto for packet 2. But for packet 3, node 4 finds that its queue for node 7 is shortest and so queues packet 3 for that node. So the packets, each with the same destination address, do not all follow the same route. Furthermore, it is just possible that packet 3 will beat packet 2 to node 6. Thus it is possible that the packets will be delivered to *E* in a different sequence from the one in which they were sent. It is up to *E* to figure out how to reorder them. In this technique each packet, treated independently, is referred to as a datagram.

In the *virtual circuit* approach, a *logical* connection is established before any packets are sent. For example, suppose that *A* has one or more messages to send to *E*. It first sends a Call Request packet to 4, requesting a connection to *E*. Node 4 decides to route the request *and* all subsequent data to 5, which decides to route the request and all subsequent data to 6, which finally delivers the Call Request packet to *E*. If *E* is prepared to accept the connection, it sends out a Call Accept packet to 6. This packet is passed back through nodes 5 and 4 to *A*. Stations *A* and *E* may now exchange data over the logical connection or virtual circuit that has been established. Each packet now contains a virtual circuit identifier as well as data. Each node on the preestablished route knows where to direct such packets; no routing decisions are required. Thus every data packet from *A* traverses nodes 4, 5, and 6; every data packet from *E* traverses nodes 6, 5, and 4. Eventually, one of the stations terminates the connection with a Clear Request packet. At any time, each station can have more than one virtual circuit to any other station and can have virtual circuits to more than one station.

So the main characteristic of the virtual-circuit technique is that a route between stations is set up prior to data transfer. Note that this does *not* mean that there is a dedicated path, as in circuit switching. A packet is still buffered at each node, and queued for output over a line. The difference from the datagram approach is that the node need not make a routing decision for each packet. It is made only once for each connection.

If two stations wish to exchange data over an extended period of time, there are certain advantages to virtual circuits. They all have to do with relieving the stations of unnecessary communications processing functions. A virtual circuit facility may provide a number of services, including sequencing, error control, and flow control. We emphasize the word "may" because not all virtual circuit facilities will provide all these services completely reliably. With that proviso, we define terms. *Sequencing* refers to that fact that, since all packets follow the same route, they arrive in the original order. *Error control* is a service that assures not only that packets arrive in proper sequence, but that all packets arrive correctly. For example, if a packet in a sequence fails to arrive at node 6, or arrives with an error, node 6 can request a retransmission of that packet from node 4. Finally, *flow control* is a technique for assuring that a sender does not overwhelm a receiver with data. For example, if station E is buffering data from A and perceives that it is about to run out of buffer space, it can request, via the virtual circuit facility, that A suspend transmission until further notice.

One advantage of the datagram approach is that the call setup phase is avoided. Thus if a station wishes to send only one or a few packets, datagram delivery will be quicker. Another advantage of the datagram service is that, because it is more primitive, it is more flexible. For example, if congestion develops in one part of the network, incoming datagrams can be routed away from the congestion. With the use of virtual circuits, packets follow a predefined route, and thus it is more difficult for the network to adapt to congestion. A third advantage is that datagram delivery is inherently more reliable. With the use of virtual circuits, if a node fails all virtual circuits that pass through that node are lost. With datagram delivery, if a node is lost, packets may find alternate routes.

7-5

COMPARISON OF SWITCHED COMMUNICATION TECHNIQUE

We have briefly described three techniques for communication switching: circuit switching, message switching, and packet switching. In this section we present a brief comparison of the three methods, looking first at the important issue of performance, and then examining other characteristics.

Performance

A simple comparison of the various techniques is illustrated in Figure 7-5. The figure depicts the transmission of a message across four nodes, from a source station attached to node 1 to a destination station attached to node 4. In this figure, we are concerned with three types of delay:

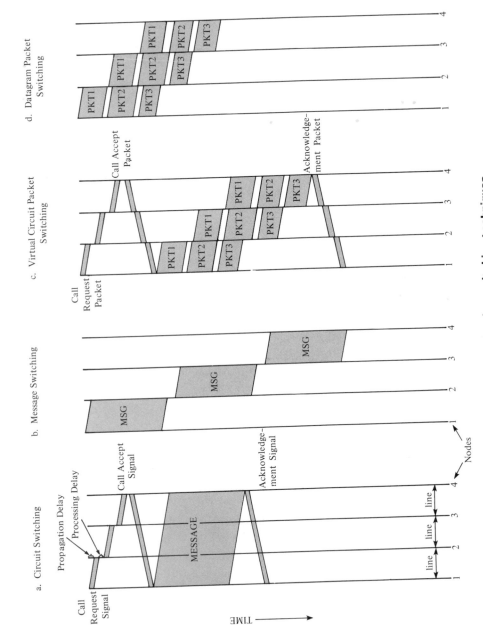

a. Circuit Switching

b. Message Switching

c. Virtual Circuit Packet Switching

d. Datagram Packet Switching

FIGURE 7-5. Event timing for various communication switching techniques.

- *Propagation delay:* the time it takes a signal to propagate from one node to the next. This time is generally negligible. The speed of electromagnetic signals through a hardwire medium, for example, is typically 2×10^8 m/s.
- *Transmission time:* the time it takes for a transmitter to send out a block of data. For example, it takes 1 s to transmit a 10,000-bit block of data onto a 10-kbps line.
- *Node delay:* the time it takes for a node to perform the necessary processing as it switches data.

For circuit switching (Figure 7-5a), there is a certain amount of elapsed time before the message can be sent. First, a call request signal is sent through the network, to set up a connection to the destination. If the destination station is not busy, a call accepted signal returns. Note that a processing delay is incurred at each node during the call request; this time is spent at each node setting up the route of the connection. On the return, this processing is not needed since the connection is already set up. After the connection is set up, the message is sent as a single block, with no noticeable delay at the switching nodes.

Message switching (Figure 7-5b) does not require a call setup. However, the entire message must be received at each node before that node begins to retransmit. Thus the total delay using message switching is almost always significantly longer than for circuit switching.

Datagram packet switching (Figure 7-5d) also does not require a call setup. Comparing Figure 7-5b and d, one can see a dramatic improvement in performance. What has changed? The difference is that each node along the route may begin transmission of each packet as soon as that packet arrives. It need not wait for the entire message. Thus datagram packet switching is almost always significantly faster than message switching.

Virtual circuit packet switching (Figure 7-5c) appears quite similar to circuit switching. A virtual circuit is requested using a call-request packet, which incurs a delay at each node. The virtual circuit is accepted with a call-accept packet. In contrast to the circuit-switching case, the call acceptance also experiences node delays, even though the virtual circuit route is now established. The reason is that this packet is queued at each node and must wait its turn before retransmission.

Once the virtual circuit is established, the message is transmitted in packets. It should be clear that this phase of the operation can be no faster than circuit switching, for comparable networks. This is because circuit switching is an essentially transparent process, providing a constant data rate across the network. Packet switching requires some node delay at each node in the path. Worse, this delay is variable and will increase with increased load.

Figure 7-5 is intended only to suggest what the relative performance of the techniques might be; however, actual performance depends on a host of factors, including:

- Number of stations.
- Number and arrangement of nodes.
- Total load on system.
- Length (in time and data) of typical exchange between two stations.
- Processing speed of the nodes.
- Packet size.

Given the problems of fairly comparing these methods, we will not attempt an analytic comparison. The interested reader is referred to [ROSN82], [SAND80],

TABLE 7-2 Comparison of Communication Switching Techniques

Circuit Switching	Message Switching	Datagram Packet Switching	Virtual-Circuit Packet Switching
Dedicated transmission path	No dedicated path	No dedicated path	No dedicated path
Continuous transmission of data	Transmission of messages	Transmission of packets	Transmission of packets
Fast enough for interactive	Too slow for interactive	Fash enough for interactive	Fast enough for interactive
Messages are not stored	Messages are filed for later retrieval	Packets may be stored until delivered	Packets stored until delivered
The path is established for entire conversation	Route established for each message	Route established for each packet	Route established for entire conversation
Call setup delay Negligible transmission delay	Message transmission delay	Packet transmission delay	Call setup delay Packet transmission delay
Busy signal if called party busy	No busy signal	Sender may be notified if packet not delivered	Sender notified of connection denial
Overload may block call setup; no delay for established calls	Overload increases message delay	Overload increases packet delay	Overload may block call setup; increases packet delay
Electromechanical or computerized switching nodes	Message switch center with filing facility	Small switching nodes	Small switching nodes
User responsible for message loss protection	Network responsible for messages	Network may be responsible for individual packets	Network may be responsible for packet sequences
Usually no speed or code conversion	Speed and code conversion	Speed and code conversion	Speed and code conversion
Fixed bandwidth transmission	Dynamic use of bandwidth	Dynamic use of bandwidth	Dynamic use of bandwidth
No overhead bits after call setup	Overhead bits in each message	Overhead bits in each packet	Overhead bits in each packet

[KUMM80], and [MIYA75]. For purposes of this discussion, we hazard a few observations.

- For interactive traffic, message switching is not appropriate.
- For light and/or intermittent loads, circuit switching is the most efficient, since the public telephone system can be used, via dial-up lines.
- For very heavy and sustained loads between two stations, a leased circuit-switched line is the most cost effective.
- Packet switching is to be preferred when there is a collection of devices that must exchange a moderate to heavy amount of data; line utilization is most efficient with this technique.
- Datagram packet switching is good for short messages and for flexibility.
- Virtual circuit packet switching is good for long exchanges and for relieving stations of processing burden.

As a final point, we mention one common means of making packet-switched networks cost effective, and that is to provide a public connection service. Examples of such networks in the United States are TELENET and TYMNET. The network consists of nodes owned by the network service provider and linked together by leased channels from common carriers such as AT&T. Subscribers pay fees for attaching to the network and for transmitting packets through it. Whereas individual subscribers may not have sufficient traffic to make a packet switched network economically feasible, the total demand of all subscribers justifies the network. These networks are referred to as *value-added networks* (VANs) because they take a basic long-haul transmission service (e.g., AT&T) and add value (the packet-switching logic). In most other countries, there is a single national-monopoly VAN, called a *public data network* (PDN).

Other Characteristics

Besides performance, there are a large number of other characteristics that may be considered in comparing the four techniques we have been discussing. Table 7-2 summarizes the most important of these. Most of these characteristics have already been discussed. A few additional comments follow.

As we mentioned, circuit-switching is an essentially transparent service. Once a connection is established, a constant data rate is provided to the connected stations. This is not the case with message and packet switching; these services introduce variable delay so that data arrives in a choppy manner. Indeed, with message switching and datagram packet switching, data may arrive in a different order from the way they were transmitted.

An additional consequence of transparency is that there is no "overhead" required to accommodate circuit switching. Once a connection is established, the analog or digital data are passed through as is from source to destination. For message and packet switching, the data are organized into digital blocks. Thus, analog data must be converted to digital before being transmitted. In addition, each message or packet includes "overhead bits," such as the destination address.

7-6

BROADCAST NETWORKS

Types of Broadcast Networks

The principal alternative to the use of a switched communication network is broadcasting. Broadcast networks share the following characteristics:

- For the basic architecture, there are no switching devices (although extended networks might consist of basic networks linked via switches).
- Data transmitted by one station is received by many, and often all, of the other stations on the network.
- Stations share a common transmission medium, and therefore some access control technique is required.

We will be concerned in this book with three types of broadcast networks:

- Packet radio networks (Chapter 10)
- Satellite networks (Chapter 10)
- Local networks (Chapter 11)

Two similar types of broadcast networks are packet radio and satellite networks. In both cases, stations transmit and receive via antenna, and all stations share the same channel or radio frequency. In a *packet radio network* (Figure 7-4a), stations are within transmission range of each other, and broadcast directly (from one station to all other stations). In a *satellite network* (Figure 7-4b), data are not transferred directly from transmitter to receiver but are relayed via satellite: Each station transmits to the satellite; the satellite repeats the transmission and it is received by multiple stations.

A *local network* is a communication network confined to a small area, such as a single building or a small cluster of buildings. In a bus local network (Figure 7-4c), all stations are attached to a common wire or cable in a multipoint configuration. A transmission by any one station propagates the length of the medium in both directions and can be received by all other stations. The ring local network (Figure 7-4d) consists of a closed loop, with each station attached to a simple repeating element. A transmission from any station circulates around the ring past all other stations, and can be received by each station as it goes by.

The two parameters that serve best to differentiate among these three types of networks are the data rate and distances between stations. The reader will recall that these two parameters define a third one, a, which was introduced in Chapter 5 and found to be an important factor in performance. The relevance of a to broadcast networks is explored in Chapter 10. Figure 7-6 depicts the range of data

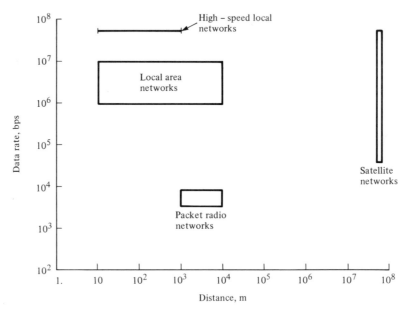

FIGURE 7-6. Data rates and distances for broadcast networks.

rates and distances applicable to the various broadcast networks. For local networks two subcategories are used, which will be explained in Chapter 11.

Medium Access Control Techniques

With all broadcast networks, the key technical issue is that of access control. Since only one device can successfully transmit on the shared medium at a time, an access control technique is required. The key parameters in any medium access control technique are where and how. "Where" refers to whether control is exercized in a centralized or distributed fashion. In a centralized scheme, a controller is designated that has the authority to grant access to the network. A station wishing to transmit must wait until it receives permission from the controller. In a decentralized network, the stations collectively perform a medium access control function to dynamically determine the order in which stations transmit.

A centralized scheme has certain advantages, such as,

- It may afford greater control over access for providing such things as priorities, overrides, and guaranteed bandwidth.
- It allows the logic at each station to be as simple as possible.
- It avoids problems of coordination.

Its principal disadvantages include:

- It results in a single point of failure.
- It may act as a bottleneck, reducing efficiency.
- If propagation delay is high, the overhead may be unacceptable.

The pros and cons for distributed control are mirror images of the points made above.

The second parameter, "how," is constrained by the topology and is a trade-off among competing factors: cost, performance, and complexity. In general, we can categorize access control techniques as being either synchronous or asynchronous. With synchronous techniques, a specific capacity is dedicated to a connection. We see this in circuit switching, FDM, and synchronous TDM. Such techniques are not optimal in broadcast networks because the needs of the stations are generally unpredictable. It is preferable to be able to allocate capacity in an asynchronous (dynamic) fashion, more or less in response to immediate needs. The asynchronous approach can be further subdivided into three categories:

- Round-robin
- Reservation
- Contention

Round-robin techniques are conceptually simple, being based on the philosophy of "give everybody a turn." Each station in turn is given an opportunity to transmit. During that opportunity the station may decline to transmit or may transmit subject to a certain upper bound, usually expressed as a maximum amount of data or time for this opportunity. In any case, the station must then relinquish its turn, and the right to transmit passes to the next station in logical sequence. Control of turns may be centralized or distributed. Polling on a multidrop line is an example of a centralized technique. Various distributed techniques have been used for local networks, and are described in Chapter 11.

TABLE 7-3 Asynchronous Access Control Techniques

	Centralized	Distributed	
Round-robin	Polling	Token bus	
		Token ring	
		Collision avoidance	
Reservation	Centralized reservation	Distributed reservation	
Contention	—	ALOHA	Slotted ring
		CSMA	Register insertion
		CSMA/CD	

When many stations have data to transmit over an extended period of time, round-robin techniques can be very efficient. If only a few stations have data to transmit at any give time, other techniques may be preferable, largely depending on whether the data traffic is "stream" or "bursty." *Stream traffic* is characterized by lengthy and fairly continuous transmissions. Examples are voice communication, telemetry, and bulk file transfer. *Bursty traffic* is characterized by short, sporadic transmissions. Interactive terminal-host traffic fits this description.

For stream traffic, *reservation* techniques are well-suited. In general for these techniques, time on the medium is divided into slots, much as with synchronous TDM. A station wishing to transmit reserves future slots for an extended or indefinite period. Again, reservations may be made in either a centralized or distributed fashion.

For bursty traffic, *contention* techniques are usually appropriate. With these techniques, no control is exercised to determine whose turn it is; all stations contend for time in a way that can be, as we shall see, rather rough and tumble. These techniques are of necessity distributed in nature. Their principal advantage is that they are simple to implement and, under light to moderate load, efficient. For some of these techniques, however, performance tends to collapse under heavy load.

The discussion above has been somewhat abstract, and should become clearer as specific techniques are discussed in Chapters 10 and 11. For future reference, Table 7-3 places the techniques that will be discussed into the classification just outlined. Table 7-4 shows which of these techniques are used with which types of broadcast networks.

TABLE 7-4 Applicability of Access Control Techniques

Packet radio	Local networks
ALOHA	CSMA/CD
CSMA	Slotted ring
	Register insertion
	Token bus
Satellite	Token ring
ALOHA	Collision avoidance
Centralized reservation	Polling
Distributed reservation	Centralized reservation
	Distributed reservation

RECOMMENDED READING

References to most of the topics discussed in this chapter are provided in the remainder of Part II. The exception is message switching, which is not further pursued. [MART76] and [DAVI73] provide good discussions of message switching. A good example of a message-switched network is the U.S. military network, AUTODIN [PAOL75]. An interesting discussion of message switching architectural issues can be found in [HOPE73].

PROBLEMS

7-1 Define the following parameters for a switching network:
- N: number of hops between two given stations
- L: message length, bits
- B data rate, in bps, on all links
- P: packet size, bits
- H: overhead (header) bits per packet
- S: call setup time (circuit-switched or virtual circuit) in seconds
- D: propagation delay per hop, in seconds

a. For $N = 4$, $L = 3200$, $B = 9600$, $P = 1024$, $H = 16$, $S = 0.2$, $D = 0.001$, compute the end-to-end delay for circuit switching, message switching, virtual circuit packet switching, and datagram packet switching. Assume that there is no node delay.

b. Derive general expressions for the four techniques, taken two at a time (six expressions in all) showing the conditions under which the delays are equal.

7-2 What value of P, as a function of N, B, and H results in minimum end-to-end delay on a datagram network? Assume that L is much larger than P, and that D is zero.

7-3 Two stations communicate via a 1-Mbps satellite link. The satellite serves merely to retransmit data received from one station to the other, with negligible delay. The up-and-down propagation delay for a synchronous orbit is 270 ms. Using HDLC frames of length 1024 bits, what is the maximum possible data throughput (not counting overhead bits)?

7-4 Consider a packet-switched network of N nodes connected by the following topologies
(a) Star: one central node with no attached stations; all other nodes attach to the central node.
(b) Loop: each node connects to two other nodes to form a closed loop
(c) Fully connected.
For each, give the average number of hops between stations.

7-5 Consider a binary tree topology for a packet-switched network. The root node connects to two other nodes. All intermediate nodes connect to one node in the direction toward the root, and two in the direction away from the root. At the bottom are nodes with just one link back toward the root. If there are $2^N - 1$ nodes, derive an expression for the mean number of hops per packet for large N, assuming that all node pairs are equally likely. $2N - 4$

7-6   A disadvantage of the contention approach for broadcast networks is the capacity wasted due to multiple stations attempting to access the channel at the same time. Suppose that time is divided into discrete slots with each of N stations attempting to transmit with probability p during each slot. What fraction of the slots are wasted due to multiple transmission attempts?

exactly 1 station to transmit a slot $P_1 = N_p (1 - p)^{N-1}$

no station $P_0 = (1 - p)^N$

more than 1 station $P_n = 1 - P_0 - P_1 =$
$$= 1 - N_p (1 - p)^{N-1} - (1 - p)^N$$

CHAPTER 8

Circuit Switching

Any treatment of the technology and architecture of circuit-switched networks must of necessity focus on the internal operation of a single switch. This is in contrast to packet-switched networks, which are best explained by the collective behavior of the set of switches that make up a network.

A single switch with a number of attached devices may function as a one-node network. Thus the chapter begins by summarizing the characteristics of such a network. Then we look at the digital switching concepts that underlie this type of network. Next we look at the devices most commonly used to build circuit-switched local networks (although these are rarely thought of as "true" local networks): digital data switches. We are then ready to look at the computerized branch exchange, which supports both digital data devices and telephones. Finally, the concepts of a multinode circuit-switched network are discussed using the public telecommunications network as an example.

8-1

ONE-NODE NETWORKS

A network built around a single circuit-switching node consists of a collection of devices or stations attached to a central switching unit. Circuit switching is used; the central switch establishes a dedicated path between any two devices that wish to communicate.

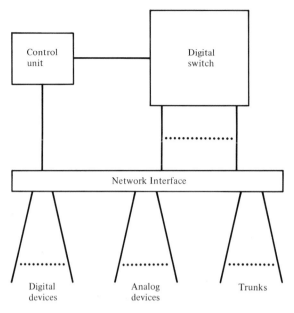

FIGURE 8-1. Elements of a one-node circuit switch.

Figure 8-1 depicts the major elements of such a one-node network. The heart of a modern system is a digital switch. The advent of digital switching technology has dramatically improved the cost, performance, and capability of circuit-switched networks. Key to the operation of such a system are that (1) all signals are represented digitally, and (2) synchronous time-division multiplexing (TDM) techniques are used.

The network interface element represents the functions and hardware needed to connect digital devices, such as data processing devices and digital telephones, to the network. Analog telephones can also be attached if the network interface contains the logic for converting to digital signals. Trunks to external systems may also be attached. These may include analog voice trunks and digital TDM lines.

The control unit performs three general tasks. First, it establishes connections. This is generally done on demand, that is, at the request of an attached device. To establish the connection, the control unit must handle and acknowledge the request, determine if the intended destination is free, and construct a path through the switch. Second, the control unit must maintain the connection. Since the digital switch uses time-division principles, this may require ongoing manipulation of the switching elements. However, the bits of the communication are transferred transparently. This is in contrast to packet-switching networks, which are sensitive to the transmission protocol (i.e., address and other control information in each packet must be processed) and can be considered content dependent. Third, the control unit must tear down the connection, either in response to a request from one of the parties or for its own reasons.

The switch may be either one-sided or two-sided. In a one-sided system, all attachment points are viewed the same: A connection can be established between any two devices. In a two-sided system, attachment points are grouped into two classes and a connection can be established only between two devices from different classes. A typical application of the latter is the connection of a set of terminals to a set of computer ports; in many cases, only terminal-to-port connections are allowed.

An important characteristic of a circuit-switching device is whether it is blocking or nonblocking. Blocking occurs when the network is unable to connect two stations because all possible paths between them are already in use. A blocking network is one in which such blocking is possible. Hence a nonblocking network permits all stations to be connected (in pairs) at once and grants all possible connection requests as long as the called party is free. When a network is supporting only voice traffic, a blocking configuration is generally acceptable, since it is expected that most phone calls are of short duration and that, therefore, only a fraction of the telephones will be engaged at any time. However, when data processing devices are involved, these assumptions may be invalid. For example, for a data entry application, a terminal may be continuously connected to a computer for hours at a time. Hence there is a desire for a nonblocking or "nearly nonblocking" (very low probability of blocking) configuration.

DIGITAL SWITCHING CONCEPTS

The technology of switching has a long history, most of it covering an era when analog signal switching predominated. With the advent of PCM and related techniques, both voice and data can be transmitted via digital signals. This has led to a fundamental change in the design and technology of switching systems. Instead of dumb space-division systems, modern digital switching systems rely on intelligent control of space- and time-division elements.

This section looks at the concepts underlying contemporary digital switching (good discussions can be found in [SKAP79], [JOEL77], and [JOEL79a,b]).

We begin with a look at space-division switching, which was originally developed for the analog environment and has been carried over into digital technology. Then the various forms of time-division switching, which were developed specifically to be used in digital switches, are examined. Later sections discuss how these concepts are implemented in data switching devices and CBXs.

Space-Division Switching

The *space-division switch* is, as its name implies, one in which paths between pairs of devices are divided in space. Each connection requires the establishment of a physical path through the switch that is dedicated solely to the transfer of signals between the two endpoints. The basic building block of the switch is a metallic crosspoint or semiconductor gate [ABBO84] that can be opened and closed by a control unit.

Figure 8-2a shows a simple crossbar matrix with n inputs and m outputs. Interconnection is possible between any input line and any output line by engaging the appropriate crosspoint. The crossbar depicts a bilateral arrangement: There is a distinction between input and output. For example, input lines may connect to terminals, while output lines connect to computer ports. The crossbar switch is said to perform concentration, distribution, or expansion according as $n > m$, $n = m$, or $n < m$.

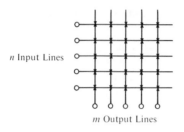

n Input Lines

m Output Lines

(a) Crossbar Matrix

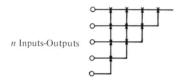

n Inputs-Outputs

(b) Triangular Switch

FIGURE 8-2.   Single-stage space-division switch.

The crossbar matrix makes a distinction between input and output: Any input can connect to any output. It requires $n \times m$ crosspoints. However, if there is no distinction between inputs and outputs, then $n = m$ and the requirement is that any end point can connect to any other endpoint. This requires only a triangular array of $n(n - 1)/2$ crosspoints (Figure 8-2b) and is referred to as a "folded" configuration.

The crossbar switch has a number of limitations or disadvantages:

• The number of crosspoints grows with n^2. This is costly for large n, and results in high capacitive loading on any message path.
• The loss of a crosspoint prevents connection between the two devices involved.
• The crosspoints are inefficiently utilized (at most n out of n^2).

To overcome these limitations, multiple stage switches are employed. The N input lines (inlets) are broken up into N/n groups of n lines. Each group of lines goes into a first-stage matrix. The outputs of the first stage matrices become inputs to a group of second-stage matrices, and so on. Figure 8-3 depicts a three-stage network of switches that is symmetric; that is, the number of inlets to the first stage equals the number of outlets from the last stage. There are k second-stage matrices, each with N/n inlets and N/n outlets. Each first-stage matrix has k outlets so that it connects to all second-stage matrices. Each second-stage matrix has N/n outlets so that it connects to all third-stage matrices.

This type of arrangement has several advantages over the simple crossbar switch:

• The number of crosspoints is reduced (see below), increasing crossbar utilization.
• There is more than one path through the network to connect two endpoints, increasing reliability.

Of course, a multistage network requires a more complex control scheme. To establish a path in a single-stage network, it is only necessary to open a single gate. In a multistage network, a free path through the stages must be determined and the appropriate gates opened.

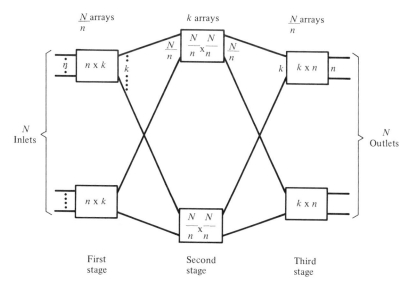

FIGURE 8-3. Three-stage space-division switch.

A consideration with a multistage space-division switch is that it may be block-ing. It should be clear from Figure 8-2a that a crossbar matrix is nonblocking; that is, a path is always available to connect an input to an output. That this is not always the case with a multiple-stage switch can be seen in Figure 8-4. The figure shows a three stage switch with $N = 9$, $n = 3$, and $k = 3$. The heavier lines indicate lines that are already in use. In this state, input line 9 cannot be connected to either output line 4 or 6, even though both of these output lines are available.

It should be clear that by increasing the value of k (the number of outlets from each first-stage switch and the number of second stage switches), the probability of blocking is reduced. What value of k is required for a nonblocking three-stage switch? The answer is depicted in Figure 8-5. Consider that we wish to es-tablish a path from input line a to output line b. The worst case situation for

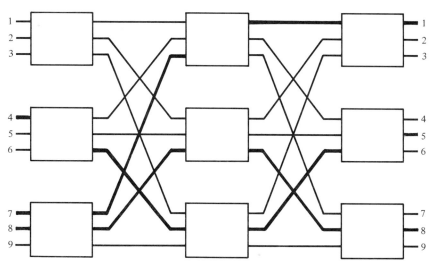

FIGURE 8-4. Example of blocking in a three-stage switch.

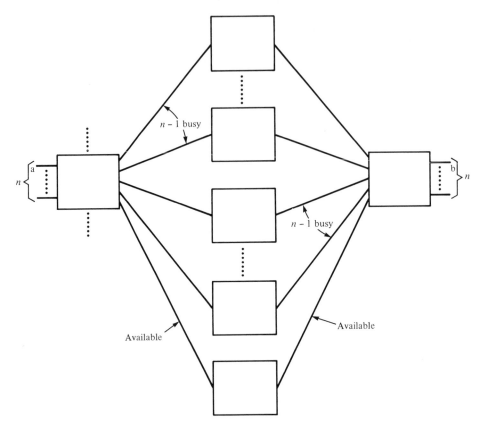

FIGURE 8-5. Nonblocking three-stage switch.

blocking occurs if all of the remaining $n - 1$ input lines and $n - 1$ output lines are busy and are connected to different center-stage switches. Thus a total of $(n - 1) + (n - 1) = 2n - 2$ center switches are unavailable for creating a path from a to b. However, if one more center-stage switch exists, the appropriate links must be available for the connection. Thus, a three-stage network will be non-blocking if

$$k = 2n - 1 \qquad (8\text{-}1)$$

We now return to our claim that a multiple-stage switch requires fewer crosspoints than a single-stage switch. From Figure 8-3, the total number of crosspoints N_x in a three-stage switch is

$$N_x = 2Nk + k\left(\frac{N}{n}\right)^2 \qquad (8\text{-}2)$$

Substituting Equation (8-1) into (8-2),

$$N_x = 2N(2n - 1) + (2n - 1)\left(\frac{N}{n}\right)^2 \qquad (8\text{-}3)$$

for a nonblocking switch. The actual value as a function of N depends on the number of switches (N/n) in the first and third stages. To optimize, differentiate N_x with respect to n and set the result to 0. For large N, the result converges to

TABLE 8-1 Number of Crosspoints in a Nonblocking Switch

Number of Lines	Number of Crosspoints for Three-Stage Switch	Number of Crosspoints for Single-Stage Switch
128	7,680	16,384
512	63,488	262,144
3,048	516,096	4.2×10^6
8,192	4.2×10^6	6.7×10^7
32,768	3.3×10^7	1×10^9
131,072	2.6×10^8	1.7×10^{10}

$n = (N/2)^{1/2}$. Substituting into (8-3),

$$N_x = 4N(\sqrt{2N} - 1)$$

Table 8.1 compares this value with the number of crosspoints in a single-stage switch. As can be seen, there is a savings, which grows with the number of lines.

Time-Division Switching

In contrast to space-division switching, in which dedicated paths are used, *time-division switching* involves the partitioning of a lower-speed data stream into pieces that share a higher-speed data stream with other data pieces. The individual pieces or slots are manipulated by the control logic to route data from input to output. Three concepts comprise the technique of time-division switching

- TDM bus switching
- Time-slot interchange (TSI)
- Time-multiplex switching (TMS)

TDM Bus Switching.   As discussed in Chapter 6, TDM is a technique that allows multiple signals to share a single transmission line by separating them in time. In this chapter we are concerned primarily with synchronous TDM, that is, a situation in which time slots are preassigned so that few or no overhead bits are required. We will see that this technique permits multiple channels of data to be handled efficiently within switching systems as well as on transmission systems.

Let us briefly review synchronous TDM. As shown in Figure 8-6a, synchronous TDM was designed to permit multiple low-speed streams to share a high-speed line. A set of inputs is sampled in turn. The samples are organized serially into slots (channels) to form a recurring frame of n slots. A slot may be a bit, a byte, or some longer block. An important point to note is that with synchronous TDM, the source and destination of the data in each time slot are known. Hence there is no need for address bits in each slot.

The mechanism for synchronous TDM may be quite simple. For example, each input line deposits data in a buffer; the multiplexer scans these buffers sequentially, taking fixed size chunks of data from each buffer and sending them out on the line. One complete scan produces one frame of data. For output to the lines, the reverse operation is performed, with the multiplexer filling the output line buffers one by one.

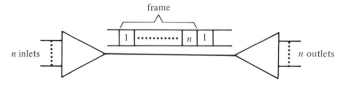

(a) Synchronous Time Division Multiplexing

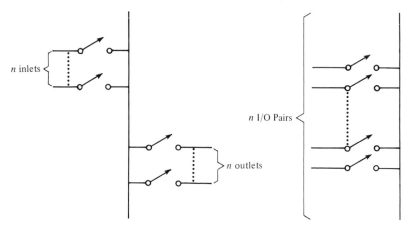

(b) A Simple Time-Division Switch

(c) A Simple Folded Time-Division Switch

FIGURE 8-6. TDM bus switching.

The I/O lines attached to the multiplexer may be synchronous or asynchronous; the multiplexed line between the two multiplexers is synchronous and must have a data rate equal to the sum of the data rates of the attached lines. Actually, the multiplexed line must have a slightly higher data rate, since each frame will include some overhead bits (headers and trailers) for synchronization.

The time slots in a frame are assigned to the I/O lines on a fixed, predetermined basis. If a device has no data to send, the multiplexer must send empty slots. Thus the actual data transfer rate may be less than the capacity of the system.

Figure 8-6b shows a simple way in which this technique can be adapted to achieve switching. A set of buffered input and output lines are connected through controlled gates to a high-speed digital bus. Each input line is assigned a time slot. During that time, that line's gate is opened, allowing a small burst of data onto the bus. For that same time slot, one of the output line gates is also opened. Since the opening and closing of gates is controlled, the sequence of input and output line activations need not be in the same order. Hence a form of switching is possible. Curiously, this technique has no specific name; we shall refer to it as TDM bus switching.

Of course, such a scheme need not be two-sided. As shown in Figure 8-6c, a "folded" switch can be devised by attaching n I/O pairs to the bus. Any attached device achieves full duplex operation by transmitting during one assigned time slot and receiving during another. The other end of the connection is an I/O pair for which these time slots have the opposite meanings.

The TDM bus switch has an advantage over a crossbar switch in terms of efficient use of gates. For N devices, the TDM bus switch requires $2N$ gates or switch points, whereas the most efficient multistage crossbar network requires on the order of $N \sqrt{N}$ switch points.

Let us look at the timing involved a bit more closely. First, consider a nonblocking implementation of Figure 8-6c. There must be N repetitively occurring time slots, each one assigned to an input and an output line. We will refer to one iteration for all time slots as a frame. The input assignment may be fixed; the output assignments vary to allow various connections. When a time slot begins, the designated input line may insert a burst of data onto the line, where it will propagate to both ends past all other lines. The designated ouput line will, during that time, copy the data if any as they go by. The time slot, then, must equal the transmission time of the input line plus the propagation delay between input and output lines. In order to keep the successive time slots uniform, time slot length should be defined as transmission time plus the end-to-end bus propagation delay. For efficiency, the propagation delay should be much less than the transmission time, and in practice this is so. Note that only one time slot or burst of data may be on the bus at a time.

To keep up with the input lines, the slots must recur sufficiently frequently. For example, consider a system connecting full-duplex lines at 19.2 kbps. Input data on each line are buffered at the gate. The buffer must be cleared, by opening the gate, fast enough to avoid overrun. So if there are 100 lines, the capacity of the bus must be at least 1.92 Mbps. Actually, it must be higher than that to account for the wasted time due to propagation delay.

These considerations determine the traffic-carrying capacity of a blocking switch as well. For a blocking switch, there is no fixed assignment of input lines to time slots; they are allocated on demand. The data rate on the bus dictates how many connections can be made at a time. For a system with 200 devices at 19.2 kbps and a bus at 2 Mbps, about half of the devices can be connected at any one time.

The TDM bus switching scheme can accommodate lines of varying data rates. For example, if a 9600-bps line gets one slot per frame, a 19.2-kbps line would get two slots per frame. Of course, only lines of the same data rate can be connected.

Several questions may occur to you. For one, is this circuit switching? Circuit switching, recall, was defined as a technique in which a dedicated communications path is established between devices. This is indeed the case in Figure 8-6b and c. To establish a connection between an input and output line, the controller dedicates a certain number of time slots per frame to that connection. The appropriate input and output gates are opened during those time slots to allow data to pass. Although the bus is shared by other connections, it is nevertheless used to create a dedicated path between input and output. Another question: Is this synchronous TDM? Synchronous TDM is generally associated with creating permanent dedicated time slots for each input line. The scheme depicted in Figure 8-6b and c can assume a dynamic character, with the controller allocating available time slots among connections. Nevertheless, at steady state (a period when no connections are made or broken) a fixed number of slots is dedicated per channel and the system behaves in a manner similar to a synchronous time-division multiplexer.

The control logic for the system described above requires the opening of two gates to achieve a connection. This logic can be simplified if the input burst into a time slot contains destination address information. All output devices can then always connect to the bus and copy the data from time slots with their address. This scheme blurs the distinction between circuit switching and packet switching.

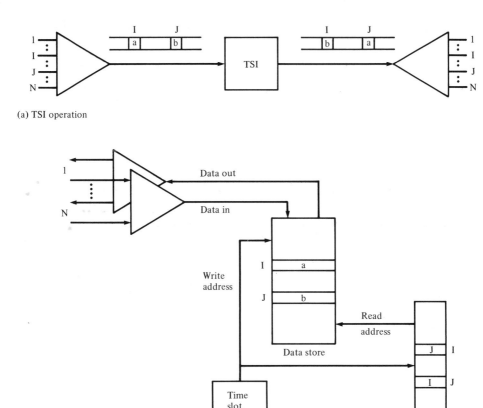

(a) TSI operation

(b) TSI mechanism

FIGURE 8-7. Time-slot interchange (TSI).

Time-Slot Interchange.   The basic building block of many time-division switches is the *time-slot interchange* (TSI) mechanism. A TSI unit operates on a synchronous TDM stream of time slots, or channels, by interchanging pairs of slots to achieve full-duplex operation. Figure 8-7a shows how the input line of device I is connected to the output line of device J, and vice versa.

We should note several points. The input lines of N devices are passed through a synchronous multiplexer to produce a TDM stream with N slots. To achieve interconnection, the slots corresponding to two inputs are interchanged. This results in a full-duplex connection between two lines. To allow the interchange of any two slots, the incoming data in a slot must be stored until they can be sent out on the right channel in the next frame cycle. Hence the TSI introduces a delay and produces output slots in the desired order. These are then demultiplexed and routed to the appropriate output line. Since each channel is provided a time slot in the frame, whether or not it transmits data, the size of the TSI unit must be chosen for the capacity of the TDM line, not the actual data transfer rate.

Figure 8-7b depicts a mechanism for TSI. Individual I/O lines are multiplexed and demultiplexed. These functions can be integrated as part of the switch itself, or they may be implemented remotely, as a device clustering mechanism. A random-access data store whose width equals one time slot of data and whose length equals the number of slots in a frame is used. An incoming TDM frame is written sequentially, slot by slot, into the data store. An outgoing TDM frame is created by reading slots from memory in an order dictated by an address store that reflects the existing connections. In the figure, the data in channels *I* and *J* are interchanged, creating a full-duplex connection between the corresponding stations.

TSI is a simple, effective way of switching TDM data. However, the size of such a switch, in terms of number of connections, is limited by the memory access speed. It is clear that, in order to keep pace with the input, data must be read into and out of memory as fast as they arrive. So, for example, if we have 24 sources operating at 64 kbps each, and a slot size of 8 bits, we would have an arrival rate of 192,000 slots per second (this is like the structure of the PCM T1 carrier). For each time slot, both a read and a write are required. Thus memory access time would need to be $1/(192,000 \times 2)$, or about 2.6 µs.

Let us look more closely at the operation of the data store; in particular, we need to view it as a function of time. As an example [DAVI73], consider a system with eight input/output lines, in which the following connections exist: 1-2, 3-7, and 5-8. The other two stations are not in use. Figure 8-8 depicts the contents of the data store over the course of one frame (eight slots). During the first time slot, data are stored in location 1 and read from location 2. During the second time slot, data are stored in location 2 and read from location 1. And so on.

As can be seen, the write accesses to the data store are cyclic, that is, accessing successive locations in sequential order, whereas the read accesses are acyclic, requiring the use of an address store. The figure also depicts two frames of the input and output sequences and indicates the transfer of data between channels 1 and 2. Note that in half the cases, data slots move into the next frame.

As with the TDM bus switch, the TSI unit can handle inputs of varying data rates. Figure 8-9 suggests a way in which this may be done. Instead of presenting the input lines to a synchronous multiplexer, they are presented to a selector device.

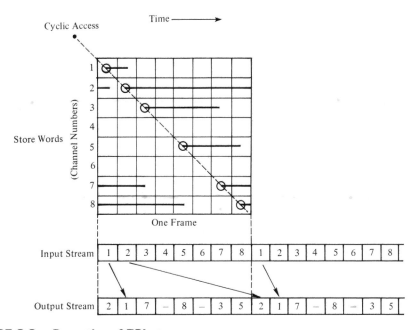

FIGURE 8-8.   Operation of TSI store.

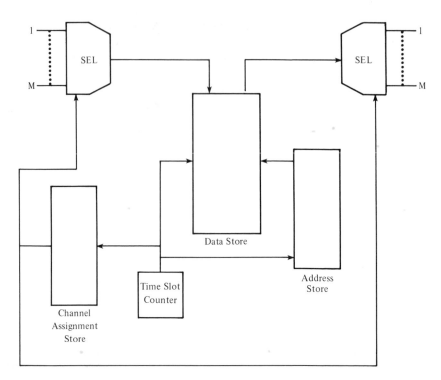

FIGURE 8-9. TSI operation with variable-rate input.

This device will select an input line based on a channel assignment provided from a store controlled by the time slot counter. Hence, instead of sampling equally from each input, it may gather more slots from some channels than others.

Time-Multiplexed Switching. As we have seen, a TSI unit can support only a limited number of connections. Further, as the size of the unit grows, for a fixed access speed, the delay at the TSI grows. To overcome both of these problems, multiple TSI units are used. Now, to connect two channels entering a single TSI unit, their time slots can be interchanged. However, to connect a channel on one TDM stream (going into one TSI) to a channel on another TDM stream (going into another TSI), some form of space division multiplexing is needed. Naturally, we do not wish to switch all of the time slots from one stream to another; we would like to do it one slot at a time. This technique is known as *time-multiplexed switching* (TMS).

Multiple-stage networks can be built up by concatenating TMS and TSI stages. TMS stages, which move slots from one stream to another, are referred to as S, and TSI stages are referred to as T. Systems are generally described by an enumeration of their stages from input to output, using the symbols T and S. Figure 8-10 is an example of a two-stage TS network. Such a network is blocking. For example, if one channel on input stream 1 is to be switched to the third channel in output stream 1, and another channel on input stream 1 is to be switched to the third channel on output stream 2, one of the connections is blocked.

To avoid blocking, three or more stages are used. Some of the more common structures used in commercially available systems are [SKAP79]:

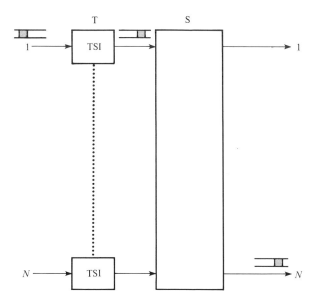

FIGURE 8-10.   Two-stage digital switch.

- TST.
- TSSST.
- STS.
- SSTSS.
- TSTST.

The requirements on the TMS unit are stringent. The unit must provide space-division connections between its input and output lines, and these connections must be reconfigured for each time slot. This requires, in effect, a control store whose width is sufficient to handle the number of ingoing and outgoing lines and whose length equals the number of time slots in a frame.

One means of implementing the TMS stage is the crossbar switch discussed earlier. This requires that the crosspoints be manipulated at each time slot. More commonly, the TMS stage is implemented by digital selectors (SEL) which select only one input at a time on a time-slot basis. These SEL devices are the same as those described in the preceding section, except that here each of their inputs is a TDM stream rather than a single line. Figure 8-11 shows STS and TST networks implemented with the SEL units.

In an STS network, the path between an incoming and outgoing channel has multiple possible physical routes equal to the number of TSI units but only one time route. For a fully nonblocking network, the number of TSI units must be double the number of incoming and outgoing TDM streams. On the other hand, the multiple routes between two channels in a TST network are all in the time domain; there is only one physical path possible. Here, too, blocking is a possibility. One way to avoid blocking is by expanding the number of time slots in the space stage. In all multistage networks, whether space- or time-division, a path-search algorithm is needed to determine the route from input to output.

It is interesting to compare the TDM bus switch with TSI and TMS. It does not exactly fit into either category. Compare it to a space switch. The TDM bus switch

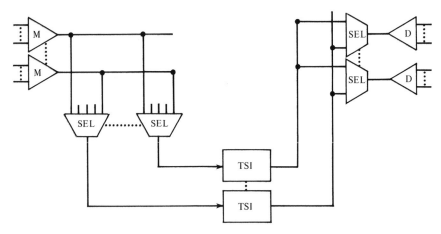

(a) Space-Time-Space Network

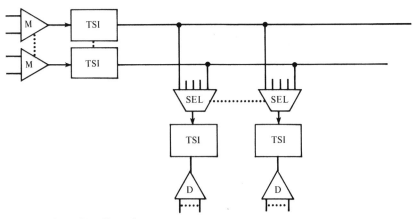

(b) Time-Space-Time Network

FIGURE 8-11. Three-stage TDM switches.

does connect any input with any output, as in a crossbar or SEL switch. The space switch operates simultaneously on all inputs, whereas the TDM bus switch operates on the inputs sequentially. However, because the frame time on the bus is less than the slot time of any input, the switching is effectively simultaneous. On the other hand, a comparison of Figures 8-7 and 8-6b reveals the similarity between TSI and TDM bus switching.

Modular Switch Architecture

The discussion so far has concerned what might be termed "traditional" digital switch architecture. More recently, a modular switch architecture has been developed based on the use of one module type for all switching stages [KAJI83]. A single module contains both time and space switching.

A major motivation for going to a modular architecture is to overcome some inherent disadvantages of the traditional multistage time-and-space switch. With the traditional switch, the designer must decide in advance the maximum exchange size in order to determine the number of stages and the switch size at each stage. These decisions, in turn, determine a lower size limit. In addition, central control is needed to set up and tear down paths through the switch. As the size of the switch grows, this task becomes increasingly complex. The modular architecture does not possess these disadvantages, as we shall see.

We can contrast the modular switch to the traditional digital switch by listing some of the advantages of the former:

- *Flexible size:* The modules serve as building blocks, allowing a large number of different switch sizes, ranging from very small to very large.
- *Simplified control:* Path setup and tear down is distributed. Each module is intelligent and control is provided via the data path.
- *Simplified manufacturing, testing, and maintenance:* There are fewer parts to build and install.

The principal disadvantage of the modular architecture is potentially increased propagation delay. Each module performs a TSI function. In a large switch, a circuit may pass through multiple modules, and the TSI delays can become substantial.

In the remainder of this section, we briefly describe one example of a modular architecture, the ITT 1240 [COTT81]. For another example, the reader is referred to [CHAR79].

The basic building block of the ITT switch is depicted in Figure 8-12. This module is a plug-in printed circuit board which carries 16 identical LSI *switch ports* interconnected by a TDM bus switch. Each port has an incoming and an outgoing synchronous TDM line. Each line has a data rate of 4.096 Mbps and carries 32 channels. Each channel is used for either digital data or PCM voice. One TDM frame consists of 16 bits from each of the 32 channels. Eight of these bits are control or unused bits. A little arithmetic reveals that each channel is therefore 64 kbps.

There is no common mechanism or control processor to control the modules. Each module is controlled by the individual switch ports acting together over the TDM bus to make and break connections. The receive (incoming) side of each switch port is in essence a synchronous demultiplexer. It sends the channel data, along with destination port number and channel number, out in 16-bit chunks onto the bus during assigned time slots. The transmit (outgoing) side recognizes its port number on the bus and places each slot of data in the appropriate frame slot of the outgoing line. Since the slots are then transmitted in a (possibly) different order than that in which they were received from the bus, the switch port performs, in effect, a TSI operation. With this architecture, any channel on any of the 16 incoming lines can be connected to any of the 512 (16×32) outgoing channels. Thus the module provides a combination of time and space switching.

To begin, let us consider the operation of the simplest switch, depicted in Figure 8-13. Individual terminals (digital data or PCM voice) attach to a *terminal control element* (TCE), which produces two 32-channel TDM streams destined for the switch. Similarly, the TCE receives two 32-channel streams from the switch. Thus the TCE is nothing more than a synchronous TDM multiplexer/demultiplexer. Up to 60 terminals attach to the switch (the extra channels are used for control). The switch in this case consists of two modules which in this context are called *access switches*, with one full-duplex 32-channel link from each TCE going to each module. The use of two modules provides redundancy in the case of failure. Thus any two of the 60 devices on the TCE can be connected via the switch.

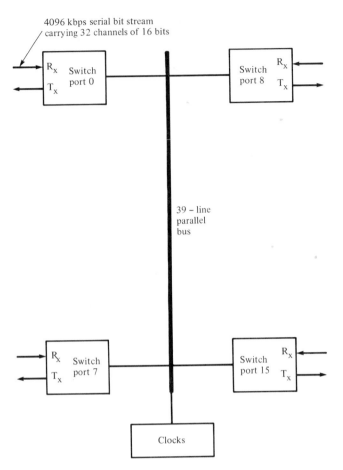

4096 kbps serial bit stream
carrying 32 channels of 16 bits

R_x Switch
   port 0
T_x

Switch R_x
port 8 T_x

39 – line
parallel
bus

R_x Switch
   port 7
T_x

Switch R_x
port 15 T_x

Clocks

FIGURE 8-12. Digital switch module.

Note that one TCE uses up only one port on each of the access switches. The switches support up to 12 TCEs using 12 of the available 16 ports. The remaining ports are unused in this configuration. Thus the simplest one-stage switch consists of two modules and supports 720 terminals. Switching is accomplished as follows. When a terminal requests a connection, and if the destination terminal is attached to the same TCE, the TCE completely implements the connection without involving an access switch. Otherwise, the TCE selects an available outgoing channel (out of the 64) and transmits a path setup request over that channel, which includes the destination address. The access switch responds by selecting an available channel going to the appropriate TCE.

The way in which a switch may be expanded, and the operation of a multistage switch, can be explained with reference to Figure 8-14. The single-stage switch is enclosed in a box labeled *A*. For a first expansion, up to three more pairs of access switches may be added to the first stage, all interconnected by a second stage of switching. The four unused ports on each access switch (32 in all) connect to a second-stage switch called a *group switch*. This stage consists of up to four modules, with eight ports on each module utilized. The four ports on each access switch attach, one each, to the four modules of stage 2. Thus full connectivity is achieved.

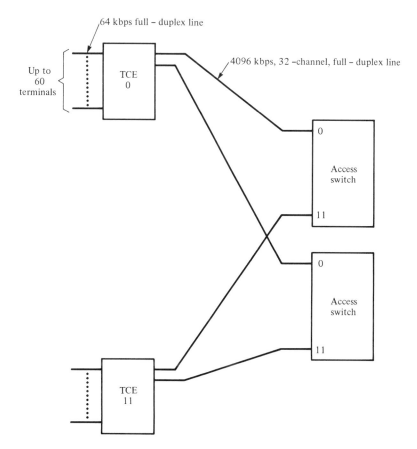

FIGURE 8-13. **Single-stage modular switch.**

The full switch can now handle a total of 2880 terminals. Switching is accomplished as follows. If two terminals connect via TCEs to the same access switch, a path is set up that "reflects back" through the access switch without going to the second stage. Addresses have a hierarchical format, so it is easy for a module to determine if reflection is allowed. If not, an available channel to the stage 2 switch is selected and that switch in turn reflects back to a different access switch that connects to the TCE of the destination terminal.

The two-step configuration is labeled *B* in the diagram. Further expansion proceeds similarly. The eight unused ports on each second stage module are used to connect to up to eight third-stage switches. Reflection can occur at stage 1, 2, or 3 (boxes *C* and *D*). The maximum configuration consists of four stages and supports over 100,000 terminals.

8-3

DIGITAL DATA SWITCHING DEVICES

The techniques discussed in the preceding section have been used to build a variety of digital switching products designed for digital data-only applications. These

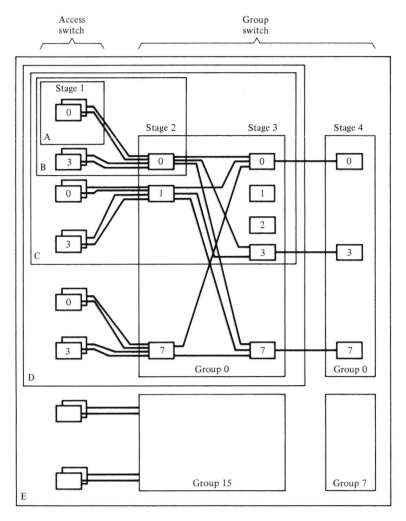

FIGURE 8-14. Modular switch architecture.

devices do not provide telephone service and are generally cheaper than a CBX for comparable capacity.

The variety of devices is wide and the distinction between types is blurred. For convenience, we categorize them as follows:

- Terminal/port-oriented switch
- Data switch
- Switching statistical multiplexer

In what follows we will look at the functions performed by each type of device, and suggest an architecture that supports those functions. Keep in mind that usually any of the techniques in Section 8-2, or any combination, may be used to implement any of these switches. The discussion here is intended only to give examples.

Before turning to the specific device types, let us look at the requirements for data switching.

Data Switching Requirements

For any circuit-switching system used to connect digital data transmitting devices, certain generic requirements can be defined. These requirements apply both to pure digital data switching devices and to CBX systems. We begin first by looking briefly at the data transmission techniques that must be supported by a data switch, and then look at the functions to be performed.

The devices attached to a data switch will use either asynchronous or synchronous transmission. Asynchronous transmission, recall, is character-at-a-time. Each character consists of a start bit, 5 to 8 data bits, a parity bit, and a stop signal, which may be 1, 1.5, or 2 bit times in length. Logic is available which can automatically determine character length, parity, and even bit rate. Hence it is a relatively easy matter for a data switch to handle asynchronous transmission. On input, data are accumulated a character at a time, and transmitted internally using synchronous transmission. At the other end of the connection, they are buffered and transmitted a character at a time to the output line. This applies to any switch using time-division switching techniques. Of course, a pure space-division switch need not concern itself with such matters: A dedicated physical path is set up and bits are transmitted transparently.

Synchronous transmission represents a greater challenge. Synchronous communication requires either a separate clock lead from the transmission point to the reception point or the use of a self-clock encoding scheme, such as Manchester. The latter technique is typical. With synchronous communication, the data rate must be known ahead of time, as well as the synchronization pattern (bits or characters used to signal the beginning of a frame). Thus there can be no universal synchronous interface (until a universal synchronous transmission technique is standardized).

Of course, for either synchronous or asynchronous transmission, full duplex operation is required. Typically, this requires two twisted pairs (known as a twin pair) between a device and the switch, one for transmission in each direction. This is in contrast to the case with analog signaling where a single twisted-pair suffices (see Figure 3-6). Recently, however, some vendors have begun to offer full-duplex digital signaling on a single twisted pair, using a *ping-pong protocol*. In essence, data are buffered at each end and sent across the line at double the data rate with the two ends taking turn. So, for example, two devices may communicate, full duplex, at 56 kbps if they are attached to a 112-kbps line and the line drivers at each end buffer the device data and transmit, alternately, at 112 kbps. In fact, an even higher data rate is required to account for propagation delay and control signals.

We turn now to the functions to be provided by a data switch. The most basic, of course, is the making of a connection between two attached lines. These connections can be preconfigured by a system operator, but more dynamic operation is often desired. This leads to two additional functions: port contention and port selection. *Port contention* is a function that allows a certain number of designated ports to contend for access to a smaller number of ports. Typically, this is used for terminal to host connection to allow a smaller number of host ports to service a larger number of terminal ports. When a terminal user attempts to connect, the system will scan through all the host ports in the contention group. If any of the ports is available, a connection is made.

Port selection is an interactive capability. It allows a user (or an application program in a host) to select a port for connection. This is analogous to dialing a number in a phone system. Port selection and port contention can be combined by allowing the selection, by name or number, of a contention group. Port selection devices are becoming increasingly common. A switch without this capability only allows connections that are preconfigured by a system operator. If one knows in advance what interconnections are required, fine. Otherwise, the flexibility of port selection is usually worth the additional cost.

An interactive capability carries with it an additional responsibility: The control unit of the switch must be able to talk to the requesting port. This can be done in two ways. In some cases, the manufacturer supplies a simple keypad device that attaches to and shares the terminal's line. The user first uses the keypad to dial a connection; once the connection is made, communication is via the terminal. As an alternative, the connection sequence can be effected through the terminal itself. A simple command language dialogue is used. However, this technique requires that the system understand the code and protocol being used by the terminal. Consequently, this feature is generally limited to asynchronous ASCII devices.

Terminal/Port-Oriented Switches

The devices discussed in this section were designed to address a specific problem: the connection of interactive terminals to computer ports. In many computer sites with one or more time-sharing systems and a population (usually growing) of terminals, means must be found for interconnection.

One means of connection is simply to assign each terminal to a specific computer port, even when not active. This is expensive in terms of computer ports, since generally only a fraction of the terminals are logged on. Further, the user cannot change to a different computer without making cable changes. Another approach is to use multiple dial-up telephone rotaries, for each computer and each transmission speed. The rotary allows a user to call a single number and gain access to one of several autoanswer modems; if all modems are busy, the rotary returns a busy signal. The approach ties up telephones lines for extended periods and requires the use of modems.

One early solution that avoids some of the expenses mentioned above was the patch panel. This device enabled manual connection of two lines and could also provide some system monitoring and diagnostics. The addition of intelligence to this type of device to eliminate the manual connection function has resulted in a variety of intelligent terminal/port-oriented switches. A variety of names are used, depending partly on function, including intelligent patch panel, port selector, and port contention device.

At a minimum, these devices permit a set of connections to be set up and periodically updated by a system operator. Port selection and port contention functions are also provided on many products.

Figure 8-15 is an example of a noninteractive (without port selection) system. The system allows connection of one I/O port to any other I/O port on the same or a different port card. Connections are set up at system initialization time and may be changed dynamically by the system operator (not the user). The means of establishing connections is simple. Each port has associated with it a destination address register. To connect two ports, the address of each is placed in the other. To transmit data, the sending device puts its data (8 bits) and the destination address (8 bits) on the bus. All devices continually monitor the bus for their own address.

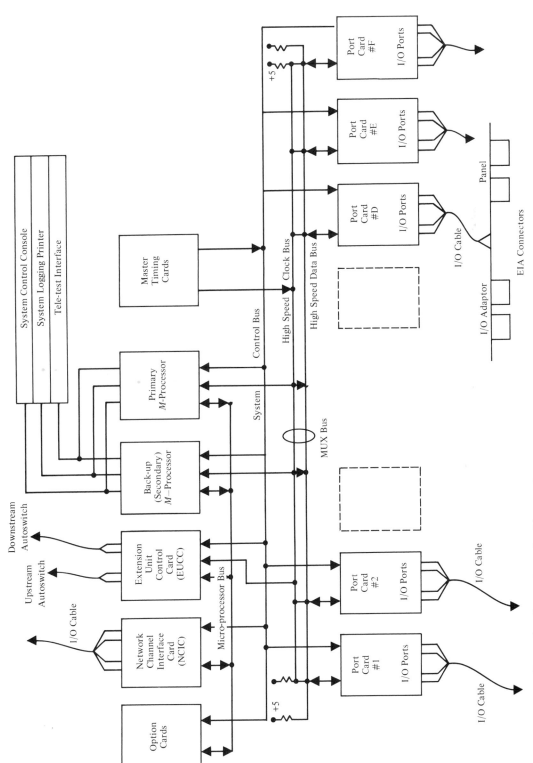

FIGURE 8-15. Example of a port contention system.

229

The switch is nonblocking, allowing the preassignment of time slots to transmitting devices. Receiving devices need not know the time slot for reception since they are looking for an address. Thus, at the cost of 100% overhead, the control logic is greatly simplified.

Figure 8-16 is an example of a port selection system. A collection of line modules are scanned to produce a TDM stream which is passed over a bus to a switch module. The output of the switch module is a switched set of time slots that are directed to the proper port. Note the redundant architecture for reliability.

Data Switches

There is little additional that need be said about these devices. No distinction is made between terminal lines and ports. The switch simply has a set of I/O lines and is capable of establishing connections between lines. Any or a combination of the digital switching techniques described in Section 8-2 may be used. Some or all of the functions described above may be provided.

Switching Statistical Multiplexers

There is one device that is quite different from the other types that we have been discussing: the *switching statistical multiplexer*. Unlike the synchronous TDM techniques used in most digital switches, the switching statistical multiplexer uses asynchronous or statistical TDM and has a switching capability [SCHO81].

The switching multiplexer uses the same technique as a statistical multiplexer (Chapter 6), with two additions:

- There may be more than one multiplexed line.
- There is sufficient intelligence to permit any form of routing through the multiplexer.

As with a statistical multiplexer, the switching multiplexer can provide a full-duplex connection between a line and a channel on a multiplexed line (usually referred to as a *trunk*). For line-to-trunk traffic, data are buffered and sent out in fixed-size chunks with an address appended. For trunk-to-line, each slot of incoming data is handled separately; the address is stripped off and the data chunk is routed to the appropriate output line.

This capability is not limited to trunk-line interaction. Two lines can be connected, with data exchanged between them, without addressing. Two channels on separate trunks can be connected; each slot of incoming data on a designated channel is routed, address and all, to the other trunk.

Figure 8-17 summarizes the connection possibilities of the switching multiplexer. Statistical TDM frames are used on the trunks. Connected lines may be synchronous or asynchronous and of varying speeds. Some type of control unit is needed to control the routing.

Figure 8-18 is a conceptual architecture that suggests how a switching multiplexer might be implemented. There are a number of I/O logic units for the lines and trunks. Each unit is capable of receiving and buffering data and transferring it to a data store; on output, it can accept data from the data store and transmit. Areas of the data store serve as dedicated buffers for the I/O units. As data accumulate, they must be transferred to the appropriate I/O unit for transmission. This is done

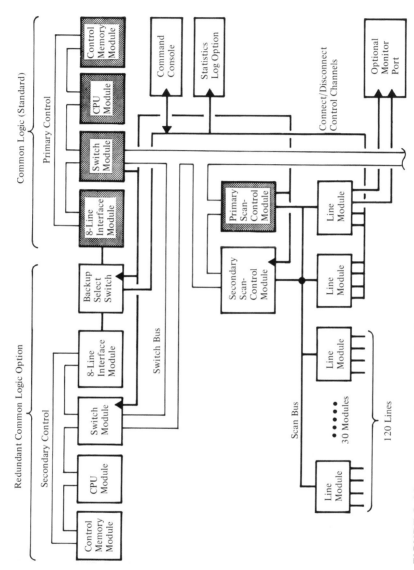

FIGURE 8-16. Example of a port selection system.

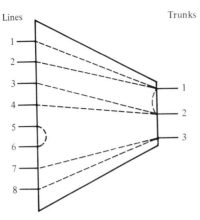

FIGURE 8-17.   Connection possibilities in a switching statistical multiplexer.

under control of the control unit, which uses information in the routing table to determine the routing.

The switching multiplexer can perform all of the data switching functions described in previous sections, although generally on a smaller scale. Preconfigured connections can be set up. The device can have sufficient intelligence to support on-demand port selection and port contention. A mixture of fixed and demand-assigned connections can be provided.

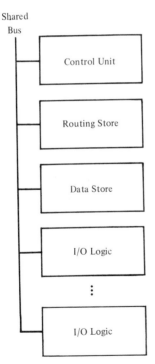

FIGURE 8-18.   Conceptual architecture of a switching statistical multiplexer.

THE COMPUTERIZED BRANCH EXCHANGE

Evolution of the CBX

The CBX is a marriage of two technologies: digital switching and telephone exchange systems. The forerunner of the CBX is the private branch exchange (PBX). A PBX is an on-premise facility, owned or leased by an organization, which interconnects the telephones within the facility and provides access to the public telephone system. Typically, a telephone user on the premises dials a three- or four-digit number to call another telephone on the premises, and dials one digit (usually 8 or 9) to get a dial tone for an "outside line," which allows the caller to dial a number in the same fashion as a residential user.

The original private exchanges were manual, with one or more operators at a switchboard required to make all connections. Back in the 1920s, these began to be replaced by automatic systems, called *private automatic branch exchanges* (PABXs), which did not require attendant intervention to place a call. These "first-generation" systems used electromechanical technology and analog signaling. Data connections could be made via modems. That is, a user with a terminal, a telephone, and a modem or acoustic coupler in the office could dial up an on-site or remote number that reached another modem and exchange data.

The "second-generation" PBXs were introduced in the middle 1970s. These systems use electronic rather than electromagnetic technology and the internal switching is digital. Such a system is referred to as digital PBX, or computerized branch exchange (CBX). These systems were designed primarily to handle analog voice traffic, with the codec function built into the switch so that digital switching could be used internally. The systems were also capable of handling digital data connections without the need of a modem.

The "third-generation" systems are touted as "integrated voice/data" systems, although the differences between third generation and upgraded second generation are rather blurred. Perhaps a better term is "improved digital PBX." Some of the characteristics of these systems that differ from those of earlier systems include:

- *The use of digital phones:* This permits integrated voice/data workstations.
- *Distributed architecture:* Multiple switches in a hierarchical or meshed configuration with distributed intelligence provides enhanced reliability.
- *Nonblocking configuration:* Typically, dedicated port assignments are used for all attached phones and devices.

Mention should be made of two systems that do not fall cleanly into the categories listed above. One is AT&T's Dimension PBX, which is not, as some people think, a digital PBX. (However, a digital version known as Dimension 85 has now been developed.) Whereas digital PBXs use PCM digital voice signals, Dimension PBX uses pulse amplitude modulation (PAM). However, because PAM involves the use of discrete voltage pulses, TDM techniques can be used for switching.

Another AT&T offering is Centrex, in which the switching facility for a site may be located remotely, so as to serve a number of customers. The user, however, can still dial other local users with an extension number. Hence, Centrex gives the appearance of a PBX.

It is worthwhile to summarize the main reasons why the evolution described above has taken place. To the untrained eye, analog and digital PBXs would seem to offer about the same level of convenience. The analog PBX can handle telephone sets directly and uses modems to accommodate digital data devices; the digital PBX can handle digital data devices directly and uses codecs to accommodate telephone sets. Some of the advantages of the digital approach are

- *Digital technology:* By handling all internal signals digitally, the digital PBX can take advantage of low-cost LSI and VLSI components. Digital technology also lends itself more readily to software and firmware control.
- *Time-division multiplexing:* Digital signals lend themselves readily to TDM techniques, which provide efficient use of internal data paths, access to public TDM carriers, and TDM switching techniques, which are more cost effective than older, crossbar techniques.
- *Digital control signals:* Control signals are inherently digital and can easily be integrated into a digital transmission path via TDM. The signaling equipment is independent of the transmission medium.
- *Encryption:* This is more easily accommodated with digital signals.

Telephone Call Processing Requirements

The characteristic that distinguishes the CBX from a digital data switch is its ability to handle telephone connections. Freeman [FREE80] lists eight functions required for telephone call processing:

- Interconnection.
- Control.
- Attending.
- Busy testing.
- Alerting.
- Information receiving.
- Information transmitting.
- Supervisory.

The interconnection function encompasses three contingencies. The first contingency is a call originated by a station bound for another station on the CBX. The switching technologies that we have discussed are used in this context. The second contingency is a call originated by a CBX station bound for an external recipient. For this, the CBX must not only have access to an external trunk, but must perform internal switching to route the call from the user station to the trunk interface. The CBX also performs a line to trunk concentration function to avoid the expense of one external line per station. The third contingency is a call originated externally bound for a CBX station. Referred to as *direct inward dialing*, this allows an external caller to use the unique phone number of a CBX station to establish a call without going through an operator. This requires trunk-to-line expansion plus internal switching.

The control function includes, of course, the logic for setting up and tearing down a connection path. In addition, the control function serves to activate and control all other functions and to provide various management and utility services, such as logging, accounting, and configuration control.

The CBX must recognize a request for a connection; this is the attending function. The CBX then determines if the called party is available (busy testing) and, if so, alerts that party (alerting). The process of setting up the connection involves an exchange of information between the CBX and the called and calling parties.

Finally, a supervisory function is needed to determine when a call is completed and the connection may be released, freeing the switching capacity and the two parties for future connections.

Let us look more closely at the sequence of events required to complete a call successfully. First, consider an internal call from extension 226 to extension 280. The following steps occur:

1. 226 goes off-hook (picks up the receiver). The control unit recognizes this condition.
2. The control unit finds an available digit receiver and sets up a circuit from 226 to the digit receiver. The control unit also sets up a circuit from a dial-tone generator to 226.
3. When the first digit is dialed, the dial-tone connection is released. The digit receiver accumulates dialed digits (280).
4. After the last digit is dialed, the connection to the digit receiver is released. The control unit examines the number for legitimacy. If it is not, the caller is informed by some means, such as connection to a rapid busy signal generator. Otherwise, the control unit then determines if 280 is busy. If so, 226 is connected to a busy-signal generator.
5. If 280 is free, the control unit sets up a connection between 226 and a ring-back-tone generator and a connection between 280 and a ringer. A connection path between 226 and 280 is reserved.
6. When 280 answers by going off-hook, the ringing and ring-back connections are dropped and a connection is set up between 226 and 280.
7. When either 280 and 226 goes on-hook, the connection between them is dropped.

For outgoing calls, the following steps are required.

1–3. As above. In this case the caller will be dialing an access code number (e.g., the single digit 9) to request access to an outgoing trunk.
4. The control unit releases the connection to the digit receiver and finds a free trunk group and sends out an off-hook signal.
5. When a dial tone is returned from the central office, the control unit repeats steps 2 and 3.
6. The control unit releases the connection to the digit receiver and sends the number out to the trunk and makes a connection from the caller to the trunk.
7. When either the caller or the trunk signals on-hook, the connection between them is dropped.

There are variations on the foregoing sequence. For example, if the CBX performs least-cost routing, it will wait until the number is dialed and then select the appropriate trunk.

Finally, incoming calls, when direct inward dialing is supported, proceed as follows.

1. The control unit detects a trunk seizure signal from the central office, sets up a path from the trunk to a digit receiver, and sends a start-dialing signal out on that trunk.
2. The control unit releases the receiver path and examines the dialed number and checks the called station for busy, in which case a busy signal is returned.

3. If the called number is free, the control unit sets up a ringing connection to the called number and a ring-back connection to the trunk. It monitors the called station for answer and the trunk for abandon.
4. When the called station goes off-hook, the ringing and ring-back connections are dropped and a connection is set up between the trunk and the called station.
5. When either the trunk or called station signals on-hook, the connection between them is dropped.

Data Switching Requirements

The data switching requirements for a CBX are the same as those for a digital switch. Typically, a terminal user will be requesting connection to a computer port. The same issues of speed, asynchronous/synchronous, and calling technique arise.

There are several new wrinkles. The CBX may support a voice/data workstation with one twisted pair for the phone and two pairs for the terminal. In such arrangements, the destination port may be selected from the phone rather than the terminal or a keypad.

The CBX has the advantage of direct connect to outgoing telephone lines. The terminal user who wishes to access an external computer need not have a telephone and a modem; the CBX can provide the link-up service. Typically, the connection is to an outgoing analog voice line. To provide the proper service, the CBX maintains a pool of modems that can be used by any data device to communicate over the external lines.

The exact implementation of the modem pool depends on the architecture of the CBX, but some strange contortions may be required. Consider the case of a CBX whose switching capability consists of a TDM bus switch. Figure 8-19 illustrates this. A device wishing to communicate outside will be connected to an available modem in the pool. The modem produces analog signals which must be switched

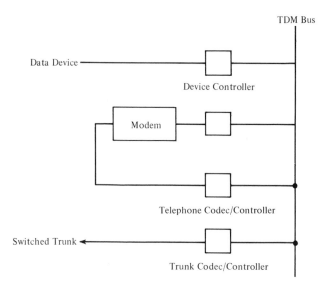

FIGURE 8-19. Use of a modem in a CBX.

to an outgoing trunk. But the CBX switches only digital signals! Therefore, the modem output is routed to a codec, which digitizes the data and puts them back onto the TDM bus. They are then routed to a trunk interface, where the signal is converted back to analog and sent on its way.

An important feature of a CBX is the internal integration of data and digitized voice. The same switching mechanism is used for both. It is therefore easier if both conform to common slot size and timing conventions. This is a consideration not faced by the digital switch designer.

CBX Architecture

A variety of architectures have been developed by CBX manufacturers. Since these are proprietary, the details are not generally known in most cases (but see [KASS79a]). In this section we attempt to present the general architectural features common to all CBX systems.

CBX Components. Figure 8-20 presents a generic CBX architecture. You should find it quite similar to the data switching architecture that we have discussed. Indeed, since the requirements for the CBX are a superset of those for the data switch, a similar architecture is not surprising.

As always, the heart of the system is some kind of digital switching network. The switch is responsible for the manipulation and switching of time multiplexed digital signal streams, using the techniques described in Section 8-2. The digital

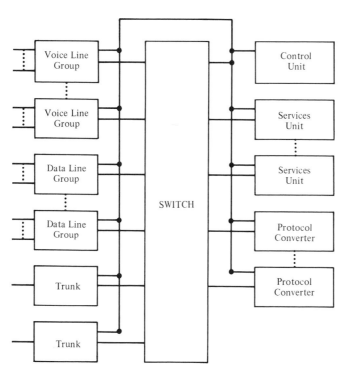

FIGURE 8-20. Generic CBX architecture.

switching network consists of some number of space and time switching stages. Many of the CBXs are not sufficiently large, in terms of lines or capacity, to require complex switching networks. Indeed, some have no network as such, but simply use a TDM bus switch [KASS79a].

Attached to the switch are a set of interface units, which provide access to/from the outside world. Typically, an interface unit will perform a synchronous time-division multiplexing function in order to accommodate multiple incoming lines. On the other side, the unit requires two lines into the switch for full duplex operation.

It is important to understand that the interface unit is performing synchronous and not statistical TDM, even though connections are dynamically changing. On the input side, the unit performs a multiplex operation. Each incoming line is sampled at a specified rate. For n incoming lines each of data rate x, the unit must achieve an input rate of nx. The incoming data are buffered and organized into chunks of time-slot size. Then, according to the timing dictated by the control unit, individual chunks are sent out into the switch at the internal CBX data rate, which may be in the range 50 to 100 Mbps. In a nonblocking switch, n time slots are dedicated to the interface unit for transmission, whether or not they are used. In a blocking switch, time slots are assigned for the duration of a connection. In either case, the time-slot assignment is fixed for the duration of the connection, and synchronous TDM techniques may be used.

On the output side, the interface unit accepts data from the switch during designated time slots. In a nonblocking switch these may be dedicated (requiring more than a simple TDM bus switch), but are in any case fixed for the duration of the connection. Incoming data are demultiplexed, buffered, and presented to the appropriate output port at its data rate.

Several types of interface unit are used. A data line group unit handles data devices, providing the functions described in Section 8-3. An analog voice line group handles voice input/ output over a number of twisted-pair phone lines. The interface unit must include codecs for digital-to-analog (input) and analog-to-digital (output) conversion. A separate type of unit may be used for integrated digital voice/data workstation, which present digitized voice at 64 kbps and data at the same or a lower rate. The range of lines accommodated by interface units is typically 8 to 24.

In addition to multiplexing interface units that accommodate multiple lines, trunk interface units are used to connect to off-site locations. These may be analog voice trunks or digital trunks, which may carry either data or PCM voice. Whereas a line interface unit must multiplex incoming lines to place on the switch, and demultiplex switch traffic to send to the lines, the trunk unit may have to demultiplex and multiplex in both directions (see Figure 8-21). Consider an incoming digital line with n channels of time-multiplexed data (the argument is the same for an analog trunk, which presents n channels of frequency-multiplexed voice). These data must be demultiplexed and stored in a buffer of length n units. Individual units of the buffer are then transmitted out to the switch at the designated time slots. Question: Why not pass the TDM stream directly from input to the bus, filling n contiguous time slots? Actually, in a nonblocking dedicated port system, this is possible. But for a system with dynamic time-slot assignment, the incoming data must be buffered and sent out on time slots that vary as connections are made and broken.

The other boxes in Figure 8-20 can be explained briefly. The control unit operates the digital switch and exchanges control signals with attached devices. For this

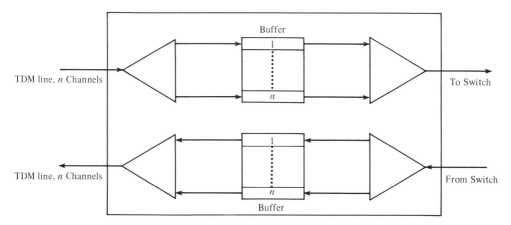

FIGURE 8-21. Operation of trunk interface unit.

purpose, a separate bus or other data path may be used or the control signals may propagate through the switch itself. As part of this or a separate unit, network administration and control functions are implemented. Service units would include such things as tone and busy-signal generators and dialed-digit registers. Some CBX systems provide protocol convertors for connecting dissimilar lines. A connection is made from each line to the protocol convertor.

It should be noted that this generic architecture lends itself to a high degree of reliability. The failure of any interface unit means the loss of only a small number of lines. Key elements such as the control unit can be made redundant.

Distributed Architecture. For reasons of efficiency and reliability, many CBX manufacturers offer distributed architectures for their larger systems. The CBX is organized into a central switch and one or more distributed modules, with twisted pair, coaxial cable, or fiber optic cable between the central switch and the modules, in a two-level hierarchical star topology.

The distributed modules off-load at least some of the central-switch processor's real-time work load (such as off-hook detection). The degree to which control intelligence is off-loaded varies. At one extreme, the modules may be replicas of the central switch, in which case they function almost autonomously with the exception of certain overall management and accounting functions. At the other extreme, the modules are as limited as possible.

A distributed architecture means that it will often be necessary to concatenate several connections to achieve a connection between two devices. Consider Figure 8-22. A connection is desired between lines *a* and *b*. In module *A*, a connection is established between line *a* and one channel on a TDM trunk to the central switch. In the central switch, that channel is connected to a channel on a TDM trunk to module *B*. In module *B*, that channel is connected to line *b*.

There are several advantages to a distributed architecture:

- It permits growth beyond the practical size of a single digital switch.
- It provides better performance by off-loading of functions.
- It provides higher reliability: the loss of a single module need not disable the entire system.
- It reduces twisted-pair wiring distances.

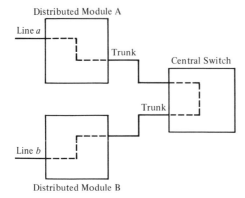

Line *a*

Distributed Module A

Trunk

Central Switch

Trunk

Line *b*

Distributed Module B

FIGURE 8-22. Circuit establishment in a distributed CBX.

8·5

THE PUBLIC TELECOMMUNICATIONS NETWORK

By far the largest circuit-switched network is the public telecommunications network—the telephone network. This is actually a collection of national networks interconnected to form an international service. Although originally designed and implemented to service analog telephone subscribers, it handles substantial data traffic via modem, and is gradually being converted to a digital network.

Architecture

The public telecommunications network, as with any communications network, can be described using four generic architectural components.

- *Stations:* generally denoted as *subscribers*, these are the devices that attach to the network.
- *Interfaces:* the interface between the stations and the network, referred to in the phone system as the *local loop*.
- *Nodes:* the *switching centers* in the network.
- *Links:* the branches between nodes, referred to as *trunks*.

Most of the *subscribers* on the network are telephones. The telephone contains a transmitter and receiver for converting back and forth between analog voice (sound waves) and analog (voice-frequency) electrical signals. With the introduction of the digital data system (DDS), some subscribers that transmit digital signals have been incorporated into the network (see Chapter 6).

The *local loop* is a pair of wires, generally twisted pair, that connects a subscriber to one of the nodes in the network. It is a dc loop that supplies a metallic path for the following [FREE80]:

- Voltage potential for the telephone transmitter. This is supplied over the line from the switching center and is used to convert acoustic energy into electric energy.
- An ac ringing voltage for the bell on the telephone instrument supplied from the switching center.

- Current to flow through the loop when the telephone instrument is taken out of its cradle (''off hook''), telling the serving switch that it requires access.
- The telephone dial or keypad which is used to signal to the switch the number of the destination subscriber.

The local loop generally covers a distance of a few kilometers to a few tens of kilometers at most. More detail on telephone transmission over the local loop can be found in [ATT61].

A two wire connection is inherently half-duplex; that is, it can carry voice in one direction at a time only. Similarly, it can carry digital signals in one direction at a time only. For full-duplex DDS connections, two twisted-pair links are generally used.

Each subscriber connects via local loop to a *switching center*, known as an end office. Typically, an end office will support many thousands of subscribers in a localized area. There are over 19,000 end offices in the United States, so it is clearly impractical for each end office to have a direct link to each other end office; this would require on the order of 2×10^8 links. Rather, intermediate switching nodes are used. Designers have found it convenient to organize these nodes into a hierarchy or tree topology (Figure 8-23), consisting of five classes of switching centers or nodes [BELL77]:

- *Class 1:* regional center.
- *Class 2:* sectional center.
- *Class 3:* primary center.
- *Class 4:* toll center.
- *Class 5:* end office.

Subscribers connect directly to an end office, which must perform the same functions listed earlier for a PBX. The remaining centers simply serve the function of concentrating traffic so as to reduce transmission facility requirements.

The switching centers are linked together by *trunks*. These trunks are designed to carry multiple voice-frequency circuits using either FDM or synchronous TDM. These were referred to as carrier systems in Chapter 6, where they are described.

Two additional elements are needed to complete the picture. In addition to the five classes of switching centers listed above, the network is augmented with additional switching nodes called *tandem switches*. These are used to interconnect adjacent end offices as explained under Routing, below. Finally, PBX facilities connect to the network not via local loop but via trunk. Since the PBX services multiple subscribers, a multiplexed link is needed to the end office. Generally, this link has lower capacity than the total number of PBX subscribers, reflecting the fact that, at any given time, only a fraction of the subscribers will be engaged in external calls.

Routing

The structure depicted in Figure 8-23 was referred to as having a tree topology. Actually, it is a set of 10 trees, each rooted in a regional center. The 10 regional centers are meshed together (45 full-duplex links) to provide full connectivity. If this were the extent of the architecture, routing would be quite simple. Consider a request from one subscriber to establish a connection with another. The following rules would apply:

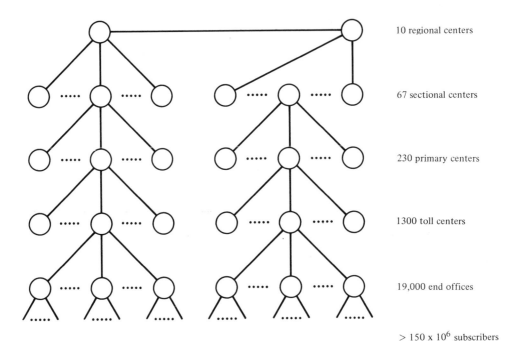

FIGURE 8-23. U.S. public circuit-switched network organization.

1. If both subscribers attach to the same end office, that end office makes the connection.
2. If (1) fails, the subscribers attach to different end offices. If those end offices attach to the same toll center, a connection is established between end offices via the toll center.

And so on. The search continues up the hierarchy until a common node is reached. If the two subscribers are under the aegis of different regional centers, the circuit will involve a trunk between regional centers, for a total of nine trunks in the path between the subscribers.

This architecture has several drawbacks. First, a tremendous amount of traffic must be carried at the upper levels of the hierarchy. Second, the loss or saturation of a single switching center decouples the network into isolated subnetworks. Finally, signal quality degrades as the number of switches and trunks increases (for analog transmission).

To compensate for these problems, a large number of *high-usage trunks* augment the basic architecture. High-usage trunks are used for direct connection between switching centers with high volumes of internode traffic. Traffic is always routed through the lowest available level of the network. Figure 8-24 shows the basic order of selection for alternate routes. The high-usage trunks are depicted as dashed lines, and the backbone hierarchical network as shown with solid lines.

Consider again two subscribers attached to different end offices. The calling subscriber's end office will determine if a direct trunk exists to the called end office. If not, or if that trunk is fully loaded, the call is routed up to a toll center. The toll center will try to find an available direct route to a center in the immediate hierarchy of the called end office. Failing that, the call is switched up to a primary

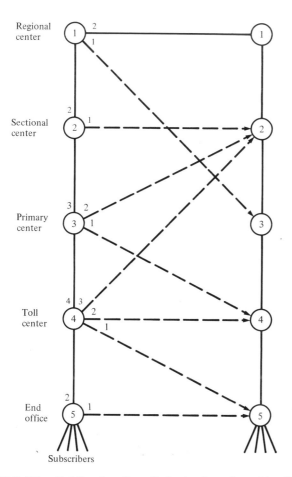

FIGURE 8-24. Public circuit-switched network routing (North America).

center, and so on. This process is dynamic and depends on the availability of high-usage trunks at the time the call is placed. Thus calls between two subscribers might follow different routes at different times. The routing algorithm is driven by the seven- or ten-digit telephone number, which uniquely identifies a subscriber and the centers in its direct hierarchy [FREE80].

The tandem switches mentioned above provide additional linkages between end offices that are closely located. Tandem switches are part of what is referred to as an *exchange area*. Typically, all calls within an exchange area are local calls (no long-distance charges).

8-6

RECOMMENDED READING

As befits its age, circuit switching has inspired a voluminous literature. Good recent books on the subject are [BELL82b], [HOBB81], and [INOS79]. The first of these is particularly lucid and comprehensive. Worthwhile accounts may also be found in [FREE80] and [DAVI73]. [BROO83] discusses alternative internal organizations for a switch.

[VONA80] describes and discusses port selection and port contention devices. [SCHO81] describes the switching statistical multiplexer. A general survey of digital data switching devices can be found in [KANE80a].

A very clear discussion of the PBX and CBX appears in [MART76, Chap. 22], which also describes a large list of features and services found in a modern CBX. A good recent paper is [GOEL83]. The architecture of a CBX is discussed in [KASS79b] and [JUNK83].

8-7

PROBLEMS

8-1 Demonstrate why there is a high probability of blocking in a two-stage switch such as Figure 8-10.

8-2 What is the magnitude of delay through a TSI stage?

8-3 In Figure 8-19, why is it not possible to route the digital data coming from the device directly to an outgoing trunk, where it will be converted to analog by the codec for transmission?

8-4 Assume that the velocity of propagation on a TDM bus is $0.7c$, its length is 10 m, and the data rate is 500 Mbps. How many bits should be transmitted in a time slot to achieve a bus efficiency of 99%?

8-5 Demonstrate that in a TSI data store, at most, only half of the memory is usefully occupied at any one time. Devise a means of reducing the TSI memory requirement while maintaining its nonblocking property.

8-6 Consider the use of a 500-ns memory in a TSI device. How many full-duplex voice channels can be supported, if the voice is encoded using PCM?

8-7 Determine the number of crosspoints and the total number of memory bits required for a TST switch defined as follows:

- Number of lines = 32.
- Single stage space switch.
- Number of channels per frame = 30.
- Time expansion = 2.

8-8 How many bits of memory are needed in a TSI unit for a 60-channel signal with nine bits per time slot?

8-9 Is the ITT switch nonblocking?

8-10 Consider a simple telephone network consisting of two end offices and one toll center with a 1-MHz full-duplex trunk between each end office and the toll center. The average telephone is used to make four calls per 8-hour workday, with a mean call duration of six minutes. Ten percent of the calls are long distance. What is the maximum number of telephones an end office can support?

CHAPTER 9

Packet Switching

In Chapter 7, we introduced the concept of packet switching, and the subordinate concepts of datagrams and virtual circuits. The purpose of this chapter is to explore in more detail the mechanisms by which packet-switched networks provide datagram and virtual-circuit services. The key elements of a packet switched network are these:

- *Routing:* Since the source and destination station are not directly connected, the network must route each packet, from node to node, through the network.
- *Traffic control:* The amount of traffic entering and transiting the network must be regulated for efficient, stable, and fair performance.
- *Error control:* Inevitably, packets will be lost in the network. Some networks ignore this contingency; most take measures to at least partially alleviate the suffering of the attached stations.

The behavior of a packet-switched network is amazingly complex. In this chapter we do not attempt a definitive treatment. Rather the key features in each of the areas above are presented, and the discussion is supported by examples from specific systems currently in operation. Four systems will be repeatedly used throughout the chapter. A discussion of these is presented first.

Throughout this chapter, examples will be given of the operation of various algorithms. Figure 9-1 is a simple instance of a packet-switched network that will be used for many of these examples.

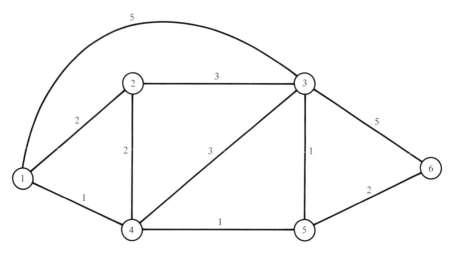

FIGURE 9-1. Example packet-switched network.

EXAMPLE SYSTEMS

Perhaps the clearest way to present the concepts and techniques of packet switching is by example. In this section we present an overview of four quite different packet-switched systems. The two best-documented communications networks are ARPANET/DDN and TYMNET. In addition, we present two commercially available computer network packages: IBM's SNA and DEC's DNA. These are not pure communications networks, but they are the most widely used computer systems for constructing user-controlled packet-switched networks.

ARPANET/DDN

The ARPA computer network (ARPANET) began under the sponsorship of the Advanced Research Projects Agency (ARPA) to study and demonstrate computer resource sharing [ROBE70, ROBE74]. By 1975, this network had many operational users and was no longer an experimental network, so responsibility for its operation transferred to the Defense Communications Agency. Today ARPANET is an operational network of many nodes and host computers and supports a large number of DOD and non-DOD projects. ARPANET has recently been split into an R&D network, which retains the name ARPANET, and the Defense Data Network (DDN), using the same technology on both. The DDN is designed to meet DOD needs for both a secure command and control communications network and for ordinary unclassified communications [WALK82, DCA82].

TYMNET

TYMNET was originally developed to provide cost-effective connection of terminals to central time-sharing computers [TYME71]. Both access and internode speeds were rather limited. As the system grew, higher data rates were provided and the system evolved into TYMNET II [KOPF77]. TYMNET II, although still terminal-oriented, provides a general-purpose packet-switched service for terminal-host and host-host transfers.

SNA

Both ARPANET and TYMNET originally became operational in 1969. Both are, in our terminology, communication networks that are independent of the attached hosts. As the technology of packet switching evolved, computer vendors realized that they could provide not only the endpoint computer functions, but the switching functions as well. The era of computer vendor-based network architectures began with the announcement in 1974 by IBM of its systems network architecture (SNA).

SNA was developed by IBM to protect its customer base and allow its customers to take advantage of new IBM offerings. The problem was that there was a proliferation of communications protocols and user access methods on IBM machines. Customers developed complex applications and were unable to easily incorporate new computers into their operation. Many of the communications techniques were inefficient and a flourishing business in front-end processors developed among minicomputer and communications vendors. These factors led to the development of a network architecture that would provide efficient user access to a network of computers. We will briefly return to SNA in the context of computer network architecture in Chapter 12. For now, we are only concerned with its packet-switching capability.

DNA

In 1975, Digital Equipment Corporation (DEC) announced its digital network architecture (DNA), whose original goals were quite different from those of SNA. SNA was originally concerned with providing uniform, efficient access to host-centered terminal networks. As a minicomputer manufacturer, DEC was concerned with resource sharing in a distributed environment. Thus DNA from the beginning was intended to provide decentralized and distributed networking capability.

9-2

VIRTUAL CIRCUITS AND DATAGRAMS

External and Internal Operation

One of the most important characteristics of a packet-switched network is whether it uses datagrams or virtual circuits. Actually, there are two levels or dimensions of this characteristic, as illustrated in Figure 9-2. At the interface between station and network node, a network may provide either a virtual circuit or datagram service. With a virtual-circuit interface, the user performs a call request to set up a virtual circuit and uses sequence numbers to exercise flow control and error control. The network attempts to deliver the packets in sequence. With datagram service, the network only agrees to handle packets independently. Internally, the network may actually construct a dedicated path between endpoints (virtual circuit) or not. These internal and external design decisions need not coincide:

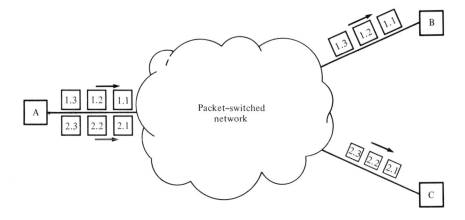

(a) External virtual circuit. A logical connection is set up between two stations. Packets are labeled with a virtual circuit number and a sequence number. Packets arrive in sequence.

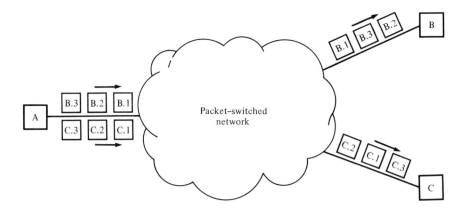

(b) External datagram. Each packet is transmitted independently. Packets are labeled with a destination address and may arrive out of sequence.

FIGURE 9-2. External and internal virtual circuits and datagrams.

- *External virtual circuit, internal virtual circuit:* When the user requests a virtual circuit a dedicated route through the network is constructed. All packets will follow that same route.
- *External virtual circuit, internal datagram:* The network handles each packet separately. Thus different packets for the same virtual circuit may take different routes. However, the network endeavors to deliver packets to the destination in sequence. Typically, the network will buffer packets at the destination node so that they may be ordered properly for delivery.
- *External datagram, internal datagram:* Each packet is treated independently from both the user's and the network's point of view.
- *External datagram, internal virtual circuit:* This combination makes little sense,

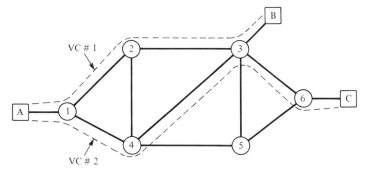

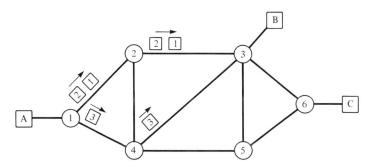

(c) Internal virtual circuit. A route for packets between two stations is defined and labeled. All packets for that virtual circuit follow the same route and arrive in sequence.

(d) Internal datagram. Each packet is treated independently by the network. Packets are labeled with a destination address and may arrive at the destination node out of sequence.

FIGURE 9-2. (continued)

since one incurs the cost of a virtual circuit implementation but gets none of the benefits.

The question arises as to the choice of virtual circuits or datagrams, both internally and externally. This will depend on the specific design objective of the communication network and the cost factors that prevail. So here we offer only a few general comments.

First, consider internal datagram and virtual circuit mechanisms. A major advantage of a datagram mechanism is its robustness and flexibility. If nodes or links in the network are unavailable, datagrams can be routed around the affected area. On the other hand the loss of a node or link could destroy some virtual circuits. Similarly, the datagram mechanism can react more quickly to congestion by making routing decisions on a per-packet basis. With virtual circuits, routing decisions are usually made only at setup time. Of course, virtual circuit routes can be changed dynamically at the cost of processing overhead. An advantage of the virtual circuit mechanism is that it minimizes per-packet overhead; routing decisions need only be made once per virtual circuit. Also, internal virtual circuits provide sequenced delivery, which is an asset if the external service is virtual circuit.

With respect to the external service, the following observations apply. The datagram service allows for efficient use of the network: no call setup or disconnection, and no need to hold up packets while a packet in error is retransmitted. This latter

TABLE 9-1 Virtual Circuit and Datagram Implementations

| | | Internal Operation | |
		Datagram	Virtual Circuit
External Service	**Datagram**	DNA ARPANET (packet)	—
	Virtual Circuit	ARPANET (message, packet)	TYMNET (packet multiplexing) SNA (virtual and explicit routes)

feature is desirable in some real-time applications. The virtual circuit service can provide end-to-end sequencing, flow control, and error control. However, in many cases, these services are provided by a higher-layer protocol and need not be duplicated by the network service.

Again, depending on circumstances, any of the three combinations listed above may be the most appropriate and all have been used. Table 9-1 compares the four example networks in terms of these combinations.

The discussion in Chapter 7 and the treatment in this chapter are concerned with the internal operation of the network. How the network appears to an attached station is determined by the network access protocol that is used. Such protocols will be discussed in Chapter 13.

Example Systems

ARPANET. Externally, ARPANET offers both datagram and virtual circuit service. When datagram service is used, the attached station (called a host) may transmit packets containing up to 991 bits of data to its local node (called an interface message processor or IMP). The node routes this packet through the network to its destination with no guarantee of delivery or of maintaining sequencing. Using the virtual circuit service, a host may establish a connection with another host and then send a sequence of messages, each containing up to 8063 bits of data. ARPANET guarantees that it will deliver all messages and that they will be delivered in sequence.

Internally, ARPANET functions as a datagram network with an unusual two-level structure. For the datagram service, the network simply treats each incoming datagram independently. For the virtual circuit service, when a message is received by a node for transmission, the message is broken up into as many as eight packets, each containing a maximum of 1008 user data bits. These packets are treated internally as datagrams and are routed independently to the node of the destination station. At the destination node, the packets are buffered until all of the packets of a single message arrive. They are then reassembled into a message and delivered to the destination host. This seemingly curious technique facilitates an effective form of traffic control, as explained below.

TYMNET. TYMNET uses virtual circuits both internally and externally, based on a technique that might be called *packet multiplexing* [RIND79a]. In essence, TYMNET views each station as a source of a character stream rather than a packet stream. As data come in from a station to a local node, they are buffered and then sent along a fixed route to the destination. The amount of data that is packetized for node-to-node hops is variable. Thus an initial burst of data may become spread out across several nodes in transit. Alternatively, characters that are transmitted later by a station may catch up with earlier characters in the network and end up exiting as a block at the destination. Furthermore, a single packet transmitted between two nodes may contain data for more than one virtual circuit.

To support virtual circuits, each node is equipped with a buffer pool, and a number of index vectors, two for each link to an adjacent node. Each of these links supports a fixed number of channels, using a statistical TDM protocol. We use the following notation:

$$R_n(l,c) = \text{read vector of node } n \text{ for channel } c \text{ of link } l$$
$$W_n(l,c) = \text{write vector of node } n \text{ for channel } c \text{ of link } l$$

Figure 9-3 illustrates the use of these vectors to construct a virtual circuit between a terminal attached to node 1000 and a host attached to node 5. When the virtual circuit is constructed, buffer space is allocated in each node along the route and a channel between each pair of these nodes is dedicated to that circuit. Figure 9-3 illustrates the buffers and the write vectors. Data from the terminal are stored in buffer 4 of node 1000. The node has $R_{1000}(112,2)$ set to 4. Thus the node will read data from buffer 4 to transmit on channel 2 to node 112. At node 112, $W_{112}(1000,2) = 200$. This instructs the node to store data on channel 2 from node 1000 in buffer 200. These data are subsequently transmitted to node 5 on channel 1. Finally, the data are directed to buffer 8 of node 5, which is dedicated to output to the attached host.

The assignment of buffers and channels to a virtual circuit is done by a central node, the supervisor. Details are provided below. Note that in this scheme, it is not necessary for the nodes to have knowledge of the overall virtual circuit. They merely need to keep track of local buffer/channel assignments.

Data are transmitted between links in frames, using the format of Figure 9-4.

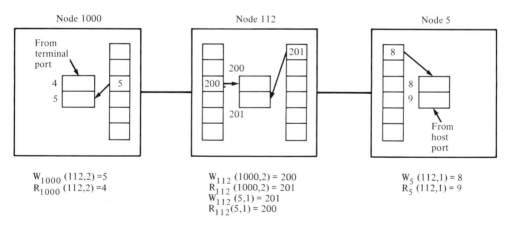

$$W_{1000}(112,2) = 5$$
$$R_{1000}(112,2) = 4$$

$$W_{112}(1000,2) = 200$$
$$R_{112}(1000,2) = 201$$
$$W_{112}(5,1) = 201$$
$$R_{112}(5,1) = 200$$

$$W_5(112,1) = 8$$
$$R_5(112,1) = 9$$

FIGURE 9-3. A virtual circuit in TYMNET.

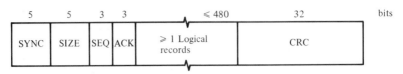

5	5	3	3	≤ 480	32	bits
SYNC	SIZE	SEQ	ACK	≥ 1 Logical records	CRC	

(a) Physical record (frame)

8	8	≤ 464
Channel number	Byte count	Data

(b) Logical record (packet)

FIGURE 9-4. TYMNET internode frame format.

Transmission is done via a character-oriented synchronous protocol, using 3-bit sequence numbers and acknowledgments. Each frame contains one or more packets of data, and each packet contains data for one channel. Note the similarity between Figures 9-4 and 6-13; the internode communication is clearly a form of statistical TDM. Each physical record is formed by picking up data from various channels using the read vector. At the receiving end, the record is unpacked and data are stored in buffers as dictated by the write vector. Note that these data, all of which came in on one link, may now fan out to various links based on the virtual circuit routing. This technique is very similar to that of the switching statistical multiplexer discussed in the preceding chapter. The strength of this technique, in terms of routing and traffic control, will become evident in due course.

SNA.   Initially, SNA was structured with a host-centered, host-controlled philosophy, but it is gradually evolving toward a more flexible approach tailored to true distributed systems [CYPS78]. Figure 9-5 presents those aspects of SNA relevant to the present discussion. The communication network is formed by *subarea nodes*, each of which may be a host or a communications controller. *Peripheral nodes*, such as terminals and terminal concentrators, attach to subarea nodes. The link between adjacent subarea nodes consists of one or more transmission groups. A *transmission group* is either a single physical link or multiple links used for parallel transmission. SNA provides a virtual-circuit service using a two-level internal virtual-circuit implementation. Between each pair of subarea nodes, a number of *explicit routes* are predefined. Each route consists of a sequence of transmission groups forming a path between the two nodes. A *virtual route* is simply a source-destination node pair assigned dynamically to an explicit route. The details are provided below, in the discussion of routing.

Note that in Figure 9-5, the identities of nodes and stations have merged. Each subarea node is a communications node capable of performing switching. It may also be a network station that supports users or applications that use the network.

DNA.   Unlike SNA, DNA does not distinguish node types with respect to the network [WECK80]. The network has no inherent notion of a separate communication network. Each node may perform both switching functions and applications functions. The service provided is datagram, using datagrams internally.

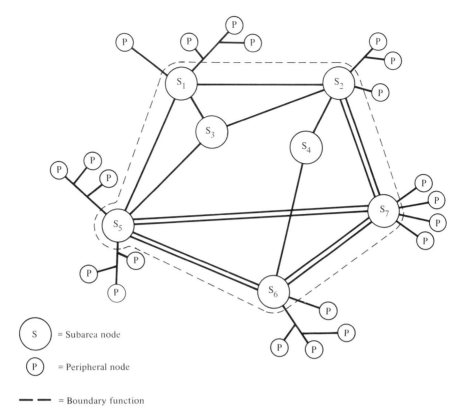

FIGURE 9-5. An example SNA network configuration.

ROUTING

In Chapter 8 we discussed the function of routing in a circuit-switched tele-communications network. Because of the hierarchical topology of the network and the numbering scheme used, this function was easily explained. With packet-switched networks, the routing function is both more complex and more difficult to explain. The chief reason for this is the relatively undifferentiated nature of the network. Packet-switched networks tend to be flat rather than hierarchical, having a number of alternative routes between endpoints, with no obvious preferred routes. This section will highlight the major elements of the routing function and give examples. The interested reader may pursue the topic in several survey articles [SCHW80, RUDI76], and in specific chapters on the subject in a number of books [ROSN82, GERL81, MART81, TANE81a, DAVI79, CYPS78].

Characteristics

The primary function of a packet-switched network is to accept packets from a source station and deliver them to a destination station. To accomplish this, a path or route through the network must be selected; generally, more than one route is possible. Thus a routing function must be performed. [TANE81a] suggests a number of desirable attributes of the routing function: correctness, simplicity, robustness, stability, fairness, and optimality. To this one might also add efficiency.

The first two items on the list are self-explanatory. Robustness has to do with the ability of the network to deliver packets via some route in the face of localized failures and overloads. Ideally, the network can react to such contingencies without loss of packets or the breaking of virtual circuits. The designer who seeks robustness must cope with the competing claims for stability. Techniques that react to changing conditions have an unfortunate tendency to either react too slowly to events or to experience unstable swings from one extreme to another. For example, the network may react to congestion in one area by shifting most of the load to a second area. Now the second area is overloaded and the first is underutilized, causing a second shift. During these shifts, packets may travel in loops through the network.

A trade-off also exists between fairness and optimality. Some performance criteria may favor the exchange of packets between nearby stations and discourage the exchange between distant stations. This policy will appear unfair to the station which primarily needs to communicate with distant stations. Finally, any routing technique involves some processing overhead at each node and often a transmission overhead as well. The penalty of such overhead needs to be less than the benefit accrued based on some reasonable metric, such as increased robustness or fairness.

With these attributes in mind, we turn to the techniques of routing that can be employed. Table 9-2 lists the elements or dimensions of the routing task. These elements are not completely orthogonal and may not even encompass all aspects of this complex problem. Nevertheless, they serve to clarify and organize routing concepts. First, we comment briefly on each of these dimensions; several are then explored in detail.

The selection of a route is generally based on some *performance criterion*. The simplest criterion is to choose the "shortest" route (one that passes through the least number of nodes) through the network. This results in the least number of hops per packet (one hop = traversal of one node-to-node link). A generalization

TABLE 9-2   Elements of Routing Techniques

Performance criterion	Network information source
Number of hops	None
Cost	Local
Delay	Adjacent nodes
Throughput	Nodes along route
Decision time	All nodes
Packet (datagram)	Routing strategy
Session (virtual circuit)	Fixed
Decision place	Flooding
Each node (distributed)	Random
Central node (centralized)	Adaptive
Originating node	Adaptive routing update time
	Continuous
	Periodic
	Major load change
	Topology change

of the shortest-route criterion is least-cost routing. In this case, a cost is associated with each link, and the route through the network that accumulates the least cost is sought. For example, the costs in the network of Figure 9-1 are shown as numeric labels on the links. The shortest path from node 1 to node 6 is 1-3-6, but the least cost path is 1-4-5-6. The cost assignment is intended to support one or more design objectives. For example, the cost could be related to the capacity of the link (i.e., the higher the capacity, the lower the cost), or the current queueing delay to use the link. In the first case, the least-cost route should provide the highest throughput. In the second case, the least-cost route should minimize delay.

So, to deliver a packet from one station to another, a routing decision is made based on some performance criterion. Key characteristics of this decision are the time and place of the decision. The *decision time* is either at the packet or virtual-circuit level. When the internal operation of the network is datagram, a routing decision is made individually for each packet. For internal virtual-circuit operation, a routing decision is made at the time that the circuit is established. All subsequent packets using that virtual circuit follow the same route. Note that we are here talking about an internal virtual circuit. For some networks, the routing strategy permits the route of individual packets of an external virtual circuit to vary. This is the case when the network uses datagrams internally but provides an external virtual circuit.

The *decision place* also varies among networks. In some networks, each node has the responsibility of selecting an output link for routing packets as they arrive (distributed routing). The principal alternative is for the routing decision to be made by a central node, such as a network control center (centralized routing). The danger of the latter approach is that the loss of the network control center may block the operation of the network. The distributed approach is perhaps more complex, but is also more robust. An infrequently used alternative is for the originating node to select the route (source node routing). Observe that the decision time and decision place are independent. Again referring to Figure 9-1, suppose that the decision place is each node and that the values depicted are the costs at a given instant in time; the costs may change. If a packet is to be delivered from node 1 to node 6, it might follow the route 1-4-5-6, with each leg of the route determined locally by the transmitting node. Now suppose that the values change such that 1-4-5-6 is no longer the optimum route. In a datagram network, the next packet may follow a different route, again determined by each node along the way. In a virtual circuit network, each node will remember the routing decision that was made when the virtual circuit was established, and simply pass on the packets without making a new decision.

The next element of routing, *network information source*, depends on the performance criterion, decision place, and routing strategy. It is nevertheless worth calling out separately. The information referred to is information about the topology of the network, traffic load, and cost. Surprisingly, some strategies use no information at all and yet manage to get packets through; flooding and some random strategies (discussed below) are in this category. With distributed routing (decision place = each node), the individual node may make use of only local information, such as the cost of each outgoing link or the queue size for each outgoing link. The node might also collect information from adjacent nodes. Finally, there are algorithms that allow the node to gain information from all nodes on any potential route of interest. Examples of all these are provided below. With centralized routing, the central node may use information obtained from all nodes. As you might expect, the more information used, the more likely the network is to make good routing decisions. On the other hand, the transmission of that information consumes network resources.

A related concept is that of information update time, which is a function of both the information source and the routing strategy. Clearly, if no information is used, there is no update. If the only information used is local, the update is essentially continuous. That is, the local node always knows the current local conditions. For all other information source categories (adjacent nodes, nodes along route, all nodes), the update time is a function of the routing strategy. For a fixed strategy, the information is never updated, except when there is a topology change. For an adaptive strategy, information update time is expressed as an *adaptive routing update time*, as described below. Again, you should expect that increased frequency of update improves the routing decision at the expense of increased overhead.

Finally, a large number of *routing strategies* have evolved. These are discussed below, after an explanation of least-cost routing algorithms.

Least-Cost Algorithms

Virtually all packet-switched networks base their routing decision on some form of least-cost criterion. If the criterion is to minimize the number of hops, each link has a value of 1. More typically, the link value is inversely proportional to the link capacity, proportional to the current load on the link, or some combination. In any case, the assignment of value is of no concern to the *least-cost routing algorithm*, which can be simply stated as:

> Given a network of nodes connected by bidirectional links, where each link has a cost associated with it in each direction, define the cost of a path between two nodes as the sum of the costs of the links traversed. For each pair of nodes find the path with least cost.

Note that the cost of a link may differ in the two directions. This would be true, for example, if the cost of the link equaled the length of the queue of packets awaiting transmission from each of the two nodes on the link. In what follows, we assume for simplicity that the cost of a link is the same in each direction.

Most least-cost routing algorithms in use in packet-switched networks are variants of one of two common algorithms which we will refer to as the forward-search and backward-search algorithms [SCHW80]. These algorithms are defined in this section. Later sections show their application in a variety of routing strategies.

The *forward-search algorithm*, due to Dijkstra [DIJK59] can be stated as: Find the least-cost path from a given source node to all other nodes. The algorithm proceeds in stages. By the kth stage, the shortest paths to the k nodes closest to (least cost away from) the source node have been determined; these nodes are in a set M. At the $(k + 1)$st stage, that node not in M that has the shortest path from the source is added to M. As nodes are added to M, their path from the source is defined. The algorithm can be formally defined as follows. Define:

N = set of nodes in the network
S = source node
M = set of nodes so far incorporated by the algorithm
$l(i,j)$ = link cost from node i to node j; the cost is ∞ if the nodes are not directly connected

TABLE 9-3 Example of Least-Cost Routing Algorithms (using Figure 9-1)

(a) Forward-Search Algorithm ($S = 1$)

Iteration	M	$C_1(2)$, Path		$C_1(3)$, Path		$C_1(4)$, Path		$C_1(5)$, Path		$C_1(6)$, Path	
1	{1}	2	1-2	5	1-3	1	1-4	∞	—	∞	—
2	{1, 4}	2	1-2	4	1-4-3	1	1-4	2	1-4-5	∞	—
3	{1, 2, 4}	2	1-2	4	1-4-3	1	1-4	2	1-4-5	∞	—
4	{1, 2, 4, 5}	2	1-2	3	1-4-5-3	1	1-4	2	1-4-5	4	1-4-5-6
5	{1, 2, 3, 4, 5}	2	1-2	3	1-4-5-3	1	1-4	2	1-4-5	4	1-4-5-6
6	{1, 2, 3, 4, 5, 6}	2	1-2	3	1-4-5-3	1	1-4	2	1-4-5	4	1-4-5-6

(b) Backward-Search Algorithm ($D = 1$)

Iteration	$C_2(2)$, Path		$C_2(3)$, Path		$C_2(4)$, Path		$C_2(5)$, Path		$C_2(6)$, Path	
1	∞		∞		∞	—	∞	—	∞	—
2	2	2-1	5	3-1	1	4-1	2	5-4-1	4	6-5-4-1
3	2	2-1	3	3-5-4-1	1	4-1	2	5-4-1	4	6-5-4-1
4	2	2-1	3	3-5-4-1	1	4-1	2	5-4-1	4	6-5-4-1

$C_1(n)$ = cost of the least cost path from S to n that is currently known to the algorithm

The algorithm has three steps:

1. Set $M = \{S\}$. For each node $n \in N - S$, set $C_1(n) = l(S,n)$
2. Find $W \in N - M$ such that $C_1(W)$ is minimum and add to M. Then set $C_1(n) = \text{MIN}[C_1(n), C_1(W) + l(W,n)]$ for each node $n \in N - M$. If the latter term is minimum, the path from S to n is now the path from S to W concatenated with the link from W to n.
3. Repeat step 2 until $M = N$.

Table 9-3a shows the result of applying this algorithm to Figure 9-1, using $S = 1$. Note that at each step the total cost plus the path is generated for each destination node. After the final iteration, the least-cost path to each node and the cost of that path has been developed. The same procedure can be used with node 2 as source node, and so on.

The *backward-search algorithm*, presented in [FORD62] can be stated as: Find the least-cost path to a given destination node from all other nodes. This algorithm also proceeds in stages. At each stage, the algorithm considers each node, other than the destination node, in turn. For each node a path and a cost to the destination node has been defined (initially a null path with infinite cost). The algorithm determines if a lower-cost path can be constructed by changing the first hop. This process is repeated until there are no changes during one stage. The algorithm can be formally defined as follows. Define:

N = set of nodes in the network
D = destination node
$l(i,j)$ = as above
$C_2(n)$ = cost of least-cost path from n to D that is currently known to the algorithm

The algorithm has three steps:

1. Set $C_2(D) = 0$. For each node $n \in N - D$, set $C_2(n) = \infty$.
2. For each node $n \in N - D$, set $C_2(n) = $ MIN $W \in N$ $[C_2(n), C_2(W) + l(n,W)]$. If the latter term is the minimum, then the path from n to D is now the link from n to W concatenated with the path from W to D.
3. Repeat step 2 until none of the costs change.

Table 9-3b shows the result of applying this algorithm to Figure 9-1, using $D = 1$. At each step, the total cost plus the path is generated from each source node. After the final iteration, the least-cost path from each node and the cost of that path has been developed. Note that the results agree with the forward-search algorithm.

Several points of comparison can be made. The forward-search algorithm seems better suited to centralized routing and the backward-search to distributed routing. Consider that, in the case of the backward-search algorithm, each node n maintains a set of costs $C_2(n)$ and associated paths, one for each destination. Suppose further that this information is exchanged with its neighbors from time to time. Each node can therefore use the expression in step 2 of the backward-search algorithm, based only on information from its neighbors, to update its costs and paths. This simple procedure is not as easily implemented with the forward-search algorithm.

Evaluation of the relative merits of the two algorithms should be done with respect to the desirable attributes listed earlier. The evaluation will depend on the implementation approach, as indicated by the various categories in Table 9-1, and the specific implementation.

Finally, we note that these algorithms are known to converge under static conditions of topology and link costs and will converge to the same solution. If the link costs change over time, the algorithm will attempt to catch up with these changes. However, if the link cost depends on traffic, which in turn depends on the routes chosen, then a feedback situation exists, and instabilities may result.

Routing Strategies

Fixed Routing. One of the simplest routing strategies is fixed routing. In this case, a route is selected for each source-destination pair of nodes in the network. Either of the least-cost routing algorithms described above could be used. The routes are fixed, or at least only change when there is a change in the topology of the network. Thus the costs used in designing routes cannot be based on any dynamic variable such as traffic. It could, however, be based on cost or expected traffic.

Figure 9-6 suggests how fixed routing might be implemented. A central routing directory is created, to be stored perhaps at a network control center. Note that it is not necessary to store the route for each possible pair of nodes. Rather, it is sufficient to know, for each pair of nodes, the identity of the first node on the route. To see this, consider that the least-cost route from X to Y begins with the X-A link. Call the remainder of the route, which is the part from A to Y, R_1. Call the least-cost route for A to Y, R_2. Now, if the cost of R_1 is greater than R_2, then the X-Y route can be improved by using R_2 instead. If the cost of R_1 is less than R_2, then R_2 is not the least-cost route from A to Y. Thus, at each point along a route, it is only necessary to know the identity of the next node, not the entire

CENTRAL ROUTING DIRECTORY

To Node

From Node	1	2	3	4	5	6
1	–	2	4	4	4	4
2	1	–	3	4	4	4
3	5	2	–	5	5	5
4	1	2	5	–	5	5
5	4	4	3	4	–	6
6	5	5	5	5	5	–

Node 1 Directory

Destination	Next node
2	2
3	4
4	4
5	4
6	4

Node 2 Directory

Destination	Next node
1	1
3	3
4	4
5	4
6	4

Node 3 Directory

Destination	Next node
1	5
2	2
4	5
5	5
6	5

Node 4 Directory

Destination	Next node
1	1
2	2
3	5
5	5
6	5

Node 5 Directory

Destination	Next node
1	4
2	4
3	3
4	4
6	6

Node 6 Directory

Destination	Next node
1	5
2	5
3	5
4	5
5	5

FIGURE 9-6. Fixed routing (using Fig. 9-1).

route. Because of this, each node need only store a single row of the routing directory. The node's directory shows the next node to take for each destination.

With fixed routing, there is no difference between routing for datagrams and virtual circuits. All packets from a given source to a given destination follow the same route. The advantage of fixed routing is its simplicity, and it should work well in a reliable network with a steady load. Its disadvantage is its lack of flexibility. It does not react to network congestion or failures.

A refinement to fixed routing that would accommodate link and node outages would be to supply the nodes with an alternate next node for each direction. For example, the alternate next nodes in the node 1 directory might be 4, 3, 2, 3, 3.

Flooding. Another simple routing technique is flooding. This technique requires no network information whatsoever, and works as follows. A packet is sent by a source node to every one of its neighbors. At each node, an incoming packet is retransmitted on all outgoing links except for the link that it arrived from. Again as an example, consider Figure 9-1. If node 1 has a packet to send to node 6, it sends a copy of that packet to nodes 2, 3, and 4. Node 2 will send a copy to nodes 3 and 4. Node 4 will send a copy to nodes 2, 3, and 5. And so it goes. Eventually, a number of copies of the packet will arrive at node 6. The packet must have some unique identifier (e.g. source node, sequence number; or virtual circuit number, sequence number) so that node 6 knows to discard all but the first copy.

It is clear that unless something is done to stop the incessant retransmission of packets, the number of packets in circulation just from a single source packet grows

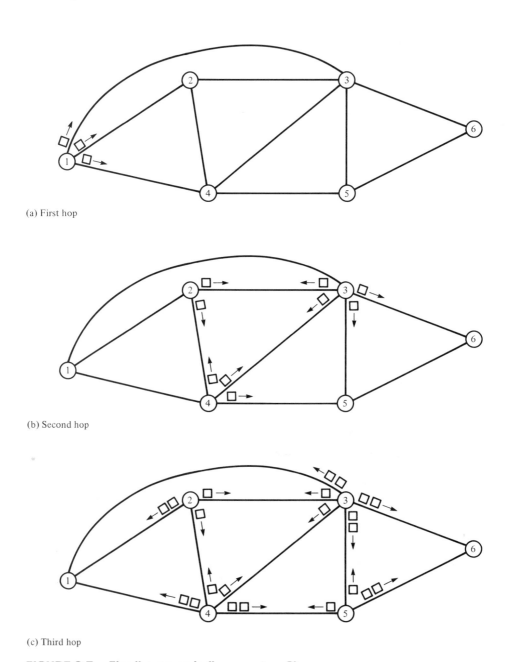

(a) First hop

(b) Second hop

(c) Third hop

FIGURE 9-7. Flooding example (hop count = 3).

without bound. One way to prevent this is for each node to remember the identity of those packets it has already retransmitted. When duplicate copies of the packet arrive, they are discarded. A simpler technique is to include a hop count field with each packet. The count can be originally set to some maximum value, such as the ''diameter'' of the network. Each time a node passes on a packet, it decrements the count by one. When the count reaches zero, the packet is discarded.

An example of this latter tactic is shown in Figure 9-7. Again, assume that a packet is to be sent from node 1 to node 6. On the first hop, three copies of the packet are created. For the second hop of all these copies, a total of nine copies are created. One of these copies reaches node 6, which absorbs it and does not retransmit. However, the other nodes generate a total of 22 new copies for their third and final hop. Note that if a node is not keeping track of packet identifiers, it may generate multiple copies at this third stage. After the third hop is completed, all packets are destroyed. Node 6 has received four additional copies of the packet.

The flooding technique has two remarkable properties:

- All possible routes between source and destination are tried. Thus, no matter what link or node outages have occurred, a packet will always get through as long as at least one path between source and destination exists.
- Because all routes are tried, at least one copy of the packet to arrive at the destination will have used a minimum-hop route.

Because of the first property, the flooding technique is highly robust and could be used to send high-priority messages. An example application is a military network that is subject to extensive damage. Because of the second property, flooding might be used to initially set up the route for a virtual circuit. On the other hand, the principal disadvantage of flooding is the total traffic load that it generates, which is directly proportional to the connectivity of the network. This increased load will increase delay for all subsequent traffic if the network load is nontrivial.

Random Routing. Random routing has the simplicity and robustness of flooding with far less traffic load. With random routing, a node selects only one outgoing path for retransmission of an incoming packet. The outgoing link is chosen at random, generally excluding the link on which the packet arrived. If all links are equally likely to be chosen, then a simple implementation is for a node to utilize outgoing links in a round-robin fashion.

A refinement of this technique is to assign a probability to each outgoing link and to select the link based on that probability. The probability could be based on data rate, in which case we have

$$P_i = \frac{R_i}{\Sigma_j R_j}$$

where

P_i = probability of selecting i

R_j = data rate on link j

The sum is taken over all candidate outgoing links. This scheme should provide good traffic distribution. The probabilities could also be based on fixed link costs.

Like flooding, random routing requires the use of no network information. Because the route taken is a random one, the actual route will typically not be the least-cost route nor the minimum hop-count route. Thus the network must carry a higher than optimal traffic load, although not nearly as high as for flooding. Because of the unpredictability of the delay in delivering packets and the increased traffic load, random routing is not in common use.

Adaptive Routing. The routing strategies discussed so far do not react to changing conditions within the network, or at most react infrequently as the result of some system operator action. This characteristic is not necessarily a bad one. Consider these drawbacks of an adaptive strategy:

- The routing decision is more complex; therefore, the processing burden on the network increases.
- In most cases, adaptive strategies depend on status information that is collected at one place but used at another; therefore, the traffic burden on the network increases.
- An adaptive strategy may react too quickly, causing congestion-producing oscillation, or too slowly, being irrelevant.

Despite these real dangers, adaptive routing strategies are by far the most prevalent, for two reasons:

- An adaptive routing strategy can improve performance as seen by the network user.
- An adaptive strategy can aid in traffic control, discussed later.

These benefits may or may not be realized, depending on the soundness of design and the nature of the load. By and large, it is an extraordinarily complex task to perform properly. Proof of this is seen in the fact that our two example communication networks, ARPANET and TYMNET, have both endured major overhauls of their routing strategy. In the former case the change was largely made to correct design flaws; in the latter it was to adapt to a changing traffic mix.

Adaptive routing strategies can be characterized by the fact that they adapt to measurable changing conditions and by the other elements listed in Table 9-2. Those elements that serve most directly to differentiate the various strategies are the decision place and the network information source. Based on those two parameters, virtually all strategies are in one or a hybrid combination of the following categories:

- *Isolated adaptive:* local information, distributed control.
- *Distributed adaptive:* information from adjacent nodes, distributed control.
- *Centralized adaptive:* information from all nodes, centralized control.

A simple isolated adaptive scheme is for a node to route each packet to the outgoing link with the shortest queue length, Q. This would have the effect of balancing the load on outgoing links. However, outgoing paths may not be headed in the correct general direction. An improvement can be obtained by also taking into account preferred directions, much as with random routing. In this case, each link emanating from the node would have a bias B_i for each destination i. For each incoming packet headed for node i, the node would choose the outgoing link that minimizes $Q + B_i$. Thus a node would tend to send packets in the right direction, with a concession made to current traffic delays.

As an example, Figure 9-8 shows the status of node 4 of Figure 9-1 at a certain point in time. Node 4 has links to four other nodes. A fair number of packets have been arriving and a backlog has built up, with a queue of packets waiting for each of the outgoing links. A packet arrives from node 1 destined for node 6. Question:

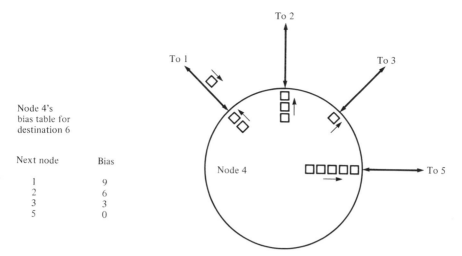

Node 4's
bias table for
destination 6

Next node	Bias
1	9
2	6
3	3
5	0

FIGURE 9-8. Example of isolated adaptive routing.

To which outgoing link should the packet be routed? Based on current queue lengths and the values of bias (B_6) for each outgoing link, the minimum value of $Q + B_6$ is four, on the link to node 3. Thus the packet is routed through node 3.

Isolated adaptive schemes are not in general use since they make little use of available information. The other two adaptive strategies are commonly found. Both take advantage of the information that each node has about the delays and outages that it experiences. In the distributed adaptive case, each node exchanges this delay information with other nodes. Based on this incoming information, a node tries to estimate the delay situation throughout the network, and applies one of the routing algorithms discussed earlier. In the case of a centralized adaptive algorithm, each node reports its information to a central node, which designs routes based on this incoming information and sends the routing information back to the nodes. In the next section we examine several examples of each approach.

Example Systems

Let us now examine the routing techniques used in the four example networks introduced earlier. Table 9-4 summarizes key characteristics of each approach.

ARPANET. The ARPANET routing algorithm is in its second generation. It is instructive to describe both algorithms. The original routing algorithm was a distributed adaptive algorithm using estimated delay as the performance criterion and a version of the backward-search algorithm. For this algorithm, each node maintains two vectors:

$$D_i = \begin{bmatrix} d_{i1} \\ \cdot \\ \cdot \\ \cdot \\ d_{iN} \end{bmatrix} \qquad S_i = \begin{bmatrix} s_{i1} \\ \cdot \\ \cdot \\ \cdot \\ s_{iN} \end{bmatrix}$$

TABLE 9-4 Routing Techniques for Some Networks

	Original ARPANET	Revised ARPANET	TYMNET I	TYMNET II	SNA	DNA
Performance criterion	Delay	Delay	Data rate, overload	Data rate, load, link and traffic types	User-defined	User-defined
Decision time	Packet	Packet	Session	Session	Session	Packet
Decision place	Each node	Each node	Central node	Central node	Originating node	Each node
Information source	Adjacent nodes	All nodes	All nodes	All nodes	User-defined	Adjacent nodes
Routing strategy	Adaptive	Adaptive	Adaptive	Adaptive	User-defined	Adaptive
Update time	Periodic	Periodic	Load change	Load change	Topology change	Topology change
Routing algorithm	Backward-search	Forward-search	Backward-search	Forward-search	User-defined	Backward-search

where

D_i = delay vector for node i

d_{ij} = current estimate of minimum delay from node i to node j ($d_{ii} = 0$)

N = number of nodes in the network

S_i = successor node vector for node i

s_{ij} = the next node in the current minimum-delay route from i to j

Periodically (every 128 ms), each node exchanges its delay vector with all of its neighbors. On the basis of all incoming delay vectors, a node k updates both of its vectors as follows:

$$d_{kj} = \text{Min } i \in A \ [d_{i,j} + l_{ki}]$$
$$s_{kj} = i \quad \text{using } i \text{ that minimizes the expression above}$$

where

A = set of neighbor nodes for k

l_{ki} = current estimate of delay from k to i

Figure 9-9 provides an example of the original ARPANET algorithm, again using Figure 9-1 as the network. Figure 9-9a shows the routing table for node 1 at a given instant in time. For each destination, a delay is specified, and the next node on the route that produces that delay. At some point, new delay vectors arrive from each of node 1's neighbors. Node 1 now discards its current routing table and builds a new one, based solely on the incoming delay vectors and its own estimate of link delay to each of its neighbors. The result is shown in Figure 9-9c.

The estimated link delay is simply the queue length for that link. Thus in building a new routing table, the node will tend to favor outgoing links with shorter queues. This tends to balance the load on outgoing links. However, because queue lengths vary rapidly with time, the distributed perception of the shortest route could change while a packet is en route. This could lead to a thrashing situation in which a packet continues to seek out areas of low congestion rather than aiming at the destination.

Desti-nation | Delay | Next Node

(a) Node 1's routing table before update

Destination	Delay	Next Node
1	0	–
2	2	2
3	5	3
4	1	4
5	6	3
6	8	3

D_1 S_1

(b) Delay vectors sent to node 1 from neighbor nodes

D_2	D_3	D_4
2	3	1
0	3	2
3	0	2
2	2	0
3	1	1
5	3	3

(c) Node is routing table after update and link costs used in update

Destination	Delay	Next Node
1	0	–
2	2	2
3	3	4
4	1	4
5	2	4
6	4	4

$i_{1,2} = 2$

$i_{1,3} = 5$

$i_{1,4} = 1$

FIGURE 9-9. Original ARPANET routing algorithm.

After some years of experience and several minor modifications, the original routing algorithm was replaced by a quite different one [MCQU80]. The major shortcomings of the old algorithm were these:

- The algorithm did not consider line speed, merely queue length. Thus higher-capacity links were not given the favored status they deserved.
- Queue length is, in any case, an artificial measure of delay, since some variable amount of processing time elapses between the arrival of a packet at a node and its placement in an outbound queue.
- The algorithm was not very accurate. In particular, it responded slowly to congestion and delay increases.

The new algorithm is also a distributed adaptive one, using delay as the performance criterion, but the differences are significant. Rather than using queue length as a surrogate for delay, the delay is measured directly. At a node, each incoming packet is timestamped with an arrival time. A departure time is recorded when the packet is transmitted. If a positive acknowledgment is returned, the delay for that packet is recorded as the departure time minus the arrival time plus transmission time and propagation delay. The node must therefore know link data rate and propagation time. If a negative acknowledgment comes back, the departure time is updated and the node tries again, until a measure of successful transmission delay is obtained.

Every 10 s, the node computes the average delay on each outgoing link. If there are any significant changes in delay, the information is sent to all other nodes using flooding. Each node maintains an estimate of delay on every network link. When new information arrives, it recomputes its routing table using the forward-search algorithm.

Experience with this new strategy indicates that it is more responsive and stable than the old one. The overhead induced by flooding is moderate since each node does this at most once every 10 s.

TYMNET Routing. As with ARPANET, the TYMNET routing algorithm has gone through two major versions. The first version [RIND77, RAJA78], used with TYMNET I, made use of a simple cost allocation based on link capacity and load. The cost table is depicted in Table 9-5. With each link, a fixed cost is associated that is a decreasing function of the data rate of the link. If the link is overloaded in one direction, a penalty cost of 16 is added; if it is overloaded in both directions, a penalty cost of 32 is added. An overload is defined as a condition in which it takes a node more than 0.5 s to service a virtual circuit; this is, in effect, a queueing delay. The last row of the table refers to a composite node made up of individual nodes connected with very high speed DMA links. Such composite nodes are required where large numbers of transmission lines converge.

TYMNET is a centralized network with a central node known as the supervisor responsible for routing. The supervisor knows the fixed cost of each link. When an overload condition exists, this is reported by the affected node to the supervisor which increases the assigned cost to the appropriate link. The cost is decreased when the node reports that the overload condition no longer exists. Thus, with only minor delay, the supervisor has a global picture of network status.

The supervisor performs routing on a virtual-circuit basis. When a virtual circuit is requested, the supervisor determines the least cost route between source and destination using a version of the backward search algorithm. The supervisor then passes the necessary routing information for this virtual circuit to each node on the route. When the virtual circuit terminates, the supervisor informs each node on the route. During the life of the virtual circuit, the route is fixed. If an outage occurs, the source and destination stations are required to construct a new virtual circuit. If the supervisor fails, one of three backup nodes assumes responsibility.

The TYMNET I technique had several useful features. Under light loading, the highest-capacity links are preferred. As the load increases, the algorithm tends to spread out the traffic nicely. Also, the processing burden on each node is minimal.

As the network grew, the TYMNET designers upgraded the routing function to improve efficiency and handle a wider variety of traffic [TYME81]. Whereas TYMNET I handled primarily interactive traffic over low-speed (up to 9600 bps) lines, TYMNET II also handles computer-to-computer traffic and has higher-speed links, including satellite links. In TYMNET II, link cost is based on data rate, load factor, satellite versus land-based link, and traffic type. For example, if the station

TABLE 9-5 Link Costs in TYMNET

Line Type	Line Not Overloaded	Line Overloaded One Way	Line Overloaded Both Ways
9600 bps	10	26	42
7200 bps	11	27	43
4800 bps	12	28	44
2400 bps	16	32	48
Memory shuffler	1	17	33

is a low-speed interactive terminal, a 9600-bps land link is assigned a lower cost than a 56-kbps satellite link because of the added delay of the satellite. If the virtual circuit is to be used for host-to-host file transfer, the satellite link has the lower cost; throughput is more important than response time.

As before, virtual circuits routes are established by the supervisor, which now uses a forward-search algorithm, deemed more efficient. Now, instead of transmitting routing information to each node, the supervisor sends a "needle" to the source node, containing the route as an ordered list of nodes. The needle threads its way along the designated route, depositing routing information as it goes. If an outage is encountered, the needle retraces to the origin and the supervisor is informed. This overcomes a problem in TYMNET I in which proper operation depended on each node successfully receiving routing information from the supervisor.

The recovery procedure is also improved. If an outage destroys a route, the supervisor finds another route for the virtual circuit. Lost packets must be recovered by an end-to-end protocol, but the virtual circuit is not lost.

SNA Routing.   The routing function in SNA is to some extent left up to the system user. What SNA provides is a foundation upon which a routing technique can be built [CYPS78, ATKI80]. To begin with, multiple physical links between nodes are provided for. This provision is to facilitate load leveling, availability, and provision for various classes of traffic. On top of this, SNA defines two types of routes: explicit and virtual. The explicit routes are predetermined fixed paths between source and destination. A number of these will exist for each source-destination pair. Virtual routes are station-visible routes between source and destination and map onto explicit routes in a precalculated way.

The separation of routes into two levels (virtual, explicit) has some advantages. The routing algorithm need not be concerned with the physical details of the network and is therefore simpler. Only the source and destination node are concerned with the identity of the virtual route. Packets in transit contain an explicit route number. Thus intermediate nodes have a simple, static routing table.

Virtual routes are defined by service class. Examples of service class are interactive, remote job entry, file transfer, secure, real time, and so on. These, of course, are user definitions. SNA simply knows that there are different classes of virtual routes and that each virtual route maps to a specific explicit route. Between any pair of nodes, up to three classes of virtual routes may be defined, with up to eight virtual routes per class, for a total of 24 virtual routes. More than one virtual route may map into a single explicit route. The virtual routes are listed in order of preference within a class. For example, high-speed satellite links may be preferred for file transfer service. Multiple sessions may use the same virtual route.

When a source station requests a session with a destination station, a service class is specified. The local node will attempt to establish a session over one of the virtual routes. If the underlying physical route is inoperative, the virtual route is rejected. Also, opportunity exists for load leveling by considering the current load on each virtual route within the service class. If an outage occurs during the session, the opportunity exists to reestablish the session by requesting a different virtual route within the class.

The SNA approach has some similarity with the TYMNET II approach. In both cases, different types of traffic can be provided with different routes based on link properties. In the case of TYMNET, the supervisor may construct a new route in response to an outage. In SNA, this task is performed by the source node.

TABLE 9-6 DNA Routing Tables (for node 1 of Figure 9-1)

		(a) Hops Next Node					(b) Cost Next Node		
		2	3	4			2	3	4
	2	1	2	2		2	2	8	3
Destination Node	3	2	1	3	Destination Node	3	5	5	3
	4	2	3	1		4	4	7	1
	5	3	2	2		5	5	6	2
	6	4	3	3		6	7	8	4

DNA Routing. The DNA routing function is essentially the same as the original ARPANET scheme. As with ARPANET, a distributed adaptive strategy is used. DNA adds a feature designed to test for reachability. Other differences are that the cost function with DNA is user defined, and that updates are triggered only by topology changes.

Table 9-6 depicts the routing tables maintained at each node. There are two matrices:

$$HOPS(i, l)$$
$$COST(i, l)$$

where

i = destination node, $i = 1, N$ for network with N nodes
l = adjacent node, $l \in$ set of adjacent nodes

$HOPS(i, l)$ is the estimate of the number of hops required to reach a destination i if node l is the next node on the route, and $COST(i, l)$ is the corresponding cost. Cost is user defined and may be based on such parameters as delay, link data rate, error rate, and node capacity. A node will send its tables to its neighbors whenever an event occurs that potentially changes routes. The primary event causing a change is a link or node going down or coming up. If a node detects such a change, it recomputes its HOPS and COST matrices. If any of the least-cost routes are changed, the node transmits this information to its neighbors, who update their tables. If this new information involves a change, the node that received the new tables must in turn issue its own new tables.

The HOPS information is needed to prevent a loop in the routing algorithm. The problem is this: If a node becomes unreachable, updated delay information will circulate around the network, with each node adding to the delay. By adding a hop count, and setting an upper limit equal to the maximum path length in the network, this condition can be detected.

9-4

TRAFFIC CONTROL

As with routing, the concept of traffic control in a packet-switched network is complex, and a wide variety of approaches have been proposed. Following the pattern of Section 9-3, we present the major elements of traffic control, provide a brief description of the most important strategies, and present examples. The interested reader may pursue the topic in several survey articles [GERL80, POUZ81], and in specific chapters on the subject in a number of books [GERL81, TANE81a, MART81, DAVI79].

Two related topics should be mentioned. Traffic control, as we use it here, deals with the control of the number of packets entering and using the network. It is concerned with preventing the network from becoming a bottleneck and in using it efficiently. It does not directly serve the end user (i.e., the stations attached to the network). The end users are in need of end-to-end flow control; this is provided at a higher level, and is discussed in Part III. Second, note that many of the adaptive routing techniques attempt to balance traffic throughout the network. This is not traffic control per se and cannot substitute for traffic control. At most, adaptive routing can smooth out temporary problems and defer an overload condition.

Types of Traffic Control

Table 9-7 summarizes the key elements or characteristics of traffic control in a packet-switched network. We briefly discuss each in turn.

Traffic control mechanisms are of three general types, each with different objectives. *Flow control* is used to regulate the flow of data between two points. We have seen examples of flow control in Chapter 5 for the case of two points that are directly connected. Flow control can also be used between indirectly connected points, such as two nodes in a packet-switched network that are the endpoints of a virtual circuit. The basic purpose of flow control is to allow the receiver to control the rate at which it receives data, so that it is not overwhelmed. Flow control techniques are also used to implement the other types of traffic control, as we shall see.

A quite different type of traffic control is *congestion control*. The objective here is to maintain the number of packets within the network or a region of the network below the level at which queueing delays blow up. In essence, a packet-switched network is a network of queues. At each node, there is a queue of packets for each outgoing channel. If the rate at which packets arrive and queue up exceeds the rate at which packets are transmitted, the queue size grows without bound and the delay experienced by a packet goes to infinity. Even if the packet arrival rate is less than the packet transmission rate, queue length will grow dramatically as the arrival rate approaches the transmission rate. We saw this kind of behavior in Figure 6-14. As a rule of thumb, when the line for which packets are queueing becomes more than 80% utilized, the queue length grows at an alarming rate [MART72].

Figure 9-10 shows the effect of congestion in general terms. Figure 9-10a plots the throughput of a network (number of packets delivered to destination stations) versus the offered load (number of packets transmitted by source stations). Both

TABLE 9-7 Elements of Traffic Control Techniques

Type	Scope	Level
Flow control	Packet (datagram)	Hop
Congestion control	Stream (virtual circuit)	Network access
Deadlock avoidance		Entry-to-exit

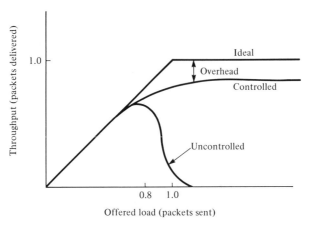

(a) Throughput

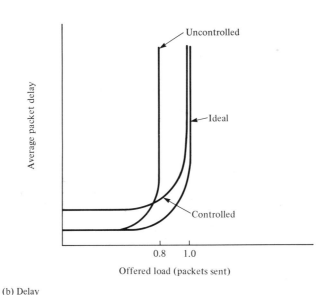

(b) Delay

FIGURE 9-10.   The effects of congestion.

axes are normalized to the maximum capacity of the network, which can be expressed as the rate at which the network is theoretically capable of handling packets. In the ideal case, throughput and hence network utilization increases to accommodate an offered load up to the maximum capacity of the network. Utilization then remains at 100%. The ideal case, of course, requires that all stations somehow know the timing and rate of packets that can be presented to the network, which is impossible. If no congestion control is exercised, we have the curve labeled "uncontrolled." As the load increases, utilization increases for a while. Then as the queue lengths at the various nodes begins to grow, throughput actually drops. The reason for this is that the buffers at each node are of finite size. When a node's buffers are full, it must discard packets. Thus the source stations must retransmit the discarded packets in addition to the new packets. This only exacerbates the situation: As more and more packets are retransmitted, the load on the system grows, and more buffers become saturated. While the system is trying desperately to clear the backlog, stations are pumping old and new packets into the system. Even successfully delivered packets may be retransmitted because it takes so long to acknowledge them: The sender assumes that the packet did not go through. Under these circumstances, the effective capacity of the system is virtually zero.

It is clear that these catastrophic events must be avoided, which is the task of congestion control. The object of all congestion control techniques is to limit queue lengths at the nodes so as to avoid traffic collapse. This control involves some unavoidable overhead. Thus a congestion control technique cannot perform as well as the theoretical ideal. However, a good congestion control strategy will avoid throughput collapse and maintain a throughput that differs from the ideal by an amount roughly equal to the overhead of the control.

Figure 9-10b points out that no matter what technique is used, the average delay experienced by packets grows without bound as the load approaches the capacity of the system. Note that initially the uncontrolled policy results in less delay than a controlled policy, because of its lack of overhead. However, the uncontrolled policy will saturate at lower load.

A problem equally serious to that of congestion is deadlock, a condition in which a set of nodes are unable to forward packets because no buffers are available. This condition can occur even without a heavy load. *Deadlock avoidance* techniques are used to design the network in such a way that deadlock cannot occur. We briefly describe three types of deadlock to which a packet-switched network may be prone.

The simplest form of deadlock is *direct store-and-forward deadlock* and can occur if a node uses a common buffer pool from which buffers are assigned to packets on demand. Figure 9-11a shows a situation in which all of the buffer space in node A is occupied with packets destined for B. The reverse is true at B. Neither node can accept any more packets since their buffers are full. Thus neither node can transmit or receive on any link.

Store-and-forward deadlock can be prevented by not allowing all buffers to be dedicated to a single link. A more subtle form of deadlock, *indirect store-and-forward deadlock*, is illustrated in Figure 9-10b. For each node, the queue to the adjacent node in one direction is full with packets destined for the next node beyond.

Finally, there is *reassembly deadlock*, which is peculiar to ARPANET and like networks. Figure 9-10c shows a situation in which node C has three of four packets from message 1 and one from message 3. All of its buffers are full, so it can accept no more packets. Yet, because it has no complete message, it cannot reassemble packets and deliver them to the host.

Techniques

Traffic control techniques can be categorized also by their scope of application. Packet techniques are concerned with controlling the flow of individual packets. This is all that is allowed in a datagram network, and is sometimes used in virtual circuit networks. Stream techniques have to do with controlling the stream of packets flowing through a virtual circuit.

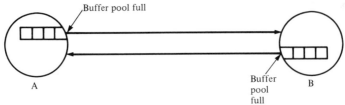

(a) Direct store – and – forward deadlock

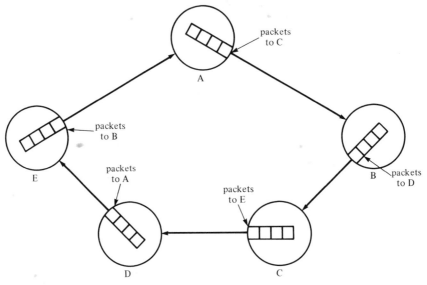

(b) Indirect store – and – forward deadlock

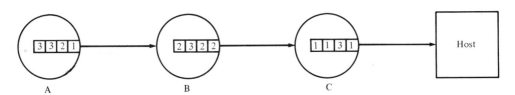

(c) Reassembly deadlock

FIGURE 9-11. Types of deadlock

A third dimension of traffic control is the level, or where is it applied. The hop level is concerned with controls exerted between adjacent nodes. These typically have to do with congestion control or deadlock avoidance. Network access controls limit the number of packets being transmitted by a particular station. That is, they control the number of new packets entering the network. These typically are used in congestion control. Finally, entry-to-exit controls are concerned with the flow of packets between two endpoints.

Table 9-8 summarizes the traffic control techniques of our example networks;

TABLE 9-8 Traffic Control Techniques for Some Networks

Scope	Hop	Network Access	Entry-to-Exit
Packet	DNA (channel queue limit)	DNA (channel queue limit)	
Stream	TYMNET (quota) SNA (pacing)	TYMNET (quota) ARPANET (RFNM)	ARPANET (window, reassembly buffer allocation) SNA (pacing)

these are described below. For more detail on traffic control techniques in general, the reader is referred to the references listed above.

Example Systems

ARPANET. For its virtual-circuit service, ARPANET provides two levels of traffic control [BBN81]. One is an entry-to-entry technique. Recall that a virtual circuit is used to send a sequence of numbered messages between hosts. ARPANET enforces a limit of eight messages in transit between any pair of hosts. This window mechanism with window size of eight is used to prevent any host from flooding the network.

Of more serious concern is a situation of reassembly lockup, as described earlier. ARPANET's solution is to require that a source node reserve space for each message in advance with a "request for buffer space" packet. When a destination node receives this request, and has available eight buffers for the eight packets that the message might contain, it returns an "allocation" packet. After the entire message is received and reassembled, the receiving node sends back an acknowledgment known as *ready for next message* (RFNM). If the node has buffer space for an additional message, it piggybacks an allocation packet with the RFNM. Thus, during stream transmission, the source node need not send request packets. A time may come when the source has no messages to send but has collected one or more allocation permits. The source node is then obligated to send a "give back" packet to free up buffer space at the destination.

For datagram service, no positive flow control is enforced. Rather, a destination node will discard datagrams for which it has no free buffer space. It is up to the source station to determine from the destination station if the datagram did not get through and to resend it if necessary.

TYMNET. It is in the area of traffic control that the real strength of the TYMNET approach is seen. The TYMNET traffic control mechanism has the following positive features.

- It is simple.
- It requires very little overhead.
- Deadlocks cannot occur and therefore no mechanisms are needed to avoid it.
- Under conditions of heavy load, virtual circuits with low data rate requirements get all the capacity they need; circuits with high data rate requirements get at least some of what they need. Thus no active circuit is denied service.

Traffic control in TYMNET is on a virtual-circuit basis and includes both network access and hop-level mechanisms [RIND79b, TYME81]. The network access flow control is based on the establishment of the virtual circuit. When the supervisor sets up a virtual circuit, it assigns a quota of buffer space for each channel used along the circuit. The quota is based on throughput class. A node can only transmit data on a particular channel until the quota is exhausted. It must then wait for the next node to refresh its quota. Every half-second, each node sends a "backpressure vector" to each adjacent node. The vector contains one bit for each channel on the link. If a bit is set to 1, the sending node may reset the quota for the corresponding buffer. Otherwise, the sending node continues to decrement the quota for a particular channel for each character that is transmitted. The result is a backpressure mechanism that eventually works its way back to the sending host.

For example, in Figure 9-3, suppose that the terminal connected to node 1000 is 10 characters per second (cps) and the host is connected to node 5 over a 30-cps virtual-circuit link. As characters arrive from the host they start to flow through the virtual circuit. The characters arrive at node 1000 at 30 cps but can leave at only 10 cps. After the number of characters buffered in node 1000 exceeds the quota of 30, the bit for channel 2 in the backpressure vector is set to zero. Thus node 1000 will have at most 60 characters buffered for this circuit. Now node 112 will go through the same process resulting in at most 60 characters in its buffer. Now the buffer in node 5 begins to grow and, when it reaches 30, the host will be requested to stop transmitting. This request may be in the form of an HDLC RNR (receiver not ready) packet. When the number of characters in node 1000's buffer drops below 30, data again begin to flow from 112 to 1000, from 5 to 112, and finally from the host.

Two refinements help to reduce congestion further. A situation may arise when a station wishes to abort a transmission; for example, a terminal user realizes that what is printing on the screen is of no interest and wishes to stop it with an abort command. To clear out the characters in transit, the host can send a *character gobbler*. This is a PACman-like device that ignores backpressure and goes through the circuit at full speed, gobbling all characters in front of it. A second refinement: When a virtual circuit is terminated, a *circuit zapper* is sent which not only gobbles characters, but releases the buffer pairs and clears the table entries to free up these resources for new circuits.

We have discussed how flow control is performed at the virtual circuit level using a backpressure mechanism. Since TYMNET uses a statistical TDM technique at the hop level (Figure 9-4), there remains the question of how capacity is allocated to the active channels on a link. Frames are constructed using a round robin technique among all active channels. A node sends frames as fast as possible over each link. Each frame contains one or more packets, each corresponding to a different channel. To construct a frame, a node cycles through all channels, picking up packets, until it has a total of 480 bits of data or until it has completed a full cycle. The frame is then sent and a new frame constructed. For each channel visited, the amount of data collected is

$$MIN(Q, D, F)$$

where

Q = quota for that channel
D = amount of data in the read buffer of that channel
F = amount of data space remaining in the frame

Thus, when bandwidth is oversubscribed, channels that only need little get what they want with little or no queueing delay, whereas channels that want all they can get share the remaining bandwidth fairly.

The TYMNET approach is a powerful one that possesses the positive characteristics listed above. The only disadvantage is the packets are torn down and reconstructed at each node, which increases processing requirements.

SNA. Traffic control in SNA [ATKI80, GEOR82] is an interesting hybrid [ATKI80]. The control is exercised on a virtual circuit (virtual route) basis. This control may be triggered by either the destination node, to avoid overflow, or by an intermediate node to reduce congestion. In the case of the endpoint, control is selectively exercised on a particular virtual circuit. In the case of an intermediate node, the node will exercise control on all virtual circuits that pass through a congested link.

The technique is known as pacing, and is similar to the sliding-window technique. When a virtual route is established, a maximum WS-MAX and minimum WS-MIN window size are defined. WS-MIN is equal to the hop count of the explicit route. WS-MAX is a system-defined multiple, typically three times the hop count. Each sender maintains a window size WS and a pacing count PC, which is the number of additional packets it may send; both are initialized to WS-MIN.

First consider the use of pacing for entry-to-exit flow control. The sending node sends a virtual route pacing request (VRPRQ) bit in the first packet of a window (i.e., when PC = WS). When the receiving node gets the request, and when it has buffer space, it returns a virtual route pacing response (VRPRS) packet, which allows the sender to increment PC by WS. Since the sender decrements PC by 1 with each packet sent, the maximum value of PC is 2WS-1. Thus the receiving node can exercise flow control by simply withholding the VRPRS.

To improve throughput, the sending node is allowed to increment its window size by 1, up to WS-MAX, if its pacing count has gone to 0 by the time it receives VRPRS. The assumption is that the receiving node could handle packets at a faster rate. Unfortunately, the opposite may be true: The receiving node is withholding its VRPRS because it is getting too many packets! To account for this contingency, the receiver may set a change window reply indicator (CWRI) bit or a reset window indicator (RWI) bit on its next VRPRS. The former requests that the sender decrement WS by 1 (down to a minimum of WS-MIN). The latter requests that WS be reset to WS-MIN.

These techniques are also used to relieve congestion in the network. If a node suffers minor congestion on an outgoing link (i.e., queue length is beginning to grow), it sets the change window indicator (CWI) bit on all packets on all virtual routes going out that link. When the receiver gets a packet with CWI set, it sets CRWI on its next VRPRS. Thus, all sending nodes whose virtual routes go through the complaining node will decrement their window size and relieve the congestion. If severe congestion occurs (i.e., buffer saturation), the intermediate node takes more drastic action to relieve the problem. Instead of acting on packets going out the congested link, it sets the RWI bit on all packets coming in on that link. Thus all sending nodes will quickly reset their window sizes to their minimum value.

Each sending node dynamically adjusts its window size based on pacing controls set both in data packets and VRPRS packets. Figure 9-12 is a flowchart of the algorithm. Thus a single, relatively simple technique provides a unified flow control and congestion control mechanism.

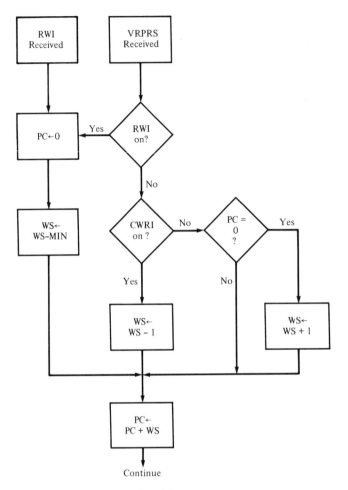

FIGURE 9-12. SNA pacing algorithm.

DNA. The principal virtue of the DNA traffic control mechanism is its simplicity. Furthermore, measurements using the mechanism verify that it is effective in preventing buffer saturation and network congestion [WECK80].

The basic mechanism is a channel queue limit technique. When the length of an output channel queue exceeds a specified threshold, input packets (packets originating at this node) are delayed at the user source, and transit packets (this node is neither source nor destination) are discarded. The threshold, proposed in [IRLA78], is equal to the total number of buffers divided by the square root of the number of output lines. Thus no output link ever uses more than that fraction of the buffers. This was found to provide close to optimal performance for the case in which all buffers are pooled and dynamically allocated to output links.

To supplement the foregoing policy, DNA also uses a hop count mechanism. Each time a packet makes a hop, its count is incremented. If the hop count exceeds the maximum allowed, the node discards it. This eliminates packets caught in a temporary loop formed in the routing path.

ERROR CONTROL

Requirements

A final function of packet-switched networks, which we discuss briefly, is error control. A number of contingencies may arise which result in the loss of a packet in the network:

- A packet may be discarded in the aid of traffic control.
- A link may fail.
- A node may fail.
- The destination station may fail.

The latter three contingencies are partially handled by the data link control mechanisms between nodes or between a node and a station. But even this is not enough to ensure that a packet makes it through the network. For example, a node along the route of a packet may accept a packet and return an acknowledgment. If the node then fails before it can forward the packet, the network as a whole does not know that the packet is lost.

Ideally, no packets are lost despite congestion or failures. In relation to this, certain requirements may be placed on the network, in increasing order of difficulty:

1. If a link or node outage occurs, the network can route subsequent packets around the outage.
2. If a link or node fails, all virtual circuits that pass through the outage are automatically rebuilt. Some packets may be lost, and the station is responsible for sorting that out.
3. If a link or node fails, all affected virtual circuits are rebuilt and packets are recovered by the network, not the station.
4. No packet is ever lost in a datagram network.

Virtually all networks satisfy requirement 1. Most networks with a virtual-circuit service satisfy requirement 2, and some satisfy requirement 3. As yet, no network satisfies requirement 4.

Example Systems

We now briefly mention the error control techniques used in our example systems. In ARPANET, no error control is exercised for datagram service. Error control is provided at the message level [BBN81]. When a source node transmits a message (in up to eight packets) it retains a copy of that message, including its sequence number. If the acknowledgment (RFNM) is not received within a certain time, the source node inquires of the destination node whether the full message was received. It might be that the message got through, but the RFNM did not. If the source node gets a negative reply, it retransmits the message. If the source node fails to get a response from the destination node in a reasonable time, it returns an incomplete transmission message to its host. It is then up to the host to decide a course of action. Finally, we note that because ARPANET uses datagrams internally, virtual circuits are maintained as long as there is some route from source to destination.

TYMNET meets requirements 1 and 3 listed above [RIND79]. When a node or link outage occurs, this fact is reported to the supervisor by neighboring nodes. The supervisor clears out all tables and buffers for each affected virtual circuit and notifies both endpoints. For each destroyed virtual circuit, the originating node automatically requests a new virtual circuit. The supervisor then rebuilds all virtual circuits that were broken. This action preserves all end-to-end connections, but more is needed to preserve the data that were in transit.

Data are preserved in TYMNET in the following fashion. As we described earlier, there is a buffer dedicated to a virtual circuit at each node along its route. The source node is given this information and thus knows the maximum number of characters that may be in transit. The source node maintains two items:

- A circular buffer equal to the maximum number of characters in transit. Once the buffer is full, it always contains the last N characters transmitted, where N is the maximum number of characters in transit.
- A running count of the number of characters transmitted since the virtual circuit was established.

The destination endpoint maintains a running count of the number of characters received. (Of course, virtual circuits are full duplex, so these mechanisms are needed in both directions.) When a failed virtual circuit is rebuilt, the endpoint nodes exchange running count values. Each node then retransmits the lost characters. Thus both the virtual circuit and the data are preserved, with no involvement of the attached stations.

In SNA, the failure of a node or link will destroy an explicit route. The originating node of each affected virtual route is notified, and promptly selects an alternative explicit route to maintain the connection. The responsibility for lost packets is beyond the scope of the communication network function and is handled at a higher (station) level within SNA.

DNA makes no attempt to recover lost datagrams as part of its communications network function. As with SNA, this is left to a higher level.

9-6

RECOMMENDED READING

The literature on packet switching is enormous. We mention here only a few of the many worthwhile references. A number of survey articles were written in the early days of packet switching; among the most interesting are [KIMB75], [GREE77], and [KLEI78]. Surveys of specific networks include [WOOD84b], [ROBE78], and [SCHW72]. Books with good treatments of this subject include [ROSN82] and [DAVI79]. There is also a large body of literature on performance. Good summaries are to be found in [KLEI76] and [SCHW77]. [AHUJ82] provides a mathematical analysis of performance and reliability aspects of traffic control and routing. [MARU83] is an exhaustive analysis of the performance of virtual-circuit-based routing algorithms. [HSIE84] compares the routing algorithms of ARPANET, TYMENET, SNA, and DNA.

9-7

PROBLEMS

9-1 In step 2 of the forward-search algorithm, the least-cost path values are only updated for nodes not yet in M. Is it not possible that a shorter path could be found to a node already in M? If so, demonstrate by example. If not, provide reasoning as to why not.

9-2 Using the forward-search algorithm, generate a least-cost route to all other nodes for nodes 2 through 6 of Figure 9-1. Display the results as in Table 9-3a. Do the same for the backward-search algorithm.

9-3 In Figure 9-1, node 1 sends a packet to node 6 using flooding. Counting the transmission of one packet across one link as a load of one, what is the total load generated if:
a. Each node discards duplicate incoming packets?

b. A hop count field is used and is initially set to 5?

9-4 It was shown that flooding can be used to determine the minimum-hop route. Can it be used to determine the minimum delay route?

9-5 With random routing, only one copy of the packet is in existence at a time. Nevertheless, it would be wise to utilize a hop count field. Why?

9-6 Using Table 9-6 as a model, construct the routing tables for all other nodes of Figure 9-1.

9-7 Another adaptive routing scheme is known as *backward learning*. As a packet is routed through the network, it carries not only the destination address, but the source address plus a running hop count that is incremented for each hop. Each node builds a routing table that gives the next node and hop count for each destination. How is the packet information used to build the table? What are the advantages and disadvantages of this technique?

9-8 Suggest a technique for avoiding indirect store-and-forward deadlock.

9-9 Explain why deadlock cannot occur in TYMNET.

9-10 A proposed traffic control measure is known as *isarithmic* control. In this method, the total number of packets in transit is fixed by inserting a fixed number of permits into the network. These permits circulate through the network at random. Whenever a node wants to send a packet just given to it by a station, it must first capture and destroy a permit. When the packet reaches the destination node, that node reissues the permit.
a. What type of traffic control is this?

b. List three potential problems with this technique.

9-11 What is the maximum number of packets that may be in transit at any one time on an ARPANET virtual circuit?

9-12 Consider the following network of nodes:
C is the capacity of a link in packets per second. Node A presents a constant load of 0.8 packet per second destined for A'. Node B presents a load λ destined for B'. Node S has a common pool of buffers that it uses for traffic to both A' and B'. When the buffer is full, packets are discarded, and are later retransmitted by the

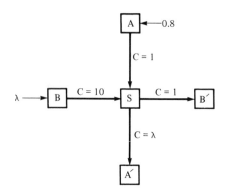

PROBLEM 9-12.

host. Plot the total throughput (i.e., the sum of $A - A'$ and $B - B'$ delivered traffic) as a function of λ. What fraction of the throughput is $A - A'$ traffic for $\lambda > 1$?

9-13 Assuming no malfunction in any of the stations or nodes of a network, is it possible for a packet to be delivered to the wrong destination?

CHAPTER 10

Radio and Satellite Networks

In this chapter we begin our discussion of packet broadcasting networks. Recall that such networks share the following characteristics:

- Packet transmission.
- No switching.
- Reception by many or all stations.
- Common transmission medium.

In contrast to the case with the packet-switched networks of Chapter 9, issues such as routing, traffic control, and error control are of less concern here. Rather, the key issue is transmission capacity allocation.

This chapter deals with packet radio and satellite networks, which exhibit a number of similarities. The characteristics of local networks are quite different, and that topic is reserved for Chapter 11. For both packet radio and satellite networks, we begin with a discussion of architectural issues, and then look at medium access control protocols. Appendix 10A explores the subject of broadcast network performance, which is relevant to both this chapter and the next.

10-1

PACKET-RADIO ARCHITECTURE

The architecture of packet-radio networks can be classified as centralized or distributed (Figure 10-1). In a centralized network, there is one central transmitter/

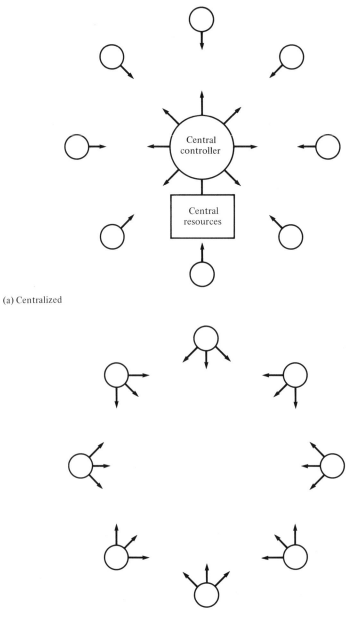

(a) Centralized

(b) Distributed

FIGURE 10-1.   Basic packet radio architecture.

receiver, attached to a central resource. All other nodes communicate only with the central node. Node-to-node communication is indirect, mediated by the central node. The earliest networks followed this model, and were designed primarily to provide terminal access to a central timesharing system. In a centralized system, two radio channels are required. Individual nodes send packets to the central node on one channel, and the central node broadcasts packets on another. Since radio transmission is omnidirectional, packets transmitted by the central node are heard by all the other nodes. Thus the configuration is logically equivalent to a multipoint line with a primary and a number of secondaries (Figure 5-2).

The centralized network is not appropriate for the more common situation today of a collection of microcomputers that wish to exchange data, messages, programs, and so forth. The distributed architecture takes full advantage of the omnidirectional property of radio. One channel is used for all transmissions and each transmission is heard by all other nodes. This configuration is logically equivalent to a local area network (Chapter 11).

Figure 10-1 and the discussion above assumes line-of-sight propagation. From Equation (2-1), recall that the maximum distance between transmitter and receiver is slightly more than the line of sight, or a distance of $7.14 \sqrt{Kh}$ in kilometers, where h is the height of both antennas in meters, and K reflects a refraction effect. For example, with two antennas at a height of 10 m, and using a nominal value of $K = 4/3$, the maximum range is 26 km. This represents the maximum radius of a centralized system, and the maximum diameter of a distributed system.

To overcome this geographic limitation, a store-and-forward repeater is used (Figure 10-2). A repeater performs much the same task as a node in a packet-

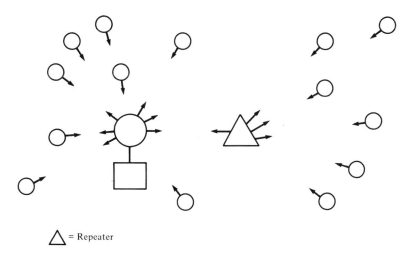

△ = Repeater

(a) Centralized

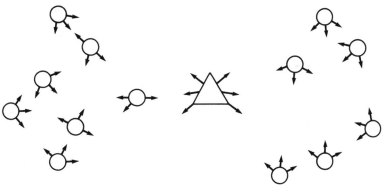

(b) Distributed

FIGURE 10-2. Packet radio networks with repeaters.

switched network except that it works with broadcast links rather than point-to-point links. In a centralized system, the repeater accepts packets from the central node and retransmits them to remote nodes. It also accepts packets from these remote nodes and forwards them to the central node. In a distributed system, the repeater acts as a switch between two sets of nodes, accepting packets from one set for retransmission to the other, and vice versa.

We now turn to a more detailed description of these two configurations, using ALOHANET [ABRA70, BIND75a] as our example of a centralized system, and MP-Net [ROUL81] as our example of a distributed system.

Centralized Networks: ALOHANET

The first packet radio network, ALOHANET, was developed by the University of Hawaii and became operational in 1970. Its principal objective was to allow user terminals in widely scattered locations to access the university computer system. Traffic was primarily terminal-to-host, but terminal-to-terminal traffic could be routed via the central node, called the *menehune* (Hawaiian for "imp"). Remote units were of two types. The *terminal control unit* (TCU) operated with a simple half-duplex terminal and included a buffer, control logic, and transceiver. The *programmable control unit* (PCU) was a microprocessor-based device for terminal concentration and/or a computing station.

As a centralized system, ALOHANET requires two channels. PCU- and TCU-to-menehune traffic are on channel f_1, using a frequency of 407.35 MHz; traffic from the menehune is carried on channel f_2, at a frequency of 413.475 MHz. Both channels have a bandwidth of 100 kHz and, using PSK, a data rate of 9600 bps. Transmission on both channels uses packets with the following format:

- *SYNC (100 bits):* A fairly lengthy synchronization pattern was deemed advisable to minimize errors.
- *Header (32 bits):* The header includes the user address (8 bits), repeater address (6 bits), packet type (3 bits), packet length (8 bits), and various other control bits.
- *CRC (16 bits):* The header is protected with its own error-detecting code.
- *Data (640 bits):* A maximum of 80 characters can be transmitted.
- *CRC (16 bits):* The data are protected with another error-detecting code.

The f_1 (user) channel uses a multiaccess contention protocol known as ALOHA. Each station transmits a packet when it has data to send. It then expects to hear an acknowledgment (ACK) from the menehune. However, since each station transmits at will, it is possible that two transmissions will overlap. This is known as a *collision*; the result is that the menehune receives a garbled transmission. To account for transmission errors and collisions, a user node retransmits a packet if no ACK is received during a random timeout interval. The random time interval avoids a second collision between packets that had originally collided. The time is uniformly distributed in an interval with a minimum of 0.2 s, chosen to allow time for receipt of the ACK, and a maximum of 1.5 s. The lower bound is increased for nodes transmitting through repeaters, to account for the repeater delay in both directions.

The f_2 channel is used primarily for two types of packets: acknowledgment packets and data packets from the central resource. Because the timing of ACKs

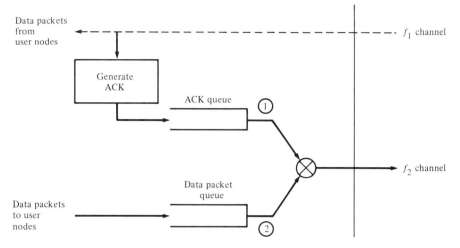

Data packets from user nodes

Generate ACK

ACK queue ①

f_1 channel

f_2 channel

Data packet queue

Data packets to user nodes

②

FIGURE 10-3. ALOHANET broadcast channel multiplexing.

is critical, acknowledgment packets have absolute priority. Two queues of packets waiting to be transmitted are maintained by the menehune, one for ACKs and one for all other packets (Figure 10-3). As long as the ACK queue is not empty, the next packet is transmitted from that queue.

In the original implementation, packets from the menehune were not acknowledged by the user nodes, for two reasons. First, since the f_2 channel was noncontention, there was a high probability of successful transmission. Second, ACKs would increase the congestion of the contention-based f_1 channel. Later on, ACKs were added for selected applications, such as file transfer.

The repeaters in ALOHANET also use channels f_1 and f_2. Each repeater has a list of addresses of nodes with which it can communicate. Packets on f_1 from a user node within the address range are repeated on f_1 to the menehune or to the next repeater in the case of cascaded repeaters. Packets on f_2 addressed to a user node within the address range are repeated on f_2 in the opposite direction. The process is depicted in Figure 10-4a, which shows a repeater that communicates with a central controller (C) and a defined set of user nodes (A). Since radio transmission is omnidirectional, it is clear that the menehune and a repeater should not transmit on f_2 at the same time. To avoid this, the menehune will pause after transmission of a packet to a repeater long enough for the packet to be forwarded.

Two more elements of ALOHANET that need to be described are the strategies for routing and flow control. Routing is required if a packet-radio network has more than one repeater. In the case of ALOHANET, a fixed routing strategy is used. The system is set up so that the ranges of addresses for the various repeaters do not overlap. In a system with many repeaters, a more complex routing strategy would be indicated.

Flow control on f_2 requires that the menehune know the input characteristics of the user node. In essence, the menehune waits sufficient time for a node to absorb a packet of data before sending another. Flow control on f_1 is normally not a problem. For lengthy transfers from a PCU, a go-ahead packet mechanism is used. The PCU can only send a certain amount of data and then has to wait for the go-ahead packet.

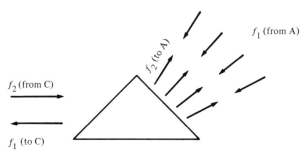

(a) Centralized network

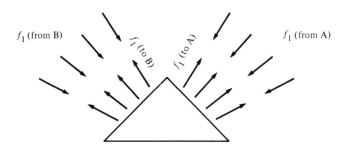

(b) Distributed network

FIGURE 10-4.   Function of a radio packet repeater.

Distributed Networks: MP-Net

A distributed packet radio network that is representative of what is likely to become an increasingly common application is MP-Net. Developed and operated by the Montreal Amateur Radio Club, MP-Net has been in operation in the Montreal area since 1978. Its objectives are to provide distributed networking among microcomputers plus remote access to computing resources.

As a distributed system, MP-Net uses a single frequency; all stations transmit and receive on 223.050 MHz, using FSK, at a data rate of 4800 bps. The network is organized into clusters connected by repeaters. As with ALOHANET, a fixed routing scheme is used. Hence, each repeater needs two sets of addresses, for the two clusters that it joins. At each node, there must be a table that shows, for each other node, whether it is in the local cluster or the identity of the repeater through which packets must be routed.

Packets are transmitted using a contention protocol known as nonpersistent CSMA, which is explained below. The packet format is as follows:

- *SYN SYN (2 bytes):* two-byte synchronization pattern.
- *SOH (1 byte):* start of header.
- *Length (1 byte):* length of packet in bytes, starting with length byte and ending with last byte of FCS.

- *Destination (6 bytes):* callsign (address) of destination station.
- *Destination repeater (1 byte):* address of a store-and-forward repeater.
- *Origin (6 bytes):* callsign (address) of sending station.
- *Origin repeater (1 byte):* address of a store-and-forward repeater.
- *Sequence number (1 byte):* is the number of this packet using a sliding window with a range 0 to 254. The last packet in a stream is always numbered 255.
- *Flags (1 byte):* indicated what kind of packet this is. Five binary flags are currently in use:

  A: This packet is an ACK.
  R: This packet has been processed by a repeater.
  F: This packet is part of a file transfer and is numbered.
  B: The data field is binary instead of ASCII.
  E: The data field is neither binary nor ASCII.

- *Space (1 byte):* reserved for future network control functions.
- *Data:* from 0 to 236 bytes.
- *FCS (2 bytes):* frame check sequence using CRC.

Notice the resemblance to DDCMP (Figure 5.18).

The sequence number is used for both flow control and error control, as explained in Chapter 5. Since there is only one sequence number field, acknowledgments cannot be piggybacked. Acknowledgment packets therefore have a zero-length data field. As with ALOHANET, a timeout is used for retransmission of unacknowledged packets. That is, a node will wait a predefined length of time after transmitting a packet for an acknowledgment. If no acknowledgment to that packet is received within the time limit, the packet is retransmitted. When a repeater is used, the timeout interval is suitably lengthened.

A repeater will ignore all packets that do not contain its address in the destination repeater field. If its address is present, the repeater then checks that the destination field contains one of the allowable destination addresses. If so, the repeater sets the R bit, recomputes the CRC, and retransmits the packet. A station receiving a packet with a repeater address without the R flag set will ignore it. This avoids the station receiving duplicate packets, one from the source and one from the repeater. This is possible since line-of-sight transmission radii of necessity overlap. The source repeater field is used in the case of cascaded repeaters. Figure 10-4b shows the use of a repeater to link two sets of user nodes (*A* and *B*).

Routing

In packet radio networks with a small number of repeaters, such as ALOHANET and MP-Net, a fixed routing scheme is adequate. As the use of packet radio grows, we are more likely to see networks with a large number (>10) of repeaters and with at least some of the stations being mobile. Military requirements clearly reflect this architecture. Figure 10-5 illustrates the types of configurations of multirepeater networks. In a centralized network, the routing problem is to find a route between the central node *F* and all other nodes. In a distributed network, we have the apparently more difficult problem of finding a route between each pair of repeaters. Note also that in a distributed network, one would need some sort of two level address for each station of the form (repeater, station), where ''repeater'' identifies

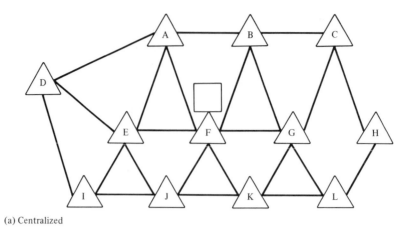

(a) Centralized

(b) Distributed

Lines indicate repeaters
within range of each other.

FIGURE 10-5. Packet radio networks with many repeaters.

the cluster of stations local to a particular repeater. This section presents an over-view of the routing problem for such networks and is based primarily on [CARP81].

A multirepeater packet radio network is topologically similar to the type of packet-switched network discussed in Chapter 9. Each repeater is equivalent to a node, and the local cluster of each repeater is equivalent to multiple stations at-tached to a node. Because of the similarities, one might think that the routing algorithms discussed previously would be applicable to multirepeater packet radio networks. However, there are differences, due to the transmission characteristics of the two networks, and the fact that some packet radio nodes may be mobile. We can group those differences between the two types of networks that affect routing strategy into two categories: link reliability effects and common channel effects.

Link reliability effects are those due to the fact that radio links are less reliable than hardwire links. They are subject to fading, multipath, and noise interference and, in a hostile environment, to jamming. Lower reliability suggests:

- *More frequent monitoring of link status:* This is required to assure reliable communication. If overhead packets for this purpose are exchanged on a regular basis, routing information could be added (piggybacking).
- *Variable data rate links:* Data link error detection and control techniques contribute to transmission overhead and thus reduce the effective data rate. Some radio designs allow these techniques, and thus the effective data rate, to vary significantly in response to link quality variations. This affects the selection of minimum delay routes.
- One-way links: This would result from different ambient noise levels, jamming, or different antenna characteristics at two radios. Most distributed routing techniques require information from any node to which a packet might be sent, but it is unclear how a sender can even learn the existence of an outgoing one-way link.

Common channel effects are those produced by the fact that all links use the same shared transmission channel. In Figure 10-5, for example, stations *G, K,* and *L* are in range of each other. Only one of the three may transmit at a time. A transmission from one is heard by the other two as well as any other repeaters within range of the transmitter (e.g., *G*'s transmission is heard by *K* and *L*, and also by *B, C,* and *F*). The implications of this situation are:

- *Link delays are the same for all output links:* With point to point links, each node has a queue of packets for each link and knows the length of its queues. With broadcast links, these local queues are not independent; there is, in effect, one large distributed queue of packets waiting to use the common channel. This will affect routing strategies that use queueing delay as a parameter.
- *Links are not independent:* The amount of traffic (and hence delay) between one pair of repeaters will affect the delay on other pairwise links. This is not taken into account by most algorithms for globally generating all routes through the network.
- *Routing overhead packets need be sent only once:* Many distributed routing strategies require that routing information be sent by a node to each of its neighbors. This would require only one radio broadcast.

It should be clear that the problem of routing in a packet radio network is even more complex than in a conventional packet-switched network. As yet, there has been little experience or research in this area. As examples, we mention two approaches.

Because of the problems of unreliable links and mobile nodes, it is clear that a highly robust routing algorithm is required. Flooding comes to mind, but is the most wasteful of bandwidth. However, from the point of view of the individual repeater, flooding is required! Even if a packet transmitted by a repeater includes a destination repeater address field (e.g., MP-Net), that packet will be received by all other repeaters within range. One way to reduce waste with a flooding approach would be to try to minimize the number of repeaters that actually do retransmit [LIUJ80]. The procedure works as follows. When a repeater receives a packet to rebroadcast, it waits a random length of time before doing so. If it receives another copy of the packet before its own broadcast, it discards the packet. Thus if two or more neighbors hear the same broadcast, only one of them will relay it. This reduces but does not eliminate packet duplication. In Figure 10-5, for example, if repeater *H* broadcasts a packet, both *C* and *L* will receive it. Since *C* and *L* are not within range of each other, both will rebroadcast it.

Another way to reduce duplicate packets is for each repeater to only forward a packet when it is closer to the destination than the repeater from which it received the packet [GITM76]. Suppose that each repeater knew its hop-count distance from every other repeater. Then the process would work as follows. When a repeater receives a packet from a station for forwarding, it adds a distance field whose value is the number of hops to the destination repeater, and then broadcasts the packet. When a repeater receives a packet from another repeater, it does the following:

- If the packet is for a station in the local cluster, broadcast it.
- If the packet is to be forwarded, check the distance field. If this repeater is closer to the destination than the last repeater, update the distance field and transmit.

In Figure 10-5b, for example, suppose that *K* broadcasts a packet with a destination of *D* and a distance of 3. Repeaters *J, F, G,* and *L* receive the transmission, but only *J* and *F* have a hop count to *D* of less than 3. They both broadcast a packet with a distance of 2. Repeaters *I, E, A, B, G, K,* and *J* get one or two copies of the packet. Of these only *I, E,* and *A* are closer to *D,* and they all send a packet to *D*.

This seems to work fine. The question is how each repeater may determine its hop count to every other repeater. This could be done in several ways. Each station could maintain a distance table which is periodically exchanged with its numbers, much like DNA and the original ARPANET algorithm. Another alternative is a backward learning algorithm. When a repeater receives a packet for the first time, that packet will have traversed the shortest route from the original repeater. This information could be used to update the distance table in the destination repeater.

10-2

PACKET RADIO ACCESS PROTOCOLS

As was mentioned in Chapter 7, a medium access control protocol is needed for a multiaccess network. Such protocols are designed to address the problem of how to share a common broadcast channel: the "Who goes next?" problem. The techniques that have been used for packet radio networks can be termed *random access* or *contention* techniques. They are random access in the sense that there is no predictable or scheduled time for any station to transmit: Stations generate packets for transmission at random times. They are contention in the sense that no central control is exercised to determine whose turn it is: All stations contend for time on a network.

In this section we introduce and discuss three contention protocols appropriate for packet radio networks: ALOHA, slotted ALOHA, and *carrier sense multiple access* (CSMA). ALOHA and CSMA have enjoyed extensive use in packet radio networks; slotted ALOHA is a refinement of ALOHA. We will see that these as well as other contention protocols exhibit an inherent instability: as the load on the network increases, a saturation point is reached, beyond which throughput collapses.

ALOHA

The earliest of the contention techniques, known as *ALOHA*, was developed for packet radio networks [ABRA70]. However, it is applicable to any transmission medium shared by uncoordinated users. ALOHA, or *pure ALOHA* as it is sometimes called, is a true free-for-all. Whenever a station has a packet to send, it does so. The station then listens for an amount of time equal to the maximum possible round-trip propagation time on the network (twice the time it takes to send packet between the two most widely separated stations). If the station hears an acknowledgment during that time, fine; otherwise, it resends the packet. After repeated failures, it gives up. A receiving station determines the correctness of an incoming packet by examining the FCS. If the packet is valid, the station acknowledges immediately. The packet may be invalid, due to noise on the channel or because another station transmitted a frame at about the same time. In the latter case, the two frames may interfere with each other so that neither gets through; this is known as a *collision*. In either case, the receiving station simply ignores the frame.

ALOHA is as simple as can be, and pays a penalty for it. To get at the performance of this protocol, we first present results based on the assumption that there are an infinite number of stations. This may strike the reader as an absurd tactic, but, in fact, it leads to analytically tractable equations that are, up to a point, very close to reality. We will define that point shortly. For now, we state the infinite-source assumption precisely: There are an infinite number of stations, each generating an infinitely small rate of packets such that the total number of packets generated per unit time is finite.

Some additional assumptions are needed. We use the following notation, which is discussed in some detail in Appendix 10A:

- S: the throughput of the network; the total rate of data being transmitted between stations (carried load). S is usually normalized to be expressed as a fraction of network capacity.
- G: the total rate of data presented to the network for transmission (offered load), also usually normalized.
- I: the total rate of data generated by the stations (input load), also usually normalized.
- D: the average delay that occurs between the time a packet or frame is ready for transmission from a station, and the completion of successful transmission.

The assumptions are:

1. All packets are of constant length. In general, such packets give better average throughput and delay performance than do variable-length packets. In some analyses, an exponential distribution of packet length is used.
2. The channel is noise-free.
3. Packets do not collect at individual stations; that is, a station transmits each packet before the next arrives, hence $I = S$. This assumption weakens at higher loads, where stations are faced with increasing delays for each packet.
4. G, the offered load, is Poisson distributed.

These assumptions do not reflect accurately any actual system. For example, higher-order moments or even the entire probability distribution of packet length or G may be needed for accurate results. These assumptions do provide analytic tractability, enabling the development of closed-form expressions for performance. Thus they provide a common basis for comparing a number of protocols and they allow the development of results that give insight into behavior of systems.

To begin, let us consider the centralized network of Figure 10-1a and assume that all stations are equidistant from the central node. Traffic is generated as so many packets per second. It is convenient to normalize this to using the packet transmission time; then we can view S as the number of packets generated per packet time. Since the capacity of the channel is one packet per packet time, S also has a meaning of throughput as a fraction of capacity.

The total traffic on the channel will consist of new packets plus packets that must be retransmitted because of collision:

$$G = S + \text{(number of retransmitted packets per unit time)}$$

Now, a packet must be retransmitted if it suffers a collision. Thus we can express the rate of retransmissions as $G \times \text{Pr}$ [individual packet suffers a collision]. Note that we must use G rather than S in this expression.

To determine the probability of collision, consider Figure 10-6a, which shows three stations that transmit packets at random times. Each transmission takes a normalized transmission time of 1. A packet generated by any station reaches the central node after a constant propagation delay (equidistant stations). Now, if two stations begin to transmit at exactly the same time, their packets will arrive at the controller at the same time and suffer a collision. Moreover, a packet transmitted by station A will suffer a collision if B begins transmission prior to A but within a time period 1 of the beginning of A's transmission, or if B begins transmission after A within a time period 1 of the beginning of A's transmission. Thus the vulnerable period is of length 2.

We have assumed that G is Poisson distributed. For a Poisson process with rate λ, the probability of transmission in a period of time t is $1 - e^{-\lambda t}$. Thus the probability of transmission during the vulnerable period is $1 - e^{-2G}$. Therefore, we have

$$G = S + G(1 - e^{-2G})$$

So

$$\text{ALOHA: } S = Ge^{-2G} \qquad (10\text{-}1)$$

This derivation assumes that G is Poisson, which is not the case even for I Poisson. However, studies indicate that this is a good approximation [SCHW77]. Also, deeper analysis indicates that the infinite population assumption results closely approximate finite population results at reasonably small numbers: say, 50 or more stations [KLEI76].

Another way of deriving (10-1) is to note that S/G is the fraction of offered packets that are transmitted successfully, which is just the probability that for each packet, no additional packets arrive during the vulnerable period, which is e^{-2G}.

One question that might be asked on the basis of Equation (10-1) is: What is the maximum possible throughput using ALOHA? If we differentiate Equation (10-1) with respect to G and set it equal to zero, we find that the maximum occurs at $G = 0.5$ and that $S = 1/2e = 0.18$. That is, the maximum throughput is only 18% of capacity. For example, ALOHANET uses a data rate of 9600 bps. Using the ALOHA scheme, the maximum total throughput (the sum of the data arriving from all user nodes) is only $0.18 \times 9600 = 1728$ bps. Furthermore, this capacity of 1728 bps must be shared among all user nodes.

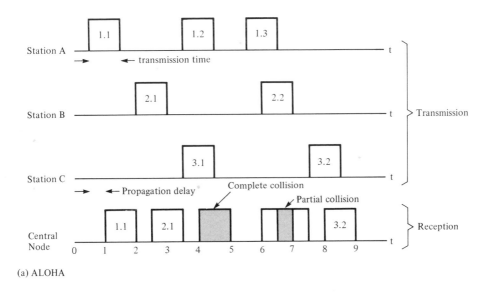

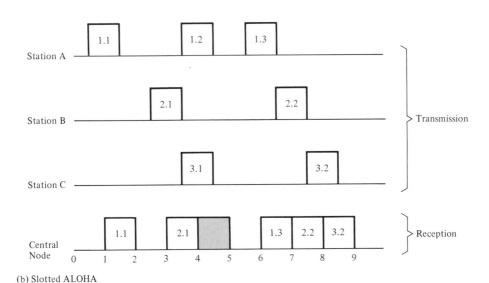

FIGURE 10-6. Behavior of ALOHA and slotted ALOHA in a centralized packet radio network.

Delay is more difficult to calculate, but the following reasoning gives a good approximation. We define delay as the time interval from when a user node is ready to transmit a packet until when it is successfully received by the central node. This delay is simply the sum of queueing delay, propagation delay, and transmission time. In ALOHA, the queueing delay is 0; that is, a node transmits immediately when it has a packet to transmit. However, because of collisions, we may consider the queueing delay time to be the total time consumed prior to successful transmission, (i.e., the total time spent in unsuccessful transmissions). To get at this, we need to know the expected number of transmissions per packet. A little

is $\frac{G}{S}$

thought shows that this is simply G/S. So the expected number of retransmissions per packet is just $G/S - 1 = e^{2G} - 1$. The delay, D, can then be expressed as

$$D = (e^{2G} - 1)\,\delta + a + 1$$

where δ is the average delay for one retransmission and a is the normalized propagation delay (see Appendix 10A). A common normalized algorithm used for ALOHA is to retransmit after a time selected from a uniform distribution of from 1 to K packet-transmission times. This minimizes repeated collisions. The average delay is then $(K + 1)/2$. To this, we must add the amount of time a station must wait to determine that its packet was unsuccessful. This is just time it would take to complete a transmission $(1 + a)$ plus the time it would take for the receiver to generate an acknowledgment (w) plus the propagation time for the acknowledgment to reach the station (a). For simplicity, we assume that acknowledgment packets do not suffer collisions. Thus

$$ALOHA: D = (e^{2G} - 1)\left(1 + 2a + w + \frac{k + 1}{2}\right) + a + 1 \quad (10\text{-}2)$$

Now let us consider the distributed packet radio network. Behavior in this case is slightly different and it will be instructive here for the reader to ponder Figure 10-6a and Appendix 10A. The difference is this: If the propagation delay between stations A and B is a, then a packet transmitted by A will suffer a collision if B begins transmission prior to A but within a time period $1 + a$ of the beginning of A's transmission or if B begins transmission after A within a time period $1 + a$ of the beginning of A's transmission. Thus the vulnerable period is of length $2(1 + a)$. Some calculation reveals that this alters Equations (10-1) and (10-2) as follows:

$$S = Ge^{-2(1+a)G} \quad (10\text{-}3)$$

$$D = (e^{2(1+a)G} - 1)\left(1 + 2a + w + \frac{k + 1}{2}\right) + a + 1 \quad (10\text{-}4)$$

For the typical packet radio network, a is extremely small, 10^{-3} or less. Thus we may safely ignore this refinement. However, we will find that it is relevant in the case of satellite and local networks.

Before attempting to discuss the results obtained so far, let us consider an improved version of ALOHA, namely slotted ALOHA.

Slotted ALOHA

We have seen that the maximum throughput with ALOHA is only 0.18. To improve efficiency, a modification of ALOHA [ROBE75], slotted ALOHA (S-ALOHA), was developed in which time on the channel is organized into uniform slots whose size equals the packet transmission time. Some central clock or other technique is needed to synchronize all stations. Transmission is permitted only to begin at a slot boundary. Thus packets that do overlap will do so totally (see Figure 10-6b).

Throughput for slotted ALOHA is also easily calculated. All packets begin transmission on a slot boundary. Thus the number of packets that are transmitted during a slot time is equal to the number that was generated during the previous slot and await transmission. So the probability that an individual packet suffers collision is

$1 - e^{-G}$. Thus we have:

$$\text{S-ALOHA: } S = Ge^{-G} \tag{10-5}$$

Differentiating (10-5) with respect to G, we have that the maximum possible value for S is $1/e = 1/0.37$. Thus the effective throughput of a packet radio network is doubled by this simple refinement.

Equations (10-1) and (10-5) are plotted in Figure 10-7, which provides insight into the nature of the instability problem with contention protocols. As offered load increases, so does throughput until, beyond its maximum value, throughput actually declines as G increases. This is because there is an increased frequency of collisions: More packets are offered, but fewer successfully escape collision. Worse, this situation may persist even if the input to the system drops to zero! Consider: For high G, virtually all offered packets are retransmissions and virtually none get through. So, even if no new packets are generated, the system will remain occupied in an unsuccessful attempt to clear the backlog; the effective capacity of the system is virtually zero. Thus, even in a moderately loaded system, a temporary burst of work could move the network into the high-collision region permanently.

Delay for S-ALOHA may be estimated in a similar fashion to that of ALOHA. The main difference now is that there is a delay, averaging half a slot time, between the time a node is ready to send a frame and the time the next slot begins:

$$\textit{S-ALOHA: } D = (e^G - 1)\left(1 + 2a + w + \frac{k + 1}{2}\right) + 1.5a + 1.5 \tag{10-6}$$

These formulas confirm the instability of contention-based protocols under heavy load. As the rate of new packets increases, so does the number of collisions. We can see that both the number of collisions and the average delay grow exponentially with G. Thus there is not only a trade-off between throughput (S) and delay (D), but a third factor enters the trade-off: stability. Figure 10-8 illustrates this point. Figure 10-8a shows that delay increases exponentially with offered load. But Figure 10-8b is perhaps more meaningful. It shows that delay increases with throughput up to the maximum possible throughput. Beyond that point, although throughput declines because of increased numbers of collisions, the delay continues to rise.

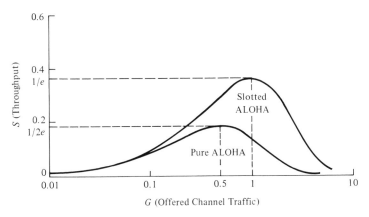

FIGURE 10-7. Performance of ALOHA, S-ALOHA with $a = 0$.

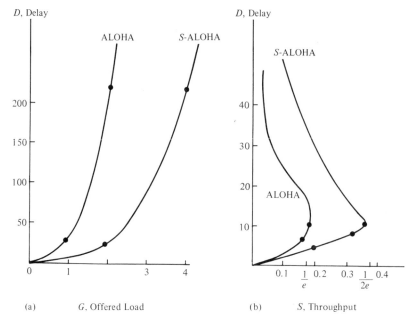

FIGURE 10-8.   Delay as a function of G and S (a = 0, K = 5).

It is worth pondering Figures 10-7 and 10-8 to get a better feeling for the behavior of contention channels. Recall that we mentioned that both S and G are "derived" parameters, and what we would really like to estimate is the actual traffic generated by network devices, the "input load" I. As long as the input load is less than the maximum potential throughput, $\text{Max}_G(S)$, then $I = S$. That is, the throughput of the system equals the input load. Therefore, all packets get through. However, if $I > \text{Max}_G(S)$, Figures 10-7 and 10-8 no longer apply. The system cannot transmit packets as fast as they arrive. The result: If I remains above the threshold indefinitely, then D goes to infinity, S goes to zero, and G grows without bound.

Figure 10-8b shows that, for a given value of S, there are two possible values of D. How can this be? In both cases, $I = S$, and the system is transmitting all input packets. The explanation is as follows: As the input, $I = S$, approaches the saturation point, the stochastic nature of the input will eventually lead to a period of a high rate of collisions, resulting in decreased throughput and higher packet delays.

Finally, we mention that these results depend critically on the assumptions made. For example, if there is only one station transmitting, the achievable throughput is 1.0, not 0.18 or 0.37. Indeed, with a single user at high data rate and a set of other users at very low data rates, utilization approaching 1 can be achieved. However, the delay encountered by the other users is significantly longer than in the homogeneous case. In general, the more unbalanced the source rates, the higher the throughput [KLEI76].

As before, equations for slotted ALOHA can be derived that take into account the parameter a:

$$S = Ge^{-(1+a)G} \tag{10-7}$$

$$D = (e^{(1+a)G} - 1)\left(1 + 2a + w + \frac{k+1}{2}\right) + 1.5a + 1.5 \tag{10-8}$$

CSMA

We have seen that even with slotted ALOHA, the maximum channel utilization is only 0.37. Both of these protocols fail to take advantage of one of the key properties of packet radio networks, which is that the propagation delay between stations is insignificant compared to packet transmission time (a is very small).

Consider the following observations. If the station-to-station propagation time is large compared to the packet transmission time, then, after a station launches a packet, it will be a long time before other stations know about it. During that time, one of the other stations may transmit a packet; the two packets may interfere with each other, and neither gets through. Indeed, if the distances are great enough, many stations may begin transmitting, one after the other, and none of their packets gets through unscathed. Suppose, however, that the propagation time is extremely small compared to packet transmission time. In that case, when a station launches a packet, all the other stations know it almost immediately. So, if they had any sense, they would not try transmitting until the first station was done. Collisions would be rare since they would occur only when two stations began to transmit almost simultaneously. Another way of looking at it is that the short delay time provides the stations with better feedback about the state of the system; this information can be used to improve efficiency.

The foregoing observations led to the development of a technique known as carrier sense multiple access (CSMA) or listen before talk (LBT). A station wishing to transmit first listens to the medium to determine if another transmission is in progress. If the medium is idle, the station may transmit. Otherwise, the station backs off some period of time and tries again, using one of the algorithms explained below. After transmitting, a station waits a reasonable amount of time for an acknowledgment, taking into account the maximum round-trip propagation delay, and the fact that the acknowledging station must also contend for the channel in order to respond.

One can see how this strategy would be effective for systems in which the packet transmission time is much longer than the propagation time. Collisions can occur only when more than one user begins transmitting within a short time (within the period of propagation delay). If a station begins to transmit, and there are no collisions during the time it takes for the leading edge of the packet to propagate to the farthest station, then the station has seized the channel and the remainder of the packet will be transmitted without collision.

With CSMA, an algorithm is needed to specify what a station should do if the medium is found to be busy. Three approaches are depicted in Figure 10-9. One algorithm is *nonpersistent* CSMA, which is the algorithm used in MP-Net. A station wishing to transmit listens to the medium and obeys the following rules:

1. If the medium is idle, transmit.
2. If the medium is busy, wait an amount of time drawn from a probability distribution (the retransmission delay) and repeat step 1.

The use of random retransmission times reduces the probability of collisions. The drawback is that even if several stations have a packet to send, there is likely to be some wasted idle time following a prior transmission.

To avoid channel idle time, the *1-persistent protocol* can be used. A station wishing to transmit listens to the medium and obeys the following rules:

1. If the medium is idle, transmit.

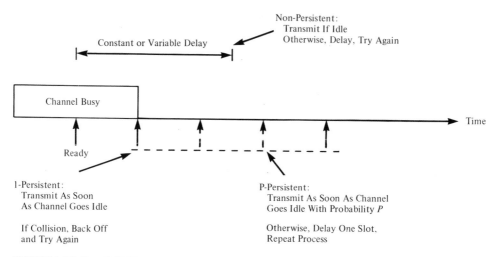

FIGURE 10-9. CSMA persistence and backoff.

2. If the medium is busy, continue to listen until the channel is sensed idle, then transmit immediately.
3. If there is a collision (determined by a lack of acknowledgment), wait a random amount of time and repeat step 1.

Whereas nonpersistent stations are deferential, 1-persistent stations are selfish. If two or more stations are waiting to transmit, a collision is guaranteed. Things only get sorted out after the collision.

A compromise that attempts to reduce collisions, like nonpersistent, and reduce idle time, like 1-persistent, is *p-persistent*. The rules are:

1. If the medium is idle, transmit with probability p, and delay one time unit with probability $(1 - p)$. The time unit is typically equal to the maximum propagation delay.
2. If the medium is busy, continue to listen until the channel is idle and repeat step 1.
3. If transmission is delayed one time unit, repeat step 1.

The question arises as to what is an effective value of p. The main problem to avoid is one of instability under heavy load. Consider the case in which n stations have packets to send while a transmission is taking place. At the end of that transmission, the expected number of stations that will attempt to transmit is np. If np is greater than 1, multiple stations will attempt to transmit and there will be a collision. What is more, as soon as all these stations realize that they did not get through, they will be back again, almost guaranteeing more collisions. Worse yet, these retries will compete with new transmissions from other stations, further increasing the probability of collision. Eventually, all stations will be trying to send, causing continuous collisions, with throughput dropping to zero. To avoid this catastrophe np must be less than one for the expected peaks of n. As p is made smaller, stations must wait longer to attempt transmission but collisions are reduced. At low loads, however, stations have unnecessarily long delays.

The performance of CSMA depends on the persistence policy. The easiest to analyze is nonpersistent CSMA, and we will be content with that. Again, we assume $a = 0$. Time on the channel consists of two types of intervals. First is a

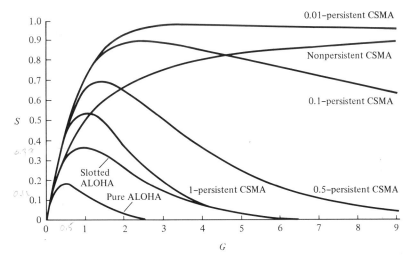

FIGURE 10-10. Throughput of various contention protocols with _a_ = 0.

transmission interval, which lasts a time period 1. Second is an idle period, which is the time between transmissions. If we assume a Poisson offered load G, the expected value of the idle period is $1/G$. Total throughput consists of the fraction of time that the channel is busy:

$$S = \frac{1}{1 + 1/G}$$

$$\text{Nonpersistent CSMA:} \quad S = \frac{G}{G + 1}$$

Figure 10-10 compares the achievable throughput for the various protocols discussed so far, assuming that $a = 0$. It is clear that dramatic improvement can be achieved using CSMA.

10-3

SATELLITE NETWORK ARCHITECTURE

We mentioned in Part I that a satellite communications link has some unique properties:

- A satellite in geosynchronous orbit is visible to about one-fourth of the earth's surface.
- Transmission cost is independent of distance, within the satellite's area of coverage.
- Both broadcast and point-to-point applications are possible.
- Very high bandwidths or data rates are available to users.
- Although satellite links are subject to periodic, short-term outages, the quality of transmission is normally extremely high.
- There is an earth-satellite-earth propagation delay of about one-fourth of a second.
- A transmitting station can in many cases receive its own transmission.

TABLE 10-1   Characteristics of Satellite Links

Configurations	Capacity Allocation
Earth stations	Access control
Fixed-assignment carrier	Centralized (satellite)
Multiplexed	Distributed (earth station)
User stations	Allocation strategy
Link configurations	FDM
Point-to-point	FDMA
Point-to-many	SCPC
Many-to-many	DAMA
Many-to-point	TDM
	TDMA
	SS-TDMA
	DAMA
	Multiple-access protocols
	Polling
	Contention
	Reservation

Satellite links are used in a wide variety of configurations, some of which are in the nature of a point-to-point link, others of which are more in the nature of a communication network. Table 10-1 summarizes some of the key characteristics of satellite communication links and groups these into a number of categories. These categories are not independent but interrelated in complex ways. In the remainder of this section we will describe these characteristics and give examples. In doing so, we will need to talk about medium access control. However, a detailed discussion of such protocols is deferred to Section 10-4.

Configurations

The first two categories in Table 10-1 deal with the types of communications configurations that are possible with a satellite link. The variety of configurations that is possible is determined primarily by the nature of the earth stations and the interconnections provided by the satellite link.

Types of Earth Stations.   Figure 10-11 depicts three general categories of earth stations; the term earth station refers to a station with a direct communications link to a satellite. By contrast, we use the term ''user station'' to refer to some endpoint station which indirectly makes use of the satellite link; the distinction should become clear soon. Figure 10-11a indicates the use of a satellite as a link for carrying bulk, long-haul transmission traffic. In this case, the satellite is being used in much the same way as a coaxial cable or terrestrial microwave link. The most common application for this type of earth station is as a component of the long-haul telecommunication network. An example of an FDM carrier providing this facility is COMSTAR-2 [BELL82a]. The satellite uses the 4/6-GHz bands and provides a 500-MHz bandwidth which is broken up into 12 40-MHz channels. Actually, the system provides 24 channels (12 full-duplex channels) by means of

 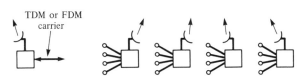

TDM or FDM carrier

TDM or FDM carrier

(a) Carrier facilities

(b) Multiplexed stations

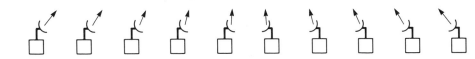

(c) Individual stations

FIGURE 10-11.   Types of satellite earth stations.

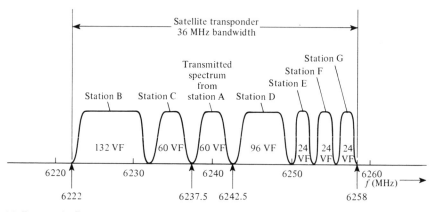

(a) Transponder Frequency Allocation

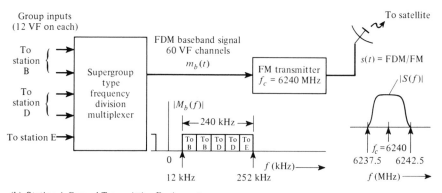

(b) Station A Ground Transmitting Equipment

FIGURE 10-12.   A fixed-assignment FDMA configuration.

frequency reuse; each frequency assignment is used by two carriers with orthogonal polarization. The 40-MHz channel includes 4 MHz of guard bands, so each channel is actually 36 MHz wide. A total of 1200 voice channels are carried in each 40-MHz channel using a second level of FDM. A similar system could be provided using a synchronous TDM scheme in each of the 40-MHz channels. For example, a 36-MHz channel may be used on the WESTAR satellite to carry one of the following:

- One 50-Mbps data stream.
- 16 channels of 1.544 Mbps each.
- 400 channels of 64 kbps each.
- 600 channels of 40 kbps each.

The discussion above suggests that the satellite is used as an intermediate device providing, in effect, a point-to-point link between two stations. Because of the wide-area coverage of the satellite, this is not necessarily the case. As an example, Figure 10-12 shows seven stations sharing a 36-MHz bandwidth. Station *A* is assigned the band of 6237.5 to 6242.5 MHz in which it can transmit 60 voice-frequency channels using FDM/FM. That is, FDM is used to carry the 60 channels, and FM is used to modulate the channels onto the carrier frequency, which is in the 6-GHz band. The figure indicates that station A has traffic for other stations as follows: 24 channels to B, 24 channels to D, and 12 channels to E. The remaining spectrum of the 36-MHz channel is divided among the other earth stations according to their traffic needs. The last example brings up several instructive points:

- The scheme described is referred to as a fixed-assignment frequency-division multiple access (FDMA) scheme. The term "fixed assignment" refers to the fact that the logical links between stations are preassigned. Thus in Figure 10-12, it appears to station A that it has three direct point-to-point links, one each to B (24 channels), D (24 channels), and E (12 channels). FDMA refers to the fact that multiple stations are accessing the satellite link by using different frequency bands.

- Although an earth station may transmit only one carrier up to the satellite (e.g., station A transmits at 6.24 GHz with a bandwidth of 5 MHz), it must be prepared to receive at least one carrier for each distant location with which it wishes to communicate (e.g., station A must receive three carriers, parts of the transmission of B, D, and E).

- The satellite performs no switching function. Although it is receiving portions of the 36-MHz channel from various sources, it simply accepts signals across that spectrum, translates them to the 4 GHz band, and retransmits them.

- Considerable bandwidth is used. For example, station A has 60 voice-frequency channels to transmit, which occupies only 240 kHz. Yet the satellite bandwidth allocation is 5 MHz. This is due to the use of FM (rather than AM) to maintain signal quality over the long distance of the satellite link and to minimize satellite power requirements.

Skipping next to Figure 10-11c, we see the extreme opposite to the use of a satellite link as a high-capacity carrier trunk. In this case multiple stations communicate directly with the satellite, functioning as both earth stations and user stations. Note the similarity to Figure 10-1a. With individual user stations functioning as earth stations we have a network in which any two stations may communicate via the satellite link. Multiple communication channels are provided with some form of either FDM or TDM. Examples will be discussed in Section 10-4.

An intermediate situation is depicted in Figure 10-10b. In this case, there are user stations, but these do not have direct links to the satellite. Rather, a group of user stations attach to an earth station which multiplexes traffic from all attached stations for transmission. Again, a variety of schemes are used. We mention two general examples.

- Any pair of these stations could have a dedicated channel between them, such as one of the 1.544 Mbps channels on a TDM channel or a 40-MHz FDM channel. This channel could then be used for a statistical TDM scheme.

- A circuit-switching capability could be provided by the satellite. Each earth station then functions in a manner analogous to a data or voice link group on a CBX and the satellite functions in a manner analogous to the central switch (Figure 8-20). This technique is examined below.

Satellite Link Characteristics. Figure 10-11 implies a symmetry between uplink and downlink transmission that is not always present. We can characterize satellite links by the number of stations transmitting on the uplink and the number of stations receiving on the downlink. Of course, this characterization depends in part on how much of the spectrum one is talking about. For example, for a satellite with a 500 MHz capacity, it is unlikely that that entire capacity would be used between two points. However, a 40-MHz channel might be so used.

Within a single channel, we have given examples of both point-to-point and many-to-many connections. An example of many-to-point might be a system that collects data from a variety of sources (e.g., sensor data) and delivers them to a single receiver. Far more common is point-to-many, and the prime example of this is TV broadcasting.

Communications satellites have been transmitting commercial broadcast and cable television programs since 1975. The TV signal is frequency modulated onto a carrier in the 6-GHz uplink band; one TV channel occupies one 40-MHz satellite channel using FM. The signal is provided to the satellite by a network or cable TV source and retransmitted on a 4-GHz downlink. The retransmissions are intended primarily for reception by central distribution hubs, such as broadcast stations and cable TV distribution centers. It is possible for people to pick up these signals, but the antennas required are large and expensive.

Another example of point-to-many video transmission, with a more sizable "many," is *direct broadcast satellite* (DBS) [GOUL84, MCDO83]. During the 1970s DBS was successfully tested on a number of experimental satellites, and this has led to design efforts that should culminate in DBS service in the mid-1980s. With this scheme, transmission is in the 12/14-GHz band at higher power; thus smaller (less than 1 meter diameter), less expensive antennas can be used, and it is feasible for people to receive signals for their TV sets directly from rooftop or backyard earth stations.

Capacity Allocation

Typically, a single satellite will handle a rather large bandwidth (e.g., 500 MHz) and divide it into a number of channels of smaller bandwidth (e.g., 40 MHz). Within each of these channels, there is a capacity allocation task to be performed. In some instances, such as TV broadcasting and a single 50 Mbps digital data stream, the entire channel is dedicated to a single user or purpose. With these exceptions, however, the cost-effective use of the satellite requires that each channel be shared by many users. In some cases, the allocation is carried out by centralized control, usually by the satellite; but in most cases, the allocation is a distributed function carried out by the earth station. We will see examples of both.

All of the allocation strategies can be categorized as either frequency-division or time-division strategies. The task is, fundamentally, one of multiplexing, and most of the schemes in use today employ variants of one or the other of the schemes discussed in Chapter 6. In some configurations, however, the satellite link takes on the character of a multipoint medium and some form of multiple access protocol is required. We will survey all these strategies in this section.

FDM. We have mentioned that FDM is almost always employed, in the sense that a satellite's total bandwidth is divided into channels. Each of these channels is, in turn, usually shared by multiple stations. When each of these stations is assigned a different carrier frequency or group of frequencies on a fixed basis, it is referred to as *frequency-division multiple access* (FDMA). Actually, all of the techniques to be discussed in this section are FDMA, since they involve access to a channel by multiple stations using FDM, but the term is generally reserved for the case of fixed assignment. Further, it is generally assumed for FDMA that each earth station supports multiple user stations on each of its assigned subchannels. Thus some further FDM or TDM technique must be used to allocate subchannel capacity.

The operation of an FDMA system is simple. The example presented earlier (Figure 10-12) is typical. A number of earth stations are assigned transmit carrier frequencies and bands. The satellite accepts signals across the entire spectrum of a channel, translates the entire channel to a different frequency, and retransmits. As an aside, we will see that a midsplit broadband local network works in much the same fashion.

The number of subchannels provided within a satellite channel via FDMA is limited by three factors:

- Thermal noise.
- Intermodulation noise.
- Cochannel interference.

We have seen (Figure 2-18) that the first two factors work in opposite directions. With too little signal strength, the transmitted signal will be corrupted by background noise. With too much signal strength, nonlinear effects in the satellite's amplifiers results in high intermodulation noise. The third factor, cochannel interference, stems from a desire to increase capacity by reusing frequencies, and limits but does not eliminate that practice. A frequency band can be reused if antennas that can radiate two polarized signals of the same frequency (cochannels) in orthogonal planes are employed. Again, if signal strength is too high, cochannel interference becomes significant.

The FDMA scheme just described is not terribly efficient. Typically, in the 6/4-GHz band, each channel has a usable bandwidth of 36 MHz. One standard FDMA scheme [FREE81] divides this into seven 5-MHz blocks, each of which carries a supergroup of 60 voice channels, for a total of 420 voice channels. When the channel is subdivided into 14 2.5-MHz channels, two groups (24 channels) are carried in each subchannel for a total of 336 channels. A more efficient utilization of the bandwidth is to avoid groupings altogether and simply to divide the 36-MHz bandwidth up into individual voice-frequency channels. This technique is known as single-channel per carrier (SCPC).

SCPC is currently provided in the 6/4-GHz band. A single 36-MHz channel is subdivided into 800 45-kHz channels, each dedicated to a simplex voice-frequency link. Analog systems use FM. There is also digital SCPC, using QPSK which provides 64-kbps service, enough for digitized voice. Both schemes use the 45-kHz bandwidth [FEHE83]. With fixed assignment, pairs of channels (for full duplex) are assigned to pairs of earth stations. Typically, each earth station is multiplexed, supporting a small number of user stations. This corresponds roughly to Figure 10-11b. With multiple user stations per earth station, a high degree of connectivity is achieved even with fixed assignment. As with conventional FDMA, the satellite accepts frequencies across the entire 36-MHz channel, translates them to the 4-GHz band, and broadcasts the channel to all stations.

SCPC is attractive for remote areas where there are few user stations near each site. Whereas FDMA is used as a trunk facility in the long-haul telecommunications system, SCPC provides direct end-user service. Although SCPC is more efficient than FDMA, it does suffer from the inefficiency of fixed assignment. This is especially unsuitable in very remote areas where it is typical that each earth station would serve one or a very few user stations (such as Figure 10-11c). To achieve greater efficiency, a technique known as demand-assignment multiple access (DAMA) is used. With DAMA, the set of subchannels in a channel is treated as a pool of available links. To establish a full-duplex link between two earth stations, a pair of subchannels is dynamically assigned on demand. This is a form of circuit switching.

The first commercially available DAMA system was SPADE (*s*ingle channel per carrier, *p*ulse code modulation, multiple-*a*ccess, *d*emand-assignment *e*quipment), introduced in the early 1970s and used on INTELSAT IVA and V satellites [EDEL72]. As with ordinary SCPC, a 36-MHz bandwidth is divided into 45-kHz subchannels. Each subchannel carries a 64-kbps QPSK signal, which occupies 38 kHz, plus a 7-kHz guardband. Typically, the signal is used to carry PCM voice traffic. With control overhead, explained below, a total of 794 subchannels are available. These subchannels are paired such that two channels 18.045 MHz apart are always used to form a full-duplex circuit (e.g.; 3-404, 4-405, 399-800). In addition, there is a 160-kHz common-signaling channel (CSC) which carries a 128 kbps PSK signal.

Demand assignment is performed in a distributed fashion, by the earth stations, using the CSC. The CSC is used to transmit a repetitive TDM frame as shown in Figure 10-13. The frame is divided into 50 slots, the first of which is devoted to a preamble pattern for synchronization. The remaining slots are permanently assigned to 49 stations. These stations have the privilege of forming full-duplex circuits on demand. This is accomplished as follows. Assume that station S_i wishes to establish a circuit with S_j. Then S_i selects a subchannel randomly from the available idle channels and transmits the subchannel identifier plus the address of station S_j in the S_i time slot. Station S_j will hear this request on the downlink about 0.25 s later. Assuming that the subchannel is still available and S_j is available, S_j transmits an acknowledgment in its own time slot, which is heard by S_i another quarter second later. When the call is complete, disconnect information is transmitted in the time slot of one of the stations to inform the others that the subchannel is again idle.

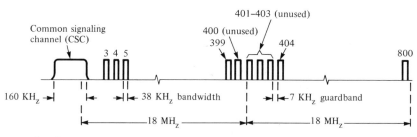

(a) Frequency allocation

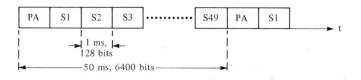

(b) CSC frame format

FIGURE 10-13. SPADE system for switched SCPC service.

Since only 49 stations can participate in this scheme, most of the subchannels are not required. These are used for ordinary fixed-assignment SCPC.

Although the SPADE system did provide the expected advantages of DAMA, the cost and complexity of the equipment at each site was considered too high and the system was discontinued. Recently, however, work has gone forward on other DAMA-SCPC schemes in the 14/12-GHz band and commercial service is likely by the late 1980s [EDEL82]. The basic concept is to develop a system that requires no switching or routing functions in either the satellite or earth stations, but to leave this task to a PBX or telephone company central office. As with fixed-assignment SCPC, each station has two dedicated subchannels for a full-duplex link. In this scheme, however, both subchannels are linked to the central earth station, which performs the circuit-switching function. The only drawback is that two hops are now required between user stations (user station 1 to central office via satellite, central office to user station 2 via satellite).

Finally, we mention that another way to increase utilization and flexibility is to have multiple stations share the same SCPC subchannel. An example of this is the ARPANET satellite IMP [WEIS78]. A number of satellite IMPs are part of the packet-switched network and share a single 64-kbps SCPC channel. Various multiple-access protocols have been tried, including slotted ALOHA and some of the protocols to be discussed in Section 10-4.

TDM. Although FDM techniques are still the most common ones in satellite transmission, TDM techniques are in increasingly widespread use. The future seems to belong to TDM for a number of reasons, including:

- The continuing drop in costs of digital components.
- The advantages of digital techniques, discussed earlier.
- The increased efficiency of TDM due to the lack of intermodulation noise.

As with FDM, all of the techniques to be discussed provide for multiple access, but the fixed-assignment technique is blessed with the name *time-division multiple access* (TDMA). TDMA is in essence the same as synchronous TDM. Transmission is in the form of a series of frames, each of which is divided into a number of slots. Each slot position across frames is dedicated to a particular transmitter. Frame lengths range from 125 s to 15 ms and consist of from 5 to 15 slots. Data rates range from 10 Mbps to over 100 Mbps.

Figure 10-14 depicts a typical frame [BELL82a] (compare Figure 6-7). The frame length is 750 μs and contains ten data bursts. The individual data bursts

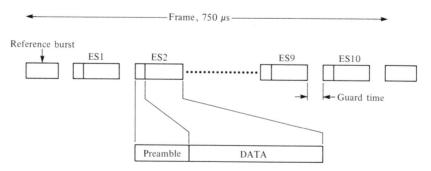

FIGURE 10-14. TDMA frame format.

may be transmitted by different stations. Each data frame begins with a *preamble* which contains a synchronization pattern and other network control data. The bursts are separated by *guard times* to ensure that there is no overlap. To synchronize the stations, each frame begins with a *reference burst* provided by a master station.

The operation of TDMA is depicted in Figure 10-15. Individual stations take turns using the uplink channel and may put a burst of data in the assigned time slot. The satellite repeats all incoming transmissions, which are broadcast to all stations. Thus all stations must know not only which time slot to use for transmissions, but which time slot to use for reception. The satellite is also repeating the reference burst, and all stations synchronize on the reception of that burst.

Each of the repetitive time slots is a subchannel and is independent of the other subchannels. Hence it can be used in any way that is deemed appropriate by the transmitting station. For example, a form of switching can be achieved by including an address field in each time slot. Thus, although the transmitting slot is dedicated, a number of stations could read the data in each slot looking for data addressed to them. Another example of a more sophisticated TDMA scheme is presented in [PONT83].

Ordinary TDMA is more efficient than ordinary FDMA because the guard times and control bits of TDMA utilize less capacity than the guard bands of FDMA. This is illustrated in Figure 10-16. Note the dramatic drop in capacity of FDMA as the number of subchannels increases. By contrast, TDMA drops much more slowly as the number of time slots (subchannels) increases. The use of a long frame time also increases efficiency. For comparison, a SCPC system provides a constant capacity of 800 channels whether its bandwidth is divided among many or a few earth stations.

Even greater efficiencies can be achieved as the newer, higher-frequency (e.g., 14/12-GHz and 30/20-GHz) bands come into use. At these frequencies, satellite transmission beams can be quite narrowly focused, allowing multiple beams on the

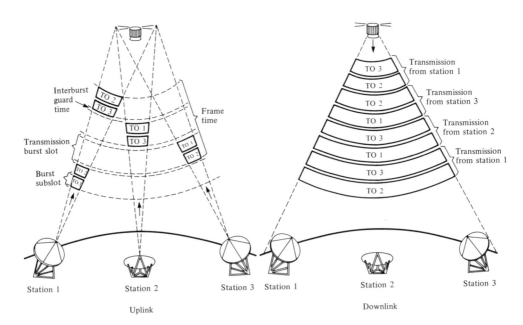

FIGURE 10-15. TDMA operation.

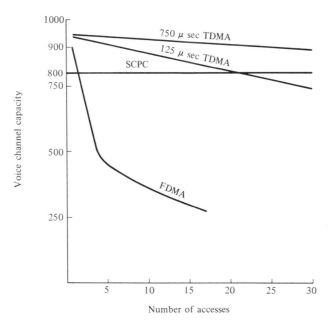

FIGURE 10-16. Relative efficiency of various satellite capacity allocation schemes. Source: [EDEL82]

same frequency to be transmitted to different areas. Thus a satellite can service a number of areas, each containing a number of earth stations. Communication among stations within a single area could be accomplished with ordinary TDMA. More-over, communication among stations in different areas can be achieved if the satellite has the capability to switch time slots from one beam to another. This is known as *satellite-switched time-division multiple access* (SS/TDMA) [SCAR83].

Figure 10-17 depicts a simple SS-TDMA system serving two areas, each with two stations. As with ordinary TDMA, only one station at a time may transmit within an area. So within area *A*, either station 1 or 2 may transmit at any one time. However, one station from area *B* may also transmit at any time. Stations from the two areas do not interfere either through the use of polarized signals or different frequencies. At the satellite, data that are received are immediately re-transmitted on a downlink frequency. Now, however, two separate downlink beams are used. The station contains a switch for interconnecting input beams and output beams. The connections through the switch may change over time. In the figure, downlink beam *A* repeats uplink beam *A* during periods 1 and 3 and repeats uplink *B* during period 2. Thus any station in any area can send data to any other station in any area.

This technique is a form of time-multiplexed switched, as described in Chapter 8. For a satellite serving *N* areas, there are *N* time-division multiplexed input streams. At any given time, the switch is configured to route these uplink beams in a particular fashion to the *N* downlink beams. Each configuration is referred to as a mode and *N*! modes are required for full connectivity. Table 10-2 shows the modes for a three-area system. For example, stations in area *A* can communicate with each other during modes 1 and 2, communicate with stations in area *B* during modes 3 and 5, and so on. The satellite will switch from mode to mode periodically. At most a mode change would occur once per slot time. The mode pattern and

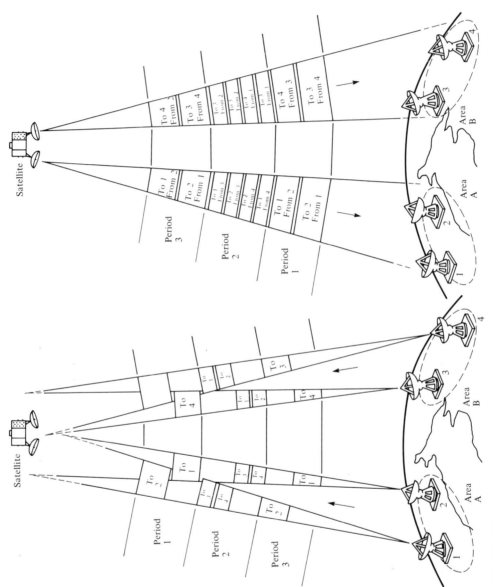

FIGURE 10-17. SS/TDMA operation.

TABLE 10-2 SS/TDMA Modes (three beams)

Input	Output					
	Mode 1	Mode 2	Mode 3	Mode 4	Mode 5	Mode 6
A	A	A	B	C	B	C
B	B	C	A	A	C	B
C	C	B	C	B	A	A

duration are normally adjustable by ground command to meet changing traffic requirements.

Finally, DAMA techniques are employed with TDM satellite schemes. The SS/TDMA system is to some extent a DAMA system if the mode pattern can be changed by ground command. More commonly DAMA in the TDM context refers to multiple-access techniques for sharing a single channel. This is the subject of our next section.

10-4

SATELLITE CHANNEL ACCESS PROTOCOLS

This section is concerned with TDM-DAMA techniques for use on a single satellite channel. In this situation, there is a single uplink channel and a single downlink channel shared by multiple earth stations. The satellite is essentially passive and performs three tasks:

- Accept all uplink signals.
- Translate signal to downlink frequency.
- Transmit downlink signals.

If two or more stations transmit simultaneously, a collision occurs. The satellite receives and retransmits garbled data. Because the satellite is passive, it is the collective responsibility of the earth stations to allocate channel capacity efficiently to maximize throughput and minimize collisions.

The situation described above is a common one, and considerable research has been done to develop suitable medium access control protocols. We begin by outlining those characteristics of a satellite network that are relevant to access control design, and then review some of the approaches that have been taken.

Characteristics

The design of a medium access control protocol for a satellite network is determined by two principal factors: the nature of the link and the nature of the users.

Let us examine the nature of the link first. The most important thing to note is that the bit length of the link is large. The up-and-down propagation delay is roughly one-fourth of a second, so the bit length is one-fourth of the data rate. SCPC channels are generally 64 kbps, which yields a length of 16,000 bits. At the upper end, a 50-Mbps channel is possible, yielding a length of 12.5 million bits! An immediate implication of the long bit length is that carrier-sense techniques will not work on a satellite network. Recall the CSMA protocol used for distributed packet-radio networks. A station refrains from transmitting if another station is already transmitting. With a satellite, a station will not know that another station is transmitting until a fourth of a second after the other starts, by which time it has long since ceased transmitting.

That's the bad news. The good news is an interesting property that satellites share with broadband local networks: A station receives its own transmissions. Thus an earth station knows, a fourth of a second after it has ceased transmitting, whether its transmission was successful or suffered a collision. This property is exploited in all of the protocols discussed below.

The other determining factor is the nature of the users of the communication service. In general, it is best to assume that there will be a variety of traffic types. For example, some of the stations may generate short, bursty traffic with modest throughput requirements but a need for a short delay time (e.g., transactions). Other stations may generate long streams of traffic that require high throughput, but they may be able to tolerate moderate delays prior to the start of a transmission (e.g., file transfers).

A fair random access scheme will not function well in these circumstances. For example, a stream transmission can cause intolerable delays for bursty traffic. If stream traffic load is stable, one solution is to dedicate certain portions of the bandwidth to various traffic types. This can be done using FDM or by dedicating certain time slots on a TDM system. However, if the stream traffic load varies, as when file transfers are made primarily at night and interactive traffic is high during the day, a fixed-allocation scheme lacks flexibility and is wasteful of bandwidth.

With these factors in mind, we can consider three generic approaches to access control: polling, contention, and reservation. Conventional polling, with a primary station and a number of secondary stations, is clearly inefficient. About a half second would elapse just in sending a poll and waiting for a response. For contention, since CSMA is impractical, ALOHA or S-ALOHA would be used. The performance calculation is the same as for a centralized packet-radio network: The maximum achievable utilization is only 0.37. Thus attention has focused on reservation schemes.

Reservation Protocols

To overcome the inherent disadvantages of polling and contention techniques for DAMA-TDMA, a number of reservation schemes have been proposed, and a few have been implemented. In this section we examine six of these schemes (Figure 10-18). These are representative and should give the reader a feeling for the nature of the trade-offs that must be made. In all of these schemes, a fixed frame length is used, which is divided into a number of time slots. (In what follows, we assume that there are K stations and M slots per frame that may be reserved.) Slots in future frames are reserved in some dynamic fashion for a specific station. The schemes differ primarily in the way in which the reservations are made and released.

Distributed Reservation. The simplest of these schemes is one proposed in [CROW73], called R-ALOHA (Figure 10-19a). In this scheme, there are generally fewer slots per frame than there are stations ($K > M$). Reservations are implicit: Successful transmission in a slot serves as a reservation for the corresponding slot in the next frame. By repeated use of that slot position, a station can transmit a long stream of data. A station wishing to transmit one or more packets (one packet per slot) of data monitors the slots in the current frame. Any slot that is empty or contains a collision is available for the next frame; the station may contend for that slot using S-ALOHA.

Several observations may be made. First, note that the frame length must be at least as long as the bit length of the link (i.e., 16,000 to 12.5 million bits for data rates of 56 kbps to 50 Mbps). This is so because a station must know the status of each slot in the most recent frame before considering its use in the next frame. Second, this approach allows a dynamic mixture of stream and bursty traffic. If the average message length (number of slots used per reservation) is long, the system behaves like a fixed-assignment TDMA scheme. If most of the traffic is bursty, the performance resembles S-ALOHA. In fact, performance could even be worse than S-ALOHA if most messages are one slot in length: After a slot is used,

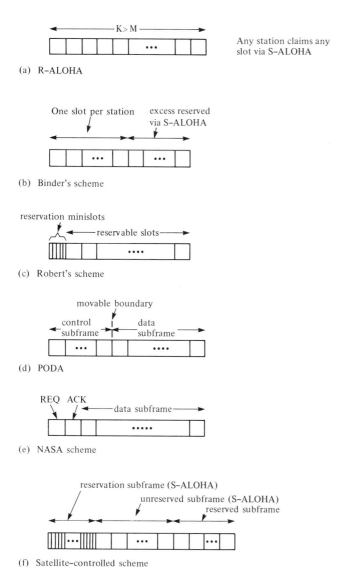

(a) R-ALOHA

(b) Binder's scheme

(c) Robert's scheme

(d) PODA

(e) NASA scheme

(f) Satellite-controlled scheme

FIGURE 10-18. Frame format for various satellite reservation protocols.

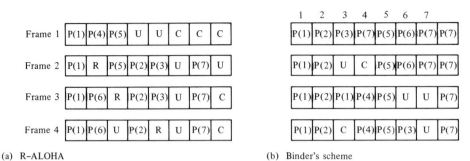

FIGURE 10-19. Implicit reservation schemes.

it will remain empty for the next frame because the stations do not realize that it is free. Performance can be improved by including an end-of-use flag with each message [LAM80]. Third, there is a basic fairness problem, since a station can capture most or all of the slots for an indefinite time; if many stations are active with long messages, average delay would be considerable.

The scheme described above will work with an unknown or dynamically varying number of stations. A scheme proposed in [BIND75b] (Figure 10-19b) requires a fixed number of stations less than or equal to the number of time slots in a frame $(K < M)$. Each station owns a particular slot position. If there are any extra slots, these are contended for by all stations using S-ALOHA. The owner may use its slot to transmit continuously. If the owner has no data to send, its slot will become empty and available for use by other stations. The owner gets its slot back simply by using it. If the transmission is successful, fine; if not, the collision causes other stations to defer and the owner reclaims its slot in the next frame. As before, the frame length must exceed the bit length.

There are two types of slots available for general use in this scheme: slots in excess of fixed-assignment slots (for K strictly less than M) and fixed-assignment slots that were unused in the previous frame. These could be allocated by S-ALOHA. Binder suggests a more complex scheme: Each station includes the length of its queue of slot-sized packets in the header of each packet that it sends. Each station keeps track of the global queue, which is the sum of the individual queues. A round-robin algorithm is used to allocate available slots to queued packets. Thus this scheme has the flavor of both an implicit and an explicit reservation protocol. A station that uses its own slot implicitly reserves it for the next frame. By broadcasting its queue length, a station is explicitly reserving future slots. This technique is superior to R-ALOHA for stream-dominated traffic, since each station is guaranteed one slot of bandwidth. However, when there are a large number of stations, this scheme can lead to a very large average delay because of the required number of slots per frame.

A different approach, proposed in [ROBE73], is to use explicit reservations exclusively. For this scheme, a frame is divided into equal-length slots, one of which is further subdivided into "minislots." The minislots, acquired via S-ALOHA, function as a common queue for all users. A station wishing to transmit must send a request packet in a minislot specifying the number of slots desired, up to some maximum number. If the reservation is successful (no collision), the station then determines which future slots it has acquired and transmits in them. To do this, the station keeps track of the current global queue length J, which is the sum of outstanding reservations. When each frame is received, the station adds to J the sum of all successful reservations (including its own, if any) and subtracts the number of slots containing data. When a reservation is successful, the station counts off J slots and then sends its data.

Figure 10-20 illustrates the operation. For lengthy streams, this scheme requires a user to contend for slots repeatedly, which results in significant delivery delay variances if there is much traffic. If the maximum reservation size is set high enough to allow complete stream transmissions, delays to begin transmission of other traffic become long. An analysis of the performance of this scheme indicates that it is a significant improvement over S-ALOHA. If the maximum number of slots that can be reserved in a single reservation is R, utilization can approach $R/(R + 1)$ for heavy loads [SCHW77].

A sophisticated scheme that combines elements of the other schemes just described is referred to as *priority-oriented demand assignment* (PODA). This approach has been implemented in SATNET, a prototype packet satellite network [JACO78]. Each frame consists of a data subframe, divided into data slots, and a control subframe divided into smaller reservation slots. A station with one or more packets to send must reserve data slots by transmitting a request during a reservation slot. A stream reservation is for one or more data slots per frame for the indefinite future. Further, once a station begins transmitting, additional reservations may be piggybacked onto a data packet.

If the number of stations is small, the control subframe consists of a fixed number of slots equal to the number of stations, and each station owns a reservation slot. For larger networks, the reservation slots are contended for using S-ALOHA. Also, the size of the control subframe decreases as the number of outstanding reservations increases, so that backlog can be cleared out.

All stations must keep track of all outstanding reservations. Each takes into account user-specified delay class and priority according to the same algorithm. For stream reservations, interpacket time is also specified. Each station automatically schedules future stream packets based on a single reservation. Additional reservations can by piggybacked on any transmission in the information subframe. These will be scheduled like reservations in the control subframe. Thus both reservation and information subframe messages must be monitored for content by every user. This places a heavy processing burden on each node.

The PODA scheme can also be used for centralized reservation. In this case the information subframe is divided into a centralized-assignment portion and a distributed-assignment portion. The reservation request mechanism does not change, but some types of requests are now filled by a central earth station.

Centralized Reservation. All of the protocols discussed so far are distributed reservation schemes (however, PODA accommodates centralized reservation). These schemes make few assumptions about traffic mix and avoid the delay that a central controller introduces. However, distributed schemes impose a greater processing burden on stations than do centralized ones, and are more vulnerable to a loss of synchronization. That is, distributed reservation schemes require that all stations

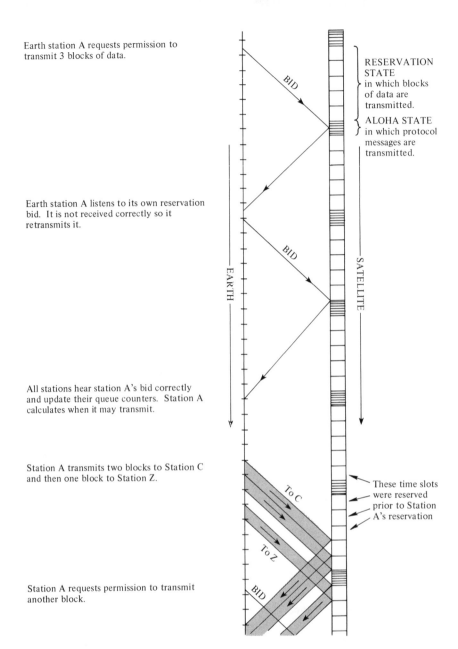

Earth station A requests permission to transmit 3 blocks of data.

BID

RESERVATION STATE in which blocks of data are transmitted.

ALOHA STATE in which protocol messages are transmitted.

Earth station A listens to its own reservation bid. It is not received correctly so it retransmits it.

BID

EARTH

SATELLITE

All stations hear station A's bid correctly and update their queue counters. Station A calculates when it may transmit.

Station A transmits two blocks to Station C and then one block to Station Z.

To C

These time slots were reserved prior to Station A's reservation

To Z

Station A requests permission to transmit another block.

BID

FIGURE 10-20. An ALOHA scheme with explicit reservations.

share the same perception of the current state (global queue status) of the system. Centralized schemes deal more easily with the problem of synchronization. Furthermore, the extra delay is generally acceptable for stream traffic.

Our first example is a centralized reservation scheme proposed to meet some unique NASA requirements [HEMM82]. The protocol was designed for a network of between 5 and 20 earth stations supporting three types of traffic: voice and telemetry (uninterruptable synchronous), file transfer (interruptable synchronous), and interactive computing and data base inquiry response (asynchronous traffic). It was felt that a SCPC system did not provide the flexibility or the high data rates needed to meet the requirements. Instead, the protocol uses a single 60-Mbps channel with reservations handled by a "reference" earth station. The reference station also supplies synchronization pulses to begin each frame.

A virtual-circuit approach is used. Each frame consists of 150 slots of 4000 bits each. (The frame length is less than the link bit length, but this is permissible in a centralized reservation scheme.) The first slot is for synchronization. The next slot is a reservation request slot that is used by an earth station to request action on one or more virtual circuits. Each action request occupies a portion of the slot and consists of the following subfields:

- *Virtual circuit number:* refers to an existing virtual circuit. If this is a circuit initiation request, the field is blank.
- *Command code:* indicates the requested action, as shown in Table 10-3.
- *Destination:* indicates destination station for a circuit initiation request.
- *Circuit type:* one of the three types of traffic listed above.
- *Error control code:* indicates the error control technique to be used.
- *Number of slots:* number of slots per frame requested.

The request slot is dedicated to one earth station per frame and is allocated in a round-robin fashion. Thus if there are K earth stations, a station may make requests once in each K frames.

The next field is the acknowledgment field and contains virtual circuit information from the reference station to a particular earth station, and again is used in round-robin fashion. The slot contains a number of subslots, each of which is a confirmation or a request. Confirmations relate to a previous request by the designated earth station. The subfields are:

- *Virtual-circuit number:* as before. If this is a reservation confirmation, an unused number is assigned.
- *Command code:* from Table 10-3. If this is a confirmation, the code from the request is repeated. Otherwise, this is a request being passed on by the reference station (see below).
- *Circuit type:* as before.
- *Error control code:* as before.
- *Starting slot:* first slot in succeeding frames to be used for this circuit.
- *Number of slots:* number of contiguous slots per frame allocated for this circuit.

Figure 10-21 depicts the circuit initiation process, which requires not only a request from the sending station but an acknowledgment from the receiving station.

TABLE 10-3 Command Codes for NASA Satellite Protocol

Code	Description
Circuit initiation	Specifies the request for initiation of a new circuit
Circuit continuation	Specifies that the earth station will continue transmitting data on a previously initiated circuit, for the next set of frames
Circuit suspension	Suspends transmission of a virtual circuit temporarily
Circuit reactivation	Reactivates the use of a previously suspended circuit
Circuit termination	Indicates that the earth station wants to stop using a circuit
Ready	Informs the reference station that the earth station is ready to perform any of the functions above that were previously requested by the reference station

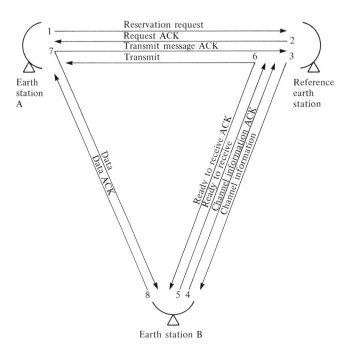

FIGURE 10-21.   Circuit initiation process.

There is clearly quite a bit of overhead and delay built in, but this is acceptable for sustained high-throughput requirements. However, a penalty is paid for bursty traffic which, as so far described, is unacceptable. To get around this, a few permanent (or at least long-lasting) virtual circuits can be set up using only one slot per frame. Thus a few of the 147 available data slots can be dedicated to bursty traffic, with the remainder used for stream traffic.

A quite different scheme, proposed in [SUDA83], employs the satellite rather than an earth station to make reservations, and is designed to deal with a mixture of stream and bursty traffic. Each frame consists of three subframes. The *reservation subframe* consists of a set of reservation minislots. The *unreserved subframe* consists of data slots that stations contend for using S-ALOHA (and is intended for bursty traffic). The *reserved subframe* consists of data slots that may be reserved for stream traffic.

To acquire slots in the reserved frame, a station contends for a minislot, using S-ALOHA, to transmit a reservation. A reservation consists of the earth station identifier. If a reservation is successfully received at the satellite, and if at least one unreserved slot is available in the reserved subframe, the satellite immediately sends a confirmation in the same minislot. The confirmation consists of a slot position within the reserved subframe. Upon receipt of the confirmation, the earth station can then use the reserved slot in each succeeding frame until it transmits an end-of-message flag. This informs the satellite to release the slot for future use.

Two timing constraints are associated with this scheme. First, frame retransmission by the satellite is delayed by the time it takes to process a reservation minislot. Second, the unreserved subframe occurs between the reservation subframe and the unreserved subframe and must be longer than the link bit length. In this way, an earth station will know whether its reservation was successful before the beginning of the reserved subframe in the same frame. This results in more efficient use of reserved slots.

Whereas the proposed NASA scheme is optimized for stream traffic, the scheme in [SUDA83] provides acceptable service for both stream and bursty traffic. A similar philosophy is used in a scheme proposed in [NG77].

10-5

RECOMMENDED READING

Two worthwhile surveys of packet radio are [KAHN78] and [NIEL84]. [BIND75a] is a detailed description of ALOHANET plus a commentary on its evolution as lessons were learned. MP-Net is described in [ROUL81]. [KAHN77] is an interesting discussion of various design issues relating to a packet radio network with repeaters.

Martin is up to his usual standard with his book on satellites [MART78]. A good technical treatment is [SPIL77]. [PICK83b] is a reasonably up-to-date survey of most of the satellite concepts discussed in this chapter. [BIND81] presents performance results for multiple-access satellite protocols. [TOBA80] is a survey of performance results for a variety of multiple-access protocols, applicable to satellite, packet radio, and local networks.

10-6

PROBLEMS

10-1 Assume the usual ALOHANET system, with a data rate of 9600 bps and a packet size of 804 bits. If $G = 0.75$, what is the load on the system in packets/second?

10-2 In MP-Net, the last packet in a multipacket transfer is given the sequence number 255. Is there any problem with that?

10-3 In MP-Net, the repeater checks both the destination repeater address and the destination address to determine whether the packet should be ignored. Would it not be sufficient to just check the destination address?

10-4 A packet is sent from J to C, as depicted in Figure 10-5. What is the total number of packets transmitted between repeaters, assuming no collisions, using each of the two routing techniques described in Section 10-1? For the modified flooding technique, assume a maximum hop count of 3.

10-5 Calculate a value of a for ALOHANET and MP-Net. Assume a maximum radius of 30 km for ALOHANET and a maximum diameter of 60 km for MP-Net.

10-6 Consider a S-ALOHA system with a finite number of stations N and $a = 0$. The offered load from each station is G_i, the throughput S_i. Derive an equation for S_i as a function of G_i. Next, assume that the G_i are identical; what is the equation for $S = \Sigma S_i$? Verify that this approaches Ge^{-G} as $N \to \infty$. Above what value of N is the difference negligible?

10-7 A group of N stations shares a 9600-bps ALOHA channel. Each station outputs a 1000-bit packet at an average rate of one every 100 s. What is the maximum useful value of N?

10-8 Consider two stations that have been using a terrestrial 4800-bps leased line with a 10^{-5} error rate. Data are transmitted in packets of 1024 bits each, and a selective repeat error control scheme is used. An equivalent satellite link with a 10^{-7} error rate is available. Which of the two has the highest effective throughput?

10-9 Figure 10-12b shows a FDM/FM earth station for a satellite communication system. Find the peak frequency deviation that achieves the allocated spectral bandwidth for the 6.24-GHz signal.

10-10 For each of the satellite reservation schemes depicted in Figure 10-18, suggest a way in which different stations could be assigned different priorities.

10-11 Consider the satellite-controlled central reservation scheme (Figure 10-18f). Would it not be simpler to divide the bandwidth into two frequency bands, one for slotted ALOHA, and the other for reservations?

10-12 Consider Figure 10-21. Assuming negligible processing time at each station, what is the minimum amount of elapsed time between a circuit initiation request by station A and its receipt of permission to transmit? How many frame times is that?

APPENDIX 10A

PERFORMANCE CONSIDERATIONS FOR BROADCAST NETWORKS

The key characteristics of packet broadcasting networks that structure the way their performance is analyzed are that there is a shared access medium, requiring a medium access control protocol, and that packet transmission is used. These characteristics are shared by packet radio, satellite, and local networks. It follows that the basic performance considerations, and the approaches to performance analysis, will be the same for all. With the foregoing points in mind, this appendix explores these basic considerations. The section begins by defining the basic measures of performance, then reviews the key parameter for determining performance, which was introduced in Chapter 5. The final topic is a discussion of the interrelationship of the various factors that affect performance.

10A-1 Measures of Performance

Three measures of performance are commonly used:

- D: the delay that occurs between the time a packet is ready for transmission from a station, and the completion of successful transmission.
- S: the throughput of the network; the total rate of data being transmitted between stations (carried load).
- U: the utilization of the medium; the fraction of total capacity being used.

These measures concern themselves with performance within the network. Actual end-to-end performance is also dependent on processing delays within the endpoint stations.

The parameter S is often normalized and expressed as a fraction of capacity. For example, if over a period of 1 s, the sum of the successful data transfers between nodes is 1 Mb on a 10-Mbps channel, then $S = 0.1$. Thus S can also be interpreted as utilization. The analysis is commonly done in terms of the total number of bits transferred, including overhead (headers, trailers) bits; the calculations are a bit easier, and this approach isolates performance effects due to the network alone. One must work backward from this to determine effective throughput.

Results for S and D are generally plotted as a function of the offered load G, which is the actual load or traffic demand presented to the network. We will find that S and G differ. The total load on the network depends in part on the medium access control technique. In some techniques "control packets" are employed; from time to time, packets are transmitted that carry no station data, but are used in the control of the medium. Also, in contention techniques, a "collision" is possible. A collision occurs when two packets are transmitted from two different stations at the same time; the packets interfere with each other and neither is successfully received. Thus S is the normalized rate of data packets successfully transmitted; G is the total number of packets offered to the network, and may include control packets and/or collisions. G, too, is often expressed as a fraction of capacity. Intuitively, we would expect D to increase with G: The more traffic competing for transmission time, the longer the delay for any individual transmission. S should also increase with G, up to some saturation point, beyond which the network cannot handle more load.

Figure 10-22 shows the ideal situation: Channel utilization increases to accommodate load up to an offered load equal to the full capacity of the system; then utilization remains at 100%. Of course, any overhead or inefficiency will cause performance to fall short of the goal. The depiction of S versus G is a reasonable one from the point of view of the network itself. It shows the behavior of the system based on the actual load on it. But from the point of view of the user or the attached station, it may seem strange. Why? Because the offered load includes

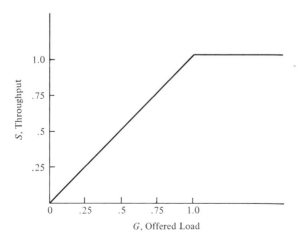

FIGURE 10-22. Ideal channel utilization.

TABLE 10-4 Example Relationship of Broadcast Network Measures of Performance[a]

I	S	G	D	U
100	100	101	0.0505	0.1
500	500	505	0.2525	0.5
990	990	1000	0.5	0.99
1000	990	—	—	0.99
2000	990	—	—	0.99

[a]I, input load (packets/s); S, throughput (packets/s); G, offered load (packets/s) (assumes 1% retransmission rate); D, delay (s); U, utilization (fraction of capacity). Capacity is 1000 packets/s.

not only original transmissions but also acknowledgments and, in the case of errors or collisions, retransmissions. The user may want to know the throughput and the delay characteristics as a function of the device-generated data to be put through the system: the "input load." Or if the network is the focus, the analyst may want to know what the offered load is given the input load. We will return to this discussion later.

In summary, we have introduced two additional parameters:

- G: the offered load to the network; the total rate of data presented to the network for transmission.
- I: the input load; the rate of data generated by the stations attached to the network.

Table 10-4 is a very simplified example to show the relationship between these parameters. Here we assume a network with a capacity of 1000 packets/s. For simplicity, I, S, and G are expressed in packets/s. It is assumed that 1% of all transmitted packets are lost and must be repeated. Thus at an input $I = 100$ packets/s, on the average 1 packet/s will be repeated. Thus $S = 100$ and $G = 101$. Assume that the input load arrives in batches, once per second. Hence, on average, with $I = 100$, $D = 0.0505$ s. The utilization is defined as $S/C = 0.1$.

The next two entries are easily seen to be correct. Note that for $I = 990$, the entire capacity of the system is being used ($G = 1000$). If I increases beyond this point, the system cannot keep up. Only 1000 packets/s will be transmitted. Thus S remains at 990 and U at 0.99. But G and D grow without bound as more and more backlog accumulates; there is no steady-state value. This pattern will become familiar in this chapter and Chapter 11.

10A-2 The Effect of Propagation Delay and Transmission Rate

In Chapter 5 we introduced the parameter a defined as

$$a = \frac{\text{Propagation Time}}{\text{Transmission Time}}$$

In that context, we were concerned with a point-to-point link, with a given propagation time between the two endpoints and a transmission time for either a fixed or average frame size. It was shown that a could be expressed as

$$a = \frac{\text{Length of Data Link (Bits)}}{\text{Length of Frame (Bits)}}$$

This parameter is also important in the broadcast network context, and in fact determines an upper bound on the utilization of the network. Consider a perfectly efficient access mechanism that allows only one transmission at a time. As soon as one transmission is over, another station begins transmitting. Furthermore, the transmission is pure data: no overhead bits. What is the maximum possible utilization of the network? It can be expressed as the ratio of total throughput of the system to the capacity or bandwidth:

$$U = \frac{\text{Throughput}}{\text{Capacity}} \tag{10-9}$$

Now define as before (as in Chapter 5):

$$B = \text{capacity of network}$$
$$d = \text{maximum distance between any two stations}$$
$$V = \text{velocity of signal propagation}$$
$$L = \text{average or fixed packet length}$$

The throughput is just the number of bits transmitted per unit time. A packet contains L bits, and the amount of time devoted to that packet is the actual transmission time (L/B) plus the propagation delay (d/V) Thus

$$\text{Throughput} = \frac{L}{d/V + L/B} \tag{10-10}$$

But, by our first definition of a, above:

$$a = \frac{d/V}{L/B} = \frac{Bd}{LV} \tag{10-11}$$

Substituting (10-10) and (10-11) into (10-9)

$$U = \frac{1}{1 + a} \tag{10-12}$$

Note that this differs from Equation (5-2). This is because the latter assumed a half-duplex protocol (no piggybacked acknowledgments).

So utilization varies inversely with a. This can be grasped intuitively by studying Figure 10-23. This figure shows two stations as far apart as possible (worst case) that take turns sending packets. If we normalize time such that the packet transmission time $= 1$, the sequence of events can be expressed as follows.

1. A station begins transmission at t_0.
2. Reception begins at $t_0 + a$.
3. Transmission is completed at $t_0 + 1$.
4. Reception ends at $t_0 + 1 + a$.
5. The other station begins transmitting.

Event 2 occurs *after* event 3 if $a > 1.0$. In any case the total time for one "turn" is $1 + a$, but the transmission time is only 1, for a utilization of $1/(1 + a)$.

The implication of Equation (10-12) for throughput is shown in Figure 10-24. The ideal case is $a = 0$, which allows 100% utilization. As offered load increases, throughput remains equal to offered load up to the full capacity of the system

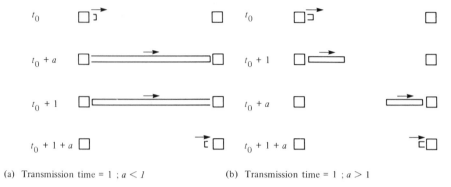

(a) Transmission time = 1 ; $a < 1$ (b) Transmission time = 1 ; $a > 1$

FIGURE 10-23.   The effect of _a_ on utilization.

$(S = G = 1)$ and then remains at $S = 1$. For any positive value of a, the system saturates at $S = 1/(1 + a)$.

So we can say that an upper bound on the utilization or efficiency of a broadcast network is $1/(1 + a)$, regardless of the medium access protocol used. Two caveats: First, this assumes that the maximum propagation time is incurred on each transmission. Second, it assumes that only one transmission may occur at a time. These assumptions are not always true; nevertheless, the formula $1/(1 + a)$ is almost always a valid upper bound, because the overhead of the medium access protocol more than makes up for the lack of validity of these assumptions.

The overhead is unavoidable. Frames must include address and synchronization bits. There is administrative overhead for controlling the protocol. In addition, there are forms of overhead peculiar to one or more of the protocols. We highlight these briefly for the most important protocols. (*Note:* On a first reading, some of these terms have not yet been defined. The reader is encouraged to refer back to this section after reading Chapter 11.)

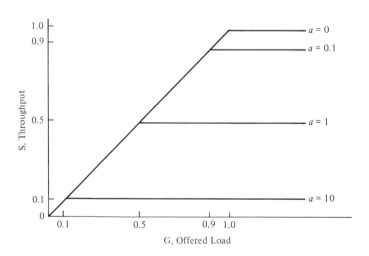

FIGURE 10-24.   Utilization as a function of _a_.

- *Contention protocols (ALOHA, S-ALOHA, CSMA, CSMA/CD):* time wasted due to collisions; need for acknowledgment frames. S-ALOHA requires that slot size equal transmission plus maximum propagation time.
- *Collision avoidance:* time spent waiting to see if other stations have data to send; acknowledgment frames.
- *Token bus:* token transmission; acknowledgment frames.
- *Token ring:* time waiting for token if intervening stations have no data to send.
- *Slotted ring:* time waiting for empty slot if intervening stations have no data to send.
- *Register insertion:* delay at each node of time equal to address length. From the point of view of a single station, the propagation time and hence *a* may increase due to insertion of registers on the ring.
- *Explicit reservation:* reservation transmission, acknowledgments.
- *Implicit reservation:* overhead of protocol used to establish reservation, acknowledgments.

There are two distinct effects here. One is that the efficiency or utilization of a channel decreases as *a* increases. This, of course, affects throughput. The other effect is that the overhead attributable to a protocol wastes bandwidth and hence reduces effective utilization and effective throughput. By and large, we can think of these two effects as independent and additive. However, we shall see that, for contention protocols, there is a strong interaction such that the overhead of these protocols increases as a function of *a*.

In any case, it would seem desirable to keep *a* as low as possible. Looking back to the defining formula [Equation 10-11], for a fixed network, *a* can be reduced by increasing packet size. This will only be useful if the length of messages produced by a station is an integral multiple of the packet size (excluding overhead bits). Otherwise, the large packet size is itself a source of waste. Furthermore, a large packet size increases the delay for other stations. This leads us to the next topic: the various factors that affect performance.

10A-3 Factors That Affect Performance

We list here those factors that affect the performance of a broadcast network. We are concerned here with that part which is independent of the attached devices: those factors that are exclusively under the control of the network designer. The chief factors are:

- Capacity.
- Propagation delay.
- Number of bits per frame.
- Medium access protocol.
- Offered load.
- Number of stations.
- Error rate.

The first three terms have already been discussed; they determine the value of *a*.

Next is the medium access protocol, which can have a significant effect on network performance. We can think of the first three factors listed above as characterizing the network; they are generally treated as constants or givens. The medium access protocol is the focus of the design effort: the choice that must be made. The next two factors, offered load and the number of stations, are generally treated as the independent variables. The analyst is concerned with determining performance as a function of these two variables. Note that these two variables must be treated separately. Certainly, it is true that for a fixed offered load per station, the total offered load increases as the number of stations increase. The same increase could be achieved by keeping the number of stations fixed but increasing the offered load per station. However, as we shall see, the network performance will be different for these two cases.

A final factor is error rate. An error in packet transmission necessitates a retransmission. Error rates are highly variable and will not be treated directly in any of our estimates of performance.

Local Networks*

In this chapter we complete our discussion of packet-broadcasting networks by looking at local networks. One class of local network, which uses circuit-switching rather than packet broadcasting, includes the digital switch and the CBX and was covered in Chapter 8.

The nature of a local network is determined primarily by three factors: transmission medium, topology, and medium access control protocol. The bulk of the chapter is devoted to these topics, together with a look at local network performance. Throughout, reference is made to standards developed for local networks by two committees: IEEE 802 and ANS X3T9.5. These are described briefly at the end of the chapter.

11-1

LOCAL NETWORK TECHNOLOGY

The principal technology alternatives that determine the nature of a local network are the transmission medium and topology of the network [ROSE82]. Together, they in large measure determine the type of data that may be transmitted, the speed and efficiency of communications, and even the kinds of applications that a network may support.

*This chapter is based on [STAL84e], with permission from the Association for Computing Machinery.

This section surveys the transmission media and topologies that, within the state of the art, are appropriate for local networks. Based on these two technologies, three classes of local networks are defined.

Transmission Media

Table 11-1 lists characteristics of the transmission media most appropriate for local networks. The media are twisted pair, coaxial cable, and optical fiber. The characteristics listed in the table serve to distinguish the performance and applicability of the various media.

One of the most common communications transmission media, and one that is certainly applicable to local networks, is twisted pair wiring. Although typically used for low speed transmission, data rates of up to a few Mbps can be achieved. Twisted pair is relatively low cost and is typically preinstalled in office buildings. It is the most cost-effective choice for single-building, low-traffic requirements.

Higher performance requirements can best be met by coaxial cable, which provides higher throughput, can support a larger number of devices, and can span greater distances than twisted pair. Two transmission methods, baseband and broadband, can be employed on a coax cable; these are explained below. Baseband systems are typically from 1 to 10 Mbps and are generally limited to a single building. However, by limiting the distance covered and the number of devices attached, data rates of 50 Mbps can be achieved. Broadband systems are also typically in the range of 1 to 10 Mbps for a single data path, with 20 Mbps representing a practical upper limit. However, as explained below, broadband can support multiple data paths in contrast to the single data path of baseband. Broadband systems use CATV (Community Antenna Television) cable, which is suitable for outdoor as well as indoor environments. Hence interbuilding and even intracity networks can be supported.

Optical fiber has even greater capacity than coaxial cable and is a promising candidate for future local network installations. However, it has been little used so far due to cost and technical limitations [RAWS79, ALLA83]. Optical fiber is well suited to point-to-point configurations which, as described below, are used in ring networks. As the cost of optical fiber transmission components drops, this configuration will become practical. For the more common multipoint configurations, the problem of insertion tap loss must be overcome to exploit fully the tremendous

TABLE 11-1   Transmission Media for Local Networks

	Signaling Technique	Maximum Data Rate (Mbps)	Maximum Range at Maximum Data Rate (km)	Practical Number of Devices
Twisted Pair	Digital	1–2	Few	10's
Coaxial cable (50Ω)	Digital	10	Few	100's
Coaxial cable (75Ω)	Digital	50	1	10's
	Analog with FDM	20	10's	1,000's
	Single-channel Analog	50	1	10's
Optical fiber	Analog	10	1	10's

capacity of optical fiber. Present multipoint systems support only a few tens of devices at distances of up to about 1 km [RAWS78, JONE83, FREE83].

Topologies

Local networks are frequently characterized in terms of their topology. Three topologies are common: star, ring, and bus or tree (Figure 11-1).

In a *star* topology, a central switching element is used to connect all the nodes in the network. The central element uses circuit switching to establish a dedicated path between two stations wishing to communicate. Twisted pair is used to link the stations to the central switch.

The *ring* topology consists of a closed loop, with each node attached to a repeating element. Data circulate around the ring on a series of point-to-point data links between repeaters. A station wishing to transmit waits for its next turn and then sends data out onto the ring in the form of a packet. The packet contains source and destination address fields as well as data. As the packet circulates, the destination station copies the data into a local buffer. The packet continues to circulate until it returns to the source station, providing a form of acknowledgment. A distributed control protocol is used to determine the sequence in which nodes transmit.

Because the ring is constructed as a series of point-to-point links, almost any transmission medium can be used. Twisted pair, at rates up to 10 Mbps, is common. Coaxial cable is used to achieve higher data rates. Fiber optics could be used to achieve very high data transfer rates.

The *bus* or *tree* topology is characterized by the use of a multipoint medium.

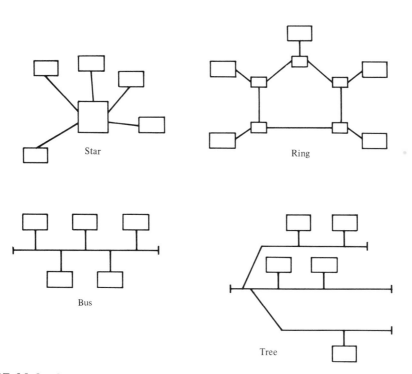

FIGURE 11-1.   Local network topologies.

The bus is simply a special case of the tree, in which there is only one trunk, with no branches. Because all devices share a common communications medium, only one pair of devices on a bus or tree can communicate at a time. A distributed medium access protocol is used to determine which station may transmit next. As with the ring, transmission employs a packet containing source and destination address fields. Each station monitors the medium and copies packets addressed to itself.

Bus/tree topology networks typically use coax cable or twisted pair. Optical fiber would provide greater capacity, but with current technology, it is not practical as a multipoint medium.

Classes of Local Networks

This section classifies local networks into three categories: local area network (LAN), high-speed local network (HSLN), and digital switch/computerized branch exchange (CBX). Table 11-2 summarizes representative characteristics. This classification was introduced in [STAL83b] and, as with any classification, is useful to the extent that it provides a clear differentiation among categories and serves to organize the field in a meaningful way. The three classifications were chosen on the following grounds:

- *Technology:* The architectural and design issues differ significantly for the three classes. This will be seen in such areas as performance, communication protocols, switching technique, and hardware/software interface, as well as transmission media and topologies.
- *Applications:* Although there is some overlap, the three classes of local networks have by and large been developed independently to meet different sets of requirements.
- *Standards:* Communication protocol standards are being developed separately for the three classes.

Local Area Network.   The term *local area network* (LAN) is generally used to refer to a general-purpose local network that can serve a wide variety of devices. LANs support minis, mainframes, terminals, and other peripherals. In many cases, these networks can carry not only data, but voice, video, and graphics.

The most common type of LAN is a bus or tree using coaxial cable. Rings using

TABLE 11-2   Classes of Local Networks

	Local Area Network	High-Speed Local Network	Computerized Branch Exchange
Transmission medium	Twisted pair, coax (both), fiber	CATV coax	Twisted pair
Topology	Bus, tree, ring	Bus	Star
Transmission speed	1–20 Mbps	50 Mbps	9.6–64 kbps
Maximum distance	25km	1km	1km
Switching technique	Packet	Packet	Circuit
Number of devices supported	100's–1000's	10's	100's–1000's
Attachment cost	$500–$5000	$40k–$50k	$250–$1000

twisted pair, coax, or even fiber are an alternative. The data transfer rates on LANs (1 to 20 Mbps) are high enough to satisfy most requirements and provide sufficient capacity to permit large numbers of devices to share the network.

The LAN is probably the best choice when a variety of devices and a mix of traffic types are involved. The LAN, alone or as part of a hybrid local network with one of the other types, will become a common feature of many office buildings and other installations.

High-Speed Local Network.   The *high-speed local network* (HSLN) is designed to provide high end-to-end throughput between expensive, high-speed devices, such as mainframes and mass storage devices.

Although other media and topologies are possible, work on HSLNs has concentrated on the bus topology using coaxial cable. Very high data rates are achievable—50 Mbps is standard—but both the distance and the number of devices are limited.

The HSLN is typically found in a computer room setting. Its main function is to provide I/O channel connections among a number of devices. Typical uses include file and bulk data transfer, automatic backup, and load leveling. Because of the current high prices for HSLN attachment, they are generally not practical for minicomputers, micros, and less expensive peripherals.

Digital Switch/Computerized Branch Exchange.   In contrast to the LAN and HSLN, which use packet transmission, the digital switch and CBX use circuit switching. Data rates to individual endpoints are typically low, but bandwidth is guaranteed and there is essentially no network delay once a connection has been made. The CBX is well suited to voice traffic, and to both terminal-to-terminal and terminal-to-host data traffic. As these devices have been covered in Chapter 8, this chapter will focus on the LAN and HSLN.

11-2

THE BUS/TREE TOPOLOGY

So far, the bus and tree topologies have been the most common ones used to implement both LANs and HSLNs. Ethernet [METC76] was one of the earliest local networks and is still the best known; it uses a baseband bus architecture. MITREnet [HOPK79] is an early bus/tree broadband system that has been the basis of much U.S. government-sponsored research and development. Many of the popular low-cost, twisted-pair LANs for microcomputers use a bus topology. Finally, the oldest and most popular HSLN, HYPERchannel [CHRI79], uses a baseband bus architecture.

In this section we first describe key characteristics common to all bus and tree configurations, and then look in more detail at baseband and broadband LAN systems.

Characteristics of Bus/Tree LANs and HSLNs

Of the topologies discussed in the preceding section, only the bus/tree topology is a multipoint medium. That is, there are more than two devices connected to the medium and capable of transmitting on the medium. Because multiple devices

TABLE 11-3 Bus/Tree Transmission Techniques

Baseband	Broadband
Digital signaling	Analog signaling (requires RF modem)
Entire bandwidth consumed by signal—no FDM	FDM possible—multiple data channels, video, audio
Bidirectional	Unidirectional
Bus topology	Bus or tree topology
Distance: up to a few kilometers	Distance: up to tens of kilometers

share a single data path, only one may transmit at a time. A station usually transmits data in the form of a packet containing the address of the destination. The packet propagates throughout the medium and is received by all other stations. The addressed station copies the packet as it goes by.

Two transmission techniques are in use for bus/tree LANs and HSLNs: baseband and broadband. Baseband, using digital signaling, can be employed on twisted pair or coaxial cable. Broadband, using analog signaling in the RF range, employs coaxial cable. Some of the differences are highlighted in Table 11-3, and the following two subsections explore the two methods in some detail. There is also a variant known as "single-channel broadband" that has the signaling characteristics of broadband but some of the restrictions of baseband; this is also covered below.

The multipoint nature of the bus/tree topology gives rise to several rather stiff problems. First is the problem of determining which station on the medium may transmit at any point in time. With point-to-point links (only two stations on the medium), this is a fairly simple task. If the line is full-duplex, both stations may transmit at the same time. If the line is half-duplex, then a rather simple mechanism is needed to ensure that the two stations take turns. Historically, the most common shared access scheme has been the multidrop line, in which access is determined by polling from a controlling station (discussed in Chapter 5). The controlling station may send data to any other station, or it may issue a poll to a specific station, asking for an immediate response. This method, however, negates some of the advantages of a distributed system and also is awkward for communication between two noncontroller stations. A variety of distributed strategies, referred to as medium access control protocols, have now been developed for bus and tree topologies. These are discussed in Section 11-4.

A second problem has to do with signal balancing. When two devices exchange data over a link, the signal strength of the transmitter must be adjusted to be within certain limits. The signal must be strong enough so that, after attenuation across the medium, it meets the receiver's minimum signal strength requirements. It must also be strong enough to maintain an adequate signal to noise ratio. On the other hand, the signal must not be so strong as to overload the circuitry of the transmitter, which creates harmonics and other spurious signals. Though easily done for a point-to-point link, signal balancing is no easy task for a multipoint line. If any device can transmit to any other device, the signal balancing must be performed for all permutations of stations taken two at a time. For n stations that works out to $n \times (n-1)$ permutations. So, for a 200-station network (not a particularly large system), 39,800 signal strength constraints must be satisfied simultaneously. With interdevice distances ranging from tens to thousands of meters, this is an impossible task for any but small networks. In systems that use radio-frequency (RF) signals, the problem is compounded because of the possibility of RF signal interference across frequencies. The solution is to divide the medium into segments within which pairwise balancing is possible, using amplifiers or repeaters between segments.

Baseband Systems

A baseband LAN or HSLN is defined as one that uses digital signaling. Digital signals are inserted on the line as voltage pulses. The entire frequency spectrum of the medium is used to form the signal; hence frequency-division multiplexing (FDM) cannot be used. Transmission is bidirectional. That is, a signal inserted at any point on the medium propagates in both directions to the ends, where it is absorbed (Figure 11-2a). The digital signaling requires a bus topology; unlike analog signals, digital signals can not easily be propagated through the splitters and joiners required for a tree topology. Baseband systems can extend only a limited distance, about a kilometer at most. This is because the attenuation of the signal, which is most pronounced at higher frequencies, causes a blurring of the pulses and a weakening of the signal to the extent that communication over larger distances is impractical.

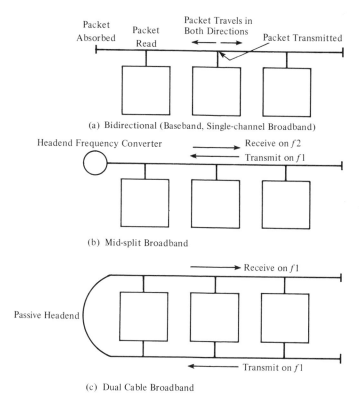

(a) Bidirectional (Baseband, Single-channel Broadband)

(b) Mid-split Broadband

(c) Dual Cable Broadband

FIGURE 11-2. Baseband and broadband transmission techniques.

Baseband Coax. The most popular form of baseband bus LAN uses coaxial cable. Unless otherwise indicated, this discussion is based on the IEEE standard [IEEE83] and the almost-identical Ethernet system [METC76, SHOC82, DIGI80].

Most baseband coax systems use a special 50-ohm cable rather than the standard CATV 75-ohm cable. This is because, for digital signals, the 50-ohm cable suffers less intense reflections from the insertion capacitance of the taps, and provides better immunity against low-frequency electromagnetic noise.

The simplest baseband coax LAN consists of an unbranched length of coax cable with a terminator at each end to prevent reflections. A maximum length of 500 m is recommended to guarantee signal quality. Stations attach to the cable by means of a tap, with the distance between any two taps being a multiple of 2.5 m; this is to ensure that reflections from adjacent taps do not add in phase. Studies have shown that if this spacing is not enforced, signal quality does suffer [YEN83]. A maximum of 100 taps is recommended. Each tap includes a transceiver, which contains the electronics for transmitting and receiving.

The specifications above are for a 10-Mbps data rate. They are based on engineering trade-offs involving data rate, cable length, number of taps, and the electrical characteristics of the transmit and receive components. For example, at lower data rates the cable could be longer.

To extend the length of the network, a repeater may be used. It consists, in essence, of two transceivers joined together and connected to two different segments of coax cable. The repeater passes digital signals in both directions between the two segments, amplifying and regenerating the signals as they pass through. A repeater is transparent to the rest of the system; since it does no buffering, it in no sense isolates one segment from another. So, for example, if two stations on different segments attempt to transmit at the same time, their packets will interfere with each other (collide). To avoid multipath interference, only one path of segments and repeaters is allowed between any two stations. A maximum of four repeaters is allowed in the path between any two stations, extending the effective cable length to 2.5 km. Figure 11-3 is an example of a baseband system with three segments and two repeaters.

Baseband coax is also used for the most widely available HSLN product, HYPERchannel [CHRI79, THOR80]. This system uses a 75-ohm CATV bus with nondirectional taps. The data rate is 50 Mbps. The vendor recommends a maximum cable length of 1.2 km with no more than 30 stations.

Twisted-Pair Baseband. A twisted-pair baseband LAN is intended for low-cost, low-performance requirements. This type of system supports fewer stations at lower speeds than a coax baseband LAN, but at far lower cost.

The components of the system are few and simple:

- Twisted-pair bus.
- Terminators.
- Controller interface.

The latter can simply be a standard two-wire I/O or communications interface. Typically, the electrical signaling technique on the cable conforms to RS-422. This is a standard, inexpensive interface.

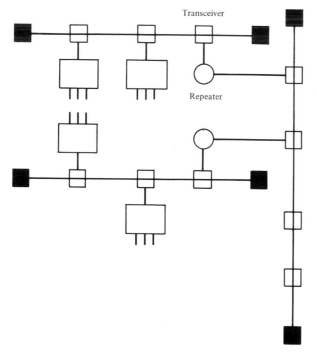

Transceiver

Repeater

FIGURE 11-3. Baseband configuration.

With this kind of network, the following parameters are reasonable:

- Length: up to 1 km.
- Data rate: up to 1 Mbps.
- Number of devices: tens.

Twisted pair is a good medium for several reasons. First, it has lower cost than coaxial cable while providing equal noise immunity. Second, virtually anyone can install the network, which consists of laying the cable and connecting the controllers. The task requires only a screwdriver and a pair of pliers, and is similar to hooking up hi-fi speakers.

Examples of these systems can be found in [MALO81], [BOSE81], and [HAHN81].

Broadband Systems

FDM Broadband LAN.   In the context of local networks, broadband refers to the use of analog signaling. Thus frequency-division multiplexing (FDM) is possible: The frequency spectrum of the cable can be divided into channels or sections of bandwidth. Separate channels can support data traffic, TV, or radio signals. Broadband components allow splitting and joining operations; hence both bus and tree topologies are possible. Much greater distances—tens of kilometers—are possible with broadband compared to baseband. This is because the analog signals that carry the digital data can propagate greater distances before the noise and attenuation damage the data.

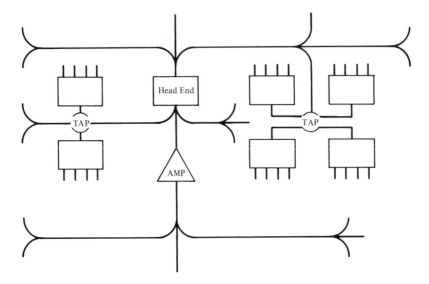

FIGURE 11-4. Broadband configuration.

Figure 11-4 shows a broadband system layout. As with baseband, stations attach to the cable by means of a tap. Unlike baseband, however, broadband is inherently a unidirectional medium; signals inserted onto the medium can propagate in only one direction. The primary reason for this is that it is infeasible to build amplifiers that will pass signals of one frequency in both directions. This unidirectional property means that only those stations "downstream" from a transmitting station can receive its signals. How, then, can full connectivity be achieved?

Clearly, two data paths are needed. These paths are joined at a point on the network known as the headend. For bus topology, the headend is simply one end of the bus. For tree topology, the headend is the root of the branching tree. All stations transmit on one path toward the headend (inbound). Signals received at the headend are then propagated along a second data path away from the headend (outbound). All stations receive on the outbound path.

Physically, two different configurations are used to implement the inbound, outbound paths (Figure 11-2). On a dual-cable configuration, the inbound and outbound paths are separate cables, with the headend simply a passive connector between the two. Stations send and receive on the same frequency.

By contrast, on the split configuration, the inbound and outbound paths are different frequencies on the same cable. Bidirectional amplifiers pass lower frequencies inbound, and higher frequencies outbound. The headend contains a device, known as a frequency converter, for translating inbound frequencies to outbound frequencies. The frequency converter at the headend can be either an analog or digital device. The analog devices simply translates signals to a new frequency and retransmits them. The digital device recovers the digital data from the headend and then retransmits the cleaned-up data on the new frequency.

Split systems are categorized by the frequency allocation to the two paths. Subsplit, commonly used by the CATV industry, provides 5 to 30 MHz inbound and 40 to 300 MHz outbound. This system was designed for metropolitan area TV distribution, with limited subscriber-to-central office communication. Midsplit, more suitable for LANs, provides an inbound range of 5 to 116 MHz and an outbound range of 168 to 300 MHz. This provides a more equitable distribution of bandwidth.

Midsplit was developed at a time when the practical spectrum of a CATV cable was 300 MHz. Spectra surpassing 400 MHz are now available, and "super-split" or "equal-split" is sometimes used to achieve even better balance by splitting the bandwidth roughly in half.

The differences between split and dual are minor. The midsplit system is useful when a single cable plant is already installed in a building. Also, the installed system is about 10–15% cheaper than a dual cable system [HOPK79]. On the other hand, a dual cable has over twice the capacity of midsplit. It does not require the frequency translator at the headend, which may need to be redundant for reliability. A further comparison is provided in [COOP83a].

Broadband systems use standard, off-the-shelf CATV components, including 75-ohm coaxial cable. All endpoints are terminated with a 75-ohm terminator to absorb signals. Broadband is suitable for tens of kilometers radius from the headend and hundreds or even thousands of devices. For all but very short distances, amplifiers are required.

The broadband LAN can be used to carry multiple channels, some used for analog signals, such as video and voice, and some for digital. Digital channels can generally carry a data rate of somewhere between 0.25 and 1 bps/Hz.

Three kinds of digital data transfer techniques are possible on a broadband cable: dedicated, switched, and multiple access (Figure 11-5). For dedicated service, a small portion of the cable's bandwidth is reserved for exclusive use by two devices. No special protocol is needed. Each of the two devices attaches to the cable through a modem; both modems are tuned to the same frequency. This technique is analogous to securing a dedicated leased line from the telephone company. Transfer rates of up to 20 Mbps are achievable. The dedicated service could be used to connect two devices when a heavy traffic pattern is expected. For example, one computer could be acting as a standby for another, and needs to get frequent updates of state information and file and data base changes.

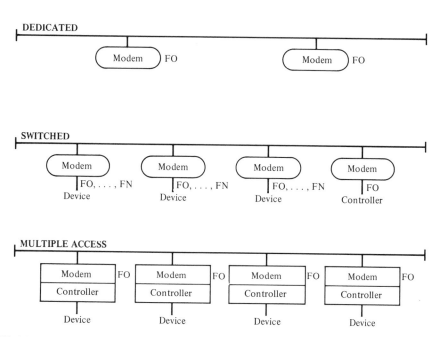

FIGURE 11-5. Broadband data transfer services.

The switched technique requires the use of a number of frequency bands. Devices are attached through "frequency agile" modems, capable of changing their frequency by electronic command. Initially, all attached devices, together with a controller, are tuned to the same frequency. A station wishing to establish a connection sends a request to the controller, which assigns an available frequency to the two devices and signals their modems to tune to that frequency. This technique is analogous to a dial-up line. Because the cost of frequency-agile modems rises dramatically with data rate, rates of 56 kbps or less are typical. This capability is available in WANG's local network [STAH82], where it is used for terminal-to-host connections. It could also be used for voice service.

Finally, the multiple access service allows a number of attached devices to be supported at the same frequency. As with baseband, some form of medium access control protocol is needed to control transmission. The multiple-access approach is the most common. It provides for distributed, peer communication among many devices, which is the primary motivation for a local network.

Discussions of broadband LANs can be found in [COOP82], [COOP83b], [DINE80], and [FORB81].

Single-Channel Broadband. An abridged form of broadband is one in which the entire spectrum of the cable is devoted to a single transmission path for analog signals. In general, a single-channel broadband LAN has the following characteristics. Bidirectional transmission, using a bus topology, is employed. Hence there can be no amplifiers, and there is no need for a headend. Some form of FSK is used, generally at a low frequency (a few megahertz). This is an advantage since attenuation is less at lower frequencies.

Because the cable is dedicated to a single task, it is not necessary to take care that the modem output is confined to a narrow bandwidth. Energy can spread over the cable's spectrum. As a result, the electronics are simple and inexpensive. This scheme would appear to give comparable performance, at a comparable price, to baseband.

The single-channel broadband approach is also used in one commercially available HSLN [HOHN80] and is the approach taken by a draft HSLN standard [ANSI82]. In both cases, a 50-Mbps data rate is used with phase-shift keying (PSK) on a 150-MHz carrier. The approach should be comparable in performance and cost to HYPERchannel.

Baseband Versus Broadband

One of the silliest aspects of the intense coverage afforded local networks in the trade and professional literature is the baseband versus broadband debate. The fact is that there is room for both technologies in the local network field. The potential customer will find himself faced with a lot of other, more complex, decisions than this one. For the interested reader, thoughtful discussions may by found in [HOPK82] and [KRUT81].

To summarize briefly, baseband has the advantage of simplicity, and, in principle, lower cost. The layout of a baseband cable plant is simple: There are just five rules for trunk layout in the Ethernet specification. A relatively inexperienced local network engineer should be able to cope.

The potential disadvantages of baseband include the limitations in capacity and distance—only disadvantages if your requirements exceed those limitations. Another concern has to do with grounding. Because dc components are on the cable, it can be grounded in only one place. Care must be taken to avoid potential shock hazards and antenna effects.

Broadband's strength is its tremendous capacity; it can carry a wide variety of traffic on a number of channels. With the use of active amplifiers, broadband can achieve very wide area coverage. Also, the system is based on a mature CATV technology. Components are reliable and readily available.

Broadband systems are more complex than baseband to install and maintain. The layout design must include cable type selection, and placement and setting of all amplifiers and taps. Maintenance involves periodic testing and alignment of all network parameters. These are jobs for experienced RF engineers. Finally, the average propagation delay between stations for broadband is twice that for a comparable baseband system. This reduces the efficiency and performance of the system.

As with all other network design choices, the selection of baseband or broadband must be based on relative costs and benefits. It is probable that some installations will have both types. Neither is likely to win the LAN war.

11-3

THE RING TOPOLOGY

The major alternative to the bus/tree topology LAN is the ring. The ring has enjoyed considerable popularity in Europe but is only slowly gaining ground in the United States, where Ethernet and MITREnet were largely responsible for shaping the early direction of activity. However, several factors suggest that the ring may become more of a competitor in the United States. IBM has conducted substantial research on ring LANs and is expected to announce a product. Also, the IEEE 802 ring LAN standard, which has lagged the bus/tree standards, is moving toward ratification.

Characteristics of Ring LANs

A ring LAN consists of a number of repeaters, each connected to two others by unidirectional transmission links to form a single closed path. Data are transferred sequentially, bit by bit, around the ring from one repeater to the next. Each repeater regenerates and retransmits each bit.

For a ring to operate as a communication network, three functions are required: data insertion, data reception, and data removal. These functions are provided by the repeaters. Each repeater, in addition to serving as an active element on the ring, serves as a device attachment point. Data insertion is accomplished by the repeater. Data are transmitted in packets, each of which contains a destination address field. As a packet circulates past a repeater, the address field is copied. If the attached station recognizes the address, the remainder of the packet is copied.

Repeaters perform the data insertion and reception functions in a manner not unlike that of taps, which serve as device attachment points on a bus or tree. Data removal, however, is another story. For a bus or tree, signals inserted onto the line propagate to the endpoints and are absorbed by terminators. Hence, shortly after transmission ceases, the bus or tree is clean of data. However, because the ring is a closed loop, a packet will circulate indefinitely unless it is removed. A packet may by removed by the addressed repeater. Alternatively, each packet could be removed by the transmitting repeater after it has made one trip around the loop. This latter approach is more desirable because (1) it permits automatic acknowledgment and (2) it permits multicast addressing: one packet sent simultaneously to multiple stations.

A variety of strategies can be used for determining how and when packets are inserted onto the ring. These strategies are, in effect, medium access control protocols, and are discussed in Section 11-4.

The repeater, then, can be seen to have two main purposes in life: (1) to contribute to the proper functioning of the ring by passing on all the data that comes its way, and (2) to provide an access point for attached stations to send and receive data. Corresponding to these two purposes are two states (Figure 11-6): the listen state and the transmit state.

In the listen state, each received bit is retransmitted with a small delay, required to allow the repeater to perform required functions. Ideally, the delay should be on the order of one bit time (the time it takes for a repeater to transmit one complete bit onto the outgoing line). These functions are:

- Scan passing bit stream for pertinent patterns. Chief among these is the address or addresses of attached stations. Another pattern, used in the token control strategy explained later, indicates permission to transmit. Note that to perform the scanning function, the repeater must have some knowledge of packet format.
- Copy each incoming bit and send it to the attached station, while continuing to retransmit each bit. This will be done for each bit of each packet addressed to this station.
- Modify a bit as it passes by. In certain control strategies, bits may be modified to, for example, indicate that the packet has been copied. This would serve as an acknowledgment.

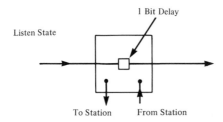

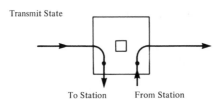

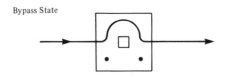

FIGURE 11-6. Ring repeater states.

When a repeater's station has data to send and when the repeater, based on the control strategy, has permission to send, the repeater enters the transmit state. In this state, the repeater receives bits from the station and retransmits them on its outgoing link. During the period of transmission, bits may appear on the incoming ring link. There are two possibilities, and they are treated differently:

- The bits could be from the same packet that the repeater is still in the process of sending. This will occur if the "bit length" of the ring is shorter than the packet. In this case, the repeater passes the bits back to the station, which can check them as a form of acknowledgment.
- For some control strategies, more than one packet could be on the ring at the same time. If the repeater, while transmitting, receives bits from a packet it did not originate, it must buffer them to be transmitted later.

These two states, listen and transmit, are sufficient for proper ring operation. A third state, the bypass state, is also useful. In this state, a bypass relay can be activated, so that signals propagate past the repeater with no delay other than medium propagation. The bypass relay affords two benefits: (1) it provides a partial solution to the reliability problem, discussed later, and (2) it improves performance by eliminating repeater delay for those stations that are not active on the network.

Twisted pair, baseband coax, and fiber optic cable can all be used to provide the repeater-to-repeater links. Broadband coax, however, could not easily be used. Each repeater would have to be capable, asynchronously, of receiving and transmitting data on multiple channels.

Potential Ring Problems

One of the principal reasons for the slow acceptance of the ring LAN in the United States is that there are a number of potential problems with this topology [SALT83]. A break in any link or the failure of a repeater disables the entire network. Installation of a new repeater to support new devices requires the identification of two nearby, topologically adjacent repeaters. Finally, because the ring is closed, a means is needed to remove circulating packets, with backup techniques to guard against error.

The last problem is a protocol issue, discussed later. The remaining problems can be handled by a refinement of the ring topology, discussed next.

The Star-Ring Architecture

Two observations can be made about the basic ring architecture described above. First, there is a practical limit to the number of stations on a ring. This limit is suggested by the reliability and maintenance problems just cited and by the accumulating delay of a large number of repeaters. A limit of a few hundred stations seems reasonable. Second, the functioning of the ring does not depend on the actual routing of the cables that link the repeaters.

These observations have led to the development of a refined ring architecture, the star-ring, which overcomes some of the problems of the ring and allows the construction of larger local networks [DIXO82]. This architecture is the basis of IBM's anticipated local network product [RAUC82] and grows out of research done at IBM [BUX82] and M.I.T. [SALT79].

As a first step, consider the rearrangement of a ring into a star. This is achieved by having the interrepeater links all thread through a single site. This *ring wiring concentrator* has a number of advantages. Because there is centralized access to the signal on every link, it is a simple matter to isolate a fault. A message can be launched into the ring and tracked to see how far it gets without mishap. A faulty segment can be disconnected and repaired at a later time. New repeaters can easily be added to the ring: simply run two cables from the new repeater to the site of ring wiring concentration and splice into the ring.

The bypass relay associated with each repeater can be moved into the ring wiring concentrator. The relay can automatically bypass its repeater and two links for any malfunction. A nice effect of this feature is that the transmission path from one working repeater to the next is approximately constant; thus the range of signal levels to which the transmission system must automatically adapt is much smaller.

The ring wiring concentrator permits rapid recovery from a cable or repeater failure. Nevertheless, a single failure could, at least temporarily, disable the entire network. Furthermore, throughput considerations still place a practical upper limit on the number of stations in a ring, since each repeater adds an increment of delay. Finally, in a spread-out network, a single wire concentration site dictates a lot of cable.

To attack these remaining problems, consider a local network consisting of multiple rings (Figure 11-7). Each ring consists of a connected sequence of wiring concentrators; the set of rings is connected by a *bridge*. The bridge routes data packets from one ring subnetwork to another based on addressing information in the packet so routed. From a physical point of view, each ring operates independently of the other rings attached to the bridge. From a logical point of view, the bridge provides transparent routing between the two rings.

The bridge must perform five functions:

- *Input filtering*: For each ring, the bridge monitors the traffic on the ring and copies all packets addressed to other rings on the bridge. This function can be performed by a repeater programmed to recognize a family of addresses rather than a single address.
- *Input buffering:* Received packets may need to be buffered, either because the interring traffic is peaking, or because the target output buffer is temporarily full.
- *Switching:* Each packet must be routed through the bridge to its appropriate destination ring.
- *Output buffering:* A packet may need to be buffered at the threshold of the destination ring, waiting for an opportunity to be inserted.
- *Output transmission:* This function can be performed by an ordinary repeater.

Two principal advantages accrue from the use of a bridge. First, the failure of a ring, for whatever reason, will disable only a portion of the network, and failure of the bridge does not prevent intraring traffic. Second, multiple rings may be employed to obtain a satisfactory level of performance when the throughput capability of a single ring is exceeded.

There are several pitfalls to be noted. First, the automatic acknowledgment feature of the ring is lost; higher level protocols must provide acknowledgment. Second, performance may not significantly improve if there is a high percentage of interring traffic. If it is possible to do so, network devices should be judiciously allocated to rings to minimize interring traffic.

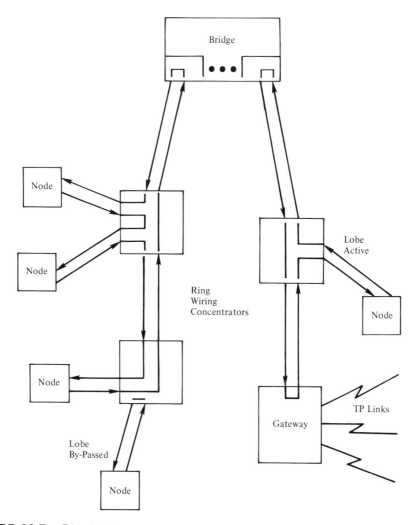

FIGURE 11-7. Ring bridge.

Bus Versus Ring

For the user with a large number of devices and high capacity requirements, the bus or tree broadband LAN seems the best suited to the requirements. For more moderate requirements, however, the choice between a baseband bus LAN and a ring LAN is not at all clear cut.

The baseband bus is the simpler system. Passive taps rather than active repeaters are used. There is no need for the complexity of bridges and ring wiring concentrators.

The most important benefit or strength of the ring is that it uses point-to-point communication links. There are a number of implications of this fact. First, because the transmitted signal is regenerated at each node, transmission errors are minimized and greater distances can be covered than with baseband bus. Broadband bus/tree can cover a similar range, but cascaded amplifiers can result in loss of data integrity at high data rates. Second, the ring can accommodate optical fiber links, which provide very high data rates and excellent electromagnetic interference

(EMI) characteristics. Finally, the electronics and maintenance of point-to-point lines are simpler than for multipoint lines.

A further discussion of ring versus bus is contained in [SALW83] and [SALT81].

11-4

MEDIUM ACCESS CONTROL PROTOCOLS

Bus/Tree LANs

Of all the local network topologies, the bus/tree topologies present the most challenges, and the most options, for medium access control. This section will not attempt to survey the many techniques that have been proposed; good discussions can be found in [LUCZ78] and [FRAN81]. Rather, the emphasis will be on the two techniques that seem likely to dominate the marketplace: CSMA/CD and token bus. Standards for these techniques have been developed by the IEEE 802 committee.

Table 11-4 compares the two techniques on a number of characteristics. The ensuing discussion should clarify its significance.

CSMA/CD. The most commonly used medium access control technique for bus/tree topologies is *carrier sense multiple access with collision detection* (CSMA/CD), also referred to as *listen while talk* (LWT). The original baseband version of this technique was developed and patented by Xerox [METC77] as part of its Ethernet local network [METC76]. The original broadband version was developed and patented by MITRE [HOPK80] as part of its MITREnet local network [HOPK79].

CSMA/CD is a refinement of the CSMA protocol described in Chapter 10. CSMA/CD attempts to overcome one glaring inefficiency of CSMA. Under CSMA, when two packets collide the medium remains unusable for the duration of transmission of both damaged packets. For packets that are long, compared to propagation time, the amount of wasted capacity can be considerable. This waste can be reduced if a station continues to listen to the medium while it is transmitting. In that case, these rules can be added to the CSMA rules:

1. If a collision is detected during transmission, immediately cease transmitting the packet, and transmit a brief jamming signal to assure that all stations know there has been a collision.
2. After transmitting the jamming signal, wait a random amount of time, then attempt to transmit again using CSMA.

TABLE 11-4 Bus/Tree Access Methods

	CSMA/CD	Token Bus
Access determination	Contention	Token
Packet-length restriction	Greater than 2 × propagation delay	None
Principal advantage	Simplicity	Regulated/fair access
Principal disadvantage	Performance under heavy load	Complexity

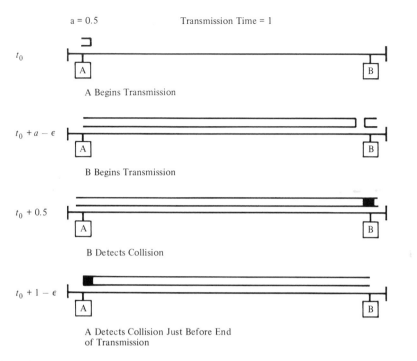

$a = 0.5$ Transmission Time $= 1$

t_0 A Begins Transmission

$t_0 + a - \epsilon$ B Begins Transmission

$t_0 + 0.5$ B Detects Collision

$t_0 + 1 - \epsilon$ A Detects Collision Just Before End of Transmission

FIGURE 11-8. For baseband CSMA/CD, packet length should be at least twice the propagation delay ($a \leq$ 0.5).

Now, the amount of wasted bandwidth is reduced to the time it takes to detect a collision. Question: How long does that take? Figure 11-8 illustrates the answer for a baseband system. Consider the worst case of two stations that are as far apart as possible. As can be seen, the amount of time it takes to detect a collision is twice the propagation delay. For broadband, the wait is even longer. The worst case is two stations close together and as far as possible from the headend. In this case the time required to detect a collision is four times the propagation delay from the station to the headend.

As with CSMA, CSMA/CD employs one of the three persistence algorithms. You may be surprised to learn that the most common choice is 1-persistent. It is used by both Ethernet and MITREnet, and is in the IEEE 802 standard. As was mentioned, the problem with the nonpersistent scheme is the wasted idle time. Though more efficient, p-persistent may still result in considerable waste. With the 1-persistent scheme, that waste is eliminated at the cost of wasted collision time.

What saves the day is that the wasted time due to collisions is mercifully short (if the packets are long relative to propagation delay, i.e., a $<<$ 1). And with random backoff, the two stations involved in a collision are unlikely to collide on their next tries. To ensure that this backoff maintains stability, a technique known as binary exponential backoff is used. A station will attempt to transmit repeatedly in the face of repeated collisions, but, after each collision, the mean value of the random delay is doubled.

Although the implementation of CSMA/CD is substantially the same for baseband and broadband, there are differences. One is the means for performing carrier sense. For baseband systems, this is done by detecting a voltage pulse train. For broadband, the RF carrier is detected.

For collision detection, baseband receivers look for voltage levels greater than would be expected from a single transmitter. Broadband receivers typically use a bit-by-bit comparison of the received data (outbound channel) with the transmitted data (inbound channel); note the similarity to a satellite link. Another approach, for midsplit systems, is for the headend to perform detection based on garbled data.

Token Bus. The token bus is a technique in which the stations on the bus or tree form a logical ring; that is, the stations are assigned positions in an ordered sequence, with the last member of the sequence followed by the first. Each station knows the identity of the stations preceding and following it (Figure 11-9).

A control packet known as the token regulates the right of access. When a station receives the token, it is granted control of the medium for a specified time. The station may transmit one or more packets and may poll stations and receive responses. When the station is done, or time has expired, it passes the token on to the next station in logical sequence. This station now has permission to transmit. Hence steady-state operation consists of alternating data transfer and token transfer phases.

Note that non-token-using stations are allowed on the bus. These stations can only respond to polls or requests for acknowledgment. It should also be pointed out that the physical ordering of the stations on the bus is irrelevant and independent of the logical ordering.

This scheme requires considerable maintenance. The following functions, at a minimum, must be performed by one or more stations on the bus:

- *Ring initialization:* When the network is started up, or after the logical ring has broken down, it must be reinitialized. Some cooperative, decentralized algorithm is needed to sort out who goes first, who goes second, and so on.
- *Addition to ring:* Periodically, nonparticipating stations must be granted the opportunity to insert themselves in the ring.
- *Deletion from ring:* A station can voluntarily remove itself from the ring by splicing together its predecessor and successor.
- *Fault management:* A number of errors can occur. These include duplicate address (two stations think it's their turn) and broken ring (no station thinks that it is its turn).

The remainder of this subsection briefly describes the approach taken for these functions in the IEEE 802 standard. To accomplish *addition to ring,* each node in

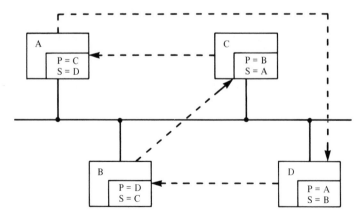

FIGURE 11-9.   Token bus.

the ring has the responsibility of periodically granting an opportunity for new nodes to enter the ring. While holding the token, the node issues a *solicit-successor* packet, inviting nodes with an address between itself and the next node in logical sequence to demand entrance. The transmitting node then waits for one response window or slot time (equal to twice the end-to-end propagation delay of the medium). If there is no response, the node passes the token to its successor as usual. If there is one response, the token holder sets its successor node to be the requesting node and transmits the token to it; the requestor sets its linkages accordingly and proceeds. If more than one node demands to enter the ring, the token holder will detect a garbled response.

The conflict is resolved by an address-based contention scheme. The token holder transmits a *resolve-contention* packet and waits four response windows. Each demander can respond in one of these windows based on the first two bits of its address. If a demander hears anything before its window comes up, it refrains from demanding. If the token holder receives a valid response, it is in business. Otherwise, it tries again, and only those nodes that responded the first time are allowed to respond this time, based on the second pair of bits in their address. This process continues until a valid response is received, no response is received, or a maximum retry count is reached. In the latter two cases, the token holder gives up and passes the token.

Deletion from ring is a much simpler process. If a node wishes to drop out, it waits until it receives the token, then sends a *set-successor* packet to its predecessor, instructing it to splice to its successor.

Fault management by the token holder covers a number of contingencies. First, while holding the token, a node may hear a packet indicating that another node has the token. If so, it immediately drops the token by reverting to listener mode. In this way, the number of token holders drops immediately to 1 or 0. A second problem may arise when, upon completion of its turn, the token holder issues a token packet to its successor. The successor should immediately issue a data or token packet. Therefore, after sending a token, the token issuer will listen for one slot time to make sure that its successor is active. This precipitates a sequence of events:

1. If the successor node is active, the token issuer will hear a valid packet and revert to listener mode.
2. If the issuer does not hear a valid packet, it reissues the token to the same successor one more time.
3. After two failures, the issuer assumes that its successor has failed and issues a *who-follows* packet, asking for the identity of the node that follows the failed node. The issuer should get back a set-successor packet from the second node down the line. If so, the issuer adjusts its linkage and issues a token (back to step 1).
4. If the issuing node gets no response to its who-follows packet, it tries again.
5. If the who-follows tactic fails, the node issues a solicit-successor packet with the full address range (i.e., every node is invited to respond). If this process works, a two-node ring is established and life goes on.
6. If two attempts of step 5 fail, the node assumes that a catastrophe has occurred; perhaps the node's receiver has failed. In any case, the node ceases activity and listens to the bus.

Logical *ring initialization* occurs when one or more stations detect a lack of bus activity of duration longer than a timeout value: The token has been lost. This can be due to a number of causes, such as the network has just been powered up, or a token-holding station fails. Once its timeout expires, a node will issue a *claim-token* packet. Contending claimants are resolved in a manner similar to the response-window process.

It should be obvious that the principal disadvantage of token bus is its complexity. The logic at each station far exceeds that required for CSMA/CD. A second disadvantage is the overhead involved. Under lightly loaded conditions, a station may have to wait through many fruitless token passes for a turn.

Indeed, at first glance it would seem difficult to make a case for this technique. Such a case can be made [MILL82], [STIE81] and it includes the following elements. First, it is possible to regulate the traffic in a number of ways. Multiple priority levels can be used, and different stations can be allowed to hold the token different amounts of time. This type of discrimination is difficult to achieve with CSMA/CD. Second, unlike with CSMA/CD, there is no minimum packet-length requirement with token bus. Third, the necessity for listening while talking imposes physical and electrical constraints on CSMA/CD systems; these do not apply to token systems where no station need listen and talk at the same time. Finally, under heavy loads, where it counts, token bus exhibits significantly superior performance to CSMA/CD, as discussed below.

Another advertised advantage of token bus is that it is "deterministic" that is, there is a known upper bound to the amount of time any station must wait before transmitting. This upper bound is known because each station in the logical ring can only hold the token for a specified time. In contrast, with CSMA/CD, the delay time can only be expressed statistically. Furthermore, since every attempt to transmit under CSMA/CD can in principle produce a collision, there is a possibility that a station could be shut out indefinitely. For process-control and other real-time applications, this "nondeterministic" behavior is undesirable. Alas, in the real world, there is always a finite possibility of transmission error, which can cause a lost token. This adds a statistical component to token bus.

Ring LANs

Over the years, a number of different algorithms have been proposed for controlling access to the ring (good surveys are [PENN79] and [LIU78]). The three most common access techniques are discussed in this section: token ring, slotted ring, and register insertion. Table 11-5 compares these three methods on a number of characteristic:

- *Transmit opportunity:* When may a repeater insert a packet onto the ring?
- *Packet purge responsibility:* Who removes a packet from a ring, to avoid its circulating indefinitely?
- *Number of packets on ring:* This depends not only on the "bit length" of the ring relative to the packet length, but on the access method.
- *Principal advantage.*
- *Principal disadvantage.*

The significance of the table entries will become clear as the discussion proceeds.

Token Ring. This is probably the oldest ring control technique, originally proposed in 1969 [FARM69] and referred to as the Newhall ring. This has become the most popular ring access technique in the United States. Prime Computer

TABLE 11-5 Ring Access Methods

	Register Insertion	Slotted Ring	Token Ring
Transmit opportunity	Idle state plus empty buffer	Empty slot	Token
Packet purge responsibility	Receiver or transmitter	Transmitter	Transmitter
Number of packets on ring	Multiple	Multiple	One
Principal advantage	Maximum ring utilization	Simplicity	Regulated/fair access
Principal disadvantage	Purge mechanism	Bandwidth waste	Token Maintenance

[GORD79] and Apollo both market token ring products, and IBM seems committed to such a product [RAUC82]. This technique is the one ring access method selected for standardization by the IEEE 802 Local Network Standards Committee [ANDR82, MARK82].

The token ring technique is based on the use of a small token packet that circulates around the ring. When all stations are idle, the token packet is labeled as a "free" token. A station wishing to transmit must wait until its detects a token passing by. It then changes the token from "free token" to "busy token" by altering the bit pattern. The station then transmits a packet immediately following the busy token (Figure 11-10).

There is now no free token on the ring, so other stations wishing to transmit must wait. The packet on the ring will make a round trip and be purged by the transmitting station. The transmitting station will insert a new free token on the ring when both of the following conditions have been met:

- The station has completed transmission of its packet.
- The busy token has returned to the station.

If the bit length of the ring is less than the packet length, the first condition implies the second. If not, a station could release a free token after it has finished transmitting but before it receives its own busy token; the second condition is not strictly necessary. However, this might complicate error recovery, since several packets will be on the ring at the same time. In any case, the use of a token guarantees that only one station at a time may transmit.

When a transmitting station releases a new free token, the next station downstream with data to send will be able to seize the token and transmit.

As with token bus, token ring requires fault management techniques. The key error conditions are no token circulating and persistent busy token. To address these problems, one station is designated as active token monitor [RAUC82]. The monitor detects the lost-token condition by using a timeout greater than the time required for the longest frame to traverse the ring completely. If no token is seen during this time, it is assumed to be lost. To recover, the monitor purges the ring of any residual data and issues a free token. To detect a circulating busy token, the monitor sets a monitor bit to 1 on any passing busy token. If it sees a busy token with a bit already set, it knows that the transmitting station failed to purge its frame. The monitor changes the busy token to a free token. Other stations on

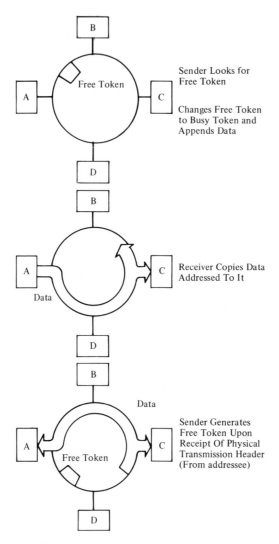

FIGURE 11-10. Token ring.

Sender Looks for
Free Token

Changes Free Token
to Busy Token and
Appends Data

Receiver Copies Data
Addressed To It

Sender Generates
Free Token Upon
Receipt Of Physical
Transmission Header
(From addressee)

the ring have the role of passive monitor. Their primary job is to detect failure of the active monitor and assume that role. A contention-resolution algorithm is used to determine which station takes over.

The token ring technique shares many of the advantages of token bus. Perhaps its principal advantage is that traffic can be regulated, either by allowing stations to transmit differing amounts of data when they receive the token, or by setting priorities so that higher-priority stations have first claim on a circulating token.

The principal disadvantage of token ring is the requirement for token maintenance. Loss of the free token prevents further utilization of the ring. Duplication of the token can also disrupt ring operation. One station must be elected monitor to assure that exactly one token is on the ring and to reinsert a free token if necessary.

Slotted Ring. The slotted ring was first developed by Pierce [PIER72], and is sometimes referred to as the Pierce loop. Most of the development work on this

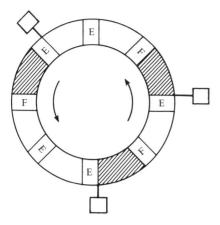

FIGURE 11-11. Slotted ring.

technique was done at the University of Cambridge in England [WILK79] and a number of British firms market commercial versions of the Cambridge ring [HEYW81].

In the slotted ring, a number of fixed-length slots circulate continuously on the ring (Figure 11-11). Each slot contains a leading bit to designate the slot as empty or full. All slots are initially marked empty. A station wishing to transmit waits until an empty slot arrives, marks the slot full, and inserts a packet of data as the slot goes by. The station cannot transmit another packet until this slot returns. The slot may also contain response bits, which can be set on the fly by the addressed station to indicate accepted, busy, or rejected. The full slot makes a complete round trip, to be marked empty again by the source. Each station knows the total number of slots on the ring and can thus clear the full/empty bit of the appropriate slot as it goes by. Once the now-empty slot goes by, the station is free to transmit again.

In the Cambridge ring, each slot contains room for one source address byte, one destination address byte, two data bytes, and five control bits for a total length of 37 bits.

The principal disadvantage of the slotted ring is that it is wasteful of bandwidth. First, a slot typically contains more overhead bits than data bits (e.g., Cambridge ring). Second, a station may send only one packet per round-trip ring time. If only one or a few stations have packets to transmit, many of the slots will circulate empty.

The principal advantage of the slotted ring appears to be its simplicity. The interaction with the ring at each node is minimized, improving reliability.

Register Insertion. This strategy was originally developed by researchers at Ohio State University [HAFN74], and is the technique used in the IBM Series 1 product [IBM82]. It derives its name from the shift register associated with each node on the ring. The shift register, equal in size to the maximum packet length, is used for temporarily holding packets that circulate past the node. In addition, the node has a buffer for storing locally produced packets.

The register insertion ring can be explained with reference to Figure 11-12, which shows the shift register and buffer at one node. First, consider the case in which the node has no data to send, but is merely handling packets of data that circulate by its position. When the ring is idle, the input pointer points to the rightmost position of the shift register, indicating that it is empty. When a packet arrives

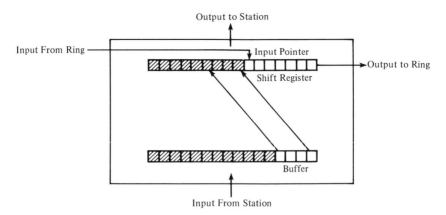

FIGURE 11-12. Register insertion ring.

along the ring, it is inserted bit by bit in the shift register, with the input pointer shifting left for each bit. The packet begins with an address field. As soon as the entire address field is in the register, the station can determine if it is the addressee. If not, the packet is forwarded by shifting one bit out on the right as each new bit arrives from the left, with the input pointer stationary. After the last bit of the packet has arrived, the station continues to shift bits out to the right until the packet is gone. If, during this time, no additional packets arrive, the input pointer will return to its initial position. Otherwise, a second packet will begin to accumulate in the register as the first is shifted out.

If the arriving packet is addressed to the node in question, it has two choices. It can erase the address bits from the shift register and divert the remainder of the packet to itself, thus purging the packet from the ring. Alternatively, it can retransmit the data as before, while copying them to the local station.

Now consider output from the station. A packet to be transmitted is placed in the output buffer. If the line is idle and the shift register is empty, the packet can be transferred immediately to the shift register. If the packet consists of some length n bits, less than the maximum frame size, and if at least n bits are empty in the shift register, the n bits are parallel-transferred to the empty portion of the shift register immediately adjacent to the full portion; the input pointer is adjusted accordingly.

The principal advantage of the register insertion technique is that it achieves the maximum ring utilization of any of the methods. A station may transmit whenever the ring is idle at its location. Thus multiple packets may be on the ring at any one time.

The principal disadvantage is the purge mechanism. Allowing multiple packets on the ring requires the recognition of an address prior to removal of a packet, whether it be removed by sender or receiver. If a packet's address field is damaged, it could circulate indefinitely. One possible solution is the use of an error-detecting code on the address field.

HSLNs

In this subsection, we review the only technique that has so far gained favor for HSLNs, known as prioritized CSMA. It is also referred to as CSMA with collision avoidance. The technique will be described in terms of the ANSI draft standard [BURR83]; the algorithm for HYPERchannel is very similar.

The protocol is based on CSMA. That is, a station wishing to transmit listens to the medium and defers if a transmission is in progress. In addition, an algorithm is used that specifically seeks to avoid collisions when the medium is found idle by multiple stations.

For this scheme, the stations or ports form an ordered sequence (PORT(1), PORT(2), . . . , PORT(N)), which need not correspond to physical position on the bus.

The scheme is initialized after each transmission by any port. Following initialization, each station, in turn, may transmit if none of the stations in sequence before it have done so. So PORT(I + 1) waits until after PORT(I) has had a chance to transmit. The waiting time consists of:

- The earliest time at which PORT(I) could begin transmitting [which depends on the transmission opportunity for PORT(I − 1)], plus
- a port delay time, during which PORT(I) has the opportunity to transmit, plus
- the propagation delay between the two ports.

As we shall see, this rather simple concept becomes complex as we consider all its refinements.

The basic rule can be described as follows. After any transmission, PORT(1) has the right to transmit. It it fails to do so in a reasonable time, PORT(2) has the chance, and so on. If any port transmits, the system reinitializes.

First refinement: We would like to permit multiframe dialogues. To accommodate this, an additional rule is added: After any transmission, the port receiving that transmission has the first right to transmit. If that port fails to transmit, it is the turn of PORT(1), and so on. This will permit two ports to seize the medium, with one port sending data frames and the other sending acknowledgment frames.

Second refinement: What happens if nobody has a frame to transmit? HYPERchannel solves this by entering a free-for-all period, in which collisions are allowed. ANSI has a more elegant solution: If none of the stations transmit when they have an opportunity, reinitialize the network and start over.

With these two refinements, we can depict the MAC protocol as a simple sequence of events:

1. Medium is active.
2. Medium Goes Idle.
      If Receiver Transmits, Then Go To 1.
                        Else Go To 3.
3. If PORT (1) Transmits, Then Go To 1.
                        ElseGo To 4.
            .
            .
            .

N + 3. If No Port Transmits, Then Go To 3.

Third refinement: Note that this scheme is biased to the lower-number ports. PORT(1) *always* gets a shot, for example. To make the scheme fair, a port that has just transmitted should not try again until everyone else has had a chance. (HYPERchannel does not have this refinement.)

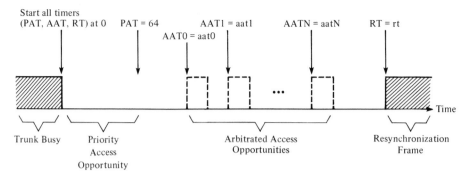

FIGURE 11-13. Operation of the ANS X 3T 9.5 medium access protocol.

To define the algorithm concisely, with these three refinements, we need to define some quantities:

- *Priority access opportunity:* a period of time granted to a port after it receives a frame. May be used to acknowledge frame and/or continue a multiframe dialogue.
- *Priority access timer (PAT):* used to time priority access opportunities—64 bit times.
- *Arbitrated access opportunity:* a period of time granted for each port in sequence, during which it may initiate a transmission—16 bit times. Assigned to individual ports to avoid collisions.
- *Arbitrated access timer (AAT):* used to provide each port with a unique, non-overlapping, arbitrated access opportunity.
- *Resynchronization timer (RT):* time by which the latest possible arbitrated transmission should have been received. Used to reset all timers.
- *Arbiter wait flag (WF):* used to enforce fairness. When a port transmits, its WF is set, so that it will not attempt another arbitrated transmission until all other ports have an opportunity.

For the timers listed, we use the convention that uppercase letters refer to the variable name, and lowercase letters to a specific value. A timer that reaches a specified maximum value is said to have expired. Figure 11-13 depicts the process.

This technique seems well suited to HSLN requirements. The provision for multiframe dialogue permits rapid transfer of large files. Typically, an HSLN will consist of only a small number of stations; under these circumstances, the round-robin access technique will not result in undue delays.

11-5

LAN PROTOCOL PERFORMANCE

The choice of a LAN architecture is based on many factors, but one of the most important is performance. Of particular concern is the behavior (throughput, response time) of the network under heavy load. In this section we provide an introduction to this topic for the two topologies and five medium access control protocols for LANs discussed earlier. A more detailed discussion can be found in [STAL84a].

As in previous chapters, we will see that the parameter a is a determining factor.

TABLE 11-6 Representative Values of *A*

Data Rate (Mbps)	Packet Size (bits)	Cable Length (km)	A
1	100	1	0.05
	1,000	10	0.05
	100	10	0.5
10	100	1	0.5
	1,000	1	0.05
	1,000	10	0.5
	10,000	10	0.05
50	10,000	1	0.025
	100	1	2.5

Table 11-6 gives some idea of the values of a that might be expected for a local network.

Simple Performance Models of Token Passing and CSMA/CD

The purpose of this section is to give the reader some insight into the relative performance of the most important LAN protocols: CSMA/CD, token bus, and token ring, by developing two simple performance models [STAL84b]. It is hoped that this exercise will aid in understanding the results of more rigorous analyses, presented later.

For these models we assume a local network with N active stations, and a maximum normalized propagation delay of a. To simplify the analysis, we assume that each station is always prepared to transmit a packet. This allows us to develop an expression for maximum achievable throughput (S). Although this should not be construed to be the sole figure of merit for a local network, it is the single most analyzed figure of merit, and does permit useful performance comparisons.

First, let us consider token ring. Time on the ring will alternate between data packet transmission and token passing. Refer to a single instance of a data packet followed by a token as a cycle and define:

C = average time for one cycle
T_1 = average time to transmit a data packet
T_2 = average time to pass a token

It should be clear that the average cycle rate is just $1/C = 1/(T_1 + T_2)$. Intuitively,

$$S = \frac{T_1}{T_1 + T_2} \tag{11-1}$$

That is, the throughput, normalized to system capacity, is just the fraction of time that is spent transmitting data.

Refer now to Figure 11-14; time is normalized such that packet transmission time equals 1 and propagation time equals a. Note that the propagation time must include repeater delays. For the case of $a < 1$, a station transmits a packet at time t_0, receives the leading edge of its own packet at $t_0 + a$, and completes transmission at $t_0 + 1$. The station then emits a token, which takes an average time a/N to reach the next station. Thus one cycle takes $1 + a/N$ and the transmission time is 1. So $S = 1/(1 + a/N)$.

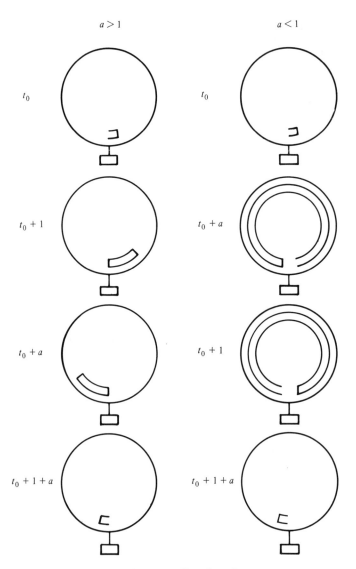

$a > 1$ $a < 1$

t_0

$t_0 + 1$

$t_0 + a$

$t_0 + 1 + a$

FIGURE 11-14. **The effect of *a* on utilization-ring.**

For $a > 1$, the reasoning is slightly different. A station transmits at t_0, completes transmission at $t_0 + 1$, and receives the leading edge of its frame at $t_0 + a$. At that point, it is free to emit a token, which takes an average time a/N to reach the next station. The cycle time is therefore $a + a/N$ and $S = 1/(a (1 + 1/N))$. Summarizing,

$$Token\ S = \begin{cases} \dfrac{1}{1 + a/N} & a < 1 \\[2ex] \dfrac{1}{a (1 + 1/N)} & a > 1 \end{cases} \tag{11-2}$$

The reasoning above applies equally well to token bus, where we assume that the logical ordering is the same as the physical ordering and that token-passing time is therefore a/N.

For CSMA/CD, we base our approach on a derivation in [METC76]. Consider time on the medium to be organized into slots whose length is twice the end-to-end propagation delay. This is a convenient way to view the activity on the medium; the slot time is the maximum time, from the start of transmission, required to detect a collision. Again, assume that there are N active stations. Clearly, if each station always has a packet to transmit, and does so, there will be nothing but collisions on the line. So we assume that each station restrains itself to transmitting during an available slot with probability P.

Time on the medium consists of two types of intervals. First is a transmission interval, which lasts $1/2a$ slots. Second is a contention interval, which is a sequence of slots with either a collision or no transmission in each slot. The throughput is just the proportion of time spent in transmission intervals [similar to the reasoning for Equation (11-1)].

To determine the average length of a contention interval, we begin by computing A, the probability that exactly one station attempts a transmission in a slot and therefore acquires the medium. This is just the binomial probability that any one station attempts to transmit and the others do not:

$$A = \binom{N}{1} P^1 (1 - P)^{N-1}$$

$$A = NP(1 - P)^{N-1}$$

This function takes on a maximum over P when $P = 1/N$:

$$A = (1 - 1/N)^{N-1}$$

Why are we interested in the maximum? Well, we want to calculate the maximum throughput of the medium. It should be clear that this will be achieved if we maximize the probability of successful seizure of the medium. This says that the following rule should be enforced: During periods of heavy usage, a station should restrain its offered load to $1/N$. (This assumes that each station knows the value of N. In order to derive an expression for maximum possible throughput, we live with this assumption.) On the other hand, during periods of light usage, maximum utilization cannot be achieved because G is too low; this region is not of interest here.

Now we can estimate the mean length of a contention interval, w, in slots:

$$E[w] = \sum_{i=1}^{\infty} i \Pr[\ i \text{ slots in a row with a collision or no transmission followed by a slot with one transmission}]$$

$$= \sum_{i=1}^{\infty} i(1 - A)^i A$$

The summation converges to

$$E[w] = \frac{1 - A}{A}$$

We can now determine the maximum utilization, which is just the length of a transmission interval as a proportion of a cycle consisting of a transmission and a contention interval:

$$\text{CSMA/CD: } S = \frac{1/2a}{1/2a + (1 - A)/A} = \frac{1}{1 + 2a(1 - A)/A} \tag{11-3}$$

Figure 11-15a shows normalized throughput as a function of a for various values of N and for both token passing and CSMA/CD. For both protocols, throughput declines as a increases. This is to be expected. But the dramatic difference between the two protocols is seen in Figure 11-15b, which shows throughput as a function of N. Token-passing performance actually improves as a function of N, because less time is spent in token passing. Conversely, the performance of CSMA/CD decreases because of the increased likelihood of collision or no transmission.

It is interesting to note the asymptotic value of S as N increases. For token:

$$\text{Token: } \lim_{N \to \infty} S = \begin{cases} 1 & a < 1 \\ \dfrac{1}{a} & a > 1 \end{cases} \quad (11\text{-}4)$$

For CSMA/CD, we need to know that $\lim (1 - 1/N)^{N-1} = 1/e$. Then CSMA/CD:

$$\lim_{N \to \infty} S = \frac{1}{1 + 3.44a} \quad (11\text{-}5)$$

Comparative Results from Analytic and Simulation Studies

Although there have been a number of performance studies focusing on a single protocol, there have been few systematic attempts to analyze the relative performance of the various local network protocols. In what follows, we look at the results of several carefully done studies that have produced comparative results.

CSMA/CD, Token Bus, and Token Ring. The first study was done by a group at Bell Labs, under the sponsorship of the IEEE 802 local network standards committee [STUC83a,b]. Naturally enough, the study analyzed the three protocols being standardized by IEEE 802: CSMA/CD, token bus, and token ring. The analysis is based on considering not only mean values but second moments of delay and message length. Two cases of message arrival statistics are employed. In the first, only 1 station out of 100 has messages to transmit, and is always ready to transmit. In such a case, one would hope that the network would not be the bottleneck, but could easily keep up with one station. In the second case, 100 stations out of 100 always have messages to transmit. This represents an extreme of congestion and one would expect that the network may be a bottleneck. In the two cases, the 1 station or 100 stations provide enough input to fully utilize the network. Hence the results are a measure of maximum potential utilization.

The results are shown in Figure 11-16. It shows the actual data transmission rate versus the transmission speed of the medium for the two cases and two packet sizes. Note that the abscissa is not offered load but the actual capacity of the medium. Three systems are examined: token ring with a one-bit latency per repeater, token bus, and CSMA/CD. The analysis yields the following conclusions:

- For the given parameters, the smaller the mean packet length, the greater the difference in maximum mean throughput rate between token passing and CSMA/CD. This reflects the strong dependence of CSMA/CD on a.
- Token ring is the least sensitive to work load.
- CSMA/CD offers the shortest delay under light load, while it is most sensitive under heavy load to the work load.

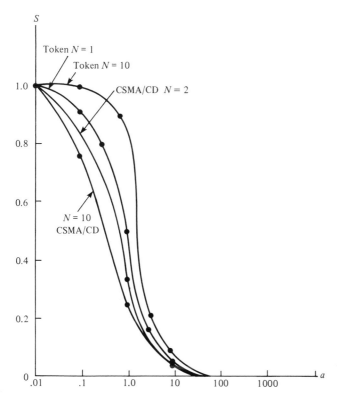

FIGURE 11-15a. Throughput as a function of *a* for token-passing and CSMA/CD.

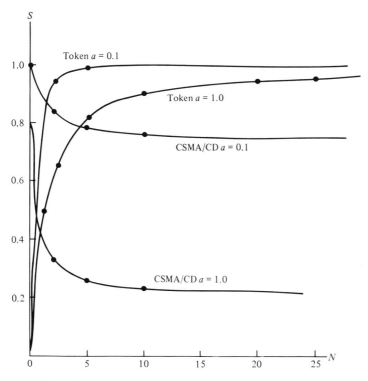

FIGURE 11-15b. Throughput as a function of *N* for token-passing and CSMA/CD.

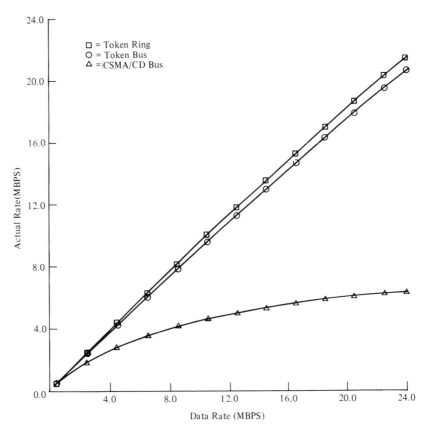

FIGURE 11-16a. Maximum potential data rate for LAN protocols: 2000 bits per packet; 100 stations active out of 100 stations total.

Note also that in the case of a single station transmitting, token bus is significantly less efficient than the other two protocols. This is so because the assumption is made that token-passing time equals the propagation delay, and that the delay in token processing is greater than for token ring.

Another phenomenon of interest is seen most clearly in Figure 11-16b. For a CSMA/CD system under these conditions, the maximum effective throughput at 5 Mbps is only about 1.25 Mbps. If expected load is, say 0.75 Mbps, this configuration may be perfectly adequate. If however, the load is expected to grow to 2 Mbps, raising the network data rate to 10 Mbps or even 20 Mbps will not accommodate the increase! The same conclusion, less precisely, can be drawn from the simple model presented earlier.

The reason for this disparity between CSMA/CD and token passing (bus or ring) under heavy load has to do with the instability of CSMA/CD. As offered load increases, so does throughput until, beyond its maximum value, throughput actually declines as G increases. This is because there is an increased frequency of collisions: More packets are offered, but fewer successfully escape collision. This same behavior was seen with other contention techniques (ALOHA, CSMA).

CSMA/CD and Ring Protocols. It is far more difficult to do a comparative performance of the three major ring protocols than to do a comparison of bus and

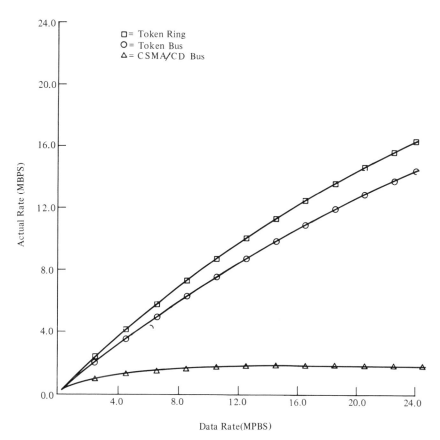

FIGURE 11-16b.   500 bits per packet; 100 stations active out of 100 stations total.

token ring protocols. The results depend critically on a number of parameters unique to each protocol. For example:

- *Token ring:* size of token, token processing time.
- *Slotted ring:* slot size, overhead bits per slot.
- *Register insertion:* register size.

Thus it is difficult to do a comparison, and although there have been a number of studies on each one of the techniques, few have attempted pairwise comparisons much less a three-way analysis. The most systematic work in this area has been done by Liu and his associates [LIU82]. Liu made comparisons based on analytic models developed by others for token ring, slotted ring, and CSMA/CD, plus his own formulations for register insertion. He then obtained very good corroboration from simulation studies.

Figure 11-17 summarizes the results. They are based on the assumption that $a = 0.005$ and that register insertion ring packets are removed by the destination station, whereas slotted ring and token ring packets are removed by the source station. This is clearly an unfair comparison since register insertion, under this scheme, does not include acknowledgments, but token ring and slotted ring do. The figure does show that slotted ring is the poorest performer, and that register insertion can carry a load greater than 1.0. This is because the protocol permits multiple packets to circulate.

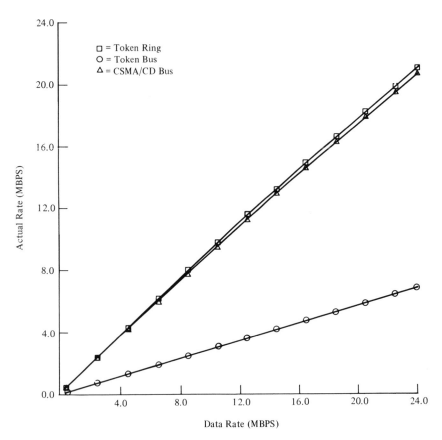

FIGURE 11-16c. **2000 bits per packet; 1 station active out of 100 stations total.**

Bux [BUX81] performed an analysis comparing token ring, slotted ring, and CSMA/CD, yielding similar results to those of Liu. This careful analysis produced several important conclusions. First, the delay-throughput performance of token ring versus CSMA/CD confirms our earlier discussion. That is, token ring suffers greater delay than CSMA/CD at light load but less delay and stable throughput at heavy loads. Further, token ring has superior delay characteristics to slotted ring. The poorer performance of slotted ring seems to have two causes: (1) the relative overhead in the small slots of a ring is very high, and (2) the time needed to pass empty slots around the ring to guarantee fair bandwidth is significant. Bux also reports several positive features of slotted ring: (1) the expected delay for a message is proportional to length (i.e., shorter packets get better service than long ones), and (2) overall mean delay is independent of packet length distribution type.

It is difficult to draw conclusions from the efforts made so far. The slotted ring seems to be the least desirable over a broad range of parameter values, owing to the considerable overhead associated with each small packet. For example, the Cambridge ring, which is the most widely available ring commercially in Europe, uses a 37 bit slot with only 16 data bits!

As between token ring and register insertion, the evidence suggests that, at least for some sets of parameter values, register insertion gives superior delay performance. Interestingly, there seems to be no commercially available register insertion product with the exception of the IBM Series 1 loop, where performance is not an issue. On the other hand, token ring in the United States, with the boost

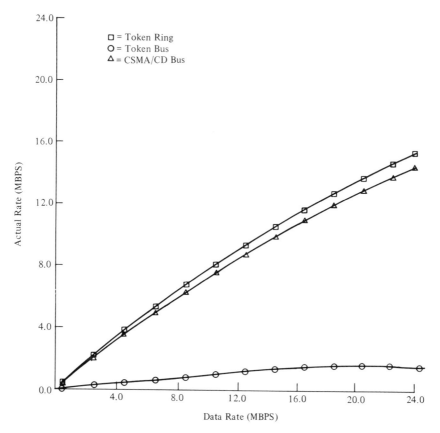

FIGURE 11-16d.   500 bits per packet; 1 station active out of 100 stations total.

from IEEE 802 and IBM, and slotted ring in Europe, where many firms have licensed the Cambridge slotted ring, seem destined to dominate the ring marketplace.

The primary advantage of register insertion is the potentially high utilization it can achieve. In contrast with token ring, multiple stations can be transmitting at a time. Further, a station can transmit as soon as a gap opens up on the ring; it need not wait for a token. On the other hand, the propagation time around the ring is not constant, but depends on the amount of traffic.

A final point in comparing token ring and register insertion. Under light loads, register insertion operates more efficiently, resulting in slightly less delay. However, both systems perform adequately. Our real interest is under heavy load. A typical local network will have $a < 1$, usually $a << 1$, so that a transmitting station on a token ring will append a token to the end of its packet. Under heavy load, a nearby station will be able to use the token. Thus almost 100% utilization is achieved, and there is no particular advantage to register insertion.

11-6

RECOMMENDED READING

Although the field of local networks is comparatively new, the literature is immense. The material in this chapter is covered in depth in [STAL84a]. [STAL83a]

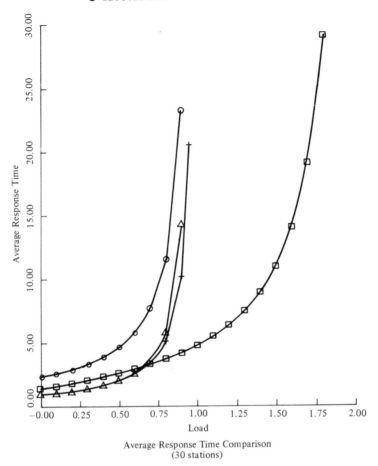

△ CSMA/CD
+ TOKEN-PASSING
□ REGISTER-INSERTION
○ SLOTTED RING

Average Response Time Comparison
(30 stations)

FIGURE 11-17. Delay for various protocols.

contains reprints of some of the key articles on local networks as well as an annotated bibliography. [DERF83] is a treatment oriented toward managers and end users. [TROP81] is a survey of performance studies.

There have been a number of survey articles; examples are [CLAR78], [COTT79], [PARK83a], [STAL84c], and [WOOD84a].

Two papers that contrast the CBX and the LAN are [PFIS82] and [RICH80].

11-8

PROBLEMS

11-1   An alternative to a local network for meeting local requirements for data processing and computer applications is a centralized time-sharing system plus a large number of terminals dispersed throughout the local area. What are the major benefits and pitfalls of this approach compared to a local network?

11-2 Could HDLC be used as a data link control protocol for a local network? If not, what is missing?

11-3 An asynchronous device, such as a teletype, transmits characters one at a time with unpredictable delays between characters. What problems, if any, do you foresee if such a device is connected to a local network and allowed to transmit at will (subject to gaining access to the medium)? How might such problems be resolved?

11-4 Consider the transfer of a file containing one million characters from one station to another. What is the total elapsed time and effective throughput for the following cases:

   a. A circuit-switched, star topology local network. Call setup time is negligible, and the data rate on the medium is 64 kbps.

   b. A bus topology local network with two stations a distance D apart, a data rate of B bps, and a packet size P with with 80 bits of overhead. Each packet is acknowledged with an 88-bit packet before the next is sent. The propagation speed on the bus is 200 m/μs. Solve for:

   (1) $D = 1$ km, $B = 1$ Mbps, $P = 256$ bits
   (2) $D = 1$ km, $B = 10$ Mbps, $P = 256$ bits
   (3) $D = 10$ km, $B = 1$ Mbps, $P = 256$ bits
   (4) $D = 1$ km, $B = 50$ Mbps, $P = 10,000$ bits

   c. A ring topology with a total circular length of $2D$, with the two stations a distance D apart. Acknowledgment is achieved by allowing a packet to circulate past the destination station, back to the source station. There are N repeaters on the ring, each of which introduces a delay of one bit time. Repeat the calculation for each of b1 through b4 for $N = 10; 100; 1000$.

11-5 A tree-topology local network is to be provided that spans two buildings. If permission can be obtained to string cable between the two buildings, one continuous tree layout will be used. Otherwise, each building will have an independent tree topology network and a point-to-point link will connect a special communications station on one network with a communications station on the other network. What functions must the communications stations perform? Repeat for ring and star.

11-6 System A consists of a single ring with 300 stations, one per repeater. System B consists of three 100-station rings linked by a bridge. If the probability of a link failure is P_1, a repeater failure is P_r, and a bridge failure is P_b, derive an expression for parts (a) through (d):

   a. Probability of failure of system A.
   b. Probability of complete failure of system B.
   c. Probability that a particular station will find the network unavailable, for systems A and B.
   d. Probability that any two stations, selected at random, will be unable to communicate, for systems A and B.
   e. Compute values for parts(a) through (d) for $P_1 = P_b = P_r = 10^{-2}$.

11-7 The binary exponential backoff algorithm is defined by IEEE 802 thus: "The delay is an integral multiple of slot time. The number of slot times to delay before the nth retransmission attempt is chosen as a uniformly distributed random integer r in the range $0 < r < 2**K$, where $K = \min(n,10)$." Slot time is, roughly, twice the round-trip propagation delay. Assume that two stations always have a frame to send. After a collision, what is the mean number of retransmission attempts before one station successfully transmits? What is the answer if three stations always have frames to send?

11-8 In what sense are the slotted ring and token ring protocols the complement of each other?

11-9 For a token ring system, suppose that the destination station removes the data frame and immediately sends a short acknowledgment frame to the sender, rather than letting the original frame return to sender. How will this affect performance?

11-10 Consider a Cambridge ring of length 10 km with a data rate of 10 Mbps and 500 repeaters, each of which introduces a 1-bit delay. How many slots are on the ring?

11-11 Define $t_{i,j}$ as the propagation delay between stations i and j on a bidirectional bus. Derive formulas for the ANS timers (Figure 11-13) using this parameter.

11-12 With continuing improvements in optical fiber transmission components, one might expect to see an HSLN using a fiber bus in the range 100 to 200 Mbps in the foreseeable future. Such a network could support a mix of stream and bursty traffic. Consider the various reservation schemes proposed in Chapter 10. Would any of these be appropriate for a fiber HSLN? Could you suggest a variation in one or more of the protocols that would be better suited?

11-13 Compare equations (10-12), (11-2), and (11-3). Under what circumstances does the throughput for the latter two equations exceed the theoretical maximum of (10-12)? Explain.

11-14 For the graphs in Figure 11-16, determine a and comment on the results.

11-15 Equations (11-2) and (11-4) are valid for token ring and for token baseband bus. What are equivalent equations for broadband bus?

APPENDIX 11A

STANDARDS

11A-1 Local Area Networks

The key to the development of the LAN market is the availability of a low-cost interface. The cost to connect equipment to a LAN must be much less than the cost of the equipment alone. This requirement, plus the complexity of the LAN protocols, dictate a VLSI solution. However, chip manufacturers will be reluctant to commit the necessary resources unless there is a high-volume market. A LAN standard would assure that volume and also enable equipment of a variety of manufacturers to intercommunicate.

This is the rationale of the IEEE 802 committee [CLAN82], which has produced a set of standards for LANs [IEEE83]. The standards are in the form of a three-layer communications architecture with a treelike expansion of options from top to bottom (Figure 11-18).

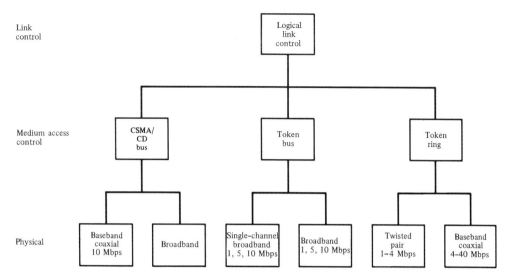

FIGURE 11-18. IEEE 802 local network standards.

The *logical link control* (LLC) layer provides for the exchange of data between service access points (SAPs), which are multiplexed over a single physical connection to the LAN. The LLC provides for both a connectionless, datagram-like, and connection-oriented, virtual-circuit-like service. Both the protocol and the frame format resemble HDLC. We will have more to say about LLC in Chapter 13.

At the *medium access control* (MAC) layer, there are three standards. CSMA/CD has converged with the Ethernet specification and is well suited to typical office applications. Both token bus and token ring have also been standardized. These are provided for time-critical applications, such as process control, as well as the office applications.

For CSMA/CD, a 10-Mbps baseband coaxial cable physical layer has been approved. Several broadband options are still under consideration, ranging from 2 to 10 Mbps. For token bus, three physical layers are provided as options. The simplest and least expensive is a single-channel broadband system using frequency-shift keying (FSK) at 1 Mbps. A more expensive version of this system runs at 5 or 10 Mbps and is intended to be easily upgradable to the final option, which is multichannel broadband. The latter provides data rates of 1, 5, and 10 Mbps. For token ring, a twisted pair standard has been defined providing data rates of 1 to 4 Mbps.

The range of options offered may seem excessive to the reader, given the alleged rationale for standards. However, the IEEE 802 committee has at least narrowed the alternatives. It is to be expected that the bulk of future LAN development work, at least in the United States, will be within the scope laid down by IEEE 802.

More detailed discussions of the standard may be found in [STAL84d], [NELS83], and [MYER82].

11A-2 High-Speed Local Networks

For HSLNs, the necessity for standards seems less compelling. Because of the high data rate requirement, the HSLN vendor must provide a high-throughput parallel interface to the attached device. Such an interface is in the range of tens of thousands of dollars, and a VLSI protocol implementation will not significantly affect the price.

A committee sponsored by the American National Standards Institute (ANSI), known as X3T9.5, has prepared a draft HSLN standard [PARK83b, ANSI82, BURR83]. The committee uses a two-layer model: The data link layer specifies a simple connectionless service. The physical layer includes the collision-avoidance protocol discussed earlier. It also specifies a single-channel phase-shift-key (PSK) scheme operating at 50 and 70 Mbps.

COMPUTER COMMUNICATIONS ARCHITECTURE

We have dealt, so far, with the technologies and techniques used to exchange data between two devices. Part I dealt with the case in which the two devices share a dedicated transmission link. Part II was concerned with the case in which a *communication network* provides a shared transmission capacity for multiple attached stations.

For voice communication, the above is adequate. However, for communication among data processing devices (computers, terminals), much more is needed. The data processing devices must implement a set of communications functions that will allow them to cooperatively perform some task. This set of functions is organized into a *communications architecture*. With these functions implemented, the network of stations and communications nodes is referred to as a *computer network*.

We begin this part with a detailed but generic look at the elements of a communications architecture (Chapter 12). The open systems interconnection (OSI) model is introduced as a model architecture and a framework for standards. Chapters 13 through 16 examine various aspects of a communications architecture, organized into four broad levels of functionality.

Finally, Chapter 17 looks at an evolving worldwide communications network, the integrated services digital network (ISDN). Although it might be argued that this topic belongs more properly in Part II, it draws on many of the concepts introduced in Part III. Furthermore, it ties together many of the concepts used throughout the book and is an appropriate culmination to our discussion of data and computer communications.

CHAPTER 12

Protocols and Architectures

The purpose of this chapter is to serve as an overview and necessary background to the detailed material that follows in the remainder of Part III. It will also serve to show how the concepts of Parts I and II fit into the broader area of computer networks and computer communications.

We begin with an exposition of the concept of a communications protocol. It is shown that protocols are fundamental to all data communications. Next, we look at a way of systematically describing and implementing the communications function by viewing the communications task in terms of a column of layers, each of which contains protocols. This is the view of the now-famous open systems interconnection (OSI) model.

Although the OSI model is almost universally accepted as the framework for discourse in this area, there is another point of view which grows out of the extensive research and practical experience of ARPANET. This viewpoint, which is characterized by a hierarchy of protocols, is also presented.

Both of the viewpoints above describe the communications function in terms of an architecture, which specifies protocols and their interrelationships. To lend concreteness to the discussion, two commercial architectures are presented: IBM's SNA and DEC's DNA.

Finally, the standards being developed by various organizations involved in protocol standardization are described briefly in Appendix 12A.

PROTOCOLS

Characteristics

The concepts of distributed processing and computer networking imply that entities in different systems need to communicate. We use the terms "entity" and "system" in a very general sense. Examples of entities are user application programs, file transfer packages, data base management systems, electronic mail facilities, and terminals. Examples of systems are computers, terminals, and remote sensors. Note that in some cases the entity and the system in which it resides are coextensive (e.g., terminals). In general, an *entity* is anything capable of sending or receiving information, and a *system* is a physically distinct object that contains one or more entities.

For two entities to successfully communicate, they must "speak the same language." What is communicated, how it is communicated, and when it is communicated must conform to some mutually acceptable set of conventions between the entities involved. The set of conventions is referred to as a *protocol*, which may be defined as a set of rules governing the exchange of data between two entities. The key elements of a protocol are:

- *Syntax:* includes such things as data format, coding, and signal levels.
- *Semantics:* includes control information for coordination and error handling.
- *Timing:* includes speed matching and sequencing.

HDLC is an example of a protocol. The data to be exchanged must be sent in frames of a specific format (syntax). The control field provides a variety of regulatory functions such as setting a mode and establishing a connection (semantics). Provisions are also included for flow control (timing). Most of Part III will be devoted to discussing other examples of protocols.

Some important characteristics of a protocol are:

- Direct/indirect.
- Monolithic/structured.
- Symmetric/asymmetric.
- Standard/nonstandard.

Communication between two entities may be *direct or indirect*. Figure 12-1 depicts the possible situations. If two systems share a point-to-point link, the entities in these systems may communicate directly; that is, data and control information pass directly between entities with no intervening active agent. The same may be said of a multipoint configuration, although here the entities must be concerned with the issue of access control, making the protocol more complex. If systems connect through a switched communication network, a direct protocol is no longer possible. The two entities must depend on the functioning of other entities to exchange data. A more extreme case is a situation in which two entities do not even share the same switched network, but are indirectly connected through two or more networks. A set of such interconnected networks is termed a *catenet*.

An important protocol design consideration is raised by the latter two configurations (Figure 12-1c and d), namely, the extent to which the entities and hence their protocol must be aware of the characteristics of intervening systems. Ideally, the intervening systems would be transparent and the protocol between the two

(a) Point–to–point

(b) Multipoint/broadcast network

(c) Switched network

(d) Catenet

FIGURE 12-1.   Means of connection of communicating systems.

entities would be the same as for a point-to-point link. We shall see that this ideal cannot be met.

Another characteristic of a protocol is whether it is *monolithic or structured*. It should become clear as Part III proceeds that the task of communication between entities on different systems is too complex to be handled as a unit. For example, consider an electronic mail package running on two computers connected by a synchronous HDLC link. To be truly monolithic, the package would need to include all of the HDLC logic. If the connection were over a packet-switched network, the package would still need the HDLC logic (or some equivalent) to attach to the network. It would also need logic for breaking up mail into packet-sized chunks, logic for requesting a virtual circuit, and so forth. Mail should only be sent when the destination system and entity are active and ready to receive. Logic is needed for that kind of coordination. And, as we shall see, the list goes on. A change in any aspect means that this huge package must be modified, with the risk of introducing difficult-to-find bugs.

An alternative is to use structured design and implementation techniques. Instead of a single protocol, there is a set of protocols that exhibit a hierarchical or layered structure. Lower level, more primitive functions are implemented in lower-level entities that provide services to higher-level entities. For example, there could be an HDLC module (entity) that is invoked by an electronic mail facility when needed. Note that this is just another form of indirection: Higher-level entities rely on lower level entities to exchange data.

Figure 12-2 suggests, in general terms, a structured set of protocols, and shows the most extreme case of two stations connected via multiple switched networks. Stations 1 and 2 each have one or more applications that wish to communicate. Between each like pair (e.g., electronic mail modules), an application-oriented protocol is needed which coordinates the activities of the two application modules, and assures common syntax and semantics. This protocol need know little about the intervening communications facility, but makes use of a network services entity that does. The network services entity will have a process-to-process protocol with a corresponding entity in the other station. This protocol might handle such matters as flow control and error control. There must also be a protocol between station 1 and network *A*, and between station 2 and network *B*. In the case of a broadcast network, this protocol would include medium access control logic. In the case of a packet-switched network, logic for virtual circuit establishment is needed. Note that a different, simpler network access protocol might be provided for less intelligent devices, such as terminals. Internal to each network, a node-to-node protocol is required between each connected pair of nodes, and an entry-to-exit protocol might also be used. Examples of these were discussed in Chapter 9. Finally, an internetwork protocol is required between networks.

Several comments are in order. In Part III we will be concerned with protocols in all of the categories above except those internal to a communication network. We are interested in computer-computer and computer-terminal communications; the internal workings of a communication network should not be visible to the attached stations. Also, the protocols exhibited in Figure 12-2 are general in nature. Typically, a protocol structure will contain more divisions, further decomposing the problem.

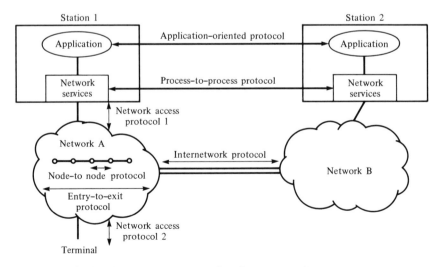

FIGURE 12-2. Relationship among communication protocols.

When structured protocol design is used, we refer to the hardware and software used to implement the communications function as a *communications architecture*. The remainder of this chapter, after this section, is devoted to this concept.

A protocol may be either *symmetric or asymmetric*. Most of the protocols that we shall study are symmetric. That is, they involve communication between peer entities. Asymmetry may be dictated by the logic of an exchange (e.g., a "user" and a "server" process), or by the desire to keep one of the entities or systems as simple as possible. An example of the latter is the normal response mode of HDLC. Typically, this involves a computer which polls and selects a number of terminals. The logic on the terminal end is quite straightforward.

Finally, a protocol may be either *standard or nonstandard*. A nonstandard protocol is one built for a specific communications situation or, at most, a particular model of a computer. Thus, if K different kinds of information sources have to communicate with L types of information receivers, $K \times L$ different protocols are needed without standards and a total of $2 \times K \times L$ implementations are required (Figure 12-3a). If all systems shared a common protocol, only $K + L$ implementations would be needed (Figure 12-3b). The increasing use of distributed processing and the decreasing inclination of customers to remain locked in to a single vendor dictate that all vendors implement protocols that conform to an agreed-upon standard. Appendix 12A lists the key organizations involved in standards development and outlines the current status of standards development.

Functions

Before turning to a discussion of communications architecture and the various levels of protocols, let us consider a rather small set of functions that form the basis of all protocols. Not all protocols have all functions; this would involve a significant duplication of effort. There are, nevertheless, many instances of the same type of function being present in protocols at different levels.

This discussion will, of necessity, be rather abstract. It does provide an integrated overview of the characteristics of functions of communications protocols. The concept of protocol is fundamental to all of the remainder of Part III, and as we proceed, specific examples of all these functions will be seen.

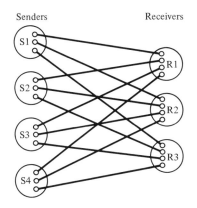

(a) Without standards: 12 different protocols, 24 protocol implementations

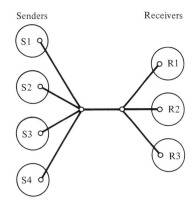

(b) With standards: 1 protocol, 7 implementations

FIGURE 12-3. The use of standard protocols.

We can group protocol functions into the following categories:

- Fragmentation and reassembly.
- Encapsulation.
- Connection control.
- Flow control.
- Error control.
- Synchronization.
- Sequencing.
- Addressing.
- Multiplexing.
- Transmission services.

Fragmentation and Reassembly. A protocol is concerned with exchanging streams of data between two entities. Usually, the transfer can be characterized as consisting of a sequence of blocks of data of some bounded size. At the application level, we refer to a logical unit of data transfer as a *message*. Now, whether the application entity sends data in messages or in a continuous stream, lower level protocols may need to break the data up into blocks of some smaller bounded size. This process is called *fragmentation*. For convenience, we shall refer to a block of data exchanged between two entities via a protocol as a *protocol data unit* (PDU).

There are a number of motivations for fragmentation, depending on the context. Among the typical reasons for fragmentation:

- The communications network may only accept blocks of data up to a certain size. ARPANET, for example, accepts messages up to 8063 bytes in length.
- Error control may be more efficient with a smaller PDU size. For example, fewer bits need to be retransmitted using smaller blocks with the selective repeat technique.
- More equitable access to shared transmission facilities, with shorter delay, can be provided. For example, without a maximum block size, one stations could monopolize a multipoint medium.
- A smaller PDU size may mean that receiving entities can allocate smaller buffers (e.g., the ARPANET entry-to-exit protocol).
- An entity may require that data transfer comes to some sort of "closure" from time to time, for checkpoint and restart/ recovery operations.

There are several disadvantages to fragmentation that argue for making blocks as large as possible:

- Each PDU, as we shall see, contains a fixed amount of control information. Hence the smaller the block, the greater the percentage overhead.
- PDU arrival may generate an interrupt that must be serviced. Smaller blocks result in more interrupts.
- More time is spent processing smaller, more numerous PDUs.

All of these factors must be taken into account by the protocol designer in determining minimum and maximum PDU size.

The counterpart of fragmentation is *reassembly*. Eventually, the fragmented data must be reassembled into messages appropriate to the application level. If PDUs arrive out of order, the task is complicated.

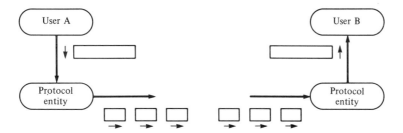

FIGURE 12-4. Fragmentation and reassembly.

Figure 12-4 illustrates the process. User *A* wishes to send a message to User *B*. *A* and *B* might be applications relying on protocol entities that communicate via a process-to-process protocol (see Figure 12-2). The figure shows that the message is fragmented into three PDUs prior to transmission and reassembled upon reception before delivery to *B*.

Encapsulation.   Each PDU contains not only data but control information. Indeed, some PDUs consist solely of control information and no data. The control information falls into three general categories:

- *Address:* The address of the sender and/or receiver may be indicated.
- *Error detecting code:* Some sort of frame check sequence is often included for error detection.
- *Protocol control:* Addition information is included to implement the protocol functions listed in the remainder of this section.

The addition of control information to data is referred to as *encapsulation*. Data are accepted or generated by an entity and encapsulated into a PDU containing that data plus control information (Figure 12-5). An example of this is the HDLC frame (Figure 5-14).

Connection Control.   An entity may transmit data to another entity in an unplanned fashion and without prior coordination. This is known as *connectionless data transfer*; an example is the use of the datagram. While this mode can be useful, it is less common than *connection-oriented data transfer*, of which the virtual circuit is an example [CHAP83].

Connection-oriented data transfer is to be preferred (even required) if stations anticipate a lengthy exchange of data and/or certain details of their protocol must

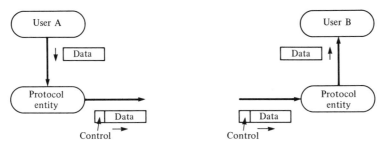

FIGURE 12-5. Encapsulation.

be worked out dynamically. A logical association, or *connection*, is established between the entities. Three phases occur (Figure 12-6):

- Connection establishment.
- Data transfer.
- Connection termination.

With more sophisticated protocols, there may also be connection interrupt and recovery phases to cope with errors and other sorts of interruptions.

During the connection establishment phase, two entities agree to exchange data. Typically, one station will issue a connection request (in connectionless fashion!) to the other. A central authority may or may not be involved. In simpler protocols, the receiving entity either accepts or rejects the request and, in the former case, away they go. In more complex proposals, this phase includes a negotiation concerning the syntax, semantics, and timing of the protocol. Both entities must, of course, be using the same protocol. But the protocol may allow certain optional features and these must be agreed upon by means of negotiation. For example, the protocol may specify a PDU size of *up to* 8000 bytes; one station may wish to restrict this to 1000 bytes.

Following connection establishment, the data transfer phase is entered. During this phase both data and control information (e.g., flow control, error control) is exchanged. Finally, one side or the other wishes to terminate the connection and does so by sending a termination request. Alternatively, a central authority might forcibly terminate a connection.

Flow Control.   Flow control was introduced in Chapter 5 and seen again in Chapter 9. In essence, flow control is a function performed by a receiving entity to limit the amount or rate of data that is sent by a transmitting entity.

The simplest form of flow control is a stop-and-wait procedure, in which each PDU must be acknowledged before the next can be sent. More efficient protocols involve some form of credit provided to the transmitter, which is the amount of data that can be sent without an acknowledgment. The sliding-window technique

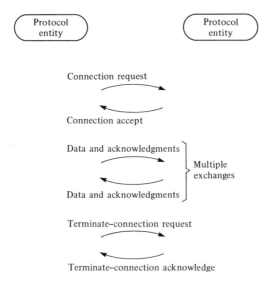

FIGURE 12-6.   The phases of a connection-oriented data transfer.

is an example of this mechanism. Closely related are SNA's pacing algorithm and ARPANET's ready-for-next-message command.

Flow control is a good example of a function that must be implemented in several protocols. Consider again Figure 12-2. Network A will need to exercise flow control over station 1's network services module via the network access protocol, in order to enforce network traffic control. At the same time, station 2's network services module has only limited buffer space and needs to exercise flow control over station 1's network services module via the process-to-process protocol. Finally, even though station 2's network service module can control its data flow, station 2's application may be vulnerable to overflow. For example, the application could be hung up waiting for disk access. Thus flow control is also needed over the application-oriented protocol.

Error Control. Another previously introduced function is error control. Techniques are needed to guard against loss or damage of data and control information. Most techniques involve error detection, based on a frame check sequence, and PDU retransmission. Retransmission is often activated by a timer. If a sending entity fails to receive an acknowledgment to a PDU within a specified period of time, it will retransmit.

As with flow control, error control is a function that must be performed at various levels of protocol. Consider again Figure 12-2. The network access protocol should include error control to assure that data are successfully exchanged between station and network. However, a packet of data may be lost inside the network, and the process-to-process protocol should be able to recover from this loss.

Synchronization. It should be apparent from the discussion so far that a protocol entity needs to remember a certain number of parameters (e.g., window size, connection phase, timer value). These parameters can be viewed as state variables and their collection defines the state of the entity. It is occasionally important that two communicating protocol entities be simultaneously in a well-defined state, for example at initialization, checkpointing, and termination. This is termed synchronization.

The difficulty with achieving synchronization is that one entity has knowledge of the state of the other only by virtue of received PDUs. These PDUs do not arrive instantly. They take some time, perhaps a variable amount of time, to traverse from sender to receiver. Furthermore, a PDU may be lost in transit.

An example from [POUZ78] illustrates the problem. Consider two entities, A and B, performing mutual data base updating. Neither should terminate until both are finished updating and the two data bases are synchronized. Question: How can the two entities be sure that both have terminated?

Figure 12-7a shows a state diagram for A. State 1 indicates that A has finished its work. When A has finished, it sends a DONE message to B. When it receives a DONE message back, A is free to terminate and disappear. However, B may finish first. To cover this contingency, let us refine the state diagram as shown in Figure 12-7b. When each station has sent and received a DONE message, in either order, it terminates.

Figure 12-7b will only work if no messages are lost. Consider: A arrives in state 3 and waits for the DONE message from B. B sends such a message but it is lost in transit. After waiting a reasonable amount of time, what should A do? Going to state 4 and terminating is risky: the two data bases may not agree; B may not yet have reached state 1 and may need A's cooperation to complete its task. On the

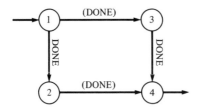

(a) Partial synchronization

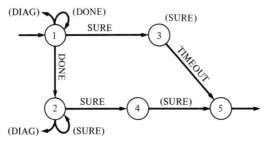

(b) Simple synchronization

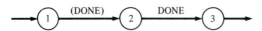

(c) Safe synchronization

(DONE): message sent   DONE: message received

FIGURE 12-7. Synchronization example.

other hand, going back to state 1 could hang *A* up, since *B* may already have gone to state 4 and vanished.

The diagram of Figure 12-7c takes errors into account. When *A* has both transmitted and received a DONE, it issues a SURE message, indicating that it knows that *B* is done. Neither entity can terminate until the other has reached state 2. In case one entity gets hung up in state 2, it at least knows that the other has reached state 1, and possibly state 5. If either entity gets hung up in state 1 or 2, it initializes a diagnostic procedure to resolve the deadlock.

This example is not meant to indicate a generally applicable solution for the synchronization problem. Rather, it serves to illustrate its complexity.

Sequencing. Sequencing is that protocol function which identifies the order in which PDUs containing data were sent by numbering them, modulo some maximum sequence number. This function only makes sense in the context of connection-oriented data transfer. Sequencing serves three main purposes:

- Ordered delivery.
- Flow control.
- Error control.

Consider first *ordered delivery*. If two entities are not directly connected, there is the risk that PDUs will not arrive in the order in which they were sent, because they may traverse different paths. In connection-oriented data transfer, it is generally required that PDU order be maintained. For example, if a file is transferred between two systems, we would like to be assured that the records of the received file are in the same order as those of the transmitted file, and not shuffled. If each PDU is given a unique sequence number, and numbers are assigned sequentially, then it is a logically simple task for the receiving entity to reorder received PDUs on the basis of sequence number. The only hitch in this scheme is that sequence numbers repeat (because they are modulo some maximum number). Evidently, the maximum sequence number must be greater than the maximum number of PDUs that could be outstanding at any time. In fact, the maximum sequence number may need to be *twice* the maximum number of PDUs that could be outstanding (e.g., selective-repeat ARQ; see Chapter 5).

The application of sequencing to *flow control* and *error control* was illustrated in Chapter 5 with the discussion of HDLC. Both flow control and error control depend on being able to uniquely identify individual PDUs.

Addressing. For two entities to communicate, other than over a point-to-point link, they must somehow be able to identify each other. For example, on a broadcast network each station looks for packets that contain its identifier. On a switched network, the network needs to know the identity of the destination station in order to properly route data or set up a connection.

A distinction is generally made among names, addresses, and routes [SHOC78]. A name specifies what an object is; an address specifies where it is; and a route indicates how to get there. For our purposes, it is more useful to draw a distinction suggested in [POUZ78]:

- *Local name:* the name by which an entity is identified within its own system.
- *Global name:* the name by which an entity is known outside its own system.

There are several points of importance here. First, it is desirable to distinguish between local names and global names. Communication may involve a variety of systems of different types and from different vendors. Each system likes to have its own naming convention, and it seems hopeless to attempt to enforce uniform local naming rules. On the other hand, no entity or system can be expected to deal with a variety of name lengths, formats, and global conventions. Thus both local and global names are needed. Second, an address is a form of global name. However, and third, there may not be a unique global name for an entity. If the entity is mobile, its address changes. If it attaches directly to more than one network, each may have its own address for the entity.

The problem of naming and addressing of entities admits of no unique solution. In the remainder of this subsection, we outline some approaches and considerations. During the discussion, we refer to the entities in Figure 12-8. The following topics are considered:

- Name structure.
- Name knowledge.
- Connection names.
- Port names.
- Group names.

The *name structure* used for global names can be either hierarchical or flat. A hierarchical name would have the structure SYSTEM.ENTITY, or in the case of multiple networks, NETWORK.SYSTEM.ENTITY. The fields SYSTEM and NETWORK contain global identifiers of some fixed format. ENTITY must pre-

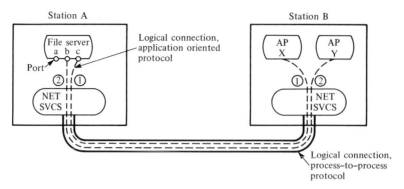

FIGURE 12-8. Example for naming conventions.

sumably be a name of some fixed maximum length. The name could have global significance, in which case the system containing that entity would have to contain a mapping from global entity identifiers to local entity identifiers. Alternatively, if all systems could live with a particular field length, local and global entity identifiers could be the same. As an example, application X in station B is identified as B.X.

A flat name structure is one in which each entity has a global name that is unique throughout the domain of communication. Names could be assigned by preallocation; that is, each system is given a set of global names, which it then assigns to its local entities. Alternatively, a mapping or directory function could be used which globally assigns names to entities.

The hierarchical structure has several advantages. It is easier to add new names to the universe of names with a hierarchical scheme, since entity names need only be unique within a system. With flat names, it must be determined that any new name added to the system is not the same as any previous name. Second, a hierarchical name is an aid to routing since it identifies the system containing the entity. Thus a hierarchical name has more the flavor of an address than does a flat name.

Regardless of name structure, there is a requirement for *name knowledge*. An entity can only send data to or request a connection with an entity whose name it knows. Consider that entity 1 in system A wishes to establish a connection with entity 2 in system B. The possibilities for naming are numerous; we mention only a few. System A could maintain a directory of global names of all entities that might be of interest. Each of these would have some identifier understandable to station A's entities. Another possibility is that entity 1 wishes access to some generic service, such as transaction processing (TP) on system B. Here there are several subpossibilities:

- A network server known to entity 1 maintains a directory mapping generic services by system onto global names.
- There is a "well-known entity" on system B. Entity 1 queries this entity for the global name of system B's TP.
- The well-known entity on system B is a log-on facility. Entity 1 logs on to system B and is then allowed access to TP.

At bottom, the problem is this: Entity 1 must know the name of entity 2 to exchange data with it, but how can it get that name unless it already knows it? The preceding should give some feel for the various approaches that can be taken.

For connectionless data transfer, a global name is used with each data transmission. For connection-oriented transfer, it is sometimes desirable to use only a *connection name* during the data transfer phase. The scenario is this: Entity 1 on system *A* requests a connection to entity 2 on system *B*, perhaps using the global address B.2. When B.2 accepts the connection, a connection name (usually a number) is provided and is used by both entities for future transmissions. As an example, two connections between applications, labeled "1" and "2," are shown in Figure 12-8. The use of a connection name has several advantages:

- *Reduced overhead:* Connection names are generally shorter than global names. For example, in the X.25 protocol (discussed in Chapter 13) used over packet-switched networks, connection request packets contain both source and destination address fields, each with a system-defined length that may be a number of bytes. After a virtual circuit is established, data packets contain just a 12-bit virtual circuit number.
- *Routing:* In setting up a connection, a fixed route may be defined (e.g. SNA and TYMNET, but not ARPANET). The connection name serves to identify the route for handling future PDUs.
- *Multiplexing:* We address this function in more general terms below. Here we note that an entity may wish to enjoy more than one connection simultaneously. Thus incoming PDUs must be identified by connection name.

Another concept often found with protocols is that of *port name*. A port name is a global entity name. If each entity has a single port name, there is not much point to the concept. However, it is often the case that multiple port names are associated with an entity. This can be used to provide multiplexing, as with connection names. For example, a file server module may be able to service a number of users simultaneously. Also, port names can indicate different entry points within an entity. For example, a file server might have a different entry point for users authorized to read and update and for users authorized only to read. In many systems, port names are unique within the system across all entities and entity names are not needed. So, for a hierarchical structure, the form NET-WORK.SYSTEM.PORT would be used. For example, the three ports depicted in Figure 12-8 are designated A.a, A.b, and A.c.

Finally, we mention the concept of *group name*, which is a name that refers to more than one entity or port. This term has been used to mean a number of things. One usage is to identify a contention group, as discussed in Chapter 8. A more meaningful use, in the present context, is that a group name identifies multiple simultaneous recipients for data. For example, a user might wish to send a memo to a number of individuals. The network control center may wish to notify all users that the network is going down. A group name may be *broadcast*, intended for all entities within a domain, or *multicast*, intended for a specific subset of entities. Table 12-1 illustrates the possibilities.

Multiplexing. We have already seen one type of multiplexing that is used with protocols: the multiplexing of data transfers into an entity. This can be accomplished using connection names, which permits multiple simultaneous connections. It can also be accomplished via port names, which also permit multiple simultaneous connections. The latter is shown in Figure 12-8, where the file server in A has two connections active at the same time. Port names also accommodate multiple connectionless transfers from different sources to the same destination. With the use of different port names, interference is avoided.

TABLE 12-1 Multicasting and Broadcasting

Destination	Network Address	System Address	Entity/Port Address
Specific	Specific	Specific	Specific
Multicast	Specific	Specific	Group
	Specific	All	Group
	All	All	Group
Broadcast	Specific	Specific	All
	Specific	All	All
	All	All	All

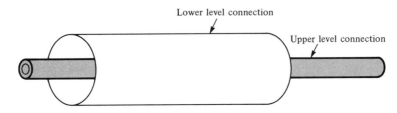

(a) One–to–one

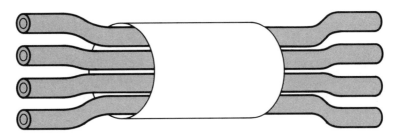

(b) Upward multiplexing

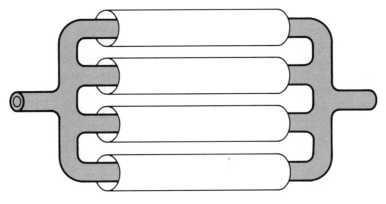

(c) Downward multiplexing

FIGURE 12-9. Multiplexing of protocol connections.

Multiplexing is used in another context as well, namely the mapping of connections from one level to another. Consider again Figure 12-2. Network A might provide a virtual circuit service. For each process-to-process connection established at the network services level, a virtual circuit could be created at the network access level. This is a one-to-one relationship, but need not be so. Multiplexing can be used in one of two directions (Figure 12-9). *Upward multiplexing* occurs when multiple higher-level connections are multiplexed on, or share, a single lower-level connection. This may be needed to make more efficient use of the lower-level service or to provide several higher-level connections in an environment where only a single lower-level connection exists. Figure 12-8 shows an example of upward multiplexing. *Downward multiplexing,* or *splitting,* means that a single higher-level connection is built on top of multiple lower-level connections, the traffic on the higher connection being divided among the various lower connections. This technique may be used to provide reliability, performance, or efficiency.

Transmission Services. A protocol may provide a variety of additional services to the entities that use it. We mention here three common examples:

- *Priority:* Certain messages, such as control messages, may need to get through to the destination entity with minimum delay. An example would be a close connection request. Thus priority could be assigned on a message basis. Additionally, priority could be assigned on a connection basis.
- *Grade of service:* Certain classes of data may require a minimum throughput or a maximum delay threshold.
- *Security:* Security mechanisms, restricting access, may be invoked.

All of these services depend on the underlying transmission system and any intervening lower-level entities. If it is possible for these services to be provided from below, the protocol can be used by the two entities to exercise those services.

12-2

THE LAYERED APPROACH: THE OSI MODEL

Motivation

When work is done that involves more than one computer, additional elements must be added to the system: the hardware and software to support the communication between or among the systems. Communications hardware is reasonably standard and generally presents few problems. However, when communication is desired among heterogeneous (different vendors, different models of same vendor) machines, the software development effort can be a nightmare. Different vendors use different data formats and data exchange conventions. Even within one vendor's product line, different model computers may communicate in unique ways.

As the use of computer communications and computer networking proliferates, a one-at-a-time special-purpose approach to communications software development is too costly to be acceptable. The only alternative is for computer vendors to adopt and implement a common set of conventions. For this to happen, a set of international or at least national standards must be promulgated by appropriate organizations. Such standards have two effects:

TABLE 12-2 Purpose of the OSI Model

The purpose of this International Standard Reference Model of Open Systems Interconnection is to provide a common basis for the coordination of standards development for the purpose of systems interconnection, while allowing existing standards to be placed into perspective within the overall Reference Model.

The term Open Systems Interconnection (OSI) qualifies standards for the exchange of information among systems that are "open" to one another for this purpose by virtue of their mutual use of the applicable standards.

The fact that a system is open does not imply any particular systems implementation, technology or means of interconnection, but refers to the mutual recognition and support of the applicable standards.

It is also the purpose of this International Standard to identify areas for developing or improving standards, and to provide a common reference for maintaining consistency of all related standards. It is not the intent of this International Standard either to serve as an implementation specification, or to be a basis for appraising the conformance of actual implementations, or to provide a sufficient level of detail to define precisely the services and protocols of the interconnection architecture. Rather, this International Standard provides a conceptual and functional framework which allows international teams of experts to work productively and independently on the development of standards for each layer of the Reference Model of OSI.

- Vendors feel encouraged to implement the standards because of an expectation that, because of wide usage of the standards, their products would be less marketable without them.
- Customers are in a position to require that the standards be implemented by any vendor wishing to propose equipment to them.

It should become clear from the ensuing discussion that no single standard will suffice. The task of communication in a truly cooperative way between applications on different computers is too complex to be handled as a unit. The problem must be decomposed into manageable parts. Hence before one can develop standards, there should be a structure or *architecture* that defines the communications tasks.

This line of reasoning led the International Organization for Standardization (ISO) in 1977 to establish a subcommittee to develop such an architecture. The result was the *Open Systems Interconnection* (OSI) reference model which is a framework for defining standards for linking heterogeneous computers. The OSI model provides the basis for connecting "open" systems for distributed applications processing. The term "open" denotes the ability of any two systems conforming to the reference model and the associated standards to connect.

Table 12-2, extracted from the basic OSI document [ISO83a] summarizes the purpose of the model.

Concepts

A widely accepted structuring technique, and the one chosen by ISO, is *layering*. The communications functions are partitioned into a vertical set of layers. Each layer performs a related subset of the functions required to communicate with another system. It relies on the next lower layer to perform more primitive functions and to conceal the details of those functions. It provides services to the next higher

TABLE 12-3   Principles Used in Defining the OSI Layers

1. Do not create so many layers as to make the system engineering task of describing and integrating the layers more difficult than necessary.
2. Create a boundary at a point where the description of services can be small and the number of interactions across the boundary are minimized.
3. Create separate layers to handle functions that are manifestly different in the process performed or the technology involved.
4. Collect similar functions into the same layer.
5. Select boundaries at a point which past experience has demonstrated to be successful.
6. Create a layer of easily localized functions so that the layer could be totally re-designed and its protocols changed in a major way to take advantage of new advances in architectural, hardware or software technology without changing the services expected from and provided to the adjacent layers.
7. Create a boundary where it may be useful at some point in time to have the corresponding interface standardized.
8. Create a layer where there is a need for a different level of abstraction in the handling of data (e.g., morphology, syntax, semantics).
9. Allow changes of functions or protocols to be made within a layer without affecting other layers.
10. Create for each layer boundaries with its upper and lower layer only.

Similar principles have been applied to sublayering:

11. Create further subgrouping and organization or functions to form sublayers within a layer in cases where distinct communication services need it.
12. Create, where needed, two or more sublayers with a common, and therefore minimal functionality to allow interface operation with adjacent layers.
13. Allow bypassing of sublayers.

layer. Ideally, the layers should be defined so that changes in one layer do not require changes in the other layers. Thus we have decomposed one problem into a number of more manageable subproblems.

The task of the ISO subcommittee was to define a set of layers and the services performed by each layer. The partitioning should group functions logically, should have enough layers to make each layer manageably small, but should not have so many layers that the processing overhead imposed by the collection of layers is burdensome. The principles by which ISO went about its task are summarized in Table 12-3. The resulting OSI reference model has seven layers, which are listed with a brief definition in Table 12-4. Table 12-5 provides ISO's justification for the selection of these layers.

Table 12-4 defines, in general terms, the functions that must be performed in a system for it to communicate. Of course, it takes two to communicate, so the same set of layered functions must exist in two systems. Communication is achieved by having corresponding (''peer'') entities in the same layer in two different systems communicate via a protocol.

Figure 12-10 illustrates the OSI model. Each system contains the seven layers. Communication is between applications in the systems, labeled AP X and AP Y in the figure. If AP X wishes to send a message to AP Y, it invokes the application layer (layer 7). Layer 7 establishes a peer relationship with layer 7 of the target machine, using a layer 7 protocol. This protocol requires services from layer 6, so the two layer 6 entities use a protocol of their own, and so on down to the physical layer, which actually passes the bits through a transmission medium.

TABLE 12-4 The OSI Layers

1. Physical	Concerned with transmission of unstructured bit stream over physical medium; deals with the mechanical, electrical, functional, and procedural characteristics to access the physical medium
2. Data link	Provides for the reliable transfer of information across the physical link; sends blocks of data (frames) with the necessary synchronization, error control, and flow control
3. Network	Provides upper layers with independence from the data transmission and switching technologies used to connect systems; responsible for establishing, maintaining, and terminating connections
4. Transport	Provides reliable, transparent transfer of data between end points; provides end-to-end error recovery and flow control
5. Session	Provides the control structure for communication between applications; establishes, manages, and terminates connections (sessions) between cooperating applications
6. Presentation	Provides independence to the application processes from differences in data representation (syntax)
7. Application	Provides access to the OSI environment for users and also provides distributed information services

Note that there is no direct communication between peer layers except at the physical layer. That is, above the physical layer, each protocol entity sends data *down* to the next lower layer in order to get the data *across* to its peer entity. Even at the physical layer, the OSI model does not stipulate that two systems be directly connected. For example, a packet-switched or circuit-switched network may be used to provide the communications link. This point should become clearer below, when we discuss the network layer.

The attractiveness of the OSI approach is that it promises to solve the heterogeneous computer communications problem. Two systems, no matter how different, can communicate effectively if they have the following in common:

- They implement the same set of communications functions.
- These functions are organized into the same set of layers. Peer layers must provide the same functions, but note that it is not necessary that they provide them in the same way.
- Peer layers must share a common protocol.

To assure the above, standards are needed. Standards must define the functions and services to be provided by a layer (but not how it is to be done—that may differ from system to system). Standards must also define the protocols between peer layers (each protocol must be identical for the two peer layers). The OSI model, by defining a seven-layer architecture, provides a framework for defining these standards.

Some useful OSI terminology is illustrated in Figure 12-11. For simplicity, any layer is referred to as the *(N) layer*, and names of constructs associated with that layer are also preceded by (N). Within a system, there are one or more active entities in each layer. An *(N) entity* implements functions of the (N) layer and also the protocol for communicating with (N) entities in other systems. An example of an entity is a process in a multiprocessing system. Or it could simply be a subroutine. There might be multiple identical (N) entities, if this is convenient or efficient

TABLE 12-5   Justification of the OSI Layers

a. It is essential that the architecture permit usage of a realistic variety of physical media for interconnection with different control procedures (e.g., V.24, V.25, X.21, etc.). Application of principles 3, 5, and 8 [Table 12-3] leads to indentification of a *Physical Layer* as the lowest layer in the architecture.

b. Some physical communication media (e.g., telephone line) require specific techniques to be used in order to transmit data between systems despite a relatively high error rate (i.e., an error rate not acceptable for the great majority of applications). These specific techniques are used in data-link control procedures which have been studied and standardized for a number of years. It must also be recognized that new physical communication media (e.g., fibre optics) will require different data-link control procedures. Application of principles 3, 5, and 8 leads to identification of a *Data Link Layer* on top of the Physical Layer in the architecture.

c. In the open systems architecture, some systems will act as the final destination of data. Some systems may act only as intermediate nodes (forwarding data to other systems). Application of principles 3, 5, and 7 leads to identification of a *Network Layer* on top of the Data Link Layer. Network oriented protocols such as routing, for example, will be grouped in this layer. Thus, the Network Layer will provide a connection path (network-connection) between a pair of transport-entities, including the case where intermediate nodes are involved.

d. Control of data transportation from source end-system to destination end-system (which is not performed in intermediate nodes) is the last function to be performed in order to provide the totality of the transport-service. Thus, the upper layer in the transport-service part of the architecture is the *Transport Layer*, on top of the Network Layer. This Transport Layer relieves higher layer entities from any concern with the transportation of data between them.

e. There is a need to organize and synchronize dialogue, and to manage the exchange of data. Application of principles 3 and 4 leads to the identification of a *Session Layer* on top of the Transport Layer.

f. The remaining set of general interest functions are those related to representation and manipulation of structured data for the benefit of application programs. Application of principles 3 and 4 leads to identification of a *Presentation Layer* on top of the Session Layer.

g. Finally, there are applications consisting of application processes which perform information processing. An aspect of these applications processes and the protocols by which they communicate comprise the *Application Layer* as the highest layer of the architecture.

---

for a given system. There might also be differing (N) entities, corresponding to different protocol standards at that level.

Each entity communicates with entities in the layers above and below it across an *interface*. The interface is realized as one or more *service access points* (SAPs), which function in the manner of ports, discussed earlier. The (N-1) entity provides *services* to an (N) entity via the invocation of *primitives*. A primitive specifies the function to be performed and is used to pass data and control information. The actual form of a primitive is implementation-dependent. An example is a subroutine call.

The OSI model is connection-oriented. Two (N) entities communicate, using a protocol, by means of an (N-1) connection. This logical connection is provided by (N-1) entities between (N-1) SAPs. ISO is currently at work on a connectionless mode, but this is not yet reflected in the model.

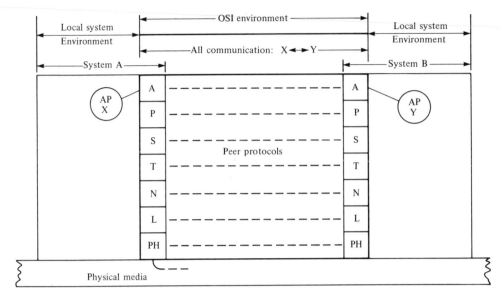

FIGURE 12-10. The OSI environment. Source: [FOLT81]

Figure 12-12 illustrates the OSI principles in operation. First, consider the most common way in which protocols are realized. When application X has a message to send to application Y, it transfers those data to an application entity in the application layer. A *header* is appended to the data that contains the required information for the peer layer 7 protocol (encapsulation). The original data, plus the header, is now passed as a unit to layer 6. The presentation entity treats the whole unit as data, and appends its own header (a second encapsulation). This process continues down through layer 2, which generally adds both a header and a trailer (e.g., HDLC). This layer 2 unit, called a *frame*, is then passed by the physical layer onto the transmission medium. When the frame is received by the target system, the reverse process occurs. As the data ascend, each layer strips off the outermost header, acts on the protocol information contained therein, and passes the remainder up to the next layer.

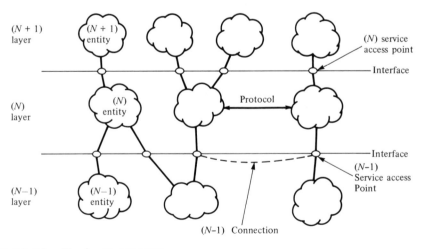

FIGURE 12-11. The layer concept.

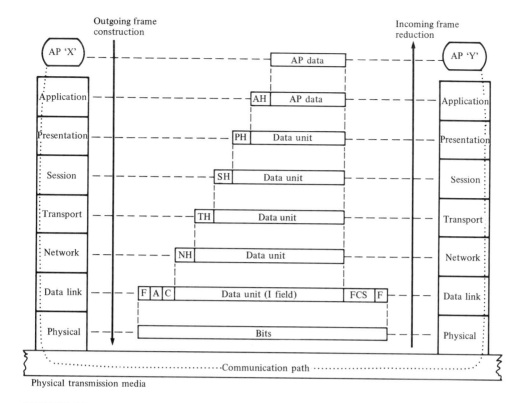

FIGURE 12-12. OSI operation. Source: [FOLT83]

At each stage of the process, a layer may fragment the data unit it receives from the next higher layer into several parts, to accommodate its own requirements. These data units must then be reassembled by the corresponding peer layer before being passed up.

When two peer entities wish to exchange data, this may be done with or without a prior connection. We have seen an example of this: virtual circuits versus datagrams. A connection can exist at any layer of the hierarchy. In the abstract, a connection is established between two (N) entities by identifying an (N-1) SAP for each (N) entity.

Layers

In this section we discuss briefly each of the layers and, where appropriate, give examples of standards for protocols at those layers.

Physical Layer. The *physical layer* covers the physical interface between devices and the rules by which bits are passed from one to another. The physical layer has four important characteristics [BERT80, MCCL83]:

- Mechanical.
- Electrical.
- Functional.
- Procedural.

We have already covered physical layer protocols in some detail in Section 4-3. Examples of standards at this layer are RS-232-C, RS-449/422/423, and portions of X.21.

Data Link Layer. While the physical layer provides only a raw bit stream service, the *data link layer* attempts to make the physical link reliable and provides the means to activate, maintain, and deactivate the link. The principal service provided by the link layer to the higher layers is that of error detection and control. Thus, with a fully functional data link layer protocol, the next higher layer may assume virtually error-free transmission over the link. However, if communication is between two systems that are not directly connected, the connection will comprise a number of data links in tandem, each functioning independently. Thus the higher layers are not relieved of an error control responsibility.

Chapter 5 was devoted to data link protocols. Examples of standards at this layer are HDLC, ADCCP, and LAP-B.

Network Layer. The basic service of the *network layer* is to provide for the transparent transfer of data between transport entities. It relieves the transport layer of the need to know anything about the underlying data transmission and switching technologies used to connect systems. The network service is responsible for establishing, maintaining, and terminating connections across the intervening communications facility.

It is at this layer that the concept of a protocol becomes a little fuzzy. This is best illustrated with reference to Figure 12-13, which shows two stations that are communicating, not via direct link, but via a packet-switched network. The stations have direct links to the network nodes. The layer 1 and 2 protocols are station-node protocols (local). Layers 4 through 7 are clearly protocols between (N) entities in the two stations. Layer 3 is a little bit of both.

The principal dialogue is between the station and its node; the station sends addressed packets to the node for delivery across the network. It requests a virtual

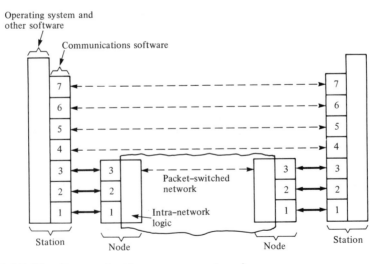

FIGURE 12-13. Communication across a network.

circuit connection, uses the connection to transmit data, and terminates the connection. All of this is done by means of a station-node protocol. However, because packets are exchanged and virtual circuits are set up between two stations, there are aspects of a station-station protocol as well.

There is a spectrum of possibilities for intervening communications facilities to be managed by the network layer. At one extreme, the simplest, there is a direct link between stations. In this case, there may be little or no need for a network layer, since the data link layer can perform the necessary functions of managing the link. Between extremes, the most common use of layer 3 is to handle the details of using a communication network. In this case, the network entity in the station must provide the network with sufficient information to switch and route data to another station. At the other extreme, two stations might wish to communicate but are not even connected to the same network. Rather, they are connected to networks which, directly or indirectly, are connected to each other. This situation is explored in some detail in Chapter 14. For now it suffices to say that one approach to providing for data transfer in such a case is to use an Internet Protocol (IP) that sits on top of a network protocol and is used by a transport protocol. IP is responsible for internetwork routing and delivery, and relies on a layer 3 at each network for intranetwork services. IP is sometimes referred to as "layer 3.5."

The best known example of layer 3 is the X.25 layer 3 standard, which will be examined in some detail in Chapter 13. The X.25 standard refers to itself as an interface between a station and a node (using our terminology). In the context of the OSI model, it is actually a station-node protocol. Another common example is the X.21 layer 3 standard, also examined in Chapter 13.

Transport Layer. Layers 4 and above of the OSI model are generally referred to as the higher layers [RAUC83]. Protocols at these levels are end-to-end and not concerned with the details of the underlying communications facility.

The purpose of layer 4 is to provide a reliable mechanism for the exchange of data between processes in different systems. The *transport layer* ensures that data units are delivered error-free, in sequence, with no losses or duplications. The transport layer may also be concerned with optimizing the use of network services and providing a requested quality of service to session entities. For example, the session entity might specify acceptable error rates, maximum delay, priority, and security. In effect, the transport layer serves as the user's liaison with the communications facility.

The size and complexity of a transport protocol depends on the type of service it can get from layer 3. For a reliable layer 3 with a virtual circuit capability, a minimal layer 4 is required. If layer 3 is unreliable and/or only supports datagrams, the layer 4 protocol should include extensive error detection and recovery. Accordingly, NBS has defined two versions of its Transport Protocol (TP): a relatively simple version for reliable networks and a more complex one for unreliable networks. The former is a subset of the latter. The more complex version is comparable in capability to another transport protocol standard, DOD's Transmission Control Protocol (TCP). ISO has gone even further and defined five classes of transport protocol, each oriented toward a different underlying service [MIER82a]. All of these standards are discussed in Chapter 15.

Session Layer. The *session layer* provides the mechanism for controlling the dialogue between applications.

At a minimum, the session layer provides a means for two application processes to establish and use a connection, called a *session*. In addition it may provide the following services:

- *Dialogue type:* This can be two-way simultaneous, two-way alternate, or one-way.
- *Recovery:* The session layer can provide a checkpointing mechanism, so that if a failure of some sort occurs between checkpoints, the session entity can retransmit all data since the last checkpoint.

Standards for this layer are still in draft form. A discussion of the principles of session protocols is presented in Chapter 16.

Presentation Layer. The *presentation layer* is concerned with the syntax of the data exchanged between application entities. Its purpose is to resolve differences in format and data representation. The presentation layer defines the syntax used between application entities and provides for the selection and subsequent modification of the representation to be used.

Examples of presentation protocols are teletext, videotex, encryption, and virtual terminal protocol. A virtual terminal protocol converts between specific terminal characteristics and a generic or virtual model used by application programs.

Application Layer. The *application layer* provides a means for application processes to access the OSI environment. This layer contains management functions and generally useful mechanisms to support distributed applications. Examples of protocols at this level are virtual file protocol and job transfer and manipulation protocol.

Summary

In a few short years, the OSI model has achieved nearly universal acceptance. It provides not only a framework for developing standards but the terms of reference for discussing communications system design. In the latter capacity, we will refer to OSI concepts repeatedly in the remainder of the book.

A question that arises naturally concerns the complexity of the model. Is it efficient to require every communication to undergo seven layers of processing, both to enter the communications process and then to leave it? In one sense, this question is no longer open to debate. Virtually all standards activities for communications are proceeding within the OSI model. Government customers and most private customers will demand OSI compatibility. The industry must conform.

This does not necessarily foreordain inefficiency. Implementers are free to use virtually null layers where appropriate, or at least very streamlined ones. We have mentioned one example: where direct connection is possible, layer 3 is not needed. As we will see, it is not really needed for local networks either. When a reliable layer 3 exists, layer 4 can be minimal. And so on.

Another point: Much of the communications processing (e.g., layers 1 through 4) can be offloaded from a host computer to a front-end processor. This is an attractive choice, given the increasing speed and declining cost of small computers.

THE HIERARCHICAL APPROACH: THE DOD MODEL

In recent years, much of the discussion and development work on communications protocols reported in the open literature has used the terminology and frame of reference of the OSI model. Remarkably, little attention has been given to a communications architecture which predates the OSI model and for which there is far more implementation and practical experience. This architecture is an outgrowth of the development of ARPANET [ROBE70] and the Defense Data Network (DDN) [WALK82]. Whereas the OSI architecture is intended to guide the future development of protocols, it is the experience already gained in the development and use of protocols within ARPANET that has led to the communications architecture we are about to describe. This architecture has only recently been articulated as such and has no universally accepted name. We refer to it as the *DOD protocol architecture* (DPA).

Both OSI and DPA deal with communications among heterogeneous computers. Both are based on the concept of protocol and have many similarities. However, there are philosophical and practical differences between the OSI model and the DPA, and the serious student of communications architecture needs to understand both.

In this section we provide an overview of the DPA. More detail is provided as various specific topics are pursued in the course of Part III.

Characteristics

The U.S. Department of Defense (DOD) is in the process of standardizing a variety of communications protocols. Its motivations are much the same as those of the ISO and any computer system customer. DOD needs to have efficient, cost-effective communications among heterogeneous computers. That DOD has chosen to develop its own protocols and architecture rather than adopt the developing international standards is for two reasons [ENNI82]:

1. DOD-specific communications requirements have a major impact on the design of protocols and an architecture. These concerns have not been uppermost in the minds of the ISO developers, and predictably are not reflected in the OSI model.
2. There are philosophic differences concerning the appropriate nature of a communications architecture and its protocols.

The first reason need not concern us in this context. The specific DOD requirements, many of which are also relevant in other contexts, include availability, survivability, security, network interoperability, and the ability to handle surge traffic. The interested reader is referred to [CERF83a].

The second reason is best explained by examining the differences between the DPA and the OSI model. There are four fundamental differences [ENNI83]:

- The concept of hierarchy versus layering.
- The importance of internetworking.
- The utility of connectionless services.
- The approach to management functions.

Hierarchy Versus Layering. The DPA recognizes that the task of communications is too complex and too diverse to be accomplished by a single unit. Accordingly, the task is broken up into modules or entities that may communicate with peer entities in another system. One entity within a system provides services to other entities and, in turn, uses the services of other entities. Good software design practice dictates that these entities be arranged hierarchically (i.e., no entity uses its own services, directly or indirectly).

The OSI model is based on the same reasoning, but takes it one step further. The next step is the recognition that, in many respects, protocols at the same level of the hierarchy have certain features in common. This yields the concept of rows or layers, and the attempt to describe in an abstract fashion what features are held in common by the protocols within a given row.

Now, as an explanatory tool, a layered model has significant value and, indeed, the OSI model is used for precisely that purpose in the remainder of this book. The objection sometimes raised by the designers of the DPA and its protocols is that the OSI model is prescriptive rather than descriptive. It dictates that protocols within a given layer perform certain functions. This may not be always desirable. It is possible to define more than one protocol at a given layer, and the functionality of those protocols may not be the same or even similar. Rather, what is common about a set of protocols at the same layer is that they share the same set of support protocols at the next lower layer.

Furthermore, there is the implication in the OSI model that, because interfaces between layers are well defined, a new protocol can be substituted for an old one at a given layer with no impact on adjacent layers (see principle 6, Table 12-3). This is not always desirable or even possible. For example, a local network lends itself easily to multicast and broadcast addressing at the link level. If the IEEE 802 link level were inserted below a network protocol entity that did not support multicasting and broadcasting, that service would be denied to upper layers of the hierarchy. To get around some of these problems, OSI proponents talk of null layers and sublayers (we will see examples). It sometimes seems that these artifacts save the model at the expense of good protocol design.

To make the points above specific, consider the following prescriptions, commonly agreed to be part of the OSI model:

- (N) entities must exchange data using services provided by (N-1) entities. Another way of saying this is that (N-1) entities must be involved in every data transfer between (N) entities.
- (N-1) entities provide their service by exchanging data units which contain (N-1) control information and data from (N) entities.
- (N) control information is passed to the remote side as (N-1) data.

The DPA is intended not to be so restrictive. As examples, the following techniques would be allowed:

- An entity may directly use the services of a hierarchically lower entity, even if it is not in an adjacent layer.
- Escape characters can be used to allow the placement of control characters within a data stream (e.g., TELNET, see Chapter 16). This situation is not correctly described by the concept of data units containing both control and higher-level data.
- Separate control and data connections may be used, in which higher-level data and control information do not share a data unit. This is useful, since one

might wish to provide different services (priority, reliability) for the different types of connections.

- Lower-level control information can be used to accomplish higher-level control. For example, the closing of a lower-level connection can implicitly close an isomorphic higher-level connection, without requiring the higher-level entity to pass control information.

- Multiple entity cooperation is allowed. For example, an application-level protocol may dictate that the services of a name server entity be employed at the start of a sequence of data transfers, but the latter entity need not be involved after transfer begins.

It may, of course, be possible to provide all of these features within the OSI model, although neither the OSI document [ISO83a] nor any of the developing protocols shows any evidence of them. The argument of the DPA proponents is not that certain things can be done in the DPA that cannot be done in the OSI model. Rather, the argument is that the DPA, by simply mandating that protocols be modular and hierarchical, give the designer more freedom to develop efficient, cost-effective, and rich protocols.

Whether the philosophical difference between hierarchy and layering results in any practical difference remains to be seen as more protocols are developed and used.

Internetworking.   An historical difference between the DPA and the ISO model is the importance that the former places on internetworking. Internetworking occurs when two communicating systems do not attach to the same network. Thus transferred data must traverse at least two networks. Further, these networks may be quite dissimilar.

The requirement for internetworking has led to the development of an Internet Protocol, discussed in Chapter 14. Such a protocol was not originally given a place within the OSI model. The current OSI document makes brief reference to the possibility of networks in tandem, and it seems likely that an internet protocol will emerge as a sublayer of the network layer (layer 3). This is not a clean solution, but it is the only one possible within the seven-layer architecture.

Connectionless Service.   A connectionless service, as the name implies, is one in which data are transferred from one entity to another without the prior mutual construction of a connection (e.g., datagrams). The DPA places equal importance on connectionless and connection-oriented services, whereas the OSI model is couched solely in terms of connection-oriented service. It is expected, however, that future versions of the OSI model will incorporate connectionless service [CHAP83].

A primary use of the connectionless service within the DPA is in internetworking. Since it is not safe to assume that all intermediate networks are reliable, a connectionless internet protocol is used, with end-to-end connectivity provided at a higher level. A name-address directory server is another example where connectionless service might be desirable.

Management Functions.   A final difference between the DPA and the OSI model is the way in which various management-related functions are treated. Examples of such functions are the naming (identification) of resources, the control of access to resources, and the accounting for resource and network usage.

The concept of management functions seems not to meld well with the OSI model, partly because these are mostly connectionless services, and partly because there's no "place" for them. It would appear that such functions must be classified according to layer and embedded as management entities within each layer. The DPA does not preclude this approach but goes further. Within the DPA, a uniform approach is taken to many of these functions and they are provided by protocols that can best be described as "session layer" protocols. This description reflects the fact that these protocols make use of transport services. This concept of session will be explored in Chapter 15.

DPA Architecture

The DPA architecture is based on a view of communication that involves three agents: processes, hosts, and networks. *Processes* are the fundamental entities that communicate. Processes execute on *hosts* (stations), which can often support multiple simultaneous processes. Communication between processes takes place across *networks* to which the hosts are attached.

These three concepts yield a fundamental principle of the DPA: the transfer of information to a process can be accomplished by first getting it to the host in which the process resides and then getting it to the process within the host. These two levels of demultiplexing can be handled independently. Therefore, a network need only be concerned with routing data between hosts, as long as the hosts agree how to direct data to processes.

With the concepts above in mind, it is natural to organize protocols into four layers. We emphasize here that the important fact is the hierarchical ordering of protocols. The designation of layers is purely for explanatory purposes. An entity in a layer may use the services of another entity in the same layer, or directly use the services of an entity in a lower but not adjacent layer. With that caveat in mind, the DPA organizes protocols into four layers (as suggested by Figure 12-2)

- Network access layer.
- Internet layer.
- Host–host layer.
- Process/application layer.

The *network access layer* contains those protocols that provide access to a communication network. Protocols at this layer are between a communications node and an attached host or its logical equivalent. A function of all these protocols is to route data between hosts attached to the same network. Other services that may be provided are flow control and error control between hosts and various quality of service features. Examples of the latter are priority and security. A network layer entity is typically invoked by an entity in either the internet or host–host layer, but may be invoked by a process/application layer entity.

The *internet layer* consists of the procedures required to allow data to traverse multiple networks between hosts. Thus it must provide a routing function. This protocol is usually implemented within hosts and gateways. A gateway is a processor connecting two networks whose primary function is to relay data between networks using an internetwork protocol.

The *host–host layer* contains protocol entities with the ability to deliver data between two processes on different host computers. A protocol entity at this level may (or may not) provide a logical connection between higher-level entities. Indeed, it is at this level that explicit connections make the most sense, with a logical

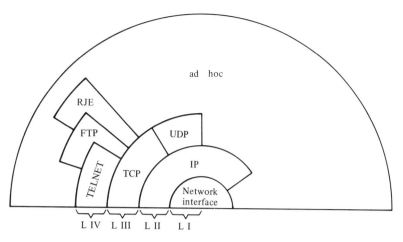

FIGURE 12-14. DOD protocol architecture.

connection being one used to exchange data between the ultimate endpoints (processes). Other possible services include error and flow control and the ability to deal with control signals not associated with a logical data connection. Four general types of protocols seem to be needed at this level [MCFA79]: a reliable connection-oriented data protocol, a datagram protocol, a speech protocol, and a real-time data protocol. Each has different services requirements:

- A reliable connection-oriented data protocol is characterized by the need for reliable, sequenced delivery of data. Many data processing applications would use such a service.
- A datagram protocol is a low-overhead, minimum functionality protocol that may be appropriate for some traffic, particularly applications that prefer to implement their own connection-oriented functionality.
- A speech protocol is characterized by the need for handling a steady stream of data with minimum delay variance.
- A real-time data protocol has the demanding characteristics of both a reliable connection-oriented protocol and a speech protocol.

The *process/application layer* contains protocols for resource sharing (e.g., computer-to-computer) and remote access (e.g., terminal-to-computer).

Figure 12-14 depicts the way in which specific DOD protocols fit into the four-layer architecture. The shape of the diagram is intended to suggest the way in which various protocols may invoke each other. For example, the file transfer protocol FTP may directly use the transmission control protocol (TCP), which provides reliable connection-oriented service, or it may use some of the services of the TELNET protocol as well. Note that "ad hoc" protocols are possible at any level.

Table 12-6 compares the four layers of the DPA to the seven of the OSI model.

12-4

EXAMPLE ARCHITECTURES

It is instructive to compare the standardization efforts underway with existing communications architectures. For this purpose, we return to two architectures intro-

TABLE 12-6 A Comparison of Communications Architectures

OSI		DPA		SNA		DNA	
7	Application	7	Process/ application	7	/////	7	User
6	Presentation	6		6	Function management data services	6	Network application
5	Session	5	Host-host	5	Data flow control	5	Network services protocol
4	Transport	4		4	Transmission control	4	
3	Network	3	Internet	3	Path control	3	Transport
2	Data link	2	Network access	2	Data link control	2	Data link
1	Physical	1		1	/////	1	Physical

duced in Chapter 9: IBM's Systems Network Architecture (SNA), and DEC's Digital Network Architecture (DNA). Table 12-6 compares these with the OSI model.

Systems Network Architecture

SNA consists of five layers [IBM81a]:

- Data link control.
- Path control.
- Transmission control.
- Data flow control.
- FMD services.

Data Link Control.   SNA does not address directly, but only implies, what OSI refers to as the physical layer. Hence the bottom layer of SNA is *data link control*. The protocol specified for this layer is SDLC. SDLC is basically a subset of HDLC, which was covered in Chapter 5.

Path Control.   The *path control* layer [ATKI80] creates logical channels between endpoints, referred to as network addressable units (NAUs). An NAU is an application-level entity capable of being addressed and of exchanging data with other entities. Thus key functions of the path control layer are routing and flow control.

Path control is based on the concepts of transmission group, explicit route, and virtual route, introduced in Chapter 9. To recall, a *transmission group* is a set of one or more physical links between adjacent nodes in the network. An *explicit route* is a path between endpoints, defined as an ordered sequence of transmission groups. A *virtual route* is a logical connection between endpoints that is dynamically assigned to an explicit route. Corresponding to these three concepts are three sublayers of the path control layer.

The primary function of the transmission group control sublayer is to make the set of links in a transmission group appear to higher layers as a single physical link. The main advantages of this are increased reliability and capacity for transmission between adjacent nodes. The protocol at this sublayer accepts data units and places them in a FIFO queue. Each data unit is sent out in turn over the next available physical link, using SDLC. Because of errors or differences in propagation delay, units may arrive out of order at the other end of the transmission group. Sequence numbers are used so that the receiving protocol entity can reorder the units. Another function performed at this sublayer is blocking. When a transmission group consists of a single link, the protocol entity may block incoming data units into a larger unit before transmission. This can increase efficiency, for example, by reducing the number of channel I/O operations that data link control needs to execute. The function of this sublayer is unusual and seems to fit best as part of layer 2 of the OSI model.

The explicit route control sublayer is primarily responsible for routing. Explicit routes are predefined in SNA and each node maintains routing information in the form of (explicit route number, next node). Thus, any incoming data must contain an explicit route number. On the basis of that number, the protocol entity selects the next node and passes the data to the transmission group control sublayer.

The virtual route control sublayer provides a logical connection on which traffic from sessions is multiplexed and on which flow control mechanisms are applied. Both entry-to-exit flow control and congestion control are exercised using the pacing algorithm described in Chapter 9. In addition, this sublayer has the ability to fragment data units from higher layers to improve efficiency. Fragmented data units must be reassembled at the other end. This sublayer and the explicit route control sublayer more or less encompass the functions of OSI's layer 3.

Transmission Control. The next higher layer of SNA is *transmission control*, which corresponds roughly to layer 4 of the OSI model. The transmission control layer is responsible for establishing, maintaining, and terminating SNA sessions. A *session*, which corresponds to OSI's transport connection is a logical relation between endpoints (NAUs). The transmission control layer can establish a session in response to a request from the next higher layer (data flow control), from an application process, or for its own control purposes.

The layer is composed of two modules: the connection point manager (CPMGR), which handles individual data transfers, and session control, which handles session-level matters. The *CPMGR* performs the following functions:

- *Routing:* This is essentially a demultiplexing function. Incoming data units are routed to the appropriate entity, which may be at the same or some higher layer.
- *Encapsulation:* Outgoing messages are encapsulated in a data unit; the header, which is appended to the data, contains control information for expedited delivery, pacing, encryption, and other control functions.
- *Pacing:* This is the same mechanism as is used on virtual routes. In this case, it is used only by the endpoints, to control the flow of data units. A fixed window size is used.

Session control is invoked to activate or deactivate a session. It is also invoked when CPMGR detects a session error, such as a missing sequence number.

Data Flow Control.   Within SNA logical connections, called sessions, may be established between applications. SNA has chosen to divide the management of sessions into two layers. The transmission control layer is transmission oriented and, as we have said, corresponds nicely of OSI's layer 4. The *data flow control* layer is end-user oriented and corresponds equally nicely to OSI's layer 5. This layer is responsible for providing session-related services that are visible and of interest to end-user processes and terminals. The principal functions are in the following categories.

- *Send/receive mode:* Three modes may be specified: full duplex, half-duplex flip-flop, and half-duplex contention. The distinction between the latter two roughly corresponds to the distinction between HDLC's normal response mode and asynchronous balanced mode.
- *Chaining:* Chaining is a mechanism to delineate transmission sequences for the purpose of recovery (as discussed under the OSI session layer, above) or quarantining. The latter function specifies that data not be delivered to the user until a certain amount (quarantine unit) has accumulated. For example, a screen-full of data may arrive in multiple blocks, but only be displayed when all the data are available.
- *Bracketing:* Whereas chaining deals with a sequence of data units transmitted in one direction, bracketing deals with a sequence of exchanges. This concept may be used to define and control transaction sequences.
- *Response options:* Three response modes may be specified. For each data unit, (1) do not send a response, (2) send a response only in case of an exception, and (3) always send a response.
- *Quiesce/shutdown:* A temporary or permanent halt to the flow of data may be requested.

Function Management Data Services.   The top layer of the SNA architecture is the *function management data (FMD) services* layer [HOBE80]. It consists of a collection of functions and services provided to the end user. It encompasses OSI's layer 6 and has some elements of layer 7.

FMD consists of two main components: session presentation services and session network services. The *session presentation services* component is essentially a presentation (6) layer, and includes the following services:

- *Format translation:* This service allows each endpoint to have a different view of the exchanged data. For example, it can be used to allow one application to handle multiple terminal types.
- *Compression and compaction:* Data can be compressed at the bit or byte level using specified procedures, to reduce transmission volume.

The *session network services* component is primarily intended to provide network management services. Since these services are directly used by an end user, such as a system manager or network operator, they best fit in OSI's layer 7. The following are included:

- *Configuration services:* allow an operator to start up or reconfigure a network by activating and deactivating links.
- *Network operator services:* include such nonconfiguration operator functions

as the collection and display of network statistics, and the communication of data from users and processes to the network operator.

- *Session services:* support the activation of a session on the behalf of end users and applications. In effect, this is the user interface to the transmission control layer.
- *Maintenance and management services:* provide for the testing of network facilities and assist in fault isolation and identification.

In addition to all of the above, reference is made in IBM documentation [IBM81a] to *application-to-application* services. These would include things such as distributed transaction processing and distributed access to data bases. However, these services are not formally a part of the layered architecture.

SNA Encapsulation. Unlike the apparent OSI policy, SNA does not require the use of a header at each layer of the hierarchy. Figure 12-15 depicts the overall SNA encapsulation strategy. The most basic piece of data in SNA is the *request/response unit* (RU), which contains either user data or network control information. A services manager creates RUs from user data. The FMD services layer may perform certain transformations on the data to accommodate presentation services or may add control information relating to chains of RUs. The latter are contained in a *FMD header*. This header is optional and, if used, may only appear occasionally (at the start of a chain or bracket); thus it is not shown in the figure.

The transmission control layer then adds a request/response header (RH), containing control information both for itself and the data flow control layer. Rather than create a separate header, the data flow control layer is content to pass parameters to the transmission control layer to include in the header that it constructs.

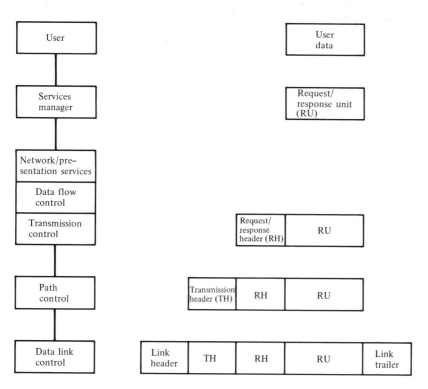

FIGURE 12-15. SNA data encapsulation. Source: [METZ83]

This seems more efficient than the OSI approach, but implies a tighter coupling between layers.

The next two layers add their own headers for their own purposes. Data link control also adds a trailer, as explained in Chapter 5.

Digital Network Architecture (DNA)

We mentioned briefly in Chapter 9 the orientation of DNA toward distributed peer resource sharing. The view coincides with the intent of ARPANET and, in fact, DNA appears to have been heavily influenced by ARPANET. Consequently, DNA is closer in spirit to DPA than to the OSI model.

DNA is composed of four layers [JOHN80]. The DNA documents, however, make explicit reference to a physical layer at the bottom and a user layer at the top. Thus, we include these in Table 12-6. The four DNA-defined layers are:

- Data link.
- Transport.
- Network services protocol.
- Network application.

Physical and Data Link Layers.   DNA recognizes the concept of a *physical* layer and allows a variety of hardware interfaces, such as RS-232-C. The discussion in Chapter 4 is applicable here. For the *data link* layer, DNA specifies DDCMP, which was described in Chapter 5.

Transport Layer.   The *transport* layer in DNA, unfortunately named, corresponds to the network layer of OSI. The transport layer provides a datagram service (neither delivery nor sequentiality is guaranteed) and performs the following functions:

- Routing.
- Congestion control.
- Packet lifetime control.
- Transport initialization.

The first two functions were discussed in Chapter 9. Packet lifetime control is used to prevent endlessly circulating packets. In the transport header, there is a hop count field that is incremented by each node that forwards the packet. When a system-defined maximum is reached, the packet is discarded.

Transport initialization procedures are used for synchronization of the transport layers in adjacent nodes. Checks are made to be sure that both nodes use the same level of transport layer protocol and that the same DDCMP block sizes are used.

Network Services.   The *network services protocol* (NSP) layer stands in the same relationship to the transport layer as the data link layer does to the physical layer. Just as the data link layer takes an unreliable physical transmission link and transforms it into a reliable data link, the NSP layer takes an unreliable network transport service and turns it into a reliable one. The NSP layer provides for the creation of logical connections between processes and corresponds roughly to OSI's layers 4 and 5.

The OSI layer-4-oriented functions performed by NSP include:

- *Connection management:* Logical connections are created and destroyed on command from the communicating processes. Endpoints are specified by node address and process name or generic service type. A logical link has two subchannels. The data subchannel carries information exchanged by user processes. The other-data subchannel is used for the transmission of interrupt messages and NSP control messages.
- *Data transfer:* Both user and interrupt/control data are transferred.
- *Error control and sequentiality:* NSP creates a sequential, no loss, no duplication service using sequence numbers and acknowledgments.
- *Flow control:* Flow control can be exercised on segments (equivalent to packets) or messages. The latter is essentially an OSI layer 5 service.
- *Segmentation reassembly:* Messages may be divided into smaller segments to conform to the requirements of the underlying network.

OSI layer 5 functions are primarily performed by a session control module, which is viewed as part of NSP [JOHN80] even though it is a separate module that interacts with the network management facility. This view of session control is much closer to that of the DPA than that of the OSI model. The session control module has a data base for translating node names into node addresses. It is invoked to manage the creation and termination of logical connections. During data transfer, it has little or no role.

Network Application. The *network application* layer contains the highest system-supplied functions in DNA. This layer provides services such as remote file access, file transfer, and remote system load. The most prominent module assigned to this layer is the *data access protocol* (DAP), which allows remote file access and manipulation. DAP includes a negotiation process to determine whether or not the two systems involved in a data exchange use the same file format. If not, one or both systems must convert to or from the defined network standard format.

It can be seen that this layer corresponds roughly to OSI's layer 6 and part of layer 7.

User. The *user* layer includes all application code and user-supplied functions. Applications executing in this layer make use of DNA services through the network application layer or by directly invoking the session control module.

12-5

RECOMMENDED READING

An excellent and still valid tutorial on the subject of protocols is [POUZ78]. Other worthwhile surveys are [FALK83], [GREE80], and [MCQU78].

A discussion of protocols using the OSI model can be found in [TANE81a], which averages about one chapter per layer. A more informal amount can be found in [MART81]. Good articles on the subject are [TANE81b] and [FOLT81]. A more formal description of the OSI model can be found in [DAY83] and the almost-identical [ZIMM80]. An interesting breakdown of functions by layer is contained in [BOWE83].

The DOD reference model is described in [ENNI82], available from its author, and in [CERF83b]. Two companion papers, [SELV82] and [CORR82], describe the DOD standardization program. A spirited advocacy of the DPA is contained in [PADL83].

[MELJ82] contains surveys of both SNA and DNA, together with thoughtful comparisons with the OSI model. The same topics are covered, more briefly, in [KONA83]. [CYPS78] is an exhaustive look at SNA; however, it does not reflect the many changes and improvements made since its publication. More current references are [BAER83] and [METZ83]. [WECK80] is a lengthy survey of DNA; [LOVE79] is a more cursory overview.

12-6

PROBLEMS

12-1   List the major disadvantages with the layered approach to protocols.

12-2   Based on the principles enunciated in Table 12-3, design an architecture with eight layers and make a case for it. Design one with six layers and make a case for that.

12-3   Two blue armies are each poised on opposite hills preparing to attack a single red army in the valley. The red army can defeat either of the blue armies separately but will fail to defeat both blue armies if they attack simultaneously. The blue armies communicate via an unreliable communications system (a foot soldier). The commander, with one of the blue armies, would like to attack at noon. His problem is this: If he sends a message ordering the attack, he cannot be sure it will get through. He could ask for acknowledgment but *that* might not get through. Is there a protocol that the two blue armies can use to avoid defeat?

12-4   In Figure 12-12, exactly one protocol data unit (PDU) in layer N is encapsulated in a protocol data unit at layer (N-1). It is also possible to break one N-level PDU into multiple (N-1)-level PDUs (fragmentation) or to group multiple N-level PDUs into one (N-1)-level PDU (blocking). (a) In the case of fragmentation, is it necessary that each (N-1)-level fragment contain a copy of the N-level header? (b) In the case of blocking, is it necessary that each N-level PDU retain its own header, or can the data be consolidated into a single N-level PDU with a single N-level header?

12-5   Discuss the need or lack of need for a network layer (OSI layer 3) in a broadcast network.

12-6   Compare SNA and DNA to the OSI and DPA frameworks. To which is each closest philosophically? Discuss similarities and differences.

12-7   What must be added to the OSI model to reconcile the differences with DPA?

APPENDIX 12A

STANDARDS

Section 1-6 described the most important standard-making organizations and Table 1-4 (repeated here as Table 12-7 for convenience) lists some of the standards and OSI layers of principal interest to these organizations. Remember that the OSI layers are not standards; they merely provide a framework for standards.

ISO, of course, continues to play the key role in the evolution of the OSI model.

TABLE 12-7 Standards and Standards—Making Organizations

Organization	Areas of Interest	Standards
International Organization for Standardization (ISO)	OSI model, layers 4–7	Transport, session
International Telegraph and Telephone Consultative Committee (CCITT)	Communications networks, telematics	X.25, X.75, X.21
National Bureau of Standards (NBS)	Layers 2–7	Transport
Defense Communications Agency (DCA)	Layers 3–7	TCP, IP
Institute of Electrical and Electronic Engineers (IEEE)	Layers 1 and 2	IEEE 802
American National Standards Institute (ANSI)	Layers 1–7	ANS X379.5
Electronics Industries Association (EIA)	Layer 1	RS-232-C, RS-449
Federal Telecommunications Standards Committee (FTSC)	Layers 1–3	Encryption
European Computer Manufacturers Association (ECMA)	Layers 1–7	Input to ISO

Their interest in individual standards has focused on layer 4 and above. Recently, ISO issued international standards (the last step in formal standardization)for transport and session protocols.

CCITT has been concerned with defining access protocols to public communication networks. It has developed standards for connecting *data terminal equipment* (DTE) to a packet-switched network that provides *data circuit-terminating equipment* (DCE). These terms correspond to the stations and nodes of Figure 7-2. The standard, X.25, specifically addresses layer 3 and subsumes standards for layers 2 and 1. Layer 2 is referred to as LAP-B (Link Access Protocol—Balanced) and is almost identical with ISO's HDLC (High-Level Data Link Control) and ANSI's ADCCP (Advanced Data Communication Control Procedures). A corresponding standard, X.21, has been developed for circuit-switched networks. CCITT is also the controlling organization for developing ISDN standards, discussed in Chapter 17. CCITT is also concerned with the area known as *telematics*, which covers user-oriented information transmission services. Teletex (communication among office word processing systems), videotex (interactive information retrieval), and facsimile (imagery transmission) are included under this term.

NBS works closely with ISO and with interested U.S. organizations. Their intent is to issue federal standards that are compatible with international standards. In some cases, they add or delete features to bring international standards more in line with U.S. standards. NBS has issued a transport standard and endorsed both X.25 and the IEEE 802 (described below) standards for federal standards.

DCA is the issuing agency for communications standards for DOD. They have promulgated the Transmission Control Protocol (TCP) as a transport protocol standard and the Internet Protocol (IP) for internetworking. In addition they have issued standards at higher layers. All of these protocols, unfortunately, differ from planned and issued standards from ISO and NBS.

For the type of local network that we refer to as a *local area network* (LAN), the Institute of Electrical and Electronics Engineers (IEEE), through its 802 committee, has developed a three-layer architecture that corresponds to layers 1 and 2 of the OSI model. A number of standards have been developed by the committee for these layers. Similarly, a subcommittee responsible to the American National Standards Institute (ANSI), known as ANS X3T9.5, has developed standards for the type of local network we refer to as a *high speed local network* (HSLN). These standards, one per layer, correspond nicely to layers 1 and 2 of the OSI model.

This narrative may be disheartening, given the alleged benefit of standards, which is to put everyone on the same road. There is certainly room for pessimism. The DOD-NBS disparity makes a uniform federal government position unlikely. For LANs, the 802 committee has produced a number of options and alternatives at each layer, to come up with an astoundingly thick volume for their standard.

The picture, however, is far from bleak. Tremendous progress has been made toward the development and issuance of standards. Most organizations are cooperating to reduce the incidence of duplicate, competing standards. And while vendors and customers are faced in some areas with multiple standards, the customer at least is far better off than in the 1970s, when virtually no standards existed above layer 1, and those that did were frequently ignored.

CHAPTER 13

Network Access Protocols

Both the Open Systems Interconnection (OSI) model and the DOD protocol architecture (DPA) agree that the details of the intervening data transmission system should be kept hidden from the end-to-end protocols that manage communications between stations or endpoints. In the case of the OSI model, these details are handled by layers 1 to 3; in the case of the DPA, a network access layer is designated.

For now, let us think of the end-to-end service as being provided by a transport protocol. We would like lower layer protocols to provide the required services for transmitting data between two transport entities, such that the transport protocol can be designed without knowledge of the underlying transmission system. Five cases need to be distinguished. The transport entities may be in separate stations connected by a:

- Circuit-switched network.
- Packet-switched network.
- Broadcast network.
- Point-to-point link.
- Multiple networks.

The first three cases are sufficiently distinct that significantly different approaches are commonly taken. We will examine each by discussing the most widely accepted approach in each case. The fourth case, point-to-point link, is a special case of a broadcast network. Finally, the task of communication across multiple networks is sufficiently complex to warrant a separate chapter.

We begin, however, with a brief examination of the nature of the network interface.

13-1

THE NETWORK INTERFACE

Communication across a network between two processes in separate systems can be thought of as involving two types of entities: the systems that contain the processes and the systems that manage communications across the network. These are depicted in Figure 7-2 as stations and nodes, respectively, and we have consistently used that terminology.

Consider now the nature of the interaction between a node and a station. In OSI terms, the transport layer is "station-oriented," providing an end-to-end service. The network layer is responsible for making use of the network facilities to route data from source to destination. Thus this layer is station-oriented in the sense that it is concerned with transferring data between source and destination stations, and it is node-oriented in the sense that it deals with the actions of the node to which the station is attached. How do these concepts relate to the node-station interaction?

Figure 13-1 shows, in general terms, two ways in which protocols may be structured for station-node attachment. In the first instance, the node may function

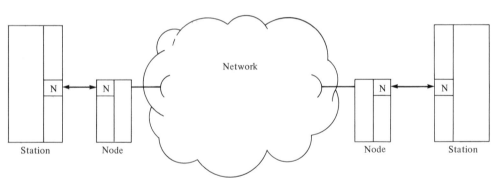

(a) The node as gateway (protocol mode)

(b) The node as front–end network processor (interface mode)

FIGURE 13-1. Node–station interaction.

as a *gateway*. A gateway is a device for connecting two systems that use different protocols: a protocol converter, if you like. In this case the node contains logic for communicating with the attached station using some protocol native to that device; the level of communication is at some layer N. The node converts between that protocol and that of the communications network.

Compare this architecture with Figure 12.13, which relates to a packet-switched network. In that figure the level of communication between the station and node is at layer 3. The operation is as follows. The data that originate at the application layer, plus all the headers generated by layers 7 through 4, are treated as a unit of data by layer 3. Layer 3 has the responsibility of routing this data unit to the destination station. It does this by means of a protocol with the *local* node at layer 3. Of course, to transmit a layer 3 data unit from station to node, a logical link (layer 2) over a physical link (layer 1) is needed. Hence the station-node conversation consists of protocols at layers 1, 2, and 3. Now, the node uses a different set of protocols to route the data unit through the network to the destination node, which in turn has a layer 1, 2, 3 protocol conversation with the destination station. The result is that a layer 4 data unit has been routed from source to destination through gateways which convert the protocols up through layer 3.

As an alternative, the node can function as a front-end network processor (FNP). An FNP provides communications services to an attached information processor. In contrast to a gateway, which *converts* from one set of protocols to another, the FNP *replaces* the protocols that might be found in the attached device. This is depicted in Figure 13-1b. The attached station contains layers 7 down through N. There is an N/N − 1 interface to the node which contains layers N − 1 to 1; these lower layers act as intranetwork protocols.

As with the gateway approach, there must be some means of communicating across the station-node interface. One possibility is to exchange data over a communications link using a layer 2 protocol. The other possibility is for the node to be integrated into the station. Data could then be exchanged via high-speed direct memory access (DMA).

The gateway mode is the most familiar one (indeed, it is the only mode discussed in most accounts). It is the natural mode to use when the communications network is owned by a different entity than the attached stations. This is the case with many packet-switched and circuit-switched networks. Thus the stations are physically distinct systems owned by different organizations. A standard protocol is defined to allow these devices to operate together.

With local networks, however, it is usually the case that both the network and attached devices are owned by the same organization. This allows a greater degree of integration between nodes and stations, and an interface specification rather than a protocol seems more appropriate.

A detailed discussion of this topic can be found in [STAL84a]. It is also addressed in [MOLD81].

13-2

CIRCUIT-SWITCHED NETWORK ACCESS

Requirements

Let us consider what is required, in terms of functions, for two devices to communicate across a circuit-switched network, and relate that to the OSI model. There are two phases of operation that are of interest: the call establishment phase and the data transfer phase.

For the *data transfer phase*, recall that a circuit-switched network provides a transparent data path between communicating stations. To the attached stations, it appears that they have a direct full-duplex link. They are free to use their own formats, protocols, and frame synchronization. This situation is depicted in Figure 13-2a. Each station is attached to a node of the communication network (example: a modem). The dashed line indicates the path of the data and the elements through which it passes. Data from the source station pass through that node, one or more intermediate nodes, and finally through the node to which the destination station is connected. Because the connection is transparent, the protocol from station to node is just at the physical level. Each node acts as a relay, passing on data from input to output. The intermediate nodes perform a switching function but, again, simply relay the data transparently.

The *call establishment phase* is more complex. Both calling and called stations have a dialogue with an element of the network:

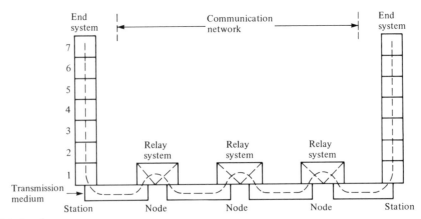

(a) Data transfer

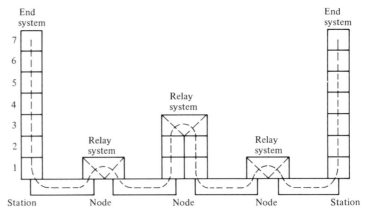

(b) Call establishment

FIGURE 13-2.   OSI configurations for circuit-switched communication. Source: [FOLT83].

- *Calling station:* sends a call request to the network identifying the called station; receives call progress signals from the network.
- *Called station:* receives call request from network; sends call acceptance to network.

This dialogue is, in OSI terms, a layer 3 protocol. Figure 13-2b depicts this protocol as taking place between the station and some intermediate node which performs a network exchange function. This node can be considered to represent all of the switching nodes involved in setting up the connection. Note that this node still performs a relay function, but this now occurs at layer 3. Thus two general types of functions are performed by the network.

- It relays call request and call accepted signals between stations.
- It has a dialogue with each station to establish the call.

Once the call is established, there is no need for an active network role, other than at the physical layer. Thus the configuration of Figure 13-2a obtains. All protocols, down through layer 2, are end-to-end.

A Circuit-Switched Network Access Standard: X.21

CCITT has developed a standard, X.21, referred to as an interface between *data terminal equipment* (DTE) and *data circuit terminating equipment* (DCE) [FOLT80a]. The terms DTE and DCE correspond roughly to our concepts of station and node. Figure 13-3 depicts the interface, showing the interchange circuits defined in Chapter 4.

X.21 actually consists of three parts, which correspond functionally to OSI layers 1 to 3. The physical layer of X.21 was described in Chapter 4. It provides a general-purpose interface that can be used for station attachment to a circuit-switched or

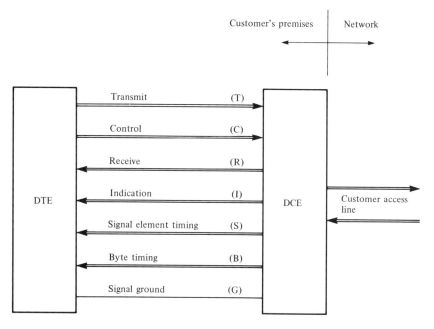

FIGURE 13-3.   X.21 interface.

packet-switched network. The remaining two layers are specifically provided for automatic call establishment over a circuit-switched network.

Data Link Layer. The data link layer in X.21 is specifically concerned with the transfer of control information between DTE and DCE over the transmit (T) and receive (R) circuits. A synchronous character-oriented protocol is specified. Control information is exchanged in sequences of control characters, using the CCITT International Alphabet Number 5, which is virtually identical to ASCII.

Synchronization is provided in two ways. Each control sequence is preceded by two SYN characters (as in BSC and DDCMP, Figures 5-17 and 5-18). Synchronization may optionally be achieved by the byte timing (B) circuit. This circuit provides an indication of the last bit of each 8-bit byte, and is transmitted as a pulse by the DCE. It is used to align characters transmitted over both the T and R circuits. Even when the B circuit is used, DTEs and DCEs must still preface control sequences with SYN SYN, so that older equipment is interoperable with newer equipment.

A final provision of this layer, for error control, is that the eighth bit of each byte be an odd parity bit.

It is important to distinguish between the X.21 specification for character alignment and error control from the data link control protocols described in Chapter 5. The "data link layer" of X.21 applies only to control characters during call establishment. X.21 does not encapsulate data being transmitted to the network nor decapsulate data coming from the network. As befits an interface defined for a circuit-switched network, X.21 passes data transparently so that once a connection is established it functions as a direct point-to-point link. This state of affairs is depicted in Figure 13-4. Once a circuit is established, the DTEs may use a data link control protocol (e.g., HDLC) for end-to-end data transfer. The data link layer and the network layer of X.21 (described next) are invoked only to set up a call. Then X.21 functions simply as a physical layer protocol on top of which the DTEs impose their own higher layer protocol.

Thus X.21 does not fit cleanly into the OSI view. We have, in effect, a dynamic change in the protocol architecture determined by the state of communications between the endpoints.

Network Layer. The network layer protocol defines the procedures for identifying DTEs and requesting, establishing, and terminating data connections. Figure 13-5 is a state diagram of the call establishment phase. Figure 13-6 shows the

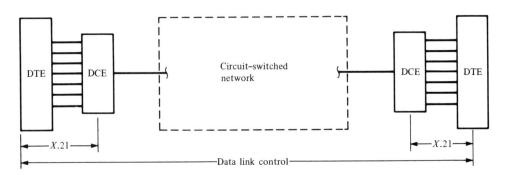

FIGURE 13-4.   DTE to DTE data link control in a circuit-switched network.

sequence of events in a successful call establishment and clear. As an example, we follow the sequence of events of the latter figure.

For call establishment to begin, both the DTE and its DCE must be in the Ready state. In this state the DTE is sending a stream of 1 bits over the T circuit and holding C at OFF, while the DCE is sending 1 bits over the R circuit and holding I off.

First, consider events from the perspective of the calling DTE. The DTE makes a Call Request by stopping the transmission of 1 bits and setting the C circuit to

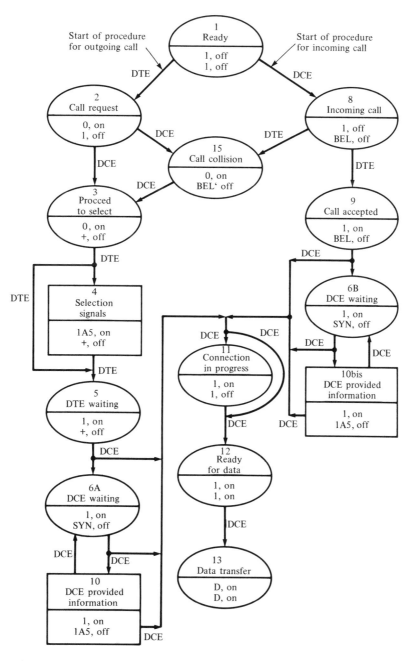

FIGURE 13-5.   State diagram for call establishment phase.

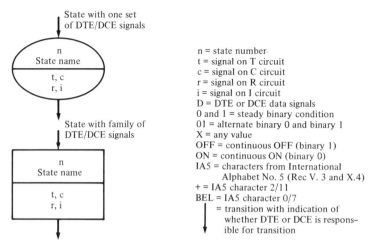

n = state number
t = signal on T circuit
c = signal on C circuit
r = signal on R circuit
i = signal on I circuit
D = DTE or DCE data signals
0 and 1 = steady binary condition
01 = alternate binary 0 and binary 1
X = any value
OFF = continuous OFF (binary 1)
ON = continuous ON (binary 0)
IA5 = characters from International
      Alphabet No. 5 (Rec V. 3 and X.4)
+ = IA5 character 2/11
BEL = IA5 character 0/7
     = transition with indication of
       whether DTE or DCE is respons-
       ible for transition

FIGURE 13-5 (continued).

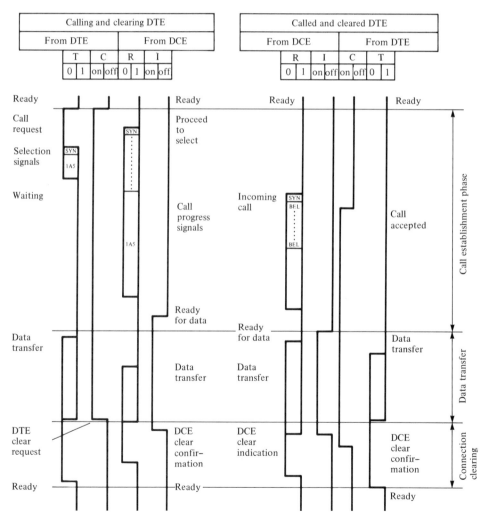

FIGURE 13-6. Sequence of events for successful call and clear. (X.21).

ON. If the DCE is processing an incoming call at the time, it will signal a call collision and then allow the DTE to proceed. Otherwise, it simply signals Proceed To Select by transmitting a sequence of " + " characters. The DTE can then proceed with the Selection Signals sequence. This is a sequence of control characters that includes the number of the called DTE plus any requested facilities for this call. These optional facilities are specified by CCITT X.2 (Table 13-1) and are requestable on a per call basis. As shown, other options may be preselected. This state may be bypassed if a predefined destination address is known to the DCE (e.g., a "hot line" service).

The DTE then enters a waiting state while the DCE attempts to place the call. The DCE indicates that it is waiting for the network to complete the call by sending SYN characters over the R circuit. If the call is successfully completed in good order, the DCE transmits 1 bits on the R circuit and sets the I circuit to ON to indicate that it is ready for data. However, if there is difficulty, the DCE will keep the DTE informed by sending call progress characters over the R circuit. These are defined in a separate standard, X.96 (Table 13-2). After call progress signals, or if there are no call progress signals, the DCE will provide called line identification if this user facility is in effect.

Once the DCE signals Ready For Data, the data transfer phase is entered and

TABLE 13-1 Optional Circuit-Switched User Facilities (X.2)

Assigned for an Agreed Contractual Period

Direct call	Connection to predesignated address
Closed user group	Communication only among designated group
Closed user group with outgoing access	Group that can be accessed by DTE
Closed user group with incoming access	Group that can access DTE
Incoming calls barred in closed user group	
Outgoing calls barred in closed user group	
Calling line identification	DTE is notified of the originating DTE address
Called line identification	DTE is notified of the destination DTE address
Bilateral closed user group	
Bilateral closed user group with outgoing access	
Incoming calls barred	
Reverse charging acceptance	
Connect when free	Camp-on facility
Waiting allowed	
Redirection of calls	Incoming calls directed to another address
On-line facility registration	Change user facilities
DTE inactive registration	Change user facilities

Requested by DTE on a per-call basis

Direct call	
Abbreviated address calling	Using predefined address abbreviation
Multiaddress calling	Conference or broadcast type of call
Reverse charging	Collect call
RPOA selection	Recognized private operating agency
Charging information	Provided to DTE after call

TABLE 13-2 Circuit-Switched Call Progress Signals (X.96)

Signal	Description
Terminal Called	Call signaled to destination DTE
Redirected Call	Call has been redirected
Connect when Free	Call is queued for busy destination DTE
Registration/Cancellation Confirmed	Requested facility registration/cancellation confirmed by network
Redirection Facility Active	
Redirection Facility Not Active	
No Connection	Cause unspecified
Selection Signal transmission Error	Transmission error detected in DTE's selection signal
Local Procedure Error	DTE procedure error
Network Congestion	Call prevented by network congestion
Invalid Facility Request	
RPOA Out of Order	
Changed Number	Called DTE has new number
Not Obtainable	Address unassigned or unknown
Access Barred	
Incompatible User Class of Service	Incompatibility between calling and called DTE
Out of Order	Called DTE out of order
Network Fault in the Local Loop	
DCE Power Off	Called DCE powered off
Uncontrolled Not Ready	DTE unable to enter operational state
Controlled Not Ready	DTE operational, but unable to accept call
Number Busy	
Call the Information Service	DTE unobtainable; call network service for details
Long Term Network Congestion	Major shortage of network resources

data is transparently transmitted from and received by the DTE over the T and R circuits.

From the perspective of the called DTE, an incoming call request is signaled by the arrival of a sequence of BEL characters over the R circuit. The DTE signals acceptance by setting the C circuit to ON. The DCE passes this acceptance back through the network and enters a waiting state. If the appropriate user facility is in force, the DCE will provide calling line identification. When the call is completed, the DCE signals Ready For Data.

The call is terminated when one of the DTEs signals Clear Request. The DCE responds with a Clear Confirmation. On the other side, the DCE signals Clear Indication and the DTE responds with Clear Confirmation. These actions terminate the circuit, after which both DTEs and both DCEs return to the Ready state.

Summary. X.21 has been designed to exploit digital circuit-switched network technology and the new services that such networks can provide (as reflected in the user facilities and call progress information). The transition to this standard is slow because of the tremendous investment required to create these new networks. The main attraction of X.21 is, of course, that it allows full use of these networks. Other strengths:

- *Simplified interface:* Although X.21 is functionally serving as OSI layers 1 to 3, the interface is very simple. Furthermore, during data transfer, the protocol does not get in the way of the data.
- *Simplified clearing procedure:* We will see the X.25 requires a clearing procedure at each of three levels. X.21 uses a single physical layer procedure to clear a circuit and at the same time clear the underlying physical link.
- *Flexibility:* It is easy to add new functions and information services by defining additional control character sequences.

13-3

PACKET-SWITCHED NETWORK ACCESS

Requirements

Unlike a circuit-switched network, a packet-switched network is not transparent to attached stations, even during the data transfer phase. Stations must break up their data into packets. The station-node protocol must perform the following functions:

- Flow control.
- Error control.
- Multiplexing.

Flow control is needed in both directions. The network must protect itself from congestion, and to do this may need to limit the flow of packets from the attached stations. Similarly, a station needs to be able to control the rate at which the network delivers packets to it. These considerations did not apply in the case of circuit switching. The circuit-switched network provides a transparent path of constant data rate. The network allocates resources to maintain that data rate. The stations may use flow control end-to-end or at the data link level to limit data flow.

Since station and node are exchanging control information as well as data, some form of *error control* is needed to assure that all of the control information is received properly.

Finally, most packet-switched networks provide a *multiplexing* service. With this service, a station can establish multiple virtual circuits with other stations at the same time.

Figure 13-7 depicts the protocol architecture implied by the above requirements. Each node, including intermediate nodes, performs functions up through layer 3. We now turn to a specific example that should help clarify this figure.

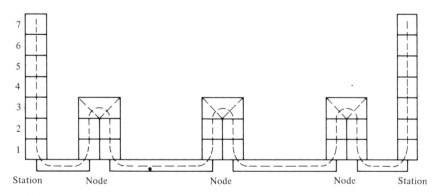

FIGURE 13-7. OSI configuration for packet-switched communication.

A Packet-Switched Network Access Standard: X.25

Perhaps the best known and most widely used protocol standard is X.25, which was originally approved in 1976 (and has been revised twice since). As with X.21, this standard specifies a DTE-DCE "interface." In the case of X.25 the DCE provides access to a packet-switched network. The standard specifically calls out three levels (Figure 13-8):

- Physical level.
- Link access level.
- Packet level.

For the physical level, the physical level portion of X.21 is specified. Optionally (and at present more commonly), X.21 *bis* may be used; this is similar to RS-232-C. The link access level is LAP-B, which is a subset of the asynchronous balanced mode (ABM) of HDLC. This section will be devoted to a discussion of the packet level.

The packet level specifies a *virtual-circuit service*. A variety of packet types are used (Table 13-3), all using the same basic format, with variations (Figure 13-9).

The virtual circuit service of X.25 provides for two types of virtual circuit: virtual call and permanent virtual circuit. A *virtual call* is a dynamically established virtual circuit using a call setup and call clearing procedure analogous to that of X.21. A *permanent virtual circuit* is a permanent, network-assigned virtual circuit. Data transfer occurs as with virtual calls, but no call setup or clearing is required.

The X.25 virtual-circuit service is quite complex. We begin by describing a typical sequence of events for the progress of a virtual call. Then we examine each of the key features of X.25.

Virtual Calls. Figure 13-10 shows a typical sequence of events in a virtual call. The left-hand part of the figure shows the packets exchanged between DTE A and its DCE; the right-hand part shows the packets exchanged between DTE B

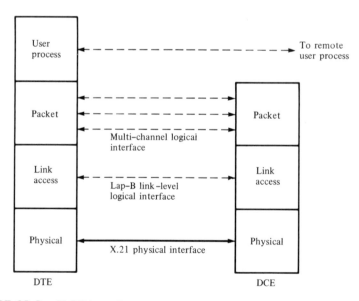

FIGURE 13-8. X.25 interface.

TABLE 13-3 X.25 Packet Types

Packet Type		Service	
From DCE to DTE	From DTE to DCE	VC	PVC
Call Setup and Clearing			
Incoming call	Call request	X	
Call connected	Call accepted	X	
Clear indication	Clear request	X	
DCE clear confirmation	DTE clear confirmation	X	
Data and Interrupt			
DCE data	DTE data	X	X
DCE interrupt	DTE interrupt	X	X
DCE interrupt confirmation	DTE interrupt confirmation	X	X
Flow Control and Reset			
DCE RR	DTE RR	X	X
DCE RNR	DTE RNR	X	X
	DTE REJ	X	X
Reset indication	Reset request	X	X
DCE reset confirmation	DTE reset confirmation	X	X
Restart			
Restart indication	Restart request	X	X
Diagnostic			
Diagnostic		X	X

and its DCE. The routing of packets between the DCEs is the responsibility of the internal logic of the network.

The sequence of events is as follows:

1. *A* requests a virtual circuit to *B* by sending a Call Request packet to its DCE. The packet includes a virtual circuit number (group, channel), as well as source and destination addresses. Future incoming and outgoing data transfers will be identified by the virtual circuit number.
2. The network routes this call request to *B*'s DCE.
3. *B*'s DCE receives the call request and sends a Call Indication packet to *B*. This packet has the same format as the Call Request packet but a different virtual circuit number, selected by *B*'s DCE from the set of locally unused numbers.
4. *B* indicates acceptance of the call by sending a Call Accepted packet specifying the same virtual circuit number as that of the Call Indication packet.
5. *A* receives a Call Connected packet with the same virtual circuit number as that of the Call Request packet.
6. *A* and *B* send data and control packets using their respective virtual circuit numbers.
7. *A* (or *B*) sends a Clear Request packet to terminate the virtual circuit and receives a local Clear Confirmation packet.
8. *B* (or *A*) receives a Clear Indication packet and transmits a Clear Confirmation packet.

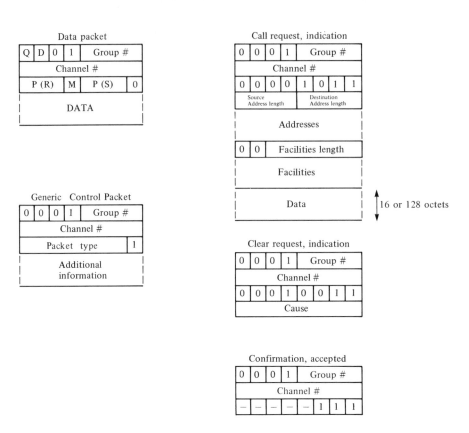

FIGURE 13-9.   X.25 packet formats.

We point out that this DTE-DCE interface is asymmetric. That is, only selected layer 3 protocol information is transferred end-to-end between subscriber DTEs. Much of the information, such as flow control and acknowledgment, usually has only local significance. However, see below.

The way in which data are encapsulated is of some interest. The transmitting DTE must break its data up into units of some maximum length. X.25 specifies that network must support a maximum user field length of at least 128 octets (i.e., the user data field may be some number of bits up to the maximum). In addition, the network may allow selection of some other maximum field length in the range 16 to 1024 octets. The length may differ for the two ends of the virtual circuit. The DTE constructs control packets and encapsulates data in data packets. These are then transmitted to the DCE via LAP-B. Thus the packet is encapsulated in a layer 2 frame (one packet per frame). The DCE strips off the layer 2 header and trailer and may encapsulate the packet according to some internal network protocol.

The description above is the essence of the X.25 virtual circuit service. We now turn to the details, in the following categories:

- Multiplexing.
- Flow control.
- Packet sequences.
- Reset and restart.
- Interrupt packets.
- Call progress signals.
- User facilities.

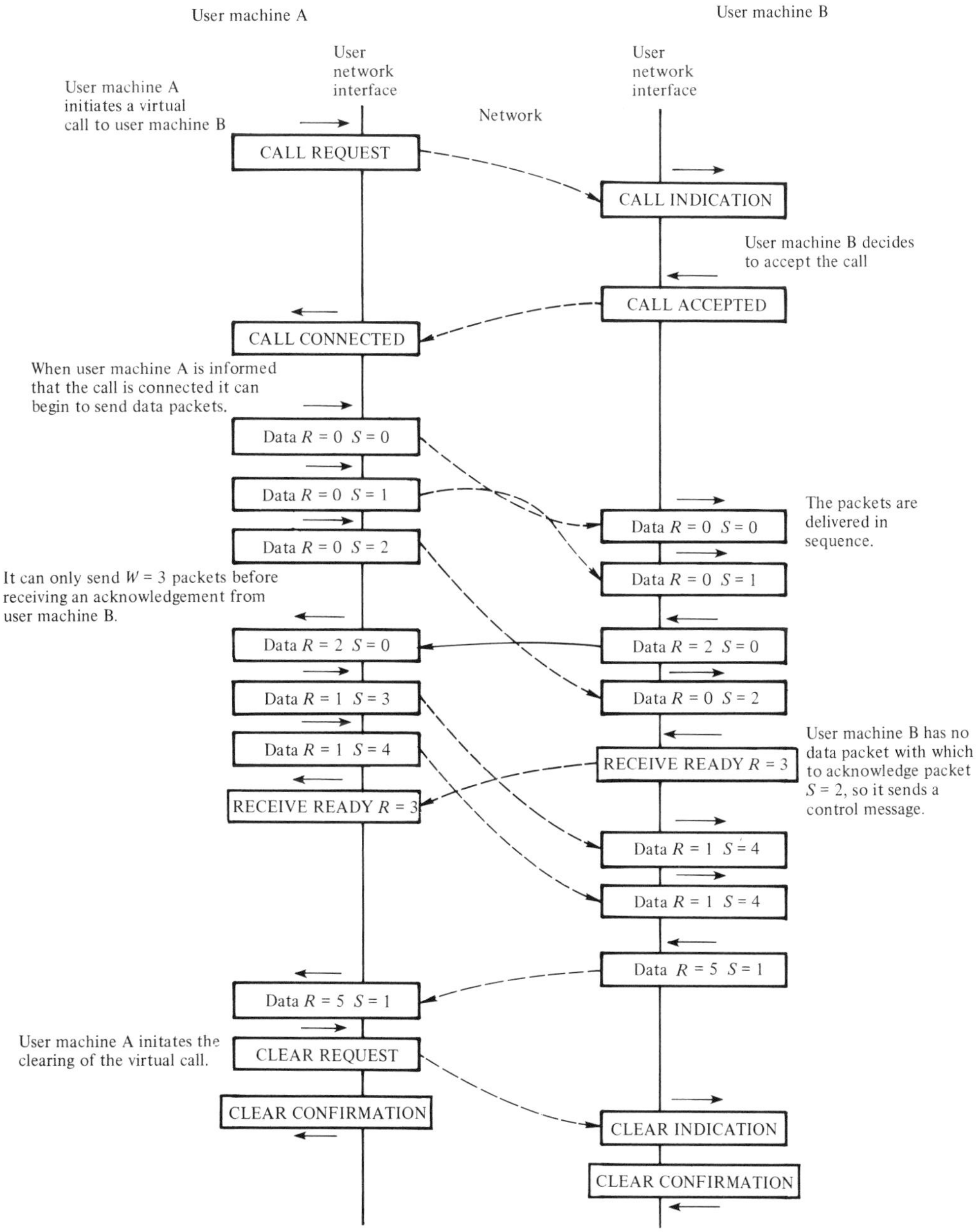

FIGURE 13-10.   Sequence of events—X.25 virtual call.

User machine A

User machine B

User
network
interface

User
network
interface

Network

User machine A
initiates a virtual
call to user machine B

CALL REQUEST

CALL INDICATION

User machine B decides
to accept the call

CALL ACCEPTED

CALL CONNECTED

When user machine A is informed
that the call is connected it can
begin to send data packets.

Data $R = 0$ $S = 0$

Data $R = 0$ $S = 1$

Data $R = 0$ $S = 0$

The packets are
delivered in
sequence.

Data $R = 0$ $S = 2$

Data $R = 0$ $S = 1$

It can only send $W = 3$ packets before
receiving an acknowledgement from
user machine B.

Data $R = 2$ $S = 0$

Data $R = 2$ $S = 0$

Data $R = 1$ $S = 3$

Data $R = 0$ $S = 2$

Data $R = 1$ $S = 4$

RECEIVE READY $R = 3$

User machine B has no
data packet with which
to acknowledge packet
$S = 2$, so it sends a
control message.

RECEIVE READY $R = 3$

Data $R = 1$ $S = 4$

Data $R = 1$ $S = 4$

Data $R = 5$ $S = 1$

Data $R = 5$ $S = 1$

User machine A initates the
clearing of the virtual call.

CLEAR REQUEST

CLEAR CONFIRMATION

CLEAR INDICATION

CLEAR CONFIRMATION

Multiplexing.   Perhaps the most important service provided by X.25 is multiplexing. A DTE is allowed by its DCE to establish up to 4095 simultaneous virtual circuits with other DTEs over a single physical DTE-DCE link. The DTE can internally assign these circuits in any way it pleases. Individual virtual circuits could correspond to applications, processes, or terminals for example. The DTE-DCE link provides full-duplex statistical multiplexing. That is, at any time a packet associated with a given virtual circuit can be transmitted in either direction.

To sort out which packets belong to which virtual circuit, each packet contains a 12-bit virtual circuit number (expressed as a 4-bit logical group number plus a 8-bit logical channel number). The assignment of virtual-circuit numbers follows the convention depicted in Figure 13-11. Number zero is always reserved for restart and diagnostic packets. If only a single virtual circuit is allowed (no multiplexing), number 1 is used. Otherwise, contiguous ranges of numbers are allocated for four categories of virtual circuits. Permanent virtual circuits are assigned numbers beginning with 1. The next category is one-way incoming virtual calls. This means that only incoming calls from the network can be assigned these numbers; the circuit, however, is two-way. When a call request comes in, the DCE selects an unused number from this category and places it in the Call Indication packet that it sends to the DTE.

The last category, one-way outgoing virtual calls, is used by the DTE to initiate virtual calls via Call Request packets. Again, the DTE selects an unused number for each new call request. This separation of categories is intended to avoid the simultaneous selection of the same number for two different virtual circuits by the DTE and DCE.

The two-way virtual call category provides an overflow for allocation shared by DTE and DCE. This allows for peak differences in traffic flow.

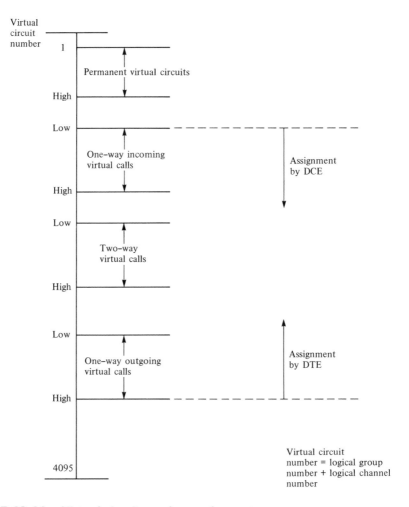

FIGURE 13-11. Virtual circuit number assignment.

Flow Control.   Flow control at the X.25 packet level is virtually identical in format and procedure to flow control at the link access layer. A sliding window protocol is used (see Chapter 5). Each data packet includes a 3-bit packet send sequence number, P(S), and a 3-bit packet receive sequence number, P(R). P(S) is assigned by the DTE on outgoing packets on a virtual circuit basis. The default window size is 2, but it may be set as high as 7 with the 3-bit field or as high as 127 using a 7-bit field. Incoming data packets on each virtual circuit contain a P(R) which is the number of the next packet expected to be received from the DTE on that virtual circuit. When there are no data packets available for piggybacking, receive ready (RR) and receive not ready (RNR) control packets may be used, with the same meaning as for HDLC. Additionally, X.25 specifies an optional DTE REJ packet.

Acknowledgment (in the form of the P(R) field or RR, RNR packets) and hence flow control may have either local or end-to-end significance, based on the setting of the D bit. When D = 0 (the usual case), acknowledgment is being exercised between the DTE and the network. This is used by the DCE and/or the network to acknowledge receipt of packets and control the flow from the DTE into the network. Note from Figure 13-12a that the acknowledgment may be from the attached DCE or from the remote DCE. In either case, the acknowledgment is said to have "local" (network) significance. When D = 1, acknowledgments come from the remote DTE.

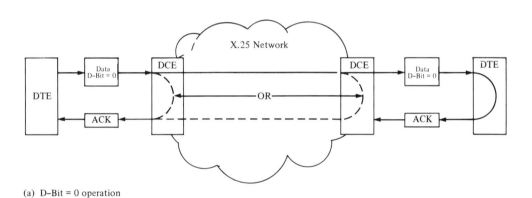

(a) D–Bit = 0 operation

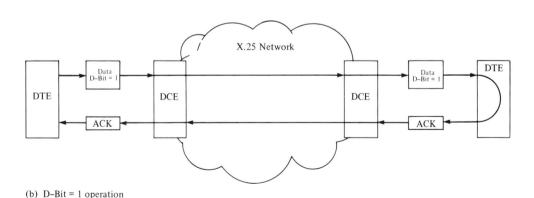

(b) D–Bit = 1 operation

FIGURE 13-12.   Treatment of acknowledgments for data packets.

Packet Sequences. X.25 provides the capability to identify a contiguous sequence of packets, which is called a *complete packet sequence*. This feature has several uses. It can provide a service to higher layers within the DTE. For example, a process may need to fragment messages to get down to the allowable packet size, but wishes to keep track of data on a message basis. This technique is also used when the DCE blocks or fragments data to conform to network packet size restrictions; this can be useful in internetworking when networks with different packet sizes are connected.

To specify this mechanism, X.25 defines two types of packets: A packets and B packets. An *A packet* is one in which the M bit is set to 1, the D bit is set to zero, and the packet is full (equal to the maximum packet length). A *B packet* is any packet that is not an A packet. Now, a complete packet sequence consists of zero or more A packets followed by a B packet. The network can combine this sequence to make one larger packet. The network may also fragment a B packet into smaller packets to produce a complete packet sequence.

The way in which the B packet is handled depends on the setting of the M and D bits. If D = 1, an end-to-end acknowledgment is sent by the receiving DTE to the sending DTE. This is in effect an acknowledgment of the entire complete packet sequence. M = 1 indicates that there are additional complete packet sequences to follow. This enables the formation of subsequences as part of a larger sequence, so that end-to-end acknowledgment can occur before the end of the larger sequence.

Figure 13-13 shows examples of these concepts. Note that it is the responsibility of the DCEs to reconcile the changes in sequence numbering that fragmentation and assembly cause.

Reset and Restart. X.25 provides two facilities for recovering from errors. The reset facility is used to reinitialize a virtual circuit. This means that the sequence numbers on both ends are set to zero. Any data or interrupt packets in transit are lost. It is up to a higher-level protocol to recover from the loss of packets.

A reset can be triggered by a number of error conditions including loss of a packet, sequence number error, congestion, or loss of the network's internal virtual

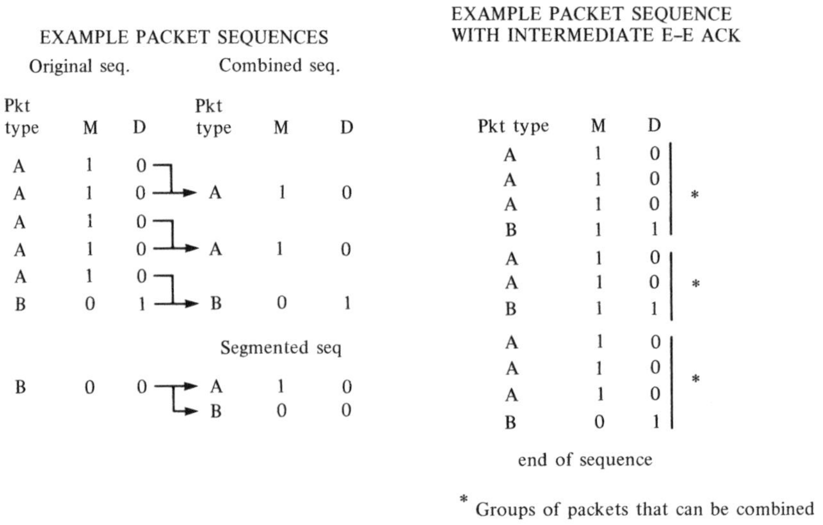

FIGURE 13-13. X.25 packet sequences.

circuit. In this latter case, the two DCEs must rebuild the internal virtual circuit to support the still-existing X.25 DTE-DTE virtual circuit.

Either a DTE or DCE can initiate a reset, with a Reset Request or Reset Indication. The recipient responds with a Reset Confirmation. Regardless of who initiated the reset, the DCE is responsible for informing the other end.

A more serious error condition calls for a restart. The issuance of a Restart Request packet is equivalent to sending a Clear Request on *all* active virtual calls and a Reset Request on all active permanent virtual circuits. Again, either DTE or DCE may initiate action. An example of a condition warranting restart is temporary loss of access to the network.

Interrupt Packets. A DTE may send an interrupt packet that bypasses the flow control procedures used for data packets. The interrupt packet carries only one byte of user data, and is to be delivered to the destination DTE by the network at a higher priority than data packets in transit. An example of the use of this service is to transmit a terminal break character.

Call Progress Signals. As with X.21, X.25 includes provision for call progress signals, and these are defined by X.96 (Table 13-4). However, in contrast to X.21,

TABLE 13-4 Packet-Switched Call Progress Signals (X.96)

| Signal | Applicable to:[a] | | Usage[b] | Description |
	VC	PVC		
Local Procedure Error	X	X	C, R	Procedure error caused by local DTE
Network Congestion	X	X	C, R	Temporary network congestion or fault
Invalid Facility Request	X		C	
RPOA Out of Order	X		C	
Not Obtainable	X		C	Called DTE address unassigned or unknown
Access Barred	X			
Reverse Charging Acceptance Not Subscribed	X		C	Called DTE will not accept charges on collect call
Fast Select Acceptance Not Subscribed	X		C	Called DTE does not support fast select
Incompatible Destination	X		C, R	The remote DTE does not have a function used or a facility requested
Out of Order	X	X	C, R	Remote DTE out of order
Number Busy	X		C	
Remote Procedure Error	X	X	C, R	Procedure error caused by remote DTE
Network Operational	X	X	R	Network ready to resume after temporary failure or congestion
Remote DTE Operational		X	R	Remote DTE ready after temporary failure
DTE Originated	X	X	C, R	Remote DTE has refused call or requested reset

[a]VC, virtual call; PVC, permanent virtual circuit.

[b]C, clearing call progress signal; R, resetting call progress signal.

call progress signals are not used only during the call establishment phase. The call progress signals fall into two general and overlapping categories for X.25. *Clearing call progress signals* are used to indicate the reason why a CALL REQUEST is denied; they are also used to indicate the reason for a CLEAR REQUEST. In both cases, the signal is carried in a CLEAR INDICATION packet.

Resetting call progress signals are used to indicate the reason why a virtual circuit is being reset. The code is contained in a RESET REQUEST or RESET INDICATION packet.

User Facilities.   Another type of service found in both by X.21 and X.25 is the optional user facilities service. Again, these are defined by X.2. A large list of facilities is included in X.2; Table 13-5 only lists those deemed essential for X.25. These facilities may be specified as part of the Call Request and Call Indication packets.

Fast Select Facility.   The X.25 standard was initially intended to be purely a virtual-circuit service. In response to demand for connectionless network service, two capabilities were included in the 1980 standard: datagram service and the fast select facility. Because of a complete lack of support for the datagram service, it was subsequently dropped in the 1984 edition of the standard.

The fast select facility is designed to handle transaction-oriented applications in which at least one and sometimes only one inquiry and response take place. The virtual call mechanism is used with the following adjustment. To use fast select, a DTE requests the fast select facility in the facilities field of the Call Request packet. The normal Call Request packet allows only 16 octets of data, but when the fast select facility is employed, 128 octets are allowed. These data are delivered to the destination DTE in a Call Indication packet.

The calling DTE must also specify an unrestricted or restricted response option (Figure 13-14). If the restricted option is selected, the destination DTE must respond to the Call Indication with a Clear Request packet, which may also contain up to 128 octets of user data. Thus a virtual circuit has been created and destroyed with one exchange, and 128 octets have been transmitted in both directions.

TABLE 13-5   Optional Packet-Switched User Facilities (X.2)

Signal	Usage[a]	Description
Throughput Class Negotiation	A, P	Expected throughput; measure of network resources devoted to virtual call
Packet Retransmission	A	Permits use of REJECT packet
Incoming Calls Barred	A	
Outgoing Calls Barred	A	
One-Way Logical Channel Outgoing	A	Restricts use of a range of channels to outgoing calls
Closed User Group	A, P	Communication only among designated group
Flow Control Parameter Designation	P	Selection of packet and window sizes

[a]A, assigned for an agreed contractual period; P, requested on a per call basis.

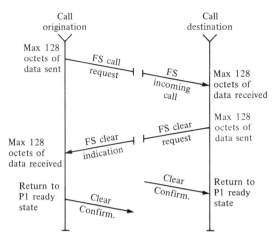

(a) Restricted

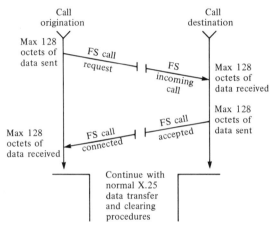

(b) Unrestricted

FIGURE 13-14. Fast select operation.

If the response is unrestricted, the destination DTE may respond as above. Alternatively, the destination DTE may respond with a Call Accepted packet, augmented with 128 octets of user data. A virtual circuit has now been established and functions as usual.

Summary. The X.25 standard was developed prior to the OSI model and does not fit cleanly into the model. It is tempting to equate the three levels of X.25 with layers 1 to 3 of the OSI model, but there are difficulties with this assignment.

Levels 1 and 2 of X.25 clearly correspond to layers 1 and 2 of the OSI model. The packet level of X.25 appears to encompass most if not all of the functions of OSI layer 3. However, when the D bit is used, the X.25 packet level provides some end-to-end functionality that appears more typical of a transport protocol. However, we shall see in Chapter 15 that X.25 does not encompass all of the functions one might like in a transport protocol.

BROADCAST NETWORK ACCESS

We turn now to the third type of network discussed in Part II: broadcast networks. As might be expected, the access method for broadcast networks must reflect requirements that are different from those of either circuit-switched or packet-switched networks. The key difference is that, typically, broadcast networks do not require the routing function. The only systematic work on standards that has been done in this area is for local networks. We will examine one of these standards: the IEEE 802 Logical Link Control (LLC) standard. We begin by looking at the architecture of the IEEE 802 standard, and then turn to a consideration of LLC.

IEEE 802 Architecture

The IEEE 802 Committee has developed a three-layer architecture for local network access that, in their view, corresponds to layer 1 and 2 of the OSI model. Before considering their reasoning, let us look at the functions, in terms of OSI layers, that are required to communicate across a local network.

What OSI layers are needed? Layer 1, certainly. Physical connection is required. Layer 2 is also needed. Data transmitted across the network must be organized into frames and control must be exercised. But what about layer 3? The answer is yes and no. If we look at the functions performed by layer 3, the answer would seem to be no. First, there is routing. But with a direct link available between any two points, this is not needed. The other functions (addressing, sequencing, flow control, error control, etc.) are, we learned, also performed by layer 2. The difference is that layer 2 performs these functions across a single link, whereas layer 3 may perform them across the sequence of links required to traverse the network. But since only one link is required to traverse the network, these layer 3 functions are redundant and superfluous!

From the point of view of an attached station, the answer would seem to be yes, the network must provide layer 3. The station sees itself attached to an access point into a network supporting communication with multiple devices. The layer for assuring that a message sent across that access point is delivered to one of a number of end points would seem to be a layer 3 function. Thus two or three OSI layers are required, depending on how you look at it.

With the points made above in mind, let us now think about the functional requirements for controlling a local network and examine these from the top down. We follow the reasoning, illustrated in Figure 13-15, used by the IEEE 802 committee [IEEE83].

At the highest level are the functions associated with accepting transmissions from and delivering receptions to attached stations. These functions include:

- Provide one or more service access points. A service access point (SAP), recall, is a logical interface between two adjacent layers.
- On transmission, assemble data into a frame with address and CRC fields.
- On reception, disassemble frame, perform address recognition and CRC validation.
- Manage communication over the link.

These are the functions typically associated with layer 2, the data link layer. The

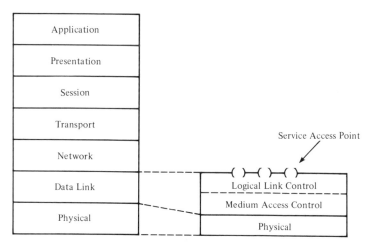

FIGURE 13-15. IEEE 802 reference model relationship to OSI model.

first three, and related functions, are grouped into a logical link control (LLC) layer by IEEE 802. The last function is treated as a separate layer, called medium access control (MAC). This is done for the following reasons:

- The logic required to manage access to a multiple-source, multiple-destination link is not found in traditional layer 2 link control.
- For the same LLC, several MAC options are provided, as was shown in Figure 11-18.

Finally, at the lowest layer, are the functions generally associated with the physical layer. These include:

- Encoding/decoding of signals.
- Preamble generation/removal (for synchronization).
- Bit transmission/reception.

As with the OSI model, these functions are assigned to a physical layer in the IEEE 802 standard.

Logical Link Control

The IEEE 802 Committee defined not only the LLC protocol, which we may think of as a DCE-DCE protocol, but also an interface for a higher layer. This interface provides the network access mechanism. The logical configuration is depicted in Figure 13-16 and can be seen to be equivalent to Figure 13-1b. That is, access to the network is provided by means of an *interface* to LLC. This is in contrast to X.25, where access is provided by a packet level *protocol* (Figure 13-1a). Thus it is sufficient to examine the interface that LLC provides to higher-level protocols. It is also of some interest to examine the LLC protocol itself, even though this is an intranetwork protocol. We begin by looking at the general link layer requirements for local networks, and then turn to the IEEE 802 specification.

Principles. The link layers for LANs should bear some resemblance to the more common link layers extant. Like all link layers, the LAN link layer is con-

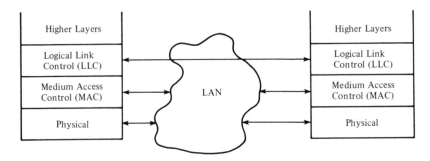

FIGURE 13-16. A LAN communication architecture.

cerned with the transmission of a frame of data between two stations, with no intermediate switching nodes.

It differs from traditional link layers in three ways:

- It must support the multiaccess nature of the link (this differs from multidrop in that there is no primary node).
- It is relieved of some details of link access by the medium access control (MAC) layer.
- It must provide some layer 3 functions.

At a minimum, the link layer should perform those functions normally associated with that layer:

- *Error control:* end-to-end error control and acknowledgment. The link layer should guarantee error-free transmission across the LAN.
- *Flow control:* end-to-end flow control.

These functions can be provided in much the same way as for HDLC and other point-to-point link protocols: by the use of sequence numbers.

It has already been mentioned that because of the lack of intermediate switching nodes, a LAN does not require a separate layer 3; rather, the essential layer three functions can be incorporated into layer 2:

- *Connectionless:* Some form of connectionless service is needed for efficient support of highly interactive traffic.
- *Connection-oriented:* A connection-oriented service is also usually needed.
- *Multiplexing:* Generally, a single physical link attaches a station to a LAN; it should be possible to provide data transfer with multiple endpoints over that link.

Because there is no need for routing, the above functions are easily provided. The connectionless service simply requires the use of source and destination address fields. The station sending the frame must designate the destination address, so that the frame is delivered properly. The source address must also be indicated so that the recipient knows where the frame came from.

Both the connection-oriented and multiplexing capabilities can be supported with the concept of the service access point (SAP), introduced in Chapter 12. An example may make this clear. Figure 13-17 shows three stations attached to a LAN. Each station has an address. Further, the link layer supports multiple SAPs, each with its own address. The link layer provides communication between SAPs. As-

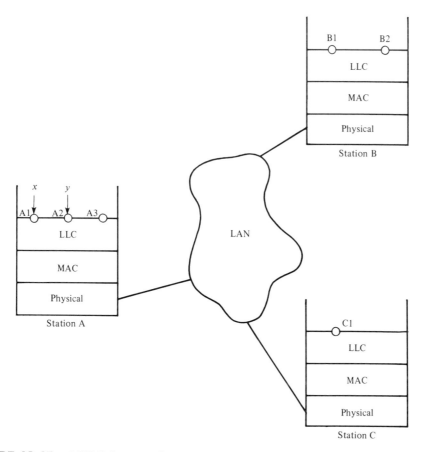

FIGURE 13-17. LAN link control scenario.

sume that a process or application X in station A wishes to send a message to a process in station C. X may be a report generator program in minicomputer A. C may be a printer and a simple printer driver. X attaches itself to SAP 1 and requests a connection to station C, SAP 1 (station C may have only one SAP if it is a single printer). Station A's link layer then sends to the LAN a "connection-request" frame which includes the source address (A,1), the destination address (C,1), and some control bits indicating that this is a connection request. The LAN delivers this frame to C, which, if it is free, returns a "connection-accepted" frame. Henceforth, all data from X will be assembled into a frame by A's LLC, which includes source (A,1) and destination (C,1) addresses. Incoming frames addressed to (A,1) will be rejected unless they are from (C,1); these might be acknowledgment frames, for example. Similarly, station C's printer is declared busy and C will only accept frames from (A,1).

Thus a connection-oriented service is provided. At the same time, process Y could attach to (A,2) and exchange data with (B,1). This is an example of multiplexing. In addition, various other processes in A could use (A,3) to send datagrams to various destinations.

One final function of the link layer should be included, to take advantage of the multiple-access nature of the LAN:

- *Multicast, broadcast:* The link layer should provide a service of sending a message to multiple stations or all stations.

With these requirements in mind, we turn to the 802 specification.

LLC Services. LLC provides two services:

- *Unacknowledged connectionless service:* This service simply allows for sending and receiving frames. It supports point-to-point, multipoint, and broadcast.
- *Connection-oriented service:* This provides a logical connection between service access points. It provides flow control, sequencing, and error recovery.

These services are specified in terms of primitives which can be viewed as commands or procedure calls with parameters. Table 13-6 summarizes the LLC primitives.

The Unacknowledged Connectionless Service provides for only two primitives across the interface between the next highest layer and LLC. L-DATA.request is used to pass a frame to LLC for transmission. L-DATA.indication is used to pass a frame up from LLC upon reception.

The Connection-Oriented Service includes L-DATA-CONNECT.request and L-DATA-CONNECT.indication, with meanings analogous to those above, plus L-DATA-CONNECT.confirm, which conveys the result (acknowledged, failure) of the previous associated L-DATA-CONNECT.request. In addition, a station, through an SAP, must be able to establish and tear down a connection and receive an acknowledgment of this action from the remote SAP. Finally, link resetting and flow control services are provided.

LLC Protocol. The LLC frame consists of four fields:

- Destination service access point (1 octet).
- Source service access point (1 octet).
- Control (1 octet).
- Data

The source and destination are uniquely specified by a (node, service access point) pair. However, the node address is also used by MAC and is included in the outer MAC frame.

The LLC protocol is modeled after the HDLC balanced mode, and has similar formats and functions. These similarities are summarized briefly in this section. The reader should be able to see how this protocol supports the LLC services defined above.

First, the address fields. Both the DSAP and SSAP fields actually contain 7-bit addresses. The least significant bit of DSAP indicates whether this is an individual or group address. The least significant bit of SSAP indicates whether this is a command or response frame.

The format of the LLC control field is identical to that of HDLC (Figure 5-14). The functioning of LLC is essentially the same as that of HDLC, with three exceptions. First, LLC only makes use of the asynchronous balanced mode of operation, and does not employ normal response mode or asynchronous response mode. This mode is used to support connection-oriented service. The set asynchronous balanced mode (SABM) command is used to establish a connection, and disconnect (DISC) is used to terminate the connection.

TABLE 13-6 Logical Link Control Primitives

Unacknowledged connectionless service:

    L-DATA.request

    L-DATA.indication

Connection-Oriented Service:

    L-DATA-CONNECT.request

    L-DATA-CONNECT.indication

    L-DATA-CONNECT.confirm

    L-CONNECT.request

    L-CONNECT.indication

    L-CONNECT.confirm

    L-DISCONNECT.request

    L-DISCONNECT.indication

    L-DISCONNECT.confirm

    L-RESET.request

    L-RESET.indication

    L-RESET.confirm

    L-CONNECTION-FLOWCONTROL.request

    L-CONNECTION-FLOWCONTROL.indication

Second, LLC supports connectionless service by using the unnumbered information (UI) frame.

Finally, LLC permits multiplexing by the use of service access points.

13-5

RECOMMENDED READING

A good account of the network and link layer functionality of X.21 can be found in [FOLT80a]. [MEIJ82], [CYPS78], and [MART81] also contain good descriptions. [YANO81] is a discussion of the practical application of X.21.

There is a large literature on X.25. [RYBC80] and [FOLT80b] together provide a thorough account. [MEIJ82], [CYPS78], and [MART81] again are additional useful sources. [BURG83] is a discussion of the practical application of X.25.

The IEEE 802 LLC is discussed in more detail in [STAL84a] and [STAL84d].

An abstract discussion of OSI layer 3 functionality is presented in [WARE83].

13-6

PROBLEMS

13-1   Consider Figure 13-1a and assume that $N = 1$; that is, the station-node protocol is only at the physical level. Suggest a mechanism by which the node will know which destination is desired for any unit of data.

13-2   Consider Figure 13-1b and assume that $N = 3$ and that layer 2 is IEEE 802 LLC. Describe, with an example, how the station's layer 3 software could make use of the layer 2 service to transmit data to a destination node.

13-3 X.25 specifies X.21 as the physical level. Could the link or packet level of X.25 be simplified by using more of the X.21 functionality? Make suggestions.

13-4 Which portion of Figure 13-2 seems most appropriate for the call termination phase? Explain.

13-5 X.21 does not provide for multiplexing at layer 3. Why?

13.6 Flow control mechanisms are used at both levels 2 and 3 of X.25. Are both necessary or is this redundant? Explain.

13-7 A DTE wishes to send X octets of data to another DTE using X.25. Its choices are (a) permanent virtual circuit, (b) virtual call, and (c) fast select. What is the total number and percentage of overhead bits? Answer for $X = 128$, 1280, and 12,800 bytes.

13-8 When an X.25 DTE and DCE both decide to put a call through at the same time, a call collision occurs and the incoming call is canceled. When both sides try to clear simultaneously, the clear collision is resolved without canceling either request. Do you think that simultaneous resets are handled like call collisions or clear collisions? Why?

13-9 What arguments or parameter do you think are necessary for each of the LLC primitives in Table 13-6?

13-10 Show, with an example, how the LLC protocol provides LLC services as defined by the LLC primitives.

CHAPTER 14

Internetworking

Packet-switched and packet broadcasting networks grew out of a need to allow the computer user to have access to resources beyond that available in a single system. In a similar fashion, the resources of a single network are often inadequate to meet users' needs. Because the networks that might be of interest exhibit so many differences, it is impractical to consider merging them into a single network. Rather, what is needed is the ability to interconnect various networks so that any two stations on any of the constituent networks can communicate.

An interconnected set of networks is referred to as a *catenet*, and the concept is illustrated in Figure 14-1. Each constituent network supports communication among a number of attached devices. In addition, networks are connected by devices that we will refer to generically as *gateways*. Gateways provide a communication path so that data can be exchanged between networks.

We begin our examination of internetworking with a discussion of the principles that underlie all forms of internetworking facilities. We then examine examples of the three principal architectural approaches to internetworking. The bridge is a simplified gateway that has been developed for use with homogeneous local networks. X.75 is a standard for a protocol that provides virtual circuit service across multiple X.25 networks. The internet protocol (IP) is a general-purpose connectionless protocol for interconnecting multiple packet-switched and/or packet broadcast networks. These three approaches are explored in some detail. Finally, a promising approach for interconnecting local networks is examined.

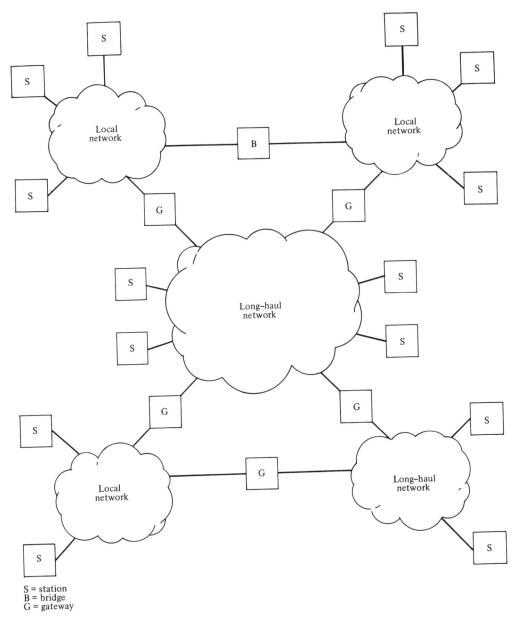

S = station
B = bridge
G = gateway

FIGURE 14-1. A catenet.

PRINCIPLES OF INTERNETWORKING

Requirements

Although a variety of approaches have been taken to provide internetwork service, the overall requirements on the internetworking facility can be stated in general. These include:

1. Provide a link between networks. At minimum, a physical and link control connection is needed.
2. Provide for the routing and delivery of data between processes on different networks.
3. Provide an accounting service that keeps track of the use of the various networks and gateways and maintains status information.
4. Provide the services listed above in such a way as not to require modifications to the networking architecture of any of the constituent networks. This means that the internetworking facility must accommodate a number of differences among networks. These include:

   a. *Different addressing schemes:* The networks may use different endpoint names and addresses and directory maintenance schemes. Some form of global network addressing must be provided, as well as a directory service.

   b. *Different maximum packet size:* Packets from one network may have to be broken up into smaller pieces for another. This process is referred to as fragmentation.

   c. *Different network access mechanisms:* The network access mechanism between station and network may be different for stations on different networks.

   d. *Different timeouts:* Typically, a connection-oriented transport service will await an acknowledgment until a timeout expires, at which time it will retransmit its segment of data. In general, longer times are required for successful delivery across multiple networks. Internetwork timing procedures must allow successful transmission that avoids unnecessary retransmissions.

   e. *Error recovery:* Intranetwork procedures may provide anything from no error recovery up to reliable end-to-end (within the network) service. The internetwork service should not depend on nor be interfered with by the nature of the individual network's error recovery capability.

   f. *Status reporting:* Different networks report status and performance differently. Yet it must be possible for the internetworking facility to provide such information on internetworking activity to interested and authorized processes.

   g. *Routing techniques:* Intranetwork routing may depend on fault detection and congestion control techniques peculiar to each network. The internetworking facility must be able to coordinate these to adaptively route data between stations on different networks.

   h. *User access control:* Each network will have its own user access control technique (authorization for use of the network). These must be invoked by the internetwork facility as needed. Further, a separate internetwork access control technique may be required.

   i. *Connection, connectionless:* Individual networks may provide connection-oriented (e.g., virtual circuit) or connectionless (datagram) service. It may be desirable for the internetwork service not to depend on the nature of the connection service of the individual networks.

These points are worthy of further comment but are best pursued in the context of specific architectural approaches. We outline these approaches next, and then turn to a more detailed discussion of each approach.

Architectural Approaches

We have said that some kind of gateway function is needed to interconnect networks. The key issue in designing such a gateway deals with the communications architecture that is used. There are essentially two dimensions that determine this architecture:

- The nature of the interface.
- The nature of the transmission service.

There are two choices for the interface: two networks interface at either the node (network, DCE) or station (attached device, DTE) level (Figure 14-2). An interface at the node level implies, at minimum, that the networks have a common network access interface (e.g. X.25). It does not necessarily imply that the networks have the same internal protocols. In any case, there is a standardized format for packets entering and leaving each network. The principal advantage of this approach is that, with the exception of an expanded address space, the stations are not aware

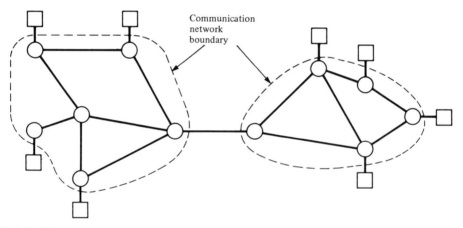

(a) Node–level interface

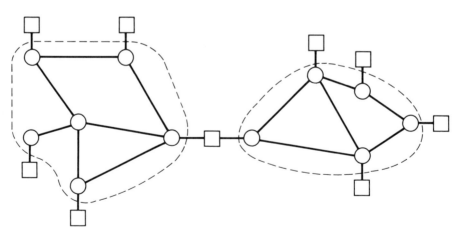

(b) Station–level interface

FIGURE 14-2. Internetwork interfacing.

that there are multiple networks. If the system is designed properly, no changes need be made in the station software. If two stations can connect over a single network, they can connect via multiple networks with the same network access interface.

If it is not possible to standardize the network access interface, some form of protocol translation, or at least manipulation, is needed. At the worst, a specialized gateway for each pair of networks must be constructed. A better approach, as we shall see, is to standardize the objects that pass between networks. In any case, this function is performed by a station that attaches to two networks.

The other dimension for characterizing internetwork architecture is the nature of the transmission service, which can be either end to end or network by network. The end-to-end approach assumes only that all networks offer at least an unreliable datagram service; that is, if a sequence of packets is sent from one station to another on the same network, some but not necessarily all will get through, and there may be duplications and reordering of the sequence. The transmission across multiple networks requires a common end-to-end protocol for providing reliable end-to-end service. In the network-by-network approach, the technique is to provide reliable service within each network and then to splice together individual network connections across multiple networks.

Table 14-1 lists possible realizations of the four architectures that result from the 2×2 combination of interface and transmission service. One architecture that has been frowned on is network-by-network station level. The only way to achieve internetworking is for each gateway to be a true protocol translator between its two attached networks. This is generally an exercise in special-purpose software of little interest to the present discussion. However, this approach has recently received attention as a means of interconnecting local networks, and will be discussed later in this chapter.

The only type of approach that seems to fit neatly into the end-to-end node-level architecture is a configuration of multiple homogeneous networks. In this case, the internetworking task is rather simple, and the gateway device is referred to as a bridge. This mechanism is most commonly used to connect multiple homogeneous local networks.

The two remaining architectures are represented by radically different approaches taken by standards organizations. An example of a network-by-network node-level architecture is the X.75 standard, designed as an extension to X.25. X.75 specifies a protocol for exchange of packets between networks to allow a series of intranetwork X.25 virtual circuits to be spliced together. To two stations on different networks, it appears that they have a single virtual circuit connecting them. In fact, the virtual circuits terminate at the node gateways, which maintain the status information required to connect separate virtual circuits.

The end-to-end station-level architecture is implemented using a protocol above the network layer, called *Internet Protocol* (IP). IP was initially developed for the DARPA Internet Project and has been standardized by the Defense Department. A similar IP standard is being developed within ISO.

TABLE 14-1 Alternative Internetworking Approaches

	Station (DTE) Level	Node (DCE) Level
Network-by-network	Protocol translator	X.75
End-to-End	Internet Protocol (IP)	Bridge

TABLE 14-2 Comparative Features of IP and X.75

IP	X.75
Station-level gateway	Node-level gateway
Datagram service	Virtual circuit service
Gateway must know IP, two network access schemes	Gateway must maintain state information about all virtual circuits
Adaptive routing easily implemented	Fixed routing typically; adaptive routing more difficult
All stations must have IP, may need common layer 4	All networks must be X.25

Table 14-2 compares IP and X.75 on a number of features. Because IP places no significant restrictions on internal network protocols, it is the more flexible approach.

Figure 14-3 depicts the protocol architecture that seems to be required for each of these four approaches. The figure depicts the gateway as a single system which implements protocols appropriate to two networks. In fact, the gateway function is often split between two devices, although logically this is immaterial.

Let us briefly describe what is happening in this figure. In each case, we have two stations that wish to communicate across three networks by establishing a transport connection. In the first case, we assume that the networks differ and that the two stations have different transport protocols. Station *A* establishes a transport connection with gateway *a*. Each uses the network access protocols for network 1(N1, L1, P1). Gateway *a* must use another transport connection to gateway *b*. Gateway *a* also includes a relay mechanism (R12) that converts between the transport protocols of network 1(T1) and network 2(T2). This process continues on across to station *B*.

In the second case, we assume that stations *A* and *B* share a common transport protocol (*T*). Both stations and all gateways share a common internet protocol (I). Data units are transmitted from station 1 to gateway *a* across network 1, using that network's access protocols (N1, L1, P1). Gateway *a* takes the internet-level data unit and retransmits it across network 2.

In the first case (protocol translator), we are in effect, splicing together transport connections. In the second case (internet protocol), there is a single transport connection, supported by a connectionless internet protocol that routes data units through the catenet. Now consider the third case (bridge), in which all the networks are homogeneous. A relay function is used to, in effect, splice together the networks at the link level.

Finally, X.75 assumes that all networks use X.25 as the network access standard. Virtual circuits are set up across each network and spliced together at the gateways by a relay mechanism.

14-2

THE BRIDGE

As was mentioned, the bridge is a simplified gateway that can be used to connect homogeneous networks. Such networks exhibit the same interface to attached sta-

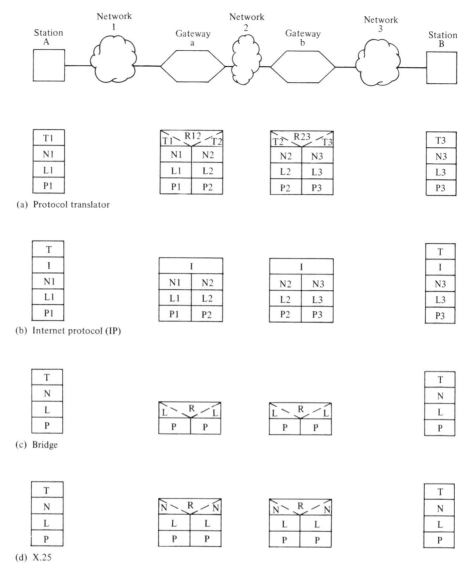

FIGURE 14-3. Internetwork architectures.

tions and use the same internal protocols. The bridge has found use in connecting local networks.

A simple example of this principle is the repeater used on baseband networks. However, this is not a true multiple network system. The repeater is merely used to extend the length of the baseband cable. It amplifies and retransmits all signals, including collisions. Thus the system behaves, from virtually all points of view, as a single network.

A system with truly separate but homogeneous networks requires a bridge to connect them. This concept was introduced in Chapter 11 as a means of linking multiple rings. To summarize again the main functions of a bridge, consider a connection between networks *A* and *B*. The bridge must do the following:

- Read all frames transmitted on *A*, and accept those addressed to *B*.
- Using the medium access control protocol for *B*, retransmit the frames onto *B*.
- Do the same for *B*-to-*A* traffic.

In addition to these basic functions, there are some interesting design considerations, which are outlined below:

1. The bridge makes no modifications to the content or format of the frames it receives, nor does it encapsulate them with an additional header. If any modifications or additions are made, we are dealing with a more complex device: a gateway. This is discussed in later sections.
2. Despite item 1, the bridge can be conceived internally as using another protocol. Figure 14-4 shows a bridge consisting of two units connected by a point-to-point link, which might be an HDLC link. For purposes of crossing that link, one or more LAN frames will be wrapped in an HDLC frame.
3. The bridge should contain enough buffer space to meet peak demands. Over a short period of time, frames may arrive faster than they can be retransmitted.
4. The bridge must contain addressing and routing intelligence. At a minimum, the bridge must know which addresses are on each network in order to know which frames to pass. Further, there may be more than two networks in a sort of cascade configuration. The bridge must be able to pass along frames addressed for networks further on.
5. A bridge may connect more than two networks.

Figure 14-5 depicts the operation of a bridge.

Having described this rather simple device, we should address the subject of why bridges are used. The principle reasons are:

- *Reliability:* The danger in connecting all data processing devices in an organization to one network is that a fault on the network disables all communications. By using bridges, the network can be partitioned into self-contained units.

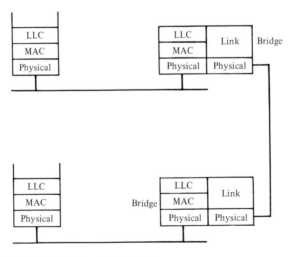

FIGURE 14-4. LAN-to-LAN bridge.

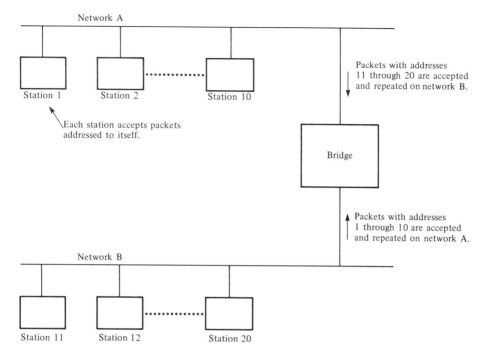

FIGURE 14-5. Bridge operation.

- *Performance:* In general, performance on a LAN or HSLN declines with an increase in the number of stations or the length of the medium. A number of smaller networks will give improved performance if devices can be clustered so that intranetwork traffic significantly exceeds internetwork traffic.
- *Security:* A bridge architecture can enhance network security, by isolating portions of the network.
- *Convenience:* It may simply be more convenient to have multiple networks. For example, if a broadband local network is to be installed in two buildings separated by a highway, it may be far easier to use a microwave point-to-point bridge link than to attempt to string coaxial cable between the two buildings.
- *Geographic coverage:* A corporation may install homogeneous LAN systems in a number of cities and wish them to function as a single integrated network. Bridges with the architecture of Figure 14-4 can be used to link widely separated networks.

The description above has applied to the simplest sort of bridge; examples of such devices are found in [THOR83] and [ESTR82]. The bridge can be more sophisticated. For example, the Ungermann-Bass product [MARS83] includes the following additional functions:

- Each bridge maintains status information on other bridges, together with the cost and number of network hops required to reach each network. This information is updated by periodic exchanges of information among bridges. This allows the bridges to perform a dynamic routing function.
- A control mechanism manages packet buffers in each bridge to overcome congestion. Under saturation conditions, the bridge gives precedence to en-

route packets over new packets just entering the catenet from an attached local network, thus preserving the investment in line bandwidth and processing time already made in the enroute packet.

Another example of a more complex bridge is contained in [SUNS83].

14-3

X.75

The X.75 standard was developed by CCITT as a supplement to X.25. It is designed for use between public X.25 networks and is not likely to be used or even allowed as an interface between public and private networks. However, it could also be used to connect a collection of private X.25 networks in a catenet that does not include public networks.

Figure 14-6 depicts the principle of X.75. As shown, X.25 specifies an interface between host equipment (DTE) and network equipment (DCE) that encompasses layers 1 through 3 and permits the set up, maintenance, and termination of virtual circuits between two DTEs. X.75 specifies signal terminating equipment (STE) that act as DCE-level gateways to connect two X.25 networks.

We begin with a description of the operation of an X.75 catenet. We then look at some of the specific packet level and link level characteristics of the standard.

Internetwork Operation

The interconnection of X.25 networks via X.75 provides a DTE-DTE virtual circuit that is spliced together from a series of virtual circuits:

- DCE to STE (intranetwork)
- STE to STE (internetwork)
- 0 or more:
  STE to STE (intranetwork)
  STE to STE (internetwork)
- STE to DCE

Each section is a distinct entity with a separate virtual circuit, flow control, and error control.

From the point of view of the DTE, however, it merely sees an enlarged X.25 network; X.75 is invisible. The DTE-DCE interface is still defined by X.25. As before, intranetwork protocols are undefined by the standard. The internetwork STE-STE interface is defined by X.75.

The transmission of a packet between two hosts can be explained with reference to Figure 14-6b. Station A sends an X.25 data packet to its DCE with the virtual circuit number (group, channel) that it associates with a connection to B. This packet is transmitted via network C to an STE. The STE uses the same format (Figure 14-7b), but modifies the virtual circuit number and flow control information for the appropriate STE-STE virtual circuit. The receiving STE then sends the packet to B's DCE, which presents a packet to B with the virtual circuit number that B associates with a connection to A. Three important points about this process:

- There is no encapsulation by the STEs. The same layer 3 header format is reused.

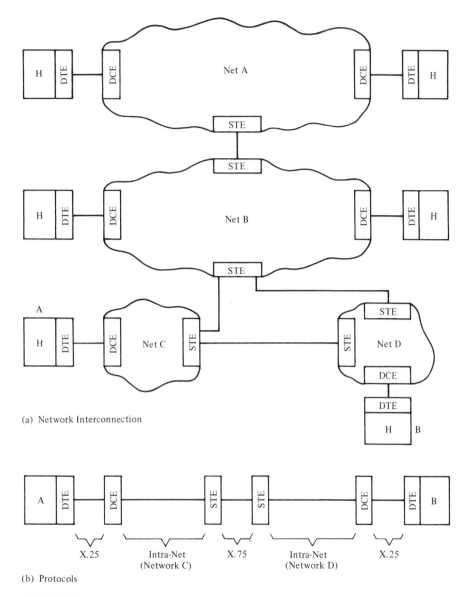

(a) Network Interconnection

(b) Protocols

FIGURE 14-6. **Interconnection of X.25 networks via X.75.**

- There is no end-to-end protocol. As in a single X.25 network, all information has local significance only (except when the D bit is set).
- Because of the 12-bit field, an STE-STE internet link can handle a maximum of 4096 connections.

Call request and clear request are handled step by step but must propagate end to end. Routing information must exist within DCEs and STEs to accomplish this. For example, a Call Request packet from *A* triggers the set up of a DCE-STE virtual circuit. Using the X.75 control packet format, which differs from X.25 only in the addition of a network-level utilities field, an STE-STE virtual circuit is set up between networks *C* and *D*. The Call Request packet then propagates to *B*'s

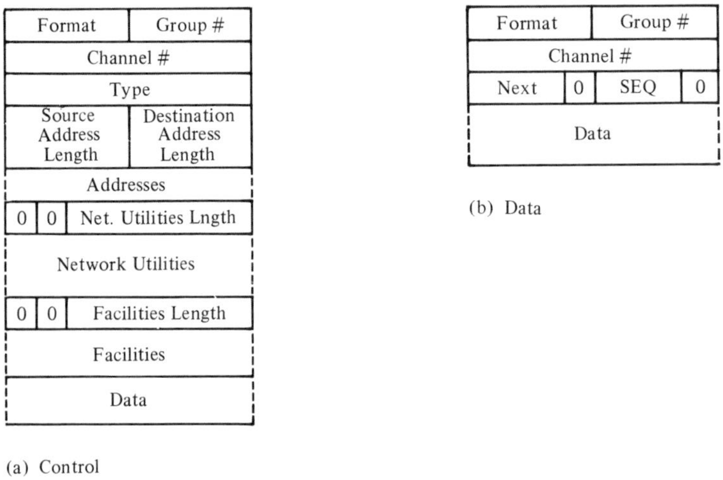

(a) Control

Format	Group #
Channel #	
Type	
Source Address Length	Destination Address Length
Addresses	
0 0	Net. Utilities Lngth
Network Utilities	
0 0	Facilities Length
Facilities	
Data	

(b) Data

Format	Group #		
Channel #			
Next	0	SEQ	0
Data			

FIGURE 14-7. X.75 packet formats.

DCE, setting up another virtual circuit. Finally, a Call Indication packet is delivered to *B*. The same procedure is used for Call Accepted and Clear Request packets.

Packet Level

The specification of the packet level of X.75 is almost identical to that of X.25. The only differences are those needed to accommodate internetwork administration and management functions of the STE. We will consider these differences by examining the three phases of a virtual call:

- Call establishment.
- Data transfer.
- Call reset or termination.

At present, X.75 does not offer permanent virtual circuit service.

Call establishment is initiated by an STE using the CALL REQUEST packet. This packet, recall, contains information being propagated from the calling DTE to the called DTE. This includes, in particular, the facilities information. To accommodate STE-STE facilities, a utilities field is added to the packet (Figure 14-7a). The facilities that can be requested are:

- Transit network identification.
- Call identifier.
- Throughput class indication.
- Window size indication.
- Packet size indication.
- Fast select indication.
- Closed user group indication.
- Closed user group with outgoing access indication.
- Reverse charging indication.
- Traffic class indication.
- Estimated transit delay.
- Tariff.

The called STE responds with a Call Connected packet.

The *data transfer* phase consists primarily of the exchange of data packets between STEs. These packets are, of course, intended for some destination DTE. Flow control is exercised by piggybacking and by using RR and RNR packets. If the D bit of a data packet is set to zero, acknowledgment has local significance: it is used to regulate STE-STE flow on a virtual circuit basis. However, if the sending DTE sets the D bit to one, that bit remains set as the data packet propagates through the catenet, and acknowledgment has end-to-end significance.

Finally, *call reset and termination* is accomplished in the same manner as for X.25. Clear Request and Clear Confirmation packets are used to terminate a virtual call. Reset Request and Reset Confirmation reinitialize a virtual call by setting sequence numbers to zero in both directions. Restart Request and Restart Confirmation reset all active virtual calls. X.75 specifies only local significance of these actions but, presumably, they correspond to global clear or reset events.

Link Level

At the link level, X.75 defines both a *single link procedure* (SLP) and a *multilink procedure* (MLP) that allows the interface to operate over multiple lines and achieve greater reliability and throughput. The SLP is defined to be LAP-B. When multiple links exist between STEs, each link is governed by the SLP LAP-B.

When multiple links exist, the set of links is used as a pooled resource for transmitting packets, regardless of virtual circuit number. When a packet is presented to MLP for transmission, any available link may be chosen. Indeed, the MLP may assign one packet to several links to satisfy throughput or availability constraints.

To keep track of packets, a special MLP frame is defined, which consists of the packet and a 2-octet multilink control (MLC) field (Figure 14-8). The MLC contains a 12-bit sequence number which is unique (modulo 2^{12}) across all links. Once an MLP frame is constructed, it is assigned to a particular link, and further encapsulated in an SLP frame. The SLP frame includes, as usual, a sequence number unique to that link.

There are two principal reasons for needing an MLP sequence number. First, frames sent out over different links may arrive in a different order from that in which they were first constructed by the sending MLP. The destination MLP will buffer incoming frames and reorder them according to MLP sequence number. Second, if repeated attempts to transmit a frame over one link fails, the STE will send the frame over one or more other links. The MLP sequence number is needed for duplicate detection in this case.

The MLP mechanism is logically equivalent to the transmission group control mechanism in SNA's path control layer. The 1984 revision of X.25 has adopted the MLP as an option for DTE-DCE links.

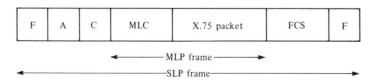

FIGURE 14-8. X.75 multilink frame format.

INTERNET PROTOCOL (IP)

The Internet Protocol (IP) is the name given to a protocol standard developed by DOD [DOD83a] as part of the DARPA Internet Project. Figure 14-9 shows the extent of the DARPA Internet as of late 1983, and Table 14-3 lists characteristics of the constituent networks [HIND83]. A protocol similar to IP is under development within ISO. We begin with a description of the operation of IP and a discussion of key design issues, before turning to specific protocol details.

Operation of an IP Catenet

IP provides a connectionless or datagram service between stations. This contrasts with the connection-oriented X.75 service. There are a number of advantages to the connectionless approach:

- A connectionless internet facility is flexible. It can deal with a variety of networks, some of which are themselves connectionless. In essence, IP requires very little of the constituent networks.
- A connectionless internet service can be made highly robust. This is basically the same argument made for a datagram network service versus a virtual circuit service. For a further discussion, the reader is referred to Section 9-2.
- A connectionless internet service is best for connectionless transport protocols. The use of such protocols is discussed in Chapter 15.

As an example, Figure 14-10 depicts the operation of IP for data exchange between station *A* on a LAN 1 and station *B* on a LAN 2 through a long-haul X.25

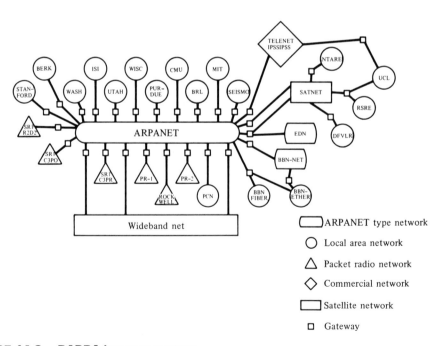

FIGURE 14-9. DARPA internet system.

TABLE 14-3 DARPA INTERNET Network Characteristics

Network Type	Message Size (Octets)	Speed[a]	Delay[b]	Guaranteed Delivery	Notes
ARPANET	1008	Medium	Medium	Yes	
SATNET	256	Low	High	No	Satellite network
Pronet	2048	High	Low	Yes	Local area network
Ethernet	1500	High	Low	Yes	Local area network
Telenet	128	Low	Medium	Yes	
Packet radio	254	Medium	Medium	No	Varying topology
Wideband	2000	High	High	No	Satellite Network

[a]Low speed is <100 kbps; medium speed is 100 kbps to 1 Mbps; high speed is >1 Mpbs.
[b]Low delay is <50 ms; medium delay is 50 to 500 ms; high delay is >500 ms.

packet-switched network. These two stations share a common transport protocol. The data to be sent by *A* are encapsulated in a datagram with an IP header specifying a global network address (station *B*). This datagram is then encapsulated with the LAN 1 protocol and sent to a gateway that strips off the LAN 1 header. The datagram is then encapsulated with the X.25 protocol and transmitted across the network to a gateway. The gateway strips off the X.25 fields and recovers the datagram, which is then wrapped in LAN 2 headers and sent to *B*. If a connection-oriented service is required, *A* and *B* must share a common layer 4 protocol.

With this example in mind, we describe briefly the sequence of steps involved in sending a datagram between two hosts on different networks. The process starts in the sending station. The station wants to send an IP datagram to a station in another network. The IP module in the station constructs the datagram with a global network address and recognizes that the destination is on another network. So the first step is to send the datagram to a gateway (example: station *A* to gateway 1 in Figure 14-10). To do this, the IP module appends to the IP datagram a header appropriate to the network that contains the address of the gateway. For example, for an X.25 network, a layer 3 packet encapsulates the IP datagram to be sent to the gateway.

Next, the packet travels through the network to the gateway, which receives it via a DCE-DTE protocol. The gateway unwraps the packet to recover the original datagram. The gateway analyzes the IP header to determine whether this datagram contains control information intended for the gateway, or data intended for a station farther on. In the latter instance, the gateway must make a routing decision. There are four possibilities:

1. The destination station is attached directly to one of the networks to which the gateway is attached. This is referred to as "directly connected." For example, in Figure 14-11, all stations labeled S0 are directly connected to gateway G1.
2. The destination station is on a network that has a gateway that directly connects to this gateway. This is known as a "neighbor gateway." In Figure 14-11, G2 is a neighbor gateway of G1, and all stations labeled S1 are one "hop" from G1.
3. To reach the destination station, more than one additional gateway must be traversed. This is known as a "multiple-hop" situation. In Figure 14-11, all stations labeled S2 are in this category.
4. The gateway does not know the destination address.

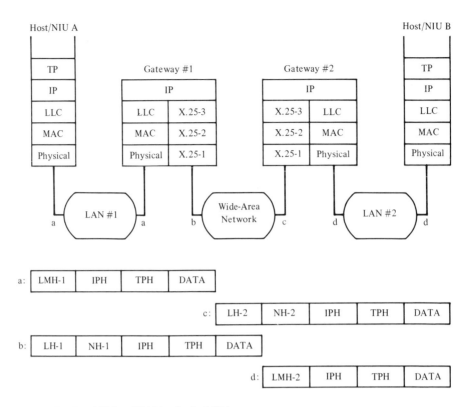

LMH-*i* : Combined LLC and MAC header for LAN i
LH-*j* : Link Header (X.25 Layer 2) for DTE = Gateway *j*
NH-*k* : Network Header (X.25 Layer 3) for DTE = Gateway k
IPH : Internet Protocol Header
TPH : Transport Protocol Header

FIGURE 14-10.   Data encapsulation—IP approach.

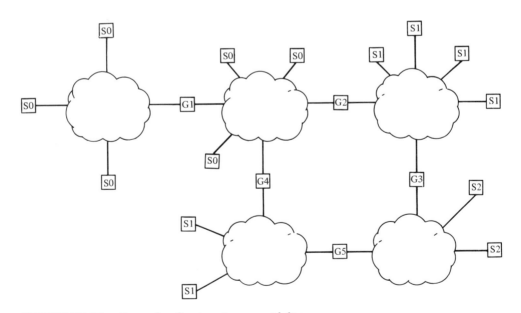

FIGURE 14-11.   Example of catanet connectivity.

INTERNETWORKING

In case 4, the gateway returns an error message to the source of the datagram. For cases 1 through 3, the gateway must select the appropriate route for the data, and insert them into the appropriate network with the appropriate address. For case 1, the address is the destination station address. For cases 2 and 3, the address is a gateway address. Remember, we are speaking here of a lower layer address, usually a layer 3 address or, in the case of local networks, a layer 2 address.

Before actually sending data, however, the gateway may need to fragment the datagram to accommodate a smaller maximum packet size limitation on the outgoing network. Each fragment becomes an independent IP datagram. Each new datagram is wrapped in a lower layer packet for transmission. The gateway then queues each packet for transmission. It may also enforce a maximum queue-length size for each network to which it attaches to avoid having a slow network penalize a faster one. In any case, once the queue limit is reached, additional datagrams are simply dropped.

The process described above continues through zero or more gateways until the datagram reaches the destination station. As with a gateway, the destination station recovers the IP datagram from its network wrapping. If fragmentation has occurred, the IP module in the destination station buffers the incoming data until the original data field is reassembled. It then passes this block of data to a higher layer. The higher layer (e.g., transport) is responsible for the proper sequencing of a stream of datagrams and for end-to-end error and flow control.

Design Issues

With that thumbnail sketch of the operation of an IP-controlled catenet, we can now go back and examine some design issues in greater detail:

- Addressing.
- Routing.
- Fragmentation and reassembly.
- Datagram lifetime.
- Error control.
- Flow control.

As we proceed with this discussion, the reader will note many similarities with the design issues and techniques relevant to packet-switched networks. To see the reason for this, consider Figure 14-12, which compares an internet architecture with a packet-switched network architecture. The gateways (G1, G2, G3) in the internet correspond to the packet-switched nodes (P1, P2, P3) in the network, and the networks (N1, N2, N3) in the internet correspond to the transmission links (T1, T2, T3) in the networks. The gateways perform essentially the same functions as packet-switched nodes, and use the intervening networks in a manner analogous to transmission links.

Addressing.   Recall from Chapter 12 that a distinction is generally made among names, addresses, and routes. A name specifies what an object is; an address specifies where it is, and a route indicates how to get there. The distinction between names and addresses can be a useful concept, but it is also an arbitrary one. For a single network, an application program uses a name to identify a referent (process, station); the station translates the name into an address understood by the network; and the network may utilize a route to reach the referent.

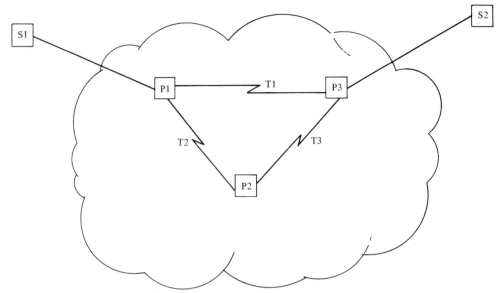

(a) Packet–switched network architecture

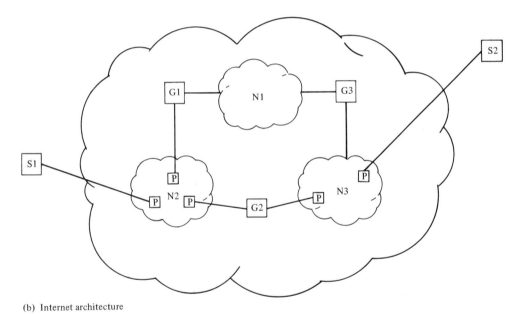

(b) Internet architecture

FIGURE 14-12. The inernet as a network.

In a catenet, the distinction is less clear. Applications continue to use names and individual networks continue to use addresses and, if necessary, routes. To transfer data through a gateway, two entities must be identified: the destination network and the destination station. The gateway requires a network address in order to perform its function. This address can be specified in a number of ways:

- The application can refer to a network by a unique number; in effect, the name and address are the same.
- The internet logic in the station can translate a network name into a network address.

- A global station addressing scheme can be used. That is, there is a unique identifier for each station in the catenet. For routing purposes, each gateway would need to derive network addresses from host addresses.

Surprisingly, the latter technique has been proposed by the developers of Ethernet [DALA81]. They recommend a 48-bit station address. This is an address space sufficient to accommodate over 10^{14} unique referents, so it is likely to be sufficient for the foreseeable future. The primary advantages of this approach are that it permits stations to move from one network to another and that it allows address recognition at the station to be "hardwired." The main disadvantages are that some central facility must manage the assignment of names and that unnecessarily long address fields must be carried across multiple networks. Given the proliferation of local networks, this unique address approach does not seem feasible.

So, typically, a gateway will receive an internet packet with a referent in the form *Net.Station*, where Net is a network address. The identifier *Station* is usually both a name and an address. To the higher-layer software in the station that generated the packet, *Station* is an address, translated from an application-level name. However, when it comes time for a gateway to deliver a datagram to a station on an attached network, *Station* must be translated into a layer 3 or 2 network address. This is so because different networks will have different address field lengths. Hence *Station* is treated as a name by the gateway.

The referent *Net.Station* can be considered a two-level hierarchical identifier of a host in the catenet. The Ethernet developers (interestingly, the same ones interested in global station addresses) have proposed a third level of addressing to identify, at the internet level, an individual service access point (SAP) at a host [BOGG80, DALA82]. Thus the internet identifier would be of the form *Net.Station.SAP*. With this identifier, an internet protocol can be viewed as process to process rather than station to station. With *SAP* in the internet layer, the internet protocol is responsible for multiplexing and demultiplexing datagrams for software modules that use the internet service. The advantage of this approach is that the next-higher layer could be simplified, a useful feature for small microprocessor devices. There are some problems in this approach, particularly when local networks are involved, where there is likely to be a proliferation of station types. Perhaps the most significant problem relates to the use of "well-known" ports, which allow ready access to common services. For example, TCP port 23 is the remote login service. Devices not using TCP, but using some other higher-level protocol, would have other well-known ports. If ports were implemented as SAPs at the IP level, the assignment of well-known ports would have to be centralized. For a further discussion, see [CLAR82].

Finally, an important service that must somehow be provided in the catenet is a directory service. The station software must be able to determine the *Net.Station* identifier of a desired destination. One or more directory servers are needed, which themselves are well known. Each server would contain part or all of a name/address directory for catenet stations.

Routing.   Routing is generally accomplished by maintaining a routing table in each station and gateway that gives, for each possible destination network, the next gateway to which the IP datagram should be sent.

Table 14-4 shows the routing table for the BBN gateway, which is part of the DARPA catenet. If a network is directly connected, it is so indicated. Otherwise, the datagram must be directed through one or more gateways (one or more hops).

TABLE 14-4 INTERNET Routing Table[a]

Network Name	Net Address	Route[b]
SATNET	4	Directly connected
ARPANET	10	Directly connected
BBN-NET	3	1hop via RCC 10.3.0.72 (ARPANET 3/72)
Purdue-Computer Science	192.5.1	2 hops via Purdue 10.2.0.37 (ARPANET 2/37)
INTELPOST	43	2 hops via Mills 10.3.0.17 (ARPANET 3/17)
DECNET-TEST	38	3 hops via Mills 10.3.0.17 (ARPANET 3/17)
Wideband	28	3 hops via RCC 10.3.0.72 (ARPANET 3/72)
BBN-Packet Radio	1	2 hops via RCC 10.3.0.72 (ARPANET 3/72)
DCN-COMSAT	29	1 hop via Mills 10.3.0.17 (ARPANET 3/17)
FIBERNET	24	3 hops via RCC 10.3.0.72 (ARPANET 3/72)
Bragg-Packet Radio	9	1 hop via Bragg 10.0.0.38 (ARPANET 0/38)
Clark Net	8	2 hops via Mills 10.3.0.17 (ARPANET 3/17)
LCSNET	18	1 hop via MIT LCS 10.0.0.77 (ARPANET 0/77)
BBN-Terminal Concentrator	192.1.2	3 hops via RCC 10.3.0.72 (ARPANET 3/72)
BBN-Jericho	192.1.3	3 hops via RCC 10.3.0.72 (ARPANET 3/72)
UCLNET	11	1 hop via UCL 4.0.0.60 (SATNET 60)
RSRE-NULL	35	1 hop via UCL 4.0.0.60 (SATNET 60)
RSRE-PPSN	25	2 hops via UCL 4.0.0.60 (SATNET 60)
San Francisco-Packet Radio-2	6	1 hop via C3PO 10.1.0.51 (ARPANET 1/51)

[a]Network table for BBN gateway.
[b]Names and acronyms identify gateways in the INTERNET system.
Source: [SHEL82].

The table indicates the identity of the next gateway on the route (which must share a common network with this gateway or host) and the number of hops to the destination.

The routing table may be static or dynamic. A static table, however, could contain alternate routes if a gateway is unavailable. A dynamic table is more flexible in responding both to error and congestion situations. In the DARPA catenet, for example, when a gateway goes down, all of its neighbors will send out a status report, allowing other gateways and hosts to update their routing tables. A similar scheme can be used to control congestion. This latter is particularly important because of the mismatch in capacity between local and long-haul networks. The interested reader may consult [DARP81], which specifies a variety of internet control messages used to facilitate routing.

Routing tables may also be used to support other internet services, such as security and priority. For example, individual networks might be classified to handle data up to a given security classification. The routing mechanism must assure that data of a given security level is not allowed to pass through networks not cleared to handle such data.

Another routing technique is source routing. The source station specifies the route by including a sequential list of gateways in the datagram. This, again, could be useful for security or priority requirements.

Finally, we mention a service related to routing: route recording. To record a route, each gateway appends its address to a list of addresses in the datagram. This feature is useful for testing and debugging purposes.

Fragmentation and Reassembly. Individual networks within a catenet will generally be diverse and, in particular, specify different maximum (and sometimes minimum) packet sizes. It would be inefficient and unwieldy to try to dictate uniform packet size across networks. Thus gateways may need to fragment incoming datagrams into smaller pieces before transmitting on to the next network.

If datagrams can be fragmented (perhaps more than once) in the course of their travels, the question arises as to where they should be reassembled. The easiest solution is to have reassembly performed at the destination only. The principal disadvantage of this approach is the packets can only get smaller as data moves through the catenet. This may seriously impair the efficiency of some networks (e.g., CSMA/CD LANs). On the other hand, if intermediate gateway reassembly is allowed, the following disadvantages result:

1. Large buffers are required at gateways, and there is a potential for reassembly deadlock.
2. All fragments of a datagram must pass through the same gateway. This inhibits the use of dynamic routing.

IP specifies an efficient technique for fragmentation. The technique requires the following fields in the datagram header:

- ID.
- Length.
- Offset.
- More flag.

The *ID* is some means of uniquely identifying a station-originated datagram. In IP, it consists of the source and destination addresses, an identifier of the protocol layer that generated the data, and a sequence number supplied by that protocol layer. The *Length* is the length of the data field in octets, and the *Offset* is the position of a fragment in the original datagram in multiples of 64 bits.

The source station IP layer creates a datagram with Length equal to the entire length of the data field, with Offset = 0, and a More Flag set to False. To fragment a long packet, an IP module in a gateway performs the following tasks:

1. Create two new datagrams and copy the header fields of the incoming datagram into both.
2. Divide the data into two approximately equal portions along a 64-bit boundary, placing one portion in each new datagram. The first portion must be a multiple of 64 bits.
3. Set the Length field of the first datagram to the length of the inserted data, and set the More Flag to True. The Offset field is unchanged.
4. Set the Length field of the second datagram to the length of the inserted data, and add the length of the first data portion divided by eight to the Offset field. The More Flag remains the same.

Table 14-5 gives an example. The procedure can be generalized to an *n*-way split.

To reassemble a datagram, there must be sufficient buffer space at the reassembly point. As fragments with the same ID arrive, their data fields are inserted in the proper position in the buffer until the entire datagram is reassembled, which is achieved when a contiguous set of data exists starting with an *Offset* of zero and ending with data from a fragment with a false *More Flag*.

TABLE 14-5 Fragmentation Example

Original datagram
      Length = 472
      Offset = 0
      More   = 0

First Fragment
      Length = 240
      Offset = 0
      More   = 1

Second fragment
      Length = 232
      Offset = 30
      More   = 0

Datagram Lifetime. If dynamic or alternate routing is used, the potential exists for a datagram or some of its fragments to loop indefinitely through the catenet. This is undesirable for two reasons. First, an endlessly circulating packet consumes resources. Second, we will see in Chapter 15 that a reliable transport protocol depends on there being an upper bound on datagram lifetime. To avoid these problems, each datagram can be marked with a lifetime. Once the lifetime expires, the datagram is discarded.

A simple way to implement lifetime is to use a hop count. Each time that a datagram passes through a gateway, the count is decremented. Alternatively, the lifetime could be a true measure of time. This requires that the gateways must somehow know how long it has been since the datagram or fragment last crossed a gateway, in order to know by how much to decrement the lifetime field. This would seem to require some global clocking mechanism.

The advantage of using a true time measure is that it can be used in the reassembly algorithm. When a datagram is being reassembled from fragments, the buffer will be cleared of a partially reconstructed datagram if its lifetime expires.

Error Control. The internetwork facility does not guarantee successful delivery of every datagram. When a datagram is discarded by a gateway, the gateway should attempt to return some information to the source, if possible. The source internet protocol entity may use this information to modify its transmission strategy and may notify higher layers. To report that a specific datagram has been discarded, some means of datagram identification is needed.

Datagrams may be discarded for a number of reasons, including lifetime expiration, congestion, and FCS error. In the latter case, notification is not possible since the source address field may have been damaged.

Flow Control. Internet flow control allows gateways and/or receiving stations to limit the rate at which they receive data. For the connectionless type of service we are describing, flow control mechanisms are limited. The best approach would seem to be to send flow control packets, requesting reduced data flow, to other gateways and source stations.

Protocol Description

As with any protocol, IP can best be described in three parts:

- The interface with a higher layer (e.g., DOD's TCP) specifying the services that IP provides.
- The IP protocol, specifying host-gateway and gateway-gateway interaction.
- The interface with a lower layer, specifying required services.

IP Services. IP provides a connectionless data transfer service to IP users (e.g., TCP) in hosts attached to networks of the catenet. Two primitives are defined at the user-IP interface. The Send primitive is used to request transmission of a data unit. The Deliver primitive is used by IP to notify a user of the arrival of a data unit. Although not part of the standard, IP is expected to use some sort of Error primitive to notify a user of failure in providing the requested service. This service is not assumed to be reliable; that is, there is no guarantee that errors will be reported.

The Send primitive includes the following parameters:

- *Source address:* internetwork address of sending IP entity.
- *Destination address:* internetwork address of IP entity to receive data.
- *Protocol:* identifies the recipient protocol entity (an IP user).
- *Type of service indicators:* used to specify the treatment of the data unit in its transmission through component networks. The indicators are precedence (eight levels), reliability (two levels), delay (two levels), and throughput (two levels). *Precedence* attempts preferential treatment for high importance datagrams. *Reliability* attempts to minimize data loss and error rate. *Delay* and *throughput* attempt to minimize delay or maximize throughput, respectively. To the extent possible, these parameters are passed on to the individual networks for their use. Of course, if a particular network supports only a single grade of service, this parameter has no effect for that leg of the journey.
- *Identifier:* is used, along with the source and destination addresses and user protocol, to identify the data unit uniquely. This parameter is needed for reassembly and error reporting.
- *Don't fragment identifier:* indicates whether IP can fragment data to accomplish delivery.
- *Time to live:* measured in network hops.
- *Data length:* length of data being transmitted.
- *Option data:* options requested by the IP user.
- *Data:* user data to be transmitted.

The *options* feature allows for future extensibility and for inclusion of parameters that are not present with every data unit. The currently defined options are:

- *Security:* The security parameter allows each data unit to be labeled with a security label (e.g., SECRET, CONFIDENTIAL). Compartments are used to specify user groups authorized to access information (i.e., have a "need to know").
- *Source routing:* A sequenced list of gateway addresses specifies the route. Routing may be strict (only identified gateways may be visited) or loose (other intermediate gateways may also be visited).
- *Record routing:* A field is allocated to record the route of the datagram through a sequence of gateways. The field should be large enough to prevent overflow.

- *Stream identification:* Reserved resources used for stream service are named. This service provides special handling for volatile periodic traffic (e.g., voice). IP must endeavor to maintain a constant delay per datagram.
- *Timestamp:* The source internet protocol entity and some or all intermediate gateways add a timestamp (accurate to milliseconds) to the data unit as it goes by.

The Deliver primitive includes the following parameters

- Source address.
- Destination address.
- Protocol.
- Type of service indicators.
- Data length.
- Option data.
- Data.

IP Protocol. The protocol between IP entities is best described by defining the IP datagram format, which is shown in Figure 14-13a. The fields are:

- *Version (4 bits):* version number, included to allow evolution of the protocol. Either header format or semantics might change.
- *Internet header length (IHL) (4 bits):* length of header in 32-bit words. The minimum value is five. Thus a header is at least 20 octets long.
- *Type of service (8 bits):* specifies reliability, precedence, delay, and throughput parameters.
- *Total length (16 bits):* total data unit length, including header, in octets.
- *Identifier (16 bits):* together with source address, destination address, and user protocol, intended to uniquely identify a datagram. Thus the identifier must

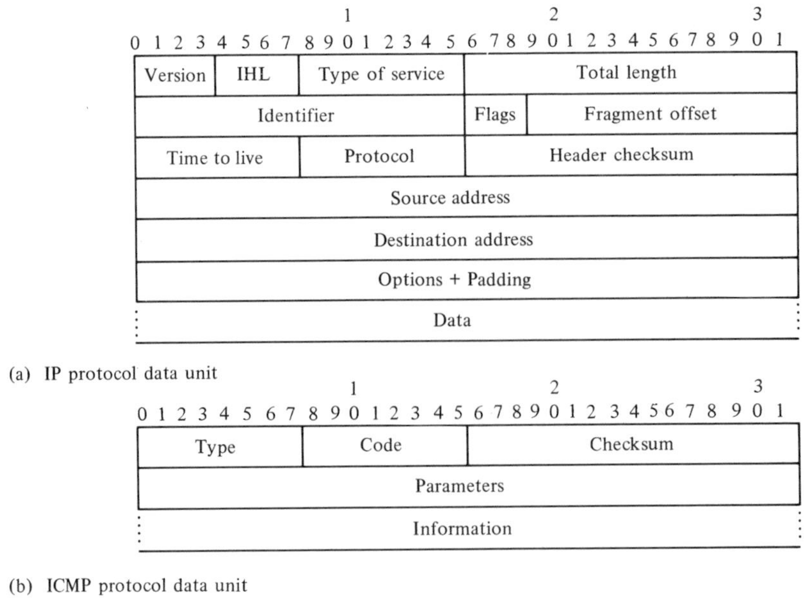

(a) IP protocol data unit

(b) ICMP protocol data unit

FIGURE 14-13.   Internet protocol formats.

be unique for the datagram's source, destination, and user protocol for the time during which the datagram will remain in the catenet.

- *Flags (3 bits):* one bit, the More flag, used for fragmentation and reassembly. Another bit, if set, prohibits fragmentation. This facility may be useful if it is known that the destination does not have the capability to reassemble fragments. An example is to down-line load a small microprocessor. However, if this bit is set, the datagram may be discarded if it exceeds the maximum size of an en route network. When the bit is set, it may be advisable to use source routing to avoid networks with small maximum packet sizes. The third bit is currently not used.
- *Fragment offset (13 bits):* indicates where in the datagram this fragment belongs. It is measured in 64-bit units. This implies that fragments (other than the last fragment) must contain a data field that is a multiple of 64 bits long.
- *Time to live (8 bits):* measured in gateway hops.
- *Protocol (8 bits):* indicates the next level protocol which is to receive the data field at the destination.
- *Header checksum (16 bits):* frame check sequence on the header only. Since some header fields may change (e.g., time to live, fragmentation-related fields), this is reverified and recomputed at each gateway. The checksum field is the 16-bit one's complement of all 16 bit words in the header. For purposes of computation, the checksum field itself is considered to have a value of zero.
- *Source address (32 bits):* coded to allow a variable allocation of bits to specify the network and the station within the specified network (7 and 24, 14 and 16, or 21 and 8).
- *Destination address (32 bits):* as above.
- *Options (variable):* encodes the options requested by the sender.
- *Padding (variable):* used to ensure that the internet header ends on a 32-bit boundary.
- *Data (variable):* the data field must be a multiple of eight bits in length. Total length of data field plus header is a maximum of 65,535 octets.

It should be easy to see how the services specified above map into the fields of the IP data units.

IP-Network Interface. IP is designed to operate in a catenet consisting of diverse individual networks. Therefore, only a minimum level of service is expected and the requirement is only for an unreliable datagram service. The IP layer in a host or gateway may choose to take advantage of a greater degree of service if it is available on a particular network. For example, two gateways on the same X.25 network may choose to maintain a virtual circuit between them if they expect to exchange a lot of traffic.

The specific format and content of the IP-network primitives will depend on the nature of the network interface. Thus the IP layer in each host and gateway must be tailored to the network or networks to which it is attached. The following minimum service is specified:

- SEND [local destination address, type of service indicators, length, data].
- DELIVER [data].

The destination address field specifies the correspondent IP entity attached to this network. The type-of-service parameter is passed down from the IP user, and the data field is the IP datagram. Note that the destination host is not assumed to be able to use any but the most essential parameters.

Internet Control Message Protocol

DOD has defined an *internet control message protocol* (ICMP) which is a required companion to IP. Basically, ICMP provides feedback about problems in the communication environment. Examples of its use are: When a datagram cannot reach its destination, when the gateway does not have the buffering capacity to forward a datagram, and when the gateway can direct the station to send traffic on a shorter route.

Although ICMP is, in effect, at the same level as IP, it is a user of IP. An ICMP message is constructed and then passed on to IP, which encapsulates the message with an IP header and then transmits it to the destination gateway or station. Figure 14-13b shows the general format of ICMP messages. The fields are:

- *Type (8 bits):* specifies the type of ICMP message.
- *Code (8 bits):* used to specify parameters of the message that can be encoded in one or a few bits.
- *Checksum (16 bits):* checksum of the entire ICMP message.
- *Parameters (32 bits):* used to specify more lengthy parameters.
- *Information (variable):* provides additional information related to the message.

Nine types of ICMP messages have been defined:

- Destination unreachable.
- Time exceeded.
- Parameter problem.
- Source quench.
- Redirect.
- Echo.
- Echo reply.
- Timestamp.
- Timestamp reply.

The *destination unreachable* message covers a number of contingencies. A gateway may return this message if it does not know how to reach the destination network. In some networks, an attached gateway may be able to determine if a particular station is unreachable, and return a message. The station itself may return this message if the user protocol or some higher-level service access point is unreachable. If the datagram specifies a source route that is unusable, a message is returned. Finally, if a gateway must fragment a datagram but the Don't Fragment flag is set, a message is returned. The message includes, in the information field, the entire IP header plus the first 64 bits of the original datagram.

A gateway will return a *time exceeded* message if the lifetime of the datagram expires. A station will send this message if it cannot complete reassembly within a time limit. The original header plus 64 bits are returned.

A syntactic or semantic error in an IP header will cause a *parameter problem* message to be returned. The parameter field contains a pointer to the octet in the original header where the error was detected. The original header plus 64 bits are sent.

The *source quench* message provides a rudimentary form of flow control. Either a gateway or a station may send this message to a station, requesting the source station to reduce the rate at which it is sending traffic to the internet destination. The original header plus 64 bits of the datagram which triggered the complaint are returned.

The gateway sends a *redirect* message to a station in the following situation. A gateway, G1, receives an internet datagram from a station on a network to which the gateway is attached. The gateway, G1, checks its routing table and obtains the address of the next gateway, G2, on the route to the datagram's internet destination network, X. If G2 and the station identified by the internet source address of the datagram are on the same network, a redirect message is sent to the station. The redirect message advises the station to send its traffic for network X directly to gateway G2 as this is a shorter path to the destination. The gateway forwards the original datagram's data to its internet destination. The address of G2 is contained in the parameter field. The original header plus 64 bits of the datagram are returned.

The *echo* and *echo reply* messagers provide a mechanism for testing that communication is possible between two entities. The recipient of an echo message is obligated to return the message in an *echo reply* message. The parameters field may be used to hold an identifier that will be returned.

The *timestamp* and *timestamp reply* messages provide a mechanism for sampling the delay characteristics of the catenet. The sender of a timestamp message may include an identifier in the parameters field and place the time that the message is sent (originate timestamp) in the information field. The receiver appends a receive timestamp and transmit timestamp and returns the message as a timestamp reply.

14-5

PROTOCOL TRANSLATION

Until recently, the use of a protocol translation technique for internetworking has been frowned upon (e.g., [SUNS77], [CERF78], and [WARN80]). With the growing use of local networks and the need to interconnect them, the issue has been reexamined [CHER83, SCHN83]. To understand this renewed interest in protocol translation, we will explore the following:

1. The problems encountered in using protocol translation for internetworking.
2. The problems encountered in using an internetwork protocol for a catenet, including local networks.
3. A protocol-translation approach that solves the problems in item 2 while avoiding those in item 1.

Problems with the Protocol-Translation Approach

The protocol-translation approach is illustrated in Figure 14-3a. As was mentioned before, a protocol translator serves as a link between two dissimilar connections. Across multiple hops, different translators might be needed to link different pairs of connections.

A major objection to this approach is its special-purpose nature. If individual networks or communities of stations are allowed to define their own connection-oriented protocol, a great number of unique protocol translators must be implemented. At the worst, if there are N communities of stations, each with a unique connection-oriented protocol, and full connectivity is required, then the number of unique protocol translators is

$$\binom{N}{2} = \frac{N!}{(N-2)!2} = \frac{N(N-1)}{2}$$

Thus the number of translators grows with the square of the number of communities.

A second problem is that it may be difficult to match differing control mechanisms and services. For example, protocol A may allow interrupt packets, which are to be delivered as soon as possible, bypassing packets already en route. If protocol B does not provide this service, there is not much an A-B translator can do about it. In effect, the use of protocol translation reduces service to the least common denominator of all protocols in a path between endpoints.

A third problem is that there is no corrective end-to-end mechanism. Once a path through a series of gateways is set up, there appears to be no easy way to recover from a gateway failure. IP, in contrast, adapts readily to such an event.

Problems with the IP Approach

Because of the difficulties of using protocol translators, internetworking protocols such as IP and X.75 have been developed and are widely used. Because of the flexibility of IP, this and similar protocols have been used extensively for linking local networks together. Figure 14-10 illustrates the protocol architecture involved.

This approach presents difficulties, stemming from the distinct differences between local and long-haul networks. The two key differences are:

- *Speed:* Local network links are typically in the range of 1 to 50 Mbps. Long-haul links are often 56 kbps or less.
- *Outstanding packets:* The local network link is generally direct—no intermediate switches—and fast enough that one packet is delivered before another is sent out. On a long-haul network, there may be a number of packets outstanding between stations.

Let us consider these differences in the context of Figure 14-14. With the use of IP, packets sent from A may arrive at C out of order—either because multiple routes are used or because a packet is lost. It is up to a higher-layer protocol (transport) in the station to buffer the packets and pass them on to the application in correct order. This places a burden on local networks heretofore not required.

Next, consider that with IP both error and flow control may be handled simply by discarding packets. The transport layer is expected to exercise end-to-end flow control and to recover from errors via the sequence number mechanism. Because of the mismatch in speed between local and long-haul networks, this lack of hop-by-hop control is undesirable. If a local network floods a long haul gateway, which simply discards the overflow, a positive feedback mechanism may arise, in which the local network continues to send new packets to the gateway and retransmits old ones.

Finally, note that the use of the IP approach suggests that both IP and the complex transport protocol needed for reliable internet communication are also used for intranetwork communication (A-to-B) traffic in Figure 14-14). However, to exploit

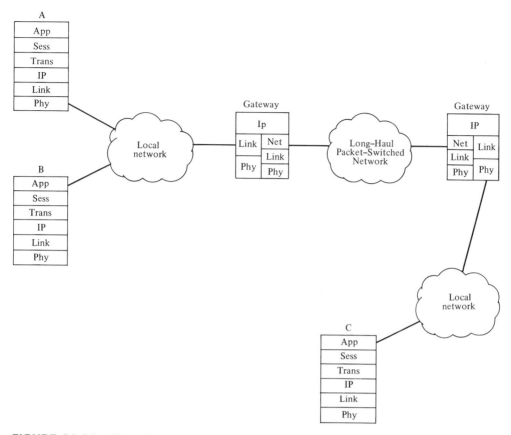

FIGURE 14-14. Use of IP to interconnect local networks.

fully the high speed of the local network for distributed processing, the protocol processing burden needs to be minimized. Speedups by factors of up to 30 by reducing the protocol overhead to the bare minimum have been reported [SPEC82]. Thus the use of IP and a complex transport protocol for intranetwork traffic imposes an unnecessary penalty on the local network.

Standardized Protocol Translation

As the preceding discussion indicates, the architecture of Figure 14-14 may not be desirable. As an alternative, consider the architecture suggested by Figure 14-15. For intra-local-network communication (*A-B*), a minimal communication architecture is used. Each station contains the functionality to control the local network (physical, link). In addition, there is a stripped-down session/transport protocol that provides the basic connection service for applications. This architecture takes advantage of the properties of the local network, including reliability and sequenced delivery.

Now consider the need for stations in two different local networks (*A-C*, *B-C*) to communicate across one or more intermediate networks. Communication is achieved as follows (using *A-C* in Figure 14-16 as an example):

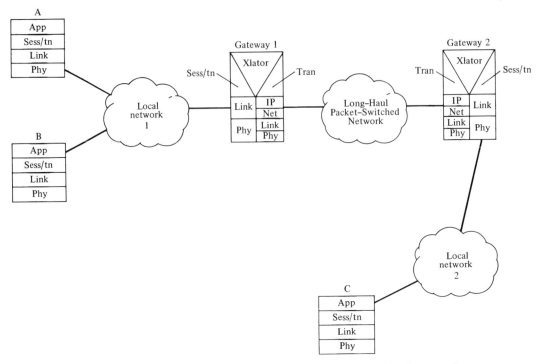

FIGURE 14-15. Use of a protocol translator to interconnect local networks.

1. The application in station *A* requests a connection to the application in station *C*.
2. The address specified is off-network, so the request is delivered to gateway 1.
3. The translator at gateway 1 sets up a reliable connection to gateway 2 using a full-blown transport protocol and IP (there may be multiple intermediate networks).
4. Gateway 2 establishes a local network connection with station *C*.

Thus there are three reliable connections strung together: a local network connection from *A* to 1, a transport connection from 1 to 2, and a local network connection from 2 to *C*. To the application in *A*, it appears that a single session/transport connection has been made to *C*. In fact, that connection terminates at gateway 1, with the translator acting as a surrogate application; that is, the translator represents an application that executes on a remote local network.

The key to making this scheme work is that there is only one local network session/transport protocol, used by all stations on all local networks, and that all gateways communicate using the same transport and internet protocols. This approach overcomes the difficulties cited earlier:

- There is only one protocol translator, not $N(N-1)/2$ of them.
- If the long-haul transport protocol is "full service," it can provide all the services requested locally.

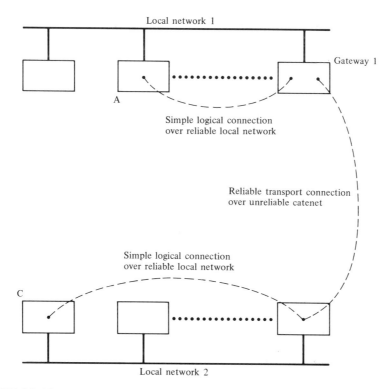

Local network 1

Gateway 1

A

Simple logical connection
over reliable local network

Reliable transport connection
over unreliable catenet

Simple logical connection
over reliable local network

C

Local network 2

FIGURE 14-16.   Logical structure of a connection using protocol translators.

- The intermediate portion of the connection uses IP for robustness and a transport protocol for end-to-end reliability.

It should be kept in mind, however, that this approach is tailored to intercommunication among stations attached to local networks. In the more general case, a station attached to a local network will require communication to some stations on the catenet that are not themselves connected to a local network. These stations will not share the simplified protocol suite of the local network stations. For this more general case, the IP type of approach is, at present, the most appropriate.

14-6

RECOMMENDED READING

The best overall discussion of internetworking is [CERF78]. [UNSO81] contains a description of X.75. A good general discussion of the IP approach is presented in [NBS80a]. Other useful discussions: [DRIV79], [POST81], [SHEL82], and [HIND83]. A comparison of X.75 and IP can be found in [POST80]. [CALL83] looks at internetworking from an OSI perspective.

For local networks, specific discussions of internetworking can be found in [STAL83c], [STAL84a], and [WAIN83]. [WARN80] lists some of the problems of including local networks in an IP catenet. [DALA82] is a readable and thorough discussion of the Ethernet approach. [SUNS79] is an interesting checklist of design issues. [MARS83] and [STEW84] describes the bridge mechanism.

PROBLEMS

14-1 Compare X.75 and IP. What are the principal strengths and weaknesses of each?

14-2 X.75 does not include the following packet types: Call Indication, Call Accepted, and Clear Indication. Why not?

14-3 Assume a local network is to be attached to a long-haul X.25 network via a single station which appears to the X.25 network as a single DTE. What gateway logic in the station would allow other local network stations to have access to the X.25 network?

14-4 An IP datagram is to be fragmented. Which options in the option field need to be copied into the header of each fragment, and which need only be retained in the first fragment?

14-5 Because of fragmentation, an IP datagram can arrive in pieces, not necessarily in the right order. The IP layer at the receiving host must accumulate these fragments until the original datagram is reconstituted.
  a. Consider that the IP layer creates a buffer for assembling the datagram. As assembly proceeds the buffer will consist of data and "holes" between the data. Describe an algorithm for reassembly based on this concept.
  b. For the algorithm above, it is necessary to keep track of the holes. Describe a simple mechanism for doing this.

14-6 A transport layer message consisting of 1500 bits of data and 160 bits of header is sent to an internet layer which appends another 160 bits of header. This is then transmitted through two networks, each of which uses a 24-bit packet header. The destination network has a maxium packet size of 800 bits. How many bits, including headers, are delivered to the network layer protocol at the destination?

14-7 The ICMP format includes the first 64 bits of the datagram data field. What might be the purpose of including these bits?

14-8 The architecture suggested by Figure 14-14 is to be used. What functions could be added to the gateways to alleviate some of the problems caused by the mismatched local and long-haul networks?

CHAPTER 15

Transport Protocols

The transport protocol is the keystone of the whole concept of a computer-communications architecture. Lower-layer protocols are needed, to be sure, but they are less important pedagogically and to designers for a number of reasons. For one thing, lower-level protocols are better understood and, on the whole, less complex than transport protocols. Also, standards have settled out quite well for most kinds of layer 1 to 3 transmission facilities, and there is a large body of experience in their use.

Viewed from the other side, upper level protocols are also of lesser importance. The transport protocol provides the basic end-to-end service of transferring data between users. Any process or application can be programmed to access directly the transport services without going through session and presentation layers. Indeed, this is the normal mode of operation for DOD's transport protocols.

The author's conviction of the importance of the transport protocol, together with the remarkable complexity of such protocols, has led to a rather long chapter. For this, the reader's indulgence is begged. We begin by looking at the services that one might expect from a transport protocol. Next, we examine the protocol mechanisms required to provide these services. We find that most of the complexity relates to connection-oriented services. As might be expected, the less the network service provides, the more the transport protocol must do. We then look briefly at the types of network services that might be provided. Finally, two sets of protocol standards are examined.

TRANSPORT SERVICES

We begin by looking at the kinds of services that a transport protocol can or should provide to higher-level protocols. Figure 15-1 places the concept of transport services in context. In a system, there is a transport entity which provides services to transport users, which might be an application process or a session protocol entity. This local transport entity communicates with some remote transport entity, using the services of some lower layer, such as the network layer.

We have already mentioned that the general service provided by a transport protocol is the end-to-end transport of data in a way that shields the user from the details of the underlying communications systems. To be more specific, we must consider the specific services that a transport protocol can provide. The following categories of service, based on [NBS80b], are useful for describing the transport service:

- Type of service.
- Grade of service.
- Data transfer.
- User interface.
- Connection management.
- Expedited delivery.
- Status reporting.
- Security.

Type of Service

Two basic types of service are possible: connection-oriented and connectionless or datagram service. A connection-oriented service provides for the establishment,

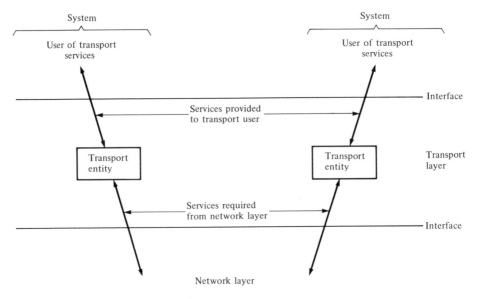

FIGURE 15-1. Transport entity context.

maintenance, and termination of a logical connection between transport users. This has, so far, been the most common type of protocol service available and has a wide variety of applications. The connection-oriented service generally implies that the service is reliable.

The strengths of the connection-oriented approach are clear. It allows connection-related features such as flow control, error control, and sequenced delivery. Connectionless service, however, is more appropriate in some contexts. At lower layers (internet, network), connectionless service is more robust (e.g., see discussion in Section 9-2). In addition, it represents a "least common denominator" of service to be expected at higher layers. Further, even at transport and above there is justification for a connectionless service. There are instances in which the overhead of connection establishment and maintenance is unjustified or even counterproductive. Some examples, listed in [CHAP82]:

- *Inward data collection:* involves the periodic active or passive sampling of data sources, such as sensors, and automatic self-test reports from security equipment or network components. In a real-time monitoring situation, the loss of an occasional data unit would not cause distress, since the next report should arrive shortly.
- *Outward data dissemination:* includes broadcast messages to network users, the announcement of a new node or the change of address of a service, and the distribution of real-time clock values.
- *Request-response:* applications in which a transaction service is provided by a common server to a number of distributed users, and for which a single request-response sequence is typical. Use of the service is regulated at the application level, and lower level connections are often unnecessary and cumbersome.
- *Real-time applications:* such as voice and telemetry, involving a degree of redundancy and/or a real-time transmission requirement. These must not have connection-oriented functions such as retransmission.

Thus, there is a place at the transport level for both a connection-oriented and a connectionless type of service.

Grade of Service

The transport protocol entity should allow the transport user to specify the grade or quality of transmission service to be provided. The transport entity will attempt to optimize the use of the underlying link, network, and catenet resources to the best of its ability, to provide the collective requested services.

Examples of services that might be requested:

- Acceptable error and loss levels.
- Desired average and maximum delay.
- Desired average and minimum throughput.
- Priority levels.

Of course, the transport entity is limited to the inherent capabilities of the underlying service. For example, IP does provide a grade of service parameter. It allows specification of eight levels of precedence or priority, and a binary specification for normal or low delay, normal or high throughput, and normal or high reliability. Thus, the transport entity can "pass the buck" to the internetwork entity, which is still dependent on the underlying transmission facilities. Another example: X.25 provides for throughput class negotiation as an optional user facility. The network may alter flow control parameters and the amount of network resources allocated on a virtual circuit to achieve desired throughput.

The transport layer may also resort to other mechanisms to try to satisfy user requests, such as splitting one transport connection among multiple virtual circuits to enhance throughput.

The user of the grade of service feature needs to recognize that:

- Depending on the nature of the transmission facility, the transport entity will have varying degrees of success in providing a requested grade of service.
- There is bound to be a trade-off among reliability, delay, throughput, and cost of services.

Nevertheless, certain applications would benefit from, or even require, certain grades of service and, in a hierarchical or layered architecture, the easiest way for an application to extract this grade of service from a transmission facility is to pass the request down to the transport protocol.

Examples of applications that might request particular grades of service:

- A file transfer protocol might require high throughput. It may also require high reliability to avoid retransmissions at the file transfer level.
- A transaction protocol (e.g., data-base query) may require low delay.
- An electronic mail protocol may require multiple priority levels.

One approach to providing a variety of grades of service is to include a grade of service facility within the protocol. We have seen this with IP and will see that transport protocols to be discussed later follow the same approach. An alternative is to provide a different transport protocol for different classes of traffic. Four types of transport protocol are suggested in [MCFA79]:

- A reliable connection-oriented protocol.
- A less reliable connectionless protocol.
- A speech protocol, requiring sequenced, timely delivery.
- A real-time protocol that requires high reliability and timeliness.

Data Transfer

The whole purpose, of course, of a transport protocol is to transfer data between two transport entities. Both user data and control data must be transferred, either on the same channel or separate channels. Full-duplex service must be provided. Half-duplex and simplex modes may also be offered to support peculiarities of particular users.

User Interface

It is not clear that the exact mechanism of the user interface to the transport protocol should be standardized. Rather, it should be optimized to the station environment. As examples, a transport entity's services could be invoked by:

- Procedure calls.
- Passing of data and parameters to a process through a mailbox.

- Use of direct memory access (DMA) between a host user and a front-end processor containing the transport entity.

A few characteristics of the interface may be specified however. For example, a mechanism is needed to prevent the user from swamping the transport entity with data. A similar mechanism is needed to prevent the transport entity from swamping a user with data. Another aspect of the interface has to do with the timing and significance of confirmations. Consider: A transport user passes data to a transport entity to be delivered to a remote user. The local transport entity can acknowledge receipt of the data immediately, or it can wait until the remote transport entity reports that the data have made it through to the other end. Perhaps the most useful interface is one that allows immediate acceptance or rejection of requests, with later confirmation of the end-to-end significance.

In discussing the interaction between a transport entity and its user, it is useful to think in terms of primitives and parameters being exchanged, and to depict them as shown in Figure 15-2. The generic primitives shown are:

- *Request:* initiated by the transport user to activate a particular service.
- *Indication:* provided by the transport entity to advise of the activation of a particular service.
- *Response:* provided by a transport user in reply to an indication primitive.
- *Confirmation:* returned to the requesting transport user upon completion of a requested service.

The layout in Figure 15-2 suggest the typical time ordering of these events. We shall have occasion to use this notation in what follows.

Connection Management

When connection-oriented service is provided. The transport entity is responsible for establishing and terminating connections. A symmetric connection establishment procedure should be provided, which allows either user to initiate connection establishment. An asymmetric procedure may also be provided to support simplex connections.

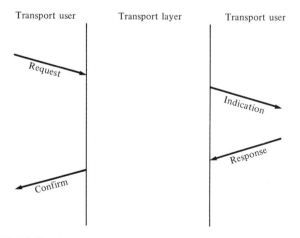

FIGURE 15-2. Interaction primitives.

Connection termination can be either abrupt or graceful. With an abrupt termination, data in transit may be lost. A graceful termination prevents either side from shutting down until all data have been delivered.

Expedited Delivery

A service similar to that provided by priority classes is the expedited delivery of data. Some data submitted to the transport service may supersede data submitted previously. The transport entity will endeavor to have the transmission facility transfer the data as rapidly as possible. At the receiving end, the transport entity will interrupt the user to notify it of the receipt of urgent data. Thus the expedited data service is in the nature of an interrupt mechanism, and is used to transfer occasional urgent data, such as a break character from a terminal or an alarm condition. In contrast, a priority service might dedicate resources and adjust parameters such that, on average, higher priority data are delivered more quickly.

Status Reporting

A status reporting service allows the transport user to obtain or be notified of information concerning the condition or attributes of the transport entity or a transport connection. Examples of status information:

- Performance characteristics of a connection (e.g., throughput, mean delay).
- Addresses (network, transport).
- Class of protocol in use.
- Current timer values.
- State of protocol "machine" supporting a connection.
- Degredation in requested grade of service.

Security

The transport entity may provide a variety of security services. Access control may be provided in the form of local verification of sender and remote verification of receiver. The transport service may also include encryption/decryption of data on demand. Finally, the transport entity may be capable of routing through secure links or nodes if such a service is available from the transmission facility.

15-2
PROTOCOL MECHANISMS

It is the purpose of this section to make good on our claim that a transport protocol may need to be very complex. For purposes of clarity we present the transport protocol mechanisms in an evolutionary fashion. We begin with a network service that makes life easy for the transport protocol and define the required mechanisms. As the network service is made progressively less capable, the transport protocol becomes progressively more complex.

The ISO has defined three types of network service [ISO83b]:

- *Type A:* network connections with acceptable residual error rate and acceptable rate of signaled failures.
- *Type B:* network connections with acceptable residual error rate but unacceptable rate of signaled failures.
- *Type C:* network connections with residual error rate not acceptable to the transport service user.

In this context, an error is defined as a lost or duplicated network protocol data unit. If the error is caught and corrected by the network service in a fashion that is transparent to the transport entity, no damage is done. If the network service detects an error, cannot recover, and signals the transport entities, this is known as a signaled failure. An example would be the notification by X.25 that a RESET has occurred. Finally, there are residual errors—those which are not corrected and for which the transport entity is not notified.

Type A provides a reliable network service. This makes life easy for the transport protocol designer. It is well to examine this case, because it helps to clarify the basic transport mechanisms. We will then see that most of the complexity of a transport protocol occurs when the underlying service is unreliable.

Following [MCQU78], we consider three subcases of Type A, which present progressively greater difficulties to the transport service:

- Reliable, sequencing network service with arbitrary message size.
- Reliable, nonsequencing network service with arbitrary message size.
- Reliable, nonsequencing network service with maximum message size.

An example of the first case would be reliable X.25 service. The second and third cases might, for example, be reliable datagram services.

In what follows, we will concern ourselves primarily with the most stringent requirement for a transport protocol: The user of the transport service requires a reliable, sequenced, connection-oriented service. It should be clear to the reader what the implications would be of less stringent requirements.

We now consider each of the five types of network service (three subcases of Type A; Type B; Type C).

Reliable Sequencing Network Service

In this case, we assume that the network service will accept messages of arbitrary length and will, with virtually 100% reliability, deliver them in sequence to the destination. These assumptions allow the development of the simplest possible transport protocol. Four issues need to be addressed:

- Addressing.
- Multiplexing.
- Flow Control.
- Connection establishment/termination.

Addressing. The issue concerned with addressing is simply this: a user of a given transport entity wishes to either establish a connection with or make a connectionless data transfer to a user of some other transport entity. The target user needs to be specified by all of the following.

- User identification.
- Transport entity identification.
- Station address.
- Network number.

Recalling our discussion in Section 12-1, user addresses can be either flat or hierarchical. Regardless, the transport protocol must be able to derive the information listed above from the user address. Typically, the user address is specified as (*Station*, *Port*). The *Port* variable represents a particular user. Generally, there will be a single transport entity at each station, so a transport entity identification is not needed. If more than one transport entity is present, there is usually only one of each type. In this latter case, the address should include a designation of the type of transport protocol (e.g., TCP, User Datagram). In the case of a single network, *Station* identifies an attached network device. In the case of a catenet, Station subsumes a network number which can be derived at the internet layer.

Since routing is not a concern of the transport layer, it simply passes the Station portion of the address down to the network service. Port is included in a transport header, to be used at the destination by the destination transport protocol.

One question remains to be addressed: How does the initiating transport user know the address of the destination transport user? We discussed this problem briefly in Section 12-1, and elaborate here. Two static and two dynamic strategies suggest themselves:

1. The user must know the address it wishes to use ahead of time. This is basically a system configuration function.
2. Some commonly used services are assigned "well-known addresses."
3. A name server is provided. The user requests a service by some generic or global name. The request is sent to the name server, which does a directory lookup and returns an address. The transport entity then proceeds with the connection.
4. In some cases, the target user is to be a process that is spawned at request time. The initiating user can send a process request to a well known address. The user at that address is a privileged system process that will spawn the new process and return an address.

To see that these are distinct cases, we give an example of each:

1. A process may be running that is only of concern to a limited number of transport users. A process in a station may collect statistics on performance. From time to time, a central network management routine connects to the process to obtain the statistics. These processes generally are not, and should not be, well known and accessible to all.
2. Examples of commonly used services are time sharing and word processing.
3. Some services may be commonly used, but their location may change from time to time. For example, a data entry process may be moved from one station to another on a local network to balance load. The names of such "movable" processes can be kept in a directory, with the addresses updated when a move occurs.
4. A programmer has developed a private application (e.g., a simulation program) that will execute on a remote mainframe but be invoked from a local minicomputer. An RJE-type request can be issued to a remote job-management process which spawns the simulation process.

Multiplexing. We now turn to the concept of multiplexing, which also was discussed in general terms in Section 12-1. With respect to the interface between the transport protocol and higher-level protocols, the transport protocol performs a multiplexing/ demultiplexing function. That is, multiple users employ the same transport protocol, and are distinguished by port numbers or service access points.

The transport entity may also perform a multiplexing function with respect to the network services that it uses. Recall that we defined upward multiplexing as the multiplexing of multiple (N) connections on a single (N-1) connection, and downward multiplexing as the splitting of a single (N) connection among multiple (N-1) connections.

Consider, for example, a transport entity making use of an X.25 service. Why should the transport entity employ upward multiplexing? There are, after all, 4095 virtual circuits available. In the typical case, this is more than enough to handle all active transport users. However, most X.25 networks base part of their charge on virtual circuit connect time, since each virtual circuit consumes some node buffer resources. Thus, if a single virtual circuit provides sufficient throughput for multiple transport users, upward multiplexing is indicated.

On the other hand, downward multiplexing or splitting might be used to improve throughput. If, for example, each X.25 virtual circuit is restricted to a 3-bit sequence number, only seven packets can be outstanding at a time. A larger sequence space might be needed for high-delay networks. Of course, throughput can only be increased so far. If there is a single station-node link over which all virtual circuits are multiplexed, the throughput of a transport connection cannot exceed the data rate of that link.

Flow Control. The ISO document [ISO83a] defines flow control as a function for the control of the data flow within a layer or between adjacent layers. Whereas flow control is a relatively simple mechanism at the link layer, it is a rather complex mechanism at the transport layer, for two main reasons:

- Flow control at the transport level involves the interaction of transport users, transport entities, and the network service.
- The transmission delay between transport entities is generally long compared to actual transmission time and, what is worse, variable.

Figure 15-3 illustrates the first point. Transport user A wishes to send data to transport user B over a transport connection. We can view the situation as involving four queues. A generates data and queues it up to send. A must wait to send that data until

- It has permission from B (peer flow control), and,
- It has permission from its own transport entity (interface flow control).

As data flows down from A to transport entity a, a queues the data until it has permission to send it on from b and the network service. The data are then handed to the network layer for delivery to b. The network service must queue the data until it receives permission from b to pass them on. Finally, b must await B's permission before delivering the data to their destination.

To see the effects of delay, consider the possible interactions depicted in Figure 15-4. When a user wishes to transmit data, it sends these data to its transport entity (e.g., using a SEND call). This triggers two events. The transport entity generates one or more transport protocol data units (TPDUs) and passes these on to the

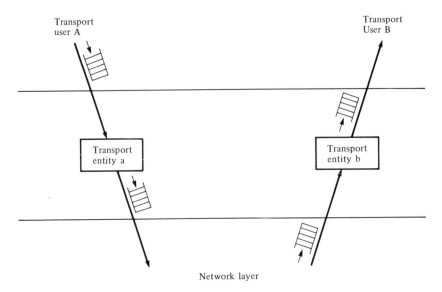

FIGURE 15-3. Queuing representation of connection-oriented data transfer.

network service. It also in some way acknowledges to the user that it has accepted the data for transmission. At this point, the transport entity can exercise flow control across the user-transport interface by simply withholding its acknowledgment. The transport entity is most likely to do this if the entity itself is being held up by a flow control exercised by either the network service or the target transport entity.

In any case, once the transport entity has accepted the data, it sends out a TPDU. Some time later, it receives an acknowledgment that the data have been received at the remote end. It then sends a confirmation to the sender.

At the receiving end, a TPDU arrives at the transport entity. It unwraps the data and sends them on (e.g., by an Indication primitive) to the destination user. When the user accepts the data, it issues an acknowledgment (e.g., in the form of a RESPONSE primitive). The user can exercise flow control over the transport entity by withholding its response.

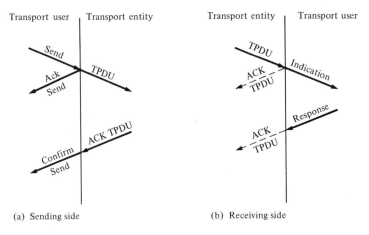

FIGURE 15-4. User—transport interaction.

Now, the target transport entity has two choices regarding acknowledgment. Either it can issue an acknowledgment as soon as it has correctly received the TPDU (the usual practice), or it can wait until it knows that the user has correctly received the data before acknowledging. The latter course is the safer. In the latter case, the send confirmation is in fact a confirmation that the destination user received the data. In the former case, it merely confirms that the data made it through to the remote transport entity.

With the discussion above in mind, we can cite two reasons why one transport entity would want to restrain the rate of TPDU transmission over a connection from another transport entity:

- The user of the receiving transport entity cannot keep up with the flow of data.
- The receiving transport entity itself cannot keep up with the flow of TPDUs.

How do such problems manifest themselves? Well, presumably a transport entity has a certain amount of buffer space. Incoming TPDUs are added to the buffer. Each buffered TPDU is processed (i.e., examine the transport header) and the data are sent to the user. Either of the two problems mentioned above will cause the buffer to fill up. Thus the transport entity needs to take steps to stop or slow the flow of TPDUs to prevent buffer overflow. This requirement is not so easy to fulfill, because of the annoying time gap between sender and receiver. We return to this point in a moment. First, we present four ways of coping with the flow control requirement. The receiving transport entity can:

1. Do nothing.
2. Refuse to accept further TPDUs from the network service.
3. Use a fixed sliding-window protocol.
4. Use a credit scheme.

Alternative 1 means that the TPDUs that overflow the buffer are discarded. The sending transport entity, failing to get an acknowledgment, will retransmit. This is a shame, since the advantage of a reliable network is that one never has to retransmit. Furthermore, the effect of this maneuver is to exacerbate the problem! The sender has increased its output to include new TPDUs plus retransmitted old TPDUs.

The second alternative is a backpressure mechanism that relies on the network service to do the work. When a buffer of a transport entity is full, it refuses additional data from the network service. This triggers flow control procedures within the network that throttle the network service at the sending end. This service, in turn, refuses additional TPDUs from its transport entity. It should be clear that this mechanism is clumsy and coarse-grained. For example, if multiple transport connections are multiplexed on a single network connection (virtual circuit), flow control is exercised only on the aggregate of all transport connections. Remarkably, there is at least one transport protocol that uses this strategy: the EHKP4 protocol standard developed in West Germany [MEIJ82].

The third alternative is already familiar to you from our discussions of link layer protocols. The key ingredients, recall, are:

- The use of sequence numbers on data units.
- The use of a window of fixed size.
- The use of acknowledgments to advance the window.

With a reliable network service, the sliding window technique would actually work quite well. For example, consider a protocol with a window size of 7. Whenever the sender receives an acknowledgment to a particular TPDU, it is automatically authorized to send the succeeding seven TPDUs (of course, some may already have been sent). Now, when the receiver's buffer capacity gets down to seven TPDUs, it can withhold acknowledgment of incoming TPDUs to avoid overflow. The sending transport entity can send at most seven additional TPDUs and then must stop. Since the underlying network service is reliable, the sender will not time out and retransmit. Thus, at some point, a sending transport entity may have a number of TPDUs outstanding for which no acknowledgment has been received. Since we are dealing with a reliable network, the sending transport entity can assume that the TPDUs will get through and that the lack of acknowledgment is a flow control tactic. This tactic would not work well in an unreliable network, since the sending transport entity would not know whether the lack of acknowledgment is due to flow control or a lost TPDU.

The fourth alternative, a credit scheme, provides the receiver with a greater degree of control over data flow. Although it is not strictly necessary with a reliable

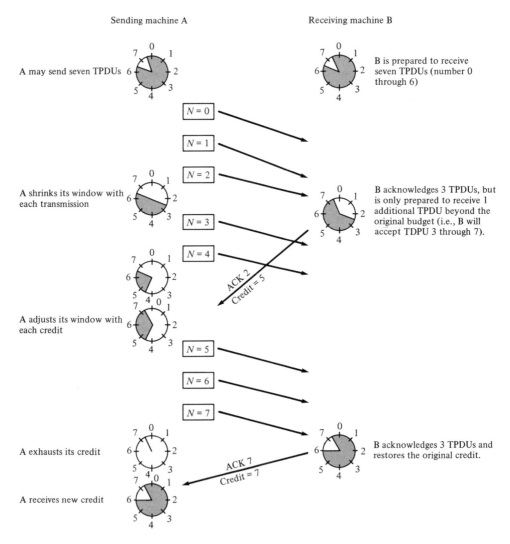

FIGURE 15-5.   Example of a credit allocation protocol.

network service, a credit scheme should result in a smoother traffic flow. Further, it is a more effective scheme with an unreliable network service, as we shall see.

The credit scheme decouples acknowledgment from flow control. In fixed sliding-window protocols, such as X.25, the two are synonymous. In a credit scheme, a TPDU may be acknowledged without granting new credit, and vice versa. Figure 15-5 illustrates the protocol (compare Figure 5-7). For simplicity, we show a data flow in one direction only. In this example, TPDUs are numbered sequentially modulo 8. Initially, through the connection establishment process, the sending and receiving sequence numbers are synchronized and A is granted a credit allocation of 7. A advances the trailing edge of its window each time that it transmits, and advances the leading edge only when it is granted credit.

In both the credit allocation scheme and the sliding window scheme, the receiver needs to adopt some policy concerning the amount of data it permits the sender to transmit. The conservative approach is to only allow new TPDUs up to the limit of available buffer space. If this policy were in effect in Figure 15-5, the first credit message implies that B has five free buffer slots, and the second message that B has seven free slots.

A conservative flow control scheme may limit the throughput of the transport connection in long-delay situations. The receiver could potentially increase throughput by optimistically granting credit for space it does not have. For example, if a receiver's buffer is full but it anticipates that it can release space for two TPDUs within a round-trip propagation time, it could immediately send a credit of 2. If the receiver can keep up with the sender, this scheme may increase throughput and can do no harm. If the sender is faster than the receiver, however, some TPDUs may be discarded, necessitating a retransmission. Since retransmissions are not otherwise necessary with a reliable network service, an optimistic flow control scheme will complicate the protocol.

Connection Establishment and Termination. Even with a reliable network service, there is a need for connection establishment and termination procedures to support connection-oriented service. Connection establishment serves three main purposes:

- It allows each end to assure that the other exists.
- It allows negotiation of optional parameters (e.g., TPDU size, window size, grade of service).
- It triggers allocation of transport entity resources (e.g., buffer space, entry in connection table).

Connection establishment is by mutual agreement and can be accomplished by a simple set of user commands and control TPDUs, as shown in the state diagram of Figure 15-6. To begin, a user is in an IDLE state (with respect to the transport entity). The user can signal that it will passively wait for a request with a LISTEN command. A server program, such as time sharing or a file transfer application, might do this. The user may change its mind by sending a CLOSE command.

After the LISTEN command is issued, the transport entity creates a connection object of some sort (i.e., a table entry) that is in the LSTN state. If a RFC (request for connection) TPDU is received that specifies the listening user, then a connection is opened. To do this, the transport entity:

- Signals the user that a connection is open.
- Sends an RFC as confirmation to the remote transport entity.
- Puts the connection object in an OPEN state.

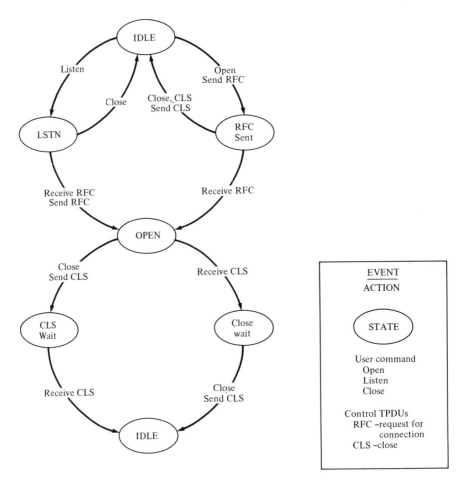

FIGURE 15-6. Simple connection state diagram.

A user may open a connection by issuing an OPEN command, which triggers the transport entity to send an RFC. The reception of a matching RFC establishes the connection. The connection is prematurely aborted if the local user issues a CLOSE command or the remote transport entity refuses the connection by sending a CLS TPDU.

Figure 15-7 shows the robustness of this protocol. Either side can initiate a connection. Further, if both sides initiate the connection at about the same time, it is established without confusion.

The reader may ask what happens if an RFC comes in while the requested user is idle (not listening). Three courses may be followed:

- The transport entity can reject the request by sending a CLS.
- The request can be queued until a LISTEN is issued by the user.
- The transport entity can interrupt or otherwise signal the user to notify it of a pending request.

Note that if the latter mechanism is used, a Listen command is not strictly necessary, but may be replaced by an Accept command, which is a signal from the user to the transport entity that it accepts the request for connection.

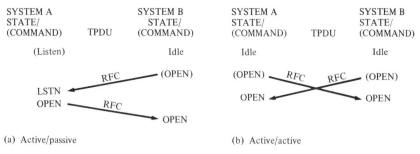

FIGURE 15-7. **Connection establishment sequence of events.**

Connection termination is handled similarly. Either side, or both sides, may initiate a close. The connection is closed by mutual agreement. This strategy allows for either abrupt or graceful termination. To achieve the latter, a connection in the CLS WAIT state must continue to accept data TPDUs until a CLS is received.

Reliable Nonsequencing Network Service

In this case, we assume that the network service will accept messages of arbitrary length and will, with virtually 100% reliability, deliver them to the destination. However, we now assume that the TPDUs may arrive out of sequence. This seemingly trivial change has a number of consequences.

The first consequence is that sequence numbers are required on TPDUs for connection-oriented service. We employ them with a reliable sequencing network service for flow control purposes. Here they are required to permit the transport entity to deliver data in sequence.

Equally important, the transport entity must keep track of control TPDUs, both in relationship to each other and to data TPDUs. Examples of this requirement are seen in flow control and in connection establishment and termination.

First, consider flow control. A transport entity may sometimes find it desirable to decrease outstanding offered credit on a connection, because expected resources did not become available, or because resources had to be reallocated to serve another connection. If sequencing is not guaranteed, a situation such as that shown in Figure 15-8 might arise. After transport entity A has sent TPDU 1, B responds with a new credit allocation of 5. A short time later, and before additional TPDUs arrive, B discovers a potential shortfall and sends a reduced credit allocation of 3. However, this allocation overtakes the earlier one and arrives first. It appears to A that B has initially granted an allocation of 3 and then obtained additional resources, and increased the allocation to 5. Thus, while B is not prepared to receive any more TPDUs at this point, A feels entitled to send two additional TPDUs. The solution to this problem is to number credit allocations sequentially.

Now consider connection establishment. Figure 15-6 shows that after a transport entity has sent an RFC, it expects to receive either a CLS (connection reject) or RFC (connection accept) from the target entity. The target transport entity, having received the opening RFC, might respond with RFC, followed by a number of TPDUs. One of these TPDUs could arrive back at the initiating entity prior to the RFC. The best policy would seem to be for the initiating transport entity to queue these TPDUs until the RFC is received that confirms the connection.

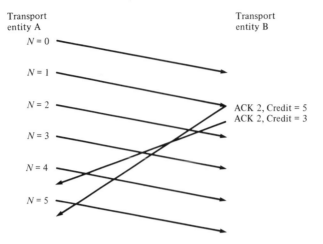

Transport
entity A

Transport
entity B

$N = 0$

$N = 1$

$N = 2$ ACK 2, Credit = 5
                 ACK 2, Credit = 3

$N = 3$

$N = 4$

$N = 5$

FIGURE 15-8. Example of flow control with a nonsequenced network service.

Just as data may arrive before a connection is officially open, they may also arrive after the connection has closed. The following may occur. After a transport entity has sent its last data TPDU, it sends a CLS. The CLS may arrive before the last data TPDU. One way to avoid a problem is for the CLS TPDU to contain the next sequence number after the last data TPDU sent on this connection. Then, the receiving transport entity, upon receiving a CLS, will wait if necessary for late-arriving data TPDUs before closing the connection.

Reliable Nonsequencing Network Service with Maximum TPDU Size

We now add another limitation to the capability of the network service: It will only accept TPDUs of some maximum size for transfer. Presumably, this size is chosen to optimize network performance.

We need to distinguish two types of data transfer required by the user: stream oriented and block oriented. A stream-oriented interface between transport and the user accepts data as if they were a continuous stream of bits and reproduces the stream at the other end without conveying any information about the breakpoints in the stream submitted by the sender. This interface might serve voice and real-time applications.

A more common occurrence is a transport user that sends data in blocks. For convenience, we refer to a block of data presented to transport as a *letter*. If a letter exceeds the maximum allowable TPDU size, the transport entity must fragment the letter before transmission, to be reassembled at reception prior to delivery to the user. Because our network is nonsequencing, fragments may arrive out of order. Worse, fragments from different letters may be interchanged en route.

A simple solution to this problem is to number each letter sequentially and to number each fragment sequentially within each letter. This, however, is an unnecessary duplication of the TPDU sequence numbering function. A moment's thought should make it clear that all that is required is an end-of-letter (EOL) flag. As TPDUs arrive at the destination transport entity, they are reordered. Each sequential set of TPDUs, starting with the first TPDU after an EOL, and including all TPDUs through the next EOL, are treated as a unit. The data from this unit, stripped of transport headers, are delivered as a single letter to the user.

A variation on the foregoing approach is to apply the sequence numbers to the data rather than the TPDUs. An example of this was discussed in Chapter 14, namely the fragmentation and reassmbly technique for IP.

Failure-Prone Network Service

We now turn to what may strike the reader as an unusual sort of network. This is a connection-oriented network service and, while it delivers data reliably (though not necessarily in sequence), it suffers from network failures that cause it to reset or restart network connections. Thus TPDUs may be lost, but the loss is reported to the transport entities affected. The reader might visualize an X.25 network service being provided by a relatively unreliable underlying network.

In any case, the transport entity must now cope with the problem of recovering from known loss of data and/or network connections. The sequence numbering scheme provides an effective tool. In the normal course of events, TPDUs need not be acknowledged, since the network service is reliable. However, acknowledgment takes place from time to time in connection with the flow control scheme. We show this mechanism also deals with network failure.

First, consider a connection reset, such as the X.25 RESET command will cause. The network service will signal the transport entity that a reset has occurred on one or more transport connections. The transport entity realizes that it has perhaps lost some incoming TPDUs in transit, and that some already-transmitted TPDUs may not reach their destination. Two actions are indicated:

- Issue a control TPDU to the other end that acknowledges a reset condition and gives the number of the last TPDU received.
- Refrain from issuing new data TPDUs until a corresponding reset control TPDU is received from the other end.

A more serious condition is the loss of an underlying network connection, such as an X.25 RESTART causes. In this case, the side that first initiated the connection should issue a request to the network service for a new network connection and then issue a control TPDU to the other side that identifies the new network connection for the ongoing transport connection. Following this, both sides must resynchronize with the use of reset control TPDUs.

Unreliable Network Service

The most difficult case for a transport protocol is that of an unreliable network service. The problem is not just that TPDUs are occasionally lost, but that TPDUs may arrive out of sequence due to variable transit delays. As we shall see, elaborate machinery is required to cope with these two interrelated network deficiencies. We shall also see that a discouraging pattern emerges. The combination of unreliability and nonsequencing creates problems with every mechanism we have discussed so far. Generally, the solution to each problem raises new problems. Although there are problems to be overcome for protocols at all levels, it seems that there are more difficulties with a reliable connection-oriented transport protocol than any other sort of protocol.

Six issues need to be addressed:

- Retransmission strategy.
- Duplicate detection.
- Flow control.
- Connection establishment.
- Connection termination.
- Crash recovery.

Retransmission Strategy. Two events necessitate the retransmission of a TPDU. First, the TPDU may be damaged in transit but nevertheless arrive at its destination. If a frame check sequence is included with the TPDU, the receiving transport entity can detect the error and discard the TPDU. The second contingency is that a TPDU fails to arrive. In either case, the sending transport entity does not know that the TPDU transmission was unsuccessful. To cover this contingency, we require that a positive acknowledgment (ACK) scheme be used: The receiver must acknowledge each successfully received TPDU. For efficiency, we do not require one ACK per TPDU. Rather, a cumulative acknowledgment can be used, as we have seen many times in this book. Thus the receiver may receive TPDUs numbered 1, 2, and 3, but only send ACK 3 back. The sender must interpret ACK 3 to mean that number 3 and all previous TPDUs have been successfully received.

If a TPDU does not arrive successfully, no ACK will be issued and a retransmission is in order. To cope with this situation, there must be a timer associated with each TPDU as it is sent. If the timer expires before the TPDU is acknowledged, the sender must retransmit.

So the addition of a timer solves that problem. Next problem: At what value should the timer be set? If the value is too small, there will be many unnecessary retransmissions, wasting network capacity. If the value is too large, the protocol will be sluggish in responding to a lost TPDU. The timer should be set at a value a bit longer than the round trip delay (send TPDU, receive ACK). Of course this delay is variable even under constant network load. Worse, the statistics of the delay will vary with changing network conditions.

Two strategies suggest themselves. A fixed timer value could be used, based on an understanding of the network's typical behavior. This suffers from an inability to respond to changing network conditions. If the value is set too high, the service will always be sluggish. If it is set too low, a positive feedback condition can develop, in which network congestion leads to more retransmissions, which increase congestion.

An adaptive scheme has its own problems. Suppose that the transport entity keeps track of the time taken to acknowledge data TPDUs and sets its retransmission timer based on the average of the observed delays. This value cannot be trusted for three reasons:

- The peer entity may not acknowledge a TPDU immediately. Recall that we gave it the privilege of cumulative acknowledgments.
- If a TPDU has been retransmitted, the sender cannot know whether the received ACK is a response to the initial transmission or the retransmission.
- Network conditions may change suddenly.

Each of these problems is a cause for some further tweaking of the transport algorithm, but the problem admits of no complete solution. There will always be some uncertainty concerning the best value for the retransmission timer.

TABLE 15-1 Transport Protocol Timers

Retransmission timer	Retransmit an unacknowledged TPDU
Reconnection timer	Minimum time between closing one connection and opening another with the same destination address
Window timer	Maximum time between ACK/CREDIT TPDUs
Retransmit-RFC timer	Time between attempts to open a connection
Give-up timer	Abort connection when no TPDUs are acknowledged

Incidentally, the retransmission timer is only one of a number of timers needed for proper functioning of a transport protocol. These are listed in Table 15-1, together with a brief explanation. Further discussion will be found in what follows.

Duplicate Detection. If a TPDU is lost and then retransmitted, no confusion will result. If however, an ACK is lost, one or more TPDUs will be retransmitted and, if they arrive successfully, be duplicates of previously received TPDUs. Thus the sender must be able to recognize duplicates. The fact that each TPDU carries a sequence number helps but, nevertheless, duplicate detection and handling is no easy thing. There are two cases:

- A duplicate is received prior to the close of the connection.
- A duplicate is received after the close of the connection.

Notice that we say "a" duplicate rather than "the" duplicate. From the sender's point of view, the retransmitted TPDU is the duplicate. However, the retransmitted TPDU may arrive before the original TPDU, in which case the receiver views the original TPDU as the duplicate. In any case, two tactics are needed to cope with a duplicate received prior to the close of a connection:

- The receiver must assume that its acknowledgment was lost and therefore must acknowledge the duplicate. Consequently, the sender must not get confused if it receives multiple ACKs to the same TPDU.
- The sequence number space must be long enough so as not to "cycle" in less than the maximum possible TPDU lifetime.

Figure 15-9 illustrates the reason for the latter requirement. In this example, the sequence space is of length 8. For simplicity, we assume a sliding-window protocol with a window size of 3. Suppose that A has transmitted TPDUs 0, 1, and 2 and receives no acknowledgments. Eventually, it times out and retransmits TPDU 0. B has received 1 and 2, but 0 is delayed in transit. Thus B does not send any ACKs. When the duplicate TPDU 0 arrives, B acknowledges 0, 1, and 2. Meanwhile, A has timed out again and retransmits 1, which B acknowledges with another ACK 2. Things now seem to have sorted themselves out and data transfer continues. When the sequence space is exhausted, A cycles back to sequence number 0 and continues. Alas, the old TPDU 0 makes a belated appearance and is accepted by B before the new TPDU 0 arrives.

It should be clear that the untimely emergence of the old TPDU would have caused no difficulty if the sequence numbers had not yet wrapped around. The problem is: How big must the sequence space be? This depends on, among other things, whether the network enforces a maximum packet lifetime, and the rate at which TPDUs are being transmitted. Fortunately, each addition of a single bit to

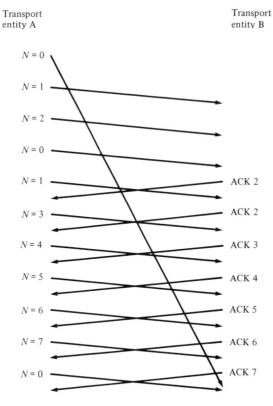

Transport
entity A

Transport
entity B

$N = 0$

$N = 1$

$N = 2$

$N = 0$

$N = 1$ ACK 2

$N = 3$ ACK 2

$N = 4$ ACK 3

$N = 5$ ACK 4

$N = 6$ ACK 5

$N = 7$ ACK 6

$N = 0$ ACK 7

FIGURE 15-9. Example of incorrect duplicate detection.

the sequence number field doubles the sequence space, so it is rather easy to select a safe size. As we shall see, the standard transport protocols allow stupendous sequence spaces.

A more subtle problem is posed by TPDUs that continue to rattle around after a transport connection is closed. If a subsequent connection is opened between the same two transport entities, a TPDU from the old connection could arrive and be accepted on the new connection! Similarly, a delayed ACK can enter a new connection and cause problems.

There are a number of approaches to this particular problem. We mention several of the more promising. First, the sequence numbering scheme can be extended across connection lifetimes. This requires that a transport entity remember the last sequence number that it used on transmission for each terminated connection. Then, when a new connection to a transport entity is attempted, the RFC contains the sequence number to be used to begin data transfer. Of course, this procedure is symmetric, with each side responsible for declaring the sequence number with which it will commence transmission.

A second approach is to provide a separate transport connection identifier, and use a new identifier with each new connection.

The procedures above work fine unless a system crash occurs. In that case, the system will not remember what sequence number or connection identifier was used last. An alternative is to simply wait a sufficient time between connections to assure that all old TPDUs are gone. Then, even if one side has experienced a crash, the other side can refuse a connection until the reconnection timer expires. This, of course, may cause unnecessary delays.

Flow Control.   The credit allocation flow control mechanism described earlier is quite robust in the face of an unreliable network service and requires little enhancement. We assume that the credit allocation scheme is tied to acknowledgments in the following way: To both acknowledge TPDUs and grant credit, a transport entity sends a control TPDU of the form (ACK N, CREDIT M), where ACK N acknowledges all data TPDUs through number N, and CREDIT M allows TPDUs number N + 1 though N + M to be transmitted. This mechanism is quite powerful. Consider that the last control TPDU issued by B was (ACK N, CREDIT M). Then:

- To increase or decrease credit to X when no additional TPDUs have arrived, B can issue (ACK N, CREDIT X).
- To acknowledge a new TPDU without increasing credit, B can issue (ACK N + 1, CREDIT M - 1).

If an ACK/CREDIT TPDU is lost, little harm is done. Future acknowledgments will resynchronize the protocol. Further, if no new acknowledgments are forthcoming, the sender times out and retransmits a data TPDU, which triggers a new acknowledgment. However, it is still possible for deadlock to occur. Consider a situation in which B sends (ACK N, CREDIT 0), temporarily closing the window. Subsequently, B sends (ACK N, CREDIT M), but this TPDU is lost. A is awaiting the opportunity to send data and B thinks that it has granted that opportunity. To overcome this problem, a window timer can be used. This timer is reset with each outgoing ACK/CREDIT TPDU. If the timer ever expires, the protocol entity is required to send an ACK/CREDIT TPDU, even if it duplicates a previous one. This breaks the deadlock and also assures the other end that the protocol entity is still alive.

An alternative or supplemental mechanism is to provide for acknowledgments to the ACK/CREDIT TPDU. With this mechanism in place, the window timer can have a quite large value without causing much difficulty.

Connection Establishment.   As with other protocol mechanisms, connection establishment must take into account the unreliability of a network service. Recall that a connection establishment calls for the exchange of RFCs, a procedure sometimes referred to as a *two-way handshake*. Suppose that A issues an RFC to B. It expects to get an RFC back, confirming the connection. Two things can go wrong: A's RFC can be lost or B's answering RFC can be lost. Both cases can be handled by use of a retransmit-RFC timer. After A issues an RFC, it will reissue the RFC when the timer expires.

This gives rise, potentially, to duplicate RFCs. If A's initial RFC was lost, there are no duplicates. If B's response was lost, then B may receive two RFCs from A. Further, if B's response was not lost, but simply delayed, A may get two responding RFCs. All of this means that A and B must simply ignore duplicate RFCs once a connection is established.

Now, consider that a duplicate RFC may survive past the termination of the connection. Figure 15-10 depicts the problem that may arise. An old RFC X (request for connection, sequence number begins at X) arrives at B after the con-

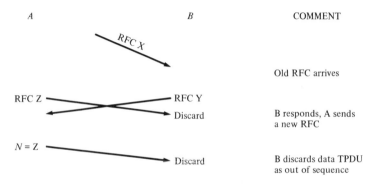

FIGURE 15-10. Example of a two-way handshake.

nection is terminated. *B* assumes that this is a fresh request and responds with RFC Y. Meanwhile, *A* has decided to open a new connection with *B* and sends RFC Z. *B* discards this as a duplicate. Subsequently, *A* initiates data transfer with a TPDU numbered Z. *B* rejects the TPDU as being out of sequence.

The way out of this problem is for each side to acknowledge explicitly the other's RFC and sequence number. The procedure is known as a *three-way handshake* [TOML75]. The revised connection state diagram is shown in the upper part of Figure 15-11. A new state (RFC Received) is added. In this state, the transport entity hesitates during connection opening to assure that any RFC which was sent has also been acknowledged before the connection is declared open. In addition to the new state, there is a new control TPDU (RST) to reset the other side when a duplicate RFC is detected.

Figure 15-12 illustrates typical three-way handshake operations. Under normal conditions, an RFC includes the sending sequence number. The responding RFC acknowledges that number and includes the sequence number for the other side. The initiating transport entity acknowledges the RFC/ACK in its first data TPDU. Next is shown a situation in which an old RFC X arrives at *B* after the close of the relevant connection. *B* assumes that this is a fresh request and responds with RFC Y, ACK X. When *A* receives this message, it realizes that it has not requested a connection and therefore sends a RST, ACK Y. Note that the ACK Y portion of the RST message is essential so that an old duplicate RST does not abort a legitimate connection establishment. The final example shows a case in which an old RFC, ACK arrives in the middle of a new connection establishment. Because of the use of sequence numbers in the acknowledgments, this event causes no mischief.

The upper part of Figure 15-11 does not include transitions in which RST is sent. This was done for simplicity. The basic rule is: Send an RST if connection state is not yet OPEN and an invalid ACK (one which does not reference something that was sent) is received. The reader should try various combinations of events to see that this connection establishment procedure works in spite of any combination of old and lost TPDUs.

Connection Termination. As with connection establishment, the connection termination procedure must cope with old and lost control TPDUs. Figure 15-11 indicates that a similar solution is adopted. Each side must explicitly acknowledge the CLS TPDU of the other. To avoid confusion, sequence numbers are used as follows:

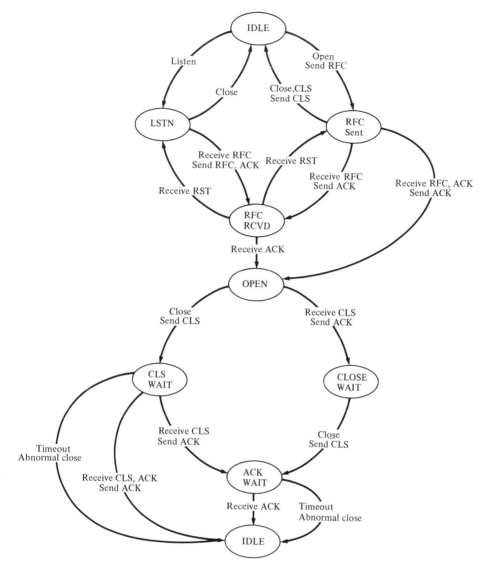

FIGURE 15-11. Revised connection state diagram.

- CLS contains the sequence number plus one of the last data TPDU sent.
- ACK contains the sequence number received in the CLS.

Timeout procedures are included to allow a transport entity to complete its closing if the other side appears uncooperative. The problem may be lost TPDUs rather than a failure at the other end. Therefore, one or more retransmissions are advisable before signaling an abnormal close.

Crash Recovery. When the system upon which a transport entity is running fails and subsequently restarts, the state information of all active connections is lost. The affected connections become "half-open" since the side that did not fail does not yet realize the problem.

The still active side of a half-open connection can close the connection using a

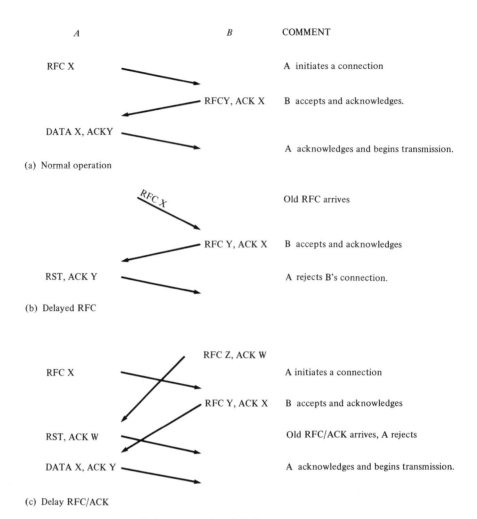

| | *A* | | *B* | COMMENT |

A RFC X → B

RFC X A initiates a connection

RFCY, ACK X B accepts and acknowledges.

DATA X, ACKY A acknowledges and begins transmission.

(a) Normal operation

RFC X Old RFC arrives

RFC Y, ACK X B accepts and acknowledges

RST, ACK Y A rejects B's connection.

(b) Delayed RFC

RFC Z, ACK W

RFC X A initiates a connection

RFC Y, ACK X B accepts and acknowledges

RST, ACK W Old RFC/ACK arrives, A rejects

DATA X, ACK Y A acknowledges and begins transmission.

(c) Delay RFC/ACK

FIGURE 15-12.   Examples of three-way handshake.

give-up timer. This timer measures the time the transport machine will continue to await an acknowledgment (or other appropriate reply) of a transmitted TPDU after the TPDU has been retransmitted the maximum number of times. When the timer expires, the transport entity assumes that the other transport entity or the intervening network has failed, closes the connection, and signals an abnormal close to the transport user.

In the event that a transport entity fails and quickly restarts, half-open connections can be terminated more quickly by the use of the RST TPDU. The failed side returns a RST X to every TPDU X that it receives. When the RST X reaches the other side, it must be checked for validity based on the sequence number X, since the RST could be in response to an old TPDU. If the reset is valid, the transport entity performs an abnormal termination.

These measures clean up the situation at the transport level. The decision as to whether to reopen the connection is up to the transport users. The problem is one of synchronization. At the time of failure, there may have been one or more outstanding TPDUs in either direction. The transport user on the side that did not fail knows how much data it has received, but the other user may not, if state information were lost. Thus, there is the danger that some user data will be lost or duplicated.

15-3

NETWORK SERVICES

To function, a transport protocol must make use of the services of some lower-level network-oriented protocol, such as X.25 or IP. Standards for such interfaces do not exist, but are at the discretion of the implementor. In this section we look first at the primitives that might be used to implement the transport/network interface, and then discuss the relationship of these primitives to the types of network service provided.

Service Primitives

Table 15-2 lists a set of primitives that might be used to provide a network service to a transport entity. This list is based on that specified by ISO [WARE83].

At minimum, the network service must provide a means of delivering TPDUs to a remote correspondent. The transport entity uses N-DATA.request to transfer data to the network service for transmission. The network service passes up received data using N-DATA.indication. If the service is not connection-oriented, address information must be included in the primitive invocation.

If the network service is connection-oriented, additional primitives are needed: N-CONNECT.request signals a request by a transport entity to open a connection.

TABLE 15-2 Network Service Primitives

Required:

    N-DATA.request ([to network address]; [from network address]; data)
    N-DATA.indication ([to network address]; [from network address]; data)

Required for connection-oriented service:

    N-CONNECT.request (to network address; from network address; security; quality of service)
    N-CONNECT.indication (to network address; from network address; security; quality of service)
    N-CONNECT.response ( )
    N-CONNECT.confirm ( )
    N-DISCONNECT.request ( )
    N-DISCONNECT.indication ( )

Additional Useful Primitives:

    N-DATA-ACKNOWLEDGE.request ( )
    N-DATA-ACKNOWLEDGE.indication ( )
    N-EXPEDITED-DATA.request (data)
    N-EXPEDITED-DATA.indication (data)
    N-RESET.request ( )
    N-RESET.indication ( )
    N-RESET.response ( )
    N-RESET.confirmation ( )

N-CONNECT.indication presents this request to the correspondent transport entity identified in the connection request. A transport entity signals its willingness to accept the connection with N-CONNECT.response. This willingness is communicated to the initiating transport entity with N-CONNECT.confirm. N-DISCONNECT.request and N-DISCONNECT.indication are used to terminate a connection. Please note that these primitives are concerned with the establishment and termination of a network connection (e.g., an X.25 virtual circuit) between two transport entities. These entities may then use this connection to establish one or more transport connections on behalf of transport users.

Additional primitives may be provided by the network service. Although not strictly necessary, these primitives enhance the capability and efficiency of the transport protocol. The N-DATA-ACKNOWLEDGE primitives permit the local exercise of flow control across the transport/network interface in both directions. N-EXPEDITED-DATA provides direct support of the transport expedited data feature. Finally, the N-RESET primitives allow the transport entity to force a reset of the network connection.

Relationship to Type of Network

It is important to realize that there is not a unique correspondence between reliability and whether a network service is connection oriented. A connection-oriented service might be reliable, in which case the techniques described above for a reliable sequencing network service would suffice for the transport protocol. On the other hand, the service might be unreliable, calling for a far more complex transport protocol.

Similarly, an unreliable connectionless service will require a complex transport protocol. However, if the connectionless service is reliable, the transport mechanisms associated with a reliable nonsequencing network service will be adequate.

15-4

THE ISO/NBS TRANSPORT STANDARDS

In this section we look at a family of transport protocols developed by ISO as an international standard [ISO83b] and accepted, with restrictions and slight modifications, by NBS as a proposed U.S. federal government standard [NBS83a]. This protocol family seems destined to achieve near-universal acceptance outside DOD.

The Transport Protocol Family

In order to handle a variety of user service requirements and available network services, ISO has defined five classes of transport protocol:

- *Class 0:* simple class.
- *Class 1:* basic error recovery class.
- *Class 2:* multiplexing class.
- *Class 3:* error recovery and multiplexing class.
- *Class 4:* error detection and recovery class.

These classes are related to the three types of network service defined in Section

TABLE 15-3 Functions of ISO Transport Protocol Classes[a]

Protocol Mechanism	Variant	0	1	2	3	4
Assignment to network connection		*	*	*	*	*
TPDU transfer		*	*	*	*	*
Segmenting and reassembling		*	*	*	*	*
Concatenation and separation			*	*	*	*
Connection establishment		*	*	*	*	*
Connection refusal		*	*	*	*	*
Normal release	Implicit	*				
	Explicit		*	*	*	*
Error release		*		*		
Association of TPDUs with transport connection		*	*	*	*	*
DT TPDU numbering	Normal		*	m(1)	m	m
	Extended			o(1)	o	o
Expedited data transfer	Network normal		m	*(1)	*	*
	Network expedited		ao			
Reassignment after failure			*		*	
Retention until acknowledgment of TPDUs	Conf. receipt		ao			
	AK		m		*	*
Resynchronisation			*		*	
Multiplexing and demultiplexing				*	*	*
Explicit flow control	With			m	*	*
	Without	*	*	o		
Checksum	Use of					m
	Nonuse of	*	*	*	*	o
Frozen references			*		*	*
Retransmission on timeout						*
Resequencing						*
Inactivity control						*
Treatment of protocol errors		*	*	*	*	*
Splitting and recombining						*

[a]Symbols used in this table are as follows:

* Procedure always included in class.

m Negotiable procedure whose implementation in equipment is mandatory.

o Negotiable procedure whose implementation in equipment is optional.

ao Negotiable procedure whose implementation in equipment is optional and where use depends on availability within the network service.

(1)Not applicable in Class 2 when nonuse of explicit flow control is selected.

15-2 as follows. Classes 0 and 2 are used with Type A networks; Classes 1 and 3 are used with Type B networks; and Class 4 is used with Type C networks. Table 15-3 lists the functions of the various protocol classes.

Class 0 was developed by CCITT and is oriented for teletex, a text-transmission upgrade to Telex (not to be confused with teletext; see Chapter 16). It provides the simplest kind of transport connection. It provides a connection with flow control based on network-level flow control, and connection release based on the release of the network connection.

Class 1 was also developed by CCITT and is designed to run on an X.25 network and provide minimal error recovery (network-signaled errors). The key difference from Class 0 is that TPDUs are numbered. This allows the protocol to resynchronize after an X.25 RESET and to reassign a transport connection after an X.25 RESTART. Flow control is still provided by the network layer. Expedited data transfer is also provided.

Class 2 is an enhancement to Class 0 that still assumes a highly reliable network service. The key enhancement is the ability to multiplex multiple transport connections onto a single network connection. A corollary enhancement is the provision of explicit flow control, since a single network connection flow control mechanism does not allow individual flow control of transport connections. A credit allocation scheme is used.

Class 3 is basically the union of the Class 1 and 2 capabilities. It provides the multiplexing and flow control capabilities of Class 2. It also contains the resynchronization and reassignment capabilities needed to cope with failure-prone networks.

Class 4 assumes that the underlying network service is unreliable. Thus most if not all of the mechanisms described in Section 15-2 must be included.

Transport Services

The transport service specification is the same for all classes. This is to be expected, since one of the main points of the transport service is to provide end-to-end data transfer independent of the nature of the underlying network. The ISO specification is in the form of just four primitive types and 10 primitives. These are listed in Table 15-4. Figure 15-13 displays the sequences in which these primitives are used. (*Note:* The use of ~ indicates the lack of a defined time relationship between two primitives.)

The first two primitive types are concerned with connection management. The T-CONNECT primitives are used to establish a connection. The quality of service parameter indicates the user's requirements for the throughput, transit delay, reli-

TABLE 15-4   ISO Transport Service Primitives

T-CONNECT.request (Called Address, Calling Address, Expedited Data Option, Quality of Service, Data)

T-CONNECT.indication (Called Address, Calling Address, Expedited Data Option, Quality of Service, Data)

T-CONNECT.response (Quality of Service, Responding Address, Expedited Data Option, Data)

T-CONNECT.confirm (Quality of Service, Responding Address, Expedited Data Option, Data)

T-DISCONNECT.request (Data)
T-DISCONNECT.indication (Disconnect Reason, Data)

T-DATA.request (Data)
T-DATA.indication (Data)

T-EXPEDITED-DATA.request (Data)
T-EXPEDITED-DATA.indication (Data)

ability, and relative priority of this connection. The data parameter can be used to send up to 32 octets of user data.

T-DISCONNECT provides for an abrupt connection termination. Termination can be initiated by either side or by one of the transport entities. T-DISCONNECT can also be used by the local transport entity or the remote addressee to reject a connection attempt.

The remaining primitives are concerned with data transfer. T-DATA and T-EXPEDITED data are used to transfer data over a transport connection. The latter attempts to expedite delivery of the data.

Protocol Formats

The ISO protocol makes use of 10 types of transport protocol data units (TPDUs):

- Connection request (CR).
- Connection confirm (CC).
- Disconnect request (DR).
- Disconnect confirm (DC).
- Data (DT).
- Expedited data (ED).
- Acknowledgment (AK).
- Expedited acknowledgment (EA).
- Reject (RJ).
- TPDU error (ER).

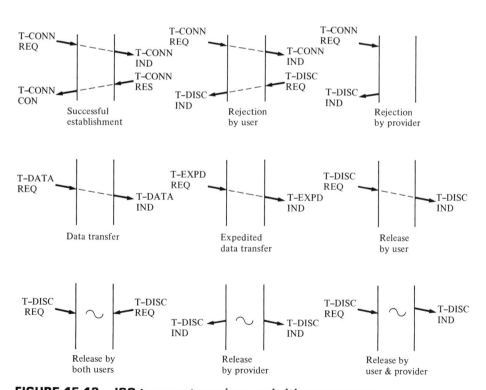

FIGURE 15-13.   ISO transport services—primitive sequences.

By this time, the use of these TPDUs should be self-explanatory. In this section we confine ourselves to a discussion of the formats and field values of the various TPDUs. In the next subsection, we discuss the protocol mechanisms that are implemented with these TPDU types.

Each TPDU consists of three parts: a fixed header, a variable header, and a data field. The latter two optionally may not be present in a TPDU. The fixed header contains the frequently occurring parameters (Figure 15-14), and the variable header contains optional or infrequently occurring parameters (Table 15-5).

The fixed headers of the various TPDU types are similar. The fields, not all of which occur in all types, can be defined briefly:

- *Length indicator (LI) (8 bits):* length of the header (fixed plus variable) excluding the LI field, in octets.

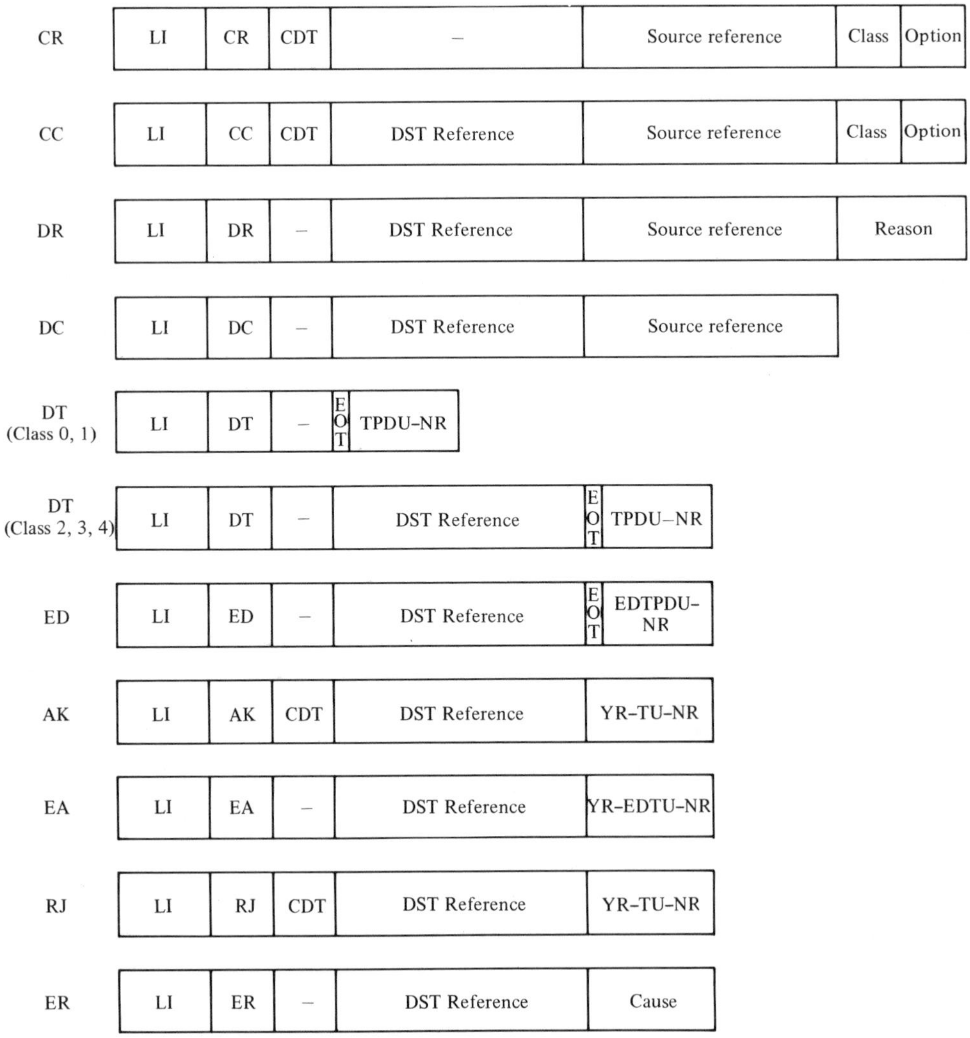

CR	LI	CR	CDT	—	Source reference	Class	Option

CC	LI	CC	CDT	DST Reference	Source reference	Class	Option

DR	LI	DR	—	DST Reference	Source reference	Reason

DC	LI	DC	—	DST Reference	Source reference

DT (Class 0, 1): LI | DT | — | EOT | TPDU–NR

DT (Class 2, 3, 4): LI | DT | — | DST Reference | EOT | TPDU–NR

ED: LI | ED | — | DST Reference | EOT | EDTPDU–NR

AK: LI | AK | CDT | DST Reference | YR–TU–NR

EA: LI | EA | — | DST Reference | YR–EDTU–NR

RJ: LI | RJ | CDT | DST Reference | YR–TU–NR

ER: LI | ER | — | DST Reference | Cause

FIGURE 15-14. ISO transport protocol fixed header formats.

TABLE 15-5   ISO Transport Protocol Variable Header Primitives[a]

	CR	CC	DR	DC	DT	ED	AK	EA	RJ	ER
Calling TSAP ID	X	X								
Called TSAP ID	X	X								
TPDU size	X	X								
Version number	X	X								
Security parameter	X	X								
Checksum	4	4	4	4	4	4	4	4		
Additional option selection	X	X								
Alternative protocol class	X	X								
Acknowledge time	4	4								
Throughput	X	X								
Residual error rate	X	X								
Priority	X	X								
Transmit delay	X	X								
Reassignment time	1, 3	1, 3								
Subsequence number							4			
Flow control confirmation							4			
Invalid TPDU										X

[a]4, class 4 only; 1, 3, classes 1 and 3 only.

- *TPDU code (4 bits):* type of TPDU.
- *Credit (CDT) (4 bits):* flow control credit allocation. Initial credit is granted in CR and CC, subsequent credit is granted in AK. As an option, a 16-bit credit field is used with AK, and is appended after the YR-TU-NR field.
- *Source reference (16 bits):* reference used by the transport entity to identify the transport connection uniquely in its own system.
- *Destination reference (16 bits):* reference used by the peer transport entity to identify the transport connection uniquely in its own system.
- *Class (4 bits):* protocol class.
- *Option (4 bits):* specifies normal (7-bit sequence number, 4-bit credit) or extended (31-bit sequence number, 16-bit credit) flow control fields. Also specifies whether explicit flow control is to be used in Class 2.
- *Reason (8 bits):* reason for requesting a disconnect or rejecting a connection request. The reasons are listed in Table 15-6.
- *EOT (1 bit):* used when a user letter has been fragmented into multiple TPDUs. It is set to 1 on the last TPDU.
- *TPDU-NR (7 bits):* send sequence number of a DT TPDU. It is normally modulo 2^7, but may be extended by three octets to be modulo 2^{31}.
- *EDTPDU-NR (7 bits):* send sequence number of a ED TPDU.
- *YR-TU-NR (8 bits):* the next expected DT sequence number.
- *YR-EDTU-NR (8 bits):* the next expected ED sequence number.
- *Cause (8 bits):* reason for rejection of a TPDU (Table 15-6).

The variable header consists of a sequence of additional parameters. Each parameter field consists of three subfields: a parameter code (8 bits), a parameter length (8 bits), and the parameter value (one or more octets). Most of the parameters are used by CC and CR in the connection establishment process. The parameters are:

TABLE 15-6 ISO Transport Parameter Values

Reason for Disconnect Request	Reason for TPDU Error
Not specified	Not specified
Congestion at TSAP	Invalid parameter code
Session entity not attached to TSAP	Invalid TPDU error
Address unknown	Invalid parameter value
Normal user-initiated disconnect	
Remote transport entity congestion	**Negotiated Options**
Connection negotiation failed	Network expedited in Class 0
Duplicate source reference	Acknowledgment in Class 1
Mismatch references	Checksum in Class 4
Protocol error	Transport expedited data service
Reference overflow	
Request refused on this network connection	
Header or parameter length invalid	

- *Calling TSAP ID:* service access point that identifies the calling transport user.
- *Called TSAP ID:* service access point that identifies the called transport user.
- *TPDU size:* maximum TPDU size in octets. The range of options is from 128 to 8192 in powers of 2.
- *Version number:* version of protocol to be followed. This accommodates future revisions to the standard.
- *Security parameter:* user-defined.
- *Checksum:* result of checksum algorithm (defined in an appendix to this chapter) for the entire TPDU. The checksum is used only for Class 4 and, within that class, it is mandatory for all CR TPDUs, and for all TPDUs when the checksum option is selected.
- *Additional option selection:* used to specify use or nonuse of certain options (Table 15-6).
- *Alternative protocol class:* specifies whether only the requested protocol class is acceptable, or that some other class is also acceptable.
- *Acknowledge time:* an estimate of the time taken by the entity to acknowledge a DT TPDU. This helps the other entity select a value for its retransmission timer.
- *Throughput:* specifies the user's throughput requirements in octets per second. Four values are specified: the target and minimum acceptable throughput in both the calling-called direction and the called-calling direction.
- *Residual error rate:* expresses the target and minimum rate of unreported user data loss.
- *Priority:* priority of this connection.
- *Transit delay:* specifies the user's delay requirements in milliseconds. Four values are specified: the target and maximum acceptable transit delay in both directions.
- *Reassignment time:* amount of time an entity will persist in attempts to reconnect after a network connection is broken.
- *Subsequence number:* number of the AK. It is used to assure that AKs with the same YR-TU-NR are processed in correct sequence.
- *Flow control confirmation:* echoes parameter values in the last AK TPDU

received. It contains the values of the YR-TU-NR, CDT, and Subsequence Number fields.

- *Invalid TPDU:* the bit pattern of the rejected TPDU up to and including the octet that caused the rejection.

Protocol Mechanisms

The purpose of this section is to highlight the key transport protocol mechanisms. Much of what was discussed in Section 15-2 is applicable, so only a brief commentary is provided. The following topics are considered:

- Connection establishment.
- Data transfer.
- Connection termination.

Connection Establishment.   The connection establishment phase requires, at minimum, the exchange of a CR and a CC TPDU (Figure 15-13). This two-way handshake suffices for Classes 0 through 3. For Class 4, a third TPDU is needed to acknowledge the CC; this may be an AK, DT, or ED.

The purpose of this phase is to establish a transport connection with agreed-upon characteristics. If the establishment attempt is successful, these characteristics are defined by the parameters of the CC. Prior to success, there may be a period of negotiation. In some cases, the calling entity specifies options (e.g., other classes are acceptable), and the called entity selects one in the CC. In other cases, the calling entity proposes a value (e.g., maximum TPDU size), and the calling entity may accept it (CC) or reject it (DR). The parameters involved in this latter process are listed in Table 15-6.

A transport connection involves four different types of identifiers:

- User identifier (service access point).
- Transport/network address.
- Transport protocol identifier.
- Transport connection identifier.

Since there may be more than one user of the transport entity, a user identifier is needed to allow the transport entity to multiplex data transfers to multiple users. This identifier must be passed down from the transport user, and included in CC and CR TPDUs. The transport/network address identifies the station on which the transport entity is located. This address, or a corresponding name, is passed down from the transport user. The address is not needed in any TPDU, but must be passed down to the network protocol entity for its use. Normally, there will be only one transport protocol entity in a station. However, more than one entity, each of a different type, might be resident in one station. In the latter case, the protocol must be identified to the network service. We saw this facility in use in IP. Finally, each transport connection is given a unique identifier (similar to an X.25 virtual-circuit number) by each of the two transport entities involved. This identifier is used in all TPDUs. It allows the transport entity to multiplex multiple transport connections on a single network connection.

Data Transfer.   Normal data transfer over a connection is accomplished using DTs. Each data unit may be self contained. Alternatively, if the user letter plus

DT header exceeds the maximum packet size, the transport entity may fragment the letter and send it out as a sequence of TPDUs. The last TPDU in sequence has the EOT bit set.

DTs are numbered sequentially. This is used in Classes 2 through 4 for flow control. A credit-allocation scheme is used. The initial credit is set in the CC and CR TPDUs. Subsequent credit is granted with an AK. Note that acknowledgments are in separate TPDUs, and never piggybacked onto DTs. At first glance, this might seem inefficient since an entire TPDU is needed for flow control. This is not so for two reasons:

- The transport entity may choose not to acknowledge every single DT, but only acknowledge in bunches. Thus no overhead for piggybacking is wasted in the DT.
- A sort of piggybacking is possible. A transport entity may concatenate multiple TPDUs (e.g., a DT and an AK) into one unit to be passed to the network service. Thus several TPDUs will be efficiently handled as a single packet by the network.

In Class 4, sequence numbers are also used for resequencing DTs that arrive out of order. Another mechanism unique to Class 4 is the DT checksum. If an error is detected, an ER is returned. Other reasons for ER, for all classes, are listed in Table 15-6.

Expedited data transfer uses the ED and EA data units. Sequence numbers are used, but only one ED may be outstanding at a time. The sender must receive an EA before sending another ED. The reader may ask how a transport entity expedites data. The answer may strike some as clumsy and inefficient, but it is just one more example of the limitations and complexities with which a transport protocol must cope. In Classes 1 through 4, an ED is sent before any DTs queued for that connection. In Class 4, we must contend with the problem that being sent out first does not mean being delivered first. Therefore, the Class 4 entity suspends the transfer of new DTs (although pending DTs will go out) until an EA is received. In effect, the connection is shut down to accommodate this one piece of data.

Connection Termination. An abrupt termination is achieved by the exchange of a DR and a DC. When a transport entity receives a disconnect request from it user, it discards any pending DTs and issues the DR. The entity that receives the DR issues a DC, discards any pending DTs, and informs its user.

The NBS Standard

The NBS transport protocol standard is both a subset and a superset of the ISO standard. (It seems that with transport protocols, nothing is ever simple!) NBS has determined that only Class 2 and Class 4 will experience significant demand in the United States. Accordingly, these are the only two classes being standardized.

The NBS and ISO standards for Classes 2 and 4 use the same formats and procedures, with some differences. The principal difference is that NBS provides a graceful close service in Class 4. This reflects a desire by NBS to encompass all transport-level DOD requirements. No similar demand has been strongly expressed in the international community.

The graceful close service seems to be one that would normally be found at the session layer or higher. If two users wish to assure that all data are delivered in both directions before a session is terminated, this is easily done at the session level, and there seems no need to repeat the capability at the transport layer. Again, this seems to have been included to match the DOD capability. DOD's TCP is typically used directly by application programs and has some "session-layer" features in it.

The foregoing difference is concerned with transport services. There are also some small differences in the transport protocols. Both NBS and ISO allow for the use of either a 7-bit or an extended 31-bit sequence space. The extended sequence space is an option that can be requested by either transport entity at connection time. ISO allows the other entity to refuse, and insist on a 7-bit sequence space. NBS, however, requires the implementation of this feature so that, if it is requested, it is always available. Given the wide variety of networks and catenets over which transport protocols are likely to be used, this seems a worthwhile requirement.

15-5
DOD TRANSPORT PROTOCOLS

The DOD transport protocols, together with IP, are the centerpiece of the DOD protocol architecture. The comments made in Chapter 12 concerning the philosophy of that model apply specifically to these protocols.

DOD has defined two transport-level protocols: the Transmission Control Protocol (TCP), which is connection-oriented, and the User Datagram Protocol (UDP), which is connectionless. As yet, UDP is little used. TCP is the principal transport protocol in the DOD world [DOD83b].

TCP Services

TCP is designed to provide reliable communication between pairs of processes (TCP users) across a variety of reliable and unreliable networks and catenets. In contrast to the ISO model, TCP is stream oriented. That is, TCP users exchange streams of data. The data are placed in allocated buffers and transmitted by TCP in segments (TPDUs). TCP supports security and precedence labeling. In addition, TCP provides two useful facilities for labeling data: push and urgent:

- *Data stream push:* Ordinarily, TCP decides when sufficient data has accumulated to form a TPDU for transmission. The TCP user can require TCP to transmit all outstanding data up to and including that labeled with a push flag. On the receiving end, TCP will deliver these data to the user in the same manner. A user might request this if it has come to a logical break in the data.
- *Urgent data signaling:* This provides a means of informing the destination TCP user that significant or "urgent" data is in the upcoming data stream. It is up to the destination user to determine appropriate action.

Tables 15-7 and 15-8 list the TCP service request (user to TCP) and service response (TCP to user) primitives. Several comments are in order.

The two passive open commands correspond to the LISTEN command of Figure 15-11. They signal the user's willingness to accept a connection request. The active open with data is analogous to the X.25 fast select facility.

Source port and *destination port* are essentially transport service access points. *Destination address* identifies the network and station address of the remote TCP entity. *Timeout* permits the user to set up a timeout for all data submitted to TCP.

TABLE 15-7   TCP Service Request Primitives

UNSPECIFIED-PASSIVE-OPEN (source-port, [timeout], [timeout-action], [precedence], [security-range])

    Listen for connection attempts at specified security and precedence levels from any remote user.

FULL-PASSIVE-OPEN (source-port, destination-port, destination-address, [timeout], [timeout-action], [precedence], [security])

    Listen for connection attempts at specified security and precedence levels from specified user.

ACTIVE-OPEN (source-port, destination-port, destination-address, [timeout], [timeout-action], [precedence], [security],)

    Request connection at particular security and precedence levels.

ACTIVE-OPEN W/DATA (source-port, destination-port, destination-address, [timeout], [timeout-action], [precedence], [security], data, data-length, push-flag, urgent-flag)

    Request connection at particular security and precedence levels and transmit data with the request.

SEND (local-connection-name, data, data length, push-flag, urgent-flag, [timeout], [timeout-action])

    Causes data to be transferred across named connection.

ALLOCATE (local-connection-name, data length)

    Issue incremental allocation for receive data to TCP.

CLOSE (local-connection-name)

    Close connection gracefully.

ABORT (local-connection-name)

    Close connection abruptly.

STATUS (local-connection-name)

    Report connection status.

If data are not successfully delivered within the timeout, TCP will abort the connection.

TCP Header Format

TCP uses only a single type of TPDU. The header is shown in Figure 15-15a. Because one header must serve to perform all protocol mechanisms, it is rather large. Whereas the ISO fixed header is from five to seven octets long, the TCP header is a minimum of 20 octets long. The fields are:

- *Source port (16 bits):* identifies source service access point.
- *Destination port (16 bits):* identifies destination service access point.
- *Sequence number (32 bits):* sequence number of the first data octet in this TPDU, except when SYN is present. If SYN is present, it is the initial sequence number (ISN) and the first data octet is ISN + 1.
- *Acknowledgment number (32 bits):* a piggybacked acknowledgment. Contains the sequence number of the next octet that the TCP entity expects to receive.

TABLE 15-8 TCP Service Response Primitives

OPEN-ID (local-connection-name, source-port, destination-port, destination address)
> Informs user of connection name assigned to pending connection requested in an OPEN primitive.

OPEN-FAILURE (local-connection-name)
> Reports failure of an active OPEN request.

OPEN-SUCCESS (local-connection-name)
> Reports completion of an active OPEN request.

DELIVER (local-connection-name, data, data-length, urgent-flag)
> Reports arrival of data.

CLOSING (local-connection-name)
> Reports that remote TCP user has issued a CLOSE.

TERMINATE (local-connection-name, description)
> Reports that connection has been terminated and no longer exists.

STATUS-RESPONSE (local-connection-name, source-port, source-address, destination-port, destination-address, connection-state, receive-window, send-window, amount-waiting-ack, amount-waiting-receipt, urgent-mode, timeout, timeout-action)
> Reports current status of connection.

- *Data offset (4 bits):* number of 32-bit words in the header.
- *Reserved (6 bits):* reserved for future use.
- *Flags (6 bits):*
  URG: urgent pointer field significant.
  ACK: acknowledgment field significant.
  PSH: push function.
  RST: reset the connection.
  SYN: synchronize the sequence numbers.
  FIN: no more data from sender.
- *Window (16 bits):* flow control credit allocation, in octets. Contains the number of data octets beginning with the one indicated in the acknowledgment field which the sender is willing to accept.
- *Checksum (16 bits):* the one's complement of the sum modulo $2^{16} - 1$ of all the 16-bit words in the TPDU.
- *Urgent Pointer (16 bits):* points to the octet following the urgent data. This allows the receiver to know how much urgent data are coming.
- *Options (Variable):* at present, only one option is defined, which specifies the maximum TPDU size that will be accepted.

The reader may feel that some items are missing, and that is indeed the case. TCP is designed specifically and exclusively to work with IP. Hence some user parameters are passed down for inclusion in the IP header. The relevant ones are:

- Precedence: a 3-bit field.
- Normal delay/low delay.
- Normal throughput/high throughput.
- Normal reliability/high reliability.
- Security: an 11-bit field.

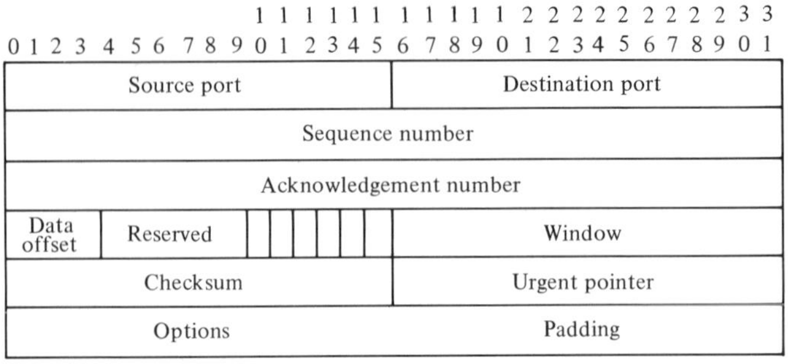

(a) Transmission control protocol (TCP)

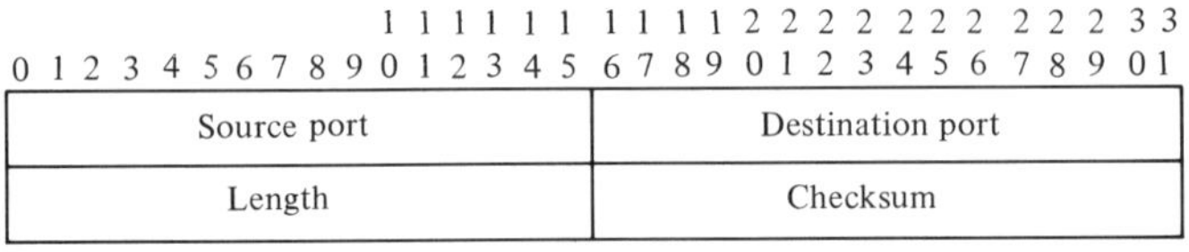

(b) User datagram protocol (UDP)

FIGURE 15-15. DOD transport protocol header formats.

It is worth observing that this TCP/IP linkage means that the required minimum overhead for every data unit is actually 40 octets.

TCP Mechanisms

Connection Establishment.   Connection establishment in TCP always uses a three-way handshake. When the SYN flag is set, the TPDU is essentially a request for connection (RFC), and functions as explained in Section 15-2. To initiate a connection, an entity sends an RFC X, where X is the initial sequence number. The receiver responds with RFC Y, ACK X by setting both the SYN and ACK flags. Finally, the initiater responds with ACK Y. If both sides issue crossing RFCs, no problem results: Both sides respond with ACKs.

Data Transfer.   Although data are transferred in TPDUs over a transport connection, data transfer is viewed logically as consisting of a stream of octets. Hence every octet is numbered, modulo 2^{32}. Each TPDU contains the sequence number of the first octet in the data field. Flow control is exercised using a credit allocation scheme in which the credit is a number of octets rather than a number of TPDUs. In principle, this numbering scheme is more flexible than the ISO/NBS approach and gives the transport entity tighter control over its buffers. In practice, the two seem to provide equivalent performance.

As was mentioned, data are buffered by the transport entity on both transmission and reception. TCP normally exercises its own discretion as to when to construct a TPDU for transmission and when to release received data to the user. The PUSH flag is used to force the data so far accumulated to be sent by the transmitter and passed on by the receiver. This serves an end-of-letter function.

The user may specify a block of data as urgent. TCP will designate the end of that block with an urgent pointer and send it out in the ordinary data stream. The receiving user is alerted that urgent data are being received.

If, during data exchange, a TPDU arrives which is apparently not meant for the current connection, the RST flag is set on an outgoing TPDU. Examples of this situation are delayed duplicate SYNs and an acknowledgment of data not yet sent.

Connection Termination. The normal means of terminating a connection is a graceful close. Each transport user must issue a CLOSE primitive. The transport entity sets the FIN bit on the last TPDU that it sends out, which also contains the last of the data to be sent on this connection.

An abrupt termination occurs if the user issues an ABORT primitive. In this case, the entity abandons all attempts to send or receive data and discards data in its transmission and reception buffers. A RST TPDU is sent to the other side.

User Datagram Protocol

The User Datagram Protocol (UDP) provides a transport-level datagram service. UDP is basically an unreliable service; delivery and duplicate protection are not guaranteed. However, this does reduce the overhead of the protocol and may be adequate in many cases.

Figure 15-15b shows the format of the UDP header. As with TCP, UDP is expected to work with IP. Although it includes a checksum, there is no provision for error reporting. A "one-way" handshake is used. That is, UDP assembles a data unit and hands it to IP for transmission. Incoming data units are checked using the checksum. An invalid data unit is discarded. A valid one is passed to the user.

15-6

RECOMMENDED READING

A good account of transport protocols can be found in [MCQU78]. Other sources are [SUNS81], [GARL77], and a chapter in [TANE81a]. [NBS80b] is a good discussion of the types of services and protocol mechanism to be looked for in a transport protocol. The serious student will be amply repaid by the effort of reading the five-volume [NBS83a].

15-7

PROBLEMS

15-1   It is common practice in most transport protocols (indeed, most protocols at all levels) for control and data to be multiplexed over the same logical channel on a per-user-connection basis. An alternative is to establish a single control transport connection between each pair of communicating transport entities. This connection would be used to carry control signals relating to all user transport connections between the two entities. Discuss the implications of this strategy.

15-2   The discussion of flow control with a reliable network service referred to a backpressure mechanism utilizing a lower-level flow control protocol. Discuss the disadvantages of this strategy.

15-3   Two transport entities communicate across a reliable network. Let the normalized time to transmit a TPDU equal 1. Assume that the end-to-end propagation delay is 3, and that it takes a time 2 to deliver data from a received TPDU to the transport user. The sender initially granted a credit of seven TPDUs. The receiver uses a conservative flow control policy, and updates its credit allocation at every opportunity. What is the maximum achievable throughput?

15-4 Draw diagrams similar to Figure 15-7 for the following (assume a reliable sequenced network service):
  a. Connection termination: active/passive.
  b. Connection termination: active/active.
  c. Connection rejection.
  d. Connection abortion: user issues an OPEN to a listening user, and then issues a CLOSE before any data are exchanged.

15-5 With a reliable sequencing network service, are TPDU sequence numbers strictly necessary? What, if any, capability is lost without them?

15-6 Consider a failure-prone network service that suffers a reset. Should the transport entity allow for the possibility of duplicate TPDUs as a result of the transport-level reset mechanism?

15-7 The discussion of retransmission strategy made reference to three problems associated with dynamic timer calculation. What modifications to the strategy would help to alleviate those problems?

15-8 If a dynamic timer calculation is used for the retransmission strategy, the following moving-average formula is suggested by NBS:

SRTD: = (ALPHA * SRTD) + ((1 - ALPHA) * RTD)
rtrans: = min(UBOUND, max (LBOUND, (BETA * SRTD)))

Where UBOUND and LBOUND are prechosen upper and lower bounds on the timer value, SRTD is the smoothed round-trip delay, and RTD is the last observed round-trip delay. What functions do ALPHA and BETA perform, and what is the effect of higher or lower values of each?

15-9 Consider a transport protocol that uses a connection-oriented network service. Suppose that the transport protocol uses a credit allocation flow control scheme, and the network protocol uses a sliding window scheme. What relationship, if any, should there be between the dynamic window of the transport protocol and the fixed window of the network protocol?

15-10 In a network that has a maximum packet size of 128 bytes, a maximum packet lifetime of 30 s, and an 8-bit packet sequence number, what is the maximum data rate per connection?

15-11 Is a deadlock possible using only a two-way handshake instead of a three-way handshake? Give an example or prove otherwise.

15-12 Why is there not a T-DATA.confirm primitive in Table 15-4?

15-13 In the ISO protocol, why is the Source Reference field included in CR, CC, DR, and DC, but not the other TPDUs?

15-14 Compare the PUSH and URGENT mechanisms of TCP with the expedited data mechanism of ISO. How do they differ?

15-15 Why is UDP needed? Why can't a user program directly access IP?

APPENDIX 15A

THE ISO CHECKSUM ALGORITHM

The Class 4 transport protocol uses a checksum algorithm originally specified in [FLET82]. The algorithm is much easier to implement in software than a CRC, yet has error-detection properties that are almost the equal of those of CRC.

The mechanism employed is a 16-bit checksum included as a parameter in each TPDU. The checksum is initially calculated by the sender and placed in the outgoing TPDU. The receiver applies the same algorithm to the entire TPDU, now including the 16-bit checksum, and should get a zero result if there are no errors.

The algorithm is as follows. For transmission, let

$$L = \text{length of TPDU in octets}$$
$$B_i = \text{value of } i^{\text{th}} \text{ octet}$$
$$n, n + 1 = \text{octet positions for checksum}$$

Initially, B_n and B_{n+1} are set to zero. Two checksum octets, R and S, are calculated by processing the B_i one at a time:

$$R_i = R_{i-1} + B_i$$
$$S_i = S_{i-1} + R_i$$

Addition is performed modulo 255 (one's complement arithmetic). On completion, we have

$$R = R_L = \sum_{i=1}^{L} B_i$$

$$S = S_i = \sum_{i=1}^{L} (L - i + 1)B_i$$

These numbers were computed with $B_n = B_{n+1} = 0$. Now we must put the appropriate values in these octets so that the algorithm yields zero on reception. Some thought reveals that we must have

$$B_n + B_{n+1} = -R$$
$$(L - n + 1)B_n + (L - n)B_{n+1} = -S$$

Solving, we obtain

$$B_n = (L - n)R - S$$
$$B_{n+1} = (L - n + 1)(-R) + S$$

CHAPTER 16

Process/Application Protocols

The transport layer, as we have seen, presents difficult technical problems. But there is universal agreement that transport protocols are needed, and, fortunately, existing standards are solidifying and being accepted. What do we have above transport? Let us consider this from the top down.

At the application level, users should be able to write their own applications that invoke the computer network functionality through a transport, session, or presentation interface, as appropriate. In addition, certain "utility-grade" applications, such as electronic mail, should be standardized and made available universally. This is widely accepted in principle. Also widely accepted, in principle, is the need for presentation services. A notable example here is a virtual terminal protocol. Some protocols seem to span both application and presentation levels. Examples are videotex, teletext, and file transfer protocols.

OSI's session layer occupies an anomalous position. The DOD reference model (DRM) sets its face against a ''session layer'' as such, feeling that some of its presumed functions (e.g., graceful close) should be performed by transport and that other functions are peculiar to the processes or applications that wish to communicate. The non-DOD standards organizations have had some trouble pinning down a session layer standard, in part because of the lack of strong motivation for its existence.

In this chapter we begin with an examination of the session protocol, recognizing that it may be the least useful component of a communications architecture. Above session, the possibilities for protocol types are manifold, and we attempt only to give the reader the flavor of this up-and-coming area with a few examples.

SESSION PROTOCOLS

Because the details of, and indeed even the requirements for, a session protocol have not yet been resolved, this section will discuss session protocols in terms of principles and objectives, rather than a specific standard. We also look at the approach taken in the context of the DOD Protocol Architecture (DPA).

Characteristics

Few session protocols exist at the present time. Much of the original work that has led to the OSI concept of a session layer was done by a group of designers at Honeywell [BACH79], in the context of OSI and Honeywell's own communications architecture [HONE82]. This same general approach is also being pursued by NBS [NBS81] and ISO [NEUM83, EMMO83] in developing a specific session protocol standard. What follows is based on the model of the session layer as reflected in the above efforts.

The essential purpose of a session protocol is to provide a user-oriented connection service. The transport protocol is responsible for creating and maintaining a connection between endpoints. A session protocol would provide a "user interface" by "adding value" to the basic connection service. Let us consider some of the value-added features. We can group them into the following categories:

- Session establishment and maintenance.
- Dialogue management.
- Recovery.

Session Establishment and Maintenance. The minimum service that a session protocol entity provides its users is the establishment, maintenance, and termination of sessions. When two users wish to establish a connection, their respective entities will create a session that is mapped onto a transport connection and negotiate the parameters of the session (e.g., data unit size; see below for further examples).

Let us refer to the unit of data exchanged between a session user and a session protocol entity as a record. Then the entity accepts records from the user and transmits the data over a transport connection in a sequence of letters. The data are received on the other side and delivered to the user in the proper order. The sending entity may, at its discretion, fragment records into multiple letters if the record size is too large. Alternatively, multiple records may be blocked into a single letter for efficiency of transmission. In any case, the receiving entity recovers the original records and passes these on to the receiving user.

The simplest relationship between sessions and transport connections is one to one. It might be desirable to multiplex multiple sessions onto a single transport connection. This reduces the processing burden and amount of state information required of the transport entity. However, caution must be observed. For example, a session supporting inquiry/response should not be multiplexed with a session supporting a file transfer, since the sending of the inquiry text may be significantly delayed when entering a long transport queue of file text from the other session.

Furthermore, if the receiving session entity is forced, for any reason, to stop receiving the file transfer text, the receiving queue may soon fill up. This will cause the source queue to fill up as well and any text from the inquiry session multiplexed with the halted session may remain trapped in it.

A session might also be split between two transport connections. This could facilitate the transfer of expedited or interrupt data.

Dialogue Management.   The session entity may impose a structure on the interaction or dialogue between users. There are three possible modes of dialogue: two-way simultaneous, two-way alternate, and one-way.

The two-way simultaneous mode is a full-duplex type of operation. Both sides can simultaneously send data. Once this mode is agreed upon in the session negotiation phase, there is no specific dialogue management task required. This would probably be the most common mode of dialogue.

Similarly, the one-way mode requires no specific dialogue management mechanism once it is established. All user data flows in one direction only. An example of this is if data are to be sent to a temporarily inactive user, and are accepted by a "receiver server," whose only task is to accept data on behalf of other local users and store them. Note that the characteristic of being one-way is not absolute. There is a two-way dialogue required to establish the session. During data transfer, the receiving session entity may transmit acknowledgments and other control information. Furthermore, the receiving session user may need to send back some interrupt data. For example, the receiver may need to halt reception temporarily because of a local system problem.

The most complex of the three modes is two-way alternate. In this case, the two sides take turns sending data. An example of the use of this mode is for inquiry/response applications. The session entity enforces the alternating interaction by informing each user when it is its turn. This is actually a three-step process:

- The user who has the turn informs its session entity when it has completed its turn.
- The sending session entity sends any outstanding data to the receiving entity and then informs the receiving entity that the turn is being passed.
- The receiving entity passes up any outstanding data to its user and then informs the user that it is its turn.

An economical means of accomplishing this process is to mark the data with a delimiter. Specifically, the sending user includes a delimiter in the last record of its turn. Let us call the sequence of records sent during one user's turn a *session interaction unit*. Then, on the last record of its turn, the user would include an end-of-interaction unit (I) delimiter. This delimiter is, in effect, a token that is passed to the other user.

With two-way alternate, the user is prevented from sending normal data unless it is its turn. However, a user may send interrupt data to, for example, demand the turn. As an example of the use of the demand-turn mechanism, consider a user who has requested data and is viewing them as they scroll onto a screen. The user may wish to abort the transmission once the first few lines have been viewed.

Recovery.   Another potential feature of a session protocol is a recovery support service similar to the checkpoint/restart mechanisms used in file management.

This feature could be provided by defining a *session recovery unit*, which corresponds to the interval between checkpoints. Each user specifies the point at which a recovery unit ends, and the recovery units are numbered sequentially. To recover lost data (e.g., following a disk fault or a paper break on a printer), a user can issue a command to recover, using the recovery unit number to identify the point to which the session should be backed up.

Once a session has been backed up, some form of recovery will generally be attempted. This is a complex function, which would doubtless extend beyond the bounds of the session layer, and will not be pursued in detail here (for a discussion of the issues, see [CHAN72] and [STAL76]).

One fundamental point does need to be mentioned, namely, the degree of responsibility of the session protocol entities. When the session is backed up to the beginning of a session recovery unit, the session protocol entities may be requested to retransmit all records from that point forward. If so, the session entity must maintain a copy of each record. To avoid unbounded storage requirements, the user should periodically issue a release command, so that some prior session recovery units can be discarded. Alternatively, the session entity might only be required to remember the records of the current recovery unit.

On the other hand, the session entity may only be required to discard outstanding records and back up its recovery-unit counter to the point indicated, with the primary recovery responsibilities being handled at higher levels. In this case, there does not seem much point in having any recovery feature in the session layer. Indeed NBS takes the position that recovery is inherently an application function and, based on the principle of functional separation of layers, should not be visible in the session layer [NBS80b].

Figure 16-1 indicates that a session recovery unit is made up of one or more records. However, there is no need for a defined relationship between session recovery units and session interaction units.

DPA Philosophy

The DOD protocol architecture views the session functionality in a completely different light than the OSI model. The generic session control functions in the OSI model (dialogue management, recovery marking) are viewed as useful but minor, and not sufficient to justify a separate layer.

Rather, the DPA envisions various specialized session entities that are amenable to standardization. These entities perform functions related to the establishment, monitoring, or termination of a user-to-user logical connection, but are not actively involved in data transfer. This view, incidentally, is reflected in DEC's DNA architecture.

We list here a few examples of session entities:

- *Name server:* allows a user to locate a service or application within the network.

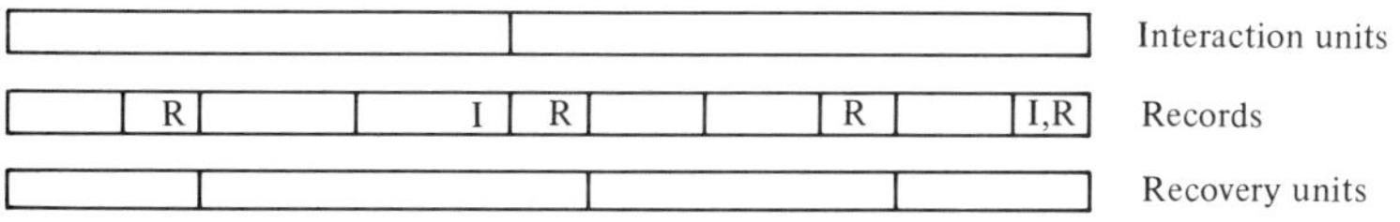

FIGURE 16-1. Session delimited data units.

- *Access control mechanism:* restricts user access to certain resources. Any user attempt to access a controlled resource triggers this entity, which mediates the establishment of a connection.
- *Preemptive mechanism:* used, for example, if a low-priority user is dominating a particular resource, and an agent of the network administration must preempt this user's communication on behalf of a user with a critical current need.
- *Statistics reporting service:* invoked at termination of a user connection to communicate usage statistics to a network accounting entity.

The two views (OSI, DPA) are certainly different, but not necessarily conflicting. One could conceive of an architecture with a session layer that includes a connection-service entity which is involved throughout data transfer and a collection of specialize entities which provide services of general utility that do not endure for the lifetime of a session. The important issue is the extent to which the services of any of these entities are needed, and how they should be integrated into a communications architecture.

VIRTUAL TERMINAL PROTOCOLS

Most of our discussion has implicitly assumed that communication is between "peer" entities, that is, entities of roughly equal capabilities that wish to do roughly similar kinds of things. There are exceptions to this rule, and perhaps the most significant is the case of terminal-to-application communication.

One's first impression is that this type of communication is outside the scope of a computer-communications architecture. In the case of a terminal directly connected to a computer, the computer will have an I/O driver that handles the terminal and a mechanism for communication between that driver and the application program. If the terminal and computer are connected via a network, the network must transparently pass the data between the terminal and a computer I/O port. This seems to be a requirement since a number of terminal devices do not have the capability of implementing the various OSI layers.

There is, however, a problem in this approach that relates to one of the advertised benefits of a computer network. Specifically, a user at a terminal would like to be able to access resources and applications on a variety of computers. Furthermore, the user does not want to be limited to using the terminals and computers of a single vendor. What does this imply? Usually, in order to be able to use a terminal from one vendor with a host from another vendor, a special host software package must be built to accommodate the foreign terminal. Now consider a network with N types of terminals and M types of hosts. For complete connectivity, each host type must contain a package for handling each terminal type. In the worst case, MN I/O packages must be developed. Furthermore, if a new type of host is acquired, it must be equipped with N new I/O packages. If a new type of terminal is acquired, each host must be equipped with a new I/O package, for a total of M new packages. This is not the type of situation designed to encourage multivendor interoperability.

To solve this problem, a universal terminal protocol is needed—one that can handle all types of terminals. Such a thing exists today in name only: *virtual terminal protocol* (VTP). However, rudimentary versions do already exist. One is the X.28/X.29/X.3 protocol, which is based on a simple parameterized model of an asynchronous terminal. The true VTP is a fundamentally different and more flexible approach. In this section we will provide an overview of both approaches.

Packet Assembler/Dissassembler (PAD)

As supplements to the X.25 standard CCITT has developed a set of standards related to a facility known as a *packet assembler/disassembler* (PAD). The PAD is designed to solve the two fundamental problems associated with the attachment of terminals to a network:

1. Many terminals are not capable of implementing the protocol layers for attaching in the same manner as a host. The PAD facility provides the intelligence for communicating with a host using the X.25 protocol.
2. There are differences among terminal types. The PAD facility provides a set of parameters to account for those differences. However, it only deals with asynchronous terminals.

Three standards define the PAD facility:

- *X.3:* describes the functions of the PAD and the parameters used to control its operation.
- *X.28:* describes the PAD-terminal protocol.
- *X.29:* describes the PAD-host protocol.

Figure 16-2a indicates the architecture for use of the PAD. The terminal attached to the PAD sends characters one at a time. These are buffered in the PAD and then assembled into an X.25 packet, and sent through the network to the host. Host packets are received at the PAD, disassembled by stripping off the X.25 header, and passed to the terminal one character at a time. Simple commands between terminal and PAD (X.28), used to set parameters and establish virtual circuits, consist of character strings. Similar host-PAD control information (X.29) is transmitted in the data field of an X.25 packet, with a bit set in the X.25 header to indicate that this is control information.

Let us look briefly at each of the three standards involved. The PAD itself is defined in X.3, which lists 18 parameters that determine the behavior of the PAD (Table 16-1). Since a PAD may serve more than one terminal (a terminal concentration function), a set of these parameters is maintained for each terminal. Most of these parameters are self-explanatory, but items 3 and 4 deserve further comment. As the PAD receives characters from a terminal, it places them in a buffer whose length equals the maximum data field size of an X.25 packet. When the buffer is full, the packet is sent. These parameters may also allow the PAD to send a packet when it receives a carriage return, another control character, or when a timeout occurs.

The interface (actually the protocol) between the PAD and a terminal is specified in X.28. There are two phases of operation. In the data transfer phase, the PAD exchanges data between the terminal and the remote DTE. In the control phase, there is a dialogue between the terminal and the PAD. Normally, the control phase is used by the terminal only to request connection to a particular DTE. In response to this request, the PAD sets up a connection to the appropriate DCE, which in turn sets up a virtual circuit to its local DTE. The control phase may also be invoked from a terminal by hitting the break key, if X.3 parameter 7 is set appro-

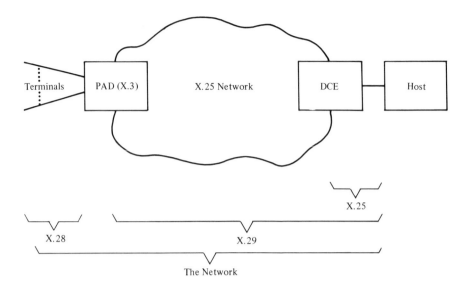

(a) Parameter-Defined Terminal

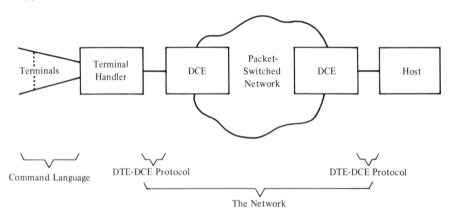

(b) Virtual Terminal Protocol

FIGURE 16-2. Two views of terminal-network architecture.

priately. Table 16-2 summarizes the terminal commands and PAD responses specified in X.28.

Control information, in *PAD messages*, is exchanged between the PAD and the remote DTE in the data field of an X.25 data packet (see Figure 13-9), as specified in X.29. When the Q bit of a data packet is set, the data are interpreted as one of the messages of Table 16-3. Otherwise, the packet contains data being exchanged between the terminal and the remote DTE. In addition, conventional X.25 packets are exchanged between the DTE and the PAD to manage the virtual circuit.

Generalized Virtual Terminal Protocols

The X.3/X.28/X.29 approach to terminal handling is an effective one for simple asynchronous terminals. Its main defect is a lack of flexibility. As more complex

TABLE 16-1   PAD Parameters (X.3)

Number	Description	Selectable Values
1	Whether terminal operator can escape from data transfer to PAD command state	0: not allowed 1: escape character 32–126: graphic characters
2	Whether PAD echoes back characters received from terminal	0: no echo 1: echo
3	Terminal characters that will trigger the sending of a partially full packet by the PAD	0: only send full packets 2: carriage return 6, 18, 126: other control characters
4	Timeout value that will trigger the sending of a partially full packet by the PAD	0: no timeout 1–255: multiple of 50 ms
5	Whether PAD can exercise flow control over terminal output, using X-ON, X-OFF	0: not allowed 1: allowed
6	Whether PAD can send service signals (control information) to terminal	0: not allowed 1: allowed
7	Action(s) taken by PAD on receipt of break signal from terminal	0: nothing 1: interrupt 2: reset 8: escape 21: discard output, send break to host
8	Whether PAD will discard DTE data intended for terminal	0: normal delivery 1: discard
9	Number of padding characters inserted after carriage return (to terminal)	0: determined by data rate 1–7: number of characters
10	Whether PAD inserts control characters to prevent terminal line overflow	0: no 1–255: yes, line length
11	Terminal speed (bps)	0–18: 50 to 64,000
12	Whether terminal can exercise flow control over PAD, using X-ON, X-OFF	0: not allowed 1: allowed
13	Whether PAD inserts line feed after carriage return sent or echoed to terminal	0: no line feed 1–7: various conditions
14	Number of padding characters inserted after line feed (to terminal)	0: no padding 1–7: number of characters
15	Whether PAD supports editing during data transfer (defined in parameters 16–18)	0: no 1: yes
16	Character delete	0–127: selected characters
17	Line delete	0–127: selected characters
18	Line display	0–127: selected characters

terminals are used, more and more parameters must be defined to deal with them. The alternative is to go to a generalized virtual terminal protocol. In this section we first discuss the characteristics of such protocols and then look at a simple but pioneering example: TELNET.

Characteristics.   As the name implies, the VTP is a protocol, a set of conventions for communication between peer entities. It includes the following functions:

TABLE 16-2   X.28 Commands and Responses

PAD Command Signal Format	Function	PAD Service Signal Sent in Response[a]
STAT	To request status information regarding a virtual call connected to the DTE	FREE or ENGAGED
CLR	To clear down a virtual call	CLR CONF or CLR ERR (in the case of local procedure error)
PAR? (list of parameter references	To request the current values of specified parameters	PAR (list of parameter references with their current values or INV)
SET? (list of parameter references and corresponding values)	To request changing or setting of the current values of the specified parameters and to request the current values of specified parameters	PAR (list of parameter references with their current values or INV)
PROF (identifier)	To give to PAD parameters a standard set of values	Acknowledgment
RESET	To reset the virtual call	Acknowledgment
INT	To transmit an *interrupt* packet	Acknowledgment
SET (list of parameters with requested values)	To set or change parameter values	Acknowledgment
Selection PAD command signal	To set up a virtual call	Acknowledgment

[a]*PAD service* signals are not sent when prameter 6 is set to 0.

- Establishing and maintaining a connection between two application-level entities.
- Controlling a dialogue for negotiating the allowable actions to be performed across the connection.
- Creating and maintaining a data structure that represents the ''state'' of the terminal.
- Translating between actual terminal characteristics and a standardized representation.

The first two functions are in the nature of session control (layer 5); the latter two are presentation control (layer 6) functions. Figure 16-2 illustrates the difference in philosophy between this approach and that of the PAD. In the VTP approach, the terminal handler, which implements the terminal side of the protocol, is considered architecturally as a host attached to the network. Thus the protocol is end-to-end in terms of reliability, flow control, and so on. By comparison, the PAD is considered part of the network, not a separate host. From the point of view of the host, the PAD facility is part of its local DCE's X.25 layer 3 functionality. Although the PAD concept affords an easily implemented capability, it does not provide the architectural base for a flexible terminal-handling facility.

The principal purpose of the VTP is to transform the characteristics of a real terminal into a standardized form or virtual terminal. Because of the wide differences in capabilities among terminals, it is unreasonable to attempt to develop a single virtual terminal type. Four classes are of interest:

TABLE 16-3 X.29 Messages

Message	Direction	Description
Set PAD	To PAD	Set selected parameters to indicated values
Read PAD	To PAD	Read values of indicated parameters
Set and read PAD	To PAD	Perform set and read functions
Parameter indication	From PAD	List of parameters and values in response to read command
Invitation to clear	To PAD	Requests the PAD to clear the virtual call
Indication of break	To or from PAD	Indication of break from DTE or terminal
Error	To or from PAD	Indicates error in previous message

- *Scroll mode:* These are terminals with no local intelligence, including keyboard-printer and keyboard-display devices. Characters are transmitted as they are entered, and incoming characters are printed or displayed as they come in. On a display, as the screen fills, the top line is scrolled off.
- *Page mode:* These are keyboard-display terminals with a cursor-addressable character matrix display. Either user or host can modify random-accessed portions of the display. I/O can be a page at a time.
- *Form/data entry mode:* These are similar to page mode terminals, but allow definition of fixed and variable fields on the display. This permits a number of features, such as transmitting only the variable part, and defining field attributes to be used as validity checks.
- *Graphics mode:* These allow the creation of arbitrary two-dimensional patterns.

Little has yet been done for graphics mode, but a number of proposals exist for the first three modes. Table 16-4 is a proposed European standard defining the primitives or commands that can be used to control the terminal and the parameters that define the terminal.

For any VTP, there are basically four phases of operation:

- *Connection management:* includes session-layer-related functions, such as connection request and termination.
- *Negotiation:* used to determine a mutually agreeable set of characteristics between the two correspondents.
- *Control:* exchange of control information and commands (e.g., defining the attributes of a field).
- *Data:* transfer of data between two correspondents.

Figure 16-3 shows two models for VTPs. In the asymmetric model, the virtual terminal is seen as a combination of the real terminal and the local mapping functions needed to adapt it to a standard language. On the other side is the host-resident application, which either "talks" VTP or must adapt its own representation to the standard language. A more general view is the symmetric one, which uses a shared presentation unit which represents the state of the virtual terminal. The presentation unit is implemented as a data structure that both sides, symmetrically, may read and update. Figure 16-4 is an example. The advantage of the symmetric

TABLE 16-4 Parameters and Primitives for VTP

Mode	Primitive	Parameter
Scroll	Agree	Terminal class
	Disagree	Line length
	Request	Erase overprint
	Indicate	Dialogue mode
	New line	Auxiliary data structure
	Start of line	
	Text segment	
	Purge	
	Asynchronous attention	
	Synchronous attention	
Paged	Scroll mode primitives	Scroll mode parameters
	Delete all	Page size
	Position	
Data entry terminal	Paged mode primitives	Paged mode parameters
	Attribute[a]	
	Delete attribute	
	Erase unprotected	
	Next unprotected field	

[a]Attributes are protected/unprotected fields, and three levels of display: nondisplay, normal, and intensified.

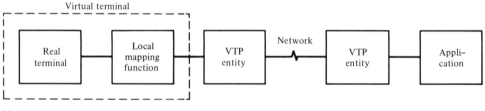

(a) Asymmetric

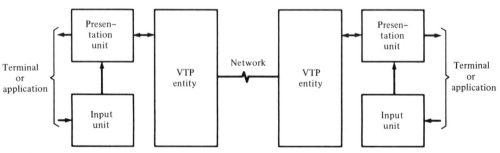

(b) Symmetric

FIGURE 16-3. Virtual terminal protocol (VTP) models.

```
type  field = record
         text: array [0 .. MaxText] of char;        {contents of the field}
         xposition: 0 .. MaxX;                       {horizontal position on screen}
         yposition: 0 .. MaxY;                       {vertical position on screen}
         size: 0 .. MaxSize;                         {size of the field}
         rendition: 0... MaxRendition;               {color, intensity, etc.}
         adjustment: (left, right);                  {positioning of text within field}
         lcletters, ucletters, numbers, space, special: boolean;   {allowed input}
         protected, EntryRequired, MustFill: boolean
end;
var   datastruct: record
         display: array [0 .. MaxField] of field;    {collection of fields}
         cursor: record x: 0 .. MaxText; y: 0 .. MaxField end;    {cursor position}
         TerminalType: (scroll, page, form);
         FlowMode: (alternating, FreeRunning);       {half or full duplex}
         turn: (mine, his);                          {who goes next (if half duplex)}
         state: (uninitialized, normal, interrupted)
end;
```

FIGURE 16-4.   A VTP data structure (from [TANE81a]).

view is that it permits terminal-to-terminal and even host-to-host, as well as terminal-to-host dialogue.

TELNET.   One of the first attempts to develop a true virtual terminal protocol is TELNET, which was developed as part of ARPANET and is still in active use. Although this protocol is currently used for scroll-mode asynchronous terminals, it embodies the principles one would expect in a VTP.

TELNET is built on three main principles:

* The concept of a *network virtual terminal* (NVT).
* A symmetric view of terminals and processes.
* The principle of negotiated options.

The first two principles are reflected in Figure 16-3b. The NVT is an imaginary device that provides an intermediate representation of a canonical terminal. If the communicating entity is a process, a module is needed (Server TELNET) to convert between the NVT representation and the process representation. If the communicating entity is a terminal, a module is needed (User TELNET) to map the characteristics of the terminal into those of NVT.

Communication can occur between two terminals, two processes, or a process and a terminal. It is expected that the communication will be over a TCP connection. TELNET enforces a two-way alternate mode of communication to accommodate half-duplex terminals. TELNET assumes that the ASCII code will be used. Table 16-5 lists the ASCII control characters that are part of the NVT keyboard.

Each TELNET connection begins with a negotiated option phase. Four commands are used in this process: WILL, WONT, DO, DONT. WILL X is sent by either party, to indicate that party's desire (offer) to begin performing option X; DO X and DONT X are positive and negative acknowledgments, respectively. Similarly, DO X is sent to indicate a desire (request) that the other party begin performing option X; WILL X and WONT X are the positive and negative acknowledgments. This mechanism is a general one and can be used to negotiate any sort of option. Certain options are considered common enough to be ''registered'' and assigned codes (Table 16-5). Additional options may be encoded at the discretion of individual communicating entities. The registered options fall into three general classes of control:

TABLE 16-5 TELNET Parameters

ASCII Control Codes		Registered Options	
Null		0	Binary transmission
Line feed		1	Echo
Carriage return		2	Reconnection
Bell		3	Suppress go ahead
Backspace		4	Approximate message size
Horizontal tab		5	Status
Vertical tab		6	Timing mark
Form feed		7	Remote-controlled transmission and echoing
TELNET Commands		8	Output line width
End of subnegotiation		9	Output page size
NOP		10	Output carriage-return disposition
Data mark		11	Output horizontal tabstops
Break		12	Output horizontal tab disposition
Interrupt process		13	Output formfeed disposition
Abort output		14	Output vertical tab stops
Are you there		15	Output vertical tab disposition
Erase character		16	Output line feed disposition
Erase line		17	Extended ASCII
Go ahead		255	Extended options list
Beginning of subnegotiation			
Will			
Wont			
Do			
Dont			
Interpret as command			

- *Physical terminal (8 to 17):* control or accommodate physical characteristics of the real terminal.
- *TELNET (0, 2, 3, 5, 255):* concerned with controlling use of TELNET connections.
- *Operating system and processes (1, 4, 6):* concerned with nonterminal users of TELNET.

Option 7 is an elaborate scheme for dealing with the propagation delays experienced with remote echoing. It combines the functions of all three option classes, and is discussed in [DAVI77].

In addition to the negotiation phase, there are other times when control information needs to be exchanged. This is achieved by the use of commands inserted into the data stream and preceded by an escape character (interpret as command). This is, unfortunately, a clumsy mechanism since it requires the NVT entity to scan all input for the escape character. Table 16-5 lists the TELNET commands. Most are self-explanatory or have already been discussed. Among the remaining commands:

- *Interrupt process:* interrupts the operation of a remote process. This function is invoked when a user believes the process is looping, or when an unwanted process has been activated.
- *Abort output:* allows a process which is generating output to run to completion without sending the output to the user's terminal. This function also clears any output already produced but not yet printed on the user's terminal.

- *Are you there:* gives the users some visible evidence that the system is still up and running.

FILE TRANSFER PROTOCOLS

The development of computer protocols has been a bottom-up affair. The most used and the most well-defined protocols exist at the lower layers of the hierarchy. At the application level, although there is a great deal of activity, few working protocols exist. The most notable exception is in the area of file transfer protocols, examples of which have been around for many years.

Architecture

The purpose of a file transfer protocol (FTP) is to transfer a file or a portion of a file from one system to another, under command of an FTP user. Depending on its scope of responsibility, the FTP may be a pure application protocol in the OSI sense, or it may also have presentation functionality, and even some elements of a session layer.

Figure 16-5 shows a view of FTP as an application-level protocol. Here, FTP is viewed as the top layer of a seven-layer communications architecture that is supported by the station's operating system. Typically, FTP is used interactively by an on-line user. The user's communication with FTP is mediated by the operating system, which contains I/O drivers. If the user on system *A* wishes access to a file on system *B*, then *A*'s FTP establishes a connection to *B*'s FTP. This is, of course, a logical connection. The actual path for control and user data is through the layers of the architecture.

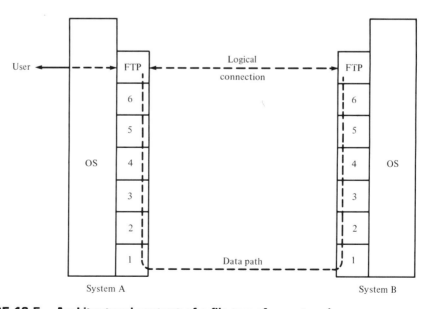

FIGURE 16-5. Architectural context of a file transfer protocol.

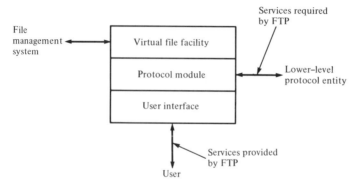

FIGURE 16-6. Generic FTP structure.

The user connects to the local FTP in order to transfer all or part of a file. There are three possibilities. The user at *A* may wish a file at *B* to be transferred to *A*. This would give the user local access to the contents of the file. The user may have prepared a file locally (at *A*) and wish it sent to *B*. Finally, the user may request that a file be exchanged between *B* and a third system, *C*. This is referred to as a third-party transfer and involves the FTP entities at *A*, *B*, and *C*.

FTP must interact with three entities, as depicted in Figure 16-6. First, there must be a user interface to accept requests from an interactive user or, possibly, a program. Of course, this interaction only takes place at the requesting system. The remote FTP in a file transfer event does not interact with a user. Second, FTP must be able to communicate with other FTPs to achieve file transfer. Typically, this is done by interfacing to a lower-level protocol entity. Finally, to transfer a file, FTP must be able to get at the file. For this, an interface is needed to the local file management system.

Consideration of this last interface reminds us that a general-purpose FTP must operate in a heterogeneous environment. Because different systems may have different file formats and structures, FTP must have knowledge of the local file system or, at least, rely on an entity that does. Before suggesting an effective way of handling this situation, let us consider what it is that is to be transferred. There are three possibilities.

- *The data in the file:* If just the actual data in the file are sent, we are not really dealing with a file transfer. This is more in the nature of a message exchange or electronic mail facility.
- *The data plus the file structure:* This, at minimum, is what is usually meant by a file transfer protocol.
- *The data, file structure, and all its attributes:* Examples of attributes are an access control list, an update history, and a list of indices for an indexed sequential file facility.

If the FTP operates somewhere on a spectrum bounded by the last two items, it must have knowledge of the local file structure and format, and it must understand the incoming file structure and format. To avoid the $M \times N$ problem discussed in the section on virtual terminal protocols, a similar solution may be adopted: the virtual file. Thus a general-purpose virtual file structure is defined. Only virtual files are exchanged between FTPs. Locally, a transformation is needed between

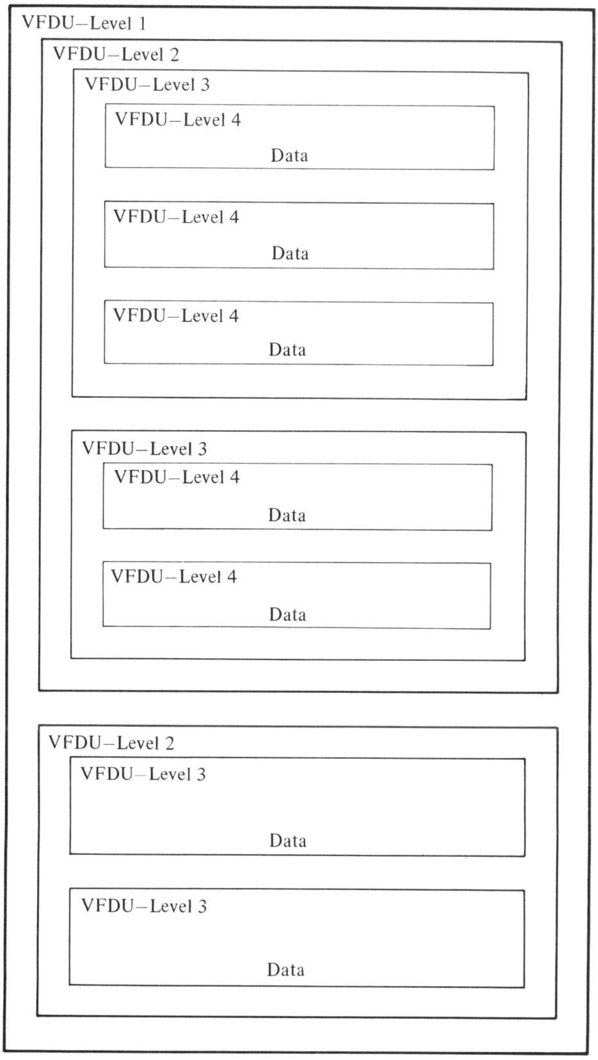

```
┌─────────────────────────────────────────────────────┐
│ VFDU–Level 1                                          │
│ ┌───────────────────────────────────────────────┐   │
│ │ VFDU–Level 2                                    │   │
│ │ ┌───────────────────────────────────────────┐ │   │
│ │ │ VFDU–Level 3                              │ │   │
│ │ │ ┌───────────────────────────────────────┐ │ │   │
│ │ │ │ VFDU–Level 4                          │ │ │   │
│ │ │ │              Data                     │ │ │   │
│ │ │ └───────────────────────────────────────┘ │ │   │
│ │ │ ┌───────────────────────────────────────┐ │ │   │
│ │ │ │ VFDU–Level 4                          │ │ │   │
│ │ │ │              Data                     │ │ │   │
│ │ │ └───────────────────────────────────────┘ │ │   │
│ │ │ ┌───────────────────────────────────────┐ │ │   │
│ │ │ │ VFDU–Level 4                          │ │ │   │
│ │ │ │              Data                     │ │ │   │
│ │ │ └───────────────────────────────────────┘ │ │   │
│ │ └───────────────────────────────────────────┘ │   │
│ │ ┌───────────────────────────────────────────┐ │   │
│ │ │ VFDU–Level 3                              │ │   │
│ │ │ ┌───────────────────────────────────────┐ │ │   │
│ │ │ │ VFDU–Level 4                          │ │ │   │
│ │ │ │              Data                     │ │ │   │
│ │ │ └───────────────────────────────────────┘ │ │   │
│ │ │ ┌───────────────────────────────────────┐ │ │   │
│ │ │ │ VFDU–Level 4                          │ │ │   │
│ │ │ │              Data                     │ │ │   │
│ │ │ └───────────────────────────────────────┘ │ │   │
│ │ └───────────────────────────────────────────┘ │   │
│ └───────────────────────────────────────────────┘   │
│ ┌───────────────────────────────────────────────┐   │
│ │ VFDU–Level 2                                    │   │
│ │ ┌───────────────────────────────────────────┐ │   │
│ │ │ VFDU–Level 3                              │ │   │
│ │ │              Data                         │ │   │
│ │ └───────────────────────────────────────────┘ │   │
│ │ ┌───────────────────────────────────────────┐ │   │
│ │ │ VFDU–Level 3                              │ │   │
│ │ │              Data                         │ │   │
│ │ └───────────────────────────────────────────┘ │   │
│ └───────────────────────────────────────────────┘   │
└─────────────────────────────────────────────────────┘
```

FIGURE 16-7. Virtual file structure.

the virtual file format and the local file format. This transformation can be implemented in the FTP or provided by a presentation protocol.

A virtual file structure should be simple enough that files can be exchanged between identical file systems with minimum overhead. On the other hand, it must be complex enough to be able to represent accurately a variety of dissimilar file systems.

A rather simple virtual file structure is shown in Figure 16-7. The key building block of a virtual file is a *virtual file data unit* (VFDU). The highest or first-level data unit encompasses the entire file. Each VFDU may contain data or other VFDUs. The lowest level VFDUs in this tree structure must contain data. The internal structure of a data VFDU (e.g., in terms of fields and groups of fields) is not specified. However, certain attributes of the file may be part of the virtual file structure. These may include access control parameters, and the identity of index keys.

Characteristics

As is usually the case with any protocol, file transfer protocols can be characterized by the services they provide and the protocol mechanisms they employ. Table 16-6 contains a list of relevant service and protocol features for file transfer protocols, suggested in [NBS80c]. We will briefly consider each feature in turn.

Service Features. In the typical computer system, there is some *access control* mechanism to protect the file system. A user must have an ID and password to gain access to the system at all. Then individual files may maintain access control lists with specific permissions (read, write) by user. This capability must be extended across the network. The simplest way, perhaps, is to require the user to do a remote login and be identified at the system. In a controlled network environment, there might be a network-wide access control mechanism. In any case, the mechanism must be mediated by the FTP.

The normal *processing mode* of a file transfer is immediate. That is, when the transfer is requested, FTP will endeavor to achieve the transfer right away and report back. If, however, the transfer is not urgent, the user could indicate that the transfer could take place in a background mode.

A *file naming* facility is needed to identify the source and destination station and the source and destination file. At a minimum, the user must specify the network name of the station and a file name that is locally significant (local to the system on which the file resides). This requires the user to know the syntax and semantics of file naming conventions at each system of interest. A better service is one that involves standardized syntax for file names, although semantics may still differ (e.g., modifiers such as SOURCE and OBJECT may have particular significance). A virtual file name would then be used, to be translated locally by FTP. Again, in a controlled network environment, one might hope for a network-wide file system, with a common syntax and semantics, in which the user need not even know the location of a file.

The basic operation of FTP is to duplicate a file and send it to another system,

TABLE 16-6   File Transfer Protocol Features

Service Features	Protocol Features
Access control	Transmission of commands
Processing mode	File attributes
File naming	Negotiation
Alternative operations	Text formatting
File management	Security
Error recovery	Statistics
Flow control	
File structuring	
Status reports	

where it is stored with a new local name. *Alternative operations* include: transfer of a portion of a file, copy a file only if an empty destination file already exists, and append a file to the contents of a destination file.

An FTP can mediate user access to certain *file management* facilities, either local or remote. Although file management is not properly a part of a file transfer protocol, certain minimal services seem warranted. The following three are found in most file transfer protocols: file allocation (define a new file and allocate space), file deletion, and listing file names in a directory.

An *error recovery* facility would provide for recovery from errors or failure in the file system or operating system. The mechanism to be used is checkpointing. Checkpoint locations are transferred along with the file. The number of unacknowledged checkpoints can be controlled by a sliding window protocol. When an error is detected, the file transfer can be backed up to any acknowledged checkpoint. This mechanism could be implemented entirely in FTP, or rely on the session layer for checkpoint transmission and acknowledgment.

A simple stop-and-wait *flow-control* scheme is a useful addition to an FTP. This mechanism allows the transfer to be temporarily halted and resumed later. This feature provides the ability to mount tapes during the transfer and allows system resources such as disks to be preempted by a higher priority task without aborting a transfer in progress.

We have already discussed the need for a *file structuring* service with an FTP. A hierarchical or tree structure file description will have the most general applicability.

File transfers can be lengthy processes, particularly if performed in background mode. *Status reports* should be provided that indicate the start and completion of a transfer. The user should be able to interrogate FTP to determine the current status of any ongoing file transfer.

Protocol Features.   A fundamental feature of a file transfer protocol is the *transmission of commands*. An FTP entity must communicate with a peer counterpart to coordinate and control the data transfer. Control information could be exchanged over the same session as the file data, or it could be accomplished over a separate session. In a third-party transfer, mechanisms must be in place to provide for the coordination among three FTP entities.

The source FTP must communicate *file attributes* to the recipient system. This is so even if a fully general virtual file structure is used. The reason is that, at the receiving end, the virtual file must be transformed into a local real file. The nature of that transformation may depend on attributes of the original source file. For example, if the destination system only uses the ASCII character code and the source file is non-ASCII text, this attribute needs to be known so that either the source or destination FTP can invoke a conversion function.

A flexible file transfer protocol is bound to have a number of options, for example, use of checkpointing, flow control, buffer size, and so on. A process of *negotiation* is required for two FTP entities to agree on a common level of service.

In text files, there will be certain control codes that affect the format of the text (e.g., vertical and horizontal spacing). A *text formatting* mechanism indicates which control codes are in the file and how they are to be interpreted. Thus systems using different text format control conventions can intelligibly exchange text files.

In addition to specific access control mechanisms that control access to files by identified users, files may be designated with a *security* label. FTP must cooperate with the file system's security mechanism to maintain security. Specifically, FTP must match the security level of the file to the security level of the session.

Finally, *statistics* can be gathered by FTP to provide information to a central control authority and to provide the user with information to be used when allocating local resources.

A Simple File Transfer Protocol

As an example, we now present a relatively simple file transfer protocol [NBS83b]. This protocol is a subset of the FTP that is moving toward standardization within ISO and NBS, and was designed specifically to provide an early practical demonstration of the forthcoming standard.

The FTP acts as a mediator between a user and a remote filestore administrator. The FTP supports a dialogue that:

- Allows the user and filestore administrator to establish each other's identity.
- Identifies the file that is needed.
- Engages in the transfer of data.

Twelve types of primitives and a total of 42 specific primitives are used as the interface between the user and FTP. These primitives are listed and defined in Table 16-7.

The parameters associated with these primitives are:

- *Called address:* identifies the filestore to which the connection is to be established.
- *Calling address:* identifies the requesting user.
- *Service subset:* indicates the options of the file service supported by the implementation.
- *Filename:* identifies the file to be transferred.
- *Originator:* indicates which side initiated an abort.
- *Diagnostic:* indicates success or failure of an operation and, if applicable, the reason for the failure.
- *Data type:* the type of the data transferred in this operation.
- *Data value:* the value of the data transferred in this operation.

Once a connection has been made, a file transfer consists of the following operations:

- A READ exchange initiated by the requestor.
- One or more DATA exchanges initiated by the responder.
- A DATA-END exchange initiated by the responder.
- A TRANSFER-END exchange initiated by the requestor.

The protocol between FTP entities is carried out, as usual, by exchanging protocol data units (PDUs). The format of each PDU is simple. The first field contains the length of the header in octets. The second field contains the PDU id. A variable number of additional fields contain qualifying information. Table 16-8 lists the FTP PDUs.

As can be seen, this is a very rudimentary protocol, with a minimal set of features. Yet it involves 42 primitives and 20 PDUs. As more features are added, the protocol can be expected to become increasingly complex.

TABLE 16-7 File Transfer Primitives and Parameters

F-CONNECT.request (Called address, Calling address, Service subset)
F-CONNECT.indication (Called address, Calling address, Service subset)
F-CONNECT.response (Called address, Calling address, Service subset)
F-CONNECT.confirm(Called address, Calling address, Service subset)

> Establishes a connection between two FTP entities, one serving the file user and one serving the filestore administrator.

F-RELEASE.request ( )
F-RELEASE.indication ( )
F-RELEASE.response ( )
F-RELEASE.confirm ( )

> Terminates a file service connection.

F-ABORT.request ( )
F-ABORT.indication (Originator, Diagnostic)

> Abruptly terminates a connection. Also used to refuse a connection request.

F-SELECT.request (Filename)
F-SELECT.indication (Filename)
F-SELECT.response (Filename, Diagnostic)
F-SELECT.confirm (Filename, Diagnostic)

> Selects an existing file.

F-DESELECT.request ( )
F-DESELECT.indication ( )
F-DESELECT.response (Diagnostic)
F-DESELECT.confirm (Diagnostic)

> Releases the association between the file service connection and the file.

F-OPEN.request ( )
F-OPEN.indication ( )
F-OPEN.response (Diagnostic)
F-OPEN.confirm (Diagnostic)

> Opens the currently selected file.

F-CLOSE.request ( )
F-CLOSE.indication ( )
F-CLOSE.response (Diagnostic)
F-CLOSE.confirm (Diagnostic)

> Closes the currently open file.

F-READ.request ( )
F-READ.indication ( )
F-READ.response (Diagnostic)
F-READ.confirm (Diagnostic)

> Specifies a transfer from the responder to the initiator of the file transfer.

F-DATA.request (Data type, Data value)
F-DATA.indication (Data type, Data value)

> Transfers file data from entity that issued the READ request.

F-DATA-END.request (Diagnostic)
F-DATA-END.indication (Diagnostic)

> Indicates the completion of a data transfer.

TABLE 16-7 (continued)   File Transfer Primitives and Parameter

F-TRANSFER-END.request (Diagnostic)
F-TRANSFER-END.indication (Diagnostic)
F-TRANSFER-END.response (Diagnostic)
F-TRANSFER-END.confirm (Diagnostic)

    Indicates end of a file transfer.

F-CANCEL.request (Diagnostic)
F-CANCEL.indication (Diagnostic)
F-CANCEL.response (Diagnostic)
F-CANCEL.confirm (Diagnostic)

    Cancels a data transfer activity.

16-4

TELETEXT AND VIDEOTEX

One of the most exciting new areas of communications is Teletext and Videotex. These are information retrieval services that display data on specially equipped TV sets of the residential or business user. Some interesting protocol standards issues arise in relation to these services. We begin with a brief description of Teletext and Videotex, and then explore presentation protocol standards, an area where much work has already been done.

TABLE 16-8   File Transfer Protocol Data Units

PDU Type	Name	Fields[a]
FCR	File connect request	67
FCC	File connect confirm	67
FRLR	File release request	0
FRLC	File release confirm	0
FSR	File select request	68
FSC	File select confirm	68, 69, 70, 71
FDSR	File deselect request	0
FDSC	File deselect confirm	69, 70, 71
FOR	File open request	0
FOC	File open confirm	69, 70, 71
FCLR	File close request	0
FCLC	File close confirm	69, 70, 71
FRR	File read request	0
FRC	File read confirm	69, 70, 71
FDR	File data request	72, 73
FDER	File data end request	69, 70, 71
FTER	File transfer end request	69, 70, 71
FTEC	File transfer end confirm	69, 70, 71
FCANR	File cancel request	69, 70, 71
FCANC	File cancel confirm	69, 70, 71

[a] 67, service subset; 68, filename; 69, error type identification; 70, error identification; 71, diagnostic string; 72, data type; 73, data value.

Description

Teletext. The simpler of the two systems is Teletext, which is depicted in Figure 16-8. Teletext is a simple one-way system that uses unallocated portions of the bandwidth of a broadcast TV signal. At the transmission end, a fixed set of pages of text is sent repeatedly in round-robin fashion. The receiver consists of a special decoder and storage unit, a keypad for user entry, and an ordinary TV set. The user keys in the number of the page desired. The decoder reads that page from the incoming signal, stores it, and displays it continuously until instructed to do otherwise. Typically, pages of teletext form a tree pattern with higher-level pages containing menus that guide the selection of lower level pages. Thus, although the system appears interactive to the user, it is actually a one-way broadcast of information.

Since only a small portion of the TV signal bandwidth is used for this purpose, the number of pages is limited by a desire to reduce access time. For example, using two lines of the vertical blanking interval, 100 pages of text can be cycled every 25 seconds.

Teletext is oriented primarily to the home market. Different sets of services could be offered on different channels. Examples of information presented by the system are stock market reports, weather reports, news, leisure information, and recipes.

Videotex. Videotex (formerly called Viewdata) is an interactive system designed to service both home and business needs. It is a general-purpose data base retrieval system that can use the public switched telephone network or an interactive metropolitan cable TV system.

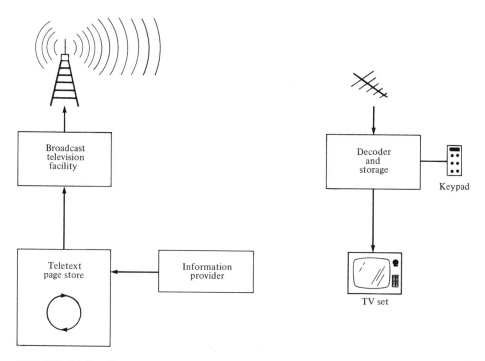

FIGURE 16-8. A typical teletext system.

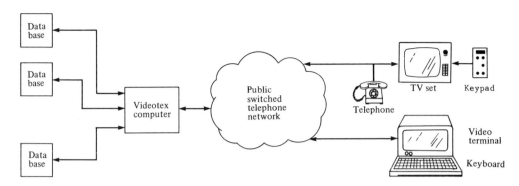

FIGURE 16-9. A typical videotex system.

Figure 16-9 depicts a typical system. The Videotex provider maintains a variety of data bases on a central computer. Some of these are public data bases provided by the Videotex system. Others are vendor-supplied services, such as a stock market advisory.

As with Teletext, Videotex presents information in pages, as requested by the user. The key differences are:

- Videotex can handle a much larger number of pages.
- With Videotex, user requests are serviced by the central computer rather than the local device.

Clearly, Videotex is a more flexible and open-ended system. Table 16-9 lists some typical services that can be made available through videotex.

Presentation Standards

A perusal of Figures 16-8 and 16-9 suggest a number of areas where standards might be appropriate. These include

- User terminal dialogue.
- Terminal-system protocol.
- Data base format.
- Display techniques.

TABLE 16-9 Typical Videotex Services

Information	Interactive	Transactive
Airline schedules	Educational activities, such as CAI	Payment of bills
Bus schedules		Stock market prices; buy and sell
Bulletin boards	Electronic message center	
Entertainment listings	Remote conferencing	Banking at home
Educational material	Video games	Purchase theater tickets
Library card catalogs	Public opinion polling	Hotel and airline reservations
Yellow pages		
News, sports, weather		Catalog shopping

Other areas are also possible. Of the possible areas, the emphasis to date has been on display techniques: How is the page of information to be constructed and formatted for display to the user? This area most properly falls into the presentation layer of the OSI model.

Unfortunately, but predictably, competing standards are evolving. The main centers of activity are Europe and North America. European standards emphasize the requirement for low-cost terminals and lean toward simple display techniques tailored to existing technology. North American standards activities stress the need for flexible, upward compatible capabilities. Although the work has primarily concerned Videotex, it is also applicable to Teletext.

At the present time, there are two popular standards: the NAPLPS (North American Presentation Level Protocol.Syntax), which is a draft proposed ANSI standard based on AT&T's Presentation Level Protocol [MOKH84, WETH832], and the CEPT (Council of European Postal and Telecommunications Authorities), which has been adopted by a consortium of 26 European nations [CHIL83]. CCITT has adopted S-100, which attempts to incorporate features of both standards.

The key difference between the European and American standards is the picture and character coding schemes used. CEPT employs alphamosaic coding and NAPLPS employs alphageometric coding.

With *alphamosaic coding*, the TV screen is divided into 24 lines of 40 spaces. For text, each space contains one character. Each character is encoded in a 7-bit code and is displayed using an 8 × 10 pattern of dots. In addition, an escape control character designates a space as being pictorial, in which case the character code is translated into a two by three pattern of squares. These patterns, extended over a number of spaces, allow crude pictorial displays to be constructed (Figure 16-10).

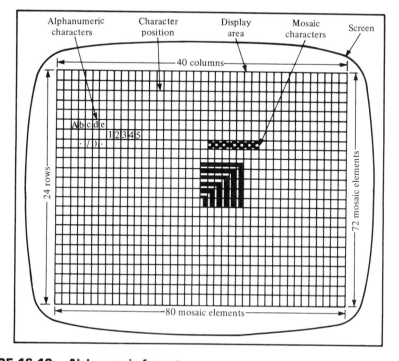

FIGURE 16-10. Alphamosaic format.

TABLE 16-10 NAPLPS Coding Scheme

a. Primary Character Set

	10	11	12	13	14	15
	2	3	4	5	6	7
0		0	@	P	`	p
1	!	1	A	Q	a	q
2	"	2	B	R	b	r
3	#	3	C	S	c	s
4	$	4	D	T	d	t
5	%	5	E	U	e	u
6	&	6	F	V	f	v
7	'	7	G	W	g	w
8	(	8	H	X	h	x
9	)	9	I	Y	i	y
10	*	:	J	Z	j	z
11	+	;	K	[	k	{
12	,	<	L	\	l	|
13	-	=	M	]	m	}
14	.	>	N	^	n	~
15	/	?	O	—	o	

b. Supplementary Character Set

	10	11	12	13	14	15
	2	3	4	5	6	7
0		°	→	—	Ω	κ
1	i	±	'	¹	AE	æ
2	¢	²	'	®	Đ	d
3	£	³	^	©	a̲	ð
4	S	×	~	TM	Ħ	ħ
5	≚	μ	‾	♪	⊞	i
6	#	¶	˘	⊟	IJ	ij
7	§	·	˙	⊔	L	l
8	¤	÷	¨	⊘	Ł	ł
9	'	'	/	⊠	Φ	υ
10	"	"	°	◤	Œ	œ
11	«	»	.	◼	ọ	β
12	←	¼	▢	⅛	ŀ	b
13	↑	½	"	⅜	Ŧ	t
14	→	¾	˝	⅝	ŋ	n
15	↓	¿	ˇ	⅞	'n	

c. Mosaic set

	10	11	12	13	14	15
	2	3	4	5	6	7

The *alphageometric coding* scheme allows the display of characters and 2 × 3 pictorial elements, but is also able to display high-resolution cartoon-like pictures created using geometric primitive instructions (e.g., point, line, arc). The mathematical description of each geometric element is encoded, and special hardware at the TV set produces the figure. Although this system produces pictures of higher quality than with the alphamosaic scheme, it still requires only voice-grade telephone lines for transmission. However, a more complex decoder unit is required.

Table 16-10 shows the coding tables for the NAPLPS. Encoding is done in 8-bit character format with escape codes to reuse the same bit patterns. The basic coding sets are:

- *Text:* The standard ASCII alphanumerics are included. In addition, a supplementary set of graphics characters are defined.
- *Mosaic graphics:* The 2 × 3 block mosaic characters are included for simple graphics and compatibility with European systems.
- *Picture description instructions:* These specify the geometric primitive as well as color.
- *Control sets:* Control set C0 is very close to the ASCII control character set. Control set C1 provides supplementary control characters.

TABLE 16-10 (continued)   NAPLPS Coding Scheme

d. Picture Description Instruction Set

	10 (2)	11 (3)	12 (4)	13 (5)	14 (6)	15 (7)
0	RESET	RECT (OUTLINED)	Numeric data			
1	DOMAIN	RECT (FILLED)				
2	TEXT	SET & RECT (OUTLINED)				
3	TEXTURE	SET & RECT (FILLED)				
4	POINT SET	POLY (OUTLINED)				
5	POINT SET (REL)	POLY (FILLED)				
6	POINT (ABS)	SET & POLY (OUTLINED)				
7	POINT (REL)	SET & POLY (FILLED)				
8	LINE (ABS)	FIELD				
9	LINE (REL)	INCR POINT				
10	SET & LINE (ABS)	INCR LINE				
11	SET & LINE (REL)	INCR POLY (FILLED)				
12	ARC (OUTLINED)	SET COLOR				
13	ARC (FILLED)	WAIT				
14	SET & ARC (OUT-	SELECT COLOR				
15	SET & ARC (FILLED)	BLINK				

e. C1 Control Set

	8 (4)	9 (5)
0	DEF MACRO	PROTECT
1	DEFP MACRO	EDC_1
2	DEFT MACRO	EDC2
3	DEF DRCS	EDC_3
4	DEF TEXTURE	EDC_4
5	END	WORD WRAP ON
6	REPEAT	WORD WRAP OFF
7	REPEAT 10 EOL	SCROLL ON
8	REVERSE VIDEO	SCROLL OFF
9	NORMAL VIDEO	UNDER LINE START
10	SMALL TEXT	UNDER LINE STOP
11	MED TEXT	FLASH CURSOR
12	NORMAL TEXT	STEADY CURSOR
13	DOUBLE WEIGHT	CURSOR OFF
14	BLANK START	BLANK STOP
15	DOUBLE SIZE	UNPROTECT

f. C0 Control Set

	0 (0)	1 (1)
0	NUL	TC_7 (DLE)
1	TC_1 (SOH)	DC_1
2	TC_2 (STX)	DC_2
3	TC_3 (ETX)	DC_3
4	TC_4 (EOT)	DC_4
5	TC_5 ENQ)	TC_8 (NAK)
6	TC_6 (ACK)	TC_9 (SYN)
7	BEL	TC_{10} ETB
8	BS APB)	CAN
9	HT (APF)	SS2
10	LF (APD)	SUB
11	VT (APU)	ESC
12	FF (CS)	FS
13	CR (APR)	SS3
14	SO	RS (APH)
15	SI	US

16-5

RECOMMENDED READING

Very little has been written about session protocols. [NBS80b] is a good general discussion. A readable discussion of X.3/X.28/X.29 is contained in [MART81]. A lengthy and quite good discussion of terminal handling and virtual terminal protocols is contained in [DAVI79]. [DAY80] and [MAGN79] also contain good discussions of virtual terminal protocols. [LOWE83] presents the current ISO view of virtual terminal services. For analyses of issues relating to file transfer protocols, see [DAY81] and [NBS80c]. [LEWA83] presents the status of the ISO file service standard. [LINN84] describes the virtual file store concept. [TYDE82] is a nontechnical but quite interesting account of Teletext and Videotex; a more technical account is [GECS83]. [BERR84] is a general discussion of upper-level protocols.

PROBLEMS

16-1 Assume that a session layer is making use of a reliable transport layer. The transport layer guarantees that data will be delivered in sequence, but makes no guarantee about timing. Thus multiple session recovery units may be outstanding. Might there be a problem when the sending user requests that the current recovery unit be cancelled?

16-2 A session recovery unit is defined by one of the two session users. Yet it would seem that recovery must involve backing up the data streams of both users. What mechanisms are required to achieve the necessary cooperation?

16-3 To which layer of the OSI model would you assign the X.3, X.28, and X.29 standards? Justify your answer in each case.

16-4 Describe how a protocol converter in a CBX architecture can be used to implement a virtual terminal protocol.

16-5 User A requests a third-party file transfer between *B* and *C*. What logical connections (e.g., *A-B, B-C, C-A*) are necessary for this transfer?

16-6 There are two file transfer protocols in use on ARPANET: the file transfer protocol (FTP) and the trivial file transfer protocol (TFTP). The former makes use of TELNET, which makes use of TCP. The latter simply makes use of the user datagram protocol (UDP). What features would you expect to be lacking in TFTP?

16-7 Consider the simple file transfer protocol defined in Section 16-3. Draw a time sequence diagram of primitives showing the sequence of events in a successful file transfer.

16-8 Indicate how the PDUs of Table 16-8 can be used to implement the primitives of Table 16-7.

CHAPTER 17

Integrated Services Digital Network

We have but one more topic to address in this book, and that topic represents in some sense a culmination of all the technologies and techniques that we have explored. The *integrated services digital network* (ISDN) is a projected worldwide public telecommunications network that will service a wide variety of user needs. The ISDN will be defined by the standardization of user interfaces, and will be implemented as a set of digital switches and paths supporting a broad range of traffic types and employing many of the concepts already discussed in this book. Actually, there will be multiple ISDNs, implemented within national boundaries, but from the user's point of view, there will be a single worldwide service.

Because the ISDN does not exist and is defined only by an evolving set of standards (being developed on a truly massive scale, both in terms of content and participants), this chapter can only suggest the probable characteristics of the future ISDN. We begin with an overview, which defines the ISDN by viewing it from several perspectives, discusses the overall ISDN architecture, and provides a brief summary of standards activities.

The next two sections concentrate on the two areas that are receiving the most attention, both technically and in terms of standards. These are the transmission structure and user access to the ISDN. Finally, a specification of the connection requirements of a user-to-user connection are defined in something known as the hypothetical reference connection.

OVERVIEW

Although both the standards for and the technology of ISDN are well-advanced, any description of the ISDN is, at present, speculative. With that in mind, we present an overview.

ISDN Concept

The concept of an ISDN is best explained by considering it from several different viewpoints:

- Evolution of the ISDN.
- The user interface.
- Objectives.
- Benefits.
- Services.

Evolution. The evolution of the existing telecommunications network, specialized carrier facilities, and value-added data communications networks to an integrated services digital network (ISDN) is based on two technological developments that we have discussed previously: digital transmission and digital switching.

Both of these developments are, of course, well established. The first T-carrier system was introduced into commercial service by AT&T in 1962, and the first large-scale time-division digital switch, the Western Electric 4ESS, was introduced in 1976. More important than the benefits of either of these two technologies however, was the revolutionary idea that the functions of transmission and switching could be integrated to form an *integrated digital network* (IDN). The idea was proposed as early as 1959 [VAUG59] and is in the process of being implemented worldwide [DORR83, COOK84].

To understand the implications of an IDN, consider Figure 17-1. Traditionally, the transmission and switching systems of a telephone network have been designed and administered by functionally separate organizations. The two systems are referred to by the operating telephone companies as outside plant and inside plant, respectively. In the analog network, incoming voice lines are modulated and multiplexed at the end office and sent out over an FDM line. As you know, the constituent signals may pass through one or more intermediate switching centers before reaching the destination end office (Figure 8-24). At each switching center, the incoming FDM carrier has to be demultiplexed and demodulated by an FDM channel bank before being switched by a space-division switch. After switching, the signals have to be multiplexed and modulated again to be transmitted. This repeated process results in an accumulation of noise, as well as cost.

When both the transmission and switching systems are digital, integration as in Figure 17-1b can be achieved. Incoming voice signals are digitized using PCM and multiplexed using TDM. Time-division digital switches along the way can switch the individual signals without decoding them. Furthermore, separate multiplex/demultiplex channel banks are not needed at the intermediate offices, since that function is incorporated into the switching system.

The conversion of telecommunications networks to digital transmission and dig-

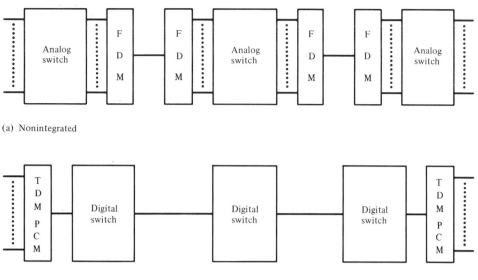

(a) Nonintegrated

(b) Integrated

FIGURE 17-1. The integration of transmission and switching.

ital switching is well under way. Much less well developed is the extension of digital service to the end user. Telephones are still sending analog data to the end office where they must be digitized. Lower-speed (<56 kbps) end-user digital service is commonly available via leased lines at present, and higher speed leased services are being introduced [HOLM83]. The provision of switched digital service over the local loop [KELC83] will eventually lead to an end-to-end switched digital telecommunications network.

This evolution has been driven by the need to provide economic voice communications. The resulting network, however, is also well suited to meet the growing variety of digital data service needs. Thus the IDN will combine the coverage of the geographically extensive telephone network with the data carrying capacity of digital data networks in a structure called the *integrated services digital network* (ISDN). In this latter context, the "integrated" of ISDN refers to the simultaneous carrying of digitized voice and a variety of data traffic on the same digital transmission links and by the same digital exchanges. The key to ISDN is the small marginal cost for offering data services on the digital telephone network, with no cost or performance penalty for voice services already carried on the IDN.

The User Interface. Figure 17-2 is a conceptual view of the ISDN from a user or customer point of view. The user has access to the ISDN by means of a local interface to a "digital pipe" of a certain bit rate. Pipes of various sizes will be available to satisfy differing needs. For example, a residential customer may require only sufficient capacity to handle a telephone and a videotex terminal. An office will undoubtedly wish to connect to the ISDN via an on-premise digital PBX, and will require a much higher capacity pipe.

At any given point in time, the pipe to the user's premises has a fixed capacity, but the traffic on the pipe may be a variable mix up to the capacity limit. Thus a user may access circuit-switched and packet-switched services, as well as other

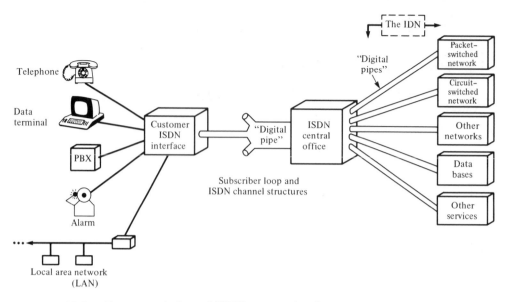

FIGURE 17-2. Conceptual view of ISDN connection features.

services, in a dynamic mix of signal types and bit rates. To provide these services, the ISDN will require rather complex control signals to instruct it how to sort out the time-multiplexed data and provide the required services. These control signals will also be multiplexed onto the same digital pipe.

An important aspect of the interface is that the user may, at any time, employ less than the maximum capacity of the pipe, and will be charged according to the capacity used rather than "connect time." This characteristic significantly diminishes the value of current user design efforts that are geared to optimize circuit utilization by use of concentrators, multiplexers, packet switches, and other line sharing arrangements.

Objectives.   Activities currently under way are leading to the development of a worldwide ISDN. This effort involves national governments, data processing and communications companies, standards organizations, and others. Certain common objectives are, by and large, shared by this disparate group. We list here the key objectives:

- *Standardization:* It is essential that a single set of ISDN standards be provided to permit universal access and to permit the development of cost-effective equipment.
- *Transparency:* The most important service to be provided is a transparent transmission service. This permits users to develop applications and protocols with the confidence that they will not be affected by the underlying ISDN.
- *Separation of competitive functions:* It must be possible to separate out functions that could be provided competitively as opposed to those that are fundamentally part of the ISDN. In most countries, a single, government-owned entity will provide all services. Some countries desire (in the case of the United States, require) that certain enhanced services be offered competitively (e.g., videotex, electronic mail). Figures 17-3 and 17-4 depict these alternative views.

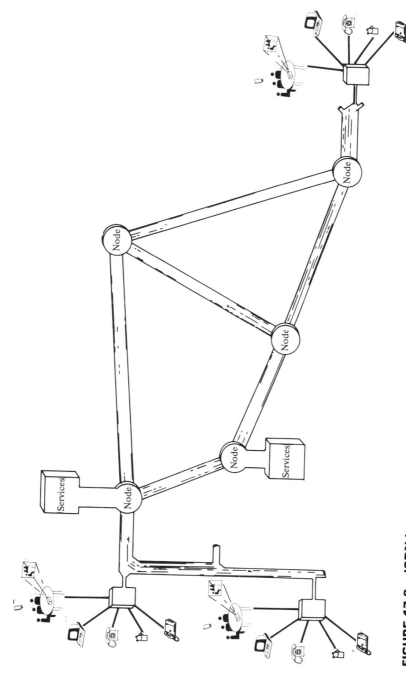

FIGURE 17-3. ISDN in a noncompetitive environment.

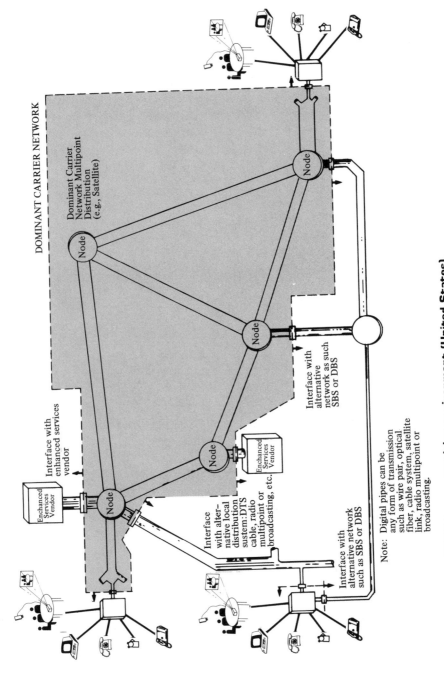

DOMINANT CARRIER NETWORK

Dominant Carrier
Network Multipoint
Distribution
(e.g, Satellite)

Interface with enhanced services vendor

Interface with alternative network such as such SBS or DBS

Enchanced Services Vendor

Enchanced Services Vendor

Interface with alternative local distribution sustem: DTS cable, radio multipoint or broadcasting, etc.

Interface with alternative network such as SBS or DBS

Note: Digital pipes can be
any form of transmission
such as wire pair, optical
fiber, cable system, satellite
link, radio multipoint or
broadcasting.

FIGURE 17-4. ISDN in a competitive environment (United States).

- *Leased and switched services:* The ISDN should provide dedicated point-to-point services as well as switched services. This will allow the user to optimize his or her implementation of switching and routing techniques.
- *Cost-related tariffs:* The price for ISDN service should be related to cost, and independent of the type of data being carried. One type of service should not be in the position of subsidizing others.
- *Smooth migration:* The conversion to ISDN will be gradual, and the evolving network must coexist with existing equipment and services. Thus ISDN interfaces should evolve from current interfaces, and provide a migration path for users.
- *Multiplexed support:* In addition to providing low-capacity support to individual users, multiplexed support must be provided to accommodate user-owned CBX and local network equipment.

There are, of course, other objectives that could be named. Those listed above are certainly among the most important and widely accepted, and help to define the character of the ISDN.

Benefits. The principal benefits to the user can be expressed in terms of cost savings and flexibility. The integration of voice and a variety of data on a single transport system means that the user does not have to buy multiple services to meet multiple needs. The efficiencies and economies of scale of an integrated network allows these services to be offered at lower cost than if they were provided separately. Further, the user needs to bear the expense of just a single access line to these multiple services.

The requirements of various users can differ greatly in a number of ways: for example, information volume, traffic pattern, response time, and interface types. The ISDN will allow the user to tailor the service purchased to actual needs to a degree not possible at present.

Services. The ISDN will provide a variety of services, supporting existing voice and data applications as well as providing for applications now being developed. The most important in the latter category are:

- *Facsimile:* service for the transmission and reproduction of graphics, hand-written, and printed material. This type of service has been available for many years, but has suffered from a lack of standardization and the limitations of the analog telephone network. Digital facsimile standards (CCITT Group 3) are now available and can be used to transmit a page of data at 64 kbps in 5 s.
- *Teletex:* service that enables subscriber terminals to exchange correspondence. Communicating terminals are used to prepare, edit, transmit, and print messages. Transmission is at a rate of one page in 2 s at 9.6 kbps.
- *Videotex:* discussed in Chapter 16. A page of data can be transmitted in one second at 9.6 kbps.

Table 17-1 shows the type of services that could be supported by ISDN. These services fall into the broad categories of voice, digital data, text, and image. Most of these services can be provided with a transmission capacity of 64 kbps or less. This rate, as we shall see, will be the standard ISDN rate offered to the user. Some services require considerably higher data rates and may be provided by high speed facilities outside the ISDN (e.g., cable TV distribution plants). However, these

TABLE 17-1 Candidate Services for Integration

Bandwidth	Service			
	Telephony	Data	Text	Image
Digital voice (64 kbps)	Telephone Leased circuits Information retrieval (by voice analysis and synthesis)	Packet-switched data Circuit-switched data Leased circuits Telemetry Funds transfer Information retrieval Mailbox Electronic mail Alarms	Telex Teletex Leased circuits Videotex Information retrieval Mailbox Electronic mail	Facsimile Information retrieval Surveillance
Wide band (>64 kbps)	Music	High-speed computer communication		TV conferencing Teletext Videophone Cable TV distribution

higher-speed services may intersect with the ISDN and make use of high-capacity ISDN links for part of a transmission path.

One of the key aspects of the ISDN will be that it is an "intelligent network." By use of a flexible signaling protocol, the ISDN will provide a variety of network facilities for each service. Table 17-2 gives some examples of planned facilities.

Architecture

Figure 17-5 is a block diagram of the ISDN. The ISDN will support a completely new physical connecter for users, a digital subscriber loop (link from end user to central or end office), and modifications to all central office equipment.

The area to which most attention has been paid by standards organizations is that of user access. A *common physical interface* will be defined to provide, in essence, a DTE-DCE connection. The same interface should be usable for telephone, computer terminal, and videotex terminal. Protocols are needed for the exchange of control information between user device and the network. Provision must be made for high-speed interfaces to, for example, a digital PBX or a LAN.

The subscriber loop portion of today's telephone network consists of twisted pair links between the subscriber and the central office, carrying 4-kHz analog signals. Under the ISDN, one or two twisted pairs will be used to provide a basic full-duplex digital communications link.

The digital central office will connect the numerous ISDN subscriber loop signals to the IDN. In addition to providing access to the circuit-switched network, the central office will provide subscriber access to dedicated lines, packet-switched networks, and time-shared transaction-oriented computer services. Multiplexed access via digital PBX and LAN must also be accommodated.

Standards

Although a number of standards organizations are involved in various aspects of ISDN, the controlling body for ISDN standards is CCITT. The CCITT defines the ISDN by describing it in terms of six attributes.

1. The ISDN is to evolve from the existing telephone networks, which themselves are evolving into integrated digital networks.
2. New services introduced into the ISDN should be compatible with the basic 64 kbps switched digital connections.
3. The ISDN will require from 10 to 20 years (from the early 1980s) for full transition.
4. During the transition, the ISDN will rely on internetworking among the national ISDNs and other non-ISDN networks (such as PDNs).
5. The ISDN will contain intelligence for the provision of service features, maintenance and system control, and network management.
6. The ISDN will use a layered functional set of integrated protocols for the various access arrangements.

With these attributes in mind, standards are being developed related to signaling, network interfaces, and protocols. This work will have a significant effect in every major area of telecommunications:

TABLE 17-2 Basic and Additional Facilities for ISDN Services

Telephony	Data	Teletex	Videotex	Facsimile
		Basic		
National toll access	Automatic dialed call	Incoming call not disturbing local mode	Information retrieval by dialogue with a database	Automatic dialed call
International toll access	Manual dialed call	Message printed on operator demand		Manual dialed call
Malicious call blocking	Automatic answer	Message presentation as in the original		Automatic answer
		Day and hour automatic indication		
		Additional		
Transfer call	Direct call	Delayed messges	Transactions (e.g. reservation, shopping)	Delayed delivery
Abbreviated dialing	Closed user group	Abbreviated address		Multiple destination
Rerouting of verbal announcements	Closed user group with outgoing access	Multiple address		
Intermediate call	Calling line identification	Charging indication	Message box service between users	Code, speed, and format conversion for different terminals
Conference call	Called line identification	Telex access		
Camp-on busy	Abbreviated address calling	Graphic mode	Loading of software from a data base to a terminal	
Barring outgoing toll traffic	Barred incoming call			
	Multiaddress calling		Loading of special character set	
Hot line	Detailed billing			
Detailed billing	Transfer call			
Automatic wake-up	Call charging indication			

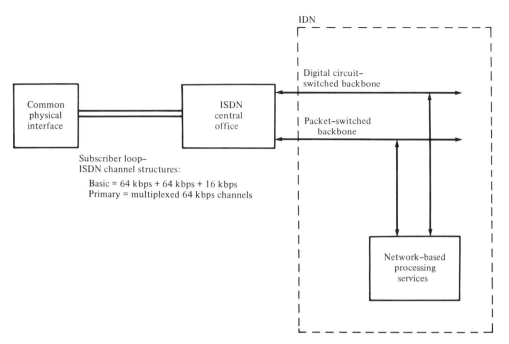

IDN

Digital circuit-
switched backbone

Common
physical
interface

ISDN
central
office

Packet-switched
backbone

Subscriber loop–
ISDN channel structures:

Basic = 64 kbps + 64 kbps + 16 kbps
Primary = multiplexed 64 kbps channels

Network–based
processing
services

FIGURE 17-5.   Block diagram of ISDN functions.

- Subscriber loop technology
- Switching technology.
- Transmission technologies.
- Signaling.
- Interfaces and protocols.
- Network management and system control.

The principal coordinating body for CCITT ISDN standards activities is Study Group XVIII, the Digital Networks study group. This group is addressing a number of specific ISDN issues. In addition, it coordinates the activities of other study groups. The most important of these are:

- *Study Group II:* telephone operation and quality of service.
- *Study Group IV:* transmission maintenance.
- *Study Group VII:* data communications networks.
- *Study Group XI:* telephone switching and signaling.
- *Study Group XVII:* data communications over the telephone network.

Table 17-3 summarizes the key areas being addressed by each of these study groups. Clearly, the ISDN standards activity is a massive effort. In the remainder of this chapter, we explore some of the most important aspects of ISDN that are subject to standardization.

17-2

TRANSMISSION STRUCTURE

ISDN Channels

The digital pipe between the central office and the ISDN user will be used to carry a number of communication channels. The capacity of the pipe, and therefore the

TABLE 17-3   CCITT ISDN Standards Effort

Study Group XVIII

General network aspects
Customer/network interface
Synchronization
Signaling for the ISDN
Switching for the ISDN
General network performance
Availability
Maintenance philosophy
Maintenance implementation
Interworking
Interfaces in digital networks
Multiplex arrangements
Network aspects in hierarchy
Non-PCM encoding methods
Digital speech interpolation
Characteristics of digital sections

Study Group II

Network management
Human factors
Nontelephone use
Alleviation of failure conditions
Traffic and operations requirements

Study Group IV

General maintenance organization
Measuring instruments
Quality of the international network
New system maintenance

Study Group VII

Call setup and cleardown time
Grade of service
DTE/DCE interface
Maintenance of PDNs
Digital data switching
Interworking of packet networks
Multiplex structure of international links
Integration of satellite systems

Study Group XI

Signaling systems
Switch design
Digital transit exchanges
Higher-level languages

Study Group XVII

Physical level interface

number of channels carried may vary from user to user. The transmission structure of any access link will be constructed from the following types of channels:

- *B channel:* 64 kbps.
- *D channel:* 16 kbps.
- *C channel:* 8 or 16 kbps.
- *A channel:* 4 kHz analog.

The B channel is the basic user channel and can carry any one of the following types of traffic:

- PCM-encoded digital voice.
- Digital data for circuit-switched or packet-switched applications.
- A mixture of lower-rate traffic, including digital data and digitized voice encoded at a fraction of 64 kbps. All traffic must be destined for the same endpoint.

The designation of 64 kbps as the standard user channel rate highlights the fundamental contradiction in standards activities. This rate was chosen as the most effective for digitized voice, yet the technology has progressed to the point at which 32 kbps or even less will produce equally satisfactory voice reproduction. To be effective, a standard must freeze the technology at some defined point. Yet by the time the standard is approved, it may already be obsolete.

The D channel serves two purposes. First, it will be used to exchange control information between user and network. Second, it will support lower-speed digital data requirements. Table 17-4 summarizes the types of data traffic to be supported on B and D channels.

TABLE 17-4   ISDN Channel Functions

B Channel (64 kbps)	D Channel (16 kbps)
Digital voice	Signaling
64 kbps PCM	Basic
Low bit rate (32 kbps)	Enhanced
High-speed data	Low-speed data
Circuit-switched	Videotex
Packet-switched	Teletex
Other	Terminal
Facsimile	Telemetry
Slow-scan video	Emergency services
	Energy management

The A channel will be used in the transitional period to carry conventional analog voice signals. Associated with the A channel, to form a hybrid access channel, is the C channel operating at either 8 kbps (United States wants) or 16 kbps (Japan wants).

These channel types are grouped into transmission structures that are offered as a package to the user. The best defined structures at this time are the basic channel structure (basic access) and the primary channel structure (primary access), which are depicted in Figure 17-6.

The basic channel structure consists of two full-duplex 64 kbps B channels and a full-duplex 16-kbps D channel. The total bit rate, by simple arithmetic, is 144 kbps. However, framing, synchronization, and other overhead bits bring the total bit rate on a basic access link to 192 kbps. Figure 17-7 shows a possible frame structure for basic access. Each frame of 24 bits includes 8 bits from each of the B channels and 2 bits from the D channel. Most of the remaining bits are used in the synchronous TDM protocol between the user and the central office.

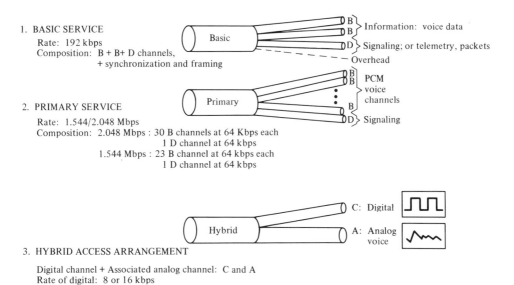

1. BASIC SERVICE
  Rate: 192 kbps
  Composition: B + B+ D channels,
       + synchronization and framing

2. PRIMARY SERVICE
  Rate: 1.544/2.048 Mbps
  Composition: 2.048 Mbps : 30 B channels at 64 Kbps each
                  1 D channel at 64 kbps
          1.544 Mbps : 23 B channel at 64 kbps each
                  1 D channel at 64 kbps

3. HYBRID ACCESS ARRANGEMENT

  Digital channel + Associated analog channel: C and A
  Rate of digital: 8 or 16 kbps

FIGURE 17-6.   ISDN channel structures.

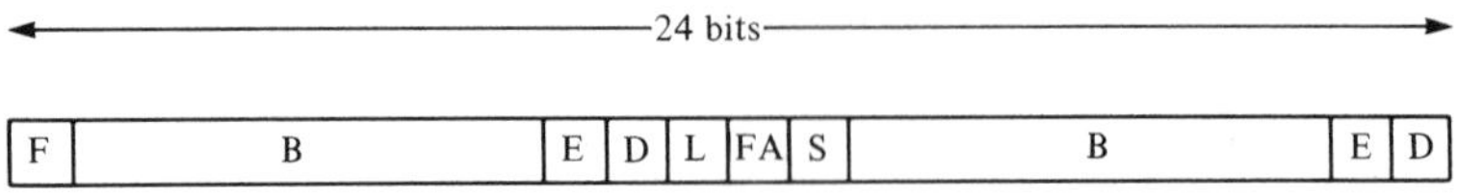

<-------------------------------24 bits------------------------------->

| F | B | E | D | L | FA | S | B | E | D |

. F, FA – Frame bits
. E – Echo D bits for contention resolution
. L – DC balancing bits
. S – Spare bits
. B – B channel bits (16 per frame)
. D – D channel bits (2 per frame)

FIGURE 17-7. Possible basic access frame structure.

The next higher level of multiplexing, primary service, may standardize on one or both of two competing proposals. The U.S. proposal, supported by Canada and Japan, calls for 23 B channels at 64 kbps plus one D channel of 64 kbps on a 1.544-Mbps link. This, of course, corresponds to the T1 transmission facility, using the DS-1 transmission format. The Europeans, of course, prefer their own 2.048-Mbps link containing 30 B channels and one D channel, each at 64 kbps.

In addition to the above, a number of other capacity services are being considered as standard offerings. These include:

- *Intermediate service:* at rates between 400 and 800 kbps, composed of 4, 6, 8, and 10 64-kbps channels have been considered.
- *Broadband service:* provides an unpartitioned 1.544- or 2.048-Mbps capacity for high-speed applications such as video teleconferencing.
- *Higher rate structures:* made available to customers with heavy loads and value-added providers. These would correspond to the higher levels of the TDM hierarchy used internally by ISDN.

Finally, we elaborate on an earlier reference to the use of a B channel to carry multiple lower-data-rate signals. For this purpose, a technique known as rate adaption is used [COLL83]. If the requested rate is an integral divisor of the basic B rate (8, 16, or 32 kbps), byte repetition is used to occupy the 64-kbps channel. For example, each byte of a 16-kbps source is repeated four times to generate a 64-kbps data stream. The repetition can be reversed at any point in the transmission path where useful for the purpose of conserving loop or trunk bandwidth. In addition, it is expected that service at 2.4, 4.8, and 9.6 kbps will be offered. These signals must go through two stages of adaption. In the first stage the signal is converted to an intermediate ISDN rate (8, 16, or 32 kbps) by bit padding: superfluous overhead bits are added. The second stage is byte repetition. A service offering rate adaption could carry a lower tariff rate reflecting the lesser bandwidth requirement.

Subscriber Loop Technology

The extension of digital links to the end users is an essential part of ISDN evolution: The subscriber loop must support the channel structure being developed.

We have already referenced an intermediate technique for providing access: the A/C channel structure. The technique used here is *data over voice*. On an analog link, voice occupies the frequency spectrum below 4 kHz. A data rate of 8 to 16 kbps can be supported by appropriate modulation of the digital signal onto a carrier at a band above 4 kHz.

To provide true full-duplex digital service, two approaches are possible. The first makes use of two twisted pairs (four-wire) per subscriber. Each twisted pair is operated in simplex fashion. This technique is technically simple, but doubles the amount of cable needed to serve hundreds of millions of residential subscribers.

An alternative approach has previously been referred to, and is known as time compression multiplexing, or the ping-pong protocol. This technique provides full-duplex data transmission over a single pair of wires. It does so by partitioning the bit stream in each direction of transmission into segments. Each segment is transmitted on the loop at approximately 2.25 times the source data rate.

17-3

USER ACCESS

One of the key objectives of the ISDN is that a uniform user access, both physically and logically, be provided. The details of user access arrangements are still evolving, but the work is sufficiently advanced to present an overview.

Access Configurations

To define the requirements for ISDN user access, an understanding of the anticipated configuration of user premises equipment and of the necessary standard interfaces is critical. The first step is to group functions that may exist on the user's premises. Figure 17-8 shows the CCITT approach to this task, using:

- *Reference points:* conceptual points used to separate groups of functions.
- *Functional groupings:* certain finite arrangements of physical equipment or combinations of equipment.

Let us consider first the functional groupings. *Network termination 1* (NT1) includes functions that may be regarded as belonging to OSI layer 1, that is, functions associated with the physical and electrical termination of the ISDN on the user's premises. The NT1 may be controlled by the ISDN provider and forms a boundary to the network. This boundary isolates the user from the transmission technology of the subscriber loop and presents a new physical connector interface for user device attachment. In addition, the NT1 will perform line maintenance functions such as loopback testing and performance monitoring.

Network termination 2 (NT2) is an intelligent device that may include, depending on the requirement, up through OSI layer 3 functionality. NT2 can perform switching, and concentration functions. Examples of NT2 are a digital PBX, a terminal controller, and a LAN.

Network termination 1, 2 (NT12) is a single device that contains the combined functions of the NT1 and NT2. This points out one of the regulatory issues associated with ISDN interface development. In many countries, the ISDN provider will own the NT12 and provide full service to the user. In the United States, there is a need for a network termination with a limited number of functions to permit competitive provision of user premises equipment. Hence the user premises network functions are split into NT1 and NT2.

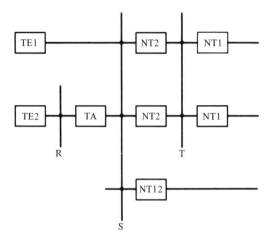

R,S,T – Reference interface points
TE1 – Subscriber terminel type 1
TE2 – Subscriber terminal type 2
TA – Terminal adapter
NT1 – Network termination 1
NT2 – Network termination 2
Nt12 – Combined network termination 1 and 2

FIGURE 17-8.   ISDN reference points and functional groupings.

Terminal equipment type 1 (TE1) refers to devices that support the standard ISDN interface. Examples are a digital telephone, integrated voice/data terminal, and digital facsimile equipment. *Terminal equipment type 2* (TE2) encompasses existing non-ISDN equipment that requires a *terminal adapter* (TA) to plug into an ISDN interface. Examples are devices with RS-232-C and X.21 interfaces.

The definitions of the functional groupings also define, by implication, the reference points. The two new ISDN reference points are S and T. A main focus of interest has been the number of wires at the S and T interfaces. The ISDN will follow the trend of X.21 and utilize few interchange circuits to provide a flexible and powerful interface. Current thinking is to use an eight-wire interface: one pair each for balanced transmission of data in each direction, and four additional wires for optional powering capabilities.

Based on the definitions above, various possible configurations for ISDN user–network interfaces have been proposed by CCITT. These are shown in Figure 17-9, but are not meant to be either exhaustive or mandatory.

Figure 17-9a shows that it is possible that a device intended to connect to an interface at point *S* could also work at an interface at point *T*. An example of this is a telephone, which can attach either to a CBX or directly to the subscriber loop terminator. Figure 17-9b extends this concept to multiple TE1s (any TE1 can be replaced by TE2 + TA) directly connected to an NT1 using a multidrop arrangement. This is not intended to require that individual terminals can talk to each other, as in a LAN, but rather that each terminal can communicate with the network.

Figure 17-9c and d provide multiple connections between TE1s and NT2. The two figures more or less correspond to CBX and LAN, respectively. Figure 17-9e shows the case of multiple NT1 equipment, whereas Figure 17-9f shows a case in which NT1 provides a layer 1 upward multiplexing of multiple connections.

The final two configurations indicate that either *S* or *T*, but not both, need not

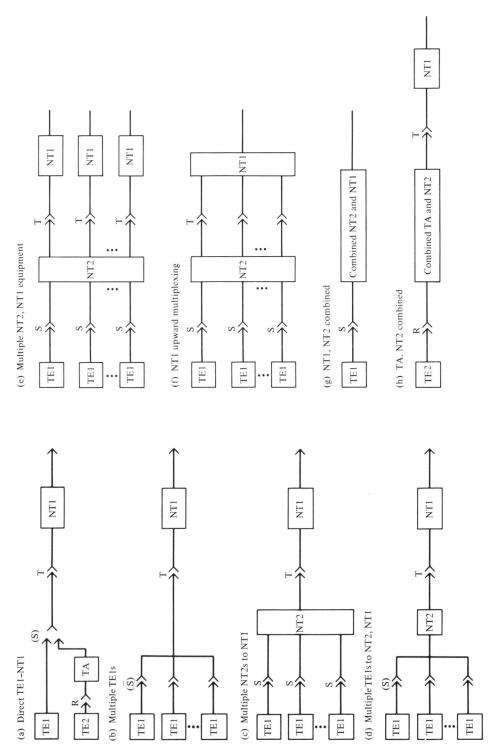

FIGURE 17-9. Possible configurations for ISDN user/network interfaces.

553

correspond to a physical interface in a particular instance. We have already referred to the combination of NT1 and NT2 as NT12. In addition, an NT2 can be equipped with the capability to attach TE2 equipment directly.

Physical Layer Functions

The ISDN physical layer is presented to the user at either reference point S or T (Figure 17-8). In either case, the following functions should be included as physical layer (OSI layer 1) functions:

- Full-duplex transmission of B-channel data and timing signals.
- Full-duplex transmission of D-channel data and timing signals.
- Activation and deactivation of the physical circuit.
- Power feeding from the network termination to the terminal.
- Terminal identification.
- Faulty terminal isolation.
- Rate adaption.
- D-channel contention access.

The first six functions are straightforward. Rate adaption was described earlier and is considered a physical layer function. The final function, also considered to be at the physical layer, is required when multiple TE1 terminals share a single D-channel line (i.e, via a multipoint configuration). The details of the access method remain to be worked out, but it will be a simple contention access protocol, perhaps incorporating priorities.

Circuit Switching

The network configuration and protocols for circuit switching involve both the B and D channels. The B channel is used for the transparent exchange of user data. The communicating users may use any protocols they wish for end-to-end communication. The D channel is used to exchange control information between the user and the network for call establishment and termination, and access to network facilities.

Figure 17-10 depicts the protocol architecture that implements circuit switching. (See Table 17-5 for a key to Figures 17-10 through 17-12.) The B channel is serviced by an NT1 or NT2 using only layer 1 functions. The end users may employ any protocol although generally, layer 3 will be null.

The interface between the user and the network on the D channel consists of three layers. The physical layer has already been discussed. For the data link layer, a protocol similar to LAP-B, known as LAP-D, is being considered. The use of LAP-D frames would allow different types of information, including control signals, to be statistically multiplexed. Each of these types of data may employ different layer 3 protocols. For control signals used in conjunction with B-channel circuit switching, a standard known as *CCITT Common Channel Signaling System No. 7* (SS7) is being considered. SS7 is actually a standard for communication between network nodes, but may also be used between a CBX and an ISDN node.

SS7 has a four-layer protocol architecture. Layers 1 through 3 are referred to collectively as the *message transfer part*. This provides a reliable mechanism for

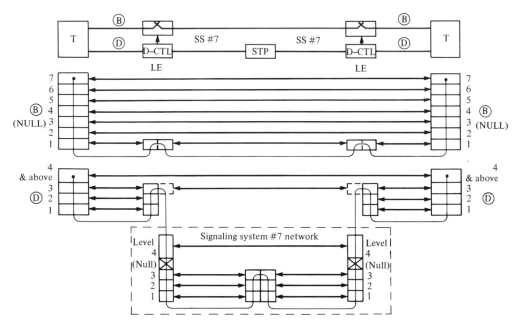

FIGURE 17-10. Network configuration and protocols for circuit switching.

the transfer of higher-level data. Above this is the user part, which corresponds roughly to OSI layers 5 through 7; there is no functionality corresponding to OSI layer 4.

Two user parts are defined. The *telephone user part* carries control data relating to telephone voice connections, including circuit identification and originating and destination exchanges. Signaling messages are defined for all foreseen events in the control of a telephonic connection and placed in a message signaling unit. The *data user part* carries control data relating to a digital data connection. The signaling messages are specific to the data environment.

TABLE 17-5   Key to Figures 17-10 Through 17-12

B =	An ISDN B channel
D =	An ISDN D channel
T =	Terminal
D-CTL =	D-channel controller
SS 7 =	CCITT signaling system 7
STP =	Signaling transfer point
(Null) =	Channel not present
7, 6, 5, 4, 3, 2, 1 =	Layers in ISO basic reference model
LEVEL =	Levels in SS 7
LE =	Local exchange
TE =	Transit exchange
PSF =	Packed-switching facility
Horizontal line =	Peer-to-peer protocol
Vertical line =	Layer-to-layer data flow

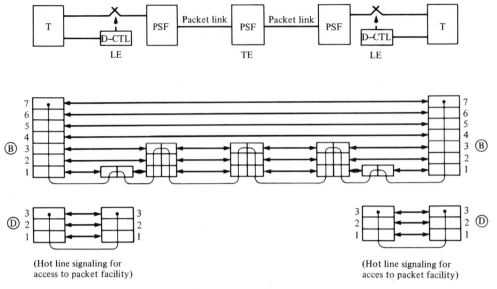

FIGURE 17-11. Network configuration and protocols for packet switching using B channel with circuit-switched access.

Packet Switching

The ISDN must also permit user access to packet-switched services for data traffic (e.g., interactive) that is best serviced by packet switching. Figures 17-11 and 17-12 show two possibilities.

The first possibility is high-speed (64 kbps) packet-switched access. Figure 17-11 depicts a scenario in which the ISDN provides a circuit-switched link to a value-added packet-switching node. The local user interface need only perform physical layer functions to maintain a transparent connection between the user and the packet-switching node. The latter two entities could communicate using X.25 layers 1-3. The D channel would still be used to set up the connection.

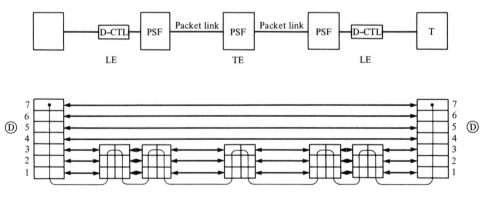

Note: There is another possibility: that LE is transparent to layer 3.

FIGURE 17-12. Network configuration and protocols for packet switching for D channel.

Figure 17-12 shows the use of D channel capacity for lower-speed packet switching. In this case, the local interface could act as an X.25 DCE. Alternatively, the local interface could support only physical layer functions.

17.4

HYPOTHETICAL REFERENCE CONNECTION

By and large, the ISDN standards are not intended to restrict the means by which ISDN providers implement network functions. However, in order to establish certain performance and error requirements, a *hypothetical reference connection* (HRX) for ISDN has been proposed. Actually, there are a set of HRXs defined between ISDN users.

Figure 17-13, page 558, depicts a maximum length international connection. The HRX is designed primarily for circuit-switched voice and data at 64 kbps. The number of intermediate switching points is to be reduced for packet-switched data.

One controversial aspect of the HRX is the proposed restriction of voice services to a single satellite hop and of data services to an as yet unspecified number of satellite hops depending on the application. Satellite service providers are understandably opposed to this restriction and would prefer that the decision be made in the marketplace [RUTK83].

The whole subject of HRXs is a subject for further study within CCITT. One can expect accommodation of the satellite point of view. Another likely addition is HRXs for primary (1.544/2.048 Mbps) as well as basic (64 kbps) service.

17-5

RECOMMENDED READING

The ISDN is such a new concept that the literature is, as yet, sparse. This situation should change dramatically in the next few years. The following provide overviews of ISDN: [DECI82a], [DORR81], [DORR83], [KOST84], [ROBI81], and [RUTK82]. [SAKA82] is a thorough discussion of the state of ISDN standards work up to 1982. [BOSI82] and [KADE81] discuss digital subscriber loop technology. [DECI82b] is a well-organized discussion of user access to ISDN. Other papers on the subject are [GERL84], [BHUS83], [BHUS84], [GRIF82], and [WABE82].

17.6

PROBLEMS

17-1   Is an IDN necessary for an ISDN? Sufficient? Explain.

17-2   An ISDN customer has offices at a number of sites. A typical office is served by two 1.544 Mbps digital pipes. One provides circuit-switched access to the ISDN; the other is a leased line connecting to another user site. The on-premises equipment

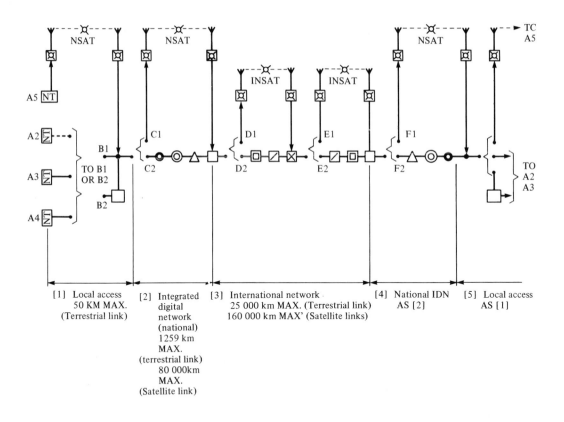

FIGURE 17-13. Proposed (maximum) ISDN hypothetical reference connection (HRX).

KEY

NT   = Network termination

LINKS

A1 = Small–dish digital satellite link
A2 = Microwave (or line–of–sight optical) link
A3 = 64 kbps digital link
A4 = Analog link
A5 = Remote ISDN termination connected to local
       exchange by way of national satellite

SATELLITES

⊠ SDS = Small–dish digital

⊠ NSAT = National

⊠ INSAT = International

{ = Choice of 2 or more options

● ISDN local exchange

▢ Remote multiplexer/demultiplexer or concentrator

○ = Primary center   ⎫
◎ = Secondary center ⎬ National network
△ = Tertiary center   ⎭

⊠ CTX   ⎫
⊠ CT1   ⎬ International
▢ CT2   ⎪ transit centers
▢ CT3 = Gateway exchange ⎭

consists of a CBX aligned with packet-switching node logic. The user has three requirements:
- Telephone service.
- A private packet-switched network for data.
- Video teleconferencing at 1.544 Mbps.

How might the user allocate capacity optimally to meet these requirements?

17-3 It was mentioned in Section 17-1 that user-implemented multidrop lines and multiplexers may disappear. Explain why.

17-4 Figure 17-7 indicates that an ISDN basic access frame has 16 B bits and 2 D bits. Suppose that more bits were used, say 160 B bits and 20 D bits per frame. Would this reduce the percentage overhead and therefore the basic access bit rate? If so, discuss any potential disadvantages.

17-5 In Figure 17-10, under what circumstances would user layer 3 on the B channel not be null?

GLOSSARY

Some of the terms in this glossary are from the *American National Dictionary for Information Processing Systems* [ANSC82], the *Vocabulary for Data Processing, Telecommunications and Office Systems* [IBM81b], or the *CCITT Sixth Plenary Assembly Orange Book, Terms and Definitions*. These are indicated in the text by ANS, IBM, and CCITT respectively.

Aloha. A medium access control technique for multiple access transmission media. A station transmits whenever it has data to send. Unacknowledged transmissions are repeated.

Alphageometric coding. A display technique for Videotex. In addition to characters, patterns built up from geometric primitives can be displayed.

Alphamosaic coding. A display technique for Teletext and Videotex. In addition to ordinary characters, geometric patterns can be displayed using a 2×3 grid within each character space.

Amplitude (IBM). The size or magnitude of a voltage or current waveform.

Amplitude modulation (CCITT). Modulation in which the amplitude of an alternating current is the characteristic varied.

Amplitude-shift keying. Modulation in which the two binary values are represented by two different amplitudes of the carrier frequency.

Analog data (ANS). Data in the form of a physical quantity that is considered to be continuously variable and whose magnitude is made directly proportional to the data or a suitable function of the data.

Analog signal.   A continuously varying electromagnetic wave that may be propagated over a variety of media.

Analog transmission.   The transmission of analog signals without regard to content. The signal may be amplified, but there is no intermediate attempt to recover the data from the signal.

Application layer.   Layer 7 of the OSI model. This layer determines the interface of the system with the user.

Asynchronous transmission (IBM).   Transmission in which each information character is individually synchronized (usually by the use of start elements and stop elements).

Attenuation (IBM).   A decrease in magnitude of current, voltage, or power of a signal in transmission between points.

Automatic repeat request (IBM).   A feature that automatically initiates a request for retransmission when an error in transmission is detected.

Balanced transmission.   A transmission mode in which signals are transmitted as a current that travels down one conductor and returns on the other. For digital signals, this technique is known as differential signaling, with the binary value depending on the voltage difference.

Bandlimited signal.   A signal all of whose energy is contained within a finite frequency range.

Bandwidth (IBM).   The difference, expressed in hertz, between the two limiting frequencies of a spectrum.

Baseband.   Transmission of signals without modulation. In a baseband local network, digital signals (1's and 0's) are inserted directly onto the cable as voltage pulses. The entire spectrum of the cable is consumed by the signal. This scheme does not allow frequency-division multiplexing.

Bit stuffing.   The insertion of extra bits into a data stream to avoid the appearance of unintended control sequences.

Bridge.   A device that links two homogeneous packet-broadcast local networks. It accepts all packets from each network addressed to devices on the other, buffers them, and retransmits them to the other network.

Broadband.   The use of coaxial cable for providing data transfer by means of analog (radio-frequency) signals. Digital signals are passed through a modem and transmitted over one of the frequency bands of the cable.

Broadcast (IBM).   The simultaneous transmission of data to a number of stations.

Broadcast address.   An address that designates all entities within a domain (e.g., network, catenet).

Broadcast communication network.   A communication network in which a transmission from one station is broadcast to and received by all other stations.

Bus. (ANS)   One or more conductors used for transmitting signals or power.

Carrier (IBM).   A continuous frequency capable of being modulated or impressed with a second (information carrying) signal.

Catenet.   A collection of packet-switched and broadcast networks that are connected together via gateways.

CATV. Community Antenna Television. CATV cable is used for broadband local networks, and broadcast TV distribution.

Cellular radio. The use of low-power radio transmitters arranged in a honeycomb pattern, to permit reuse of a frequency multiple times in a small area.

Checksum. An error-detecting code based on a summation operation performed on the bits to be checked.

Circuit switching. A method of communicating in which a dedicated communications path is established between two devices through one or more intermediate switching nodes. Unlike packet switching, digital data are sent as a continuous stream of bits. Bandwidth is guaranteed, and delay is essentially limited to propagation time. The telephone system uses circuit switching.

Coaxial cable (IBM). A cable consisting of one conductor, usually a small copper tube or wire, within and insulated from another conductor of larger diameter, usually copper tubing or copper braid.

Codec. Coder-decoder. Transforms analog data into a digital bit stream (coder), and digital signals into analog data (decoder).

Collision. A condition in which two packets are being transmitted over a medium at the same time. Their interference makes both unintelligible.

Communications architecture. The hardware and software structure that implements the communications function.

Communication network. A collection of interconnected functional units that provides a data communications service among stations attached to the network.

Computerized branch exchange (CBX). A local network based on the digital private branch exchange architecture. Provides an integrated voice/data switching service.

Connectionless data transfer. A protocol for exchanging data in a unplanned fashion and without prior coordination (e.g., datagram).

Connection-oriented data transfer. A protocol for exchanging data in which a logical connection is established between the endpoints (e.g., virtual circuit).

Contention. The condition when two or more stations attempt to use the same channel at the same time.

Crosstalk (ANS). The unwanted energy transferred from one circuit, called the disturbing circuit, to another circuit, called the disturbed circuit.

CSMA. Carrier Sense Multiple Access. A medium access control technique for multiple-access transmission media. A station wishing to transmit first senses the medium and transmits only if the medium is idle.

CSMA/CD. Carrier Sense Multiple Access with Collision Detection. A refinement of CSMA in which a station ceases transmission if it detects a collision.

Current-mode transmission. A transmission mode in which the transmitter alternately applies current to each of two conductors in a twisted pair to represent logic 1 or 0. The total current is constant and always in the same direction.

Cyclic redundancy check. An error detecting code in which the code is the remainder resulting from dividing the bits to be checked by a predetermined binary number.

Data circuit-terminating equipment (ANS). In a data station, the equipment that provides the signal conversion and coding between the data terminal equipment (DTE) and the line. The DCE may be separate equipment or an integral part of the DTE or of intermediate equipment. The DCE may perform other functions that are normally performed at the network end of the line.

Datagram (ANS). In packet switching, a self-contained packet, independent of other packets, that does not require acknowledgment, and that carries information sufficient for routing from the originating data terminal equipment (DTE), without relying on earlier exchanges between the DTEs and the network.

Data link layer. Layer 2 of the OSI model. Converts unreliable transmission channel into reliable one.

Data terminal equipment (ANS). That part of a data station that serves as a data source, data sink, or both.

Decibel. A measure of the relative strength of two signals. The number of decibels is 10 times the log of the ratio of the power of two signals, or 20 times the log of the ratio of the voltage of two signals.

Delay distortion. Distortion of a signal occurring when the propagation delay for the transmission medium is not constant over the frequency range of the signal.

Demand-assignment multiple access. A technique for allocating satellite capacity, based on either FDM or TDM, in which capacity is granted on demand.

Differential encoding. A means of encoding digital data on a digital signal such that the binary value is determined by a signal change rather than a signal level.

Digital data. Data consisting of a sequence of discrete elements.

Digital signal. A discrete or discontinuous signal, such as voltage pulses.

Digital switch. A star topology local network. Usually refers to a system that handles only data but not voice.

Digital transmission. The transmission of digital data, using either an analog or digital signal, in which the digital data is recovered and repeated at intermediate points to reduce the effects of noise.

Digitize (ANS). To express or represent in a digital form data that are not discrete data (e.g., to obtain a digital representation of the magnitude of a physical quantity from an analog representation of that magnitude).

DOD Protocol architecture. A communications architecture that has evolved from the ARPANET project and DOD standardization activities.

Encapsulation. The addition of control information by a protocol entity to data obtained from a protocol user.

Error detecting code (ANS). A code in which each expression conforms to specific rules of construction, so that if certain errors occur in an expression, the resulting expression will not conform to the rules of construction and thus the presence of the errors is detected.

Error rate (ANS). The ratio of the number of data units in error to the total number of data units.

Fast select. An option of the X.25 virtual call that allows the inclusion of data in the call setup and call clearing packets.

Flow control. The function performed by a receiving entity to limit the amount or rate of data that is sent by a transmitting entity.

Frame check sequence. An error-detecting code inserted as a field in a block of data to be transmitted. The code serves to check for errors upon reception of the data.

Frequency (IBM). Rate of signal oscillation in hertz.

Frequency-division multiple access. A technique for allocating capacity on a satellite channel using fixed-assignment FDM.

Frequency-division multiplexing (IBM). The division of a transmission facility into two or more channels by splitting the frequency band transmitted by the facility into narrower bands, each of which is used to constitute a distinct channel.

Frequency modulation (CCITT). Modulation in which the frequency of an alternating current is the characteristic varied.

Frequency-shift keying. Modulation in which the two binary values are represented by two different frequencies near the carrier frequency.

Full-duplex transmission (ANS). Data transmission in both directions at the same time.

Gateway. A device that connects two systems, especially if the systems use different protocols. For example, a gateway is needed to connect two independent local networks, or to connect a local network to a long-haul network.

Half-duplex transmission (ANS). Data transmission in either direction, one direction at a time.

HDLC (high-level data link control). A very common bit-oriented data link protocol (OSI layer 2) issued by ISO. Similar protocols are ADCCP, LAP-B, and SDLC.

Header (IBM). System-defined control information that precedes user data.

High-speed local network (HSLN). A local network designed to provide high throughput between expensive, high-speed devices, such as mainframes and mass storage devices.

Impulse noise. A high-amplitude, short-duration noise pulse.

Integrated services digital network. A planned worldwide telecommunication service that will use digital transmission and switching technology to support voice and digital data communication.

Intermodulation noise. Noise due to the nonlinear combination of signals of different frequencies.

Internet protocol. An internetworking protocol that provides connectionless service across multiple packet-switched networks.

Internetworking. Communication among devices across multiple networks.

Local area network (LAN). A general-purpose local network that can serve a variety of devices. Typically used for terminals, microcomputers, and minicomputers.

Local loop. Transmission path, generally twisted pair, between the individual subscriber and the nearest switching center of the public telecommunications network.

Local network. A communication network that provides interconnection of a variety of data communicating devices within a small area.

Longitudinal redundancy check. The use of a set of parity bits for a block of characters such that there is a parity bit for each bit position in the characters.

Manchester encoding. A digital signaling technique in which there is a transition in the middle of each bit time. A 1 is encoded with a high level during the first half of the bit time; a 0 is encoded with a low level during the first half of the bit time.

Medium access control (MAC). For broadcast networks, the method of determining which device has access to the transmission medium at any time. CSMA/CD and token are common access methods.

Message switching. A switching technique using a message store-and-forward system. No dedicated path is established. Rather, each message contains a destination address and is passed from source to destination through intermediate nodes. At each node, the entire message is received, stored briefly, and then passed on to the next node.

Microwave. Electromagnetic waves in the frequency range of about 2 to 40 GHz.

Modem. Modulator/Demodulator. Transforms a digital bit stream into an analog signal (modulator), and vice versa (demodulator).

Modulation (IBM). The process by which some characteristic of one wave is varied in accordance with another wave or signal.

Multicast address. An address that designates a group of entities within a domain (e.g., network, catenet).

Multiplexing (ANS). In data transmission, a function that permits two or more data sources to share a common transmission medium such that each data source has its own channel.

Multipoint. A configuration in which more than two stations share a transmission path.

Network layer. Layer 3 of the OSI model. Responsible for routing data through a communication network.

Noise. Unwanted signals that combine with and hence distort the signal intended for transmission and reception.

Nonreturn to zero. A digital signaling technique in which the signal is at a constant level for the duration of a bit time.

Optical fiber. A thin filament of glass or other transparent material through which a signal-encoded light beam may be transmitted by means of total internal reflection.

Packet assembler/disassembler. A device used with an X.25 network to provide service to asynchronous terminals.

Packet switching. A method of transmitting messages through a communication network, in which long messages are subdivided into short packets. The packets are then transmitted as in message switching. Usually, packet switching is more efficient and rapid than message switching.

Parity bit (ANS). A check bit appended to an array of binary digits to make the sum of all the binary digits, including the check bit, always odd or always even.

PBX. Private branch exchange. A telephone exchange on the user's premises. Provides a switching facility for telephones on extension lines within the building and access to the public telephone network. May be manual (PMBX) or automatic (PABX). A digital PBX that also handles data devices without modems is called a CBX.

Phase. The relative position in time within a single period of a signal.

Phase modulation (CCITT). Modulation in which the phase angle of a carrier is the characteristic varied.

Phase-shift keying. Modulation in which the phase of the carrier signal is shifted to represent digital data.

Physical layer. Layer 1 of the OSI model. Concerned with the electrical, mechanical, and timing aspects of signal transmission over a medium.

Piggybacking. The inclusion of an acknowledgment to a previously received packet in an outgoing data packet.

Point-to-point. A configuration in which two stations share a transmission path.

Poll and select. The process by which a primary station invites secondary stations, one at a time, to transmit (poll), and by which a primary station requests that a secondary receive data (select).

Presentation layer. Layer 6 of the OSI model. Concerned with data format and display.

Protocol (ANS). A set of rules that govern the operation of functional units to achieve communication.

Protocol data unit. A block of data exchanged between two entities via a protocol.

Public data network. A government-controlled or national monopoly packet-switched network. This service is publicly available to data processing users.

Pulse code modulation (CCITT). A process in which a signal is sampled, and the magnitude of each sample with respect to a fixed reference is quantized and converted by coding to a digital signal.

Register insertion ring. A medium access control technique for rings. Each station contains a register that can temporarily hold a circulating packet. A station may transmit whenever there is a gap on the ring and, if necessary, hold an oncoming packet until it has completed transmission.

Residual error rate (ANS). The error rate remaining after attempts at correction are made.

Ring. A local network topology in which stations are attached to repeaters connected in a closed loop. Data are transmitted in one direction around the ring, and can be read by all attached stations.

RS-232-C. A physical layer interface standard for the interconnection of equipment, established by EIA.

RS-449/422-A/423-A. A set of physical layer standards developed by EIA and intended to replace RS-232-C. RS-422-A and RS-423-A specify electrical characteristics; RS-449 specifies mechanical, functional, and procedural characteristics.

Satellite-switched time-division multiple access (SS/TDMA). A form of TDMA in which circuit switching is used to dynamically change the channel assignments.

Service access point. A means of identifying a user of the services of a protocol entity. A protocol entity provides one or more SAPs for use by higher-level entities.

Session layer. Layer 5 of the OSI model. Manages a logical connection (session) between two communicating processes or applications.

Simplex transmission (ANS). Data transmission in one preassigned direction only.

Single channel per carrier. A technique for allocating satellite capacity in which the bandwidth is divided into a number of individual voice-frequency channels.

Sliding-window technique. A method of flow control in which a transmitting station may send numbered packets within a window of numbers. The window changes dynamically to allow additional packets to be sent.

Slotted ring. A medium access control technique for rings. The ring is divided into slots, which may be designated empty or full. A station may transmit whenever an empty slot goes by, by marking it full and inserting a packet into the slot.

Space-division switching. A circuit-switching technique in which each connection through the switch take a physically separate and dedicated path.

Spectrum. Refers to an absolute range of frequencies. For example, the spectrum of CATV cable is now about 5 to 400 MHz.

Star. A topology in which all stations are connected to a central switch. Two stations communicate via circuit switching.

Statistical time-division multiplexing. A method of TDM in which time slots on a shared transmission line are allocated to I/O channels on demand.

Stop and wait. A flow control protocol in which the sender transmits a block of data and then awaits an acknowledgment before transmitting the next block.

Switched communication network. A communication network consisting of a network of nodes connected by point-to-point links. Data are transmitted from source to destination through intermediate nodes.

Synchronous time-division multiplexing. A method of TDM in which time slots on a shared transmission line are assigned to I/O channels on a fixed, predetermined basis.

Synchronous transmission (ANS). Data transmission in which the time of occurrence of each signal representing a bit is related to a fixed time frame.

TDM bus switching. A form of time-division switching in which time slots are used to transfer data over a shared bus between transmitter and receiver.

Telematics. User-oriented information transmission services. Includes Teletex, Videotex, and facsimile.

Teletex.   A text communications service that provides message preparation and transmission facilities.

Teletext.   A one-way information retrieval services. A fixed number of information pages are repetitively broadcast on unused portions of a TV channel bandwidth. A decoder at the TV set is used to select and display pages.

Thermal noise.   Statistically uniform noise due to the temperature of the transmission medium.

Time-division multiple access.   A synchronous TDM scheme for satellite capacity allocation.

Time-division multiplexing (IBM).   The division of a transmission facility into two or more channels by allotting the facility to several different information channels, one at a time.

Time-division switching.   A circuit-switching technique in which time slots in a time-multiplexed stream of data are manipulated to pass data from an input to an output.

Time-multiplexed switching (TMS).   A form of space-division switching in which each input line is a TDM stream. The switching configuration may change for each time slot.

Time-slot interchange (TSI).   The interchange of time slots within a time-division multiplexed frame.

Token bus.   A medium access control technique for bus/tree. Stations form a logical ring, around which a token is passed. A station receiving the token may transmit data, and then must pass the token on to the next station in the ring.

Token ring.   A medium access control technique for rings. A token circulates around the ring. A station may transmit by seizing the token, inserting a packet onto the ring, and then retransmitting the token.

Topology.   The structure, consisting of paths and switches, that provides the communications interconnection among nodes of a network.

Transmission medium.   The physical path between transmitters and receivers in a communications system.

Transport layer.   Layer 4 of the OSI model. Provides reliable, transparent transfer of data between endpoints.

Tree.   A local network topology in which stations are attached to a shared transmission medium. The transmission medium is a branching cable emanating from a headend, with no closed circuits. Transmissions propagate throughout all branches of the tree, and are received by all stations.

Twisted pair.   A transmission medium consisting of two insulated wires arranged in a regular spiral pattern.

Unbalanced transmission.   A transmission mode in which signals are transmitted on a single conductor. Transmitter and receiver share a common ground.

Value-added network.   A privately owned packet-switched network whose services are sold to the public.

Videotex.   A two-way information retrieval service accessible to terminals and TV sets equipped with a special decoder. Pages of information at a central resource are retrieved interactively over a switched telephone line connection.

Virtual circuit. A packet-switching service in which a connection (virtual circuit) is established between two stations at the start of transmission. All packets follow the same route, need not carry a complete address, and arrive in sequence.

X.21. A network access standard for connecting stations to a circuit-switched network. Includes OSI layers 1-3 functionality.

X.25. A network access standard for connecting stations to a packet-switched network. Includes OSI layers 1-3 functionality.

X.75. An internetworking protocol that provides virtual circuit service across multiple X.25 networks.

REFERENCES

ABBO84   Abbott, G. F. "Digital Space Division: A Technique for Switching High-Speed Data Signals." *IEEE Communications Magazine*, April 1984.

ABRA70   Abramson, N. "The ALOHA System - Another Alternative for Computer Communications." *Proceedings, Fall Joint Computer Conference*, 1970.

AHUJ82   Ahuja, V. *Design and Analysis of Computer Communication Networks*. New York: McGraw-Hill, 1982.

ALLA82   Allan, R. "Local-Area Networks Spur Moves to Standardize Data Communications Among Computers and Peripherals." *Electronic Design*, December 23, 1982.

ALLA83   Allan, R. "Local Networks: Fiber Optics Gains Momentum." *Electronic Design*, June 23, 1983.

AMOR80   Amoroso, F. "The Bandwidth of Digital Data Signals." *IEEE Communications Magazine*, November 1980.

ANDE81   Anderson, H., and Crane, R. "A Technique for Digital Information Broadcasting Using SCA Channels." *IEEE Transactions on Broadcasting*, December 1981.

ANDR82   Andrews, D. W., and Schultz, G.D. "A Token-Ring Architecture for Local Area Networks: An Update." *Proceedings, COMPCON Fall 82*, IEEE, 1982.

ANSC82   American National Standards Committee. *American National Dictionary for Information Processing Systems*. X3/TR-1-82, 1982.

ANSI82   American National Standards Institute. *Draft, Proposed American National Standard Local Distributed Data Interface*, May 1982.

ATKI80   Atkins, J. "Path Control: The Transport Network of SNA." *IEEE Transactions on Communications*, April 1980.

ATT61   American Telephone and Telegraph Co. *Principles of Electricity Applied to Telephone and Telegraph Work*, 1961.

571

BACH79 Bachman, C., and Canepa, M. *The Session Control Layer of an Open System Interconnection*. International Organization for Standardization OSIC/TG 6/79-10, 1979.

BACH83 Bachmann, L. "Statistical Multiplexers Gain Sophistication and Status." *Mini-Micro Systems*, March 1983.

BAER83 Baer, D., and Sturch, J. "An SNA Primer for Programmers, Parts 1 and 2." *Computer World*, November 14 and 21, 1983.

BBN81 Bolt, Beranek, and Newman Inc. *Specifications for the Interconnection of a Host and an IMP*. Report 1822, December 1981.

BELL77 Bell Telephone Laboratories. *Engineering and Operations in the Bell System*, 1977.

BELL82a Bell Telephone Laboratories. *Transmission Systems for Communications*, 1982.

BELL82b Bellamy, J. *Digital Telephony*. New York: Wiley, 1982.

BERR84 Berry, D. "Standardizing Upper-Level Network Protocols." *Computer Design*, February 1984.

BERT80 Bertine, H. U. "Physical Level Protocols." *IEEE Transactions on Communications*, April 1980.

BHAR83 Bhargava, V. "Forward Error Correction Schemes for Digital Communications." *IEEE Communications Magazine*, January 1983.

BHUS83 Bhusri, G. "Optimum Implementation of Common Channel Signalling in Local Networks." *Proceedings, INFOCOM 83*, 1983.

BHUS84 Bhusri, G. "Considerations for ISDN Planning and Implementation." *IEEE Communications Magazine*, January 1984.

BIND75a Binder, R.; Abramson, N.; Kuo, F.; Okinaka, A.; and Wax, D. "ALOHA Packet Broadcasting - A Retrospect." *Proceedings, National Computer Conference*, 1975.

BIND75b Binder, R. "A Dynamic Packet Switching System for Satellite Broadcast Channels." *Proceedings of the ICC*, 1975.

BIND81 Binder, R. "Packet Protocols for Broadcast Satellites." In [KUO81].

BLAC82 Black, U. "Data Link Controls: The Great Variety Calls for Wise and Careful Choices." *Data Communications*, June 1982.

BOGG80 Boggs, D.; Shoch, J.; Taft, E.; and Metcalfe, R. "Pup: An Internetwork Architecture." *IEEE Transactions on Communications*, April 1980.

BOSE81 Bosen, R. "A Low-Speed Local Net for Under $100 per Station." *Data Communications*, December 1981.

BOSI82 Bosik, B., and Kartalopoulos, S. "A Time Compression Multiplexing System for a Circuit Switched Digital Capability." *IEEE Transactions on Communications*, September 1982.

BOWE83 Bowers, A., and Connell, E. "A Checklist of Communications Protocol Functions Organized Using the Open System Interconnection Seven-Layer Reference Model." *Proceedings, COMPCON 83 Fall*, 1983.

BROD83a Brodd, W. "HDLC, ADCCP, and SDLC: What's the Difference?" *Data Communications*, August 1983.

BROD83b Brodd, W., and Boudreau, P. "Operational Characteristics: BSC Versus SDLC." *Data Communications*, October 1983.

BROO83 Broomell, G., and Heath, J. "Classification Categories and Historical Development of Circuit Switching Topologies." *ACM Computing Surveys*, June 1983.

BURG83 Burg, F. "Design Considerations for Using the X.25 Packet Layer on Data Terminal Equipment." *Proceedings, IEEE INFOCOM 83*, 1983.

BURR83 Burr, W. "An Overview of the Proposed American National Standard for Local Distributed Data Interfaces." *Communications of the ACM*, August 1983.

BUX81 Bux, W. "Local-Area Subnetworks: A Performance Comparison." *IEEE Transactions on Communications*, October 1981.

BUX82 Bux, W.; Closs, F.; Janson, P. A.; Kummerle, K.; Miller, H. R.; and Rothauser, H. "A Local-Area Communication Network Based on a Reliable Token Ring System." *Proceedings, International Symposium on Local Computer Networks*, 1982.

BYTE82 Bytex Corporation. *Autoswitch User Manual*, 1982.

CALL83   Callon, R. "Internetwork Protocols." *Proceedings of the IEEE*, December 1983.

CARL80   Carlson, D. E. "Bit-Oriented Data Link Control Procedures." *IEEE Transactions on Communications*, April 1980.

CARP81   Carpenter, R. *A Survey of Routing Algorithms for Distributed Digital Radio Networks*. MITRE Technical Report MTR-81W00074, March 1981.

CERF78   Cerf, V., and Kristein, P. T. "Issues in Packet-Network Interconnection." *Proceedings of the IEEE*, November 1978.

CERF83a   Cerf, V., and Lyons, R. "Military Requirements for Packet-Switched Networks and Their Implications for Protocol Standardization." *Computer Networks*, October 1983.

CERF83b   Cerf, V., and Cain, E. "The DOD Internet Architecture Model." *Computer Networks*, October 1983.

CHAN72   Chandy, K., and Ramamoorthy, C. "Rollback and Recovery Strategies for Computer Programs." *IEEE Transactions on Computers*, June 1972.

CHAN76   Chang, K. Y. "Transmission of Analog, Video, and Digital Signals Over Analog-Repeatered Coaxial Lines." *IEEE Transactions on Communications*, September 1976.

CHAP82   Chapin, A. "Connectionless Data Transmission." *Computer Communication Review*, April 1982.

CHAP83   Chapin, A. "Connections and Connectionless Data Transmission." *Proceedings of the IEEE*, December 1983.

CHAR79   Charransol, P.; Hauri, J.; Athenes, C.; and Hardy, D. "Development of a Time Division Switching Network Usable in a Very Large Range of Capacities." *IEEE Transactions on Communications*, July 1979.

CHER83   Cheriton, D. "Local Networking and Internetworking in the V-System." *Proceedings, Eighth Data Communications Symposium*, 1983.

CHIL83   Childs, G. "United Kingdom Videotex Service and the European Unified Videotex Standard." *IEEE Journal on Selected Areas in Communications*, February 1983.

CHOU83   Chou, W., ed. *Computer Communications, Vol. I: Principles*. Englewood Cliffs, NJ: Prentice-Hall, 1983.

CHOU84   Chou, W., ed. *Computer Communications, Vol. II: System and Applications*. Englewood Cliffs, NJ: Prentice-Hall, 1984.

CHRI79   Christensen, G. S. "Links Between Computer-Room Networks." *Telecommunications*, February 1979.

CHU73   Chu, W. "Asynchronous Time-Division Multiplexing Systems," In *Computer Communication Networks* (ed. Abramson and Kuo). Englewood Cliffs, NJ, 1973.

CLAN82   Clancy, G. J., et al. "The IEEE 802 Committee States Its Case Concerning Its Local Network Standards Efforts." *Data Communications*, April 1982.

CLAR78   Clark, D. D.; Pogran, K. T.; and Reed, D. P. "An Introduction to Local Area Networks." *Proceedings of the IEEE*, November 1978.

CLAR82   Clark, D. D. "Names, Addresses, Ports, and Routes." *Internet Protocol Implementation Guide*. Menlo Park, CA: SRI International, August 1982.

COLL83   Collie, B.; Kayser, L.; and Rybczynski, A. "Looking at the ISDN Interfaces: Issues and Answers." *Data Communications*, June 1983.

CONA80   Conard, J. "Character-Oriented Data Link Control Protocols." *IEEE Transactions on Communications*, April 1980.

CONA83   Conard, J. "Services and Protocols of the Data Link Layer." *Proceedings of the IEEE*, December 1983.

COOK84   Cooke, R. "Intercity Limits: Looking Ahead to All-Digital Networks and No Bottlenecks." *Data Communications*, March 1984.

COOP82   Cooper, E. "13 Often-Asked Questions About Broadband." *Data Communications*, April 1982.

COOP83a   Cooper, E., and Edholm, P. K. "Design Issues in Broadband Local Networks." *Data Communications*, February 1983.

COOP83b   Cooper, E. "Broadband Network Design: Issues and Answers." *Computer Design*, March 1983.

CORR82   Corrigan, M. "Defense Data Network Protocols." *Proceedings, EASCON 82*, 1982.

COTT79   Cotton, I. W. "Technologies for Local Area Computer Networks." *Proceedings, Local Area Communications Network Symposium*, 1979.

COTT81   Cotton, J.; Giesken, K.; Lawrence, A.; and Upp, D. "ITT 1240 Digital Exchange: Digital Switching Network." *Electrical Communication*, No. 2/3, 1981.

COUC83   Couch, L. *Digital and Analog Communication Systems*. New York: Macmillan, 1983.

CROC83   Crochiere, R. E., and Flanagan, J. L. "Current Perspectives in Digital Speech." *IEEE Communications Magazine*, January 1983.

CROW73   Crowther, W.; Rettberg, R.; Walden, D.; Orenstein, S.; and Heart, F. "A System for Broadcast Communication: Reservation ALOHA." *Proceedings, Sixth Hawaii International System Science Conference*, 1973.

CUNN80   Cunningham, J. E. *Cable Television*. Indianapolis: Howard W. Sams, 1980.

CYPS78   Cypser, R. *Communications Architecture for Distributed Systems*. Reading, MA: Addison-Wesley, 1978.

DALA81   Dalal, Y. K., and Printis, R. S. "48-Bit Absolute Internet and Ethernet Host Numbers." *Proceedings, Seventh Data Communications Symposium*, 1981.

DALA82   Dalal, Y. K. "Use of Multiple Networks in the Xerox Network System." *Computer*, October 1982.

DARP81   Defense Advanced Research Projects Agency. *Internet Control Message Protocol*. RFC: 792, September 1981.

DAVE72   Davey, T. "Modems." *Proceedings of the IEEE*, November 1972.

DAVI73   Davies, D. W., and Barber, D. L. *Communication Networks for Computers*. New York: Wiley, 1973.

DAVI77   Davidson, J.; Hathaway, W.; Postel, J.; Mimno, N.; Thomas, R.; and Walden, D. "The ARPANET Telnet Protocol: Its Purpose, Principles, Implementation, and Impact on Host Operating System Design." *Proceedings, Fifth Data Communications Symposium*, 1977.

DAVI79   Davies, D.; Barber, D.; Price, W.; and Solomonides, C. *Computer Networks and Their Protocols*. New York: Wiley, 1979.

DAY80   Day, J. "Terminal Protocols." *IEEE Transactions on Communications*, April 1980.

DAY81   Day, J. "Terminal, File Transfer, and Remote Job Protocols for Heterogeneous Computer Networks." In *Protocols and Techniques for Data Communication Networks* (ed. F. F. Kuo). Englewood Cliffs, NJ: Prentice-Hall, 1981.

DAY83   Day, J., and Zimmerman, H. "The OSI Reference Model." *Proceedings of the IEEE*, December 1983.

DCA82   Defense Communications Agency. *Defense Data Network Program Plan*, May 1982.

DECI82a   Decina, M. "Managing ISDN Through International Standards Activities." *IEEE Communications Magazine*, September 1982.

DECI82b   Decina, M. "Progress Towards User Access Arrangements in Integrated Services Digital Networks." *IEEE Transactions on Communications*, September 1982.

DERF83   Derfler, F., and Stallings, W. *A Manager's Guide to Local Networks*. Englewood Cliffs, NJ: Prentice-Hall/Spectrum, 1983.

DIGI80   Digital Equipment Corp.; Intel Corp.; and Xerox Corp. *The Ethernet: A Local Area Network Data Link Layer and Physical Layer Specifications*, September 30, 1980.

DIJK59   Dijkstra, E. "A Note on Two Problems in Connection with Graphs." *Numerical Mathematics*, October 1959.

DINE80   Dineson, M. A., and Picazo, J. J. "Broadband Technology Magnifies Local Network Capability." *Data Communications*, February 1980.

DIXO82   Dixon, R. C. "Ring Network Topology for Local Data Communications." *Proceedings, COMPCON Fall 82*, IEEE, 1982.

DOD83a Department of Defense. *Military Standard Internet Protocol*, MIL-STD-1777, August 12, 1983.

DOD83b Department of Defense. *Military Standard Transmission Control Protocol*, MIL-STD-1778, August 12, 1983.

DOLL78 Doll, D. R. *Data Communications: Facilities, Networks, and System Design*. New York: Wiley, 1980.

DONN74 Donnan, R., and Kersey, J. "Synchronous Data Link Control: A Perspective." *IBM Systems Journal*, May 1974.

DORR81 Dorros, I. "ISDN." *IEEE Communications Magazine*, March 1981.

DORR83 Dorros, I. "Telephone Nets Go Digital." *IEEE Spectrum*, April 1983.

DRIV79 Driver, H.; Hopewell, H.; and Iaquinto, J. "How the Gateway Regulates Information Flow." *Data Communications*, September 1979.

EDEL72 Edelson, B., and Werth, A. "SPADE System Progress and Application." *COMSAT Technical Review*, Spring 1972.

EDEL82 Edelson, B.; Marsten, R.; and Morgan, W. "Greater Message Capacity for Satellites." *IEEE Spectrum*, March 1982.

EIA69 Electronic Industries Association. *EIA Standard RS-232-C Interface Between Data Terminal Equipment and Data Communication Equipment Employing Serial Binary Data Interchange*, October 1969.

EIA71 Electronic Industries Association. *Application Notes for EIA Standard RS-232-C*, May 1971.

EMMO83 Emmons, W., and Chandler, H. "OSI Session Layer Services and Protocols." *Proceedings of the IEEE*, December 1983.

ENNI82 Ennis, G.; Kaufman, D.; and Biba, K. *DoD Protocol Reference Model*, Sytek, TR-82026, September 1982.

ENNI83 Ennis, G. "Development of the DoD Protocol Reference Model." *Proceedings, SIGCOMM '83 Symposium*, 1983.

ESTR82 Estrin, J., and Carrico, B. "Gateways Promise to Link Local Networks into Hybrid Systems." *Electronics*, September 22, 1982.

FALK83 Falk, G. "The Structure and Function of Network Protocols." In [CHOU83].

FARM69 Farmer, W. D., and Newhall, E. E. "An Experimental Distributed Switching System to Handle Bursty Computer Traffic." *Proceedings, ACM Symposium on Problems in the Optimization of Data Communications*, 1969.

FEHE83 Feher, K. "SCPC Satcom Systems for Voice and Data Services." *Telecommunications*, June 1983.

FLET82 Fletcher, J. "An Arithmetic Checksum for Serial Transmissions." *IEEE Transactions on Communications*, January 1982.

FLOO82 Floodas, J. "Cellular Radio Today." *Proceedings, Computer Networking Symposium*, 1982.

FOLT80a Folts, H. "Procedures for Circuit-Switched Service in Synchronous Public Data Networks." *IEEE Transactions on Communications*, April 1980.

FOLT80b Folts, H. "X.25 Transaction-Oriented Features—Datagram and Fast Select." *IEEE Transactions on Communications*, April 1980.

FOLT80c Folts, H. "A Powerful Standard Replaces the Old Interface Standby." *Data Communications*, May 1980.

FOLT81 Folts, H., "Coming of Age: A Long-Awaited Standard for Heterogeneous Nets." *Data Communications*, January 1981.

FOLT83 Folts, H. *OSI Workbook*. Vienna, VA: OMNICOM, Inc., 1983.

FORB81 Forbes, V. "RF Prescribed for Many Local Links." *Data Communications*, September 1981.

FORD62 Ford, L., and Fulkerson, D. *Flows in Networks*. Princeton, NJ: Princeton University Press, 1962.

FRAN81 Franta, W., and Chlamtec, I. *Local Networks*. Lexington, MA: Lexington Books, 1981.

FREE80   Freeman, R. *Telecommunication System Engineering.* New York: Wiley, 1980.

FREE81   Freeman, R. *Telecommunication Transmission Handbook.* New York: Wiley, 1981.

FREE83   Freedman, D. "Fiber Optics Shine in Local Area Networks." *Mini-Micro Systems,* September 1983.

GALL68   Gallagher, R. *Information Theory and Reliable Communication.* New York: Wiley, 1968.

GARL77   Garlick, L.; Rom, R.; and Postel, J. "Reliable Host-to-Host Protocols: Problems and Techniques." *Proceedings, Fifth Data Communications Symposium,* 1977.

GECS83   Gecsei, J. *The Architecture of Videotex Systems.* Englewood Cliffs, NJ: Prentice-Hall, 1983.

GEOR82   George, F. and Young, G. "SNA Flow Control: Architecture and Implementation." *IBM Systems Journal,* Number 2, 1982.

GERL80   Gerla, M., and Kleinrock, L. "Flow Control: A Comparative Survey." *IEEE Transactions on Communications,* April 1980.

GERL81   Gerla, M. "Routing and Flow Control." In [KUO81].

GERL84   Gerla, M. and Pazos-Rangel, A. "Bandwidth Allocation and Routing in ISDN's." *IEEE Communications Magazine,* February 1984.

GITM76   Gitman, I.; Van Slyke, R.; and Frank, H. "Routing in Packet-Switching Broadcast Radio Networks." *IEEE Transactions on Communications,* August 1976.

GODI83   Godin, R. "The Cellular Telephone Goes on Line." *Electronics,* September 22, 1983.

GOEL83   Goeller, L. F., and Goldston, J. A. "The ABCs of the PBX." *Datamation,* April 1983.

GORD79   Gordon, R.; Farr, W.; and Levine, P. "Ringnet: A Packet Switched Local Network with Decentralized Control." *Proceedings, Fourth Conference on Local Computer Networks,* 1979.

GOUL84   Gould, R. "Transmission Standards for Direct Broadcast Satellites." *IEEE Communications Magazine,* March 1984.

GRAU82   Graube, M. "Local Area Nets: A Pair of Standards." *IEEE Spectrum,* June 1982.

GRAY72   Gray, J. "Line Control Procedures." *Proceedings of the IEEE,* November 1972.

GREE77   Greene, W., and Pooch, U. "A Review of Classification Schemes for Computer Communication Networks." *Computer,* November 1977.

GREE80   Green, P. "An Introduction to Network Architectures and Protocols." *IEEE Transactions on Communications,* April 1980.

GRIF82   Griffiths, J. "ISDN Network Terminating Equipment." *IEEE Transactions on Communications,* September 1982.

HAFN74   Hafner, E.; Nenadal, Z.; and Tschanz, M. "A Digital Loop Communications System." *IEEE Transactions on Communications,* June 1974.

HAHN81   Hahn, M., and Belanger, P. "Network Minimizes Overhead of Small Computers." *Electronics,* August 25, 1981.

HASK81   Haskell, B., and Steele, R. "Audio and Video Bit-Rate Reduction." *Proceedings of the IEEE,* February 1981.

HEGG84   Heggestad, H. "An Overview of Packet-Switching Communications." *IEEE Communications Magazine,* April 1984.

HELD79   Held, G. *Data Communication Components.* Rochelle Park, NJ: Hayden, 1979.

HEMM82   Hemmat, A. "An Integrated Satellite Communications Protocol." *Proceedings, Computer Networking Symposium,* 1982.

HEYW81   Heywood, P. "The Cambridge Ring Is Still Making the Rounds." *Data Communications,* July 1981.

HIND83   Hinden, R.; Haverty, J.; and Sheltzer, A. "The DARPA Internet: Interconnecting Heterogeneous Computer Networks with Gateways." *Computer,* September 1983.

HOBB81   Hobbs, M. *Modern Communications Switching Systems.* Blue Ridge Summit, PA: TAB Books, 1981.

HOBE80   Hoberecht, V. "SNA Function Management." *IEEE Transactions on Communications,* April 1980.

HOHN80   Hohn, W. C. "The Control Data Loosely Coupled Network Lower Level Protocols." *Proceedings, National Computer Conference*, 1980.

HOLM83   Holmes, E. "A Closer Look at AT&T's New High-Speed Digital Services." *Data Communications*, July 1983.

HONE82   Honeywell Information Systems, Inc. *Distributed Systems Architecture*, CT37-01, 1982.

HOPE73   Hopewell, L.; Chou, W.; and Frank, H. "Analysis of Architectural Strategies for a Large Message-Switching Network: A Case Study." *Computer*, April 1973.

HOPK79   Hopkins, G. T. "Multimode Communications on the MITRENET." *Proceedings, Local Area Communications Network Symposium*, 1979.

HOPK80   Hopkins, G. T., and Wagner, P. E. *Multiple Access Digital Communications System*. U.S. Patent 4,210,780, July 1, 1980.

HOPK82   Hopkins, G. T., and Meisner, N. B. "Choosing Between Broadband and Baseband Local Networks." *Mini-Micro Systems*, June 1982.

HSIE84   Hsieh, W. and Gitman, I. "How Good Is Your Network Routing Protocol?" *Data Communications*, May 1984.

IBM70   IBM Corp. *General Information—Binary Synchronous Communications*, GA27-3004-2, 1970.

IBM81a   IBM Corp. *Systems Network Architecture: Concepts and Products*, GC30-3072, 1981.

IBM81b   IBM Corp. *Vocabulary for Data Processing, Telecommunications, and Office Systems*, GC20-1699-6, 1981.

IBM82   IBM Corp. *IBM Series/1 Local Communications Controller Feature Description*, GA34-0142-2, 1982.

IEEE83   Institute for Electrical and Electronic Engineers. *IEEE Project 802, Local Network Standards*, 1983.

INOS79   Inose, H. *An Introduction to Digital Integrated Communications Systems*. Tokyo: University of Tokyo Press, 1979.

IRLA78   Irland, M. "Buffer Management in a Packet Switch." *IEEE Transactions on Communications*, March 1978.

ISO83a   International Organization for Standardization. *Basic Reference Model for Open Systems Interconnection*, DIS 7498, 1983.

ISO83b   International Organization for Standardization. *Connection Oriented Transport Protocol*, DP 8073, 1983.

ITT75   International Telephone and Telegraph Corp. *Reference Data for Radio Engineers*. Indianapolis, IN: Howard W. Sams, 1975.

JACO78   Jacobs, I.; Binder, R.; and Hoversten, E. "General Purpose Packet Satellite Networks." *Proceedings of the IEEE*, November 1978.

JOEL77   Joel, A. E. "What Is Telecommunications Circuit Switching?" *Proceedings of the IEEE*, September 1977.

JOEL79a   Joel, A. E. "Circuit Switching: Unique Architecture and Applications." *Computer*, June 1979.

JOEL79b   Joel, A. E. "Digital Switching—How it Has Developed." *IEEE Transactions on Communications*, July 1979.

JOHN80   Johnson, S. "Architectural Evolution: Digital Unveils Its Decnet Phase III." *Data Communications*, March 1980.

JONE83   Jones, J. R. "Consider Fiber Optics for Local Network Designs." *EDN*, March 3, 1983.

JUNK83   Junker, S., and Noller, W. "Digital Private Branch Exchanges." *IEEE Communications Magazine*, May 1983.

KADE81   Kaderali, F., and Weston, J. "Digital Subscriber Loops." *Electrical Communication*, Vol. 56, No. 1, 1981.

KAHN77   Kahn, R. "The Organization of Computer Resources into a Packet Radio Network." *IEEE Transactions on Communications*, January 1977.

KAHN78   Kahn, R.; Gronemeyer, S.; Burchfiel, J.; and Kunzelman, C. "Advances in Packet Radio Technology." *Proceedings of the IEEE*, November 1978.

KAJI83   Kajiwara, M. "Trends in Digital Switching System Architectures." *IEEE Communications Magazine*, May 1983.

KANE80a   Kane, D. A. "Data Communications Network Switching Methods," *Computer Design*, April 1980.

KANE80b   Kaneko, H., and Ishigura, T. "Digital Television Transmission Using Bandwidth Compression Techniques." *IEEE Communications Magazine*, July 1980.

KASA83   Kasac, H.; Ohue, K.; Hoshino, T.; and Tsuyuki, S. "800 Mbit/s Digital Transmission System Over Coaxial Cable." *IEEE Transactions on Communications*, February 1983.

KASS79a   Kasson, J. M. "The Rolm Computerized Branch Exchange: An Advanced Digital PBX." *Computer*, June 1979.

KASS79b   Kasson, J. M. "Survey of Digital PBX Design." *IEEE Transactions on Communications*, July 1979.

KELC83   Kelcourse, F., and Siegel, E. "Switched Digital Capability: An Overview." *IEEE Communications Magazine*, January 1983.

KIMB75   Kimbleton, S., and Schneider, G. "Computer Communication Networks: Approaches, Objectives, and Performance Considerations." *ACM Computing Surveys*, September 1975.

KLEI76   Kleinrock, L. *Queueing Systems, Vol. II: Computer Applications*. New York: Wiley, 1976.

KLEI78   Kleinrock, L. "Principles and Lessons in Packet Communications." *Proceedings of the IEEE*, November 1978.

KONA83   Konangi, V., and Dhas, C. "An Introduction to Network Architectures." *IEEE Communications Magazine*, October 1983.

KOPF77   Kopf, J. "TYMNET as a Multiplexed Packet Network." *Proceedings, National Computer Conference*, 1977.

KOST84   Kostas, D. "Transition to ISDN—An Overview." *IEEE Communications Magazine*, January 1984.

KRUT81   Krutsch, T. E. "A User Speaks Out: Broadband or Baseband for Local Nets?" *Data Communications*, December 1981.

KUMM80   Kummede, K., and Rudin, H. "Packet and Circuit Switching: Cost/Performance Boundaries." *Computer Networks*, No. 2, 1980.

KUO81   Kuo, F. *Protocols and Techniques for Data Communication Networks*. Englewood Cliffs, NJ: Prentice-Hall, 1981.

LAM80   Lam, S. "Packet Broadcast Networks—A Performance Analysis of the R-ALOHA Protocol." *IEEE Transactions on Computers*, July 1980.

LAM83   Lam, S. "Data Link Control Procedures." In [CHOU83].

LEWA83   Lewan, D., and Long, H. "The OSI File Service." *Proceedings of the IEEE*, December 1983.

LIND73   Lindsey, W., and Simon, M. *Telecommunication Systems Engineering*. Englewood Cliffs, NJ: Prentice-Hall, 1973.

LINN84   Linnington, P. F. "The Virtual Filestore Concept." *Computer Networks*, February 1984.

LIU78   Liu, M. T. "Distributed Loop Computer Networks." In *Advances in Computers, Vol. 17* (ed. M. C. Yovits). New York: Academic Press, 1978.

LIU82   Liu, M. T.; Hilal, W.; and Groomes, B. H. "Performance Evaluation of Channel Access Protocols for Local Computer Networks." *Proceedings, COMPCON 82 Fall*, 1982.

LIUJ80   Liu, J. "Distributed Routing and Relay Management in Mobile Packet Radio Networks." *Proceedings, COMPCON FALL 80*, 1980.

LOVE79   Loveland, R. "Putting Decnet into Perspective." *Datamation*, March 1979.

LOWE83   Lowe, H. "OSI Virtual Terminal Service." *Proceedings of the IEEE*, December 1983.

Lucz78   Luczak, E. C. "Global Bus Computer Communication Techniques." *Proceedings, Computer Network Symposium,* 1978.

Magn79   Magnee, F.; Endrizzi, A.; and Day, J. "A Survey of Terminal Protocols." *Computer Networks,* November 1979.

Malo81   Malone, J. "The Microcomputer Connection to Local Networks." *Data Communications,* December 1981.

Mark82   Markov, J. D., and Strole, N. C. "Token-Ring Local Area Networks: A Perspective." *Proceedings, COMPCON FALL 82,* IEEE, 1982.

Mars83   Marshall, G. "Bridge Link LANs." *Systems and Software,* May 1983.

Mart70   Martin, J. *Teleprocessing Network Organization.* Englewood Cliffs, NJ: Prentice-Hall, 1970.

Mart72   Martin, J. *Systems Analysis for Data Transmission.* Englewood Cliffs, NJ: Prentice-Hall, 1972.

Mart76   Martin, J. *Telecommunications and the Computer, 2nd Ed.* Englewood Cliffs, NJ: Prentice-Hall, 1976.

Mart78   Martin, J. *Communications Satellite Systems.* Englewood Cliffs, NJ: Prentice-Hall, 1978.

Mart81   Martin, J. *Computer Networks and Distributed Processing.* Englewood Cliffs, NJ: Prentice-Hall, 1981.

Maru83   Maruyama, K., and Shorter, D. "Dynamic Route Selection Algorithms for Session-Based Communication Networks." *Computer Communication Review,* April 1983.

Mccl83   McClelland, F. "Services and Protocols of the Physical Layer." *Proceedings of the IEEE,* December 1983.

Mcdo83   McDougal, P. "Direct Broadcast Satellites in the USA." *Telecommunications,* June 1983.

Mcfa79   McFarland, R. "Protocols in a Computer Internetworking Environment." *Proceedings, EASCON 79,* 1979.

Mcna82   McNamara, J. E. *Technical Aspects of Data Communication.* Bedford, MA: Digital Press, 1982.

Mcqu78   McQuillan, J., and Cerf, V. *Tutorial: A Practical View of Computer Communications Protocols.* Silver Spring, MD: IEEE Computer Society Press, 1978.

Mcqu80   McQuillan, J.; Richer, I.; and Rosen, E. "The New Routing Algorithm for the ARPANET." *IEEE Transactions on Communications.* May 1980.

Meij82   Meijer, A., and Peeters, P. *Computer Network Architectures,* Rockville, MD: Computer Science Press, 1982.

Metc76   Metcalfe, R. M., and Boggs, D. R. "Ethernet: Distributed Packet Switching for Local Computer Networks." *Communications of the ACM,* July 1976.

Metc77   Metcalfe, R. M.; Boggs, D. R.; Thacker, C. P.; and Lampson, B. W. *Multipoint Data Communication System with Collision Detection. U.S. Patent 4,063,220,* 1977.

Metz83   Metz, S. "The Different Flavors of SNA Compatibility." *Data Communications,* April 1983.

Mier82a   Mier, E. "High-Level Protocols, Standards, and the OSI Reference Model." *Data Communications,* July 1982.

Mier82b   Mier, E. "Tuning into Cellular Radio." *Data Communications,* September 1982.

Mier83   Mier, E. "Bell Shines New Light on Digital Transmission Specification." *Data Communications,* April 1983.

Mier84   Mier, E. "The ABCs of FEC." *Data Communications,* May 1984.

Mill81   Miller, L. "An Analysis of Link Level Protocols for Error Prone Links." *Proceedings, Seventh Data Communications Symposium,* 1981.

Mill82   Miller, C. K., and Thompson, D. M. "Making a Case for Token Passing in Local Networks." *Data Communications,* March 1982.

Miya75   Miyahura, H.; Hasegawa, T.; and Teshigawara, Y. "A Comparative Evaluation of Switching Methods in Computer Communication Networks." *Proceedings, International Communications Conference,* 1975.

Mokh81   Mokhoff, N. "Communications: Fiber Optics." *IEEE Spectrum,* January 1981.

MOKH84   Mokhoff, N. "NAPLPS: A Standard for Drawing and Sending Pictures." *Computer Design*, April 1984.

MOLD81   Moldow, B. "Reality and the Proposed OSI Standard." *Data Communications*, June 1981.

MYER82   Myers, W. "Toward a Local Network Standard." *IEEE Micro*, August 1982.

NBS80a   National Bureau of Standards. *Features of Internetwork Protocol.* ICST/HLNP-80-8, July 1980.

NBS80b   National Bureau of Standards. *Features of the Transport and Session Protocols*, ICST/HLNP-80-1, March 1980.

NBS80c   National Bureau of Standards. *Features of the File Transfer Protocol (FTP) and the Data Presentation Protocol (DPP).* ICST/HLNP-80-6, 1980.

NBS81   National Bureau of Standards. *Specification of the Session Protocol*, ICST/HLNP-81-2, March 1981.

NBS83a   National Bureau of Standards. *Specification of a Transport Protocol for Computer Communications*, ICST/HLNP-83-1 to ICST/HLNP-83-5, January 1983.

NBS83b   National Bureau of Standards. *Multi-Vendor Demonstration File Transfer Protocol*, August 1983.

NELS83   Nelson, J. "802: A Progress Report." *Datamation*, September 1983.

NETR80   Netravali, A., and Limb, J. "Picture Coding: A Review." *Proceedings of the IEEE*, March 1980.

NEUM83   Neumann, J. "OSI Transport and Session Layers: Services and Protocol." *Proceedings, INFOCOM 83*, 1983.

NG77   Ng, S., and Mark, J. "A Multiaccess Model for Packet Switching With a Satellite Having Some Processing Capability." *IEEE Transactions on Communications*, January 1977.

NIEL84   Nielson, D. "Packet Radio: An Area-Coverage Digital Radio Network." In [CHOU84].

OETT79   Oetting, J. "A Comparison of Modulation Techniques for Digital Radio." *IEEE Transactions on Communications*, December 1979.

ONEA80   O'Neal, J. "Waveform Encoding of Voiceband Data Signals." *Proceedings of the IEEE*, February 1980.

PADL83   Padlipsky, M. "A Perspective on the ARPANET Reference Model." *Proceedings, INFOCOM 83*, 1983.

PAOL75   Paolette, L. "AUTODIN." In *Computer Communication Networks* (ed. R. L. Grimsdale and F. F. Kuo). Leyden, The Netherlands: Noordhoff International, 1975.

PARK83a   Parker, R., and Shapiro, S. "Untangling Local Area Networks." *Computer Design*, March 1983.

PARK83b   Parker, R. "Committees Push to Standardize Disk I/O." *Computer Design*, March 1983.

PENN79   Penny, B. K., and Baghdadi, A. A. "Survey of Computer Communications Loop Networks." *Computer Communications*, August and October 1979.

PETE61   Peterson, W., and Brown, D. "Cyclic Codes for Error Detection." *Proceedings of the IRE*, January 1961.

PFIS82   Pfister, G., and O'Brien, B. "Comparing the CBX to the Local Network—and the Winner Is?" *Data Communications*, July 1982.

PICK83a   Pickens, R. "Wideband Transmission Media I: Radio Communication." In [CHOU83].

PICK83b   Pickens, R. "Wideband Transmission Media II: Satellite Communication." In [CHOU83].

PICK83c   Pickens, R. "Wideband Transmission Media III: Guided Transmission: Wireline, Coaxial Cable, and Fiber Optics." In [CHOU83].

PIER72   Pierce, J. R. "Network for Block Switches of Data." *Bell System Technical Journal*, July/August 1972.

PONT83   Pontano, B.; Dicks, J.; Colby, R.; Forcina, G.; and Phiel, J. "The INTELSAT TDMA/DSI System." *IEEE Journal on Selected Areas in Communications*, January 1983.

POST80   Postel, J. B. "Internetwork Protocol Approaches." *IEEE Transactions on Communications*, April 1980.

POST81   Postel, J. B.; Sunshine, C. A.; and Cihen, D. "The ARPA Internet Protocol." *Computer Networks*, 1981.

POUZ78   Pouzin, L., and Zimmermann, H. "A Tutorial on Protocols." *Proceedings of the IEEE*, November 1978.

POUZ81   Pouzin, L. "Methods, Tools, and Observations on Flow Control in Packet-Switched Data Networks." *IEEE Transactions on Communications*, April 1981.

PRIT84   Pritchard, W. "The History and Future of Commercial Satellite Communications." *IEEE Communications Magazine*, May 1984.

RAJA78   Rajaraman, A. "Routing in TYMNET." *Proceedings, European Computing Conference*, 1978.

RAUC82   Rauch-Hindin, W. "IBM's Local Network Scheme." *Data Communications*, May 1982.

RAUC83   Rauch-Hindin, W. "Upper-Level Network Protocols." *Electronic Design*, March 3, 1983.

RAWS78   Rawson, E. G., and Metcalfe, R. M. "Fibernet: Multimode Optical Fibers for Local Computer Networks." *IEEE Transactions on Communications*, July 1978.

RAWS79   Rawson, E. G. "Application of Fiber Optics to Local Networks." *Proceedings, Local Area Communications Network Symposium*, 1979.

RICH80   Richer, J.; Steiner, M.; and Sengoku, M. "Office Communications and the Digital PBX." *Computer Networks*, December 1980.

RIND77   Rinde, J. "Routing and Control in a Centrally Directed Network." *Proceedings, National Computer Conference*, 1977.

RIND79a   Rinde, J. "Virtual Circuits in TYMNET II." *Proceedings, National Electronics Conference*, 1979.

RIND79b   Rinde, J., and Caisse, A. "Passive Flow Control Techniques for Distributed Networks." *Proceedings, IRIA Flow Control and Computer Networks Conference*, 1979.

ROBE70   Roberts, L., and Wessler, B. "Computer Network Development to Achieve Resource Sharing." *Proceedings, Spring Joint Computer Conference*, 1970.

ROBE73   Roberts, L. "Dynamic Allocation of Satellite Capacity Through Packet Reservation." *Proceedings, National Computer Conference*, 1973.

ROBE74   Roberts, L. "Data by the Packet." *IEEE Spectrum*, February 1974.

ROBE75   Roberts, L. "ALOHA Packet System With and Without Slots and Capture." *Computer Communications Review*, April 1975.

ROBE78   Roberts, L. "The Evolution of Packet Switching." *Proceedings of the IEEE*, November 1978.

ROBI81   Robin, G., and Treves, S. "An Introduction to Integrated Services Digital Networks." *Electrical Communication*, Vol. 56, No. 1, 1981.

ROCH79   Rocher, E. "Taking a Fresh Look at Local Data Distribution." *Data Communications*, May 1979.

RODE82   Roden, M. *Digital and Data Communication Systems*. Englewood Cliffs, NJ: Prentice-Hall, 1982.

ROSE82   Rosenthal, R., ed. *The Selection of Local Area Computer Networks*. National Bureau of Standards Special Publication 500-96, November 1982.

ROSN82   Rosner, R. *Packet Switching: Tomorrow's Communications Today*. Belmont, CA: Lifetime Learning, 1982.

ROUL81   Rouleau, R., and Hodgson, I. *Packet Radio*. Blue Ridge Summit, PA: TAB Books, 1981.

RUDI76   Rudin, H. "On Routing and Delta Routing: A Taxonomy and Performance Comparison of Techniques for Packet-Switched Networks." *IEEE Transactions on Communications*, January 1976.

RUSH82   Rush, J. R. "Microwave Links Add Flexibility to Local Networks." *Electronics*, January 13, 1982.

RUTK82   Rutkowski, A., and Marcus, M. "The Integrated Services Digital Network: Developments and Regulatory Issues." *Computer Communications Review,* July/October 1982.

RUTK83   Rutkowski, A. "The Role of Satellite Radiocommunication in ISDN." *Telecommunications,* June 1983.

RYBC80   Rybczynski, A. "X.25 Interface and End-to-End Virtual Circuit Service Characteristics." *IEEE Transactions on Communications,* April 1980.

SAKA82   Sakamoto, R. *CCITT Standards Activity: The Integrated Services Digital Network (ISDN).* Mitre Technical Report MTR-82W00169, September 1982.

SAIN84   Saint-Remi, J. "The Many Sounds of Voice Digitization." *Data Communications,* January 1984.

SALT79   Saltzer, J. H., and Pogran, K. T. "A Star-Shaped Ring Network with High Maintainability." *Proceedings, Local Area Communications Network Symposium,* 1979.

SALT83   Saltzer, J.; Pogran, K.; and Clark, D. "Why a Ring?" *Computer Networks,* August 1983.

SALW83   Salwen, H. "In Praise of Ring Architecture for Local Area Networks." *Computer Design,* March 1983.

SAND80   Sanders, R. "Effects of Switching Technologies on Network Delay." *Data Communications,* April 1980.

SAND82   Sanders, L. "Manchester Code Gaining on NRZ." *Electronic Design,* August 5, 1982.

SCAR83   Scarcella, T., and Abbott, R. "Orbital Efficiency Through Satellite Digital Switching." *IEEE Communications Magazine,* May 1983.

SCHN83   Schneidewind, N. "Interconnecting Local Networks to Long-Distance Networks." *Computer,* September 1983.

SCHO81   Scholl, T. H. "The New Breed—Switching Muxes." *Data Communications,* June 1981.

SCHW72   Schwartz, M.; Boorstym, R.; and Pickholtz, R. "Terminal-Oriented Computer-Communication Networks." *Proceedings of the IEEE,* November 1972.

SCHW77   Schwartz, M. *Computer-Communication Network Design and Analysis.* Englewood Cliffs, N.J.: Prentice-Hall, 1977.

SCHW80   Schwartz, M., and Stern, T. E. "Routing Techniques Used in Computer Communication Networks." *IEEE Transactions on Communications,* April 1980.

SCHW84   Schwartz, M. "Optical Fiber Transmission—From Conception to Prominence in 20 Years." *IEEE Communications Magazine,* May 1984.

SEID78   Seider, R. "How Statistical TDMs Let Network Lines Support More Terminals." *Data Communications,* September 1978.

SELV82   Selvaggi, P. "The Department of Defense Data Protocol Standardization Program." *Proceedings, EASCON 82,* 1982.

SEVE80   Severt, R. "Encoding Schemes Support High Density Digital Data Recording." *Computer Design,* May 1980.

SHEL82   Sheltzer, A.; Hinden, R.; and Brescia, M. "Connecting Different Types of Networks with Gateways." *Data Communications,* August 1982.

SHOC78   Shoch, J. F. "Internetwork Naming, Addressing, and Routing." *Proceedings, COMPCON 78,* 1978.

SHOC82   Shoch, J. F.; Dala, Y. K.; and Redell, D. D. "Evolution of the Ethernet Local Computer Network." *Computer,* August 1982.

SKAP79   Skaperda, N. J. "Some Architectural Alternatives in the Design of a Digital Switch." *IEEE Transactions on Communications,* July 1979.

SLAN81   Slana, M., and Lehman, H. "Data Communication Using the Telecommunication Network." *Computer,* May 1981.

SPEC82   Spector, A. "Performing Remote Operations Efficiently on a Local Computer Network." *Communications of the ACM,* April 1982.

SPIL77   Spilker, J. *Digital Communications by Satellite.* Englewood Cliffs, NJ: Prentice-Hall, 1977.

STAH82   Stahlman, M. "Inside Wang's Local Net Architecture." *Data Communications*, January 1982.

STAL76   Stallings, W. "An Application of Coroutines and Backtracking in Interactive Systems." *International Journal of Computer and Information Sciences*. December 1976.

STAL83a Stallings, W. *Tutorial: Local Network Technology*, Silver Spring, MD: IEEE Computer Society Press, 1983.

STAL83b Stallings, W. "Local Network Overview." *Signal Magazine*, January 1983.

STAL83c Stallings, W. "Beyond Local Networks." *Datamation*, August 1983.

STAL84a Stallings, W. *Local Networks: An Introduction*. New York: Macmillan, 1984.

STAL84b Stallings, W. "Local Network Performance." *IEEE Communications Magazine*, February, 1984.

STAL84c Stallings, W. "Local Networks." *Scientific American*, to appear.

STAL84d Stallings, W. "IEEE Project 802: Setting Standards for Local-Area Networks." *Computerworld*, February 13, 1984.

STAL84e Stallings, W. "Local Networks." *Computing Surveys*, March 1984.

STAL85   Stallings, W. *Tutorial: Computer Communications Architectures, Protocols, and Standards*. Silver Spring, MD: IEEE Computer Society Press, 1985.

STEW84   Stewart, B.; Hawe, B.; and Kirby, A. "Local Area Network Connection." *Telecommunications*, April 1984.

STIE81   Stieglitz, M. "Local Network Access Tradeoffs." *Computer Design*, October 1981.

STIF83   Stifle, J. "The Interactive Difference in Multiplexing." *Data Communications*, October 1983.

STUC83a Stuck, B. "Which Local Net Bus Access Is Most Sensitive to Congestion?" *Data Communications*, January 1983.

STUC83b Stuck, B. "Calculating the Maximum Mean Data Rate in Local Area Networks." *Computer*, May 1983.

STUT72   Stutzman, B. "Data Communication Control Procedures." *ACM Computing Surveys*, December 1972.

SUDA83   Suda, T.; Miyahara, H.; and Hasegawa, T. "Performance Evaluation of an Integrated Access Scheme in a Satellite Communication Channel." *IEEE Journal on Selected Areas in Communications*, January 1983.

SUNS77   Sunshine, C. "Interconnection of Computer Networks." *Computer Networks*, February 1977.

SUNS79   Sunshine, C. "Network Interconnection." *Proceedings of Local Area Communications Network Symposium*, 1979.

SUNS81   Sunshine, C. "Transport Protocols for Computer Networks." In [KUO81].

SUNS83   Sunshine, C.; Kaufaman, D.; Ennis, G.; and Biba, K. "Interconnection of Broadband Local Area Networks." *Proceedings, Eighth Data Communications Symposium*, 1983.

TANE81a Tanenbaum, A. *Computer Networks*. Englewood Cliffs, NJ: Prentice-Hall, 1981.

TANE81b Tanenbaum, A. "Network Protocols." *Computing Surveys*, December 1981.

THOR80   Thornton, J. E. "Back-End Network Approaches." *Computer*, February 1980.

THOR83   Thornton, J., and Christenson, G. "Hyperchannel Network Links." *Computer*, September 1983.

TOBA80   Tobagi, F. A. "Multiaccess Protocols in Packet Communications Systems." *IEEE Transactions on Communications*, April 1980.

TOML75   Tomlinson, R. "Selecting Sequence Numbers." *Proceedings ACM SIGCOMM/SIGOPS Interprocess Communication Workshop*, 1975.

TROP81   Tropper, C. *Local Computer Network Technologies*. New York: Academic Press, 1981.

TUGA82   Tugal, D., and Tugal, O. *Data Transmission: Analysis, Design, Applications*. New York: McGraw-Hill, 1982.

TYDE82   Tydeman, J.; Lipinski, H.; Adler, R.; Nyhan, M.; Zwimpfer, L. *Teletext and Videotext in the United States*. New York: McGraw-Hill, 1982.

Tyme71   Tymes, R. "TYMNET—A Terminal-Oriented Communication Network." *Proceedings, Spring Joint Computer Conference*, 1971.

Tyme81   Tymes, L. "Routing and Flow Control in TYMNET." *IEEE Transactions on Communications*, April 1981.

Unso81   Unsoy, M., and Shanahan, T. "X.75 Internetworking of Datapac and Telenet." *Proceedings, Seventh Data Communications Symposium*, 1981.

Vaug59   Vaughan, H. "Research Model for Time Separation Integrated Communication." *Bell System Technical Journal*, July 1959.

Vona80   Vonarx, M. "Controlling the Mushrooming Communications Net." *Data Communications*, June 1980.

Wabe82   Waber, K. "Considerations on Customer Access to the ISDN." *IEEE Transactions on Communications*, September 1982.

Wain83   Wainwright, P. F. "Internetworking and Addressing for Local Networks." In [IEEE83].

Walk82   Walker, S. "Department of Defense Data Network." *Signal*, October 1982.

Ware83   Ware, C. "The OSI Network Layer: Standards to Cope with the Real World." *Proceedings of the IEEE*, December 1983.

Warn80   Warner, C. "Connecting Local Networks to Long-Haul Networks: Issues in Protocol Design." *Proceedings, Fifth Conference on Local Computer Networks*, 1980.

Weck80   Wecker, S. "DNA: The Digital Network Architecture." *IEEE Transactions on Communications*, April 1980.

Weis78   Weissler, R.; Binder, R.; Bressler, R.; Rettberg, R.; and Walden, D. "Synchronization and Multiple Access Protocols in the Initial Satellite IMP." *Proceedings, COMPCON FALL 78*, 1978.

Weis83   Weissberger, A. "Bit Oriented Data Link Controls." *Computer Design*, March 1983.

Weth83   Wetherington, J. "The Story of PLP." *IEEE Journal on Selected Areas in Communications*. February 1983.

Wilk79   Wilkes, M. V., and Wheeler, D. J. "The Cambridge Digital Communication Ring." *Proceedings, Local Area Communications Network Symposium*, 1979.

Wood84a   Wood, D. C. "Local Networks." In [CHOU84].

Wood84b   Wood, D. C. "Computer Networks." In [CHOU84].

Yano81   Yanoschak, V. "Implementing the X.21 Interface." *Data Communications*, February 1981.

Yen83   Yen, C., and Crawford, R. "Distribution and Equalization of Signal on Coaxial Cables Used in 10 Mbps/s Baseband Local Area Networks." *IEEE Transactions on Communications*, October 1983.

Ziem83   Ziemer, R.; Tranter, W.; and Fannin, D. *Signals and Systems: Continuous and Discrete*. New York: Macmillan, 1983.

Zimm80   Zimmermann, H. "OSI Reference Model—The ISO Model of Architecture for Open System Interconnection." *IEEE Transactions on Communications*, April 1980.

INDEX